Dedication

To my family

TABLE OF CONTENTS

Preface

Chapter 4—General Accounting and End-of-Period Procedures: Service Business

CONTENTS

Chapter 5—Sales and Receivables: Merchandising Business

Chapter 6—Payables and Purchases: Merchandising Business

Chapter 7—General Accounting and End-of-Period Procedures: Merchandising Business

Chapter 9—Creating a Company in QuickBooks

Appendix C: QuickBooks® Pro Online Features

PREFACE

QuickBooks® Pro 2010: A Complete Course is a comprehensive instructional learning resource. The text provides training using the *QuickBooks® Pro 2010* accounting program. The text was written using QuickBooks® Pro 2010 but may be used with QuickBooks® Basic or Premier versions.

ORGANIZATIONAL FEATURES

QuickBooks® Pro 2010: A Complete Course is designed to present accounting concepts and their relationship to *QuickBooks® Pro 2010*. In addition to accounting concepts, students use a fictitious company and receive hands-on training in the use of *QuickBooks® Pro 2010* within each chapter. At the end of every chapter, the concepts and applications learned are reinforced by the completion of true/false, multiple-choice, fill-in, and essay questions plus an application problem using a different fictitious company. There are three practices sets in the text that utilize all the major concepts and transactions presented within an area of study. The third practice set is comprehensive and utilizes all the major concepts and transactions presented within the entire textbook.

The text introduces students to QuickBooks accounting for a service business, a merchandising business, payroll, and a company setup for QuickBooks. The appendices include information regarding QuickBooks Integration using: Word, Excel, and Outlook; QuickBooks Features: QuickBooks Notes, Time Tracking, Job Costing, and Price Levels; and QuickBooks Online: online updates, Internet connection, payroll services, online banking and payments, billing solutions, merchant services, online billing, online credit card billing, online backup services, direct deposit, and Google desktop features.

DISTINGUISHING FEATURES

Throughout the text, emphasis has been placed on the use of QuickBooks' innovative approach to recording accounting transactions based on a business form rather than using the traditional journal format. This approach, however, has been correlated to traditional accounting through adjusting entries, end-of-period procedures, and use of the "behind the scenes" journal.

Unlike many other computerized accounting programs, QuickBooks is user-friendly when corrections and adjustments are required. The ease of corrections and the ramifications as a result of this ease are explored thoroughly.

Accounting concepts and the use of *QuickBooks® Pro 2010* are reinforced throughout the text with the use of graphics that show completed transactions, reports, and QuickBooks screens. The text helps students transition from textbook transaction analysis to "real-world" transaction analysis.

The text provides extensive assignment material in the form of tutorials; end-of-chapter questions (true/false, multiple-choice, fill-in, and essay); practice sets for a service business, a merchandising business, and a comprehensive practice set.

Students develop confidence in recording business transactions using an up-to-date commercial software program designed for small to mid-size businesses. With thorough exploration of the program in the text, students should be able to transition from training to using *QuickBooks® Pro 2010* in an actual business.

Students will explore and use many of the features of QuickBooks as it pertains to a service business and a merchandising business, including recording transactions ranging from simple to complex, preparing a multitude of reports, closing an accounting period, compiling charts and graphs, creating a company, and preparing the payroll. The transactions entered by students begin with simple entries and become more complex as they progress through the text. Students also learn ways in which QuickBooks can be customized to fit the needs of an individual company.

COURSES

QuickBooks® Pro 2010: A Complete Course is designed for a one-term course in microcomputer accounting. This text covers a service business, a merchandising business, a sole proprietorship, a partnership, payroll, and company setup to use QuickBooks. When using the text, students should be familiar with the accounting cycle and how it is related to a business. No prior knowledge of or experience with computers, Windows, or QuickBooks is required; however, an understanding of accounting is essential to successful completion of the coursework.

SUPPLEMENTS FOR THE INSTRUCTOR

Pearson Education maintains a website where student and instructor materials may be downloaded for classroom use **www.pearsonhighered.com**. The *Instructor's Resource Center* contains:

- Master data files for all the companies in the text. These are the same as the Student Company files
- Backup company files for each chapter that may be restored to a QuickBooks company file
- An "Answer Key" containing Adobe .pdf files for all the printouts prepared in the text.
- A sample syllabus/course outline
- Lectures for each chapter with a hands-on demonstration lecture
- PowerPoint lectures with notes and accompanying Word files for each chapter
- Written exams for each area of study, a written final exam, and an exam for each practice set

- Suggestions for grading. Instructor materials include a lecture outline for each chapter
- Answers to the end-of-chapter questions
- Transmittal sheets that include the totals of reports and documents
- Excel files for all the reports prepared in the text.

ACKNOWLEDGMENTS

I wish to thank my colleagues for testing and reviewing the manuscript, the professors who use the text and share their thoughts and suggestions with me, and my students for providing me with a special insight into problems encountered in training. All of your comments and suggestions are greatly appreciated. A special thank you goes to Sally Kurz, Michael Fagan, and Barb Gillespie for their proofreading and comments. In addition, I would like to thank Jodi McPherson, Rebecca Knauer, and the production team at Pearson Education for their editorial support and assistance.

INTRODUCTION TO QUICKBOOKS® PRO 2010 AND COMPANY FILES

LEARNING OBJECTIVES

At the completion of this chapter, you will be able to:

1. Identify QuickBooks Pro desktop features, be familiar with the QuickBooks Centers, and understand the QuickBooks Home Page.
2. Recognize menu commands and use some keyboard shortcuts.
3. Recognize QuickBooks Pro forms and understand the use of lists and registers in QuickBooks Pro.
4. Access QuickBooks Pro reports and be familiar with QuickZoom.
5. Open and close QuickBooks Pro
6. Copy a company file and open a company
7. Add your name to a company name
8 Access QuickBooks Pro reports and be familiar with QuickZoom.
9 Prepare QuickBooks Pro graphs and use QuickReport within graphs.
10 Use QuickMath and the Windows Calculator.
11. Download a company file
12. Back up a company
13. Restore a company from a backup file
14. Close a company

MANUAL AND COMPUTERIZED ACCOUNTING

The work to be performed to keep the books for a business is the same whether you use a manual or a computerized accounting system. Transactions need to be analyzed, recorded in a journal, and posted to a ledger. Business documents such as invoices, checks, bank deposits, and credit/debit memos need to be prepared and distributed. Reports to management and owners for information and decision-making purposes need to be prepared. Records for one business period need to be closed before recording transactions for the next business period.

In a manual system, each transaction that is analyzed must be entered by hand into the appropriate journal (the book of original entry where all transactions are recorded) and posted to the appropriate ledger (the book of final entry that contains records for all the accounts used in the business). A separate business document such as an invoice or a check must be prepared and distributed. In order to prepare a report, the accountant/bookkeeper must go through the journal or ledger and look for the appropriate amounts to include in the report. Closing the books must be done item by item via closing entries, which are recorded in the journal and posted to the appropriate ledger accounts. After the closing entries are recorded, the ledger accounts must be ruled and balance sheet accounts must be reopened with Brought Forward Balances being entered. All of this is extremely time consuming.

When using a computerized system and a program such as QuickBooks, the transactions must still be analyzed and recorded. QuickBooks Pro operates from a business document point of view. As a transaction occurs, the necessary business document (an invoice or a check, for example) is prepared. Based on the information given on the business document, QuickBooks Pro records the necessary debits and credits behind the scenes in the Journal. If an error is made when entering a transaction, QuickBooks Pro allows the user to return to the business document and make the correction. QuickBooks Pro will automatically record the changes in the debits and credits in the Journal. If you want to see or make a correction using the actual debit/credit entries, QuickBooks Pro allows you to view the transaction register and make corrections directly in the register or use the traditional General Journal. Reports and graphs are prepared by simply clicking "Report" on the menu bar.

VERSIONS OF QUICKBOOKS®

While this text focuses on training using QuickBooks® Pro 2010, it may also be used with the Premier version of the program. The Premier version offers some additional enhancements not available in the Pro version. The Premier version of the program is also available in industry specific versions, such as, Accountant, Contractor, Healthcare, Manufacturing and Wholesale, Nonprofit, Professional Services, and Retail. There is an Online Edition of QuickBooks that is available online for a monthly fee. However, the functions available are limited and many features of QuickBooks Pro cannot be utilized. In addition, there is also the Simple Start program, which is designed for first time QuickBooks users, and Enterprise Solutions, which is designed for larger businesses that want a great deal of customization. There is even a QuickBooks program for Macs that has many of the same functions as QuickBooks Pro.

For a comparison of features available among the different versions of the QuickBooks programs, access Intuit's Web site at www.quickbooks.intuit.com.

BEGIN COMPUTER TRAINING

DO When you see the arrow, it means you will be performing a computer task. Sometimes the computer task will have several steps. Continue until all steps listed are completed.

OPEN QUICKBOOKS® PRO

Once you are in Windows, opening QuickBooks Pro is as easy as point and click.

DO Open QuickBooks Pro

Click **Start**
Point to **All Programs**

Point to **QuickBooks** (or the program name given to you by your instructor)
On the drop-down list, click **QuickBooks Pro 2010**

HOW TO OPEN A COMPANY

To explore some of the features of QuickBooks Pro, you will work with a sample company that comes with the program. The company is Larry's Landscaping & Garden Supply and is stored on the hard disk (C:) inside the computer.

DO Open a sample company

Click the **Open a sample file** button
Click **Sample service-based business**

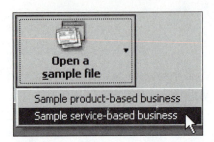

When using the sample company for training, a warning screen will appear. This is to remind you NOT to enter the transactions for your business in the sample company.

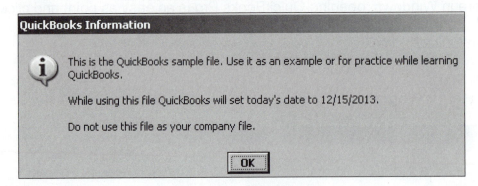

Click **OK** to accept the sample company data for use

When opening the sample company, you may get a screen for QuickBooks Learning Center. This allows you to obtain an overview of QuickBooks features and to work with tutorials regarding some of the basic areas of QuickBooks. If you do not want to see this screen every time you open QuickBooks, click the "Show this window at startup" box at the bottom of the Learning Center screen to remove the check mark. To continue, click the **Begin Using QuickBooks** button at the bottom of the Learning Center screen.

In addition to the Learning Center, you may get a screen suggesting QuickBooks Products and Services. Close this screen, and click the "Show this window at startup" box at the bottom of the screen to remove the check mark.

If the QuickBooks Coach is open on the screen you can view a tutorial and see coach tips (explanations of the icons and work flowchart on the screen). If the QuickBooks Coach is not open, it will be available on the right-side of the QuickBooks screen. If the Coach is open, it looks like the following:

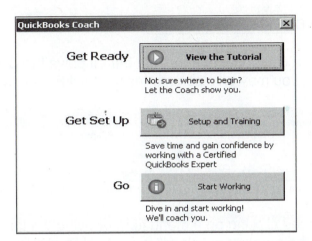

DO If the Coach is open, click the Close button (the x) on the QuickBooks Coach.

- Notice that the QuickBooks Coach is moved to the upper-right area of the screen and is available for use at any time. Simply click Maximize Coach.

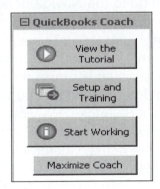

VERIFY AN OPEN COMPANY

It is important to make sure you have opened the data for the correct company. Always verify the company name in the title bar. The title bar is located at the top of the screen and will tell you the name of the company and the program.

DO Verify an open company

Check the **title bar** at the top of the QuickBooks screen to make sure it includes the company name. The title bar should show:

QUICKBOOKS® PRO DESKTOP FEATURES

Once you have opened a company, and the title bar displays the **Company Name - QuickBooks Pro 2010**, you may give commands to QuickBooks by using the:

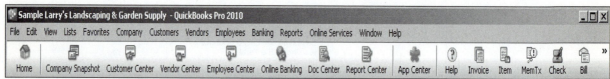

Menu bar, QuickBooks Home Icon, Company Snapshot, Command Centers, and Icon Bar

Menu bar. By pointing and clicking on a menu item or using the keyboard shortcut of Alt+ the underlined letter in the menu item you will give QuickBooks Pro the command to display the drop-down menu. For example, the File menu is used to open and close a company and may also be used to exit QuickBooks Pro.

QuickBooks Home. Below the Menu bar is a row of icons (small picture symbols). The first icon says Home and is used to go to the Navigator screen.

QuickBooks Company Snapshot

Next to Home is an icon for Company Snapshot. When you click this icon, you get information about the company. You may customize the Company Snapshot and select from among 12 different options to determine what you want displayed. These options include listings or graphs for Account Balances, Previous Year Income Comparison, Income Breakdown, Previous Year Expense Comparison, Income and Expense Trend, Top Customers by Sales, Best-Selling Items, Customers Who Owe Money, Top Vendors by Expense, Vendors to Pay, and Reminders.

QuickBooks Command Centers. Next to the Company Snapshot icon are icons for Centers. Each center goes to a specific list within the program. For example, the Customer Center displays a list of customers and their current balances.

Icon bar. This optional bar contains small pictures that may be used to give commands by pointing to a picture and clicking the primary mouse button.

MENU COMMANDS

Menu commands can be the starting point for issuing commands in QuickBooks Pro. Many commands will be the same as the ones you can give when using QuickBooks Home Page. Notice that available keyboard shortcuts are listed next to the menu item. Click outside the menu to close it.

> **DO** Access each of the menus by clicking or pointing to each menu item

File menu is used to access company files and perform several other functions—New Company, Open or Restore Company, Open Previous Company, Save Copy or Backup, Close Company, Switch to Multi-user Mode, Remote Access, Utilities, Accountant's Copy, Print Forms, Printer Setup, Send Forms, Shipping, Update Web Services, and Exit.

Edit menu is used to make changes such as: Undo, Revert, Cut, Copy, Paste, Use Register, Use Calculator, Find, and Preferences.

View menu is used to select the use of an Open Window List, Icon bar, Customize Icon bar, Add Home to the Icon Bar, Favorites Menu, and One or Multiple Windows.

Lists menu is used to show lists used by QuickBooks Pro. These lists include: Chart of Accounts (the General Ledger), Items, Fixed Asset Items, Price Level Items, Sales Tax Codes, Payroll Items, Class, Workers Comp, Other Names, Customer & Vendor Profiles, Templates, Memorized Transactions, and Add/Edit Multiple List Entries.

Favorites menu is used to place your favorite or most frequently used commands on this list. It must be selected in the View menu and may then be customized with your selected commands.

Company menu is used to access the Home Page, access the Company Snapshot, change Company Information, Advance Service Administration, Set Up Users and Passwords, Customer Credit Card Protection, Set Closing Date, Planning & Budgeting, access the To Do List, access Reminders, use the Alerts Manager, Enter Vehicle Mileage, Manage Currency, Document Management, and access the Chart of Accounts. It is also used to Make General Journal Entries, Prepare Letters with Envelopes, and Email Marketing.

Customers menu is used to access the Customer Center, enter transactions and prepare business documents such as invoices, sales receipts, credit memos/refunds, statements and statement charges, finance charges, receive payments, add credit card, mobile and electronic check processing, link payment service to company file, and email marketing. It is also used to access the Item list, and to change item prices.

Vendors menu is used to access the Vendor Center and the Item List. In addition, this menu is used to enter transactions for recording bills, paying bills, paying sales tax, creating purchase orders, receiving items, inventory activities, and printing 1099s/1096s.

Employees menu is used to access the Employee Center and the Payroll Center; pay employees; add or edit payroll schedules; edit/void paychecks; process payroll taxes and liabilities; access payroll forms; access Workers Compensation to set up Workers Comp, a Workers Comp List, and create a Workers Comp Summary; perform payroll service activities; set up payroll services; manage payroll items; and get payroll updates.

Banking menu is used to write checks, order checks and envelopes, enter credit card charges, use the check register, make deposits, transfer funds, reconcile accounts, access online banking, use the loan manager, and access the Other Names Lists.

Reports menu is used to access the Report Center, display the Company Snapshot, and to prepare reports in the following categories: Company & Financial; Customers & Receivables; Sales; Jobs, Time & Mileage; Vendors & Payables; Purchases; Inventory; Employees & Payroll; Banking; Accountant & Taxes; Budgets; and Lists. You can also create a Custom Summary Report; Custom Transaction Detail Report; Transaction History; Transaction Journal; and Memorized Reports.

Online Services menu is used for Customer Manager Online, Manage Services, Email Marketing, Websites, Search Advertising, Incorporation Services, and Set Up Intuit Sync Manager.

Window menu is used to switch between windows that have been opened and to arrange icons.

Help menu is used to access QuickBooks Help. The Help menu includes topics such as: Learning Center Tutorials, Support, Find a Local QuickBooks Expert, Send Feedback Online, Internet Connection Setup, New Business Checklist, Year-End Guide, Add QuickBooks Services, App Center: Find More Business Solutions, Update QuickBooks, Manage My License, Buy QuickBooks Premier Edition, QuickBooks Privacy Statement, About Automatic Update, About QuickBooks Pro 2010.

QUICKBOOKS® PRO HOME PAGE

The QuickBooks Home Page allows you to give commands to QuickBooks Pro according to the type of transaction being entered. The Home Page tasks are organized into logical groups (Vendors, Customers, Employees, Company, and Banking).

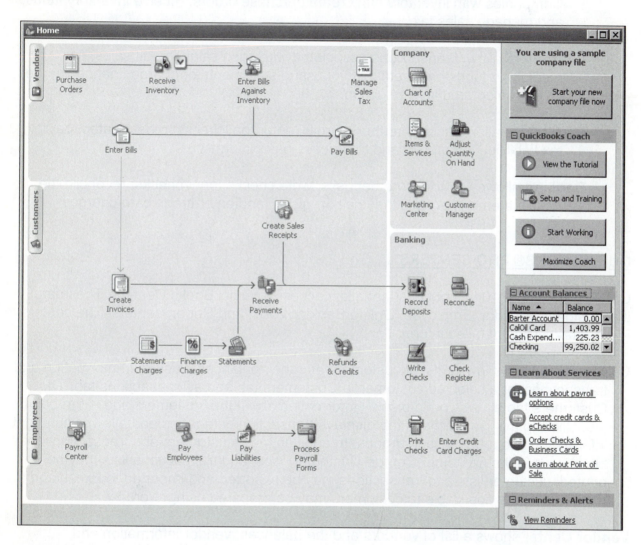

Each of the areas on the Home Page is used to enter different types of transactions. When appropriate, the Home Page shows a flow chart with icons indicating the major activities performed. The icons are arranged in the order in which transactions usually occur.

DO ▶ View each of the areas on the Home Page:

Company allows you to display information about your company. There are graphic icons used to display the Chart of Accounts, Items & Services, Adjust the Quantity on Hand, Marketing Center, and Customer Manager.

Vendors allows you to enter your bills and to record the payment of bills. Companies with inventory can create purchase orders, receive inventory items, and manage sales tax.

Customers allows transactions associated with cash sales, credit sales, cash receipts, refunds and credits. If you issue statements or charge finance charges, these are entered in this section.

Employees allows access to the Payroll Center, paychecks to be created, payroll tax liabilities to be paid, and to process payroll forms.

Banking allows you to record deposits, write checks, print checks, reconcile the bank statement, access the check register, and enter credit card charges.

QUICKBOOKS® PRO CENTERS

QuickBooks Pro 2010 has buttons that allow access to QuickBooks Centers. These are the Customer, Vendor, Employee, Online Banking, Doc, and Report centers. The centers focus on providing detailed information.

Customer Center shows a list of customers and their balances, customer information and transactions for a selected customer, a Customers tab and a Transactions tab. The Customers tab allows you to display information about the customers and is the default tab. Clicking the Transactions tab displays transaction categories and allows you to get information about transaction groups. In addition, new customers and transactions may be entered in the Customer Center. Customer, jobs, and transactions lists may be printed; customer lists and transactions may be exported and imported to Excel; and a variety of letters applicable to customers may be prepared using Word.

Vendor Center shows a list of vendors and the balances, vendor information and transactions for a selected vendor, a Vendors tab and a Transactions tab. The Vendors tab allows you to display information about the vendors and is the default tab. Clicking the Transactions tab displays transaction categories and allows you to get information about transaction groups. In addition, new vendors and transactions may be entered in the Vendor Center. The vendor, information, and transactions lists may be printed; vendor lists and transactions may be exported and imported to Excel; and a variety of letters applicable to vendors may be prepared using Word.

Employee Center shows a list of employees, employee information and payroll transactions for a selected employee, an Employees tab, a Transactions tab, and a Payroll tab. The Employees tab allows you to display information about the individual employees and is the default tab. Clicking the Transactions tab displays transaction categories and allows you to get information about transaction groups. The Payroll tab provides information regarding payroll dates, payroll taxes, and payroll forms. In addition, new employees may be entered and employee information may be managed in the Employee Center. Paychecks may be printed and paystubs may be printed or emailed. The employee list, employee information, and the employee transaction list may be printed. The employee list, transactions, and payroll data may be summarized and exported to Excel. Word may be used to prepare letters applicable to employees.

Online Banking Center allows you to perform online banking transactions through the center.

Doc Center is a subscription service that allows you to attach documents to items, scan paper documents right into QuickBooks, and store your documents online.

Report Center accesses the Reports available in QuickBooks Pro and allows all of them to be prepared. These include specific reports, such as, Profit and Loss, Balance Sheet, Tax Reports, Transaction Detail Reports, Journal, General Ledger, Trial Balance, Income Tax Summary, Income Tax Detail, and an Audit Trail. There is also a variety of reports specific to payroll, customers, vendors, inventory, purchases, banking, and taxes. Over 100 reports may be prepared in the Report Center. The Report Center lists the reports available by category. The reports may be displayed in a carousel view, a list view, or a grid view.

App Center is a link to Intuit subscription services with workplace applications such as Run My Business, Manage My Work, Grow and Manage Customers, Reduce Costs, Small Business Scheduler, Professional Services Apps, Financial Services Apps, Field Services Apps, and others.

▸ **DO** Access each of the centers by clicking the appropriate Center icon beneath the menu bar and close each Center before opening the next Center

KEYBOARD CONVENTIONS

When using Windows, there are some standard keyboard conventions for the use of certain keys. These keyboard conventions also apply to QuickBooks Pro and include:

Alt key is used to access the drop-down menus on the menu bar. Rather than click on a menu item, hold down the Alt key and type the underlined letter in the menu item name.

Close the menu by simply pressing the Alt key. *Note*: Menu items do not have an underlined letter until you press the Alt key.

Tab key is used to move to the next field or, if a button is selected, to the next button.

Shift+Tab is used to move back to the previous field.

Esc key is used to cancel an active window without saving anything that has been entered. It is equivalent to clicking the Cancel button.

▶ **DO** ▶ Practice using the keyboard conventions:

Access **Customer** menu: **Alt+U**
Access **Create Invoices**: type **I**
Press **Tab** key to move forward through the invoice
Press **Shift+Tab** to move back through the invoice
Press **Esc** to close the invoice

ICON BAR

Another way to give commands to QuickBooks Pro is to use the icon bar. If activated, the icon bar will be placed below the menu bar and next to the Centers bar. The icon bar has a list of buttons (icons) that may be clicked in order to access activities, lists, or reports. The icon bar may be turned on or off and it may be customized. If there is a double >> at the edge of the icon bar, that means that there are more icons available for use.

ON-SCREEN HELP

QuickBooks Pro has on-screen help, which is similar to having the QuickBooks Pro reference manual available on the computer screen. Help can give you assistance with a particular function you are performing. QuickBooks Pro Help also gives you information about the program using an on-screen index.

Help may be accessed to obtain information on a variety of topics, and it may be accessed in different ways:

To find out about the window in which you are working, press F1, click on the list of relevant topics displayed and read the information given; or click the Search tab, enter the topic you wish to view, and then click the Start Search button.

To learn about the new features available in QuickBooks Pro, click QuickBooks Help on the Help Menu, click the Search tab, type "New Features" in the textbox, click the Start Search button.

To get additional information on how to use QuickBooks Pro or to enter a question and get immediate answers drawn from both the QuickBooks Help system and the technical support database, click the Help menu and click Support.

When the topic for Help has been located, information about the topic is provided in the Help window. If there is more information than can be shown on the screen, scroll bars will appear on the right side of the Help screen. A scroll bar is used to show or go through information. As you scroll through Help, information at the top of the Help screen disappears from view while new information appears at the bottom of the screen.

Sometimes words appear in blue and may be underlined or be underlined and have a + sign in the QuickBooks Pro Help screen. Clicking on the blue word(s) with a + sign will give you a pop-up definition of the word, display the corresponding icon, or list items for the definition. Clicking on blue underlined words will take you to other topics.

Often, the onscreen help provides links to an external Web site. To visit these links, you must have an Internet connection and be online. Links to sites outside the QuickBooks Help are indicated with a lightning bolt symbol.

If you want to see a different topic, you may type in different key words at the top of the Search screen. Information will be provided on the new topic.

If you want to print a copy of the QuickBooks Pro Help screen, click the Printer icon at the top of the green title bar for the Help topic.

You may close a QuickBooks Pro Help screen by clicking the Close button (X) in the upper right corner of the screen.

PRACTICE USING HELP SEARCH TO FIND KEYBOARD SHORTCUTS

Frequently, it is faster to use a keyboard shortcut to give QuickBooks Pro a command than it is to point and click the mouse through several layers of menus or icons. The list of common keyboard shortcuts may be obtained by using Help.

▶ **DO** ▶ Use Help

> Click **Help** on the Menu bar
> Click **QuickBooks Help**
> Click the **Search** tab
> Type **keyboard shortcuts**
>
> Click the **Search** button
> Look at the list of topics provided

> Click **QuickBooks keyboard shortcuts**
> View the results

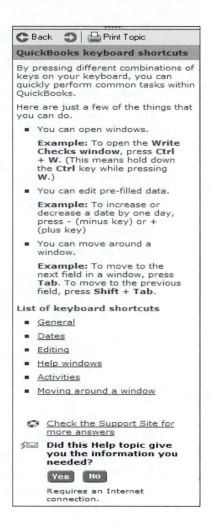

Click **General** in the list of keyboard shortcuts to see the General keyboard shortcuts

General keyboard shortcuts	
General action	**Shortcut**
To start QuickBooks without a company file	Ctrl (while opening)
To suppress the desktop windows (at Open Company window)	Alt (while opening)
Display product information about your QuickBooks version	F2
Close active window	Esc or Ctrl + F4
Record (when black border is around OK, Save and Close, Save and New, or Record)	Enter
Record (always)	Ctrl + Enter

Click the **Close** button in the upper right corner of the Help screen

QUICKBOOKS® PRO FORMS

The premise of QuickBooks Pro is to allow you to focus on running the business, not deciding whether an account is debited or credited. Transactions are entered directly onto the business form that is prepared as a result of the transaction. Behind the scenes, QuickBooks Pro enters the debit and credit to the Journal and posts to the individual accounts.

QuickBooks Pro uses several types of forms to record your daily business transactions. They are divided into two categories: forms you want to send or give to people and forms you have received. Forms to send or give to people include invoices, sales receipts, credit memos, checks, deposit slips, and purchase orders. Forms you have received include payments from customers, bills, credits for a bill, and credit card charge receipts.

You may use the forms as they come with QuickBooks Pro, you may change or modify them, or you may create your own custom forms for use in the program.

> **DO** Examine the following invoice and note the terms, icons, and buttons listed as they apply to invoices. These terms will be used throughout the text when giving instructions for entries.

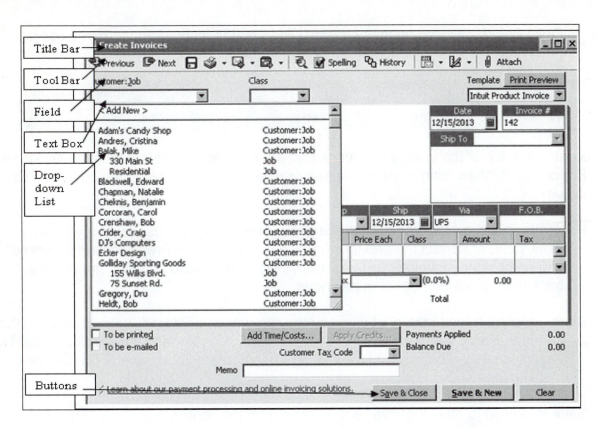

Field is an area on a form requiring information. Customer:Job is a field.

Text box is the area within a field where information may be typed or inserted. The area to be filled in to identify the Customer:Job is a text box.

Drop-down list arrow appears next to a field when there is a list of options available. On the invoice for Larry's Landscaping & Garden Supply, clicking the drop-down list arrow for Customer:Job will display the names of all customers who have accounts with the company. Clicking a customer's name will insert the name into the text box for the field.

Title bar at the top of form indicates what you are completing. In this case, it says **Create Invoices**. The title bar also contains some buttons. They include:

> **Minimize button** clicking this will remove the form from the screen but still leave it open. You may click the form on the Taskbar to re-display it.

> **Maximize** **or restore button** enlarges the form to fill the screen or restores the form to its previous size

> **Close button** closes the current screen.

- Depending on the size of your screen, the task for Create Invoices may be shown on the QuickBooks title bar. If this happens, the buttons on the title bar are applicable to the program. Clicking on the Close button on the title bar will close

QuickBooks. Clicking on the separate Close button located on the menu bar just below the one for QuickBooks will close the invoice.

Toolbar at the top of the invoice has icons that are used to give commands to QuickBooks Pro or to get information regarding linked or related transactions. Icons on the Toolbar include:

Previous is clicked to go back to the previous invoice. This is used when you want to view, print, or correct the previous invoice. Each time the Previous icon is clicked, you go back one invoice. You may click the Previous icon until you go all the way back to invoices with opening balances.

Next is clicked to go to the next invoice after the one you entered. If the invoice on the screen has not been saved, this saves the invoice and goes to the next invoice. The next invoice may be one that has already been created and saved or it may be a blank invoice.

Save is clicked to save the invoice and leave it on the screen.

Print icon is used to print the invoice on paper; to preview the invoice; to print a batch of invoices; to print packing slips, shipping labels, and envelopes; or to order business forms.

Send icon is used to e-mail invoices or to use Intuit's mail invoices subscription service.

Ship icon is used to ship merchandise via FedEx or UPS.

Find is used to find invoices previously prepared. If you are using a different business document, such as a sales receipt, Find will locate other sales receipts.

Spelling is used to check the spelling in a business document.

History allows you to view information regarding any payments that have been made on the invoice.

Letters icon is used to create letters for invoices.

Customize icon allows you to add logos and fonts, create additional customization, and manage templates.

Attach is used with a subscription to Document Management services. It allows you to attach a scanned copy of supporting documents to the invoice.

Buttons on the bottom of the invoice are used to give commands to QuickBooks Pro.

Save & Close button is clicked when all information has been entered for the invoice and you are ready for QuickBooks Pro to save the invoice and exit the Create Invoices screen.

Save & New button is clicked when all information has been entered for the invoice and you are ready to complete a new invoice.

Clear button is clicked if you want to clear the information entered on the current invoice.

QUICKBOOKS® PRO LISTS

In order to expedite entering transactions, QuickBooks Pro uses lists as an integral part of the program. Customers, vendors, sales items, and accounts are organized as lists. In fact, the chart of accounts is considered to be a list in QuickBooks Pro. Frequently, information can be entered on a form by clicking on a list item.

Most lists have a maximum. However, it's unlikely that you'll run out of room on your lists. With so many entries available, there is room to add list items "on the fly" as you work. The vendors, customers, and employees lists are all provided in the related Centers. If you open the Customer Center, the Customer List will appear on the left side of the Center as follows:

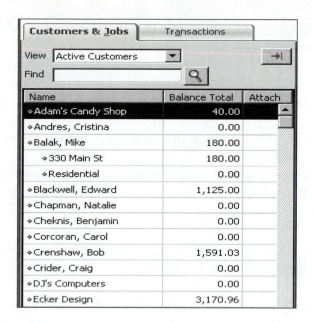

DO ▶ Examine several lists:

Click **Customer Center** to view the list of customers (in accounting concepts this is referred to as the Accounts Receivable Subsidiary Ledger), click the **Close** button to exit

Click the **Lists** menu, click **Chart of Accounts** to view the Chart of Accounts, click the **Close** button to exit

Click the **Vendor Center** to view the list of vendors (in accounting concepts this is referred to as the Accounts Payable Subsidiary Ledger), click the **Close** button to exit

QUICKBOOKS® PRO REGISTERS

QuickBooks Pro prepares a register for every balance sheet account. An account register contains records of all activity for the account. Registers provide an excellent means of looking at transactions within an account. For example, the Accounts Receivable register maintains a record of every invoice, credit memo, and payment that has been recorded for credit customers (in accounting concepts this is the Accounts Receivable account).

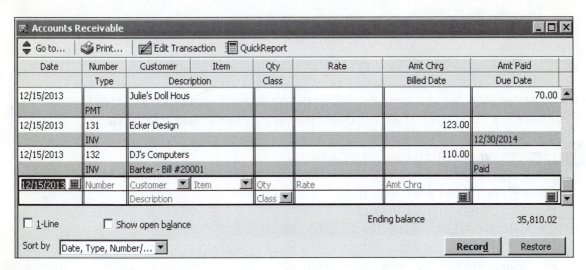

DO ▶ Examine the Accounts Receivable Register

    Click **Chart of Accounts** in the Company section of the Home Page
    Click **Accounts Receivable**
    Click the **Activities** button at the bottom of the screen
    Click **Use Register**
    Scroll through the register
    Look at the Number/Type column
    Notice the types of transactions listed:
        INV is for an invoice
        PMT indicates a payment received from a customer
    Click the **Close** button on the Register
    Click the **Close** button on the Chart of Accounts List

QUICKBOOKS® PRO REPORTS

Reports are an integral part of a business. Reports enable owners and managers to determine how the business is doing and to make decisions affecting the future of the company. Reports can be prepared showing the profit and loss for the period, the status of the Balance Sheet (assets equal liabilities plus owner's equity), information regarding accounts receivable and accounts payable, and the amount of sales for each item. QuickBooks Pro has a wide range of reports and reporting options available. Reports may be customized to better reflect the information needs of a company. Reports may be generated in a variety of ways.

Reports menu includes a complete listing of the reports available in QuickBooks Pro and is used to prepare reports including: company and financial reports such as profit and loss (income statement), balance sheet; accounts receivable reports; sales reports;

accounts payable reports; budget reports; transaction reports; transaction detail reports; payroll reports; list reports; custom reports; graphs showing graphical analysis of business operations; and several other classifications of reports.

Report Center includes a complete listing of the reports available in QuickBooks Pro. Reports may be shown in a Carousel view, a List view, and a Grid view.

▶ **DO** ▶ Prepare reports from the Reports menu

Click **Reports** on the menu bar
Point to **Company & Financial**
Click **Profit & Loss Standard**
Scroll the Profit and Loss Statement for Larry's Landscaping & Garden Supply
• Notice the Net Income for the period.
Click the **Close** button to exit the report

▶ **DO** ▶ Prepare reports using the **Report Center**

Click **Report Center** button
Click **Company & Financial** in the list of reports on the left side of the navigator if it is not already highlighted

Click the button for **List View** ▤ in the upper-right corner of the Report Center
Scroll through the list of reports available until you see Balance Sheet Standard
Click **Balance Sheet Standard**

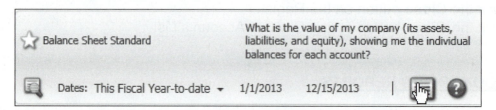

Click the **Display Report** button to view the report
Scroll through the report
• Notice that assets equal liabilities plus equity.
Do not close the report

QUICKZOOM

QuickZoom allows you to view transactions that contribute to the data on reports or graphs.

▶ **DO** Use QuickZoom

Scroll through the Balance Sheet on the screen until you see the fixed asset Truck
Position the mouse pointer over the amount for **Total Truck**

- The mouse pointer turns into 🔍.

Double-click the mouse to see the transaction detail for the Total Truck
Click the **Close** button to close the **Transactions by Account** report
Click the **Close** button to close the **Balance Sheet**
Do not close the Report Center

QUICKBOOKS® PRO GRAPHS

Using bar charts and pie charts, QuickBooks Pro gives you an instant visual analysis of different elements of your business. You may obtain information in a graphical form for Income & Expenses, Sales, Accounts Receivable, Accounts Payable, Net Worth, and Budget vs. Actual. For example, using the Report Center and Company & Financial as the type of report, clicking on Net Worth allows you to see an owner's net worth in relationship to assets and liabilities. This is displayed on a bar chart according to the month. To obtain information about liabilities for a given month, you may zoom in on the liabilities portion of the bar, double-click, and see the liabilities for the month displayed in a pie chart.

▶ **DO** View a Graph

Report Center should be on the screen
Company & Financial is the **Type of Report**
Scroll through the list of reports, click **Net Worth Graph**

Click the **Carousel View** button 🔲 to see what a Net Worth Graph looks like

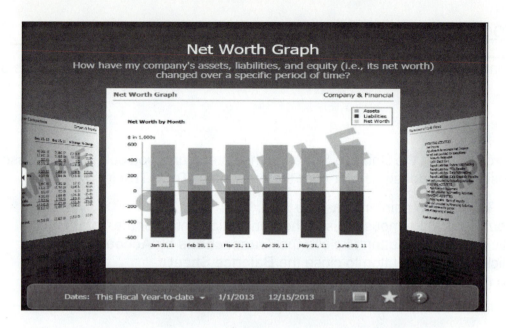

Click the **Display Report** button to display the actual report

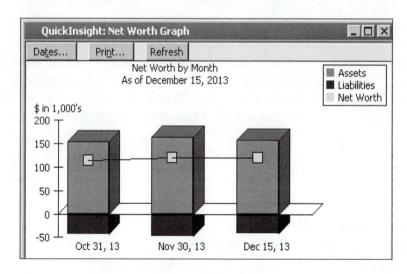

Zoom in on the Liabilities for October by pointing to the liabilities and double-clicking
View the pie chart for October's liabilities

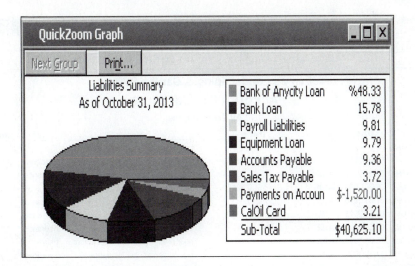

Click the **Close** button to close the pie chart
Zoom in on the Net Worth for December and double-click
View the pie chart for December's **Net Worth Summary**
Use the keyboard shortcut **Ctrl+F4** to close the pie chart
Click the **Close** button to close the **Net Worth** graph
Close the **Report Center**

QUICKREPORT

QuickReports are reports that give you detailed information about items you are viewing. They look just like standard reports that you prepare but are considered "quick" because you don't have to go through the Reports menu to create them. For example, when you are viewing the Employee List, you can obtain information about an individual employee simply by clicking the employee's name in the list, clicking the Reports button, and selecting QuickReports from the menu.

DO View a QuickReport

Click **Lists** on the menu bar
Click **Chart of Accounts**
Click **Prepaid Insurance**
Click **Reports** button at the bottom of the Chart of Accounts List
Click **QuickReport: Prepaid Insurance**

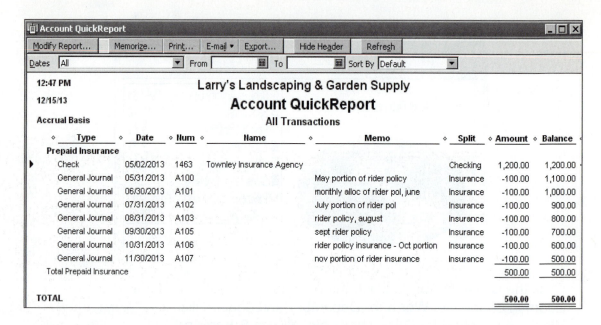

Click **Close** to close the **QuickReport**
Click **Close** to close the **Chart of Accounts**

HOW TO USE QUICKMATH

QuickMath is available for use whenever you are in a field where a calculation is to be made. Frequently, QuickBooks Pro will make calculations for you automatically; however, there may be instances when you need to perform the calculation. For example, on an invoice, QuickBooks Pro will calculate an amount based on the quantity and the rate given for a sales item. If for some reason you do not have a rate for a sales item, you may use QuickMath to calculate the amount. To do this, you tab to the amount column, type an **=** or a number and the **+**. QuickBooks Pro will show an adding machine tape on the screen. You may then add, subtract, multiply, or divide to obtain a total or a subtotal. Pressing the enter key inserts the amount into the column.

DO Use QuickMath

        Click the **Create Invoices** icon on the Home Page
        Click in the **Amount** column on the Invoice
        Enter the numbers: **123+**
                                456+
                                789

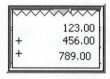

Press **Enter**
The total **1,368** is inserted into the Amount column
Click the **Clear** button at the bottom of the invoice to clear the Amount column
Press the **=** sign
Backspace to remove the **0.00** from the tape
Enter the numbers   **123+**
        456+
        789
Press **Enter**
Click **Clear** to remove the total amount of **1,368**
Click the **Close** button on the Invoice to close the invoice without saving

HOW TO USE WINDOWS® CALCULATOR

Windows includes accessory programs that may be used to complete tasks while you are working in QuickBooks. One of these accessory programs is Calculator. Using this program gives you an on-screen calculator. To use the Calculator in Windows, click Start, point to Programs, point to Accessories, click Calculator. A calculator appears on your screen. The Windows calculator is also accessible through QuickBooks.

▶ DO ▶ Access Windows Calculator through QuickBooks Pro

Click **Edit** on the menu bar
Click **Use Calculator**
Change from a standard calculator to a scientific calculator: click the **View** menu on
 the Calculator menu bar, click **Scientific**
Change back to a standard calculator: click the **View** menu on the Calculator menu
 bar, click **Standard**
Numbers may be entered by:
 Clicking the number on the calculator
 Keying the number using the numeric keypad
 Typing the keyboard numbers
 Enter the numbers: **123+**
      456+
      789+
The amount is subtotaled after each entry
 After typing 789+, the answer 1368 appears automatically
Note: Using the Windows Calculator does not insert the amount into a QuickBooks
 form.
To clear the answer, click the **C** button on the calculator
Enter: **55*6**
Press **Enter** or click **=** to get the answer 330

Click **Control menu icon** (the picture of the Calculator on the calculator title bar), click **Close** to close the **Calculator**

HOW TO CLOSE A COMPANY

The sample company—Larry's Landscaping & Garden Supply—will appear as the open company whenever you open QuickBooks Pro. In order to discontinue the use of the sample company, you must close the company. In a classroom environment, you should always back up your work and close the company you are using at the end of a work session. If you use different computers when training, not closing a company at the end of each work session may cause your files to become corrupt, your disk to fail, or leave unwanted .qbi (QuickBooks In Use) files on your data disk.

 Close a company

Click **File** menu, click **Close Company**
Close **QuickBooks**

COMPANY FILES

When working in QuickBooks, you will use files that contain data for companies that are in the text. Before beginning to use the program, you need to get a working copy of the Computer company file. This may be done by accessing the Pearson Education Web Site. Instructions follow for downloading and extracting files

DOWNLOAD COMPANY FILES

The company files for the text are available on the Prentice Hall web site
http://www.pearsonhighered.com/horne/

 Download company files

Insert your USB drive into your computer or ask you professor for specific directions to be used at your school
Open Internet Explorer
Enter the address http://www.pearsonhighered.com/horne/
Click **Company Master Files (Student Data Files)** next to the QuickBooks Pro 2010 cover image
- Note: At the time of writing, a temporary cover image was posted. The actual cover will change when the site is finalized.

- When completing the following steps, be sure to use the section for QuickBooks Pro 2010.
- Check with your instructor to determine if you will use a different procedure.

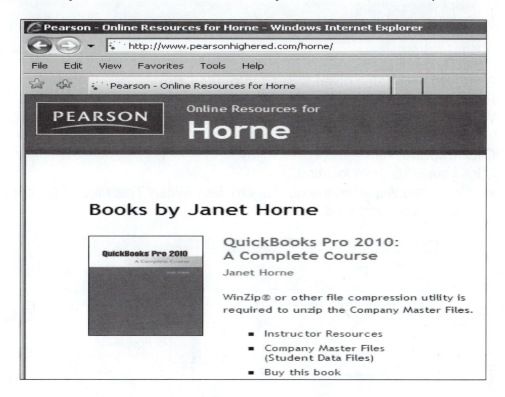

On the File Download screen, click **Save**

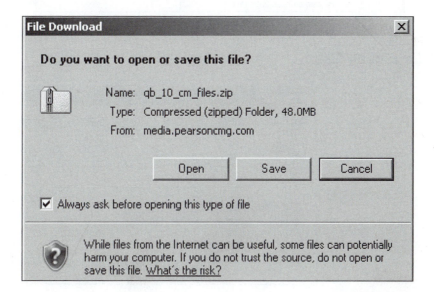

When the **Save As** screen appears, click the drop-down list arrow next to **Save In**

Click on the drive location for your USB drive
- In the example, my drive location is K:

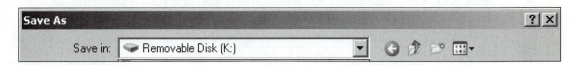

Accept the file name given **QB_10_cm_files.zip**
Click the **Save** button
When the download is complete, right-click the **Start** button in the lower-left corner of your screen
Click **Explore**
Click your USB drive location
- Notice the zipper on the qb_10_cm_files folder. This means the compressed file needs to be unzipped.

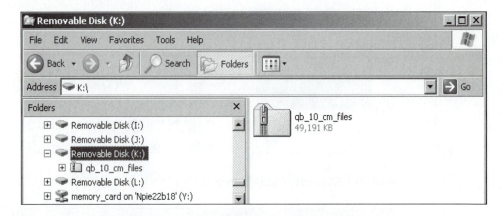

Double-click the **qb_10_cm_files** folder
Click **Extract all files**

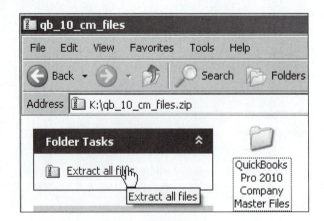

To complete the extraction Wizard, click **Next**

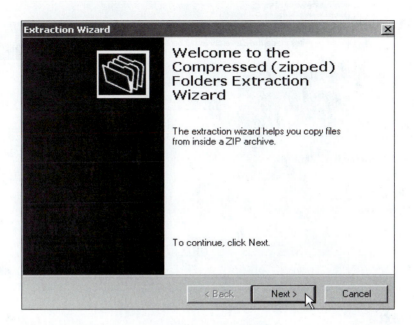

Verify the location for storage of the files, click **Next**
- In the screen shot, the files will be stored on the USB drive in location K:

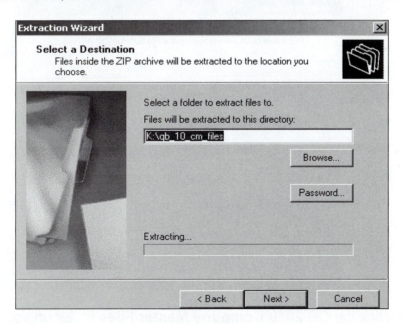

Click after K:\qb_10_cm_files, backspace until you see the letter designating your
    USB drive location

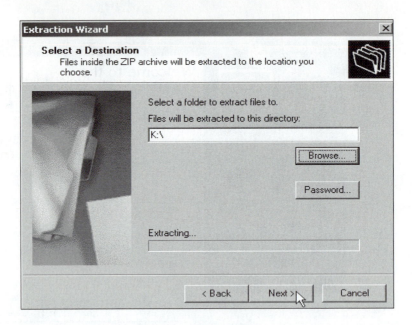

Click **Next**

When the files have been extracted, click **Finish** on the Extraction Wizard

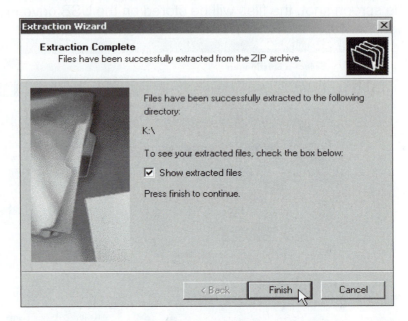

Double-click the **QB 2010 Company Master Files** folder on your USB drive

The folder will be opened and will display a list of company files

- Notice that these files are also compressed.
Double-click the file **Computer**

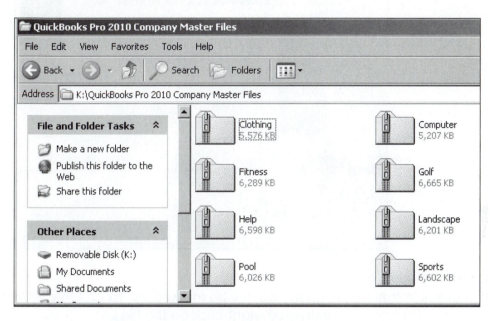

- An icon for the company file for Computer will appear.
Click the file named **Computer**, and then click **Extract all files**

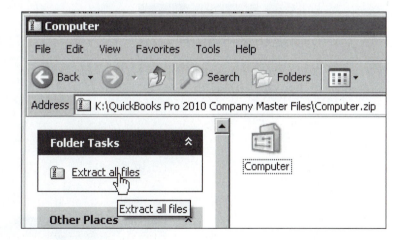

Click **Next** on the Extraction Wizard
Use the storage location shown

- This should be K:\QuickBooks Pro 2010 Company Master Files\Computer. If it is not, change the location.

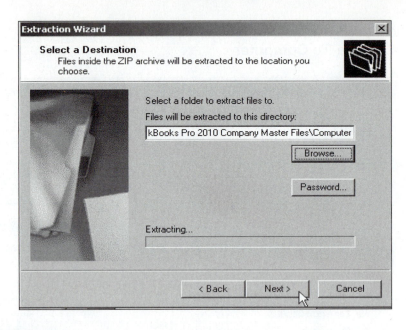

Click the **Finish** button
It is possible that the company file will be marked as "Read Only" and/or "Archive"
Once the file has been extracted, right-click on the file
Click **Properties**

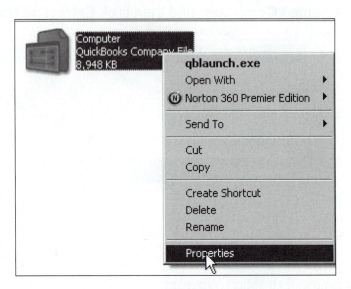

If there is a checkmark next to **Read Only** and/or **Archive**, click the check box to
    remove the mark

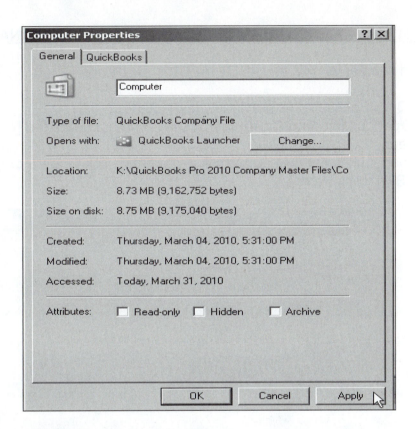

Click the **Apply** button, and then click **OK**
The file is now ready for use.

COMPUTER CONSULTING BY STUDENT'S NAME—COMPANY DESCRIPTION

In the text you will be recording transactions for a company that specializes in computer consulting. The company provides program installation, training, and technical support for today's business software as well as getting clients online and giving instruction in the use of the Internet. In addition, Computer Consulting by Student's Name will set up computer systems for customers and will install basic computer components, such as memory, modems, sound cards, disk drives, and CD and DVD drives.

This fictitious, small, sole proprietor company will be owned and run by you. You will be adding your name to the company name and equity accounts. This company will be used for training while completing Chapters 1 through 4.

OPEN A COMPANY—COMPUTER CONSULTING BY STUDENT'S NAME

DO Open a company

> Open QuickBooks Pro as previously instructed
> Click **Open an Existing Company** button at the bottom of the No Company Open screen
> The Open or Restore Company screen appears, click **Open a company file (.QBW)**, click **Next**

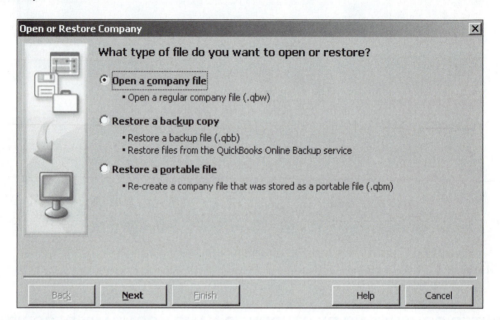

> Click the drop-down list arrow for **Look in**
> Click **Removable Disk (USB Drive Letter:)**
> Locate **Computer** (under the **Look in** text box)
> * Your company file may have an extension of **.qbw.** This is the file extension for your "QuickBooks Working" file. This is the company file that may be opened and used.
> Double-click **Computer** to open, or click **Computer** and click **Open**

VERIFYING AN OPEN COMPANY

DO ▶ Verify the title bar heading:

⚙ **Computer Consulting by Student's Name - QuickBooks Pro 2010**

Unless you tell QuickBooks Pro to create a new company, open a different company, or close the company, Computer Consulting by Student's Name will appear as the open company whenever you open QuickBooks Pro. However, when you finish a work session, you should always close the company in order to avoid problems with the file in a future work session.

SETTING UP YOUR INTUIT ACCOUNT

In QuickBooks 2010, Intuit makes it possible to setup an account used for online services including the creation of a free website, getting business advice and tips, and extra services for Google and Yahoo. Since none of the companies you use in the text are actual businesses, you should not setup an online account. If you get this screen, click the Exit or Close button.

QUICKBOOKS LEARNING CENTER

QuickBooks has an optional window that may be shown when a company is open. This is called the QuickBooks Learning Center. It contains information and short tutorials on how to use QuickBooks and lists new materials for the current version of the software. This may be shown whenever you open the company or you may select not to have it shown.

> **DO**   If the QuickBooks Learning Center is on the screen, close it and begin using QuickBooks

    If the Learning Center is on the screen, click the checkbox for **Show this window at startup** to remove the check
Click the **Go to QuickBooks** button

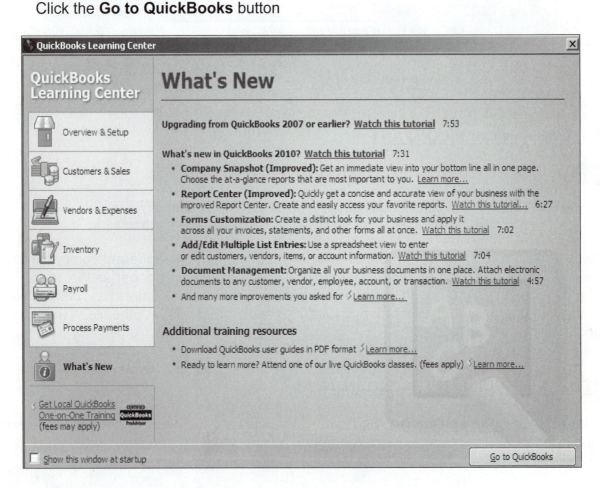

QUICKBOOKS OPENING SCREENS

Sometimes company files open with screens such as QuickBooks Products and Services, QuickBooks Alerts, QuickBooks Coach, and others. These screens provide information and/or instructions on how to use QuickBooks, how to subscribe to optional services, or give information regarding reminder alerts. In addition, QuickBooks may open business forms with wizards, questions, or tutorials regarding options, methods of work, and other items.

DO ▶ If the QuickBooks Products and Services screen appears, click the **Close** button

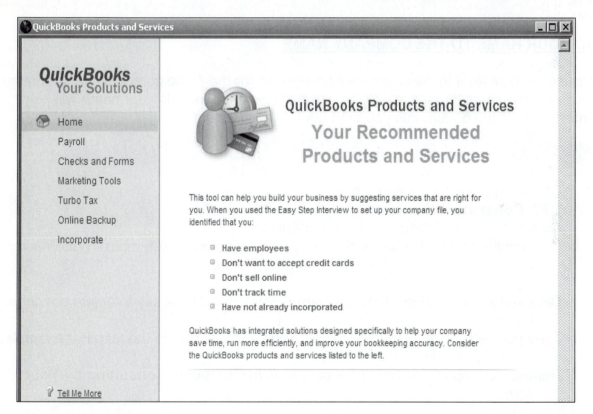

- If any other screens appear, such as setting up your internet account, click the Close button.

DO ▶ If any Alert screens appear, click **Mark as Done**

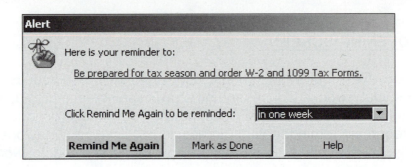

- In addition, if you open a business document, such as an Invoice, and get a payment interview, click the Close button to close the interview.

ADD YOUR NAME TO THE COMPANY NAME

Because each student in the course will be working for the same companies and printing the same documents, personalizing the company name to include your name will help identify many of the documents you print during your training.

DO Add your name to the company name

Click **Company** on the menu bar
Click **Company Information**
Click to the right of **Computer Consulting by**
Replace the words **Student's Name** by holding down the left mouse button and dragging through the "Student's Name" to highlight
OR
Click in front of the S in Student's Name, press the **Delete** key to delete one letter at a time
Type your actual name, *not* the words *Your Name* shown in the text. For example, Jeff Jones would type **Jeff Jones**
Repeat the steps to change the legal name to **Computer Consulting by Your Name**
Click **OK**

- The title bar now shows **Computer Consulting by Your Name – QuickBooks Pro 2010**

HOW TO CREATE A COMPANY BACKUP FILE

As you work with a company and record transactions, it is important to back up your work. This allows you to keep the information for a particular period separate from current information. A backup also allows you to restore information in case your data disk becomes damaged. QuickBooks Pro has a feature to make a backup copy of your company file. A condensed file is created by QuickBooks. The file contains the essential transaction and account information. This file has a **.qbb** extension and is <u>not</u> usable unless it is restored to a company file that has a **.qbw** extension. This can be an existing company file or a new company file.

In this text, you will make a backup file at the end of each chapter. It will contain all of the transactions entered up until the time you made the backup. At the end of each chapter, you will be instructed to make a backup file for the chapter. *Future transactions will not be part of the backup file unless you make a new backup file.* For example, Chapter 1 backup will not contain any transactions entered in Chapter 2. However, Chapter 2 backup will contain all the transactions for both Chapters 1 and 2. Chapter 3 backup will contain all the transactions for Chapters 1, 2, and 3, and so on.

In many classroom configurations, you will be storing your backup files onto the same USB drive that you use for the company file. In actual business practice, you should save the backup to a different location. Most likely, you will store your company file on the hard disk of the computer and the backup file will be stored on a USB drive, a network drive, or some other remote location. Check with your instructor to see if there are any other backup file locations you should use in your training.

▶ **DO** ▶ Make a QuickBooks Pro backup of the company data for Computer Consulting by Your Name.

> Click **File** on the Menu Bar
> Click **Save Copy or Back Up...**
> On the Save Copy or Backup screen, click **Backup copy**, then click the **Next** button

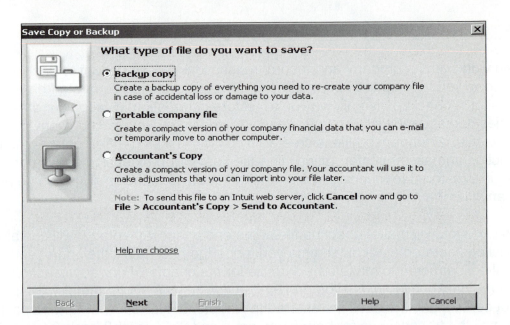

To indicate whether you want to save the backup locally or online, click **Local backup**, then click the **Next** button

You will either get a screen with **Backup Options** or a **Save Copy or Backup** screen

If you get the **Backup Options** screen, complete the following:

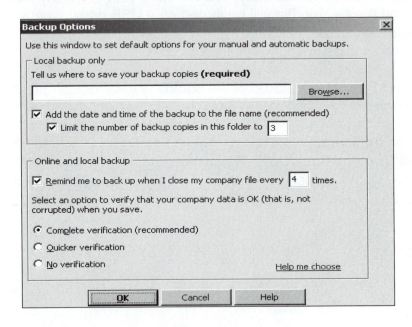

Complete the screen by indicating the USB Drive Location

• The text uses (K:\)

Click the checkboxes for **Add the date and time of the backup to the file name** and **Remind me to back up when I close my company file** to remove the check marks

Keep **Complete verification**

Click **OK**

To complete the **Save Copy or Backup** screen, click **Save it now**, then click the **Next** button

If you are saving the backup file to the same USB drive that you are using to store the company file, you will get the following screen

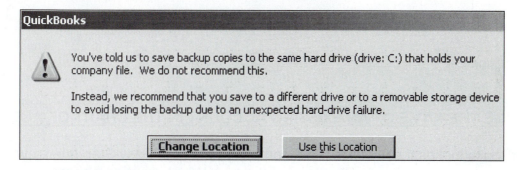

Click **Use this Location**

On the Save Backup Copy screen, **Save in:** should be **USB Drive Location**

• If necessary, click the drop-down list arrow next to Save in: and click the USB Drive Location

Change the File Name to **Computer (Backup Ch. 1)**

Save as type: **QBW Backup (*.QBB)**

Click the **Save** button

- QuickBooks Pro will back up the information for Computer Consulting by Your Name on the USB disk

When the backup is complete, you will see the following screen

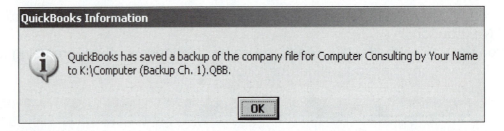

Click **OK**

CHANGE THE NAME OF AN EXISTING ACCOUNT IN THE CHART OF ACCOUNTS

QuickBooks makes it easy to set up a company using the Easy Step Interview. You will create a company for use in Chapter 9 of the text. When creating a company using QuickBooks' Easy Step Interview, account names are assigned automatically. They might need to be changed to names more appropriate to the individual company. Even if an account has been used to record transactions or has a balance, the name can still be changed.

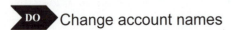 Change account names

Access the **Chart of Accounts**:
Click **Lists** on the menu bar, click **Chart of Accounts**
Scroll through accounts until you see Student's Name Capital
Click **Student's Name Capital**
Click the **Account** button at the bottom of the Chart of Accounts
Click **Edit Account**
On the **Edit Account** screen, highlight **Student's Name**
Enter y*our actual name*
Click the **Save and Close** button

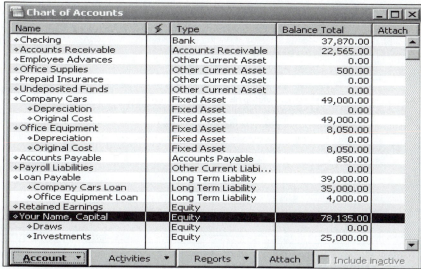

Close the **Chart of Accounts**

RESTORE A COMPANY BACKUP FILE

If you make an error in your training, you may find it beneficial to restore your .qbb backup file. The only way in which a .qbb backup file may be used is by restoring it to a .qbw company file. Using QuickBooks' Restore command on the File menu restores a backup file. A restored backup file replaces the current data in your company file with the data in the backup file so any transactions recorded after the backup was made will be erased.

DO ▶ Practice restoring a backup file after a change has been made in the company file

Click **File** on the menu bar
Click **Open or Restore Company…**
Click **Restore a backup copy**, then click the **Next** button

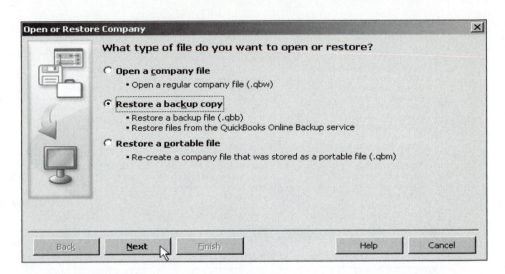

Click **Local backup**, then click the **Next** button

On the Open Backup Copy screen, make sure that Look in: shows the name of your **USB Drive** location

The File name: should be **Computer (Backup Ch. 1)**, if necessary, click the file name to insert it

Click the **Open** button

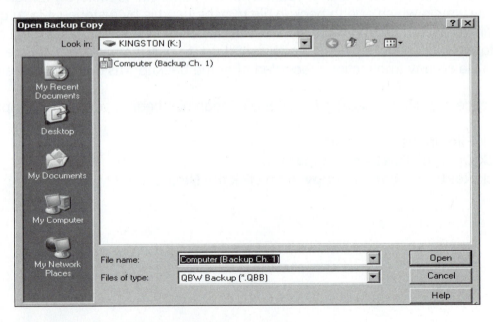

Click the **Next** button on "Where do you want to restore the file?"

Save in: should be your **USB Drive Location**

File name: should be **Computer**

Click the **Save** button

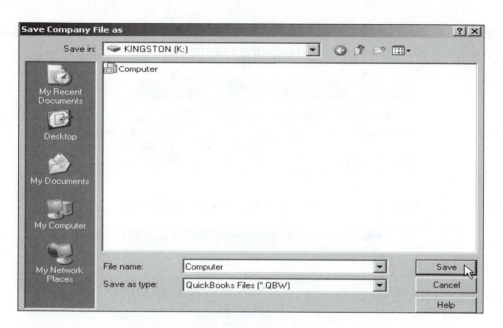

You may get a screen asking "Where do you want to restore the file?"

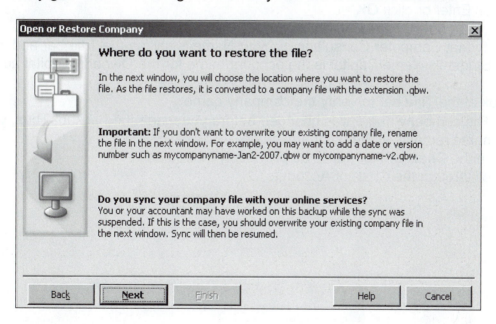

If so, click **Next**
Save in: should be the location of your USB drive (K:\)
The file name should be **Computer**
Click **Save**
Click **Yes** on the screen telling you the file already exists
• You will get a **Delete Entire File** warning screen
Enter the word **Yes** and click **OK**

- When you restore a file to an existing company file, all the data contained in the company file will be replaced with the information in the backup file.

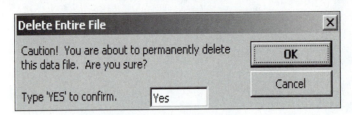

When the file has been restored, you will get the following

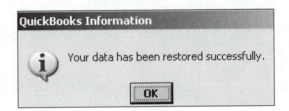

Press Enter or click **OK**

DO ▶ Verify that Computer Consulting by Your Name is still on the Title bar and that Student's Name Capital is the account name for the Owner's Capital account.

Look at the Title bar to verify the company name
- The company name was changed before you made the backup. Thus, your name remains in the company name.

Open the **Chart of Accounts** as previously instructed

Scroll through the Chart of Accounts

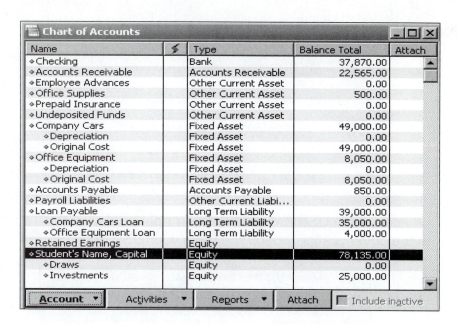

- Your Name Capital no longer shows because the company information was restored from the backup file made prior to changing the account name.

CREATE A DUPLICATE USB DRIVE

In addition to making a backup of the company file, you should always have a duplicate of the USB drive you use for your work. Follow the instructions provided by your instructor to copy your files to another USB drive.

EXIT QUICKBOOKS® PRO AND REMOVE YOUR USB DRIVE

When you complete your work, you need to exit the QuickBooks Pro program. If you are saving work on a separate data disk or USB drive, you must not remove your disk until you exit the program. Following the appropriate steps to close and exit a program is extremely important. There are program and data files that must be closed in order to leave the program and company data so that they are ready to be used again. It is common for a beginning computer user to turn off the computer without exiting a program. This can cause corrupt program and data files and can make a disk or program unusable.

DO Close the company file for Computer Consulting by Your Name, close QuickBooks, and stop the USB

Close the company file following the steps indicated earlier
Close QuickBooks by clicking the **Close** button in upper right corner of title bar

If you get a message box for Exiting QuickBooks, click **Yes**

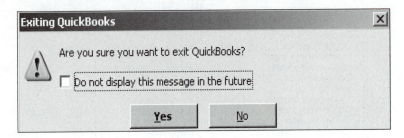

Click the icon for the USB drive in the lower right portion of the Taskbar
Click on the drive location where you have your USB drive

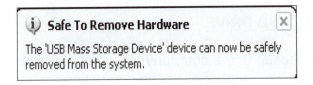

When you get the message that it is safe to remove hardware or when the light goes out on your USB drive, remove your USB

SUMMARY

Chapter 1 provides general information regarding QuickBooks Pro. In this chapter, various QuickBooks features were examined. A company file was opened, your name was added to the company name, and an account name was changed. QuickBooks backup files were made and restored. Companies were closed, QuickBooks was closed, and USB drives were removed.

END-OF-CHAPTER QUESTIONS

TRUE/FALSE

ANSWER THE FOLLOWING QUESTIONS IN THE SPACE PROVIDED BEFORE THE QUESTION NUMBER.

_____ 1. There are various methods of giving QuickBooks Pro commands, including use of QuickBooks Home Page, icon bar, menu bar, and keyboard shortcuts.

_____ 2. A company file with a .qbw extension is used to record transactions.

_____ 3. Once an account has been used, the name cannot be changed.

_____ 4. If an error is made when entering a transaction, QuickBooks Pro will not allow the user to return to the business document and make the correction.

_____ 5. In a computerized accounting system, each transaction that is analyzed must be entered by hand into the appropriate journal and posted to the appropriate ledger.

_____ 6. QuickBooks Home Page appears beneath the title bar and has a list of drop-down menus.

_____ 7. If you use QuickBooks Pro to make a backup, you are actually having QuickBooks Pro create a condensed file that contains the essential transaction and account information.

_____ 8. The Alt key + a letter are used to access the drop-down menus on the menu bar.

_____ 9. When you end your work session, you must close your company, close QuickBooks, and remove your USB drive properly.

_____ 10. QuickBooks Learning Center must be shown whenever you open the company.

MULTIPLE CHOICE

WRITE THE LETTER OF THE CORRECT ANSWER IN THE SPACE PROVIDED
BEFORE THE QUESTION NUMBER.

_____ 1. The extension for a company file that may be used to enter transactions is
   A. .qbi
   B. .qbb
   C. .qbw
   D. .qbc

_____ 2. A (n) ___ is considered to be a list in QuickBooks Pro.
   A. Invoice
   B. Chart of Accounts
   C. Company
   D. none of the above

_____ 3. QuickBooks Pro keyboard conventions ___.
   A. are keyboard command shortcuts
   B. use the mouse
   C. use certain keys in a manner consistent with Windows
   D. incorporate the use of QuickBooks Company Center

_____ 4. Buttons on the toolbar and on the bottom of an invoice are used to ___.
   A. give commands to QuickBooks Pro
   B. exit QuickBooks Pro
   C. prepare reports
   D. show graphs of invoices prepared

_____ 5. QuickMath displays ___.
   A. a calculator
   B. an adding machine tape
   C. a calculator with adding machine tape
   D. none of the above

_____ 6. QuickBooks Home Page ___.
   A. allows you to give commands to QuickBooks Pro according to the type of
       transaction being entered
   B. are icons shown in a row beneath the menu bar
   C. appears above the menu bar
   D. appears at the bottom of the screen

_____ 7. An icon is ___.
    A. a document
    B. a picture
    C. a chart
    D. a type of software

_____ 8. A way to find out the keyboard shortcuts for various commands is to look them up using ___.
    A. the Internet
    B. Help
    C. the File menu
    D. a Keyboard icon

_____ 9. A .qbb extension on a file name means that the file is ___.
    A. open
    B. the working file
    C. a restored file
    D. a backup file

_____ 10. To verify the name of the open company, look at ___.
    A. the icon bar
    B. QuickBooks Home Page
    C. the menu bar
    D. the title bar

FILL-IN

IN THE SPACE PROVIDED, WRITE THE ANSWER THAT MOST APPROPRIATELY COMPLETES THE SENTENCE.

1. Whether you are using a manual or a computerized accounting system, transactions must still be _____ and _____.

2. The _____ menu is used to open and close a company and may also be used to exit QuickBooks Pro.

3. The name of the company file in use is displayed on the _____.

4. In QuickBooks you may change the company name by clicking Company Information on the _____ menu.

5. The _____ organizes tasks into logical groups (Vendors, Customers, Employees, Company, and Banking).

SHORT ESSAY

Describe the importance of making a backup of a company file and explain what will happen to transactions entered today if a backup from an earlier date is restored.

_____
_____
_____
_____
_____
_____
_____
_____
_____
_____
_____
_____
_____
_____.

END-OF-CHAPTER PROBLEM

At the end of each chapter, you will work with a different company and enter transactions that are similar to the ones you competed in the text. Follow the instructions given for transaction entry and printing. You may refer to the chapter for assistance.

YOUR NAME LANDSCAPE & POOL SERVICE

Your Name Landscape and Pool Service is owned and operated by you. Laura Lewis and Lupe Gonzalez also work for the company. Laura manages the office and keeps the books for the business. Lupe provides lawn maintenance and supervises the lawn maintenance employees. You provide the pool maintenance. The company is located in Santa Barbara, California.

INSTRUCTIONS

▶ Download the company file for Student's Name Landscape and Pool Service, **Landscape.qbw**, as instructed in the chapter.
▶ Open the company.
▶ If the Learning Center appears, click **Show this window at start up** to remove the check mark on the QuickBooks Learning Center, and then click **Begin Using QuickBooks**.
▶ Add your name to the company name. The company name will be **Your Name Landscape and Pool Service**. (Type your actual name, *not* the words *Your Name*. Do this whenever you are instructed to add *Your Name*.)
▶ Backup your file to **Landscape (Backup Ch. 1)**
▶ Change the name of Student's Name, Capital to **Your Name, Capital**
▶ Restore the Landscape (Backup Ch 1) file.

SALES AND RECEIVABLES: SERVICE BUSINESS

LEARNING OBJECTIVES

At the completion of this chapter, you will be able to:

1. Create invoices and record sales transactions on account.
2. Create sales receipts to record cash sales.
3. Edit, void, and delete invoices/sales receipts.
4. Create credit memos/refunds.
6. Add new customers and modify customer records.
7. Record cash receipts.
8. Enter partial cash payments.
9. Display and print invoices, sales receipts, and credit memos.
10. Display and print Quick Reports, Customer Balance Summary Reports, Customer Balance Detail Reports, and Transaction Reports by Customer.
11. Display and print Summary Sales by Item Reports and Itemized Sales by Item Reports.
12. Display and print Deposit Summary, Journal Reports, and Trial Balance.
13. Display Accounts Receivable Graphs and Sales Graphs.

ACCOUNTING FOR SALES AND RECEIVABLES

Rather than use a traditional Sales Journal to record sales on account using debits and credits and special columns, QuickBooks Pro uses an invoice to record sales transactions for accounts receivable in the Accounts Receivable Register. Because cash sales do not involve accounts receivable and would be recorded in the Cash Receipts Journal in traditional accounting, the transactions are recorded on a Sales Receipt. However, all transactions, regardless of the activity, are placed in the General Journal behind the scenes.

QuickBooks Pro puts the money received from a cash sale and from a customer's payment on account into the Undeposited Funds account. When a bank deposit is made the Undeposited Funds are placed in the Checking or Cash account.

A new customer can be added on the fly as transactions are entered. Unlike many computerized accounting programs, in QuickBooks Pro, error correction is easy. A sales form may be edited, voided, or deleted in the same window where it was created. Customer information may be changed by editing the Customer in the Customer Center.

A multitude of reports are available when using QuickBooks Pro. Accounts receivable reports include Customer Balance Summary and Balance Detail reports. Sales reports provide information regarding the amount of sales by item. Transaction Reports by Customer are available as well as the traditional accounting reports such as Trial Balance, Profit and Loss, and Balance Sheet. QuickBooks Pro also has graphing capabilities so you can see and evaluate your accounts receivable and sales at the click of a button.

TRAINING TUTORIAL

The following tutorial is a step-by-step guide to recording sales (both cash and credit), customer payments, bank deposits, and other transactions for receivables for a fictitious company with fictitious employees. This company was used in Chapter 1 and is called Computer Consulting by Your Name. In addition to recording transactions using QuickBooks Pro, we will prepare several reports and graphs for the company. The tutorial for Computer Consulting by Your Name will continue in Chapters 3 and 4, where accounting for payables, bank reconciliations, financial statement preparation, and closing an accounting period will be completed.

TRAINING PROCEDURES

To maximize the training benefits, you should:

1. Read the entire chapter *before* beginning the tutorial within the chapter.
2. Answer the end-of-chapter questions.
3. Be aware that transactions to be entered are given within a **MEMO**.
4. Complete all the steps listed for the Computer Consulting by Your Name tutorial in the chapter. (Indicated by: ▶ **DO**
5. When you have completed a section, put a check mark next to the final step completed.
6. If you do not complete a section, put the date in the margin next to the last step completed. This will make it easier to know where to begin when training is resumed.
7. As you complete your work, proofread carefully and check for accuracy. Double-check amounts of money and the accounts, items, and dates used.

8. If you find an error while preparing a transaction, correct it. If you find the error after the Invoice, Sales Form, Credit Memo, or Customer:Job List is complete, follow the steps indicated in this chapter to correct, void, or delete transactions.
9. Print as directed within the chapter.
10. You may not finish the entire chapter in one computer session. Always use QuickBooks Pro to back up your work at the end of your work session as described in Chapter 1. Make a duplicate copy of your USB drive as instructed by your professor.
11. When you complete your computer session, always close your company. If you try to use a computer and a previous student did not close the company, QuickBooks Pro may freeze when you start to work. In addition, if you do not close the company as you leave, you may have problems with your company file, your USB drive may be damaged, and you may have unwanted .qbi (QuickBooks In Use) files that cause problems when using the company file.

DATES

Throughout the text, the year used for the screen shots is 2010, which is the same year as the version of the program. You may want to check with your instructor to see if you should use 2010 as the year for the transactions.

Always pay special attention to the dates when recording transactions. It is not unusual to forget to enter the date that appears in the text and to use the date of the computer for a transaction. This can cause errors in reports and other entries. There will be times when you can tell QuickBooks which date to use such as, business documents and some reports. There will be other instances when QuickBooks automatically inserts the date of the computer, and it cannot be changed. This will occur later in the chapter when you print the bank deposit summary. When this happens, accept QuickBooks' printed date.

COMPANY FILE

In Chapter 1, you began using the company. You changed the name from Computer Consulting by Student's Name to Computer Consulting by Your Name. A backup of the file was made. An account name was changed. The backup file was restored and you learned that the account name change had been replaced by the name in the backup file. During Chapters 2-4, you will continue to use the Computer.qbw file originally used in Chapter 1 to record transactions.

COMPANY PROFILE: COMPUTER CONSULTING BY YOUR NAME

As you learned in Chapter 1, Computer Consulting by Your Name is a company specializing in computer consulting. The company provides program installation, training, and technical support for today's business software as well as getting clients online and giving instruction in the use of the Internet. In addition, Computer Consulting by Your Name will set up computer systems for customers and will install basic computer components, such as memory, modems, sound cards, disk drives, and DVD and CD-ROM drives.

Computer Consulting by Your Name is located in Southern California and is a sole proprietorship owned by you. You are involved in all aspects of the business and have the responsibility of obtaining clients. There are three employees: Jennifer Lockwood, who is responsible for software training; Rom Levy, who handles hardware and network installation and technical support; and Alhandra Cruz, whose duties include being office manager and bookkeeper and providing technical support.

Computer Consulting by Your Name bills by the hour for training and hardware and network installation with a minimum charge of $95 for the first hour and $80 per hour thereafter. Clients with contracts for technical support are charged a monthly rate for service.

BEGIN TRAINING IN QUICKBOOKS® PRO

As you continue this chapter, you will be instructed to enter transactions for Computer Consulting by Your Name. As you learned in Chapter 1, the first thing you must do in order to work is boot up or start your computer, open the program QuickBooks Pro, and open the company.

▶ DO ▶Refer to Chapter 1 to Open QuickBooks Pro

OPEN A COMPANY—COMPUTER CONSULTING BY YOUR NAME

In Chapter 1, Computer Consulting by Your Name was opened and a backup of the company file was made using QuickBooks Pro. Computer Consulting by Your Name should have been closed in Chapter 1. To open the company for this work session you may click the Open an Existing Company button on the No Company Open screen or by clicking on File menu and Open Company. Verify this by checking the title bar.

▶ DO ▶Open **Computer Consulting by Your Name**

Click **Open or Restore an Existing Company** button at the bottom of the No
    Company Open screen
        OR
Click **File** on the Menu bar and click **Open or Restore Company**

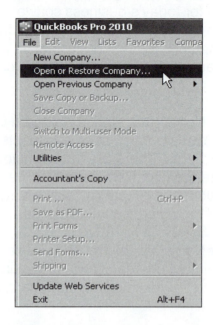

Open a Company File should be selected, click **Next**.
Click the drop-down list arrow for **Look in**
Click **Removable Disk (USB Drive Location:)**
Locate **Computer** (under the **Look in** text box)

• Your company file may have an extension of **.qbw.** This is the file extension
    for your "QuickBooks Working" file. This is the company file that may be
    opened and used. As you learned in Chapter 1, you may not use a .qbb
    (backup) file for direct entry. A backup file must be restored to a .qbw
    (company) file.

Double-click **Computer** to open, or click **Computer** and click **Open**

•   Remember, this is the same file you used in Chapter 1.

VERIFYING AN OPEN COMPANY

DO ▶ Verify the title bar heading:

> **Computer Consulting by Your Name - QuickBooks Pro 2010**

•   The title bar should show **Computer Consulting by Your Name** as the company name. (Remember you will have your actual name in the title.)
•   *Note:* Unless you tell QuickBooks Pro to create a new company, open a different company, or close the company, Computer Consulting by Your Name will appear as the open company whenever you open QuickBooks Pro. However, when you finish a work session, you should always close the company in order to avoid problems with the file in a future work session.

QUICKBOOKS® HOME PAGE AND CENTERS

The QuickBooks Home Page allows you to give commands to QuickBooks Pro according to the type of transaction being entered. The Home Page tasks are organized into logical groups (Vendors, Customers, Employees, Company, and Banking). Each of the areas on the Home Page is used to enter different types of transactions. When appropriate, the Home Page shows a flow chart with icons indicating the major activities performed. The icons are arranged in the order in which transactions usually occur and are clicked to access screens in order to enter information or transactions in QuickBooks Pro. You may also choose to use the menu bar, the icon bar, or the keyboard to give commands to QuickBooks Pro. For more detailed information regarding the QuickBooks Home Page, refer to Chapter 1. Instructions in this text will be given primarily using the QuickBooks Home Page. However, the menu bar, the icon bar, and/or keyboard methods will be used as well.

At the top of the Home Page and below the menu bar, are a series of buttons that allow access to QuickBooks Centers. These are the Vendor, Customer, Employee, Report, Banking, Online, and Apps centers. The centers focus on providing detailed information and accessing the lists associated with the center.

BEGINNING THE TUTORIAL

In this chapter you will be entering accounts receivable transactions, cash sales transactions, receipts for payments on account, and bank deposits. Much of the organization of QuickBooks Pro is dependent on lists. The two primary types of lists you will use in the tutorial for receivables are a Customers & Jobs List and a Sales Item List.

The names, addresses, telephone numbers, credit terms, credit limits, and balances for all established credit customers are contained in the Customer & Jobs List in the Customer Center. The Customer Center can also be referred to as the Accounts Receivable Ledger. QuickBooks Pro does not use this term; however, the Customer Center does function as the Accounts Receivable Ledger. A transaction entry for an individual customer is posted to the customer's account in the Customer Center just as it would be posted to the customer's individual account in an Accounts Receivable Ledger.

The balance of the Customer & Jobs List in the Customer Center will be equal to the balance of the Accounts Receivable account in the Chart of Accounts, which is also the General Ledger. Invoices and accounts receivable transactions can also be related to specific jobs you are completing for customers. To see the balance of all customers, click the Transactions tab.

You will be using the following Customers & Jobs List in the Customer Center for established credit customers.

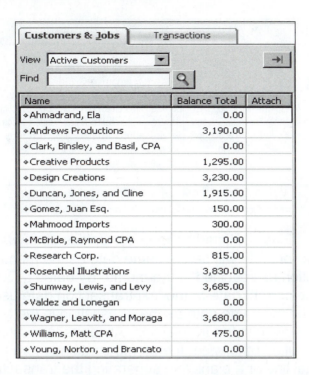

Note: When you display the Customers & Jobs list in the Customer Center, the customer names may not be displayed in full. The lists shown in the text have been formatted to show the names in full.

Various types of income are considered to be sales. In Computer Consulting by Your Name, there are several income accounts. In addition, there are categories within an income account. For example, Computer Consulting by Your Name uses Training Income to represent revenues earned by providing on-site training. The sales items used for Training Income are Training 1 for the first or initial hour of on-site training and Training 2 for all additional hours of on-site training. As you look at the Item List, you will observe that the rates for the two items are different. Using lists for sales items allows for flexibility in billing and a more accurate representation of the way in which income is earned. The following Item List for the various types of sales will be used for the company.

In the tutorial all transactions are listed on memos. Unless otherwise specified within the transaction, the transaction date will be the same date as the memo date. Always enter the date of the transaction as specified in the memo. By default, QuickBooks Pro automatically enters the current date or the last transaction date used. In many instances, this will not be the same date as the transaction in the text. Customer names, when necessary, will be given in the transaction. All terms for customers on account are Net 30 days unless specified otherwise. If a memo contains more than one transaction, there will be a horizontal line or a blank line separating the transactions.

MEMO

DATE: The transaction date is listed here

Transaction details are given in the body of the memo. Customer names, the type of transaction, amounts of money, and any other details needed are listed here.

Even when you are given instructions on how to enter a transaction step by step, you should always refer to the memo for transaction details. Once a specific type of transaction has been entered in a step-by-step manner, additional transactions will be made without having instructions provided. Of course, you may always refer to instructions given for previous transactions for ideas or for the steps used to enter those transactions. Again, always double-check the date and the year used for the transaction. QuickBooks automatically inserts the computer's current date, which will probably be quite different from the date in the text. Using an incorrect date will cause reports to have different totals and contain different transactions than those shown in the text.

ENTER SALE ON ACCOUNT

Because QuickBooks Pro operates on a business form premise, a sale on account is entered via an invoice. You prepare an invoice, and QuickBooks Pro records the transaction in the Journal and updates the customer's account automatically.

MEMO:

DATE: January 2, 2010

Bill the following: Invoice No. 1—Juan Gomez has had several questions regarding his new computer system. He spoke with you about this and has signed up for 10 hours of technical support (Tech Sup 2) for January. Bill him for this and use <u>Thank you for your business.</u> as the message.

DO ▶ Record the sale on account shown in the invoice above. This invoice is used to bill a customer for a sale using one sales item:

Click the **Create Invoices** icon on the Home Page
- A blank invoice will show on the screen.

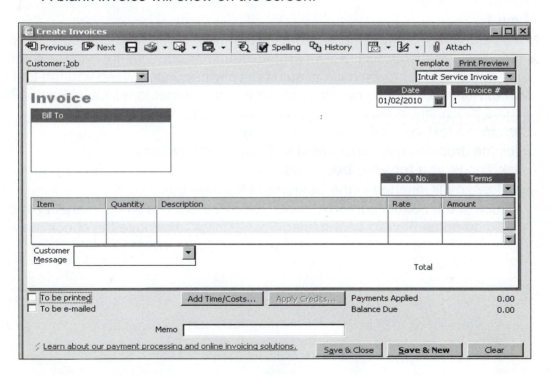

Click the drop-down list arrow next to **Customer:Job**
Click **Gomez, Juan Esq.**

- His name is entered as Customer:Job, and Bill To information is completed automatically.

Tab two times to highlight **Intuit Service Invoice**

- Intuit Service Invoice should be displayed in the text box beneath Template. If it is not, click the drop-down list arrow next to the Customize button, click **Intuit Service Invoice**.

Tab to **Date**

- When you tab to the date, it will be highlighted. When you type in the new date, the highlighted date will be overwritten.

Type **01/02/10** as the date

Invoice No. 1 should be showing in the **Invoice No.** box

- The Invoice No. should not have to be changed.

There is no PO No. (Purchase Order Number) to record

Terms should be indicated as **Net 30**

- If not, click the drop-down list arrow next to **Terms** and click **Net 30**.

Tab to or click the first line beneath **Item**

Click the drop-down list arrow next to **Item**

- Refer to the memo above and the Item List for appropriate billing information.

Click **Tech Sup 2** to bill for 10 hours of technical support

- Tech Sup 2 is entered as the Item.

Tab to or click **Qty**

Type **1**

- The quantity is one because you are billing for 1 unit of Tech Sup 2. As you can see on the Item List, Tech Sup 2 is for 10 hours of support. The total for the item and for the invoice is automatically calculated when you tab to the next item or click in a new invoice area. If you forget to tell QuickBooks Pro to use a quantity, it will automatically calculate the quantity as 1.

Click in the textbox for **Customer Message**

Click the drop-down list arrow next to **Customer Message**

Click **Thank you for your business.**

- Message is inserted in the Customer Message box.
- Look at the bottom portion of the Invoice. If there is a check mark in either the "To be printed" or To be e-mailed," boxes click to remove the check mark.

EDIT AND CORRECT ERRORS

If an error is discovered while entering invoice information, it may be corrected by positioning the cursor in the field containing the error. You may do this by clicking in the field containing the error, tabbing to move forward through each field, or pressing Shift+Tab to move back to the field containing the error. If the error is highlighted, type the correction. If the error is not highlighted, you can correct the error by pressing the backspace or the delete key as many times as necessary to remove the error, then typing the correction. (Alternate method: Point to the error, highlight by dragging the mouse through the error, then type the correction or press the Delete key to remove completely.)

▶ **DO**   Practice editing and making corrections to Invoice No. 1

Click the drop-down list arrow next to **Customer:Job**
Click **Williams, Matt CPA**
• Name is changed in Customer:Job and Bill To information is also changed.
Click to the left of the first number in the **Date**—this is **0**
Hold down primary mouse button and drag through the date to highlight.
Type **10/24/10** as the date
• This removes the 01/02/2010 date originally entered.
Click to the right of the **1** in **Quantity**
Backspace and type a **2**
Press **Tab** to see how QuickBooks automatically calculates the new total
To eliminate the changes made to Invoice No. 1, click the drop-down list arrow next to **Customer:Job**
Click **Gomez, Juan, Esq.**
Tab to the Date textbox to highlight the date
Type **01/02/10**
Click to the right of the **2** in **Quantity**
Backspace and type a **1**
Press the **Tab** key
• This will cause QuickBooks Pro to calculate the amount and the total for the invoice and will move the cursor to the Description field.
• Invoice No. 1 has been returned to the correct customer, date, and quantity. Compare the information you entered with the information provided in the memo.

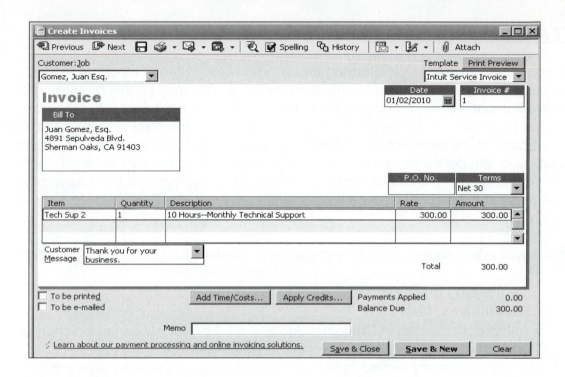

PRINT AN INVOICE

DO With Invoice No. 1 on the screen, print the invoice immediately after entering information

Click the **Print** icon (looks like a printer) at the top of the **Create Invoices** screen
- If you click the drop-down list arrow for the Print button, you will get a list of printing options. Click the **Print** option.

Check the information on the **Print One Invoice Settings** tab:

Printer name (should identify the type of printer you are using):
- This may be different from the printer identified in this text.

Printer type: Page-oriented (Single sheets)

Print on: Blank paper
- The circle next to this should be filled. If it is not, click the circle to select.

The **Do not print lines around each field** should have a check in the check box
- If there is not a check, click the Do not print lines around each field to insert a check mark.
- If there is a check in the box, lines will not print around each field.
- If a check is not in the box, lines will print around each field.

Number of copies should be 1
- If a number other than 1 shows:
  Click in the box

Drag to highlight the number

Type **1**

Collate may show a check mark

- Since the invoice is only one-page in length, you will not be using the collate feature.

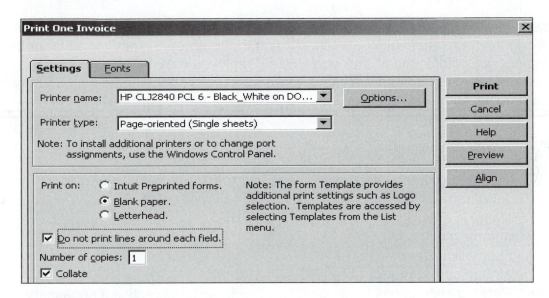

Click the **Print** button

- This initiates the printing of the invoice through QuickBooks Pro. However, because not all classroom configurations are the same, check with your instructor for specific printing instructions.
- If QuickBooks Pro prints your name on two lines, do not be concerned.

Click the **Save & New** button to save Invoice No. 1 and go to a new invoice

ENTER TRANSACTIONS USING TWO SALES ITEMS

> **MEMO:**
>
> **Date:** January 3, 2010
>
> Bill the following: Invoice No. 2—Matt Williams, CPA, spoke with you regarding the need for on-site training to help him get started using the Internet. Bill him for a 5-hour on-site training session with Jennifer Lockwood. Use Thank you for your business. as the message. (Remember to use Training 1 for the first hour of on-site training and Training 2 for all additional hours of training.)

DO ▶ Record a transaction on account for a sale involving two sales items

On Invoice No. 2, click the drop-down list arrow next to **Customer:Job**
Click **Williams, Matt, CPA**
- Name is entered as Customer:Job. Bill To information is completed automatically.
Tab to or click **Date**
Delete the current date
- Refer to instructions for Invoice No. 1 or to editing practice if necessary.
Type **01/03/10** as the date
Make sure that Invoice No. 2 is showing in the **Invoice No.** box
- The Invoice No. should not have to be changed.
There is no PO No. to record
Terms should be indicated as **Net 30**
Tab to or click the first line beneath **Item**
- Refer to Memo and Item List for appropriate billing information.
- *Note:* Services are recorded based on sales items and are not related to the employee who provides the service.
Click the drop-down list arrow next to **Item**
Click **Training 1**
- Training 1 is entered as the Item.
Tab to or click **Quantity**
Type **1**
- Amount will be calculated automatically and entered into the Amount Column when you go to the next line. Notice the amount is $95.00.
Tab to or click the second line for **Item**
Click the drop-down list arrow next to **Item**
Click **Training 2**
Tab to or click **Quantity**
Type **4**

- The total amount of training time is five hours. Because the first hour is billed as Training 1, the remaining four hours are billed as Training 2 hours. The total amount due for the Training 2 hours and the total for the invoice are automatically calculated when you go to the Customer Message box.

Click **Customer Message**

Click the drop-down list arrow next to **Customer Message**

Click **Thank you for your business.**

- Message is inserted in the Customer Message box.

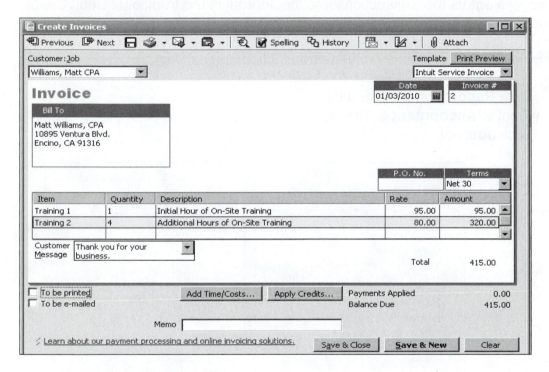

PRINT AN INVOICE

DO With Invoice No. 2 on the screen, print the invoice immediately after entering invoice information

Click **Print** button on the **Create Invoices** screen

- If you click the drop-down list arrow for the Print button, you will get a list of printing options. Click the **Print** option.

Check the information on the **Print One Invoice Settings** tab:

Printer name (should identify the type of printer you are using):

Printer type: Page-oriented (Single sheets)

Print on: Blank paper

Do not Print lines around each field check box should have a check mark

Click the **Print** button
After the invoice has printed, click the **Save & Close** button at the bottom of the
Create Invoices screen to record Invoice No. 2 and exit Create Invoices

ANALYZE TRANSACTIONS ENTERED INTO THE JOURNAL

Whenever a transaction is recorded on an invoice or any other business form,
QuickBooks enters the transactions into the Journal in the traditional Debit/Credit
format.

▶ **DO** View the Journal and verify the transaction entries

Click **Reports** on the Menu bar
Point to **Accountant & Taxes**
Click **Journal**

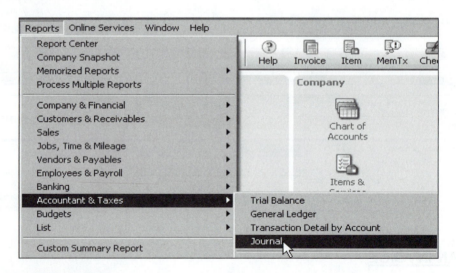

Tab to the From textbox
Enter the date **01/01/10**
Tab to the To textbox
Enter the date **01/03/10**
Press Tab to generate the report
* Notice the debit to Accounts Receivable for both Invoice No. 1 and 2.
* The credit for each invoice is to an income account. The income accounts are
  different for each invoice because the sales items are different. Technical
  Support Income is the account used when any Tech Sup sales item is used.
  Training Income is the account used when any Training sales item is used.

- In the upper-left corner of the report is the date and time the report was prepared. Your date and time will be the actual date and time of your computer. It will not match the illustration below.

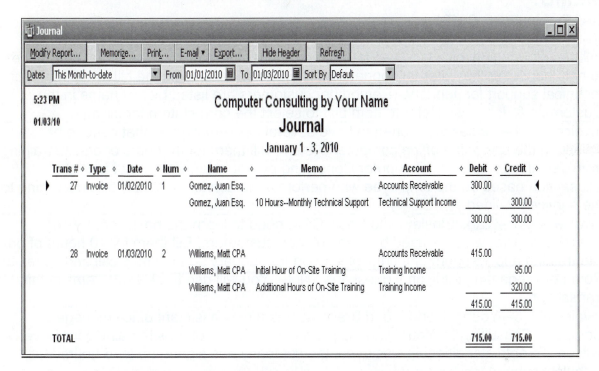

Click the **Close** button to close the report
- If you get a Memorize Report dialog box, click **No**.

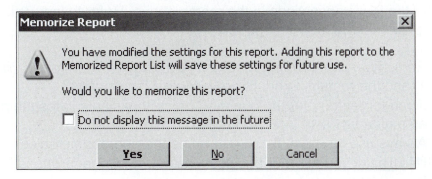

PREPARE INVOICES WITHOUT STEP-BY-STEP INSTRUCTIONS

MEMO:

DATE: January 5, 2010

Bill the following: Invoice No. 3—Ela Ahmadrand needed to have telephone assistance to help her set up her Internet connection. Prepare an invoice as the bill for 10 hours of technical support for January. (Remember customers are listed by last name in the Customers & Jobs List. Refer to Item List to select the correct item for billing.)

Invoice No. 4—Valdez and Lonegan have several new employees that need to be trained in the use of the office computer system. Bill them for 40 hours of on-site training from Jennifer Lockwood. (Computer Consulting by Your Name does not record a transaction based on the employee who performs the service. It simply bills according to the service provided.)

Invoice No. 5—Clark, Binsley, and Basil, CPA, need to learn the basic features of QuickBooks Pro, which is used by many of their customers. Bill them for 10 hours of on-site training and 15 hours of technical support for January so they may call and speak to Rom Levy regarding additional questions. (Note: You will use three sales items in this transaction.)

Invoice No. 6—Young, Norton, and Brancato has a new assistant office manager. Computer Consulting by Your Name is providing 40 hours of on-site training for Beverly Wilson. To obtain additional assistance, the company has signed up for 5 hours technical support for January.

▶DO▶ Enter the four transactions in the memo above. Refer to instructions given for the two previous transactions entered

- Remember, when billing for on-site training, the first hour is billed as Training 1, and the remaining hours are billed as Training 2.
- If you forget to enter the quantity, QuickBooks calculates the amount based on a quantity of 1.
- Always use the Item List to determine the appropriate sales items for billing.
- Use Thank you for your business. as the message for these invoices.
- If you make an error, correct it.
- Print each invoice immediately after you enter the information for it.
- To go from one invoice to the next, click the **Save & New** button.
- Click **Save & Close** after Invoice No. 6 has been entered and printed.

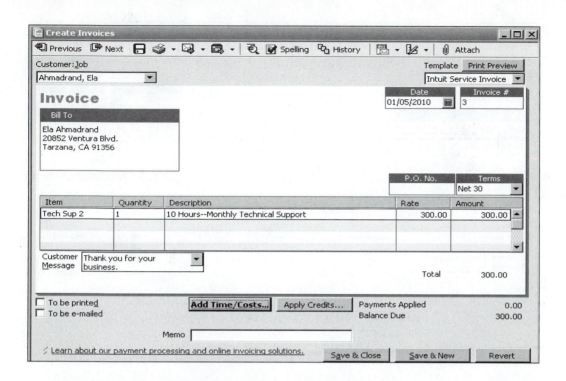

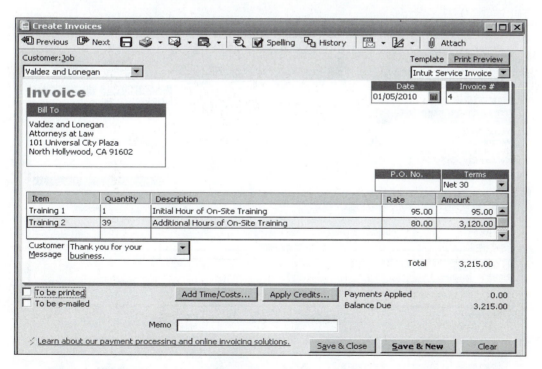

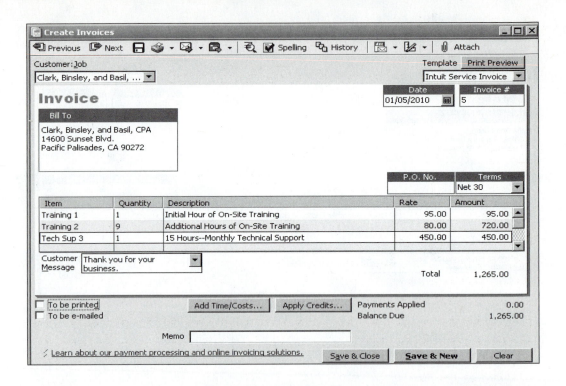

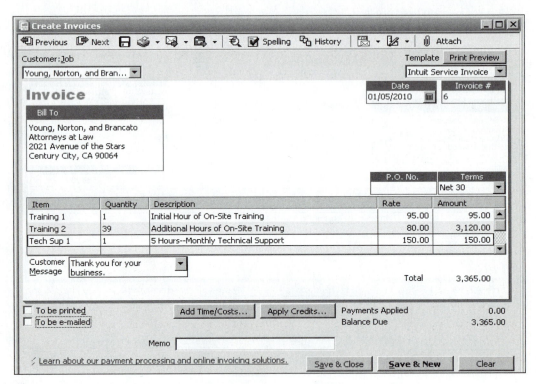

PRINT ACCOUNTS RECEIVABLE REPORTS

QuickBooks Pro has several reports available for accounts receivable. One of the most useful is the Customer Balance Summary Report. It shows you the balances of all the customers on account.

DO Print the Customer Balance Summary Report

Click **Reports** on the menu bar
Point to **Customers & Receivables**
Click **Customer Balance Summary**
- The report should appear on the screen.
- The current date and time will appear on the report. Since the dates given in the text will not be the same date as the computer, it may be helpful to remove the date and time prepared from your report.
Remove the date prepared and the time prepared from the report:
Click **Modify Report**
Click the **Header/Footer** tab
Click the check box next to **Date Prepared** to deselect this option
Click the check box next to **Time Prepared** to deselect this option
- *Note:* Some reports will also have a Report Basis—Cash or Accrual. You may turn off the display of the report basis by clicking the check box for this option.
Click **OK** on the **Modify Report** screen
- The Date Prepared and Time Prepared are no longer displayed on the report.
- The modification of the header is only applicable to this report. The next time a report is prepared, the header must once again be modified to deselect the Date Prepared and Time Prepared.
Change the Dates for the report:
Click in or tab to **From**
Enter **01/01/10**
Tab to **To**
Enter **01/05/10**
Press the Tab key
- After you enter the date, pressing the tab key will generate the report.
- This report lists the names of all customers with balances on account. The amount column shows the total balance for each customer. This includes opening balances as well as current invoices.

Computer Consulting by Your Name
Customer Balance Summary
As of January 5, 2010

	◇ Jan 5, 10 ◇
Ahmadrand, Ela	▶ 300.00 ◀
Andrews Productions	3,190.00
Clark, Binsley, and Basil, CPA	1,265.00
Creative Products	1,295.00
Design Creations	3,230.00
Duncan, Jones, and Cline	1,915.00
Gomez, Juan Esq.	450.00
Mahmood Imports	300.00
Research Corp.	815.00
Rosenthal Illustrations	3,830.00
Shumway, Lewis, and Levy	3,685.00
Valdez and Lonegan	3,215.00
Wagner, Leavitt, and Moraga	3,680.00
Williams, Matt CPA	890.00
Young, Norton, and Brancato	3,365.00
TOTAL	**31,425.00**

Click the **Print** button at the top of the Customer Balance Summary Report

Complete the information on the **Print Reports Settings** tab:

Print To: The selected item should be **Printer**

Orientation: Should be Portrait. If it is not, click **Portrait** to select Portrait orientation for this report

- Portrait orientation prints in the traditional 8 ½- by 11-inch paper size.

Page Range: **All** should be selected; if it is not, click **All**

Page Breaks: Smart page breaks (widow/orphan control) should be selected

Number of copies should be **1**

Collate is not necessary on a one-page report, it may be left with or without the check mark

If necessary, click on **Fit report to 1 page(s) wide** to deselect this item

- When selected, the printer will print the report using a smaller font so it will be one page in width.

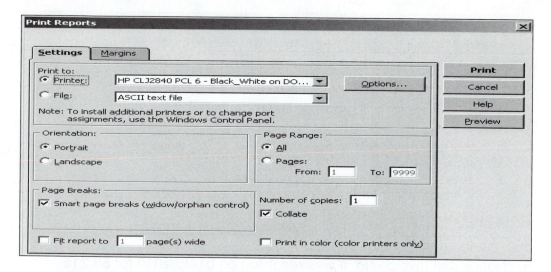

Click **Print** on the **Print Reports** screen
Do not close the **Customer Balance Summary Report**

USE THE QUICKZOOM FEATURE

You ask the office manager, Alhandra Cruz, to obtain information regarding the balance of the Valdez and Lonegan account. To get detailed information regarding an individual customer's balance while in the Customer Balance Summary Report, use the QuickZoom feature. With the individual customer's information on the screen, you can print a report for that customer.

DO ▶ Use QuickZoom

Point to the balance for **Valdez and Lonegan**

- Notice that the mouse pointer turns into a magnifying glass with a **Z** in it. 🔍
Click once to mark the balance **3,215.00**
- Notice the marks on either side of the amount.

Double-click to **Zoom** in to see the details
The report dates used should be from **01/01/10** to **01/05/10**
Remove the Date Prepared and Time Prepared from the header
- Follow the instructions previously listed for removing the date and time prepared from the header for the Customer Balance Summary Report.

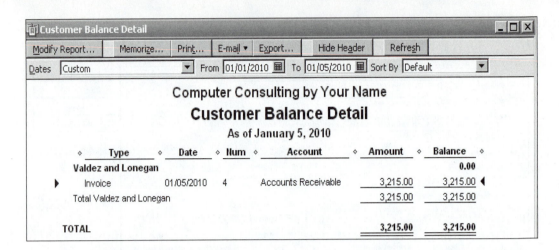

- Notice that Invoice No. 4 was recorded on 01/05/2010 for $3,215.
- To view Invoice No. 4, simply double-click on this transaction, and the invoice will be shown on the screen.

To exit Invoice No. 4 and return to the Customer Balance Detail Report, click the **Close** button on the title bar of the **Create Invoices** screen for Invoice No. 4.

Print the **Customer Balance Detail Report** for Valdez and Lonegan

- Follow the steps previously listed for printing the Customer Balance Summary Report.

Click **Close** to close **Customer Balance Detail Report**

- If you get a screen for Memorize Report, always click **No**

Click **Close** to close **Customer Balance Summary Report**

CORRECT AN INVOICE AND PRINT THE CORRECTED FORM

Errors may be corrected very easily with QuickBooks Pro. Because an invoice is prepared for sales on account, corrections may be made directly on the invoice or in the Accounts Receivable account register. We will access the invoice via the register for the Accounts Receivable account. The account register contains detailed information regarding each transaction made to the account. Therefore, anytime an invoice is recorded, it is posted to the Accounts Receivable register.

MEMO:

DATE: January 7, 2010

The actual amount of time spent for on-site training at Clark, Binsley, and Basil, CPA increased from 10 hours to 12 hours. Change Invoice No. 5 to correct the actual amount of training hours to show a total of 12 hours.

DO ▶ Correct an invoice using the Accounts Receivable Register

Correct the error in Invoice 5, and print a corrected invoice:
Click the **Chart of Accounts** icon in the Company sections of the
     Home Page
In the Chart of Accounts, click **Accounts Receivable**

Name	💲	Type	Balance Total	Attach
◇Checking		Bank	37,870.00	▲
◇Accounts Receivable		Accounts Receivable	31,425.00	
◇Employee Advances		Other Current Asset	0.00	
◇Office Supplies		Other Current Asset	500.00	
◇Prepaid Insurance		Other Current Asset	0.00	
◇Undeposited Funds		Other Current Asset	0.00	
◇Company Cars		Fixed Asset	49,000.00	
◇Depreciation		Fixed Asset	0.00	
◇Original Cost		Fixed Asset	49,000.00	▼

| Account ▾ | Activities ▾ | Reports ▾ | Attach | ☐ Include inactive |

Click the **Activities** button
Click **Use Register**
     OR
Double-click **Accounts Receivable** in the Chart of Accounts
• The Accounts Receivable Register appears on the screen with information
  regarding each transaction entered into the account.
• *Note:* This is the same as the Accounts Receivable General Ledger Account

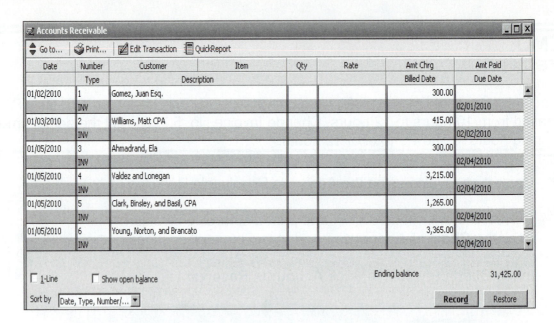

If necessary, scroll through the register until the transaction for **Invoice No. 5** is on the screen

- Look at the **Number/Type** column to identify the number of the invoice and the type of transaction.
- On the Number line you will see an invoice number or a check number.
- On the Type line, INV indicates a sale on account, and PMT indicates a payment received on account.

Click anywhere in the transaction for Invoice No. 5 to Clark, Binsley, and Basil, CPA

Click **Edit Transaction** at the top of the register

- Invoice No. 5 appears on the screen.

Click the line in the **Quantity** field that corresponds to the **Training 2** hours

Change the quantity from 9 hours to 11 hours

Position cursor in front of the 9

Press **Delete**

Type **11**

Press **Tab** to generate a new total

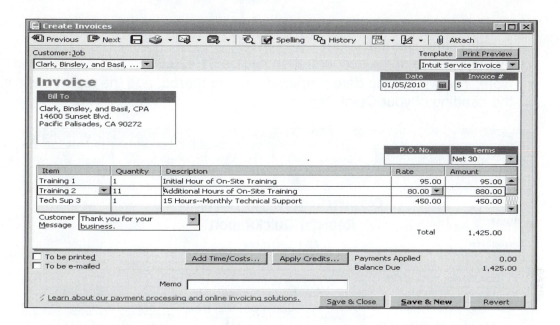

- Notice that the date remains 01/05/2010.

Click **Print** button on the **Create Invoices** screen to print a corrected invoice

If you get the Recording Transaction dialog box at this point, click **Yes**

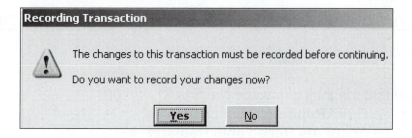

Check the information on the **Print One Invoice Settings** tab

Click **Print**

Click **Save & Close** to record changes and close invoice

If you did not get the Recording Transaction dialog box before printing and you see it now, click **Yes**

After closing the invoice, you return to the register.

VIEW A QUICKREPORT

After editing the invoice and returning to the register, you may get a detailed report regarding the customer's transactions by clicking the QuickReport button.

DO View a QuickReport for Clark, Binsley, and Basil, CPA

Click the **QuickReport** button at the top of the Register to view the **Clark, Binsley, and Basil** account

Verify the balance of the account. It should be **$1,425.00**

- *Note:* You will get the date prepared, time prepared, and the report basis in the heading of your QuickReport.

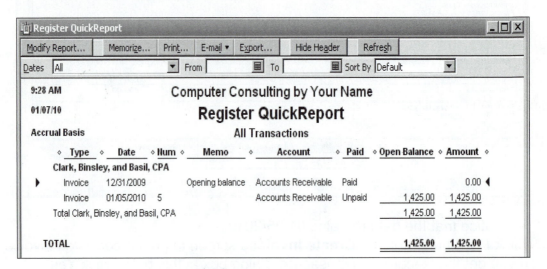

ANALYZE THE QUICKREPORT FOR CLARK, BINSLEY, AND BASIL

DO ▶ Analyze the QuickReport

Notice that the total of Invoice No. 5 is $1,425.00
Close the **QuickReport** without printing
Close the **Accounts Receivable Register**
Close the **Chart of Accounts**

VOID AND DELETE SALES FORMS

Deleting an invoice or sales receipt permanently removes it from QuickBooks Pro without leaving a trace. If you would like to correct your financial records for the invoice that you no longer want, it is more appropriate to void the invoice. When an invoice is voided, it remains in the QuickBooks Pro system with a zero balance.

VOID AN INVOICE

MEMO:

DATE: January 7, 2010

Ela Ahmadrand called to cancel the 10 hours of technical support for January. Since none of the technical support had been used, you decide to void Invoice 3.

DO Void the invoice above by going directly to the original invoice:

Use the keyboard shortcut **Ctrl+I** to open the Create Invoices screen
- Remember I stands for Invoice

Click the **Previous** button until you get to **Invoice No. 3**

With Invoice No. 3 on the screen, click **Edit** on the <u>menu</u> bar

Click **Void Invoice**

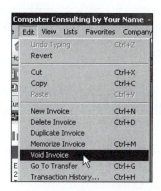

- Notice that the amount and total for the invoice are no longer 300. They are both **0.00**. Find the Memo text box at the bottom of the screen and verify that **VOID:** appears as the memo.

Click **Save & Close** on the **Create Invoices** screen

Click **Yes** on the Recording Transaction dialog box

Click the **Report Center** button above the Home Page

Click **Customers & Receivables** as the Type of Report
- The report categories are displayed on the left side of the Report Center. To prepare a report, click the desired type of report.

Click the **List View** button to select the report list
- Remember there are three ways to view a report list—carousel view, list view, and graph view.

After selecting the List view, scroll through the list of reports, and click **Transaction List by Customer** in the Customer Balance section

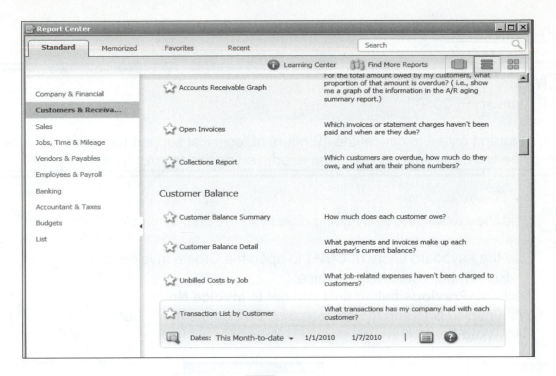

Click the **Display Report** button

Click in **From**

Enter **010110**

- Using a **/** between the items in a date is optional.

Tab to or click in **To**

Enter **010710**, press **Tab**

Remove the date prepared and the time prepared from the report heading:

    Click **Modify Report**

    Click **Header/Footer** tab

    Click the check box next to **Date Prepared** and **Time Prepared** to deselect these options

    Click **OK**

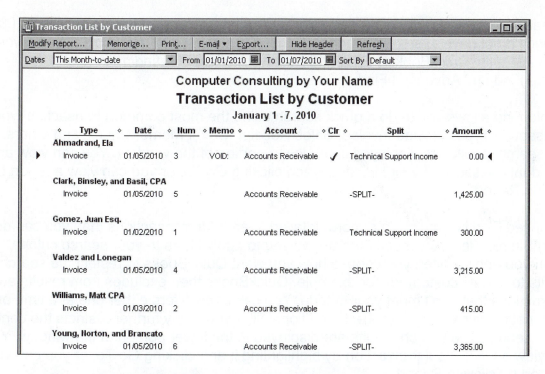

Print the **Transactions List by Customer Report** in Portrait orientation following printing instructions provided earlier in the chapter

- Do not use the option to fit the report to one-page wide. This report may print on two pages.
- This report gives the amount for each transaction with the customer.
- Notice that Invoice No. 3 is marked VOID in the Memo column and has a √ in the **Clr** (Cleared) column.
- The SPLIT column tells you which account was used to record the income. If the word **-SPLIT-** appears in the column, this means the transaction amount was split or divided among two or more accounts.

Close the **Transaction List by Customer Report**

- If you get a screen for Memorize Report, always click **No**

Close the **Report Center**

USE FIND AND DELETE AN INVOICE

When an invoice is deleted, it is permanently removed from QuickBooks. It will no longer be listed in any reports or shown as an invoice.

Find is useful when you have a large number of invoices and want to locate an invoice for a particular customer. Using Find will locate the invoice without requiring you to scroll through all the invoices for the company. For example, if customer Jimenez's transaction was on Invoice No. 3 and the invoice on the screen was Invoice No. 1,084, you would not have to scroll through 1,081 invoices because Find would locate Invoice No. 3 instantly. QuickBooks® Pro 2010 has two methods for finding transactions: Simple Find and Advanced Find.

Simple Find allows you to do a quick search using the most common transaction types. Transaction Types include Invoice, Sales Receipt, Credit Memo, Check, and others. The search results are displayed in the lower portion of the window. You can view an individual transaction by highlighting it and clicking Go To, or you can view a report by clicking Report.

Advanced Find is used to do a more detailed search for transactions than you can do using Simple Find. Advanced Find allows you to apply filters to your search criteria. When you apply a filter, you choose how you want QuickBooks to restrict the search results to certain customers, for example. QuickBooks then excludes from results any transactions that don't meet your criteria. You can apply filters either one at a time or in combination with each other. Each additional filter you apply further restricts the content of the search. The search results are displayed in the lower portion of the window. You can view an individual transaction by highlighting it and clicking Go To, or you can view a report by clicking Report.

MEMO:
DATE: January 7, 2010

Because of the upcoming tax season, Matt Williams has had to reschedule his 5-hour training session with Jennifer Lockwood three times. He finally decided to cancel the training session and reschedule it after April 15. Delete Invoice No. 2.

DO ▶ Delete Invoice No. 2 to Matt Williams, using Find to locate the invoice:

Use Simple Find by clicking **Edit** on the menu bar, clicking **Find** on the Edit menu and clicking the **Simple Find** tab
The Transaction Type should be **Invoice**.
- If it is not, click the drop-down list arrow for Transaction Type and click Invoice.
Click the drop-down list arrow for **Customer/Job:**
Click **Williams, Matt CPA**
- This allows QuickBooks Pro to find any invoices recorded for Matt Williams.
Click the **Find** button
Click the line for **Invoice No. 2**

- Make sure you have selected Invoice No. 2 and not the invoice containing the opening balance.

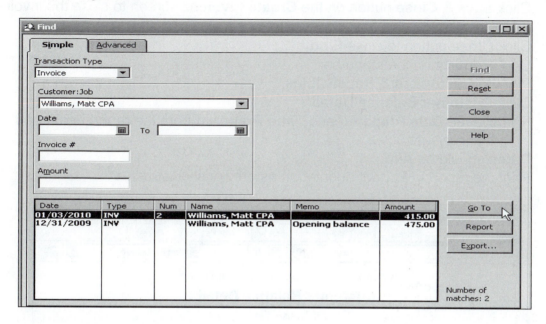

Click **Go To**

- Invoice No. 2 appears on the screen.

With the invoice on the screen, click **Edit** on the menu bar

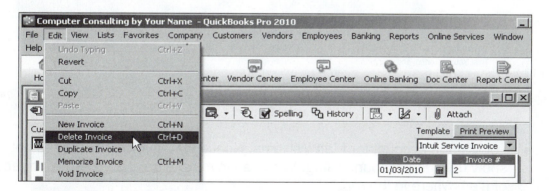

Click **Delete Invoice**

Click **OK** in the **Delete Transaction** dialog box

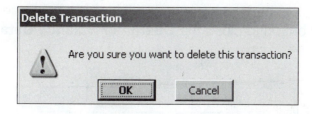

- Notice that the cursor is now positioned on Invoice No. 3 and that the voided invoice is marked Paid.

Click **Save & Close** button on the **Create Invoices** screen to close the invoice

- Notice that Invoice No. 2 no longer shows on Find.

Click **Close** button to close **Find**

Click **Reports** on the menu bar

Point to **Customers & Receivables**

Click **Customer Balance Detail**

Remove the **Date Prepared** and **Time Prepared** from the report header as previously instructed

Dates should be **All**

Print the report in Portrait orientation as previously instructed

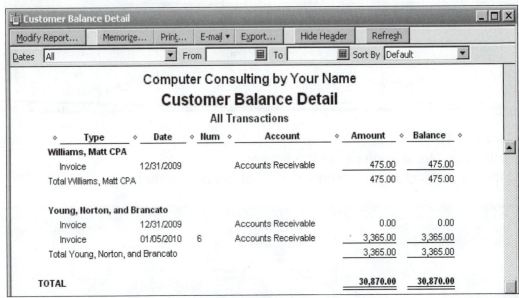

Partial Report

- Look at the account for Matt Williams. Notice that Invoice No. 2 does not show up in the account listing. When an invoice is deleted, there is no record of it anywhere in the report.
- Notice that the Customer Balance Detail Report does not include the information telling you which amounts are opening balances.
- The report does give information regarding the amount owed on each transaction plus the total amount owed by each customer.

Click the Close button to close the **Customer Balance Detail Report**

If you get a screen to Memorize a Report, always click **No**

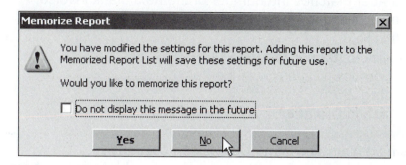

- If you want to tell QuickBooks to stop displaying the message, click **Do not display this message in the future.**

PREPARE A CREDIT MEMO

Credit memos are prepared to show a reduction to a transaction. If the invoice has already been sent to the customer, it is more appropriate and less confusing to make a change to a transaction by issuing a credit memo rather than voiding or deleting the invoice and issuing a new one. A credit memo notifies a customer that a change has been made to a transaction.

MEMO:

DATE: January 8, 2010

Prepare the following: Credit Memo No. 7—Valdez and Lonegan did not need 5 hours of the training billed on Invoice No. 4. Issue a Credit Memo to reduce Training 2 by 5 hours.

Prepare a Credit Memo

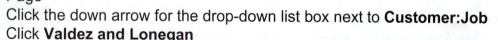

Click the **Refunds and Credits** icon in the Customers area of the Home Page

Click the down arrow for the drop-down list box next to **Customer:Job**
Click **Valdez and Lonegan**
Tab twice to **Template** textbox
- It should say **Custom Credit Memo**.
- If not, click the drop-down list arrow and click **Custom Credit Memo**.
Tab to or click **Date**
Type in the date of the credit memo: **01/08/10**
The **Credit No.** field should show the number **7**

- Because credit memos are included in the numbering sequence for invoices, this number matches the number of the next blank invoice.

There is no PO No.

- Omit this field.

Tab to or click in **Item**

Click the drop-down list arrow in the Item column

Click **Training 2**

Tab to or click in **Quantity**

Type in **5**

Click the next blank line in the Description column

Type **Deduct 5 hours of additional training, which was not required. Reduce the amount due for Invoice #4.**

- This will print as a note or explanation to the customer.

Click the drop-down list arrow next to **Customer Message**

Click **It's been a pleasure working with you!**

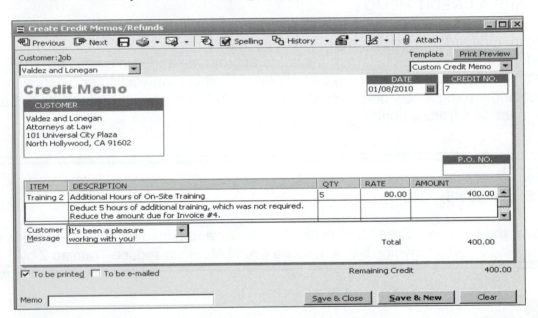

To apply the credit to an invoice, click the **Use Credit to** icon on the Icon bar

Click **Apply to invoice**

- Make sure there is a check mark for Invoice 4 on the Apply Credit to Invoices screen.

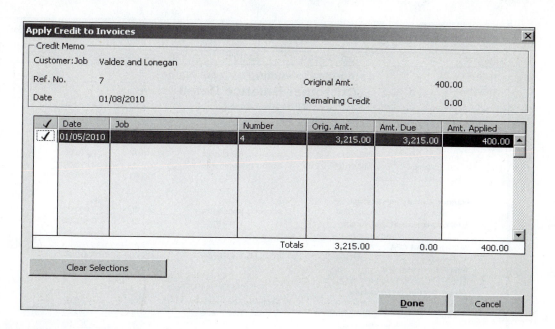

Click **Done**
Click **Print** on **Create Credit Memos/Refunds**
Click **Print** on **Print One Credit Memo**
Click the **Save & Close** button

VIEW CUSTOMER BALANCE DETAIL REPORT

Periodically viewing reports allows you to verify the changes that have occurred to accounts. The Customer Balance Detail report shows all the transactions for each credit customer. Cash customers must be viewed through sales reports.

DO View the Customer Balance Detail Report

Click the **Report Center** button
Click **Customers & Receivables** as the report type
In the Customer Balance section, double-click **Customer Balance Detail** on the
    list of reports displayed
Scroll through the report
- Notice that the account for Valdez and Lonegan shows Credit Memo No. 7 for
    $400.00. The total amount owed was reduced by $400 and is $2,815.00.

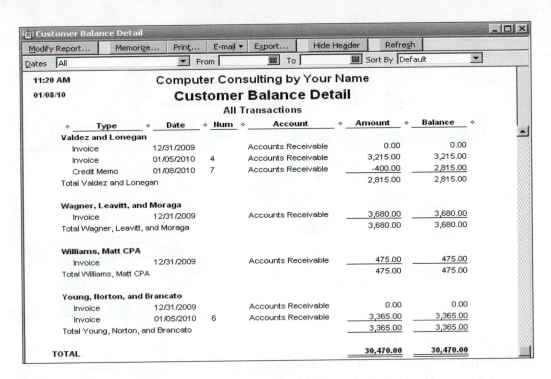

Click **Close** to close the report without printing
Close the **Report Center**

ADD A NEW ACCOUNT TO THE CHART OF ACCOUNTS

Because account needs can change as a business is in operation, QuickBooks Pro allows you to make changes to the chart of accounts at any time. Some changes to the chart of accounts require additional changes to lists.

You have determined that Computer Consulting by Your Name has received a lot of calls from customers for assistance with hardware and network installation. Even though Computer Consulting by Your Name does not record revenue according to the employee performing the service, it does assign primary areas of responsibility to some of the personnel. Rom Levy will be responsible for installing hardware and setting up networks for customers. As a result of this decision, you will be adding a third income account. This account will be used when revenue from hardware or network installation is earned. In addition to adding the account, you will also have to add two new sales items to the Item list.

MEMO:

DATE: January 8, 2010

Add a new account, Installation Income. It is a subaccount of Income.

DO Add a new income account for Hardware and Network Installation

Click the **Chart of Accounts** icon in the Company section of the Home Page
- Remember that the Chart of Accounts is also the General Ledger.

Click the **Account** button at the bottom of the Chart of Accounts screen

Click **New**

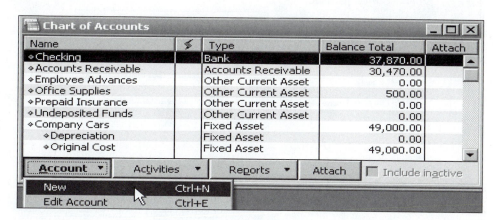

Click **Income** to choose one account type

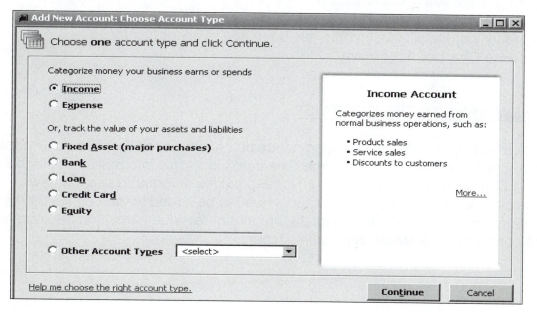

Click the **Continue** button.
Tab to or click in the text box for **Account Name**
Type **Installation Income**
Click the check box for **Subaccount of**
Click the drop-down list arrow for **Subaccount of**
Click **Income**
Tab to or click **Description**
Type **Hardware and Network Installation Income**

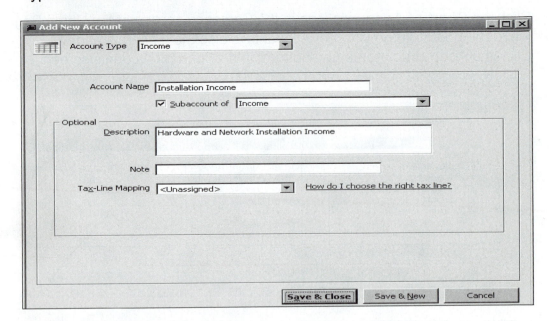

Click the **Save & Close** button
Scroll through the Chart of Accounts
Verify that Installation Income has been added under Income
Close **Chart of Accounts**

ADD NEW ITEMS TO THE ITEMS LIST

In order to accommodate the changing needs of a business, all QuickBooks Pro lists allow you to make changes at any time. The Item List stores information about the services Computer Consulting by Your Name provides. In order to use the new Installation Income account, two new items need to be added to the Item List. When these items are used in a transaction, the amount of revenue earned on the transaction will be posted to the Installation Income account.

MEMO:

DATE: January 8, 2010

Add two Service items to the Item List—Name: Install 1, Description: Initial Hour of Hardware or Network Installation, Rate: 95.00, Account: Installation Income. Name: Install 2, Description: Additional Hours of Hardware or Network Installation, Rate: 80.00, Account: Installation Income.

DO Add two new sales items

Click the **Items & Services** icon in the Company section of the Home Page
Click the **Item** button at the bottom of the **Item List** screen
Click **New**
- If you get a **New Feature** screen, click the Close button

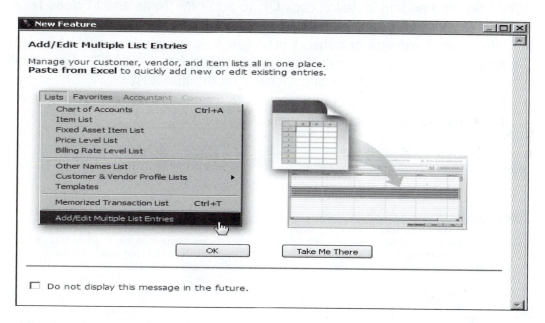

Item Type is **Service**
Tab to or click **Item Name/Number**
Type **Install 1**
Tab to or click **Description**
Type **Initial Hour of Hardware or Network Installation**
Tab to or click **Rate**
Type **95**
To indicate the general ledger account to be used to record the sale of this item,
    click the drop-down list arrow for **Account**
Click **Installation Income**

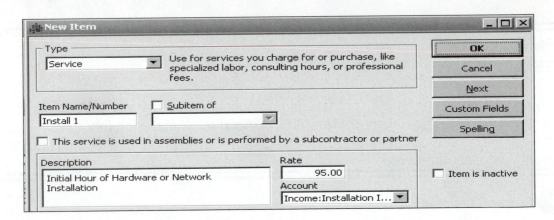

Click **Next** on the New Item dialog box

Repeat the steps above to add **Install 2**

The description is **Additional Hours of Hardware or Network Installation**

The rate is **80.00** per hour

When finished adding Install 2, click **OK** to add new items and to close **New Item** screen

- Whenever hardware or network installation is provided for customers, the first hour will be billed as Install 1, and additional hours will be billed as Install 2.

Verify the addition of Install 1 and Install 2 on the Item List

- If you find an error, click on the item with the error, click the **Item** button, click **Edit**, and make corrections as needed.

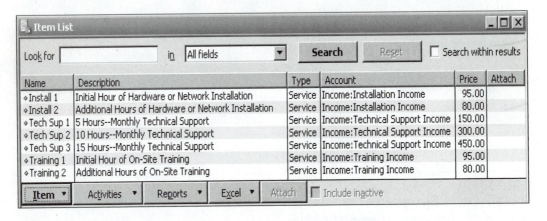

Close the **Item List**

ADD A NEW CUSTOMER

Because customers are the lifeblood of a business, QuickBooks Pro allows customers to be added "on the fly" as you create an invoice or a sales receipt. You may choose between Quick Add (used to add only a customer's name) and Set Up (used to add complete information for a customer).

MEMO:

DATE: January 8, 2010

Prepare the following: <u>Invoice No. 8</u>—A new customer, Ken Collins, has purchased several upgrade items for his personal computer but needed assistance with the installation. Rom Levy spent two hours installing this hardware. Bill Mr. Collins for 2 hours of hardware installation. His address is: 20985 Ventura Blvd., Woodland Hills, CA 91371. His telephone number is: 818-555-2058. He does not have a fax. His credit limit is $1,000; and the terms are Net 30.

DO ▶Add a new customer and record the above sale on account

  Click the **Create Invoices** icon on the Home Page
  In the Customer:Job dialog box, type **Collins, Ken**
  Press **Tab**
  • You will see a message box for **Customer:Job Not Found** with buttons for three choices:
    Quick Add (used to add only a customer's name)
    Set Up (used to add complete information for a customer)
    Cancel (used to cancel the **Customer:Job Not Found** message box)
  Click **Set Up**

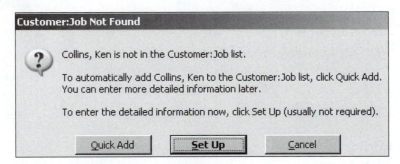

  Complete the **New Customer** dialog box
  • The name **Collins, Ken** is displayed in the Customer Name field and as the first line of Bill To in the Address section on the Address Info tab.

There is no Opening Balance, so leave this field blank

- An opening balance may be given only when the customer's account is created. It is the amount the customer owes you at the time the account is created. It is not the amount of any transaction not yet recorded.

Complete the information for the **Address Info** tab

Tab to or click in First Name, type **Ken**

Tab to or click in Last Name, type **Collins**

Tab to or click the first line for **Bill To**

If necessary, highlight **Collins, Ken**

Type **Ken Collins**

- Entering the customer name in this manner allows for the Customer:Job List to be organized according to the last name, yet the bill will be printed with the first name, then the last name.

Press **Enter** or click the second line of the billing address

Type the address **20985 Ventura Blvd.**

Press **Enter** or click the third line of the billing address

Type **Woodland Hills, CA 91371**

The Contact person is Ken Collins

Tab to or click **Phone**

Type the phone number **818-555-2058**

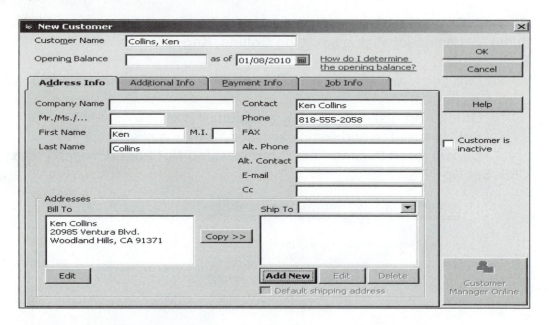

Click the **Additional Info** tab

Tab to or click **Terms**

Click the drop-down list arrow

Click **Net 30**

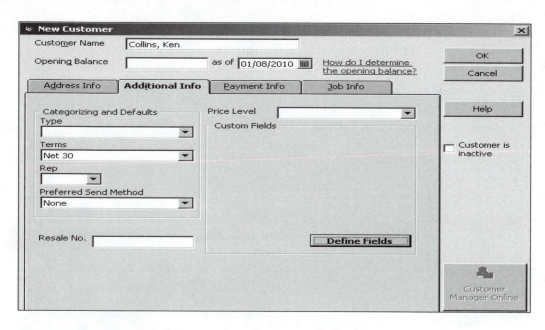

Click **Payment Info** tab
Tab to or click **Credit Limit**
Type the amount **1000**, press **Tab**

• Do not use a dollar sign. QuickBooks Pro will insert the comma for you.

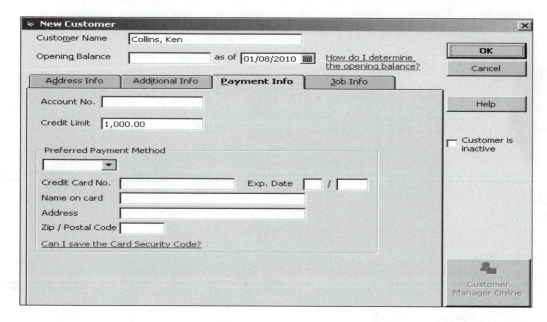

Click **OK** to return to the Invoice
Enter Invoice information as previously instructed
Date of the invoice is **01/08/10**
Invoice No. is **8**
The bill is for 2 hours of hardware installation

- Remember to bill for the initial or first hour, then bill the other hour separately. The message is **Thank you for your business.**

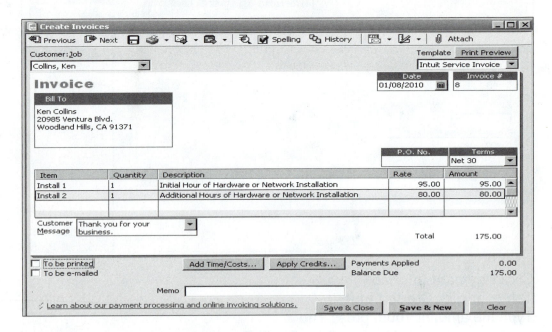

Print the invoice as previously instructed
Click **Save & Close** on the invoice to record and close the transaction

MODIFY CUSTOMER RECORDS

Occasionally, information regarding a customer will change. QuickBooks Pro allows you to modify customer accounts at any time by editing the Customer:Job List.

MEMO:

DATE: January 8, 2010

Update the following account: Design Creations has changed its fax number to 310-555-2109.

DO Edit the above account:

Access the Customer:Job List:
- There are several ways to access the Customer:Job List. Some are:
  Click the **Customer Center** icon.
  Use the keyboard shortcut: **Ctrl+J**

Click the **Customers** icon left side of the Home Page
Click **Design Creations** in the Customers & Job list in the Customer Center

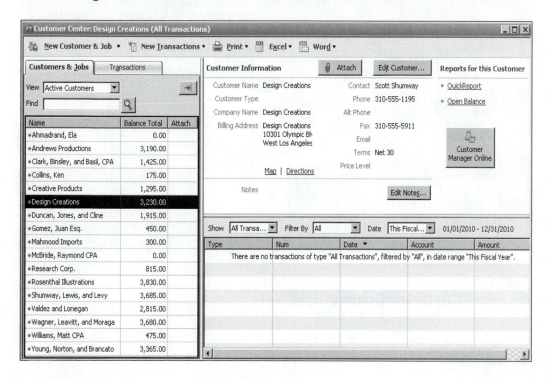

Edit the customer in one of three ways:

Click the **Edit Customer** button

Click **Design Creations** on the **Customer:Job List**. Use the keyboard
shortcut **Ctrl+E**.

Double-click **Design Creations** on the **Customer:Job List**.

• If you get a New Feature screen, click the **Close** button

Change the fax number to 310-555-2109:

Click at the end of the fax number

Backspace to delete **5911**

Type **2109**

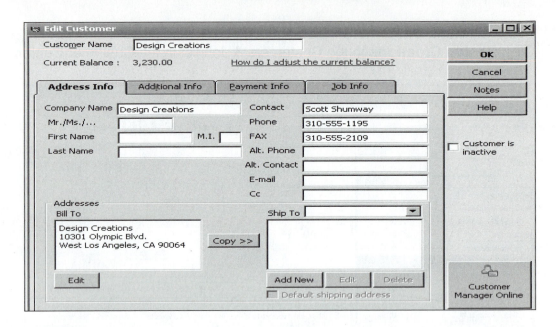

Click **OK**
Close the **Customer Center**

RECORD CASH SALES

Not all sales in a business are on account. In many instances, payment is made at the time the service is performed. This is entered as a cash sale. When entering a cash sale, you prepare a sales receipt rather than an invoice. QuickBooks Pro records the transaction in the Journal and places the amount of cash received in an account called Undeposited Funds. The funds received remain in Undeposited Funds until you record a deposit to your bank account.

MEMO:

DATE: January 10, 2010

Prepare the following to record cash sales: Sales Receipt No. 1—You provided 5 hours of on-site training to Raymond McBride, CPA, and received Ray's Check No. 3287 for the full amount due. Prepare Sales Receipt No. 1 for this transaction. Use "It's been a pleasure working with you!" as the message.

DO Record a Cash Sale

Click the **Create Sales Receipts** icon in the Customers section of the Home Page

- Refer to Appendix C for information regarding the choices shown in Accept Payments and Manage Payments section on the left side of the Sales Receipt.

Click the drop-down list arrow next to **Customer:Job**

Click **McBride, Raymond, CPA**

Tab to **Template**

- This should have **Custom Cash Sales** as the template. If not, click the drop-down list arrow and click **Custom Cash Sale**.

Tab to or click **Date**

Type **01/10/10**

- You may click on the calendar icon next to the date text box. Make sure the month is January and the year is 2010 then click **10**

Sales No. should be **1**

Tab to or click **Check No.**

Type **3287**

Click the drop-down list arrow next to **Payment Method**

Click **Check**

Tab to or click the first line for **Item**

Click the drop-down list arrow next to **Item**

Click **Training 1**

Tab to or click **Qty**

Type **1**

Tab to or click the second line for **Item**

Click the drop-down list arrow next to **Item**

Click **Training 2**

Tab to or click **Qty**

Type **4**

- The amount and total are automatically calculated when you go to the Customer Message or tab past Qty.

Click **Customer Message**

Click the drop-down list arrow for **Customer Message**

Click **It's been a pleasure working with you!**

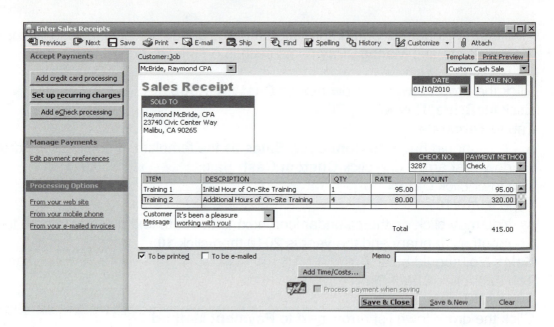

Do not close the Sales Receipt

PRINT SALES RECEIPT

DO Print the sales receipt

Click **Print** button on the top of the **Enter Sales Receipts** screen
Check the information on the **Print One Sales Receipt Settings** tab:
Printer name (should identify the type of printer you are using):
Printer type: Page-oriented (Single sheets)
Print on: Blank paper
Do not print lines around each field check box should be selected
Number of copies should be **1**
Click **Print**

• This initiates the printing of the sales receipt through QuickBooks Pro. However, since not all classroom configurations are the same, check with your instructor for specific printing instructions.

Once the Sales Receipt has been printed, click **Save & New** on the bottom of the **Enter Sales Receipts** screen

ENTER CASH SALES TRANSACTIONS WITHOUT STEP-BY-STEP INSTRUCTIONS

MEMO:

DATE: January 12, 2010

Sales Receipt No. 2—Raymond McBride needed additional on-site training to correct some error messages he received on his computer. You provided 1 hour of on-site training for Raymond McBride, CPA, and received Ray's Check No. 3306 for the full amount due. (Even though Mr. McBride has had on-site training previously, this is a new sales call and should be billed as Training 1.)

Sales Receipt No. 3—You provided 4 hours of on-site Internet training for Research Corp. so the company could be online. You received Check No. 10358 for the full amount due.

DO Record the two transactions listed above

Use the procedures given when you entered Sales Receipt No. 1:
- Remember, the first hour for on-site training is billed as Training 1 and the remaining hours are billed as Training 2.
- Always use the Item List to determine the appropriate sales items for billing.
- Use Thank you for your business. as the message for these sales receipts.
- Print each sales receipt immediately after entering the information for it.
- If you make an error, correct it.
- To go from one sales receipt to the next, click the **Save & New** button on the bottom of the **Enter Sales Receipts** screen.
- Click **Save & Close** after you have entered and printed Sales Receipt No. 3.

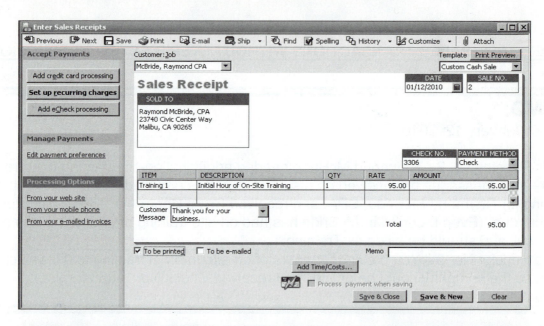

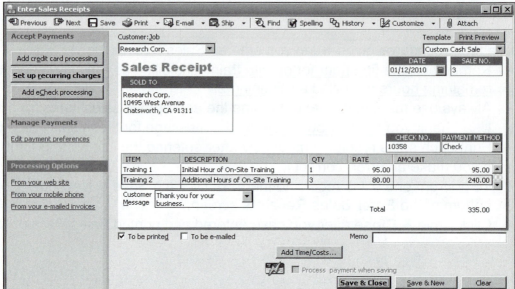

PRINT SALES BY CUSTOMER DETAIL REPORT

QuickBooks Pro has reports available that enable you to obtain sales information about sales items or customers. To get information about the total amount of sales to each customer during a specific period, print a Sales Report by Customer Detail. The total shown represents both cash and/or credit sales.

DO Prepare and print a Sales by Customer Detail Report

Click **Reports** on the menu bar

Point to **Sales**

Click **Sales by Customer Detail**

To remove the **Date Prepared**, **Time Prepared**, and **Report Basis** from the
report, click the **Modify Report** button and follow the instructions given
previously for deselecting the date prepared, time prepared, and report basis
from the Header/Footer

Change the dates to reflect the sales period from **01/01/10** to **01/14/10**

Tab to generate the report

- Notice that the report information includes the type of sales to each customer,
  the date of the sale, the sales item(s), the quantity for each item, the sales
  price, the amount, and the balance.

- The report does not include information regarding opening or previous
  balances due.

- The scope of this report is to focus on sales.

Computer Consulting by Your Name

Sales by Customer Detail

January 1 - 14, 2010

Type	Date	Num	Memo	Name	Item	Qty	Sales Price	Amount	Balance
Ahmadrand, Ela									
Invoice	01/05/2010	3	10 Hours--Monthly Technical Support	Ahmadrand, Ela	Tech Sup 2	0	300.00	0.00	0.00
Total Ahmadrand, Ela								0.00	0.00
Clark, Binsley, and Basil, CPA									
Invoice	01/05/2010	5	Initial Hour of On-Site Training	Clark, Binsley, and Basil, CPA	Training 1	1	95.00	95.00	95.00
Invoice	01/05/2010	5	Additional Hours of On-Site Training	Clark, Binsley, and Basil, CPA	Training 2	11	80.00	880.00	975.00
Invoice	01/05/2010	5	15 Hours--Monthly Technical Support	Clark, Binsley, and Basil, CPA	Tech Sup 3	1	450.00	450.00	1,425.00
Total Clark, Binsley, and Basil, CPA								1,425.00	1,425.00
Collins, Ken									
Invoice	01/08/2010	8	Initial Hour of Hardware or Network Installation	Collins, Ken	Install 1	1	95.00	95.00	95.00
Invoice	01/08/2010	8	Additional Hours of Hardware or Network Installation	Collins, Ken	Install 2	1	80.00	80.00	175.00
Total Collins, Ken								175.00	175.00
Gomez, Juan Esq.									
Invoice	01/02/2010	1	10 Hours--Monthly Technical Support	Gomez, Juan Esq.	Tech Sup 2	1	300.00	300.00	300.00
Total Gomez, Juan Esq.								300.00	300.00
McBride, Raymond CPA									
Sales Receipt	01/10/2010	1	Initial Hour of On-Site Training	McBride, Raymond CPA	Training 1	1	95.00	95.00	95.00
Sales Receipt	01/10/2010	1	Additional Hours of On-Site Training	McBride, Raymond CPA	Training 2	4	80.00	320.00	415.00
Sales Receipt	01/12/2010	2	Initial Hour of On-Site Training	McBride, Raymond CPA	Training 1	1	95.00	95.00	510.00
Total McBride, Raymond CPA								510.00	510.00
Research Corp.									
Sales Receipt	01/12/2010	3	Initial Hour of On-Site Training	Research Corp.	Training 1	1	95.00	95.00	95.00
Sales Receipt	01/12/2010	3	Additional Hours of On-Site Training	Research Corp.	Training 2	3	80.00	240.00	335.00
Total Research Corp.								335.00	335.00
Valdez and Lonegan									
Invoice	01/05/2010	4	Initial Hour of On-Site Training	Valdez and Lonegan	Training 1	1	95.00	95.00	95.00
Invoice	01/05/2010	4	Additional Hours of On-Site Training	Valdez and Lonegan	Training 2	39	80.00	3,120.00	3,215.00
Credit Memo	01/08/2010	7	Additional Hours of On-Site Training	Valdez and Lonegan	Training 2	-5	80.00	-400.00	2,815.00
Total Valdez and Lonegan								2,815.00	2,815.00
Young, Norton, and Brancato									
Invoice	01/05/2010	6	Initial Hour of On-Site Training	Young, Norton, and Brancato	Training 1	1	95.00	95.00	95.00
Invoice	01/05/2010	6	Additional Hours of On-Site Training	Young, Norton, and Brancato	Training 2	39	80.00	3,120.00	3,215.00
Invoice	01/05/2010	6	5 Hours--Monthly Technical Support	Young, Norton, and Brancato	Tech Sup 1	1	150.00	150.00	3,365.00
Total Young, Norton, and Brancato								3,365.00	3,365.00
TOTAL								**8,925.00**	**8,925.00**

Click the **Print** button on the **Sales by Customer Detail** screen

On the **Print Report** screen, check the Settings tab to verify that **Print to**: Printer is selected and that the name of your printer is correct

Click **Landscape** to change the **Orientation** from Portrait

- Landscape changes the orientation of the paper so the report is printed 11-inches wide by 8½-inches long.

Verify that the **Page Range** is **All**

Make sure **Smart page breaks** have been selected

On the **Print Report** screen, click **Print**

- Do not select **Fit** report **to one page wide**. The printed report may require more than one page.

Close the **Sales by Customer Detail Report**

- If you get a Memorize Transaction dialog box, click **No**.

CORRECT A SALES RECEIPT AND PRINT THE CORRECTED FORM

QuickBooks Pro makes correcting errors user friendly. When an error is discovered in a transaction such as a cash sale, you can simply return to the form where the transaction was recorded and correct the error. Thus, to correct a sales receipt, you would open a Sales Receipt, click the Previous button until you found the appropriate sales receipt, and then correct the error. Because cash or checks received for cash sales are held in the Undeposited Funds account until the bank deposit is made, you can access the sales receipt through the Undeposited Funds account in the Chart of Accounts as well. Accessing the receipt in this manner allows you to see all the transactions entered in the account for Undeposited Funds.

When a correction for a sale is made, QuickBooks Pro not only changes the form, it also changes all journal and account entries for the transaction to reflect the correction. QuickBooks Pro then allows a corrected sales receipt to be printed.

MEMO:

DATE: January 14, 2010

After reviewing transaction information, you realize the date for the Sales Receipt No. 1 to Raymond McBride, CPA, was entered incorrectly. Change the date to 1/9/2010.

DO Correct the error indicated in the memo above and print a corrected sales receipt

Click the **Chart of Accounts** icon on the Home Page

Click **Undeposited Funds**

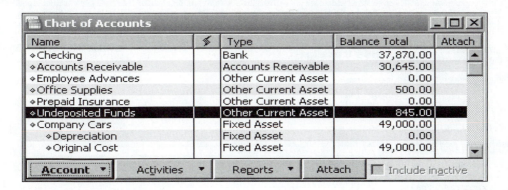

Click the **Activities** button
Click **Use Register**
- The register maintains a record of all the transactions recorded within the Undeposited Funds account.

Date	Ref	Payee		Decrease	✓	Increase	Balance
	Type	Account	Memo				
01/10/2010	1	McBride, Raymond CPA				415.00	415.00
	RCPT	-split-					
01/12/2010	2	McBride, Raymond CPA				95.00	510.00
	RCPT	Income:Training Inc					
01/12/2010	3	Research Corp.				335.00	845.00
	RCPT	-split-					

Ending balance 845.00

Click anywhere in the transaction for Sales Receipt No. 1 to Raymond McBride, CPA
- Look at the Ref/Type column to see the type of transaction.
- The number in the Ref line indicates the number of the sales receipt or the customer's check number.
- Type shows RCPT for a sales receipt.
Click the **Edit Transaction** button at the top of the register
- The sales receipt appears on the screen.
Tab to or click **Date** field
Change the Date to **01/09/10**
Tab to enter the date

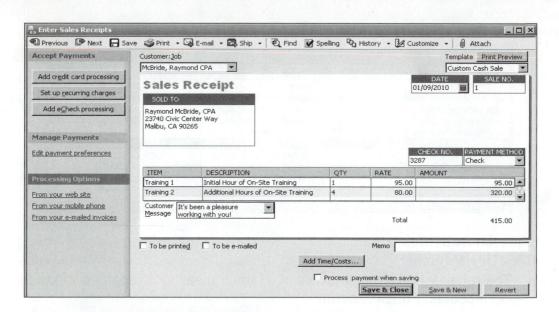

Print the Sales Receipt as previously instructed
Click **Yes** on the **Recording Transaction** dialog box
Click **Save & Close**
After closing the sales receipt, you are returned to the register for the
    Undeposited Funds account
Do not close the register

VIEW A QUICKREPORT

After editing the sales receipt and returning to the register, you may get a detailed report regarding the customer's transactions by clicking the QuickReport button.

DO Prepare a QuickReport for Raymond McBride

Click the **QuickReport** button to display the Register QuickReport for Raymond
    McBride, CPA

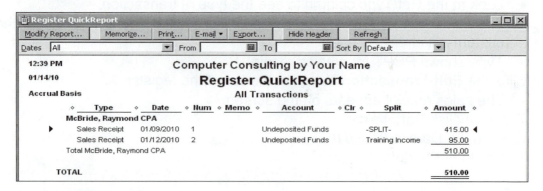

ANALYZE THE QUICKREPORT FOR RAYMOND MCBRIDE

DO Analyze the QuickReport

Notice that the date for Sales Receipt No. 1 has been changed to **01/09/2010**
- You may need to use the horizontal scroll bar to view all the columns in the report.

The account used is Undeposited Funds
The Split column contains the other accounts used in the transaction
- For Sales Receipt No. 2, the account used is **Training Income**.
- For Sales Receipt No. 1, you see the word **Split** rather than an account name.
- Split means that more than one sales item or account was used for this portion of the transaction.

View the sales items or accounts used for the Split by using QuickZoom to view the actual Sales Receipt
Use QuickZoom by double-clicking anywhere on the information for Sales Receipt No. 1
- You will see Sales Receipt 1.
- The sales items used are Training 1 and Training 2.

Close the **Sales Receipt**
Close the **Register QuickReport** without printing
Close the **Register for Undeposited Funds**
Close the **Chart of Accounts**

ANALYZE SALES

To obtain information regarding the amount of sales by item, you can print or view sales reports. Sales reports provide information regarding cash and credit sales. When information regarding the sales according to the Sales Item is needed, a Sales by Item Summary Report is the appropriate report to print or view. This report enables you to see how much revenue is being generated by each sales item. This provides important information for decision making and managing the business. For example, if a sales item is not generating much income, it might be wise to discontinue that sales item.

DO Print a summarized list of sales by item

Click the **Report Center** icon
Click **Sales** as the type of report
Double-click **Sales by Item Summary** in the Sales by Item report list
The dates of the report are from **01/01/10** to **01/15/10**
Tab to generate the report

Turn off the Date Prepared, Time Prepared, and Report Basis following
instructions given previously

Computer Consulting by Your Name
Sales by Item Summary
January 1 - 15, 2010

	Qty	Amount	% of Sales	Avg Price
		Jan 1 - 15, 10		
Service				
Install 1 ▶	1	95.00	1.1%	95.00
Install 2	1	80.00	0.9%	80.00
Tech Sup 1	1	150.00	1.7%	150.00
Tech Sup 2	1	300.00	3.4%	300.00
Tech Sup 3	1	450.00	5%	450.00
Training 1	6	570.00	6.4%	95.00
Training 2	91	7,280.00	81.6%	80.00
Total Service		8,925.00	100.0%	
TOTAL		**8,925.00**	**100.0%**	

Click **Print**
The Orientation should be **Portrait**
Click **Print** on **Print Reports** dialog box
Close the report

DO View a sales report by item detail to obtain information regarding which
transactions apply to each sales item

Double-click **Sales by Item Detail** on the Sales by Item report list
The dates of the report are from **01/01/10** to **01/15/10**
Tab to generate the report
Scroll through the report to view the types of sales and the transactions that
occurred within each category
- Notice how many transactions occurred in each sales item.

```
1:58 PM                           Computer Consulting by Your Name
01/15/10                                Sales by Item Detail
Accrual Basis                            January 1 - 15, 2010
```

◇ Type ◇	Date	◇ Num ◇	Memo	◇	Name	◇	Qty	◇ Sales Price ◇	Amount	◇ Balance
Service										
Install 1										
Invoice	01/08/2010	8	Initial Hour of Hardware or Network Installation		Collins, Ken		1	95.00	95.00	95.00
Total Install 1									95.00	95.00
Install 2										
Invoice	01/08/2010	8	Additional Hours of Hardware or Network Installation		Collins, Ken		1	80.00	80.00	80.00
Total Install 2									80.00	80.00
Tech Sup 1										
Invoice	01/05/2010	6	5 Hours--Monthly Technical Support		Young, Norton, and Brancato		1	150.00	150.00	150.00
Total Tech Sup 1									150.00	150.00
Tech Sup 2										
Invoice	01/02/2010	1	10 Hours--Monthly Technical Support		Gomez, Juan Esq.		1	300.00	300.00	300.00
Invoice	01/05/2010	3	10 Hours--Monthly Technical Support		Ahmadrand, Ela		0	300.00	0.00	300.00
Total Tech Sup 2									300.00	300.00
Tech Sup 3										
Invoice	01/05/2010	5	15 Hours--Monthly Technical Support		Clark, Binsley, and Basil, CPA		1	450.00	450.00	450.00
Total Tech Sup 3									450.00	450.00
Training 1										
Invoice	01/05/2010	4	Initial Hour of On-Site Training		Valdez and Lonegan		1	95.00	95.00	95.00
Invoice	01/05/2010	5	Initial Hour of On-Site Training		Clark, Binsley, and Basil, CPA		1	95.00	95.00	190.00
Invoice	01/05/2010	6	Initial Hour of On-Site Training		Young, Norton, and Brancato		1	95.00	95.00	285.00
Sales Receipt	01/09/2010	1	Initial Hour of On-Site Training		McBride, Raymond CPA		1	95.00	95.00	380.00
Sales Receipt	01/12/2010	2	Initial Hour of On-Site Training		McBride, Raymond CPA		1	95.00	95.00	475.00
Sales Receipt	01/12/2010	3	Initial Hour of On-Site Training		Research Corp.		1	95.00	95.00	570.00
Total Training 1									570.00	570.00

Close the report without printing
Close the **Report Center**

RECORD CUSTOMER PAYMENTS ON ACCOUNT

When you start to record a payment made by a customer who owes you money for an invoice, you see the customer's balance, any credits made to the account, and a complete list of outstanding invoices. QuickBooks Pro automatically applies the payment received to the oldest invoice. When customers make a full or partial payment of the amount they owe, QuickBooks Pro places the money received in an account called Undeposited Funds. The money stays in the account until a bank deposit is made.

MEMO:

DATE: January 15, 2010

Record the following cash receipt: Received Check No. 0684 for $815 from Research Corp. as payment on account.

DO Record the receipt of a payment on account

Click the **Receive Payments** icon on the Customers section of the Home Page

- Notice the flow chart line from Create Invoices to Receive Payments. This icon is illustrated in this manner because recording a payment receipt is for a payment made on account. This is <u>not</u> a cash sale.

Click the drop-down list arrow for **Received From**

Click **Research Corp.**

- Notice that the current date or the last transaction date shows in the **Date** column and the total amount owed appears as the balance.
- Also note that previous cash sales to Research Corp. are not listed. This is because a payment receipt is used only for payments on account.

Tab to or click **Amount**

- If you click, you will need to delete the 0.00. If you tab, it will be deleted when you type in the amount.

Enter **815**

- QuickBooks Pro will enter the **.00** when you tab to or click **Date**
- When you press Tab, QuickBooks Pro automatically places a check in the check mark column for the invoice that has the same amount as the payment. If there isn't an invoice with the same amount, QuickBooks marks the oldest invoice and enters the payment amount in the Payment column for the invoice being paid.

Tab to or click **Date**

- If you click, you will need to delete the date. If you tab, the date will be replaced when you type 01/15/10.

Type date **01/15/10**

Click the drop-down list arrow for **Pmt. Method**

Click **Check**

Tab to or click **Check No.**

Enter **0684**

Click the **Print** button and print a copy of the Payment Receipt following steps presented earlier for printing other business forms

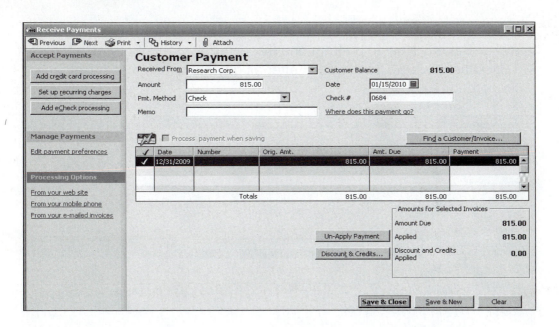

When the Payment Receipt has been printed, click **Save & New**

RECORD ADDITIONAL PAYMENTS ON ACCOUNT WITHOUT STEP-BY-STEP INSTRUCTIONS

> **MEMO:**
> **DATE:** January 15, 2010
>
> Received Check No. 1952 from Wagner, Leavitt, and Moraga for $3,680.
>
> Received Check No. 8925 for $2,000 from Rosenthal Illustrations in partial payment of account. This receipt requires a Memo notation of Partial Payment. Make sure "Leave as an underpayment" is selected in the lower portion of the Customer Payment window.
>
> Received Check No. 39251 from Matt Williams for $475.
>
> Received Check No. 2051 for $2,190 from Andrews Productions as a partial payment. Record a Memo of Partial Payment for this receipt. Leave as an underpayment.
>
> Received Check No. 5632 from Juan Gomez for $150 for payment of his opening balance
>
> Received Check No. 80195 from Shumway, Lewis, and Levy for $3,685.

DO ▶ Enter the above payments on account; if necessary, refer to the previous steps listed

- Print a Payment Receipt for each payment received
- Click **Save & New** to go from one Receive Payments Screen to the next
- Click the **Save & Close** button after all payments received have been recorded

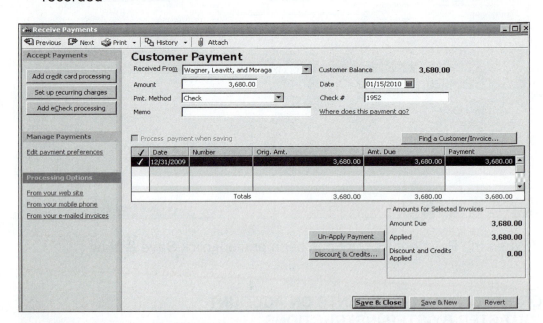

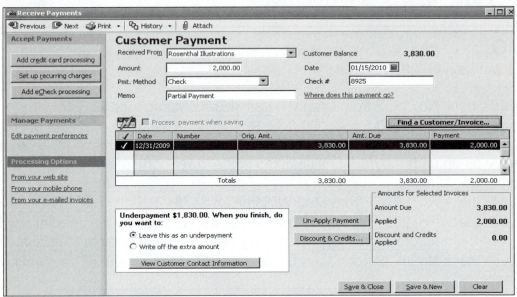

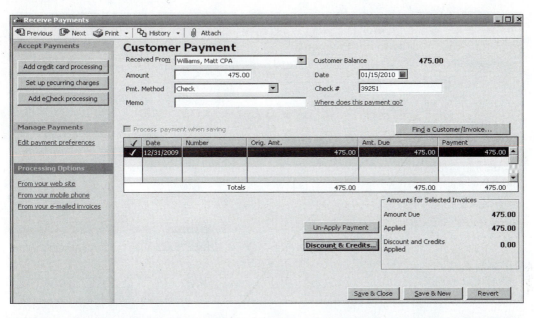

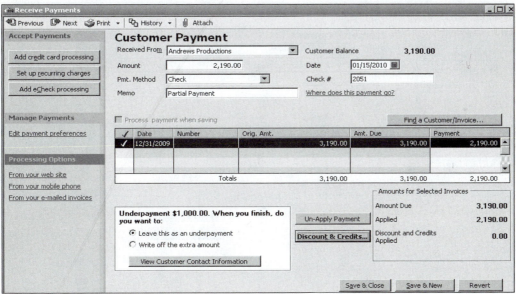

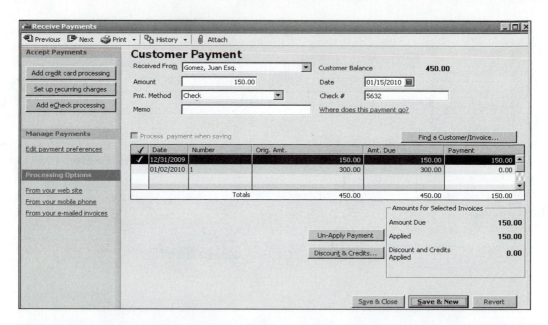

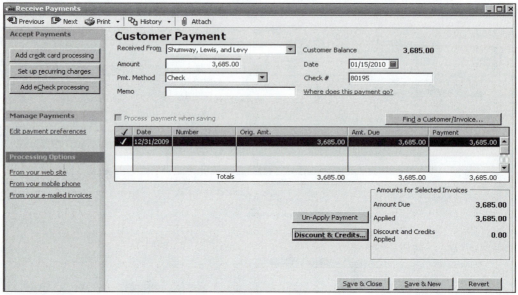

VIEW TRANSACTIONS BY CUSTOMER

In order to see the transactions for credit customers, you need to prepare a transaction report by customer. This report shows all sales, credits, and payments for each customer on account.

DO Prepare a Transaction List by Customer report

Click **Reports** on the menu bar

Point to **Customers & Receivables**
Click **Transaction List by Customer**
- Since you are only viewing the report, you do not need to remove the Date Prepared and the Time Prepared from the header

The dates are From **01/01/10** to **01/15/10**
Tab to generate the report
Scroll through the report
- Notice that information is shown for the invoices, cash sales, credit memo, and payments made on the accounts.
- Notice that the **Num** column shows the invoice numbers, sales receipt numbers, credit memo numbers, and check numbers.

2:35 PM			Computer Consulting by Your Name				
01/15/10			**Transaction List by Customer**				
			January 1 - 15, 2010				
◇ Type ◇	Date ◇	Num ◇	Memo ◇	Account	◇ Clr ◇	Split	◇ Amount ◇
Ahmadrand, Ela							
▸ Invoice	01/05/2010	3	VOID:	Accounts Receivable	✓	Technical Support Income	0.00 ◀
Andrews Productions							
Payment	01/15/2010	2051	Partial Payment	Undeposited Funds		Accounts Receivable	2,190.00
Clark, Binsley, and Basil, CPA							
Invoice	01/05/2010	5		Accounts Receivable		-SPLIT-	1,425.00
Collins, Ken							
Invoice	01/08/2010	8		Accounts Receivable		-SPLIT-	175.00
Gomez, Juan Esq.							
Invoice	01/02/2010	1		Accounts Receivable		Technical Support Income	300.00
Payment	01/15/2010	5632		Undeposited Funds		Accounts Receivable	150.00
McBride, Raymond CPA							
Sales Receipt	01/09/2010	1		Undeposited Funds		-SPLIT-	415.00
Sales Receipt	01/12/2010	2		Undeposited Funds		Training Income	95.00

Partial Report

Click the **Close** button to exit the report without printing

DEPOSIT CHECKS RECEIVED FOR CASH SALES AND PAYMENTS ON ACCOUNT

When you record cash sales and the receipt of payments on accounts, QuickBooks Pro places the money received in the Undeposited Funds account. Once the deposit has been made at the bank, it should be recorded. When the deposit is recorded, the funds are transferred from Undeposited Funds to the account selected when preparing the deposit.

MEMO:

DATE: January 15, 2010

Deposit all checks received for cash sales and payments on account.

DO Deposit checks received

Click the **Record Deposits** icon in the Banking section of the Home Page
- **Payments to Deposit** window shows all amounts received for cash sales and payments on account that have not been deposited in the bank.
- The column for **Type** contains RCPT, which means the amount is for a Sales Receipt (Cash Sale), and PMT, which means the amount received is for a payment on account.
- Notice that the √ column to the left of the Date column is empty.

Click the **Select All** button
- Notice the check marks in the √ column.

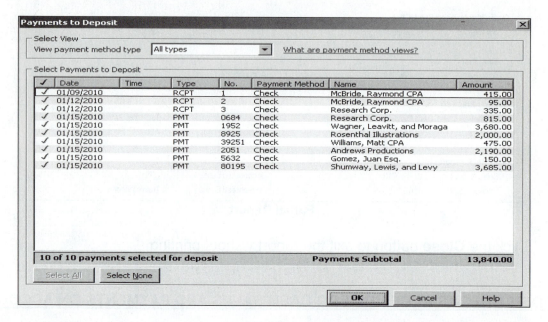

Click **OK** to close **Payments to Deposit** screen and open **Make Deposits** screen
On the **Make Deposits** screen, **Deposit To** should be **Checking**
Date should be **01/15/2010**
- Tab to date and change if not correct.

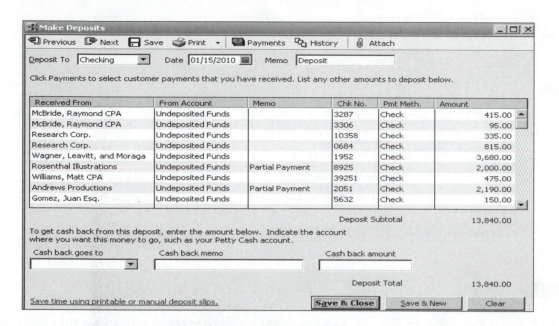

Click the **Print** button to print **Deposit Summary**
Select **Deposit summary only** on the **Print Deposit** dialog box, click **OK**

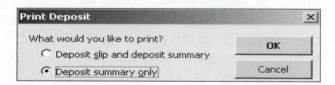

Check the **Settings** for **Print Lists**, click **Print**
* *Note:* QuickBooks Pro automatically prints the date that the Deposit Summary
  was printed on the report. It is the current date of your computer and cannot
  be changed; therefore, it may not match the date shown in the answer key.

When printing is finished, click **Save & Close** on **Make Deposits** screen to
  record and close

```
                                        Deposit Summary                              1/15/2010 3:20 PM
        Summary of Deposits to Checking on 01/15/2010
        Chk No.      PmtMethod      Rcd From                   Memo                        Amount

        3287         Check          McBride, Raymond CPA                                    415.00
        3306         Check          McBride, Raymond CPA                                     95.00
        10358        Check          Research Corp.                                          335.00
        0684         Check          Research Corp.                                          815.00
        1952         Check          Wagner, Leavitt, and Moraga                           3,680.00
        8925         Check          Rosenthal Illustrations      Partial Payment          2,000.00
        39251        Check          Williams, Matt CPA                                      475.00
        2051         Check          Andrews Productions          Partial Payment          2,190.00
        5632         Check          Gomez, Juan Esq.                                        150.00
        80195        Check          Shumway, Lewis, and Levy                              3,685.00


        Less Cash Back:


        Deposit Total:                                                                  13,840.00
```

PRINT JOURNAL

Even though QuickBooks Pro displays registers and reports in a manner that focuses on the transaction—for example, entering a sale on account via an invoice—it still keeps a Journal. The Journal records each transaction and lists the accounts and the amounts for debit and credit entries. The Journal is very useful; especially, if you are trying to find errors. Always check the transaction dates, the account names, and the items listed in the Memo column. If a transaction does not appear in the Journal, it may be due to using an incorrect date. Remember, only the transactions entered within the report dates will be displayed.

In your concepts course, you may have learned that the General Journal was where all entries were recorded in debit/credit format. In QuickBooks, you do record some non-recurring debit/credit transactions in the General Journal and then display all debit/credit entries no matter where the transactions were recorded in the Journal. (At times in the text Journal and General Journal are used synonymously to represent the report).

▶ **DO** ▶ Print the Journal

   Open the **Report Center** as previously instructed
   Click **Accountant & Taxes** as the Report type
   Double-click **Journal**
   The dates are from **01/01/10** to **01/15/10**
   Modify the Report to change the **Header/Footer** so the **Date Prepared** and **Time Prepared** are not selected, click **OK**
   Scroll through the report to view the transactions
   • You may find that your Trans # is not the same as shown. QuickBooks automatically numbers all transactions recorded. If you have deleted and re-

entered transactions more than directed in the text, you may have different transaction numbers. Do not be concerned with this.

- Also notice that not all names, memos, and accounts are displayed in full. You will learn how to change this later in training.

Click **Print**

On the **Print Reports** screen, the settings will be the same used previously except:

Click **Landscape** to select Landscape orientation

Click on **Fit report to one page wide** to select this item

- The printer will print the Journal using a smaller font so the report will fit across the 11-inch width.

Click Print

- The Journal will be several pages in length.

Computer Consulting by Your Name
Journal
January 1 - 15, 2010

Trans #	Type	Date	Num	Name	Memo	Account	Debit	Credit
41	Payment	01/15/2010	39251	Williams, Matt CPA		Undeposited Funds	475.00	
				Williams, Matt CPA		Accounts Receivable		475.00
							475.00	475.00
42	Payment	01/15/2010	2051	Andrews Productions	Partial Payment	Undeposited Funds	2,190.00	
				Andrews Productions	Partial Payment	Accounts Receivable		2,190.00
							2,190.00	2,190.00
43	Payment	01/15/2010	5632	Gomez, Juan Esq.		Undeposited Funds	150.00	
				Gomez, Juan Esq.		Accounts Receivable		150.00
							150.00	150.00
44	Payment	01/15/2010	80195	Shumway, Lewis, and Levy		Undeposited Funds	3,685.00	
				Shumway, Lewis, and Levy		Accounts Receivable		3,685.00
							3,685.00	3,685.00
45	Deposit	01/15/2010			Deposit	Checking	13,840.00	
				McBride, Raymond CPA	Deposit	Undeposited Funds		415.00
				McBride, Raymond CPA	Deposit	Undeposited Funds		95.00
				Research Corp.	Deposit	Undeposited Funds		335.00
				Research Corp.	Deposit	Undeposited Funds		815.00
				Wagner, Leavitt, and Moraga	Deposit	Undeposited Funds		3,680.00
				Rosenthal Illustrations	Partial Payment	Undeposited Funds		2,000.00
				Williams, Matt CPA	Deposit	Undeposited Funds		475.00
				Andrews Productions	Partial Payment	Undeposited Funds		2,190.00
				Gomez, Juan Esq.	Deposit	Undeposited Funds		150.00
				Shumway, Lewis, and Levy	Deposit	Undeposited Funds		3,685.00
							13,840.00	13,840.00
TOTAL							**36,560.00**	**36,560.00**

Partial Report

Close the report, do not close the Report Center

PRINT THE TRIAL BALANCE

When all sales transactions have been entered, it is important to print the Trial Balance and verify that the total debits equal the total credits.

▶ **DO** Print the Trial Balance

Click **Trial Balance** on the Report Center list of Accountant & Taxes reports
Enter the dates from **010110** to **011510**
Click the **Modify Report** button and change **Header/Footer** so **Date Prepared**,
    Time Prepared, and **Report Basis** do not print
Print the report in **Portrait** orientation
- If necessary, click on **Fit report to one page wide** to deselect this item

Computer Consulting by Your Name
Trial Balance
As of January 15, 2010

	Jan 15, 10	
	Debit	**Credit**
Checking	51,710.00	
Accounts Receivable	17,650.00	
Office Supplies	500.00	
Undeposited Funds	0.00	
Company Cars:Original Cost	49,000.00	
Office Equipment:Original Cost	8,050.00	
Accounts Payable		850.00
Loan Payable	0.00	
Loan Payable:Company Cars Loan		35,000.00
Loan Payable:Office Equipment Loan		4,000.00
Retained Earnings	0.00	
Student's Name, Capital		53,135.00
Student's Name, Capital:Investments		25,000.00
Income:Installation Income		175.00
Income:Technical Support Income		900.00
Income:Training Income		7,850.00
TOTAL	**126,910.00**	**126,910.00**

Close the report
Do not close the Report Center

GRAPHS IN QUICKBOOKS® PRO

Once transactions have been entered, transaction results can be visually represented in a graphic form. QuickBooks Pro illustrates Accounts Receivable by Aging Period as a bar chart, and it illustrates Accounts Receivable by Customer as a pie chart. For further details, double-click on an individual section of the pie chart or chart legend to create a bar chart analyzing an individual customer. QuickBooks Pro also prepares graphs based on sales and will show the results of sales by item and by customer.

PREPARE ACCOUNTS RECEIVABLE GRAPHS

Accounts Receivable graphs illustrate account information based on the age of the account and the percentage of accounts receivable owed by each customer.

DO Create graphs for accounts receivable:

> Click **Customers & Receivables** in the Report Center list to select the type of report
> Double-click **Accounts Receivable Graph** to select the report
> Click **Dates** on the QuickInsight: Accounts Receivable Graph screen
> On the **Change Graph Dates** change **Show Aging As of** to **01/15/10**
> Click **OK**
> - QuickBooks Pro generates a bar chart illustrating Accounts Receivable by Aging Period and a pie chart illustrating Accounts Receivable by Customer

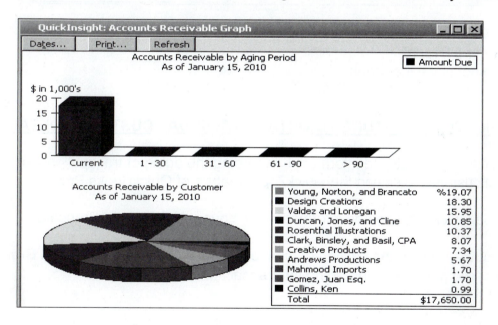

> Printing is not required for this graph
> - If you want a printed copy, click **Print** and print in Portrait mode
> Click **Dates**
> Enter **02/01/10** for the **Show Aging As of** date
> Click **OK**
> - Notice the difference in the aging of accounts.

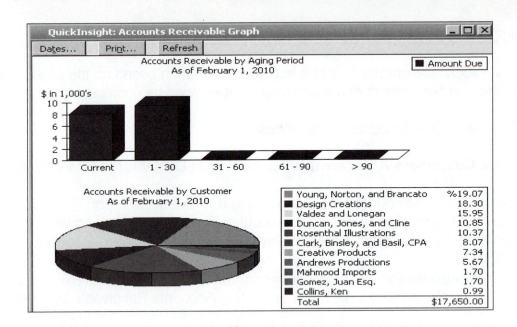

Click **Dates**
Enter **01/15/10**
Do not close the graph

USE QUICKZOOM FEATURE TO OBTAIN INDIVIDUAL CUSTOMER DETAILS

It is possible to get detailed information regarding the aging of transactions for an individual customer by using the QuickZoom feature of QuickBooks Pro.

DO Use QuickZoom to see information for Young, Norton, and Brancato

Double-click on the section of the pie chart for **Young, Norton, and Brancato**
- You get a bar chart aging the transactions of the customer.

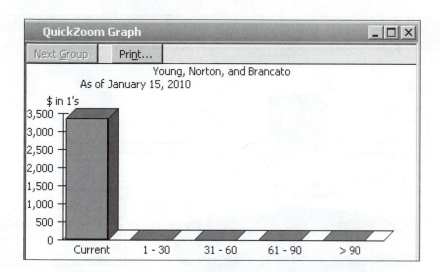

Printing is not required for this graph

Close the chart for Young, Norton, and Brancato and the Accounts Receivable graph

PREPARE SALES GRAPHS

Sales graphs illustrate the amount of cash and credit sales for a given period as well as the percentage of sales for each sales item.

DO ▸ Prepare a Sales Graph

Click **Sales** in the Report Center
Double-click **Sales Graph**
Click the **Dates** button
Click in **From**
Enter **01/01/10**
Tab to **To**
Enter **01/15/10**
Click **OK**
The **By Item** button should be indented (depressed)
- You will see a bar chart representing Sales by Month and a pie chart displaying a Sales Summary by item.
- If the **By Customer** button is indented, you will see the same bar chart but the pie chart will display a Sales Summary by customer.
- If the **By Rep** button is indented, you will see the same bar chart but the pie chart will display a Sales Summary by sales rep.

Printing is not required for this graph

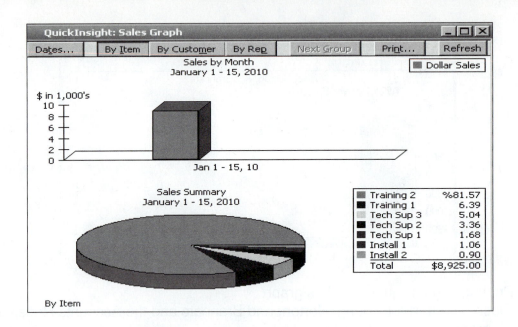

USE QUICKZOOM TO VIEW AN INDIVIDUAL ITEM

It is possible to use QuickZoom to view details regarding an individual item's sales by month.

DO ▶ Use QuickZoom to see information for Install 1

In the chart legend, double-click **Install 1**

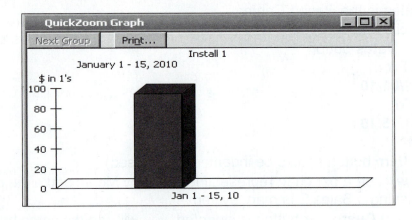

You will see the Sales by Month for Install 1
Close the graphs without printing
Close the Report Center

BACK UP AND CLOSE COMPANY

As you learned in Chapter 1, when you use QuickBooks Pro to make a back up file, the program creates a condensed file that contains all the data for the entries made up to the time of the backup file. This file has an extension **.qbb** and cannot be used to record transactions. When new transactions are recorded, a new backup file must be made. In training, it is wise to make a daily backup as well as an end-of-chapter backup. If errors are made in training, the appropriate backup file can be restored. For example, if you back up Chapter 2 and make errors in Chapter 3, the Chapter 2 backup may be restored to a company file with the extension **.qbw**. The data entered for Chapter 3 will be erased and only the data from Chapter 2 will appear.

A duplicate copy of the file may be made using Windows. Instructions for this procedure should be provided by your professor. You may hear the duplicate copy referred to as a backup file. This is different from the QuickBooks backup file.

DO ▶ Back up the company

Follow the instructions provided in Chapter 1 to make your backup
The name for the Chapter 2 backup file should be **Computer (Backup Ch. 2)**.
- Your Computer (Backup Ch. 1) file contains all of your work from Chapter 1
- Your Computer (Backup Ch. 2) file contains all your work from Chapters 1 and 2.
- The Computer (Backup Ch. 2) will not contain transactions from the work you do in Chapter 3.
- Keeping a separate backup file for each chapter is helpful for those times when you have made errors and cannot figure out how to correct them. Restoring your Chapter 2 back up file will restore your work from Chapters 1 and 2 and eliminate any work completed in Chapter 3. This will allow you to start over at the beginning of Chapter 3. If you do not have a back up file for Chapter 2, you would need to re-enter all the transactions for Chapter 2 before beginning Chapter 3.
- You may wish to make a daily back up file. If so, you should make a second backup to save your work each day. The name for the daily backup file should be **Computer (Daily Backup)**. This is helpful for those times when you have made errors and cannot figure out how to correct them but do not want to start over at the beginning of the chapter. Restoring your daily backup file will restore your work from the previous training session and eliminate the work completed in the current session.

EXIT QUICKBOOKS AND CLOSE THE COMPANY

DO After the backup file has been made, close the Company and QuickBooks

Follow the procedures given in Chapter 1 to close a company and to close QuickBooks

SUMMARY

In this chapter, cash and credit sales were prepared for Computer Consulting by Your Name, a service business, using sales receipts and invoices. Credit memos were issued. Customer accounts were added and revised. Invoices and sales receipts were edited, deleted, and voided. Cash payments were received and bank deposits were made. All the transactions entered reinforced the QuickBooks Pro concept of using the business form to record transactions rather than enter information in journals. However, QuickBooks Pro does not disregard traditional accounting methods. Instead, it performs this function in the background. The Journal was accessed and printed. The fact that the Customer:Job List functions as the Accounts Receivable Ledger and that the Chart of Accounts is the General Ledger in QuickBooks Pro was pointed out. The importance of reports for information and decision-making was illustrated. Exploration of the various sales and accounts receivable reports and graphs allowed information to be viewed from a sales standpoint and from an accounts receivable perspective. Sales reports emphasized both cash and credit sales according to the sales item generating the revenue. Accounts Receivable reports focused on amounts owed by credit customers. The traditional trial balance emphasizing the equality of debits and credits was prepared.

END-OF-CHAPTER QUESTIONS

TRUE/FALSE

ANSWER THE FOLLOWING QUESTIONS IN THE SPACE PROVIDED BEFORE THE QUESTION NUMBER.

_____ 1. A new customer can be added to a company's records on the fly.

_____ 2. In QuickBooks Pro, error correction for a sale on account can be accomplished by editing the invoice.

_____ 3. A Sales Item List stores information about products you purchase.

_____ 4. Once transactions have been entered, modifications to a customer's account may be made only at the end of the fiscal year.

_____ 5. In QuickBooks Pro all transactions must be entered using the traditional debit/credit method.

_____ 6. Checks received for cash sales are held in the Undeposited Funds account until the bank deposit is made.

_____ 7. When a correction for a transaction is made, QuickBooks Pro not only changes the form used to record the transaction, it also changes all journal and account entries for the transaction to reflect the correction.

_____ 8. QuickGraphs allow information to be viewed from both a sales standpoint and from an accounts receivable perspective.

_____ 9. QuickZoom allows you to print a report instantly.

_____10. A customer's payment on account is immediately recorded in the cash account.

MULTIPLE CHOICE

WRITE THE LETTER OF THE CORRECT ANSWER IN THE SPACE PROVIDED
BEFORE THE QUESTION NUMBER.

_____ 1. To remove an invoice without a trace, it is ___.
   A. voided
   B. deleted
   C. erased
   D. reversed

_____ 2. To enter a cash sale, ___ is completed.
   A. a debit
   B. an invoice
   C. a sales receipt
   D. receive payments

_____ 3. Two primary types of lists used in this chapter are ___.
   A. receivables and payables
   B. invoices and checks.
   C. registers and navigator
   D. customers and item

_____ 4. When you enter an invoice, an error may be corrected by ___.
   A. backspacing or deleting
   B. tabbing and typing
   C. dragging and typing
   D. all of the above

_____ 5. While in the Customer Balance Summary Report, it is possible to get an
   individual customer's information by using ___.
   A. QuickReport
   B. QuickZoom
   C. QuickGraph
   D. QuickSummary

_____ 6. Undeposited Funds represents ___.
   A. cash or checks received from customers but not yet deposited in the bank
   B. all cash sales
   C. the balance of the accounts receivable account
   D. none of the above

_____ 7. QuickBooks Pro uses graphs to illustrate information about ___.
  A. the chart of accounts
  B. sales
  C. the cash account
  D. supplies

_____ 8. Changes to the chart of accounts may be made ___.
  A. at the beginning of a fiscal period
  B. before the end of the fiscal year
  C. at any time
  D. once established, the chart of accounts may not be modified

_____ 9. To obtain information about sales by item, you can view ___.
  A. the income statement
  B. the trial balance
  C. receivables reports
  D. sales reports

_____10. When you add a customer using the Set Up method, you add ___.
  A. complete information for a customer
  B. only a customer's name
  C. the customer's name, address, and telephone number
  D. the customer's name and telephone number

FILL-IN

IN THE SPACE PROVIDED, WRITE THE ANSWER THAT MOST APPROPRIATELY
COMPLETES THE SENTENCE.

1. The report used to view only the balances on account of each customer is the
    _____.

2. The form prepared to show a reduction to a sale on account is a(n) _____.

3. The report that proves that debits equal credits is the _____.

4. QuickBooks Pro shows icons on the _____ that may be clicked to open the
    business documents used in recording transactions.

5. To verify the company being used in QuickBooks Pro, you check the _____.

SHORT ESSAY

Explain how the method used to enter an Accounts Receivable transaction in QuickBooks Pro is different from the method used to enter a transaction according to an accounting textbook.

_____
_____
_____
_____
_____

NAME_____

TRANSMITTAL

CHAPTER 2: COMPUTER CONSULTING BY YOUR NAME

Attach the following documents and reports:

Invoice No. 1: Juan Gomez
Invoice No. 2: Matt Williams
Invoice No. 3: Ela Ahmadrand
Invoice No. 4: Valdez and Lonegan
Invoice No. 5: Clark, Binsley, and Basil
Invoice No. 6: Young, Norton, and Brancato
Customer Balance Summary, January 5, 2010
Customer Balance Detail, Valdez and Lonegan
Invoice No. 5 (corrected): Clark, Binsley, and Basil
Transaction List by Customer, January 1-7, 2010
Customer Balance Detail Report
Credit Memo No. 7: Valdez and Lonegan
Invoice No. 8: Ken Collins
Sales Receipt No. 1: Raymond McBride
Sales Receipt No. 2: Raymond McBride
Sales Receipt No. 3: Research Corp.
Sales by Customer Detail Report, January 1-14, 2010
Sales Receipt No. 1 (corrected): Raymond McBride
Sales by Item Summary, January 1-15, 2010
Payment Receipt: Research Corp
Payment Receipt: Wagner, Leavitt, and Moraga
Payment Receipt: Rosenthal Illustrations
Payment Receipt: Matt Williams, CPA
Payment Receipt: Andrews Productions
Payment Receipt: Juan Gomez, Esq.
Payment Receipt: Shumway, Lewis, and Levy
Deposit Summary
Journal, January 1-15, 2010
Trial Balance, January 15, 2010

END-OF-CHAPTER PROBLEM

YOUR NAME LANDSCAPE AND POOL SERVICE

Chapter 2 continues with the entry of both cash and credit sales, receipt of payment by credit customers, credit memos, and bank deposits. In addition, reports focusing on sales and accounts receivable are prepared.

INSTRUCTIONS

Use the company file **Landscape.qbw** that you used for Chapter 1. The company name should be Your Name Landscape and Pool Service.

The invoices and sales receipts are numbered consecutively. Invoice No. 25 is the first invoice number used in this problem. Sales Receipt No. 15 is the first sales receipt number used in this problem. Each invoice recorded should be a Service Invoice and contain a message. Choose the one that you feel is most appropriate for the transaction. Print each invoice and sales receipt as it is completed. Remember that payments received on account should be recorded as Receive Payments and not as a Sales Receipt.

When recording transactions, use the following Sales Item chart to determine the item(s) billed. If the transaction does not indicate the size of the pool or property, use the first category for the item; for example, LandCom 1 or LandRes 1 would be used for standard-size landscape service. Remember that PoolCom 1 and PoolRes 1 are services for spas—not pools. The appropriate billing for a standard-size pool would be PoolCom 2 or PoolRes 2.

When printing reports, always remove the Date Prepared, Time Prepared, and Report Basis from the Header/Footer.

YOUR NAME LANDSCAPE AND POOL SERVICE
SALES ITEM LIST

ITEM	DESCRIPTION	AMOUNT
LandCom 1	Commercial Landscape Maintenance (Standard)	$150 mo.
LandCom 2	Commercial Landscape Maintenance (Medium)	250 mo.
LandCom 3	Commercial Landscape Maintenance (Large)	500 mo.
LandRes 1	Residential Landscape Maintenance (Standard)	$100 mo.
LandRes 2	Residential Landscape Maintenance (Medium)	200 mo.
LandRes 3	Residential Landscape Maintenance (Large)	350 mo.
PoolCom 1	Commercial Spa Service	$100 mo.
PoolCom 2	Commercial Pool Service (Standard)	300 mo.
PoolCom 3	Commercial Pool Service (Large)	500 mo.
PoolRes 1	Residential Spa Service	$ 50 mo.
PoolRes 2	Residential Pool Service (Standard)	100 mo.
PoolRes 3	Residential Pool Service (Large)	150 mo.
LandTrim	Trimming and Pruning	$75 hr.
LandPlant	Planting and Cultivating	50 hr.
LandWater	Sprinklers, Timers, etc.	75 hr.
LandGrow	Fertilize, Spray for Pests	75 hr.
PoolRepair	Mechanical Maintenance and Repairs	$75 hr.
PoolWash	Acid Wash, Condition	Price by the job
PoolStart	Startup for New Pools	500.00

RECORD TRANSACTIONS

January 1

► Billed Ocean View Motel for monthly landscape services and monthly pool maintenance services, Invoice No. 25. (Use a Service Invoice. Use LandCom 1 to record the monthly landscape service fee and PoolCom 2 to record the monthly pool service fee. The quantity for each item is 1.) Terms are Net 15.

► Billed Dr. Sanchez for monthly landscape and pool services at his home. Both the pool and landscaping are standard size. The terms are Net 30.

► Billed Creations for You for 2 hours shrub trimming. Terms are Net 30.

► Received Check No. 381 for $500 from Deni Anderson for pool startup services at her home, Sales Receipt No. 15.

► Received Check No. 8642 from Hiroshi Chang for $150 as payment in full on his account.

January 15

► Billed a new customer: Eric Matthews (remember to enter the last name first for the customer name and change the billing name to first name first)—10824 Hope Ranch St., Santa Barbara, CA 93110, 805-555-9825, terms Net 30—for monthly service on his large pool and large residential landscape maintenance. (If you get a message about the spelling of Lg., click Ignore All.)

► Received Check No. 6758 from Ocean View Motel in full payment of Invoice No. 25.

► Received Check No. 987 from a new customer: Wayne Childers (a neighbor of Eric Matthews) for $75 for 1 hour of pool repairs. Even though this is a cash sale, do a complete customer setup: 10877 Hope Ranch St., Santa Barbara, CA 93110, 805-555-7175, fax 805-555-5717, E-mail wchilders@abc.com, terms Net 30.

► Billed Santa Barbara Beach Resorts for their large pool service and large landscaping maintenance. Also bill for 5 hours planting, 3 hours trimming, 2 hours spraying for pests, and 3 hours pool repair services. Terms are Net 15. (If you get a message about the spelling of Lg., click Ignore All.)

January 30

► Received Check No. 1247 for $525 as payment in full from Creations for You.

► Received Check No. 8865 from Doreen Collins for amount due.

► Billed Central Coast Resorts for large pool and large landscaping maintenance. Terms are Net 15.

► Billed Anacapa Apartments for standard-size commercial pool service and standard-size commercial landscape maintenance. Terms are Net 30.

► Deposit all cash receipts (this includes checks from both Sales Receipts and Payments on Account). Print the Deposit Summary.

PRINT REPORTS AND BACKUP

▶ Customer Balance Detail Report for all transactions. Portrait orientation.
▶ Sales by Item Summary Report for 1/1/2010 through 1/30/2010. Portrait orientation.
▶ Journal for 1/1/2010 through 1/30/2010. Print in Landscape orientation, fit to one page wide.
▶ Trial Balance for 1/1/2010 through 1/30/2010. Portrait orientation.
▶ Backup your work to **Landscape (Backup Ch 2)**

NAME _____

TRANSMITTAL

CHAPTER 2: YOUR NAME LANDSCAPE AND POOL SERVICE

Attach the following documents and reports:

Invoice No. 25: Ocean View Motel
Invoice No. 26: Dr. Alex Sanchez
Invoice No. 27: Creations for You
Sales Receipt No. 15: Deni Anderson
Payment Receipt: Hiroshi Chiang
Invoice No. 28: Eric Matthews
Payment Receipt: Ocean View Motel
Sales Receipt No. 16: Wayne Childers
Invoice No. 29: Santa Barbara Beach Resorts
Payment Receipt: Creations for You
Payment Receipt: Doreen Collins
Invoice No. 30: Central Coast Resorts
Invoice No. 31: Anacapa Apartments
Deposit Summary
Customer Balance Detail
Sales by Item Summary
Journal
Trial Balance

PAYABLES AND PURCHASES: SERVICE BUSINESS

LEARNING OBJECTIVES

At the completion of this chapter you will be able to:

1. Understand the concepts for computerized accounting for payables.
2. Enter, edit, correct, delete, and pay bills.
3. Add new vendors and modify vendor records.
4. View Accounts Payable transaction history from the Enter Bills window.
5. View and/or print QuickReports for vendors, Accounts Payable Register, etc.
6. Use the QuickZoom feature.
7. Record and edit transactions in the Accounts Payable Register.
8. Enter vendor credits.
9. Print, edit, void, and delete checks.
10. Pay for expenses using petty cash.
11. Add new accounts.
12. Display and print the Accounts Payable Aging Summary Report, an Unpaid Bills Detail Report, and a Vendor Balance Summary Report.
13. Display an Accounts Payable Graph by Aging Period.

ACCOUNTING FOR PAYABLES AND PURCHASES

In a service business, most of the accounting for purchases and payables is simply paying bills for expenses incurred in the operation of the business. Purchases are for things used in the operation of the business. Some transactions will be in the form of cash purchases, and others will be purchases on account. Bills can be paid when they are received or when they are due. Rather than use cumbersome journals, QuickBooks Pro continues to focus on recording transactions based on the business document; therefore, you use the Enter Bills and Pay Bills features of the program to record the receipt and payment of bills. QuickBooks Pro can remind you when payments are due and can calculate and apply discounts earned for paying bills early. Payments can be made by recording payments in the Pay Bills window or, if using the cash basis for accounting, by writing a check. A cash purchase can be recorded by writing a check or by using petty cash. Even though QuickBooks Pro focuses on recording transactions on the business forms used, all transactions are recorded behind the scenes in the Journal. QuickBooks Pro uses a Vendor List for all vendors with which the company has an account. QuickBooks Pro does not refer to the Vendor List as the Accounts Payable Ledger; yet, that is exactly what it is. The total of the Vendor List/Accounts Payable Ledger will match the total of the Accounts Payable account in the Chart of Accounts/General Ledger. The Vendor List may be accessed through the Vendor Center.

As in Chapter 2, corrections can be made directly on the business form or within the account. New accounts and vendors may be added on the fly as transactions are entered. Reports illustrating vendor balances, unpaid bills, accounts payable aging, transaction history, and accounts payable registers may be viewed and printed. Graphs analyzing the amount of accounts payable by aging period provide a visual illustration of the accounts payable.

TRAINING TUTORIAL AND PROCEDURES

The following tutorial will once again work with Computer Consulting by Your Name. As in Chapter 2, transactions will be recorded for this fictitious company. You should enter the transactions for Chapter 3 in the same company file that you used to record the Chapter 2 transactions. The tutorial for Computer Consulting by Your Name will continue in Chapter 4, where accounting for bank reconciliations, financial statement preparation, and closing an accounting period will be completed. To maximize training benefits, you should follow the Training Procedures given in Chapter 2.

DATES

As in the other chapters and throughout the text, the year used for the screen shots is 2010, which is the same year as the version of the program. You may want to check with your instructor to see if you should use 2010 as the year for the transactions. The year you used in Chapter 2 should be the same year you use in Chapters 3 and 4.

BEGINNING THE TUTORIAL

In this chapter, you will be entering bills incurred by the company in the operation of the business. You will also be recording the payment of bills, purchases using checks, and purchases/payments using petty cash.

The Vendor List keeps information regarding the vendors with whom you do business and is the Accounts Payable Ledger. Vendor information includes the vendor names, addresses, telephone numbers, payment terms, credit limits, and account numbers. You will be using the following list for vendors with which Computer Consulting by Your Name has an account:

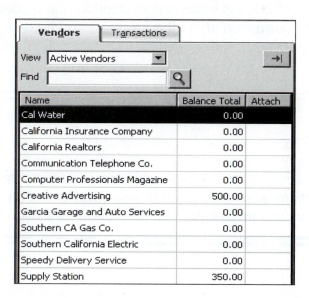

All transactions are listed on memos. The transaction date will be the same as the memo date unless specified otherwise within the transaction. Vendor names, when necessary, will be given in the transaction. Unless other terms are provided, the terms are Net 30. Once a specific type of transaction has been entered in a step-by-step manner, additional transactions of the same or a similar type will be made without having instructions provided. Of course, you may always refer to instructions given for previous transactions for ideas or for steps used to enter those transactions. To determine the account used in the transaction, refer to the Chart of Accounts. When you are entering account information on a bill, clicking on the drop-down list arrow will show a copy of the Chart of Accounts.

OPEN QUICKBOOKS® PRO AND COMPUTER CONSULTING BY YOUR NAME

 Open QuickBooks Pro and Computer Consulting by Your Name as instructed in Chapter 1 (the transactions for both Chapters 1 and 2 will be in this company file)

ENTER A BILL

QuickBooks Pro provides accounts payable tracking. Entering bills as soon as they are received is an efficient way to record your liabilities. Once bills have been entered, QuickBooks Pro will be able to provide up-to-date cash flow reports, and will remind you when it is time to pay your bills when you use the Reminders List that will be introduced in Chapter 6. A bill is divided into two sections: a vendor-related section (the upper part of the bill that looks similar to a check and has a memo text box under it) and a detail section (the area that is divided into columns for Account, Amount, and Memo). The vendor-related section of the bill is where information for the actual bill is entered, including a memo with information about the transaction. The detail section is where the expense accounts, expense account amounts, and transaction explanations are indicated.

MEMO
DATE: January 16, 2010

Record the following bill: Creative Advertising prepared and placed advertisements in local business publications announcing our new hardware and network installation service. Received Creative's Invoice No. 9875 for $260 as a bill with terms of Net 30.

DO ▶ Record a bill

Click the **Enter Bills** icon in the Vendors section of the Home Page
Verify that Bill is marked at the top of the form and complete the Vendor-section of the bill:
Click the drop-down list arrow next to **Vendor**
Click **Creative Advertising**
- Name is entered as the vendor.
Tab to **Date**
- As with other business forms, when you tab to the date, it will be highlighted.
- When you type in the new date, the highlighted date will be deleted.
Type **01/16/10** as the date
Tab to **Ref. No.**
Type the vendor's invoice number: **9875**
Tab to **Amount Due**
Type **260**
- QuickBooks Pro will automatically insert the .00 after the amount.
Tab to **Terms**
Click the drop-down list arrow next to **Terms**
Click **Net 15**
- QuickBooks Pro automatically changes the Bill Due date to show 15 days from the transaction date.
Click the drop-down list arrow for **Terms**, and click **Net 30**
- QuickBooks Pro automatically changes the Bill Due date to show 30 days from the transaction date.

- At this time nothing will be inserted as a memo in the text box between the vendor-related section of the bill and the detail section of the bill.

Complete the detail section of the bill using the **Expenses** tab

Tab to or click in the column for **Account**

Click the drop-down list arrow next to **Account**

Click **Advertising Expense**

- Based on the accrual method of accounting, Advertising Expense is selected as the account used in this transaction because this expense should be matched against the revenue of the period.

The **Amount** column already shows **260.00**—no entry required

Tab to or click the first line in the column for **Memo**

Enter the transaction explanation of **Ads for Hardware and Network Installation Services**

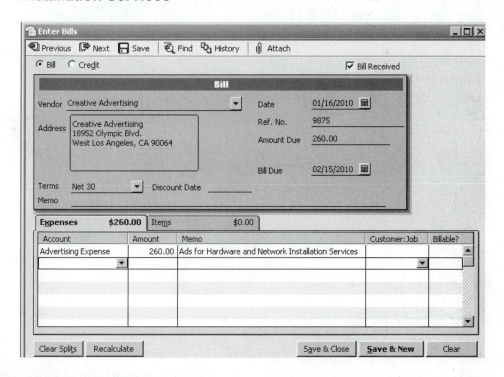

Do not click Save & Close

EDIT AND CORRECT ERRORS

If an error is discovered while you are entering information, it may be corrected by positioning the cursor in the field containing the error. You may do this by tabbing to move forward through each field or pressing Shift+Tab to move back to the field containing the error. If the error is highlighted, type the correction. If the error is not highlighted, you can correct the error by pressing the backspace or the delete key as many times as necessary to remove the error, and then type the correction. (*Alternate method:* Point to the error, highlight it by dragging the mouse through the error, and then type the correction.)

DO ▶ Practice editing and making corrections to the bill for Creative Advertising

Click the drop-down list arrow for **Vendor**
Click **Communication Telephone Co.**
Tab to **Date**
To increase the date by one day, press **+**
- You may press shift and the **=** key next to the backspace key, or you may press the **+** key on the numerical keypad.

Press **+** two more times
- The date should be **01/19/10**.

To decrease the date by one day, press **-**
- You may type a hyphen (**-**) next to the number **0**, or you may press the hyphen (**-**) key on the numerical keypad.

Press **-** two more times
- The date should be **01/16/10**.

Change the date by clicking on the calendar next to the date

←	January - 2010				→	
Su	Mo	Tu	We	Th	Fr	Sa
					1	2
3	4	5	6	7	8	9
10	11	12	13	14	15	16
17	18	19	20	21	22	23
24	25	26	27	28	29	30
31						

Click **19** on the calendar for January 2010
Click the calendar again
Click **16** to change the date back to 01/16/2010
To change the amount, click between the **2** and the **6** in **Amount Due**
Press the **Delete** key two times to delete the **60**
Key in **99** and press the **Tab** key
- The Amount Due should be **299.00**. The amount of 299.00 should also be shown in the Amount column in the detail section of the bill.

The transaction explanation was entered in the Memo column in the detail area of the bill and still shows the transaction explanation of "Ads for Hardware Installation Services."
- This memo prints on all reports that include the transaction.

- The same information should be in the Memo text box in the vendor-related area of the bill so it will appear as part of the transaction in the Accounts Payable account as well as all reports that include the transaction.

Copy **Ads for Hardware and Network Installation Services** from the Memo column to the Memo text box:

Click to the left of the letter **A** in Ads

Highlight the memo text—**Ads for Hardware and Network Installation Services**:

  Hold down the primary mouse button

  While holding down the primary mouse button, drag through the memo text **Ads for Hardware and Network Installation Services**

Click **Edit** on the menu bar

Click **Copy**

- Notice that the keyboard shortcut **Ctrl+C** is listed. This shortcut could be used rather than using the Edit menu and Copy.
- This actually copies the text and places it in a temporary storage area of Windows called the Clipboard.

Click in the **Memo** text box beneath the **Terms**

Click **Edit** on the menu bar

Click **Paste**

- Notice the keyboard shortcut **Ctrl+V**.
- This inserts a copy of the material in the Windows Clipboard into the Memo text box—**Ads for Hardware Installation Services**
- This explanation will appear in the Memo area for the transaction in the Accounts Payable account as well as in any report that used the individual transaction information.

Click the drop-down list arrow for **Vendor**

Click **Creative Advertising**

Click to the right of the last **9** in **Amount Due**

Backspace two times to delete the **99**

Key in **60**

- The Amount **Due** should once again show **260.00**
- If the terms do not show Net 30, click the **Terms** drop-down list arrow
- Click **Net 30**

Click **Save & Close** button to record the bill and return to the main screen

If you get a dialog box for **Name Information Changed**

- The dialog box states: You have changed the Terms for Creative Advertising. Would you like to have this new information appear next time?

Click **No** if the dialog box appears

PREPARE A BILL USING MORE THAN ONE EXPENSE ACCOUNT

MEMO

DATE: January 18, 2010

On the recommendation of the office manager, Alhandra Cruz, the company is trying out several different models of fax machines on a monthly basis. Received a bill from Supply Station for one month's rental of a fax machine, $25, and for fax supplies, which were consumed during January, $20, Invoice No. 1035A, Terms Net 10.

DO ▶ Record a bill using two expense accounts

Click the **Enter Bills** icon in the Vendors section of the Home Page and complete
   the vendor-related section of the bill
Click the drop-down list arrow next to **Vendor**
Click **Supply Station**
Tab to or click **Date**
• If you click in Date, you will have to delete the current date.
Enter **01/18/10**
Tab to or click **Ref. No.**
Key in the vendor's invoice number: **1035A**
Tab to or click **Amount Due**
Enter **45**
Tab to or click on the line for **Terms**
Type **Net 10** on the line for Terms, press the **Tab** key
• You will get a **Terms Not Found** message box.
Click the **Set Up** button

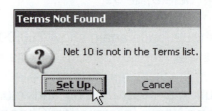

Complete the information required in the **New Terms** dialog box:
   Net 10 should appear as the Terms
   Standard should be selected
   Change the **Net due** from 0 to **10** days
   Discount percentage should be **0**
   Discount if paid within **0** days

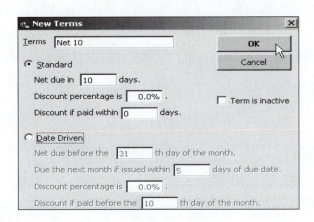

Click **OK**

Tab to or click **Memo** beneath the Terms

Enter **Fax Rental and Fax Supplies for the Month** as the transaction
description

To complete the **Detail Section** of the bill, use the Expenses tab and click the
first line for **Account**

Click the drop-down list arrow next to **Account**

Click **Equipment Rental**

- Because a portion of this transaction is for equipment that is being rented,
  Equipment Rental is the appropriate account to use.

Amount column shows **45.00**

Change this to reflect the actual amount of the Equipment Rental Expense

Tab to **Amount** to highlight

Type **25**

Tab to **Memo**

Enter **Fax Rental for the Month** as the transaction explanation

Tab to **Account**

Click the drop-down list arrow next to **Account**

Click **Office Supplies Expense**

- The transaction information indicates that the fax supplies will be used within
  the month of January. Using Office Supplies Expense account correctly
  charges the supplies expense against the period.
- If the transaction indicated that the fax supplies were purchased to have on
  hand, the appropriate account to use would be the asset Office Supplies.

The **Amount** column correctly shows **20.00** as the amount

Tab to or click **Memo**

Enter **Fax Supplies for the Month** as the transaction explanation

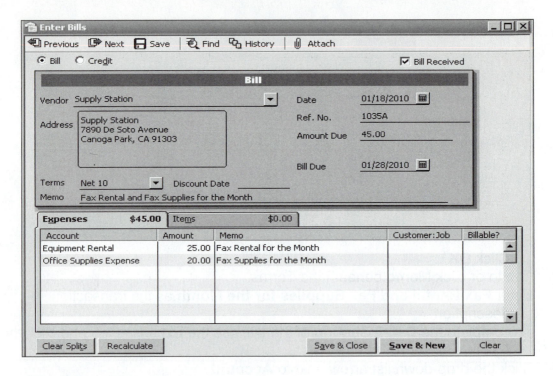

Click **Save & Close** to close the bill
- If you get a message regarding the change of Terms for Supply Station, click **No**.

PRINT TRANSACTION BY VENDOR REPORT

To obtain information regarding individual transactions grouped by vendor, you prepare a Transaction Report by Vendor. This allows you to view the vendors for which you have recorded transactions. The type of transaction is identified; for example, the word *Bill* appears when you have entered the transaction as a bill. The transaction date, any invoice numbers or memos entered when recording the transaction, the accounts used, and the transaction amount appear in the report.

DO ▶ Prepare a **Transaction by Vendor Report**

   Click the **Report Center** icon
   Click **Vendors & Payables** to select the type of report
   Double-click **Transaction List by Vendor** in the Vendor Balances Section
   Enter the Dates From **01/01/10** To **01/18/10**, press **Tab**
   Once the report is displayed, click the **Modify Report** button
   Click the **Header/Footer** tab
   Click **Date Prepared** and **Time Prepared** to deselect these features
   Click **OK**

Analyze the report:

- Look at each vendor account.
- Note the type of transaction, any invoice numbers, and memos.
- The **Account** column shows **Accounts Payable** as the account.
- As in any traditional accounting transaction recording a purchase on account, the Accounts Payable account is credited.
- The **Split** column shows the other accounts used in the transaction.
- If the word **-SPLIT-** appears in this column, it indicates that more than one account was used.
- The transaction for Supply Station has -SPLIT- in the Split Column. This is because the transaction used two accounts: Equipment Rental and Office Supplies Expense for the debit portion of the transaction.

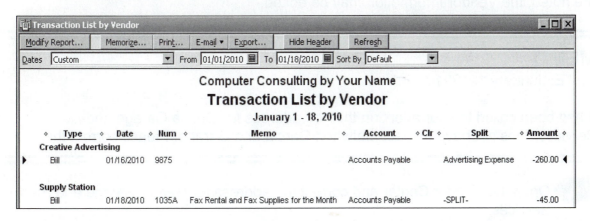

Print the report in Landscape orientation as instructed in Chapter 2
Do not close the report

USE THE QUICKZOOM FEATURE

Alhandra Cruz wants more detailed information regarding the accounts used in the Split column of the report. Specifically, she wants to know what accounts were used for the transaction of January 18, 2010 for Supply Station In order to see the account names, Alhandra will use the QuickZoom feature of QuickBooks Pro.

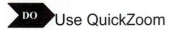Use QuickZoom

Point to the word **-SPLIT-** in the Split column
- The mouse pointer turns into a magnifying glass with a **Z** in it.
Double-click to **Zoom** in to see the accounts used in the transaction
- This returns you to the *original bill* entered for Supply Station for the transaction of 01/18/2010.

- The Expense accounts used are Equipment Rental and Office Supplies Expense.

Click **Close** button to return to the Transaction by Vendor Report

Click **Close** button to close the report

- If you get a Memorize Report dialog box, click **No**

Close the Report Center

EDIT A VENDOR

The Vendor Center contains a list of all the vendors with whom Computer Consulting by Your Name has an account. As information changes or errors in the vendor information are noted, the Vendor Information may be edited.

MEMO

DATE: January 19, 2010

It has been called to your attention that the address for Garcia Garage and Auto Services does not have a space between Garcia and Garage. Please correct this.

DO Open the Vendor Center and correct the address for Garcia Garage and Auto Services

Click the **Vendor Center** icon

Click **Garcia Garage and Auto Services** in the Vendor List

Click the **Edit Vendor** button

If you get a New Feature screen, click **Close**

In the Name and Address section, click between **Garcia** and **Garage**, press the **Space** bar

Click **OK**

View the corrected information as shown. Then, close the Vendor Center

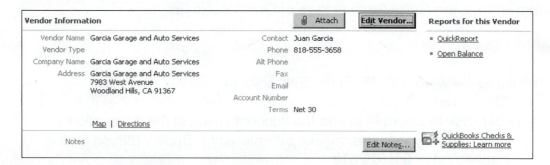

If you get a dialog box regarding sending e-mail through Outlook, click the Close button.

PREPARE BILLS WITHOUT STEP-BY-STEP INSTRUCTIONS

The accrual method of accounting matches the expenses of a period against the revenue of the period. Frequently, when in training, there may be difficulty in determining whether something is recorded as an expense or as a prepaid expense. When you pay something in advance, it is recorded as an increase (debit) to an asset rather than an increase (debit) to an expense. When you have an expense that is paid for in advance, such as insurance, it is called a prepaid expense. At the time the prepaid asset is used (such as one month's worth of insurance), an adjusting entry is made to account for the amount used during the period. Unless otherwise instructed, use the accrual basis of accounting when recording the following entries. (Notice the exception in the first transaction.)

MEMO
DATE: January 19, 2010

Received a bill from Computer Professionals Magazine for a 6-month subscription, $74, Net 30 days, Invoice No. 1579-53. (Enter as a Dues & Subscriptions expense.)

Alhandra Cruz received office supplies from Supply Station, $450, terms Net 10 days, Invoice No. 8950. These supplies will be used over a period of several months so record the entry in the asset account Office Supplies. (Note: After you enter the vendor's name, the information from the previous bill appears on the screen. As you enter the transaction, simply delete any unnecessary information. This may be done by tabbing to the information and pressing the delete key until the information is deleted or by dragging through the information to highlight, then in either method entering the new information.) If you get a Name Information Changed Dialog Box asking about Terms, do not change.

While Jennifer Lockwood was on her way to a training session at Valdez and Lonegan, the company car broke down. Garcia Garage and Auto Services towed and repaired the car for a total of $575, Net 30 days, Invoice No. 630.

Received a bill from California Insurance Company for the annual auto insurance premium, $2,850, terms Net 30, Invoice No. 3659 (Enter a memo for this bill.) (This a prepaid expense)

DO Enter the four transactions in the memo

- Refer to the instructions given for the two previous transactions entered.

- When recording bills, you will need to determine the accounts used in the transaction. Refer to the Chart of Accounts/General Ledger for account names.
- Enter information for Memos where an explanation is needed for clarification.
- To go from one bill to the next, click the **Save & New** button.
- Do not change terms for any of the vendors
- After entering the fourth bill, click **Save & Close**

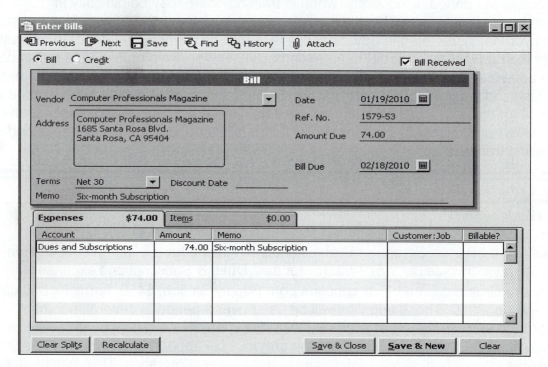

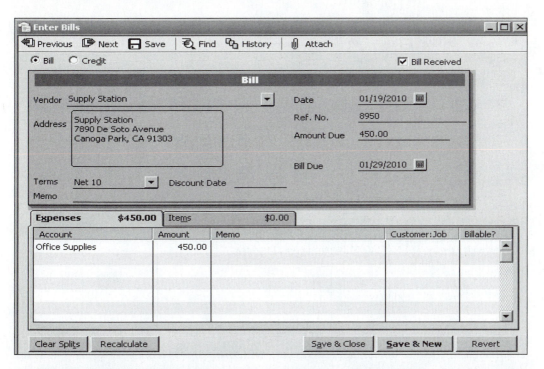

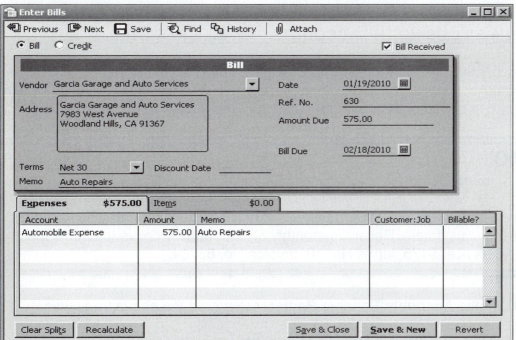

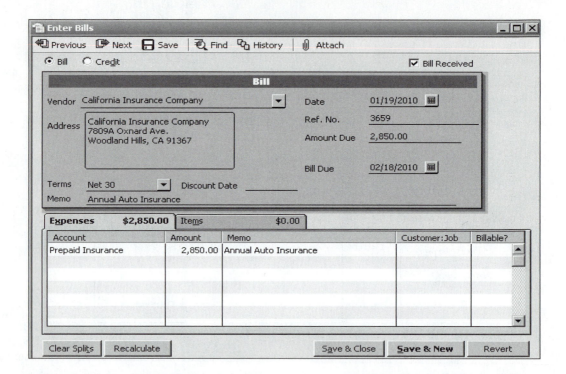

ENTER A BILL USING THE ACCOUNTS PAYABLE REGISTER

The Accounts Payable Register maintains a record of all the transactions recorded within the Accounts Payable account. Entering a bill directly into the Accounts Payable Register can be faster than filling out all of the information through Enter Bills.

MEMO

DATE: January 19, 2010

Speedy Delivery Service provides all of our delivery service for training manuals delivered to customers. Received monthly bill for January deliveries from Speedy Delivery Service, $175, terms Net 10, Invoice No. 88764.

DO Use the **Accounts Payable Register** to record the above transaction

Click the **Chart of Accounts** icon on the Home Page
   OR
Use the keyboard shortcut **Ctrl+A**
Click **Accounts Payable**

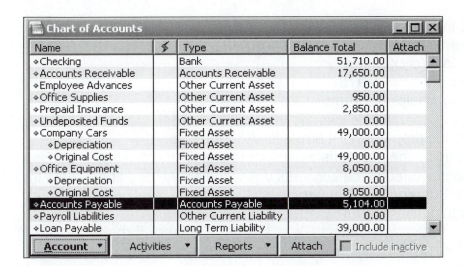

Click the **Activities** button at the bottom of the Chart of Accounts
Click **Use Register**
   OR
Use the keyboard shortcut **Ctrl+R**

The transaction date of **01/19/2010** is highlighted in the blank entry at the end of
   the Accounts Payable Register
• If it is not, click in the date column in the blank entry and key in **01/19/10**.
The word *Number* is in the next column
Tab to or click **Number**
• The word *Number* disappears.
Enter the Invoice Number **88764**
Tab to or click **Vendor**
Click the drop-down list arrow for **Vendor**
Click **Speedy Delivery Service**

Tab to or click **Due Date**
Enter the due date of **01/29/2010**
Tab to or click **Billed**
Enter the amount **175**
Tab to or click **Account**
- Note that "Bill" is inserted into the Type field
Click the drop-down list arrow for **Account**
Determine the appropriate account to use for the delivery expense
- Scroll through the accounts until you find the one appropriate for this entry.
Click **Postage and Delivery**
Tab to or click **Memo**
For the transaction memo, key **January Delivery Expense**
Click the **Record** button to record the transaction

01/19/2010	88764	Speedy Delivery Service		01/29/2010	175.00			5,279.00
	BILL	Postage and Delivery	January Delivery Expense					

Do not close the register

EDIT A TRANSACTION IN THE ACCOUNTS PAYABLE REGISTER

Because QuickBooks Pro makes corrections extremely user friendly, a transaction can be edited or changed directly in the Accounts Payable Register as well as on the original bill. By eliminating the columns for Type and Memo, it is possible to change the register to show each transaction on one line. This can make the register easier to read.

MEMO
DATE: January 20, 2010

Upon examination of the invoices and the bills entered, Alhandra Cruz discovers two errors: The actual amount of the invoice for Speedy Delivery Services was $195. The amount recorded was $175. The amount of the Invoice for *Computer Professionals Magazine* was $79, not $74. Change the transaction amounts for these transactions.

▶ DO Correct the above transactions in the Accounts Payable Register

Click the check box for **1-line** to select
- Each Accounts Payable transaction will appear on one line.
Click the transaction for *Speedy Delivery Service*
Click between the **1** and **7** in the Amount column for the transaction

Press **Delete** to delete the 7, type **9**

- The amount should be **195.00**.

Scroll through the register until the transaction for *Computer Professionals Magazine* is visible

Click the transaction for *Computer Professionals Magazine*

The **Recording Transaction** dialog box appears on the screen

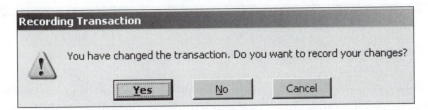

Click **Yes** to record the changes to the Speedy Delivery Service transaction

- The transaction for *Computer Professionals Magazine* will be the active transaction.

Click between the **4** and the **decimal point**

Press the **Backspace** key one time to delete the 4, type **9**

- The amount for the transaction should be **79.00**.

Click the **Record** button at the bottom of the register to record the change in the transaction

- If a Change Transaction Dialog Box appears here, you must answer Yes before you can click Record.

Accounts Payable

Go to... | Print... | Edit Transaction | QuickReport

Date	Number	Vendor	Account	Due Date	Billed	✓	Paid	Balance
12/31/2009		Creative Advertising	Uncategorized Expenses	01/30/2010	500.00			500.00
12/31/2009		Supply Station	Uncategorized Expenses	01/30/2010	350.00			850.00
01/16/2010	9875	Creative Advertising	Advertising Expense	02/15/2010	260.00			1,110.00
01/18/2010	1035A	Supply Station	-split-	01/28/2010	45.00			1,155.00
01/19/2010	1579-53	Computer Professionals Magazin	Dues and Subscriptions	02/18/2010	79.00			1,234.00
01/19/2010	630	Garcia Garage and Auto Services	Automobile Expense	02/18/2010	575.00			1,809.00
01/19/2010	3659	California Insurance Company	Prepaid Insurance	02/18/2010	2,850.00			4,659.00
01/19/2010	8950	Supply Station	Office Supplies	01/29/2010	450.00			5,109.00
01/19/2010	88764	Speedy Delivery Service	Postage and Delivery	01/29/2010	195.00			5,304.00

Splits

☑ 1-Line   ☐ Show open balance

Sort by | Date, Type, Number/... ▼

Ending balance   5,304.00

Record   Restore

Do not close the register

PREVIEW AND PRINT A QUICKREPORT
FROM THE ACCOUNTS PAYABLE REGISTER

After editing a transaction, you may want to view information about a specific vendor. This can be done quickly and efficiently by clicking the vendor's name within a transaction and clicking the QuickReport button at the top of the Register.

MEMO

DATE: January 20, 2010

Several transactions have been entered for Supply Station You like to view transaction information for all vendors that have several transactions within a short period of time.

▶ DO ▶ Prepare a QuickReport for Supply Station

Click any field in any transaction for *Supply Station*
Click the **QuickReport** button at the top of the Register
- The Register QuickReport for All Transactions for Supply Station appears on the screen.
Remove the **Date Prepared**, **Time Prepared**, and **Report Basis** as previously instructed
Click **Print**
Select Landscape orientation
Click **Preview** to view the report before printing

Computer Consulting by Your Name							
Register QuickReport							
All Transactions							
◇ Type ◇	Date ◇	Num ◇	Memo ◇	Account ◇	Paid ◇	Open Balance ◇	Amount ◇
Supply Station							
Bill	12/31/2009		Opening balance	Accounts Payable	Unpaid	350.00	350.00 ◀
Bill	01/18/2010	1035A	Fax Rental and Fax Supplies for the Month	Accounts Payable	Unpaid	45.00	45.00
Bill	01/19/2010	8950		Accounts Payable	Unpaid	450.00	450.00
Total Supply Station						845.00	845.00
TOTAL						**845.00**	**845.00**

- The report appears on the screen as a full page.
- A full-page report on the screen usually cannot be read.
To read the text in the report, click the **Zoom In** button at the top of the screen
Use the scroll buttons and bars to view the report columns
Click **Zoom Out** to return to a full-page view of the report
When finished viewing the report, click **Close**

- You will return to the **Print Reports** screen.
If the report does not fit on one page, click **Fit report to one page wide** to select
Click **Print** button on the **Print Reports** screen
Close the **Register QuickReport**, the **Accounts Payable Register**, and the
   Chart of Accounts

PREPARE UNPAID BILLS DETAIL REPORT

It is possible to get information regarding unpaid bills by simply preparing a report—no more digging through tickler files, recorded invoices, ledgers, or journals. QuickBooks Pro prepares an Unpaid Bills Report listing each unpaid bill grouped and subtotaled by vendor.

MEMO

DATE: January 25, 2010

Alhandra Cruz prepares an Unpaid Bills Report for you each week. Even though Computer Consulting by Your Name is a small business, you like to have a firm control over cash flow so you determine which bills will be paid during the week.

▶ **DO** ▶ Prepare and print an Unpaid Bills Report

Click **Unpaid Bills Detail** in the **Vendors & Payables** list on the Report Menu
   OR
Click the **Report Center** icon, click **Vendors & Payables**, and double-click
   Unpaid Bills Detail in the Vendor Balances section
Remove the Date Prepared and Time Prepared from the report header
Provide the report date by clicking in the text box for **Date**, dragging through the
   date to highlight, and typing **01/25/10**
Tab to generate the report

```
                  Computer Consulting by Your Name
                         Unpaid Bills Detail
                        As of January 25, 2010
      ◇     Type      ◇    Date    ◇  Num  ◇  Due Date  ◇ Aging ◇  Open Balance  ◇
      California Insurance Company
  ▸      Bill            01/19/2010    3659    02/18/2010                   2,850.00 ◂
      Total California Insurance Company                                    2,850.00

      Computer Professionals Magazine
         Bill            01/19/2010    1579...  02/18/2010                      79.00
      Total Computer Professionals Magazine                                    79.00

      Creative Advertising
         Bill            12/31/2009            01/30/2010                     500.00
         Bill            01/16/2010    9875    02/15/2010                     260.00
      Total Creative Advertising                                             760.00

      Garcia Garage and Auto Services
         Bill            01/19/2010    630     02/18/2010                     575.00
      Total Garcia Garage and Auto Services                                  575.00

      Speedy Delivery Service
         Bill            01/19/2010    88764   01/29/2010                     195.00
      Total Speedy Delivery Service                                          195.00

      Supply Station
         Bill            01/18/2010    1035A   01/28/2010                      45.00
         Bill            01/19/2010    8950    01/29/2010                     450.00
         Bill            12/31/2009            01/30/2010                     350.00
      Total Supply Station                                                   845.00

      TOTAL                                                                5,304.00
```

Print in Portrait orientation
Click **Close** to close the report
Click **No** if you get a Memorize Report dialog box
If necessary, click **Close** to close the **Report Center**

DELETE A BILL

QuickBooks Pro makes it possible to delete any bill that has been recorded. No adjusting entries are required in order to do this. Simply access the bill or the Accounts Payable Register and delete the bill.

MEMO

DATE: January 26, 2010

After reviewing the Unpaid Bills Report, Alhandra realizes that the bill recorded for *Computer Professionals Magazine* should have been recorded for *Computer Technologies Magazine*.

▸ DO ▸ Delete the bill recorded for Computer Professionals Magazine

Access the Chart of Accounts:
    Click the **Chart of Accounts** icon on the Home Page
        OR
    Use the keyboard shortcut **Ctrl+A**
        OR
    Use the menu bar, click **List**, and click **Chart of Accounts**
With the Chart of Accounts showing on the screen, click **Accounts Payable**
Open the Accounts Payable Register:
Use keyboard shortcut **Ctrl+R**
    OR
Click **Activities Button**, click **Use Register**
Click on the bill for *Computer Professionals Magazine*
To delete the bill:
Click **Edit** on the menu bar, click **Delete Bill**

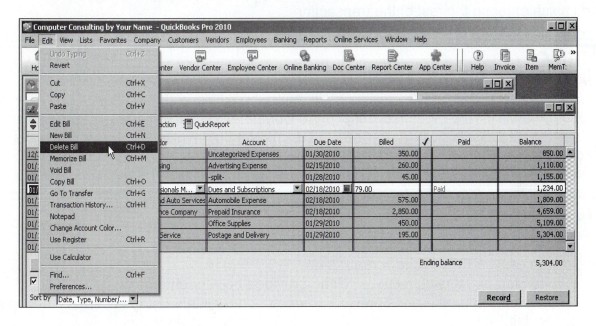

    OR
Use the keyboard shortcut **Ctrl+D**
• The **Delete Transaction** dialog box appears on the screen.

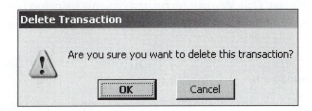

Click **OK** to delete the bill

- Notice that the transaction no longer appears in the Accounts Payable Register.

Close the **Accounts Payable Register**

Close the **Chart of Accounts**

ADD A NEW VENDOR WHILE RECORDING A BILL

When you type the first letter(s) of a vendor name on the Vendor Line, QuickBooks tries to match the name to one in the Vendor List and enter it on the Vendor line. If the vendor is not in the Vendor List, a QuickBooks Pro dialog box for Vendor Not Found appears with choices for a Quick Add—adding just the vendor name—or Set Up—adding the vendor name and all vendor account information. When the new vendor information is complete, QuickBooks Pro fills in the blanks on the bill for the vendor, and you finish entering the rest of the transaction.

MEMO

DATE: January 26, 2010

Record the bill for a 6-month subscription to *Computer Technologies Magazine*. The transaction date is 01/19/10, amount $79, Terms Net 30, Invoice No. 1579-53. This is recorded as an expense. The address and telephone for *Computer Technologies Magazine* is 12405 Menlo Park Drive, Menlo Park, CA 94025, 510-555-3829.

▶ DO Record the above transaction

Access the **Enter Bills** screen
- Step-by-step instructions will be provided only for entering a new vendor.
- Refer to transactions previously recorded for all other steps used in entering a bill.
- When you key the first few letters of a vendor name, QuickBooks Pro will automatically enter a vendor name.

On the line for Vendor, type the **C** for *Computer Technologies Magazine*
- The vendor name **Cal Water** appears on the vendor line and is highlighted and the list of Vendor names that start with C is displayed.

Type **omp**
- The vendor name changes to **Computer Professionals Magazine**.

Finish typing **uter Technologies Magazine**
- The entire Vendor List is displayed

Press **Tab**

The **Vendor Not Found** dialog box appears on the screen with buttons for:

- **Quick Add**—adds only the name to the vendor list.
- **Set Up**—adds the name to the vendor list and allows all account information to be entered.
- **Cancel**—cancels the addition of a new vendor.

Click **Set Up**

- Computer Technologies Magazine is shown in the Vendor Name text box

If necessary, highlight the Vendor Name in the Vendor Name text box

Copy the name to the Company Name textbox by using the **Ctrl+C** keyboard shortcut for copy

Click in the Company Name textbox and use **Ctrl+V** to paste the name into the textbox

Tab to or click the first line for **Address**

- Computer Technologies Magazine appears as the first line of the address.

Position the cursor at the end of the name, press **Enter** or click the line beneath the company name (Do not tab)

Type the address listed in the transaction

Press **Enter** at the end of each line

When finished with the address, tab to or click **Phone**

Enter the telephone number

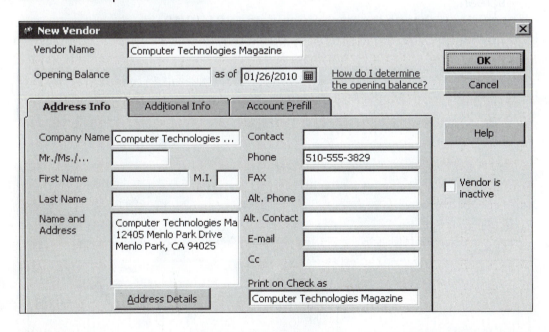

To enter the information for **Additional Info** tab, click **Additional Info** tab
Click drop-down list arrow next to **Terms**
Click **Net 30**

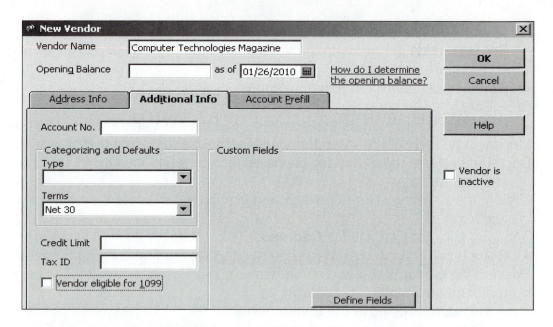

Click the **OK** button for **New Vendor** screen
- The information for Vendor, Terms, and the Dates is filled in on the Enter Bills screen.

If necessary, change the transaction date to **01/19/10**

Complete the bill using instructions previously provided for entering bills

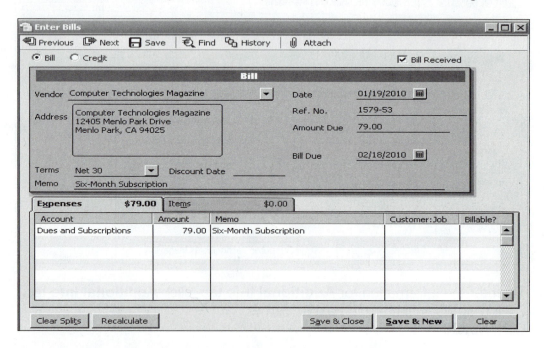

When finished, click **Save & Close** to close the bill and exit

ENTER A CREDIT FROM A VENDOR

Credit memos are prepared to record a reduction to a transaction. With QuickBooks Pro, you use the Enter Bills window to record credit memos received from vendors acknowledging a return of or an allowance for a previously recorded bill and/or payment. The amount of a credit memo is deducted from the amount owed.

MEMO
DATE: January 26, 2010

Received Credit Memo No. 789 for $5 from Supply Station for a return of fax paper that was damaged.

▶ **DO** Record the credit memo shown above

    Access the **Enter Bills** window as previously instructed

    On the **Enter Bills** screen, click **Credit** to select
* Notice that the word *Bill* changes to *Credit*.
Click the drop-down list arrow next to **Vendor**
Click **Supply Station**
Tab to or click the **Date**
Type **01/26/10**
Tab to or click **Ref. No.**
Type **789**
Tab to or click **Credit Amount**
Type **5**
Tab to or click in **Memo**
Enter **Returned Damaged Fax Paper**
Tab to or click the first line of **Account**
Click the drop-down list arrow
Because this was originally entered as an expense, click the account **Office Supplies Expense**
* The amount should show **5.00**; if not, enter **5**.
Copy the Memo to the **Memo** column

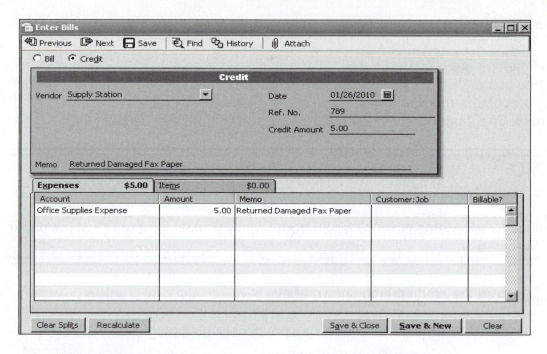

Click **Save & Close** to record the credit and exit **Enter Bills**
- QuickBooks Pro records the credit in the Accounts Payable account and shows the transaction type as BILLCRED in the Accounts Payable Register.

VIEW CREDIT IN ACCOUNTS PAYABLE REGISTER

When recording the credit in the last transaction, QuickBooks Pro listed the transaction type as BILLCRED in the Accounts Payable Register.

DO ▸Verify the credit from Supply Station

Follow steps previously provided to access the Accounts Payable Register
If a check mark shows in the **1-Line** check box, remove it by clicking the check box
- This changes the display in the Accounts Payable Register from 1-Line to multiple lines.
Look at the **Number/Type** column and verify the type **BILLCRED**

01/26/2010	789	Supply Station				5.00	5,299.00
	BILLCRED	Office Supplies Expense	Returned Damaged Fax Paper				

Close the **Accounts Payable Register**
Close the **Chart of Accounts**

PAYING BILLS

When using QuickBooks Pro, you should pay any bills entered through "Enter Bills" directly from the pay bills command and let QuickBooks Pro write your checks for you and mark the bills "Paid." If you have not entered a bill for an amount you owe, you will need to write the check yourself. If you have recorded a bill for a transaction and write the check for payment yourself, the bill will not be marked as being paid and will continue to show up as an amount due.

Using the Pay Bills window enables you to determine which bills to pay, the method of payment—check or credit card—and the appropriate account. When determining which bills to pay, QuickBooks Pro allows you to display the bills by due date, discount date, vendor, or amount. All bills may be displayed, or only those bills that are due by a certain date may be displayed.

MEMO

DATE: January 26, 2010

Whenever possible, Alhandra pays the bills on a weekly basis. With the Pay Bills window showing the bills due for payment on or before 01/31/2010, Alhandra compares the bills shown with the Unpaid Bills Report previously prepared. The report has been marked by you to indicate which bills should be paid. Alhandra will select the bills for payment and record the bill payment for the week.

▶ **DO** ▶ Pay the bills for the week

> Click the **Pay Bills** icon in the Vendors section of the Home Page to access the **Pay Bills** window
> Click **Show All Bills** to select
> Filter By should be **All Vendors**
> Sort Bills by **Due Date**
> • If this is not showing, click the drop-down list arrow next to the **Sort Bills By** text box, click **Due Date**.
> Scroll through the list of bills
> Click the drop-down list arrow next to the **Sort Bills By** text box
> Click **Vendor**
> • This shows you how much you owe each vendor.
> Again, click the drop-down list arrow next to the **Sort Bills** text box
> Click **Amount Due**
> • This shows you your bills from the highest amount owed to the lowest.
> Click drop-down list arrow next to the **Sort Bills** text box, click **Due Date**

- The bills will be shown according to the date due.

Click **Show bills due on or before** to select this option

Click in the text box for the date

Drag through the date to highlight, enter **01/31/10** as the date, press **Tab**

Scroll through the list of bills due

Select the bills to be paid

- The bills shown on the screen are an exact match to the bills you marked to be paid.

Click the **Select All Bills** button beneath the listing of bills

- To pay some of the bills but not all of them, mark each bill to be paid by clicking on the individual bill or using the cursor keys to select a bill and pressing the space bar.

The **Select All Bills** button changes to **Clear Selections** so bills can be unmarked and the bills to be paid may be selected again

Apply the $5 credit from Supply Station by clicking in the √ column for the $45 transaction for Supply Station with a due date of 01/28/2010

- This will deselect the bill

Click the √ column again to select the bill

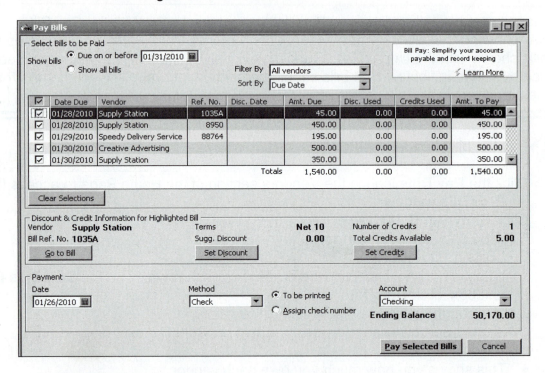

- Notice that the Set Credits button appears in bold and that a Total Credit of $5.00 is available.

Click the **Set Credits** button

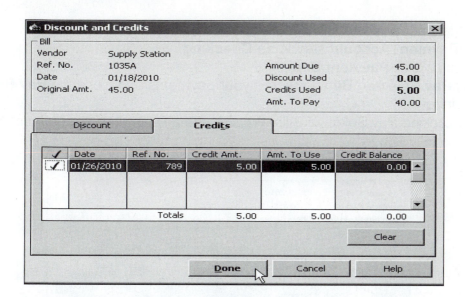

Click **Done** on the Discounts and Credits screen

- Notice that the Credits Used column for the transaction displays 5.00 and the Amt. To Pay for the bill is 40.00.

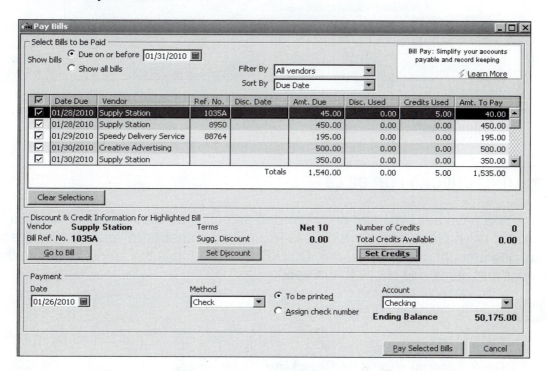

In the **Payment Method** section of the screen, enter the Payment Date of **01/26/10**

Check should be selected as the payment method

Make sure **To be printed** box has been selected

- If it is not selected, click in the circle to select

The **Payment Account** should be **Checking**

Tab to or click **Payment Date**

Click **Pay Selected Bills** to record your payments and close the **Pay Bills** window

After clicking Pay Selected Bills, you will see a Payment Summary screen.

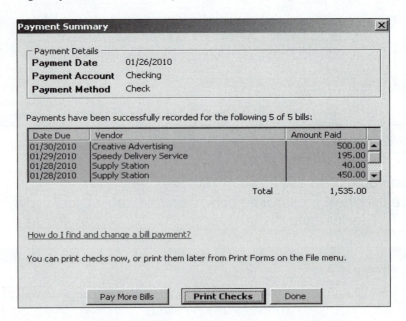

- Review the Payment Summary to see the amounts paid.

Continue with the next section

PRINTING CHECKS FOR BILLS

Once bills have been marked and recorded as paid, you may handwrite checks to vendors, or you may have QuickBooks Pro print the checks to vendors. If there is more than one amount due for a vendor, QuickBooks Pro totals the amounts due to the vendor and prints one check to the vendor.

DO ▶ Print the checks for the bills paid

Click **Print Checks**

Bank Account should be **Checking**

- If this is not showing, click the drop-down list arrow, click **Checking**.

The **First Check Number** should be **1**

- If not, delete the number showing, and key **1**.

In the √ column, the checks selected to be printed are marked with a check mark

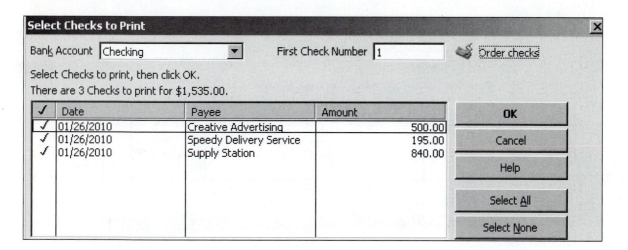

- Notice that the three bills from Supply Station have been combined into one check for payment.

Click **OK** to print the checks

- The **Print Checks** screen appears.

Verify and if necessary change information on the **Settings** tab

Printer name: The name of your printer should show in the text box

- If the correct printer name is not showing, click the drop-down list arrow, click the correct printer name.

Printer type: Page-oriented (Single sheets) should be in the text box

- If this does not show or if you use Continuous (Perforated Edge) checks, click the drop-down list arrow, click the appropriate sheet style to select.

Check style: Three different types of check styles may be used: Standard, Voucher, or Wallet

If it is not in the check style text box, click **Standard Checks** to insert

Print Company Name and Address: If the box does not have a check mark, click to select

Use Logo should not be selected; if a check mark appears in the check box, click to deselect

Click **Print** to print the checks

- All three checks will print on one page.

Print Checks - Confirmation dialog box appears

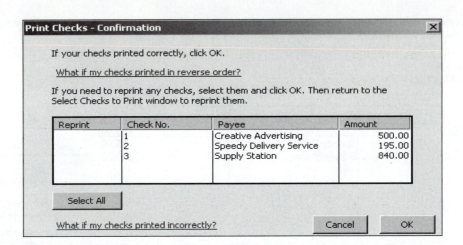

In addition to verifying the correct amount, payee, and payment date, review the checks for the following:

- The checks have the address for Computer Consulting by Your Name, the name and address of the company being paid, and the amount being paid.
- The actual checks will not have a check number printed because QuickBooks Pro is set up to work with preprinted check forms containing check numbers.
- In the memo section of the check, any memo entered on the bill shows.
- If there was no memo entered for the bill, the vendor account number appears as the memo.
- If you cannot get the checks to print on one page, it is perfectly acceptable to access the checks by clicking the **Write Checks** icon in the Banking section of the Home Page, and printing them one at a time. This method is also useful if you need to correct a check and reprint it.

If checks **printed** correctly, click **OK**

- If the checks did not print correctly, click the checks that need to be reprinted to select, and then click **OK**. Return to the Select Checks to print window and reprint them.

If you get a message box regarding purchasing checks, click **No**

REVIEW BILLS THAT HAVE BEEN PAID

In order to avoid any confusion about payment of a bill, QuickBooks Pro marks the bill PAID. Scrolling through the recorded bills in the Enter Bills window, you will see the paid bills marked PAID.

DO ▶ Scroll the **Enter Bills** window to view PAID bills

Click **Enter Bills** in the Vendors section of the Home Page
Click the **Previous** button to go back through all the bills recorded

- Notice that the bills paid for Supply Station, Speedy Delivery Service, and Creative Advertising are marked **PAID**. The Credit from Supply Station remains unmarked even though it has been used.

Click the **Close** button

PETTY CASH

Frequently, a business will need to pay for small expenses with cash. These might include expenses such as postage, office supplies, and miscellaneous expenses. For example, rather than write a check for postage due of 75 cents, you would use money from petty cash. QuickBooks Pro allows you to establish and use a petty cash account to track these small expenditures. Normally, a Petty Cash Voucher is prepared; and, if available, the receipt for the transaction is stapled to it. It is important in a business to keep accurate records of the petty cash expenditures, and procedures for control of the Petty Cash fund need to be established to prohibit access to and unauthorized use of the cash. Periodically, the petty cash expenditures are recorded so that the records of the company accurately reflect all expenses incurred in the operation of the business.

ADD PETTY CASH ACCOUNT TO THE CHART OF ACCOUNTS

QuickBooks Pro allows accounts to be added to the Chart of Accounts list at any time. Petty Cash is identified as a "Bank" account type so it will be placed at the top of the Chart of Accounts along with other checking and savings accounts.

MEMO

DATE: January 26, 2010

Occasionally, there are small items that should be paid for using cash. Alhandra Cruz needs to establish a petty cash account for $100

DO ▶ Add Petty Cash to the **Chart of Accounts**

Access **Chart of Accounts** as previously instructed
Click the **Account** button at the bottom of the Chart of Accounts, click **New**
Click **Bank** on the Add New Account: Choose Account Type screen
Click the **Continue** button

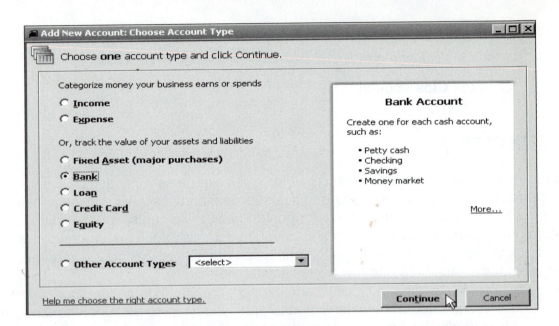

Enter **Petty Cash** in the **Account Name** text box
Leave the other items blank

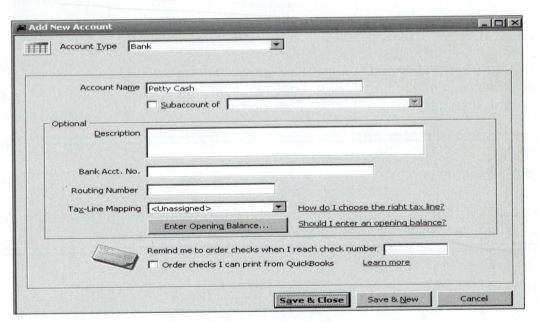

Click **Save & Close** to record the new account
Do not close the **Chart of Accounts**
- If you get a dialog box, to Set up Online Services, click **No**

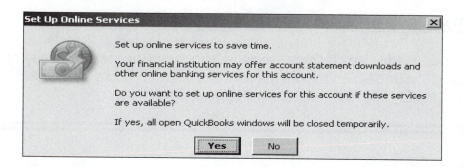

ESTABLISH PETTY CASH FUND

Once the account has been established, the petty cash fund must have money in order to pay for small expenses. A cash withdrawal from checking must be made or a check must be written and cashed to obtain petty cash funds. This may be recorded in the Checking Register.

> **DO** Record the cash withdrawal of $100 from checking to establish petty cash:

To access the **Check Register**, click the **Checking** account in the **Chart of Accounts**, click the **Activities** button, click **Use Register**
- The Check Register should be on the screen.
- If the cursor is not already in the Date column, click in the **Date** column for a new transaction at the end of the Check Register.
- The date should be highlighted; if it is not, drag through the date to highlight.

If the date is not 01/26/2010, enter **01/26/10**
Tab to or click **Number**
Enter **Cash**
Because this is a cash withdrawal, a Payee name will not be entered
Tab to or click **Payment**
Enter **100**
Tab to or click **Account**
Click the drop-down list arrow next to **Account**
Click **Petty Cash**
- The account shows Petty Cash and Type changed from CHK to TRANSFR.

Tab to or click **Memo**
Enter **Establish Petty Cash Fund**
Click **Record** button to record the withdrawal, then close the **Checking Register**

01/26/2010	Cash			100.00		50,075.00
	TRANSFR	Petty Cash	Establish Petty Cash Fund			

Do not close the **Chart of Accounts**

RECORD PAYMENT OF AN EXPENSE USING PETTY CASH

As petty cash is used to pay for small expenses in the business, these payments must be recorded. QuickBooks Pro makes it a simple matter to record petty cash expenditures directly into the Petty Cash Register.

MEMO

DATE: January 30, 2010

Alhandra Cruz needs to record the petty cash expenditures made during the week: postage due, 34 cents; purchased staples and paper clips, $3.57 (this is an expense); reimbursed Jennifer Lockwood for gasoline purchased for company car, $13.88.

▶ **DO** In the Petty Cash account, record a compound entry for the above expenditures

Click **Petty Cash** on the **Chart of Accounts**
Use the keyboard shortcut **Ctrl+R** to access the **Register**:
Click in the **Date** column, highlight the date if necessary
Type **01/30/10**
- No entry is required for Number; QuickBooks Pro inserts **1** for the number.
- No entry is required for Payee.
Tab to or click **Payment**
Enter **17.79** (you must type the decimal point)
Tab to or click in **Account** text box
Click **Splits** at the bottom of the screen
- Splits is used because the total amount of the transaction will be split among three expense accounts.
You will get an area where you can record the different accounts and amounts used in this transaction.
In the **Account** column showing on the screen, click the drop-down list arrow
Scroll until you see **Postage and Delivery**
Click **Postage and Delivery**
Tab to **Amount** column
- Using the Tab key will highlight **17.79**.
Type **.34**
- Memo notations are not necessary because the transactions are self-explanatory.
Tab to or click the next blank line in **Account**
Repeat the steps listed above to record **3.57** for **Office Supplies Expense** and **13.88** for **Automobile Expense**

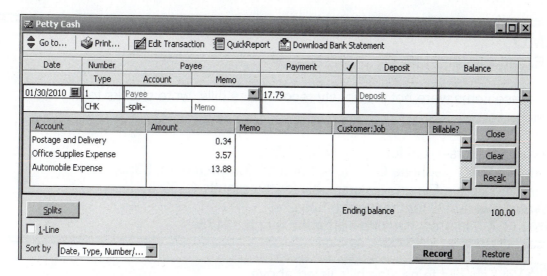

Click the **Close** button for Splits when all expenses have been recorded
Click **Record** to record the transaction

01/26/2010	Cash					100.00	100.00
	TRANSFR	Checking	Establish Petty Cash				
01/30/2010	1			17.79			82.21
	CHK	-split-					

- Notice that after the Record button has been clicked, the word "payee," the account name, and memo are removed from the transaction. Instead of showing the accounts used, **-split-** is shown.
- Verify the account Ending Balance of 82.21.

Close **Petty Cash** and the **Chart of Accounts**

PAY BILLS BY WRITING CHECKS

Although it is more efficient to record all bills in the Enter Bills window and pay all bills through the Pay Bills window, QuickBooks Pro also allows bills to be paid by writing a check to record and pay bills without entering a bill and then using the Pay Bills feature. When writing a check, the check window is divided into two main areas: the check face and the detail area. The check face includes information such as the date of the check, the payee's name, the check amount, the payee's address, and a line for a memo—just like a paper check. The detail area is used to indicate transaction accounts and amounts.

MEMO

DATE: January 30, 2010

Since these items were not previously recorded as bills, write checks to pay the following:

California Realtors—rent for the month, $1,500
Communication Telephone Co.—telephone bill for the month, $350
Southern California Electric—electric bill for the month, $250
Cal Water—water bill for the month, $35
Southern CA Gas Co.—heating bill for the month, $175

DO Write checks to pay the bills listed above

Click the **Write Checks** icon in the Banking section of the Home Page
    OR
Use the keyboard shortcut **Ctrl+W**
The bank account used for the check should be **Checking**.
- If you get a different account, Petty Cash, for example, click the drop-down list arrow for Bank Account, and click Checking.
Tab to or click **Date**
Enter **01/30/10**
To complete the check face, click the drop-down list arrow next to **Pay to the Order of**
Click **California Realtors**
Tab to or click **Amount**
Enter the amount of the rent
Tab to or click **Memo**
Enter **Monthly Rent**
- This memo prints on the check, not on reports. If you do not provide a memo on the check, QuickBooks will enter an account number, a telephone number, or a description as the memo.
Click **To Be Printed** to indicate that the check needs to be printed
- The Check Number will change from 1 to To Print, which means that the check will be printed at a later time.
Use the **Expenses** tab to complete the detail section of the check
Tab to or click the first line of **Account**
Click the drop-down list arrow for **Account**
Click **Rent**
- The total amount of the check is shown in Amount column.

- If you want a transaction description to appear in reports, enter the description in the Memo column— because these are standard transactions, no memo is entered.

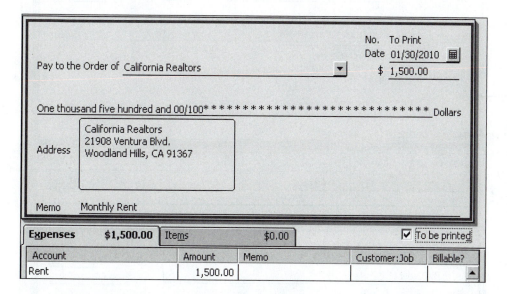

Do not print any of the checks being entered
Click **Save & New** to record the check and advance to the next check
Repeat the steps indicated above to record payment of the telephone, electric, water, and gas bills

- While entering the bills, you may see a dialog box on the screen, indicating that QuickBooks Pro allows you to do online banking. Online banking will not be used at this time. Click **OK** to close the dialog box.

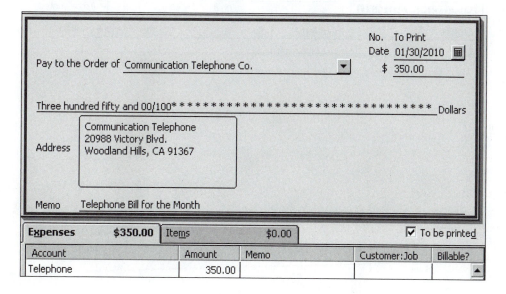

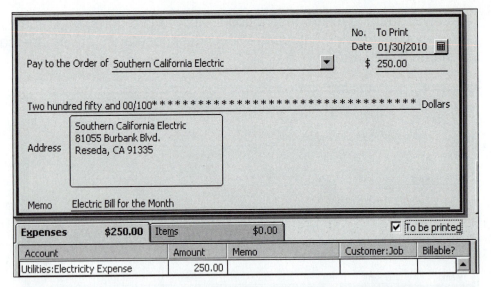

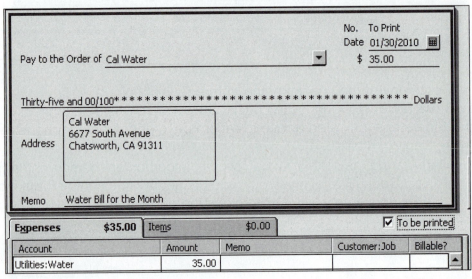

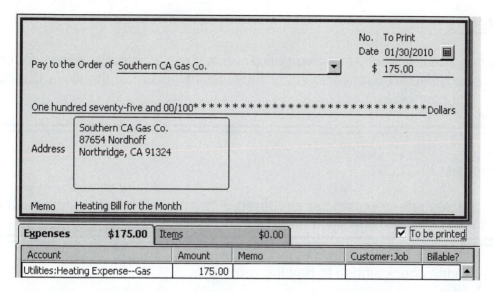

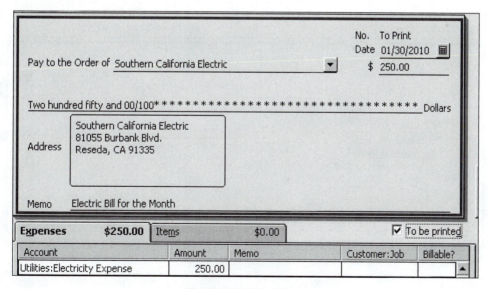

DO ► **ENTER THE CHECK FOR THE ELECTRIC BILL A SECOND TIME**

Click the drop-down list arrow and click **Southern California Electric**
- The first payment entered for the payment of the bill for electricity appears on the screen.

Duplicate Check

Click **Save & Close** to record the second payment for the electric bill and exit the **Write Checks** window

EDIT CHECKS

Mistakes can occur in business—even on a check. QuickBooks Pro allows for checks to be edited at anytime. You may use either the Check Register or the Write Checks window to edit checks.

MEMO

DATE: January 30, 2010

Once the check for the rent had been entered, Alhandra realized that it should have been for $1,600. Edit the check written to California Realtors.

DO Revise the check written to pay the rent

Open **Write Checks** as previously instructed
Click **Previous** until you reach the check for California Realtors
Click between the **1** and the **5** in the **Amount** under the Date
Press **Delete** to delete the **5**
Type **6**, press the **Tab** key

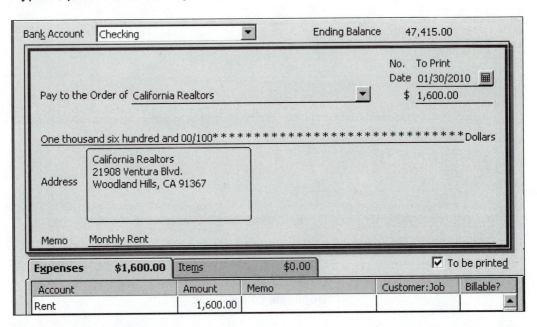

Do not print the check
Click **Save & Close**
Click **Yes** on the screen asking if you want to save the changed transaction

VOID CHECKS

QuickBooks Pro allows checks to be voided. Rather than deleting the transaction, voiding a check changes the amount of the check to zero but keeps a record of the transaction.

MEMO
DATE: January 30, 2010

The telephone bill should not have been paid until the first week of February. Void the check written for the telephone expense.

DO Use the steps given previously to access the Register for the **Checking** account

Void the check written for the telephone expense
Click anywhere in the check to Communication Telephone Co.
Click **Edit** on the menu bar at the top of the screen—not the Edit Transaction
   button
Click **Void Check**
• The amount of the check is now 0.00. The memo shows VOID:Telephone Bill
   for the Month.
Click the **Record** button
Do not close the register for checking

| 01/30/2010 | | Communication Telephone Co. | | 0.00 | ✓ | | 50,075.00 |
| | CHK | Telephone | VOID: Telephone Bill for the Month | | | | |

DELETE CHECKS

Deleting a check completely removes it and any transaction information for the check from QuickBooks Pro. Make sure you definitely want to remove the check before deleting it. Once it is deleted, a check cannot be recovered. It is often preferable to void a check than to delete it because a voided check is maintained in the company records; whereas, no record is kept in the active company records of a deleted check.

MEMO
DATE: January 30, 2010

In reviewing the register for the checking account, Alhandra Cruz discovered that two checks were written to pay the electric bill. Delete the second check.

DO   Delete the second entry for the electric bill

- Notice that there are two transactions showing for Southern California Electric.

Click anywhere in the second entry to Southern California Electric
Click **Edit** on the menu bar at the top of the screen, click **Delete Check**
    OR
Use the keyboard shortcut **Ctrl+D**

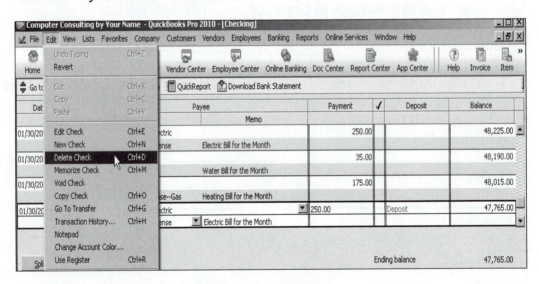

Click **OK** on the **Delete Transaction** dialog box

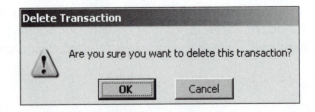

- After you have clicked the **OK** button, there is only one transaction in Checking for Southern California Electric.

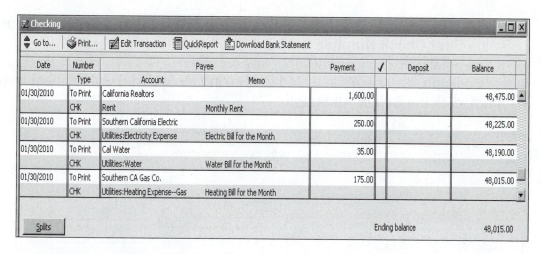

Date	Number	Payee		Payment	✓	Deposit	Balance
	Type	Account	Memo				
01/30/2010	To Print	California Realtors		1,600.00			48,475.00
	CHK	Rent	Monthly Rent				
01/30/2010	To Print	Southern California Electric		250.00			48,225.00
	CHK	Utilities:Electricity Expense	Electric Bill for the Month				
01/30/2010	To Print	Cal Water		35.00			48,190.00
	CHK	Utilities:Water	Water Bill for the Month				
01/30/2010	To Print	Southern CA Gas Co.		175.00			48,015.00
	CHK	Utilities:Heating Expense--Gas	Heating Bill for the Month				

Splits   Ending balance   48,015.00

Close the **Checking Register** and the **Chart of Accounts**

PRINT CHECKS

Checks may be printed as they are entered, or they may be printed at a later time. When checks are to be printed, QuickBooks Pro inserts the words *To Print* rather than a check number in the Check Register. The appropriate check number is indicated during printing. Because QuickBooks Pro is so flexible, a company must institute a system for cash control. For example, if the check for rent of $1,500 had been printed, QuickBooks Pro would allow a second check for $1,600 to be printed. In order to avoid any impropriety, more than one person should be designated to review checks. As a matter of practice in a small business, the owner or a person other than the one writing checks should sign the checks. Pre-numbered checks should be used, and any checks printed but not mailed should be submitted along with those for signature. Lastly, QuickBooks' audit trail feature detailing all transactions, including corrections, should be in use and the Audit Trail Report should be printed and viewed on a regular basis.

MEMO

DATE: January 30, 2010

Alhandra needs to print checks and obtain your signature so the checks can be mailed.

DO Print the checks for rent and utility bills paid by writing checks

Click the **File** menu, point to **Print Forms**, click **Checks**
Bank Account should be **Checking**
- If this is not showing, click the drop-down list arrow, click **Checking**

Because Check Nos. 1, 2, and 3 were printed previously, **4** should be the number in the **First Check Number** text box

- If not, delete the number showing, key **4**

In the √ column, the checks selected for printing are marked with a check mark

- If not, click the **Select All** button.

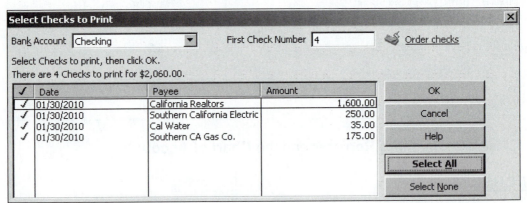

Click **OK** to print the checks

- The **Print Checks** screen appears.

Verify and if necessary change information on the **Settings** tab to use **Standard Checks** as previously shown in the chapter

Click **Print** to print the checks

Did check(s) print OK? dialog box appears

If the checks printed correctly, click **OK**

- The checks have the address for Computer Consulting by Your Name, the name and address of the company being paid, and the amount being paid. There is no check number printed on the checks because QuickBooks Pro is set up to use pre-numbered checks.

- In the memo section of the check, any memo entered when preparing the check shows. If there was no memo entered for the check, the vendor account number appears as the memo.

- If you run into difficulties or find you made an error and want to correct and/or print an individual check, you may do so by printing directly from the check.

PREPARE CHECK DETAIL REPORT

Once checks have been printed, it is important to review information about checks. The Check Detail Report provides detailed information regarding each check, including the checks for 0.00 amounts. Information indicates the type of transaction, the date, the check number, the payee, the account used, the original amount, and the paid amount of the check.

MEMO

DATE: January 30, 2010

Now that the checks have been printed, Alhandra prints a Check Detail Report. She will give this to you to examine when you sign the printed checks.

> **DO** Print a Check Detail Report

   Open the **Report Center**
   The type of report should be **Banking**
   Double-click **Check Detail** to select the report
   Remove the **Date Prepared** and **Time Prepared** from the report header
   The report is From **01/01/10** to **01/30/10**
   Tab to **generate** report
   - *Note:* You may find that the transaction for Petty Cash appears in a different order than the screen shot. The position of the transaction does not matter as long as the transaction is included in the report.
   Print the report in **Landscape** Orientation

Computer Consulting by Your Name

Check Detail

January 1 - 30, 2010

Type	Num	Date	Name	Item	Account	Paid Amount	Original Amount
▶ Check		01/30/2010	Communication Telephone Co.		Checking		0.00 ◀
TOTAL						0.00	0.00
Bill Pmt -Check	1	01/26/2010	Creative Advertising		Checking		-500.00
Bill		12/31/2009			Uncategorized Expenses	-500.00	500.00
TOTAL						-500.00	500.00
Check	1	01/30/2010			Petty Cash		-17.79
					Postage and Delivery	-0.34	0.34
					Office Supplies Expense	-3.57	3.57
					Automobile Expense	-13.88	13.88
TOTAL						-17.79	17.79
Bill Pmt -Check	2	01/26/2010	Speedy Delivery Service		Checking		-195.00
Bill	88764	01/19/2010			Postage and Delivery	-195.00	195.00
TOTAL						-195.00	195.00

Partial Report

   Click **Close** to close the report
   Do not close the Report Center

VIEW MISSING CHECKS REPORT

A Missing Checks Report lists the checks written for a bank account in order by check number. If there are any gaps between numbers or duplicate check numbers, this information is provided. The report indicates the type of transaction, Check or Bill Payment-Check, check date, check number, payee name, account used for the check, the split or additional accounts used, and the amount of the check.

MEMO

DATE: January 30, 2010

To see a listing of all checks printed, view a Missing Checks Report for all dates.

DO View a Missing Checks Report

Double-click **Missing Checks** in the Banking section to select the report being prepared
- If **Checking** appears as the account on the **Missing Checks Report** dialog box, click **OK**.
- If it does not appear, click the drop-down list arrow, click **Checking**, click **OK**.

Examine the report:

9:57 AM			Computer Consulting by Your Name				
01/30/10			**Missing Checks**				
			All Transactions				
Type	Date	Num	Name	Memo	Account	Split	Amount
Bill Pmt -Check	01/26/2010	1	Creative Advertising	1-2567135-54	Checking	Accounts Payable	-500.00
Bill Pmt -Check	01/26/2010	2	Speedy Delivery Service	January Delivery Expense	Checking	Accounts Payable	-195.00
Bill Pmt -Check	01/26/2010	3	Supply Station	456-45623	Checking	Accounts Payable	-840.00
Check	01/30/2010	4	California Realtors	Monthly Rent	Checking	Rent	-1,600.00
Check	01/30/2010	5	Southern California Electric	Electric Bill for the Month	Checking	Electricity Expense	-250.00
Check	01/30/2010	6	Cal Water	Water Bill for the Month	Checking	Water	-35.00
Check	01/30/2010	7	Southern CA Gas Co.	Heating Bill for the Month	Checking	Heating Expense--Gas	-175.00

- The **Account** in all cases is **Checking**.

- The **Split** column indicates which accounts in addition to checking have been used in the transaction.
- Look at the **Type** column.
- The checks written through Pay Bills indicate the transaction type as **Bill Pmt-Check**.
- The bills paid by actually writing the checks show **Check** as the transaction type.

Close the report without printing

VIEW THE VOIDED/DELETED TRANSACTION SUMMARY

QuickBooks has a report for all voided/deleted transactions. This report appears in the Accountant & Taxes section for reports. This report may be printed as a summary or in detail. It will show all the transactions that have been voided and/or deleted.

MEMO

DATE: January 30, 2010

In order to be informed more fully about the checks that have been written, you have Alhandra prepare the Voided/Deleted Transaction Summary Report for January.

DO Prepare the Voided/Deleted Transaction Summary report

Click **Accountant & Taxes** in the Report Center
Click **Voided/Deleted Transaction Summary** in the Account Activity section
Click the **Display Report** button
The report dates are From **01/01/2010** To **01/30/2010**

10:01 AM			Computer Consulting by Your Name					
01/30/10			**Voided/Deleted Transactions Summary**					
			Entered/Last Modified January 1 - 30, 2010					
Num	Action	Entered/Last Modified	Date	Name	Memo	Account	Split	Amount
Transactions entered or modified by Admin								
Bill 1579-53								0.00
1579-53	Deleted Transaction	01/26/2010 09:56:52						
1579-53	Changed Transaction	01/26/2010 09:56:16	01/19/2010	Computer Professionals Magazine	Six-month Subscription	Accounts Payable	Dues and Subscriptions	-79.00
1579-53	Added Transaction	01/26/2010 09:51:24	01/19/2010	Computer Professionals Magazine	Six-month Subscription	Accounts Payable	Dues and Subscriptions	-74.00
Check								0.00
	Voided Transaction	01/28/2010 09:09:55	01/30/2010	Communication Telephone Co.	VOID: Telephone Bill for the Month	Checking	Telephone	0.00
	Added Transaction	01/27/2010 10:17:40	01/30/2010	Communication Telephone Co.	Telephone Bill for the Month	Checking	Telephone	-350.00
Check								0.00
	Deleted Transaction	01/28/2010 09:14:33						
	Added Transaction	01/27/2010 10:26:56	01/30/2010	Southern California Electric	Electric Bill for the Month	Checking	Utilities:Electricity Expense	-250.00
Invoice 2								0.00
2	Deleted Transaction	01/07/2010 10:55:33						
2	Added Transaction	12/07/2009 17:20:09	01/03/2010	Williams, Matt CPA		Accounts Receivable	-SPLIT-	415.00
Invoice 3								0.00
3	Voided Transaction	01/07/2010 10:40:19	01/05/2010	Ahmadrand, Ela	VOID:	Accounts Receivable	Income:Technical Support Income	0.00
3	Added Transaction	01/03/2010 17:29:55	01/05/2010	Ahmadrand, Ela		Accounts Receivable	Income:Technical Support Income	300.00

- The Entered Last Modified column shows the actual date and time that the entry was made. The report header shows your computer's current date and time. The dates and times shown will <u>not</u> match your date and time.
- In addition, your report may not match the one illustrated if you have voided or deleted anything else during your work session.

Close the report without printing

Close the Report Center

PURCHASE AN ASSET WITH A COMPANY CHECK

Not all purchases will be transactions on account. If something is purchased and paid for with a check, a check is written and the purchase is recorded.

MEMO

DATE: January 30, 2010

Having tried out several fax machines from Supply Station on a rental basis, you decide to purchase one from them. Because the fax machine is on sale if it is purchased for cash, you decide to buy it by writing a company check for the asset for $486.

▶ **DO** Record the check written for the purchase of a fax machine

Access **Write Checks - Checking** window as previously instructed
- You wrote the check by hand. It does not need printing.

Click the **To be printed** box to deselect.
- The **No.** shows as **1**.

Because Check Nos. 1 through 7 have been printed, enter **8** for the check number

Click the drop-down list arrow for **Pay to the Order of**

Click **Supply Station**

The **Date** should be **01/30/2010**

Enter **486** for the Amount

Tab to or click **Memo**

Enter **Purchase Fax Machine**

Tab to or click **Account** on the **Expenses** tab

Click the drop-down list arrow, scroll to the top of the **Chart of Accounts**, and click **Original Cost** under **Office Equipment**
- If you get a message to Track Fixed Assets, click **NO**
- **Amount** column shows the transaction total of **486.00**. This does not need to be changed.

Click **Memo**

Enter **Purchase Fax Machine**

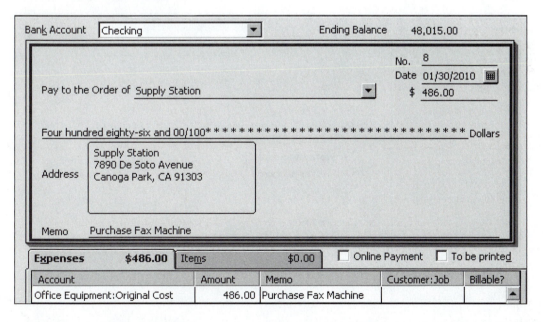

Click **Save & Close** to record the check and exit the **Write Checks - Checking** window without printing

CUSTOMIZE REPORT FORMAT

The report format used in one company may not be appropriate for all companies that use QuickBooks Pro. In order to allow program users the maximum flexibility, QuickBooks Pro makes it very easy to customize many of the user preferences of the program. For example, you may customize menus, reminder screens, and reports and graphs.

▶ DO ▶ Customize the report preferences to make permanent changes to all reports so reports are automatically refreshed, and the date prepared, time prepared, and report basis do not print on reports

Click the **Edit** menu, click **Preferences**
Scroll through the items listed on the left side of the screen until you get to Reports and Graphs
Click the **Reports and Graphs** icon   `▥ Reports & Graphs`
• If **Refresh Automatically** on the **My Preferences** tab has not been selected, click it to select
Whenever data is changed and a report appears on the screen, QuickBooks will automatically update the report to reflect the changes.

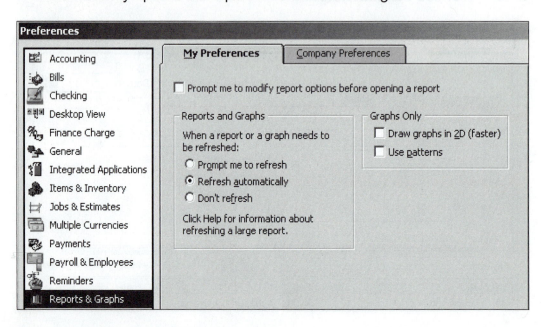

Click the **Company Preferences** tab
Click the **Format** button

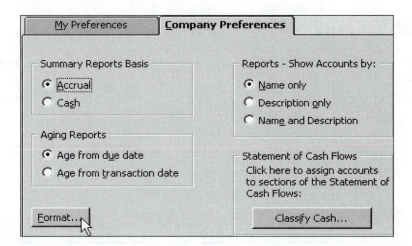

- If necessary, click the **Header/Footer** tab

Click **Date Prepared**, **Time Prepared**, and **Report Basis** to deselect

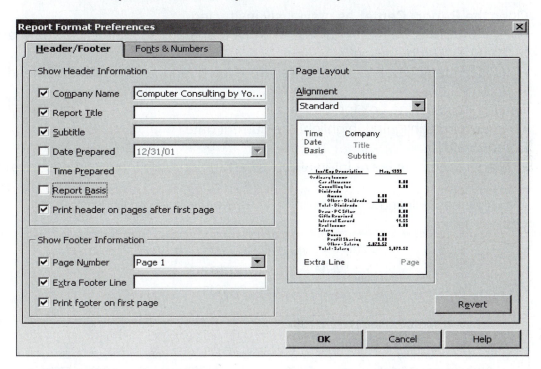

Click **OK** to save the change
Click **OK** to close **Preferences**

PRINT ACCOUNTS PAYABLE AGING SUMMARY

It is important in a business to maintain a good credit rating and to make sure that payments are made on time. In order to avoid overlooking a payment, the Accounts Payable Aging Summary lists the vendors to which the company owes money and shows how long the money has been owed.

MEMO
DATE: January 30, 2010

Prepare the Accounts Payable Aging Summary for Computer Consulting by Your Name.

DO ▶ Prepare an **Accounts Payable Aging Summary**

Open the **Report Center** as previously instructed
Click **Vendors & Payables** to select the type of report, double-click **Summary** in the **A/P Aging** section
- Notice that the date and time prepared do not appear as part of the heading information.
Tab to or click in the box for the **Date**
- If it is not highlighted, highlight the current date.
Enter **01/30/10**
- Tab through but leave Interval (days) as 30 and Through (days past due) as 90.
- The report will show the current bills as well as any past due bills.

Computer Consulting by Your Name
A/P Aging Summary
As of January 30, 2010

	Current	1 - 30	31 - 60	61 - 90	> 90	TOTAL
California Insurance Company	2,850.00	0.00	0.00	0.00	0.00	2,850.00
Computer Technologies Magazine	79.00	0.00	0.00	0.00	0.00	79.00
Creative Advertising	260.00	0.00	0.00	0.00	0.00	260.00
Garcia Garage and Auto Services	575.00	0.00	0.00	0.00	0.00	575.00
TOTAL	3,764.00	0.00	0.00	0.00	0.00	3,764.00

Follow instructions provided earlier to print the report in Portrait orientation
Close the **A/P Aging Summary** screen
Do not close the Report Center

PRINT UNPAID BILLS DETAIL REPORT

Another important report is the Unpaid Bills Detail Report. Even though it was already printed once during the month, it is always a good idea to print the report at the end of the month.

MEMO

DATE: January 30, 2010

At the end of every month, Alhandra Cruz prepares and prints an Unpaid Bills Detail Report for you.

DO ▶ Prepare and print the report

Follow instructions provided earlier in the chapter to prepare and print an **Unpaid Bills Detail Report** for **01/30/2010** in Portrait orientation

Computer Consulting by Your Name
Unpaid Bills Detail
As of January 30, 2010

Type	Date	Num	Due Date	Aging	Open Balance
California Insurance Company					
Bill	01/19/2010	3659	02/18/2010		2,850.00
Total California Insurance Company					2,850.00
Computer Technologies Magazine					
Bill	01/19/2010	1579-53	02/18/2010		79.00
Total Computer Technologies Magazine					79.00
Creative Advertising					
Bill	01/16/2010	9875	02/15/2010		260.00
Total Creative Advertising					260.00
Garcia Garage and Auto Services					
Bill	01/19/2010	630	02/18/2010		575.00
Total Garcia Garage and Auto Services					575.00
TOTAL					**3,764.00**

Close the report
- If you get a Memorize Report dialog box, remember to always click No.

Do not close the Report Center

PRINT VENDOR BALANCE SUMMARY

There are two Vendor Balance Reports available in QuickBooks Pro. There is a Summary Report that shows unpaid balances for vendors and a Detail Report that lists each transaction for a vendor. In order to see how much is owed to each vendor, prepare a Vendor Balance Summary report.

MEMO

DATE: January 30, 2010

At the end of each month, Alhandra prepares and prints a Vendor Balance Summary Report to give to you.

▶ DO ▶ Prepare and print a **Vendor Balance Summary Report**

Double-click **Vendor Balance Summary** in the Vendor Balances section
- The report should show only the totals owed to each vendor on January 30, 2010.
- If it does not, tab to or click **From**, enter **01/30/10**. Then tab to or click **To**, enter **01/30/10**.

Computer Consulting by Your Name

Vendor Balance Summary

All Transactions

	◇ Jan 30, 10 ◇
California Insurance Company	▶ 2,850.00 ◀
Computer Technologies Magazine	79.00
Creative Advertising	260.00
Garcia Garage and Auto Services	575.00
TOTAL	**3,764.00**

Follow steps listed previously to print the report in Portrait orientation
Close the report; do not close the **Report Center**

CREATE AN ACCOUNTS PAYABLE GRAPH BY AGING PERIOD

Graphs provide a visual representation of certain aspects of the business. It is sometimes easier to interpret data in a graphical format. For example, to determine if any payments are overdue for accounts payable accounts, use an Accounts Payable Graph to provide that information instantly on a bar chart. In addition, the Accounts Payable Graph feature of QuickBooks Pro also displays a pie chart showing what percentage of the total amount payable is owed to each vendor.

DO Prepare an Accounts Payable Graph

Double-click **Accounts Payable Graph** in the Vendors & Payables list of reports
Click the **Dates** button at the top of the report
Enter **01/30/10** for **Show Aging as of** in the **Change Graph Dates** text box

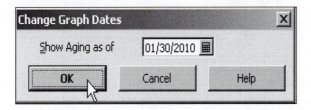

Click **OK**

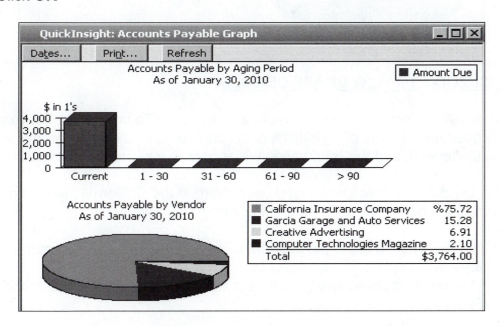

Click the **Dates** button again; enter **02/28/10** for the date
Click **OK**
- Notice that the bar moved from Current to 1-30. This means at the end of February the bills will be between 1 and 30 days overdue.

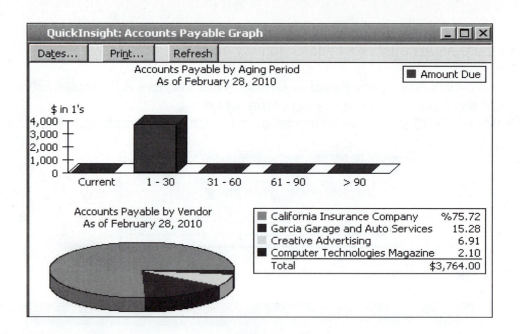

USE QUICKZOOM TO VIEW GRAPH DETAILS

To obtain detailed information from a graph, use the QuickZoom feature. For example, to see the overdue category of an individual account, double-click on a vendor in the pie chart or in the legend, and this information will appear in a separate bar chart.

DO ▶ Use QuickZoom to see how many days overdue the California Insurance Company's bill will be at the end of February

Point to the section of the pie chart for **California Insurance Company**
Double-click
- The bar chart shows the bill will be in the 1-30 day category at the end of February.

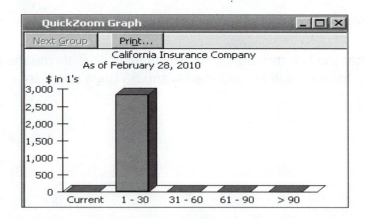

Close the QuickZoom Graph for California Insurance Company
Close the **QuickInsight: Accounts Payable Graph**

PRINT THE JOURNAL

It is always a good idea to review your transactions for appropriate amount, account and item usage. In tracing errors, the Journal is an invaluable tool. If you suspect an error, always check the transaction dates, amounts, accounts used, and items listed in the Memo column to verify the accuracy of your entry.

DO Prepare the Journal as previously instructed

The report dates are From **01/01/10** To **01/30/10**
Review the report and check the dates, amounts, accounts, and items used

Computer Consulting by Your Name
Journal
January 1 - 30, 2010

Trans #	Type	Date	Num	Name	Memo	Account	Debit	Credit
63	Check	01/30/2010	6	Cal Water	Water Bill for the Month	Checking		35.00
				Cal Water	Water Bill for the Month	Water	35.00	
							35.00	35.00
64	Check	01/30/2010	7	Southern CA Gas Co.	Heating Bill for the Month	Checking		175.00
				Southern CA Gas Co.	Heating Bill for the Month	Heating Expense--Gas	175.00	
							175.00	175.00
66	Check	01/30/2010	8	Supply Station	Purchase Fax Machine	Checking		486.00
				Supply Station	Purchase Fax Machine	Original Cost	486.00	
							486.00	486.00
TOTAL							**45,217.79**	**45,217.79**

Partial Report

- Scroll through the report. You will see all of the transactions entered for Chapters 2 and 3.

Print the Report in Landscape orientation
Close the Report Center

BACK UP COMPUTER CONSULTING BY YOUR NAME DATA AND CLOSE COMPANY

Whenever an important work session is complete, you should always back up your data. If your data disk or company file is damaged or an error is discovered at a later time, the backup file (.qbb) may be restored to the same or a new company file and the information used for recording transactions. As in previous chapters, you should close the company at the end of each work session.

▸ DO ▸ Follow the instructions given in Chapters 1 and 2 to back up data for Computer Consulting by Your Name and to close the company. Refer to the instructions provided by your professor for making a duplicate disk

Name your back up file **Computer (Backup Ch. 3)**

SUMMARY

In this chapter, bills were recorded and paid, checks were written, and reports were prepared. The petty cash fund was established and used for payments of small expense items. Checks were voided, deleted, and corrected. Accounts were added and modified. QuickReports were accessed in various ways, and QuickZoom was used to obtain transaction detail while in various reports. Reports were prepared for Missing Checks and Check Details. Unpaid Bills and Vendor Balance Summary Reports provided information regarding bills that had not been paid. The graphing feature of QuickBooks Pro allowed you to determine Accounts Payable by aging period and to see the percentage of Accounts Payable for each vendor.

END-OF-CHAPTER QUESTIONS

TRUE/FALSE

ANSWER THE FOLLOWING QUESTIONS IN THE SPACE PROVIDED BEFORE THE QUESTION NUMBER.

_____ 1. Credit Memos are prepared to record a reduction to a transaction.

_____ 2. When using QuickBooks Pro, checks may not be written in a checkbook.

_____ 3. QuickZoom is a QuickBooks Pro feature that allows detailed information to be displayed.

_____ 4. A purchase can be recorded by writing a check or by using petty cash.

_____ 5. Once a report format has been customized as a QuickBooks Pro preference for a company, QuickBooks Pro will automatically use the customized format.

_____ 6. In a service business, most of the accounting for purchases and payables is simply paying bills for expenses incurred in the operation of the business.

_____ 7. The accrual method of accounting matches the income of the period with the cash received for sales.

_____ 8. A Missing Check Report lists any duplicate check numbers or gaps between check numbers.

_____ 9. The Accounts Payable Register keeps track of all checks written in the business.

_____ 10. If a check has been edited, it cannot be printed.

MULTIPLE CHOICE

WRITE THE LETTER OF THE CORRECT ANSWER IN THE SPACE PROVIDED
BEFORE THE QUESTION NUMBER.

_____ 1. When using QuickBooks' graphs, information regarding the percentage of
accounts payable owed to each vendor is displayed as a ___.
A. pie chart
B. bar chart
C. line chart
D. both A and B

_____ 2. A check may be entered in ___.
A. the Write Checks window
B. the Check Register
C. both A and B
D. neither A nor B

_____ 3. When you enter a bill, typing the first letter(s) of a vendor's name on the
Vendor line ___.
A. enters the vendor's name on the line if the name is in the Vendor List
B. displays a list of vendor names
C. displays the Address Info tab for the vendor
D. both A and B

_____ 4. To erase an incorrect amount in a bill, you may ___, then key the correction.
A. drag through the amount to highlight
B. position the cursor in front of the amount and press the delete key until the
amount has been erased
C. position the cursor after the amount and press the backspace key until the
amount has been erased
D. all of the above

_____ 5. When a document prints sideways, it is called ___ orientation.
A. portrait
B. landscape
C. standard
D. horizontal

_C_ 6. A correction to a bill that has been recorded can be made on the bill or ___.
  A. not at all
  B. on the Accounts Payable Graph
  C. in the Accounts Payable Register
  D. none of the above

_C_ 7. When a bill is deleted, ___.
  A. the amount is changed to 0.00
  B. the word *deleted* appears as the Memo
  C. it is removed without a trace
  D. a bill cannot be deleted

_A_ 8. To increase the date on a bill by one day, ___.
  A. press the + key
  B. press the - key
  C. tab
  D. press the # key

_B_ 9. If a bill is recorded in the Enter Bills window, it is important to pay the bill by ___.
  A. writing a check
  B. using the Pay Bills window
  C. using petty cash
  D. allowing QuickBooks Pro to generate the check automatically five days before the due date

_B_ 10. When entering several bills at once on the Enter Bills screen, it is most efficient to ___ to go to the next blank screen.
  A. click Previous
  B. click Save & New
  C. click OK
  D. click Preview

FILL-IN

IN THE SPACE PROVIDED, WRITE THE ANSWER THAT MOST APPROPRIATELY COMPLETES THE SENTENCE.

1. The _____ section of a check is used to record the check date, payee, and amount for the actual check. The _____ section of a check is used to record the accounts used for the bill, the amount for each account used, and transaction explanations.

2. An Accounts Payable Graph by Aging Period shows a _____ chart detailing the amounts due by aging period and a _____ chart showing the percentage of the total amount payable owed to each vendor.

3. Three different check styles may be used in QuickBooks Pro: _____, _____, or _____.

4. The keyboard shortcut to edit or modify a vendor's record is _____.

5. Petty Cash is identified as a _____ account type so it will be placed at the top of the Chart of Accounts along with checking and savings accounts.

SHORT ESSAY

When viewing a Transaction by Vendor Report that shows the entry of a bill for the purchase of office supplies and office equipment, you will see the term **-split-** displayed. Explain what the term **Split** means when used as a column heading and when used within the Split column for the bill indicated.

_____
_____
_____
_____
_____
_____
_____

NAME_____

TRANSMITTAL

CHAPTER 3: COMPUTER CONSULTING BY YOUR NAME

Attach the following documents and reports:

Transaction List by Vendor, January 1-18, 2010
Register QuickReport, Supply Station
Unpaid Bills Detail Report, January 25, 2010
Check No. 1: Creative Advertising
Check No. 2: Speedy Delivery Service
Check No. 3: Supply Station
Check No. 4: California Realtors
Check No. 5: Southern California Electric
Check No. 6: Cal Water
Check No. 7: Southern CA Gas Co.
Check Detail Report
A/P Aging Summary, Current and Total
Unpaid Bills Detail Report, January 30, 2010
Vendor Balance Summary
Journal, January 30, 2010

END-OF-CHAPTER PROBLEM

YOUR NAME LANDSCAPE AND POOL SERVICE

Chapter 3 continues with the transactions for bills, bill payments, and purchases for Your Name Landscape and Pool Service. Cash control measures have been implemented. Sally prints the checks and any related reports; Ramon initials his approval of the checks; and you, the owner, sign the checks.

INSTRUCTIONS

Continue to use the company file that you used in Chapters 1 and 2 **Landscape.qbw**. Record the bills, bill payments, and purchases as instructed within the chapter. Always read the transactions carefully and review the Chart of Accounts when selecting transaction accounts. Print reports and graphs as indicated. If a bill is recorded on the Enter Bills screen, it should be paid on the Pay Bills screen—not by writing the check.

RECORD TRANSACTIONS

<u>January 1</u>—Use Enter Bills to record bills:

- ► Edit the vendor Communications Services. On the Address Info tab change the "Print on Check as" from Total Communications to Communications Services.
- ► Received a bill from Communications Services for cellular phone service, $485, Net 10, Invoice No. 1109, Memo: Cell Phone Services for January.
- ► Received a bill from the Office Supply Store for office supplies purchased to have on hand, $275, Net 30, Invoice No. 58-9826. (This is a prepaid expense so an asset account is used.) No memo is necessary.
- ► Received a bill from Douglas Motors for truck service and repairs, $519, Net 10, Invoice No. 1-62, Memo: Truck Service and Repairs. (Use Automobile Expense as the account for this transaction. We will change the name to something more appropriate in Chapter 4.)
- ► Received a bill from State Street Gasoline for gasoline for the month, $375, Net 10, Invoice No. 853, Memo: Gasoline for Month.
- ► Received a bill from Guy's Cooler/Heating for a repair of the office air conditioner, $150, Net 30, Invoice No. 87626, Memo: Air Conditioner Repair. (The air conditioner is part of the building.)

<u>January 15</u>—Use Enter Bills to record the following bills:

- ► Add a new expense account: Disposal Expense, Description: County Dump Charges.

▶ Received a bill from County Dump for disposing of lawn, tree, and shrub trimmings, $180, Net 30, Invoice No. 667, no memo necessary.

▶ Received a bill from Santa Barbara Water Co., $25, Net 10, Invoice No. 098-1.

▶ Change the QuickBooks Pro Company Preferences to customize the report format so that reports refresh automatically, and that the Date Prepared, the Time Prepared, and the Report Basis do not print as part of the header.

▶ Print an Unpaid Bills Detail Report for January 1-15 in Portrait orientation.

▶ Pay all bills *due on or before January 15*, print the checks. (Use Pay Bills to pay bills that have been entered in the Enter Bills window.) Print the checks using standard style.

▶ Record the receipt of a bill from Quality Equipment Maintenance. Add this new vendor as you record the transaction. Additional information needed to do a complete Set Up is: 1234 State Street, Santa Barbara, CA 93110, 805-555-0770, Net 10. The bill was for the repair of the lawn mower (equipment), $75, Invoice No. 5-1256, no memo necessary.

▶ Change the telephone number for County Dump. The new number is 805-555-3798.

▶ Prepare and print the Vendor Balance Detail Report for all transactions.

January 30—Enter the transactions:

▶ Received a $10 credit from Quality Equipment Maintenance. The repair of the lawn mower wasn't as extensive as originally estimated.

▶ Add Petty Cash to the Chart of Accounts.

▶ Use the Register for Checking to transfer $50 from Checking to Petty Cash, Memo: Establish Petty Cash Fund.

▶ Record the use of Petty Cash to pay for postage due 64 cents, and office supplies, $1.59 (this is a current expense). Memo notations are not necessary.

▶ Write Check No. 5 to Quality Equipment Maintenance to buy a lawn fertilizer spreader as a cash purchase of equipment, $349, Check Memo: Purchase of Lawn Fertilizer Spreader. Print the check. (If you get a dialog box indicating that you currently owe money to Quality Equipment Maintenance, Click **Continue Writing Check**. Remember, this is a purchase of equipment.)

▶ Print an Unpaid Bills Detail Report for January 30.

▶ Pay all bills *due on or before January 30*; print the checks. (Note: There may be some bills that were due after January 15 but before January 30. Be sure to pay these bills now. If any vendor shows a credit and has a bill that is due, apply it to the bill prior to payment. You may need to click on each bill individually in order to determine whether or not there is a credit to be applied.) Print the checks using standard style.

▶ Prepare an Accounts Payable Graph as of 1/30/2010. Do not print.

▶ Prepare a QuickZoom Graph for County Dump as of 1/30/2010. Do not print.

▶ Print the Journal for January 1-30, 2010 in Landscape orientation.

▶ Back up your data and close the company.

NAME_____

TRANSMITTAL

CHAPTER 3: YOUR NAME LANDSCAPE AND POOL SERVICE

Attach the following documents and reports:

(Note: When paying bills and printing a batch of checks, your checks may be in a different order than shown below. As long as you print the checks to the correct vendors and have the correct amounts, do not be concerned if your check numbers are not an exact match.)

Unpaid Bills Detail Report, January 15, 2010
Check No. 1: Communications Services
Check No. 2: County Dump
Check No. 3: Douglas Motors
Check No. 4: State Street Gasoline
Vendor Balance Detail
Check No. 5: Quality Equipment Maintenance
Unpaid Bills Detail Report, January 30, 2010
Check No. 6: Quality Equipment Maintenance
Check No. 7: Santa Barbara Water Co.
Journal, January 30, 2010

GENERAL ACCOUNTING AND END-OF-PERIOD PROCEDURES: SERVICE BUSINESS

4

LEARNING OBJECTIVES

At the completion of this chapter, you will be able to:

1. Complete the end-of-period procedures.
2. Change account names, delete accounts, and make accounts inactive.
3. View an account name change and its effect on subaccounts.
4. Record depreciation and enter the adjusting entries required for accrual-basis accounting.
5. Record owner's equity transactions for a sole proprietor including capital investment and owner withdrawals.
6. Reconcile the bank statement, record bank service charges, automatic payments, and mark cleared transactions.
7. Print Trial Balance, Profit and Loss Statement, and Balance Sheet.
8. Export a report to Microsoft® Excel
9. Perform end-of-period backup and close the end of a period.

GENERAL ACCOUNTING AND END-OF-PERIOD PROCEDURES

As previously stated, QuickBooks Pro operates from the standpoint of a business document rather than an accounting form, journal, or ledger. While QuickBooks Pro does incorporate all of these items into the program, in many instances they operate behind the scenes. QuickBooks Pro does not require special closing procedures at the end of a period. At the end of the fiscal year, QuickBooks Pro transfers the net income into the Retained Earnings account and allows you to protect the data for the year by assigning a closing date to the period. All of the transaction detail is maintained and viewable, but it will not be changed unless OK is clicked on a warning screen.

Even though a formal closing does not have to be performed within QuickBooks Pro, when you use accrual-basis accounting, several transactions must be recorded to reflect all expenses and income for the period. For example, bank statements must be reconciled and any charges or bank collections need to be recorded. During the business period, the CPA for the company will review things such as account names, adjusting entries, depreciation schedules, owner's equity adjustments, and so on. Sometimes the changes and adjustments will be made by the accountant in a separate file called the Accountant's Copy of the business files. This file is then imported into the company file that is used to record day-to-day business transactions, and all adjustments made by the CPA are added to the current company file. There are certain restrictions to the types of transactions that may be made on an Accountant's Copy of the business files.

Once necessary adjustments have been made, reports reflecting the end-of-period results of operations should be prepared. For archive purposes at the end of the fiscal year an additional backup disk is prepared and stored.

TRAINING TUTORIAL AND PROCEDURES

The following tutorial will once again work with Computer Consulting by Your Name. As in Chapters 2 and 3, transactions will be recorded for this fictitious company. To maximize training benefits, you should follow the steps illustrated in Chapter 2 and be sure to use the same file that you used to record transactions for Chapters 2 and 3.

OPEN QUICKBOOKS® PRO AND COMPUTER CONSULTING BY YOUR NAME

▶**DO** Open QuickBooks Pro

Open Computer Consulting by Your Name
- This file should contain all the transactions that you recorded for Chapters 2 and 3.
- To close an open company and open your copy of the company, click **File**, click **Open Company**, click **Computer.qbw**, check to make sure you are using the correct storage location, and click **Open**.

Check the title bar to verify that Computer Consulting by Your Name is the open company

DATES

As in the other chapters in the text, the year used for the screen shots is 2010, which is the same year as the version of the program. You may want to check with your instructor to see if you should use 2010 as the year for the transactions. Be sure to use the same year for all the transactions in Chapters 2, 3, and 4.

BEGINNING THE TUTORIAL

In this chapter, you will be recording end-of-period adjustments, reconciling bank statements, changing account names, and preparing traditional end-of-period reports. Because QuickBooks Pro does not perform a traditional "closing" of the books, you will learn how to assign a closing date to protect transactions and data recorded during previous accounting periods.

As in the earlier chapters, all transactions are listed on memos. The transaction date will be the same as the memo date unless otherwise specified within the transaction. Once a specific type of transaction has been entered in a step-by-step manner, additional transactions of the same or a similar type will be made without instructions being provided. Of course, you may always refer to instructions given for previous transactions for ideas or for steps used to enter those transactions. To determine the account used in the transaction, refer to the Chart of Accounts, which is also the General Ledger.

CHANGE THE NAME OF EXISTING ACCOUNTS IN THE CHART OF ACCOUNTS

Even though transactions have been recorded during the month of January, QuickBooks Pro makes it a simple matter to change the name of an existing account. Once the name of an account has been changed, all transactions using the "old" name are updated and show the "new" account name.

MEMO
DATE: January 31, 2010

Upon the recommendation from the company's CPA, you decided to change the names of several accounts: Student's Name, Capital to Your Name, Capital (Use your actual name); Company Cars to Business Vehicles; Company Cars Loan to Business Vehicles Loan; Automobile Expense to Business Vehicles Expense; Auto Insurance Expense to Business Vehicles Insurance; Office Equipment to Office Furniture & Equipment; Office Equipment Loan to Office Furniture/Equipment Loan; Loan Interest to Interest on Loans

---

DO Change the account names

Access the **Chart of Accounts** using the keyboard shortcut Ctrl+A
Scroll through accounts until you see **Student's Name, Capital**, click the account.
Click the **Account** button at the bottom of the Chart of Accounts, click **Edit Account**
OR
Use the keyboard shortcut **Ctrl+E**
On the **Edit Account** screen, highlight **Student's Name**
Enter your name
Click **Save & Close** to record the name change and to close the **Edit Account** screen

- Notice that the name of the account appears as Your Name, Capital in the Chart of Accounts and that the balance of $78,135.00 shows.
- The balances of any subaccounts of Student's Name, Capital will be reflected in the account total on the Chart of Accounts and in reports.
- While the subaccount names remain unchanged, the name of the account to which they are attached is changed.
- The account name was changed in Chapter 1; however, the backup file was restored. The backup was made before changing the account name so the account name change was eliminated.

Follow the steps above to change the names of:
Company Cars to **Business Vehicles**
Company Cars Loan to **Business Vehicles Loan**
Automobile Expense to **Business Vehicles Expense**
- Delete the Description
Auto Insurance Expense to **Business Vehicles Insurance**
Office Equipment to **Office Furniture & Equipment**
Office Equipment Loan to **Office Furniture/Equipment Loan**
- Due to exceeding the allotted number of characters in an account name, the symbol "&" was omitted and the "/" was used.
Loan Interest to **Interest on Loans**
- Leave the description as Loan Interest Expense
Do not close the **Chart of Accounts**

EFFECT OF AN ACCOUNT NAME CHANGE ON SUBACCOUNTS

Any account (even a subaccount) that uses Company Car (the master account) as part of the account name needs to be changed. When the account name of Company Car was changed to Business Vehicles, the subaccounts of Company Car automatically became subaccounts of Business Vehicles but their names did not change.

▶ **DO** ▶ Examine the Depreciation and Original Cost accounts for Business Vehicles

Click **Depreciation** under Business Vehicles
Use the keyboard shortcut **Ctrl+E**
The text box for **Subaccount of** shows as **Business Vehicles**

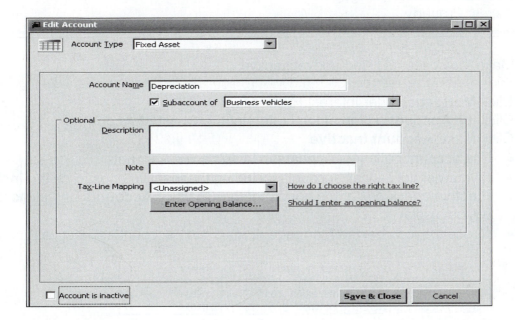

Click **Cancel**

- Repeat the above steps to examine the **Original Cost** account.
- Examine **Your Name, Capital** and **Office Furniture & Equipment** and their subaccounts.

Do not close the **Chart of Accounts**

MAKE AN ACCOUNT INACTIVE

If you are not using an account and do not have plans to use it in the near future, the account may be made inactive. The account remains available for use, yet it does not appear on your chart of accounts unless you check the Show All check box.

MEMO
DATE: January 31, 2010

At present, the company does not plan to purchase its own building. Make the following accounts inactive:
      Interest Expense: Mortgage
      Taxes: Property

DO   Make the accounts listed above inactive

Click **Mortgage** under Interest Expense
Click the **Account** button at the bottom of the **Chart of Accounts**
Click **Make Account Inactive**
- The account no longer appears in the Chart of Accounts.
- If you wish to view all accounts including the inactive ones, click the **Include Inactive** check box at the bottom of the **Chart of Accounts** and all accounts will be displayed.
- Notice the icon next to Mortgage. It marks the account as inactive.

	⋄Interest Expense	Expense
	⋄Finance Charge	Expense
	⋄Interest on Loans	Expense
✖	⋄Mortgage	Expense

Repeat the above to make **Taxes: Property** inactive

	⋄Taxes	Expense
	⋄Federal	Expense
	⋄Local	Expense
✖	⋄Property	Expense
	⋄State	Expense

DELETE AN EXISTING ACCOUNT FROM THE CHART OF ACCOUNTS

If you do not want to make an account inactive because you have not used it and do not plan to use it at all, QuickBooks Pro allows the account to be deleted at anytime. However, as a safeguard, QuickBooks Pro prevents the deletion of an account once it has been used even if it simply contains an opening or an existing balance.

MEMO
DATE: January 31, 2010

In addition to previous changes to account names, you find that you do not use nor will use the expense account: Cash Discounts. Delete this account from the Chart of Accounts. In addition, delete the Dues and Subscriptions account.

DO Delete the **Cash Discounts** expense account

Scroll through accounts until you see Cash Discounts, click **Cash Discounts**
Click the **Account** button at the bottom of the Chart of Accounts, click **Delete**
    OR
Use the keyboard shortcut **Ctrl+D**

Click **OK** on the **Delete Account** dialog box
- The account has now been deleted.

Repeat the above steps for the deletion of **Dues and Subscriptions**
- As soon as you try to delete Dues and Subscriptions, a **QuickBooks Message** appears indicating that the account has a balance or is used in a transaction, an invoice item, or your payroll setup. QuickBooks offers a solution of making the account inactive.

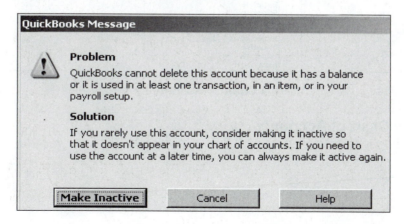

Click **Cancel**
- The account remains in the Chart of Accounts.

Name	Type	Balance Total	Attach
Checking	Bank	47,529.00	
Petty Cash	Bank	82.21	
Accounts Receivable	Accounts Receivable	17,650.00	
Employee Advances	Other Current Asset	0.00	
Office Supplies	Other Current Asset	950.00	
Prepaid Insurance	Other Current Asset	2,850.00	
Undeposited Funds	Other Current Asset	0.00	
Business Vehicles	Fixed Asset	49,000.00	
Depreciation	Fixed Asset	0.00	
Original Cost	Fixed Asset	49,000.00	
Office Furniture & Equipment	Fixed Asset	8,536.00	
Depreciation	Fixed Asset	0.00	
Original Cost	Fixed Asset	8,536.00	
Accounts Payable	Accounts Payable	3,764.00	
Payroll Liabilities	Other Current Liability	0.00	
Loan Payable	Long Term Liability	39,000.00	
Business Vehicles Loan	Long Term Liability	35,000.00	
Office Furniture/Equipment Loan	Long Term Liability	4,000.00	
Retained Earnings	Equity		
Your Name, Capital	Equity	78,135.00	
Draws	Equity	0.00	
Investments	Equity	25,000.00	
Income	Income		
Installation Income	Income		
Technical Support Income	Income		
Training Income	Income		
Other Regular Income	Income		
Reimbursed Expenses	Income		
Uncategorized Income	Income		
Advertising Expense	Expense		
Bank Service Charges	Expense		
Business Vehicles Expense	Expense		
Contributions	Expense		
Depreciation Expense	Expense		
Dues and Subscriptions	Expense		
Equipment Rental	Expense		
Insurance	Expense		
Business Vehicles Insurance	Expense		
Disability Insurance	Expense		
Liability Insurance	Expense		
Work Comp	Expense		
Interest Expense	Expense		
Finance Charge	Expense		
Interest on Loans	Expense		
Mortgage	Expense		
Licenses and Permits	Expense		
Miscellaneous	Expense		
Office Supplies Expense	Expense		
Outside Services	Expense		
Payroll Expenses	Expense		
Postage and Delivery	Expense		
Printing and Reproduction	Expense		
Professional Fees	Expense		
Accounting	Expense		
Legal Fees	Expense		
Rent	Expense		
Repairs	Expense		
Building Repairs	Expense		
Computer Repairs	Expense		
Equipment Repairs	Expense		
Janitorial Exp	Expense		
Taxes	Expense		
Federal	Expense		
Local	Expense		
Property	Expense		

Partial Chart of Accounts

Close the **Chart of Accounts**

ADJUSTMENTS FOR ACCRUAL-BASIS ACCOUNTING

As previously stated, the accrual basis of accounting matches the income and the expenses of a period in order to arrive at an accurate figure for net income. Thus, the revenue is earned at the time the service is performed or the sale is made no matter when the actual cash is received. The cash basis of accounting records income or revenue at the time cash is received no matter when the sale was made or the service performed. The same holds true when a business buys things or pays bills. In accrual-basis accounting, the expense is recorded at the time the bill is received or the purchase is made regardless of the actual payment date. In cash-basis accounting, the expense is not recorded until it is paid.

There are several internal transactions that must be recorded when you are using the accrual basis of accounting. These entries are called adjusting entries. For example, equipment does wear out and will eventually need to be replaced. Rather than wait until replacement to record the use of the equipment, one makes an adjusting entry to allocate the use of equipment as an expense for a period. This is called depreciation. Certain items used in a business are paid for in advance. These are called prepaid expenses. As these are used, they become expenses of the business. For example, insurance for the entire year would be used up month by month and should, therefore, be a monthly expense. Commonly, the insurance is billed and paid for the entire year. Until the insurance is used, it is an asset. Each month, the portion of the insurance used becomes an expense for the month.

ADJUSTING ENTRIES—PREPAID EXPENSES

During the operation of a business, companies purchase supplies to have on hand for use in the operation of the business. In accrual-basis accounting, unless the supplies are purchased for immediate use and will be used up within the month, the supplies are considered to be prepaid expenses (an asset because it is something the business owns) until they are used in the operation of the business. As the supplies are used, the amount used becomes an expense for the period. The same system applies to other things paid for in advance, such as insurance. At the end of the period, an adjusting entry must be made to allocate the amount of prepaid expenses (assets) used to expenses.

The transactions for these adjustments may be recorded in the register for the account by clicking on the prepaid expense (asset) in the Chart of Accounts, or they may be made in the General Journal.

> **MEMO**
> **DATE:** January 31, 2010
>
> Alhandra, remember to record the monthly adjustment for Prepaid Insurance. The amount we paid for the year for business vehicles insurance was $2,850. Also, we used $350 worth of supplies this month. Please adjust accordingly.

DO Record the adjusting entries for office supplies expense and business vehicles insurance expense in the General Journal.

Access the General Journal:
Click **Company** on the menu bar, click **Make General Journal Entries**
- If you get a screen regarding Assigning Numbers to Journal Entries, click **OK**
Record the adjusting entry for Prepaid Insurance
Enter **01/31/10** as the **Date**
- **Entry No.** is left blank unless you wish to record a specific number.
- Because all transactions entered for the month have been entered in the Journal as well as on an invoice or a bill, all transactions automatically have a Journal entry number.
Tab to or click the **Account** column
Click the drop-down list arrow for **Account**, click the expense account **Business Vehicles Insurance**
Tab to or click **Debit**
- The $2,850 given in the memo is the amount for the year; calculate the amount of the adjustment for the month by using QuickBooks QuickMath or the Calculator.
Use QuickBooks QuickMath
    Enter **2850** by:
        Keying the numbers on the **10-key pad** (preferred)
        - Be sure Num Lock is on. There should be a light by Num Lock on/or above the 10-key pad. If not, press Num Lock to activate.
          OR
        Typing the numbers at the top of the keyboard
    Press **/** for division
        Key **12**
    Press **Enter** to close QuickMath and enter the amount in the Debit column
Or use the Calculator
    Click **Edit** on the menu bar, click **Use Calculator**
    Enter **2850**
        Press **/** for division
        Key **12**

Press **=** or **Enter**

Click the **Close** button to close the **Calculator**

- For additional calculator instructions refer to Chapter 1.

Enter the amount of the adjustment **237.5** in the **Debit** column

- Notice that the amount must be entered by you when using Calculator; QuickBooks Math automatically enters the amount.

Tab to or click the **Memo** column

Type **Adjusting Entry, Insurance**

Tab to or click **Account**

Click the drop-down list arrow for **Account**

Click the asset account **Prepaid Insurance**

- The amount for the Credit column should be entered automatically. However, there are several reasons why an amount may not appear in the Credit column; if 237.50 does not appear, type it in the Credit column.

Tab to or click the **Memo** column, and type **Adjusting Entry, Insurance**

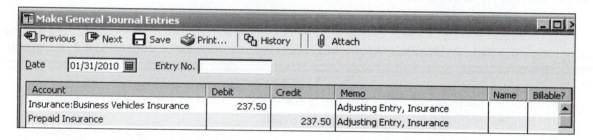

Click **Save & New** to record the adjustment and advance to the next **Make General Journal Entries** screen

Repeat the above procedures to record the adjustment for the office supplies used

Use the Memo **Supplies Used**

- The amount given in the memo is the actual amount of the supplies used in January so you will not need to use QuickMath or the calculator.
- Remember, when supplies are purchased to have on hand, the original entry records an increase to the asset Office Supplies. Once the supplies are used, the adjustment correctly records the amount of supplies used as an expense.

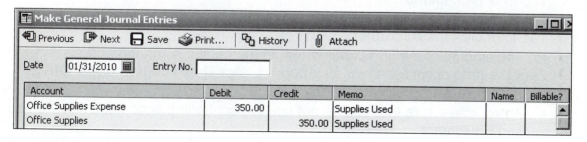

Click **Save & New**

ADJUSTING ENTRIES—DEPRECIATION

Using the accrual basis of accounting requires companies to record an expense for the amount of equipment used in the operation of the business. Unlike supplies—where you can actually see, for example, the paper supply diminishing—it is very difficult to see how much of a computer has been "used up" during the month. To account for the fact that machines do wear out and need to be replaced, an adjustment is made for depreciation. This adjustment correctly matches the expenses of the period against the revenue of the period.

The adjusting entry for depreciation can be made in the account register for Depreciation, or it can be made in the General Journal.

MEMO
DATE: January 31, 2010

Having received the necessary depreciation schedules, Alhandra records the adjusting entry for depreciation: Business Vehicles, $583 per month; Equipment, $142 per month.

DO Record a compound adjusting entry for depreciation of the equipment and the business vehicles in the **General Journal**:

If it is not automatically displayed, enter **01/31/10** as the **Date**
Entry No. is left blank
- Normally, the Debit portion of a General Journal entry is entered first. However, in order to use the automatic calculation feature of QuickBooks Pro, you will enter the Credit entries first.

Tab to or click the **Account** column
Click the drop-down list arrow for **Account**, click **Depreciation** under **Business Vehicles**
- Make sure that you do not click the controlling account, Business Vehicles

Tab to or click **Credit**, enter **583**
Tab to or click **Memo**
Enter **Adjusting Entry January**
Tab to or click the **Account** column
- The amount of the 583 credit shows in the debit column temporarily.

Click the drop-down list arrow for **Account**, click **Depreciation** under **Office Furniture & Equipment**
- Again, make sure that you do not use the controlling account, Office Furniture and Equipment.

Tab to or click **Credit**

Enter **142**
- The 583 in the debit column is removed when you tab to or click **Memo**.

Tab to or click **Memo**
Enter **Adjusting Entry January**
Tab to or click the **Account** column
Click the drop-down list arrow for **Account**
Click **Depreciation Expense**
Debit column should automatically show **725**
- If 725 does not appear, enter it in the debit column.

Tab to or click **Memo**, enter **Adjusting Entry January**

Account	Debit	Credit	Memo	Name	Billable?
Business Vehicles:Depreciation		583.00	Adjusting Entry, January		
Office Furniture & Equipment:Depreciation		142.00	Adjusting Entry, January		
Depreciation Expense	725.00		Adjusting Entry, January		

(Make General Journal Entries — Date: 01/31/2010, Entry No. ___ — Previous, Next, Save, Print..., History, Attach)

Click **Save & Close** to record the adjustment and close the **General Journal**
- If you get a message regarding Tracking Fixed Assets, click **OK.**

VIEW GENERAL JOURNAL

Once transactions have been entered in the General Journal, it is important to view them. For reports, QuickBooks Pro refers to the General Journal as the Journal and allows it to be viewed or printed at any time. Even with the special ways in which transactions are entered in QuickBooks Pro through invoices, bills, checks, and account registers, the Journal is still the book of original entry. All transactions recorded for the company may be viewed in the Journal even if they were entered elsewhere.

DO View the Journal for January

Click **Reports** on the menu bar, point to **Accountant & Taxes,** and click **Journal**
Enter the dates from **01/01/10** to **01/31/10**
Tab to generate the report
- Notice that the transactions do not begin with the adjustments entered directly into the Journal.
- The first transaction displayed is the entry for Invoice No. 1 to Juan Gomez.

- If corrections or changes are made to entries, the transaction numbers may differ from the key. Since QuickBooks assigns transaction numbers automatically, disregard any discrepancies in transaction numbers.

Scroll through the report to view all transactions recorded in the Journal

Verify the total Debit and Credit Columns of $46,530.29

- If your totals do not match, check for errors and make appropriate corrections.

Computer Consulting by Your Name
Journal
January 2010

Trans #	Type	Date	Num	Name	Memo	Account	Debit	Credit
67	General Journal	01/31/2010			Adjusting Entry, Insurance	Business Vehicles Insurance	237.50	
					Adjusting Entry, Insurance	Prepaid Insurance		237.50
							237.50	237.50
68	General Journal	01/31/2010			Supplies Used	Office Supplies Expense	350.00	
					Supplies Used	Office Supplies		350.00
							350.00	350.00
69	General Journal	01/31/2010			Adjusting Entry, January	Depreciation		583.00
					Adjusting Entry, January	Depreciation		142.00
					Adjusting Entry, January	Depreciation Expense	725.00	
							725.00	725.00
TOTAL							**46,530.29**	**46,530.29**

Partial Report

Close the report without printing

OWNER WITHDRAWALS

In a sole proprietorship an owner cannot receive a paycheck because he or she owns the business. An owner withdrawing money from a business—even to pay personal expenses—is similar to withdrawing money from a savings account. A withdrawal simply decreases the owner's capital. QuickBooks Pro allows you to establish a separate account for owner withdrawals. If a separate account is not established, owner withdrawals may be subtracted directly from the owner's capital or investment account.

MEMO
DATE: January 31, 2010

Because you work in the business full time, you do not earn a paycheck. You prepare the check for your monthly withdrawal, $2,500.

DO ▶ Write Check No. 9 to yourself for $2,500 withdrawal

Open the **Write Checks - Checking** window:
Click **Banking** on the menu bar, click **Write Checks**
> OR
Click the **Write Checks** icon in the Banking section of the Home Page
> OR
Use the keyboard shortcut **Ctrl+W**
The Check No. should be **To Print**
- If not, click the check box **To be printed**
Date should be **01/31/10**
Enter **Your Name** on the **Pay to the Order of** line
Press the **Tab** key
- Because your name was not added to any list when the company was created, the **Name Not Found** dialog box appears on the screen.

Click **Quick Add** to add your name to a list

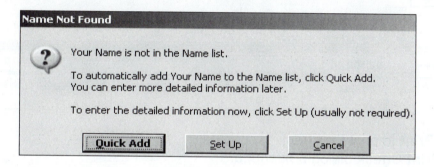

The **Select Name Type** dialog box appears
Click **Other**
- Your name is added to a list of "Other" names, which are used for owners, partners, and other miscellaneous names.

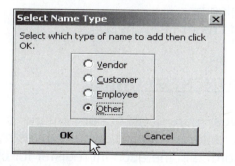

Click **OK**
Tab to or click in the area for the amount of the check
- If necessary, delete any numbers showing for the amount (0.00).
Enter **2500**

Tab to or click **Memo** on the check
Enter **Owner Withdrawal for January**
Tab to or click in the **Account** column at the bottom of the check
Click the drop-down list arrow, click the Equity account **Draws**
- The amount 2,500.00 should appear in the **Amount** column.
- If it does not, tab to or click in the **Amount** column and enter 2500.

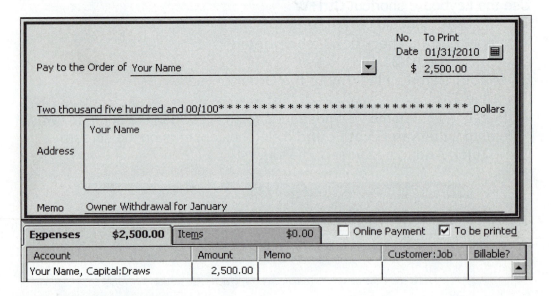

Click **Print** to print the check
The **Print Check** dialog box appears
Printed Check Number should be **9**
- If necessary, change the number to 9.
Click **OK**
Print the standard style check as previously instructed
Once the check has printed successfully, click **OK** on the **Print Checks -**
    Confirmation dialog box
Click **Save & Close** to record the check

ADDITIONAL CASH INVESTMENT BY OWNER

An owner may decide to invest more of his or her personal cash in the business at any
time. The new investment is entered into the owner's investment account and into cash.
The investment may be recorded in the account register for checking or in the register
for the owner's investment account. It may also be recorded in the General Journal.

MEMO

DATE: January 31, 2010

You received money from a certificate of deposit. Rather than reinvest in another certificate of deposit, you have decided to invest an additional $5,000 in the company.

DO ▸ Record the owner's additional cash investment in the Journal

Access the General Journal as previously instructed
The **Date** should be **01/31/10**
- Nothing is needed for Entry No.

Debit **Checking, $5,000**
The memo for both entries should be **Cash Investment**
Credit **Investments, $5,000**
- This account is listed as a subaccount of Your Name, Capital

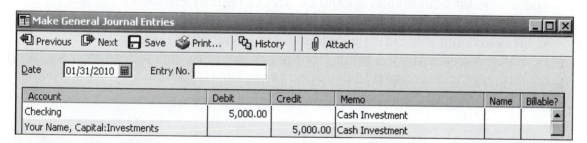

Click **Save & New** to record and go to the next blank **Make General Journal Entries** screen

---

NON-CASH INVESTMENT BY OWNER

An owner may make investments in a business at any time. The investment may be cash; but it may also be something such as reference books, equipment, tools, buildings, and so on. Additional investments by an owner(s) are added to owner's equity. In the case of a sole proprietor, the investment is added to the Capital account for Investments.

MEMO

DATE: January 31, 2010

Originally, you planned to have an office in your home as well as in the company and purchased new office furniture for your home. Since then, you decided the business environment would appear more professional if the new furniture were in the office rather than your home. You gave the new office furniture to the company as an additional owner investment. The value of the investment is $3,000.

> **DO** Record the non-cash investment in the Journal

The **Date** should be **01/31/10, Entry No**. should be blank
Debit **Office Furniture & Equipment: Original Cost, $3,000**
- Make sure you Debit the subaccount Original Cost not the controlling account Office Furniture & Equipment.
The memo for both entries should be **Investment of Furniture**
Credit **Investments, $3,000**
- This account is listed as a subaccount of Your Name, Capital
- If you wish to copy the memo for the second entry rather than retype it, drag through the memo text to highlight; press Ctrl+C; position the cursor in the memo area for the second entry; press Ctrl+V.

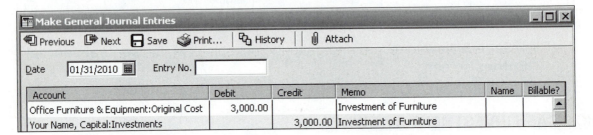

Click **Save & Close** to record and exit
- If you get a message regarding Tracking Fixed Assets, click **OK**.

VIEW BALANCE SHEET

Prior to the owner's making an additional investment in the business, there had been no withdrawals, and the drawing account balance was zero. Once the owner makes a withdrawal, that amount is carried forward in the owner's drawing account. Subsequent withdrawals are added to this account. When you view the Balance Sheet, notice the balance of the Drawing account after the check for the withdrawal was written. Also notice the Net Income account that appears in the equity section of the Balance Sheet. This account is automatically added by QuickBooks Pro to track the net income for the year.

> **DO** View a Standard Balance Sheet:

Click **Reports** on the menu bar, point to **Company & Financial**, and click
    Balance Sheet Standard
Tab to or click **As of**
Enter the date **01/31/10**
Tab to generate the report
Scroll through the report
- Notice the Equity section, especially Net Income.

Computer Consulting by Your Name
Balance Sheet
As of January 31, 2010

	Jan 31, 10
Total Liabilities	42,764.00
Equity	
Your Name, Capital	
Draws	-2,500.00
Investments	33,000.00
Your Name, Capital - Other	53,135.00
Total Your Name, Capital	83,635.00
Net Income	4,385.71
Total Equity	88,020.71
TOTAL LIABILITIES & EQUITY	130,784.71

Partial Report

Close the report without printing

BANK RECONCILIATION

Each month, the checking account should be reconciled with the bank statement to make sure that the balances agree. The bank statement will rarely have an ending balance that matches the balance of the checking account. This is due to several factors: outstanding checks (written by the business but not paid by the bank), deposits in transit (deposits that were made too late to be included on the bank statement), bank service charges, interest earned on checking accounts, collections made by the bank, and errors made in recording checks and/or deposits by the company or by the bank.

In order to have an accurate amount listed as the balance in the checking account, it is important that the differences between the bank statement and the checking account be reconciled. If something such as a service charge or a collection made by the bank appears on the bank statement, it needs to be recorded in the checking account.

Reconciling a bank statement is an appropriate time to find any errors that may have been recorded in the checking account. The reconciliation may be out of balance because a transposition was made (recording $94 rather than $49), a transaction was recorded backwards, a transaction was recorded twice, or a transaction was not recorded at all. If a transposition was made, the error may be found by dividing the difference by 9. For example, if $94 was recorded and the actual transaction amount was $49, you would subtract 49 from 94 to get 45. The number 45 can be divided by 9, so your error was a transposition. If the error can be evenly divided by 2, the transaction may have been entered backwards. For example, if you were out of balance $200, look to see if you had any $100 transactions. Perhaps you recorded a $100 debit, and it should have been a credit (or vice versa).

BEGIN RECONCILIATION

To begin the reconciliation, you need to open the Reconcile - Checking window. Verify the information shown for the checking account. The Opening Balance should match the amount of the final balance on the last reconciliation, or it should match the starting account balance.

MEMO
DATE: January 31, 2010

Received the bank statement from Sunshine Bank. The bank statement is dated January 31, 2010. Alhandra Cruz needs to reconcile the bank statement and print a Detail Reconciliation Report for you.

▶ DO ▶ Reconcile the bank statement for January

> Click the **Reconcile** icon in the Banking section of the Home Page to open the
>   **Begin Reconciliation** window and enter preliminary information
> The **Account To Reconcile** should be **Checking**
>   If not, click the drop-down list arrow, click **Checking**
> The Statement Date should be **013110**

- The Statement Date is entered automatically by the computer. If it the date is not shown at 01/31/10, change it.
- You may see several previous dates listed. Disregard them at this time.
Beginning Balance should be **12,870**
- This is the same amount as the checking account starting balance.

ENTER BANK STATEMENT INFORMATION FOR BEGIN RECONCILIATION

Some information appearing on the bank statement is entered into the Begin Reconciliation window as the next step. This information includes the ending balance, bank service charges, and interest earned.

DO ▶ Continue to reconcile the following bank statement with the checking account

SUNSHINE BANK
12345 West Colorado Avenue
Woodland Hills, CA 91377
(818) 555-3880

Computer Consulting by Your Name
2895 West Avenue
Woodland Hills, CA 91367

Acct. # 123-456-7890   January 2010

Beginning Balance 1/1/10			$12,870.00
01/02/10 Deposit	25,000.00		37,870.00
1/15/10 Deposit	13,840.00		51,710.00
1/26/10 Cash Transfer		110.00	51,600.00
1/26/10 Check 1		500.00	51,100.00
1/26/10 Check 2		195.00	50,905.00
1/26/10 Check 3		840.00	50,065.00
1/31/10 Vehicle Loan Pmt.: $467.19 Principal, $255.22 Interest		722.41	49,342.59
1/31/10 Office Equip. Loan Pmt.: $29.17 Principal, $53.39 Interest		82.56	49,260.03
1/31/10 Service Chg.		8.00	49,252.03
1/31/10 Interest	66.43		49,318.46
Ending Balance 1/31/10			49,318.46

Enter the **Ending Balance** from the Bank Statement, **49,318.46**
Tab to or click **Service Charge**

Enter **8.00**

Tab to or click Service Charge **Date**; if necessary, change to **01/31/2010**

- Don't forget to check the date. If you leave an incorrect date, you will have errors in your accounts and in your reports.

Tab to or click **Account**

Click the drop-down list arrow for **Account**

Click **Bank Service Charges**

Tab to or click **Interest Earned**, enter **66.43**

Tab to or click Interest Earned **Date**; if necessary, change to **01/31/2010**

Tab to or click **Account**

Click the drop-down list arrow for **Account**

Scroll through the list of accounts, click **Interest Income**

Begin Reconciliation			×

Select an account to reconcile, and then enter the ending balance from your account statement.

Account [Checking ▼]   last reconciled on 12/31/2009.

Statement Date   [01/31/2010 ▦]

Beginning Balance   12,870.00   What if my beginning balance doesn't match my statement?

Ending Balance   [49,318.46]

Enter any service charge or interest earned.

Service Charge   Date   Account

[8.00]   [01/31/2010 ▦]   [Bank Service Charges ▼]

Interest Earned   Date   Account

[66.43]   [01/31/2010 ▦]   [Interest Income ▼]

[Locate Discrepancies]   [Undo Last Reconciliation]   [**Continue**]   [Cancel]   [Help]

Click the **Continue** button

MARK CLEARED TRANSACTIONS FOR BANK RECONCILIATION

Once bank statement information for service charges and interest has been entered, compare the checks and deposits listed on the statement with the transactions for the checking account. Remember, the dates shown for the checks on the bank statement are the dates the checks were processed by the bank, not the dates the checks were written. If a deposit or a check is listed correctly on the bank statement and in the Reconcile - Checking window, it has cleared and should be marked. An item may be marked individually by positioning the cursor on the deposit or the check and clicking the primary mouse button. If all deposits and checks match, click the Mark All button. To remove all the checks, click the Unmark All button. To unmark an individual item, click the item to remove the check mark.

▶ **DO** Mark cleared checks and deposits

• Compare the bank statement with the **Reconcile - Checking** window
Click the items that appear on both statements
  • *Note*: The date next to the check or the deposit on the bank statement is the date the check or deposit cleared the bank, not the date the check was written or the deposit was made.
  • If you are unable to complete the reconciliation in one session, click the **Leave** button to leave the reconciliation and return to it later. Under no circumstances should you click **Reconcile Now** until the reconciliation is complete.
Make sure that the **Highlight Marked** checkbox in the lower-left corner has a check mark
  • This will change the background color of everything that you mark and make it easier to view the selections in the reconciliation.
Include the Petty Cash transaction on 1/26/10 even though the bank statement shows 110 and the check register shows 100.
  • Even though Checks 8 and 9 do not show in the following screen shot, they have been recorded. Scroll through the list of Checks and Payments in order to see them.
Look at the bottom of the **Reconcile - Checking** window
In the section labeled "Items you have marked cleared" should show the following:
3 Deposits and Other Credits for 38,840.00
  • This includes the voided check to Communication Telephone Co.
4 Checks and Payments for 1,635.00
  • This includes the $100 for petty cash.
On the right-side of the lower section next to the Modify button, the screen should show:
The Service Charge is -8.00
The Interest Earned is 66.43
The Ending Balance is 49,318.46
The Cleared Balance is 50,133.43
There is a Difference of -814.97

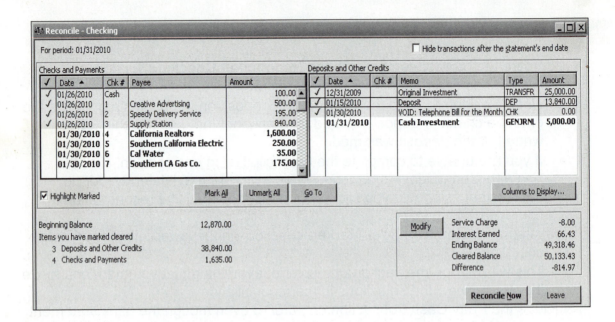

ADJUSTING AND CORRECTING ENTRIES—BANK RECONCILIATION

As you complete the reconciliation, you may find errors that need to be corrected or transactions that need to be recorded. Anything entered as a service charge or interest earned will be entered automatically when the reconciliation is complete and the Reconcile Now button is clicked. To correct an error such as a transposition, click on the entry, then click the Go To button. The original entry will appear on the screen. The correction can be made and will show in the Reconcile - Checking window. If there is a transaction, such as an automatic loan payment to the bank, you need to access the register for the account used in the transaction and enter the payment.

DO ▶ Correct the error on the transfer into Petty Cash and enter the automatic loan payments shown on the bank statement.

Correct the entry for the transfer of cash into Petty Cash:
In the section of the reconciliation for **Checks and Payments**, click the entry for **Cash** made on **01/26/10**
Click the **Go To** button

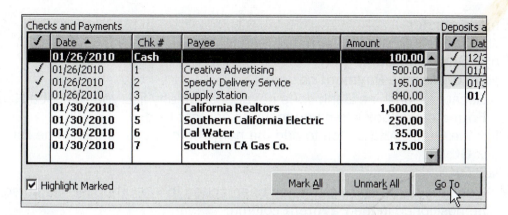

Change the amount on **Transfer Funds Between Accounts** from 100 to **110**

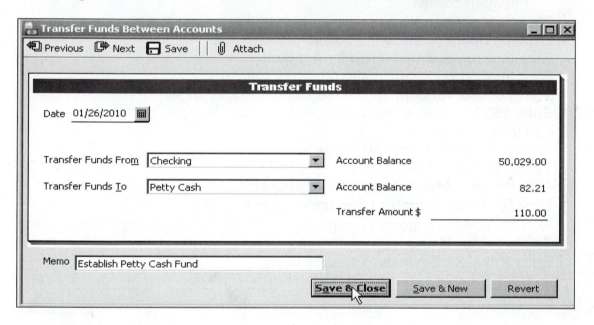

Click **Save & Close**

Click **Yes** on the **Change Transaction** dialog box

• Notice that the amount for the Petty Cash transaction now shows 110.

If necessary, click the Petty Cash transaction to mark it.

• The amount shown at the bottom of the Reconcile window for the 4 Checks and Payments, shows 1,645.00

With the **Reconcile - Checking** window still showing, enter the automatic loan payments:

To enter the automatic payments, access the Checking Account Register by using the keyboard shortcut **Ctrl+R**

In the blank transaction at the bottom of the Checking register enter the **Date**, **01/31/10**

Tab to or click **Number**

Enter **Transfer**

Tab to or click **Payee**

Enter **Sunshine Bank**

Tab to or click the **Payment** column

- Because Sunshine Bank does not appear on any list, you will get a **Name Not Found** dialog box when you move to another field.

Click the **Quick Add** button to add the name of the bank to the Name list

Click **Other**

Click **OK**

- Once the name of the bank has been added to the Other list, the cursor will be positioned in the **Payment** column.

Enter the amount of the Business Vehicles Loan payment of **722.41** in the
   Payment column

Click the **Account** column

Click the **Splits** button at the bottom of the register

Click the drop-down list arrow for **Account**

Click **Interest on Loans** under Interest Expense

Tab to or click **Amount**, delete the amount 722.41 shown

Enter **255.22** as the amount of interest

Tab to or click **Memo**

Enter **Interest Business Vehicles Loan**

Tab to or click **Account**

Click the drop-down list arrow for **Account**

Click **Business Vehicles Loan** under Loan Payable

- The correct amount of principal, 467.19, should be showing for the amount.

Tab to or click **Memo**

Enter **Principal Business Vehicles Loan**

Account	Amount	Memo	Customer:Job	Billable?	
Interest Expense:Interest on Loans	255.22	Interest Business Vehicles Loan			Close
Loan Payable:Business Vehicles Loan	467.19	Principal Business Vehicles Loan			Clear

Click the **Close** button in the Splits window

- This closes the window for the information regarding the way the transaction is to be "split" between accounts.

For the **Memo** in the Checking Register, record **Loan Pmt., Business Vehicles**

Click the **Record** button to record the transaction

- Because the **Register** organizes transactions according to date and the transaction type, you will notice that the loan payment will not appear as the last transaction in the Register. You may need to scroll through the Register to see the transaction since transfers are shown before other transactions entered on the same date.

01/31/2010	Transfer	Sunshine Bank		722.41			46,796.59
	CHK	-split-	Loan Pmt., Business Vehicles				

Repeat the procedures to record the loan payment for office equipment
- When you enter the Payee as Sunshine Bank, the amount for the previous transaction (722.41) appears in Amount.

Enter the new amount, **82.56**
Click **Splits** button
Click the appropriate accounts and enter the correct amount for each item
- *Note*: The amounts for the previous loan payment automatically appear. You will need to enter the amounts for both accounts in this transaction.
- Refer to the bank statement for details regarding the amount of the payment for interest and the amount of the payment applied to principal.

Account	Amount	Memo	Customer:Job	Billable?	
Interest Expense:Interest on Loans	53.39	Interest Office Equipment Loan			Close
Loan Payable:Office Furniture/Equipment Loan	29.17	Principal Office Equipment Loan			Clear

Click **Close** to close the window for the information regarding the "split" between accounts
Enter the transaction Memo **Loan Pmt., Office Equipment**
Click **Record** to record the loan payment

01/31/2010	Transfer	Sunshine Bank		82.56			46,714.03
	CHK	-split-	Loan Pmt., Office Equipment				

Close the **Checking** Register
- You should return to **Reconcile - Checking**.

Scroll to the top of **Checks and Payments**
- Notice the two entries for the payments in **Checks and Payments**.

Mark the two entries
- At this point, the **Ending Balance** and **Cleared Balance** should be equal— $49,318.46 with a difference of 0.00.

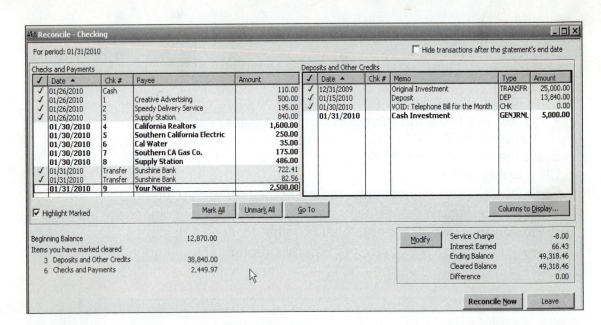

If your entries agree with the above, click **Reconcile Now** to finish the reconciliation

- If your reconciliation is not in agreement, do not click **Reconcile Now** until the errors are corrected.
- Once you click **Reconcile Now**, you may not return to this **Reconciliation - Checking** window.
- If you get an Information screen referring to online banking, click **OK**

PRINT A RECONCILIATION REPORT

As soon as the Ending Balance and the Cleared Balance are equal or when you finish marking and click Reconcile Now, a screen appears allowing you to select the level of Reconciliation report you would like to print. You may select Summary and get a report that lists totals only or Detail and get all the transactions that were reconciled on the report. You may print the report at the time you have finished reconciling the account or you may print the report later by returning to the Reconciliation window. QuickBooks Pro keeps your last two reconciliation reports in memory. If you think you may want to print the report again in the future, print the report to a file to save it permanently.

DO Print a **Detail Reconciliation Report**

On the **Select Reconciliation Report** screen, click **Detail**

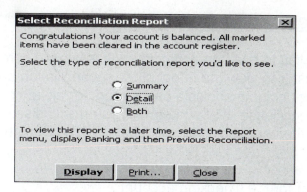

To view the report before you print, click Display; or click Print to display without viewing

Computer Consulting by Your Name
Reconciliation Detail
Checking, Period Ending 01/31/2010

Type	Date	Num	Name	Clr	Amount	Balance
Beginning Balance						12,870.00
Cleared Transactions						
Checks and Payments - 7 items						
Bill Pmt -Check	01/26/2010	3	Supply Station	✓	-840.00	-840.00 ◄
Bill Pmt -Check	01/26/2010	1	Creative Advertising	✓	-500.00	-1,340.00
Bill Pmt -Check	01/26/2010	2	Speedy Delivery Service	✓	-195.00	-1,535.00
Transfer	01/26/2010	Cash		✓	-110.00	-1,645.00
Check	01/31/2010	Transfer	Sunshine Bank	✓	-722.41	-2,367.41
Check	01/31/2010	Transfer	Sunshine Bank	✓	-82.56	-2,449.97
Check	01/31/2010			✓	-8.00	-2,457.97
Total Checks and Payments					-2,457.97	-2,457.97
Deposits and Credits - 4 items						
Transfer	12/31/2009			✓	25,000.00	25,000.00
Deposit	01/15/2010			✓	13,840.00	38,840.00
Check	01/30/2010		Communication Telephone Co.	✓	0.00	38,840.00
Deposit	01/31/2010			✓	66.43	38,906.43
Total Deposits and Credits					38,906.43	38,906.43
Total Cleared Transactions					36,448.46	36,448.46
Cleared Balance					36,448.46	49,318.46

Partial Report

- The uncleared information may be different than the report printed in the answer key. This is due to the fact that your computer's date may be different than January 31, 2010. As long as the cleared balance is $49,318.46, your report should be considered correct.

Click the **Print** button

Print as previously instructed:

    Printer should be default printer

    Orientation is **Portrait**

    Page Range is **All**

If your report printed correctly, close the report

VIEW THE CHECKING ACCOUNT REGISTER

Once the bank reconciliation has been completed, it is wise to scroll through the Checking account register to view the effect of the reconciliation on the account. You will notice that the check column shows a check mark for all items that were marked as cleared during the reconciliation. If at a later date an error is discovered, the transaction may be changed, and the correction will be reflected in the Beginning Balance on the reconciliation.

DO View the register for the Checking account

Access the register as previously instructed
To display more of the register, click the check box for **1-Line**
Scroll through the register
- Notice that the transactions are listed in chronological order and that cleared transactions have a check mark.

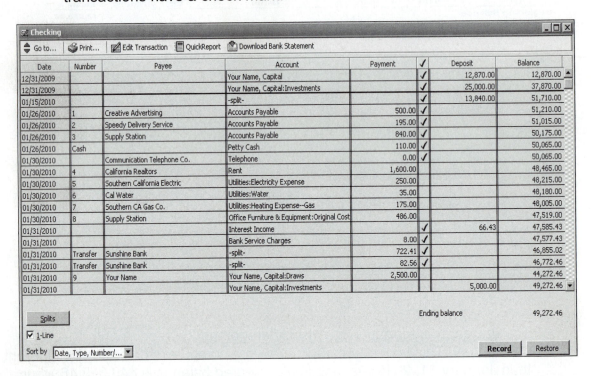

EDIT CLEARED TRANSACTIONS

DO Edit a transaction that was marked and cleared during the bank reconciliation:

Edit the **Petty Cash** transaction:
Click in the entry for the transfer of funds to **Petty Cash** on January 26

Change the **Payment** amount to **100**
Click the **Record** button

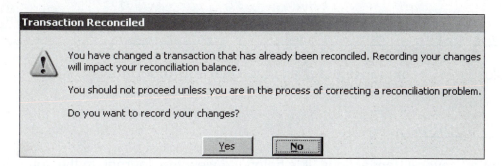

Click **Yes** on the **Transaction Reconciled** dialog box
- The transaction amount has been changed.
Close the **Checking Register** and return to the Chart of Accounts
View the effects of the change to the Petty Cash transaction in the Begin
    Reconciliation window:
Display the **Begin Reconciliation** window by:
Making sure **Checking** is highlighted, clicking the **Activities** button, and clicking
    Reconcile
- Notice that the Opening Balance has been increased by $10 and shows
    $49,328.46.

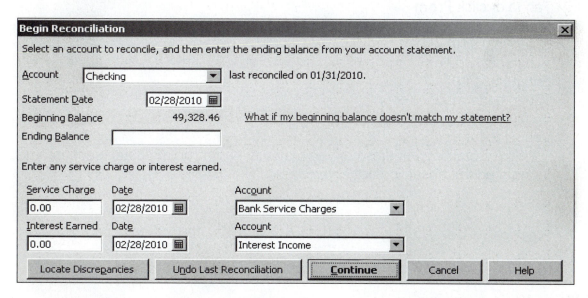

Click the **Cancel** button on the bottom of the **Begin Reconciliation** screen and
    return to the Chart of Accounts
Open the **Checking** account register
Change the amount for the **Petty Cash** transaction back to **110**
Click **Record** to record the change

Click **Yes** on the **Transaction Reconciled** dialog box

01/26/2010	3	Supply Station	Accounts Payable	840.00	✓		50,175.00
01/26/2010	Cash		Petty Cash	110.00	✓		50,065.00
01/30/2010		Communication Telephone Co.	Telephone	0.00	✓		50,065.00

Close the **Checking Register** and the **Chart of Accounts**

VIEW THE JOURNAL

After entering several transactions, it is helpful to view the Journal. In the Journal, all transactions, regardless of the method of entry are shown in traditional debit/credit format. (Remember, you may have learned this as the General Journal in your concepts course.)

 View the **Journal** for January

Click the **Report Center** button, use the view of your preference, click **Accountant & Taxes** as the type of report, and double-click **Journal**
- If you will be preparing several reports, using the Report Center is much more efficient.

Tab to or click **From**
- If necessary, delete existing date.

Enter **01/01/10**

Tab to or click **To**

Enter **01/31/10**

Tab to generate the report

Scroll through the report

Verify the total of $57,919.69
- If your total does not match, you may have an error in a date used, an amount entered, a transaction not entered, etc.

Computer Consulting by Your Name

Journal

January 2010

Trans #	Type	Date	Num	Name	Memo	Account	Debit	Credit
73	Check	01/31/2010	Transfer	Sunshine Bank	Loan Pmt., Business Vehicles	Checking		722.41
				Sunshine Bank	Interest Business Vehicles Loan	Interest on Loans	255.22	
				Sunshine Bank	Principal Business Vehicles Loan	Business Vehicles Loan	467.19	
							722.41	722.41
74	Check	01/31/2010	Transfer	Sunshine Bank	Loan Pmt., Office Equipment	Checking		82.56
				Sunshine Bank	Interest Office Equipment Loan	Interest on Loans	53.39	
				Sunshine Bank	Principal Office Equipment Loan	Office Furniture/Equipment Loan	29.17	
							82.56	82.56
75	Check	01/31/2010			Service Charge	Checking		8.00
					Service Charge	Bank Service Charges	8.00	
							8.00	8.00
76	Deposit	01/31/2010			Interest	Checking	66.43	
					Interest	Interest Income		66.43
							66.43	66.43
TOTAL							57,919.69	57,919.69

Partial Report

Close the **Journal** without printing
Do not close the Report Center

PREPARE TRIAL BALANCE

After all adjustments have been recorded and the bank reconciliation has been completed, it is wise to prepare the Trial Balance. As in traditional accounting, the QuickBooks Pro Trial Balance proves that debits equal credits.

MEMO

DATE: January 31, 2010

Because adjustments have been entered, prepare a Trial Balance.

▶ DO   Prepare a Trial Balance

Double-click **Trial Balance** on the Accountant & Taxes report
Enter the dates from **01/01/10** to **01/31/10**
Tab to generate the report
Scroll through the report and study the amounts shown
- Notice that the final totals of debits and credits are equal: $138,119.07.

Computer Consulting by Your Name
Trial Balance
As of January 31, 2010

	Jan 31, 10	
	Debit	Credit
Your Name, Capital		53,135.00
Your Name, Capital:Draws	2,500.00	
Your Name, Capital:Investments		33,000.00
Income:Installation Income		175.00
Income:Technical Support Income		900.00
Income:Training Income		7,850.00
Advertising Expense	260.00	
Bank Service Charges	8.00	
Business Vehicles Expense	588.88	
Depreciation Expense	725.00	
Dues and Subscriptions	79.00	
Equipment Rental	25.00	
Insurance:Business Vehicles Insurance	237.50	
Interest Expense:Interest on Loans	308.61	
Office Supplies Expense	368.57	
Postage and Delivery	195.34	
Rent	1,600.00	
Telephone	0.00	
Utilities:Electricity Expense	250.00	
Utilities:Heating Expense--Gas	175.00	
Utilities:Water	35.00	
Interest Income		66.43
TOTAL	138,119.07	138,119.07

Partial Report

USE QUICKZOOM IN TRIAL BALANCE

QuickZoom is a QuickBooks Pro feature that allows you to make a closer observation of transactions, amounts, and other entries. With QuickZoom you may zoom in on an item when the mouse pointer turns into a magnifying glass with a Z inside. If you point to an item and you do not get a magnifying glass with a Z inside, you cannot zoom in on the item. For example, if you point to Interest Expense, you will see the magnifying glass with the Z inside. If your Trial Balance had Retained Earnings and you pointed to the account, the mouse pointer would not change from the arrow. This means that you can see transaction details for Interest Expense but not for Retained Earnings.

▶ **DO** Use QuickZoom to view the details of Interest Expense: Interest on Loans

Scroll through the Trial Balance until you see Interest Expense: Interest on Loans
Position the mouse pointer over the amount of Interest Expense: Interest on Loans, **308.61**
- Notice that the mouse pointer changes to
Double-click the primary mouse button

- A Transactions by Account Report appears on the screen showing the payment of loan interest as of 01/31/2010.

If necessary, enter the From date **010110** and the To date **013110**

Tab to generate the report

Scroll through the report

Computer Consulting by Your Name								
Transactions by Account								
As of January 31, 2010								
Type	Date	Num	Name	Memo	Clr	Split	Amount	Balance
Interest Expense								
Interest on Loans								
Check	01/31/2010	Transfer	Sunshine Bank	Interest on Business Vehicles Loan		Checking	255.22	255.22
Check	01/31/2010	Transfer	Sunshine Bank	Interest Office Equipment Loan		Checking	53.39	308.61
Total Interest on Loans							308.61	308.61
Total Interest Expense							308.61	308.61
TOTAL							**308.61**	**308.61**

Close the Transactions by Account report without printing

PRINT THE TRIAL BALANCE

Once the Trial Balance has been prepared, it may be printed.

DO ▸ Print the Trial Balance

Click the **Print** button at the top of the **Trial Balance**

Verify the **Settings** as previously instructed to print in Portrait Orientation

Click the **Preview** button to view a miniature copy of the report

- This helps determine the orientation and whether you need to select the feature to print one page wide.

Click **Close**

Click **Print**

Close the **Trial Balance**

Do not close the **Report Center**

SELECT ACCRUAL-BASIS REPORTING PREFERENCE

QuickBooks Pro allows a business to customize the program and select certain preferences for reports, displays, graphs, accounts, and so on. There are two report preferences available in QuickBooks Pro: Cash and Accrual. You need to choose the one you prefer. If you select Cash as the report preference, income on reports will be shown as of the date payment is received and expenses will be shown as of the date you pay the bill. If Accrual is selected, QuickBooks Pro shows the income on the report as of the date of the invoice and expenses as of the bill date. Prior to printing end-of-period reports, it is advisable to verify which reporting basis is selected. If cash has been selected and you are using the accrual method, it is imperative that you change your report basis.

MEMO
DATE: January 31, 2010

Prior to printing reports, check the report preference selected for the company. If necessary, choose Accrual. After the selection has been made, print a Standard Profit and Loss and a Standard Balance Sheet for Computer Consulting by Your Name.

▶ **DO** ▶ Select **Accrual** as the **Summary Reports Basis**

> Click **Edit** on the menu bar, click **Preferences**
> Scroll through the Preferences list until you see **Reports & Graphs**
> Click **Reports & Graphs**
> Click the **Company Preferences** tab
> If necessary, click **Accrual** to select the **Summary Reports Basis**

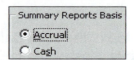

> Click **OK** to close the **Preferences** window

PREPARE AND PRINT CASH FLOW FORECAST

In planning for the cash needs of a business, QuickBooks Pro can prepare a Cash Flow Forecast. This report is useful when determining the expected income and disbursement of cash. It is important to know if your company will have enough cash on hand to meet its obligations. A company with too little cash on hand may have to borrow money to pay its bills, while another company with excess cash may miss out on investment, expansion, or dividend opportunities. QuickBooks Pro Cash Flow Forecast does not analyze investments. It simply projects the amount you will be receiving if all those who owe you money pay on time and the amounts you will be spending if you pay your accounts payable on time.

MEMO
DATE: January 31, 2010

Since this is the end of January, prepare Cash Flow Forecast for February 1-28, 2010.

DO Prepare Cash Flow Forecast for February

The Report Center should still be on the screen; if it is not, open it as previously instructed

Click **Company & Financial** in the type of reports section, scroll through the list of reports, double-click **Cash Flow Forecast**

Enter the **From** date of **02/01/10** and the **To** date of **02/28/10**

Tab to generate the report

- Notice that **Periods** show **Week**. Use Week, but click the drop-down list arrow to see the periods available for the report.
- If you are not using 2010 as the year, the individual amounts listed per week may be different from the report shown. As long as the totals are the same, consider the report as being correct.
- Analyze the report for February: The Beginning Balance for Accounts Receivable shows the amounts due from customers as of 1/31/10.
- Depending on whether or not you applied the Credit Memo to Invoice 4 in Chapter 2, you may have a $400 difference in the Accounts Receivable detail and the Projected Balance; however, the Ending Balance for Accounts Receivable and Projected Balance will still be the same.
- The amounts for A/R and A/P for the future weeks are for the customer payments you expect to receive and the bills you expect to pay. This information is based on the due dates for invoices and bills and on credit memos recorded.
- The bank account amount for future weeks is based on deposits made or deposits that need to be made.
- Net Inflows summarizes the amounts that should be received and the amounts that should be paid to get a net inflow of cash.
- The projected balance is the total in all bank accounts if all customer and bill payments are made on time.

Computer Consulting by Your Name

Cash Flow Forecast

February 2010

	Accnts Receivable	Accnts Payable	Bank Accnts	Net Inflows	Proj Balance
Beginning Balance	9,570.00	0.00	49,364.67		58,934.67
Feb 1 - 6, 10	▶ 7,905.00	◀ 0.00	0.00	7,905.00	66,839.67
Week of Feb 7, 10	175.00	0.00	0.00	175.00	67,014.67
Week of Feb 14, 10	0.00	3,764.00	0.00	-3,764.00	63,250.67
Week of Feb 21, 10	0.00	0.00	0.00	0.00	63,250.67
Feb 28, 10	0.00	0.00	0.00	0.00	63,250.67
Feb 10	8,080.00	3,764.00	0.00	4,316.00	
Ending Balance	**17,650.00**	**3,764.00**	**49,364.67**		**63,250.67**

Print the report for February in **Landscape**
Use **Preview** to determine if it is necessary to use **Fit report to one page wide**
Close the report
Do not close the Report Center

STATEMENT OF CASH FLOWS

Another report that details the amount of cash flow in a business is the Statement of Cash Flows. This report organizes information regarding cash in three areas of activities: Operating Activities, Investing Activities, and Financing Activities. The report also projects the amount of cash at the end of a period.

MEMO
DATE: January 31, 2010

Prepare Statement of Cash Flows for January 1-31, 2010.

DO Prepare Statement of Cash Flows for January

Double-click **Statement of Cash Flows** in the **Company & Financial** list of reports
Enter the **From** date of **01/01/10** and the **To** date of **01/31/10**
Tab to generate the report

```
                 Computer Consulting by Your Name
                    Statement of Cash Flows
                           January 2010
                                              ◇   Jan 10   ◇
    OPERATING ACTIVITIES
      Net Income                             ▶   4,135.53  ◀
      Adjustments to reconcile Net Income
      to net cash provided by operations:
        Accounts Receivable                       4,915.00
        Office Supplies                             -100.00
        Prepaid Insurance                        -2,612.50
        Accounts Payable                          2,914.00
    Net cash provided by Operating Activities     9,252.03

    INVESTING ACTIVITIES
      Business Vehicles:Depreciation                583.00
      Office Furniture & Equipment:Depreciation     142.00
      Office Furniture & Equipment:Original Cost  -3,486.00
    Net cash provided by Investing Activities     -2,761.00

    FINANCING ACTIVITIES
      Loan Payable:Business Vehicles Loan          -467.19
      Loan Payable:Office Furniture/Equipment Loan  -29.17
      Your Name, Capital:Draws                   -2,500.00
      Your Name, Capital:Investments              8,000.00
    Net cash provided by Financing Activities      5,003.64

    Net cash increase for period                  11,494.67

    Cash at beginning of period                   37,870.00
  Cash at end of period                           49,364.67
```

Print the report in Portrait mode following previous instructions
Close the report, do not close the Report Center

PRINT STANDARD PROFIT AND LOSS STATEMENT

Because all income, expenses, and adjustments have been made for the period, a Profit and Loss Statement can be prepared. This statement is also known as the Income Statement. QuickBooks Pro has several different types of Profit and Loss statements available: Standard—summarizes income and expenses; Detail—shows the year-to-date transactions for each income and expense account; YTD Comparison—is like the Standard Profit and Loss but summarizes your income and expenses for this month and compares them to your income and expenses for the current fiscal year; Prev Year Comparison—is like the standard statement but summarizes your income and expenses for both this month and this month last year; By Job—is like the Standard Profit and Loss statement, but has columns for each customer and job and amounts for this year to date; By Class—is like the Standard Profit and Loss statement, but has columns for each class and sub-class with the amounts for this year to date, and Unclassified—is like the Standard Profit and Loss statement, but shows how much you are making or losing within segments of your business that are not assigned to a QuickBooks class.

DO Print a **Standard Profit and Loss Report**

Double-click **Standard** as the type of Profit & Loss (Income Statement) to
   prepare in the list of Company & Financial reports
Enter the dates From **01/01/10** to **01/31/10**
Tab to generate the report
Scroll through the report to view the income and expenses listed

Computer Consulting by Your Name
Profit & Loss
January 2010

	Jan 10
Total Expense	4,855.90
Net Ordinary Income	4,069.10
Other Income/Expense	
Other Income	
Interest Income	66.43
Total Other Income	66.43
Net Other Income	66.43
Net Income	**4,135.53**

Partial Report

Print the report in **Portrait** orientation
Close the **Profit and Loss Report**
Do not close Report Center

PREPARE A STANDARD BALANCE SHEET

The Balance Sheet proves the fundamental accounting equation: Assets = Liabilities +
Owner's Equity. When all transactions and adjustments for the period have been
recorded, a balance sheet should be prepared. QuickBooks Pro has several different
types of Balance Sheet statements available: Standard—shows as of today the balance
in each balance sheet account with subtotals provided for assets, liabilities, and equity;
Detail—which is a more detailed version of the standard balance sheet report;
Summary—shows amounts for each account type but not for individual accounts; and
Prev. Year Comparison—has columns for a year ago today, $ change, and % change.
For each account, the report shows the starting balance at the beginning of last month,
transactions entered in the account for this month to date, and the ending balance as of
today.

DO ▶ Prepare a **Standard Balance Sheet Report**

Double-click **Standard** as the type of Balance Sheet to prepare in the list of
    Company & Financial reports
Tab to or click **As of**, enter **01/31/10**, tab to generate the report
Scroll through the report to view the assets, liabilities, and equities listed
• Notice the Net Income account listed in the Equity section of the report. This
  is the same amount of Net Income shown on the Profit and Loss Statement.

Computer Consulting by Your Name
Balance Sheet
As of January 31, 2010

	Jan 31, 10
Long Term Liabilities	
Loan Payable	
Business Vehicles Loan	34,532.81
Office Furniture/Equipment Loan	3,970.83
Total Loan Payable	38,503.64
Total Long Term Liabilities	38,503.64
Total Liabilities	42,267.64
Equity	
Your Name, Capital	
Draws	-2,500.00
Investments	33,000.00
Your Name, Capital - Other	53,135.00
Total Your Name, Capital	83,635.00
Net Income	4,135.53
Total Equity	87,770.53
TOTAL LIABILITIES & EQUITY	**130,038.17**

Partial Report

Do not print or close the **Standard Balance**

ADJUSTMENT TO TRANSFER NET INCOME/RETAINED EARNINGS INTO YOUR NAME, CAPITAL

Because Computer Consulting by Your Name is a sole proprietorship, the amount of net income should appear as part of your capital account rather than set aside in Retained Earnings as QuickBooks Pro does automatically. In many instances, this is the type of adjustment the CPA makes on the Accountant's Copy of the QuickBooks Pro company files. The adjustment may be made before the closing date for the fiscal year, or it may be made after the closing has been performed. Because QuickBooks Pro automatically transfers Net Income into Retained Earnings, the closing entry will transfer the net income into the Owner's Capital account. This adjustment is made in a General Journal entry that debits Retained Earnings and credits the Owner's Capital account. When you view a report before the end of the year after you enter the adjustment, you will see an amount in Net Income and the same amount as a negative in Retained Earnings. If you view a report after the end of the year, you will not see any information regarding Retained Earnings or Net Income because the adjustment correctly transferred the amount to the Owner's Capital account.

If you prefer to use the power of the program and not make the adjustment, QuickBooks Pro simply carries the amount of Retained Earnings forward. Each year net income is added to Retained Earnings. On the Balance Sheet, Retained Earnings and/or Net Income appears as part of the equity section. The owner's drawing and investment accounts are kept separate from Retained Earnings at all times.

To make the transfer of net income, you will record the entry in the General Journal. (Once the transaction is recorded in the General Journal, the entry and all other transactions will be displayed in debit/credit format in the report called the Journal.)

DO   Transfer the net income into Your Name, Capital account

Open the General Journal by clicking on **Company** on the menu bar, and clicking **Make General Journal Entries**
Enter the date of **01/31/10**
The first account used is **Retained Earnings**
Debit **Retained Earnings**, **4,135.53**
- Note: if the entire General Journal disappears during the transaction entry, simply open the Journal again and continue recording the transaction.

For the Memo record, **Transfer Net Income into Capital**
The other account used is **Your Name, Capital**
4,135.53 should appear as the credit amount for **Your Name, Capital**
Enter the same Memo

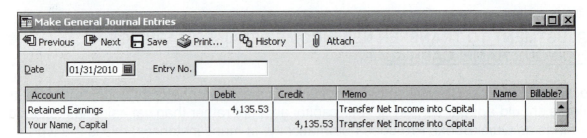

Click **Save & Close** to record and close the **General Journal**
If a Retained Earnings screen appears, click **OK**

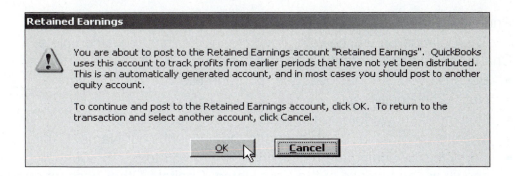

PRINT STANDARD BALANCE SHEET

Once the adjustment for Net Income/Retained Earnings has been performed, viewing or printing the Balance Sheet will show you the status of the Owner's Equity.

DO ▶ Print a **Standard Balance Sheet** for January 2010

The Standard Balance Sheet should still be showing on the screen
Scroll through the report
- Notice the Equity section, especially Retained Earnings and Net Income.
Prior to printing, change the title of the report by clicking **Modify Report**, clicking the **Header/Footer** tab, clicking at the end of **Balance Sheet** in the Report Title dialog box and keying **(After Transfer of Net Income)**, click **OK**

Computer Consulting by Your Name
Balance Sheet (After Transfer of Net Income)
As of January 31, 2010

	Jan 31, 10
Total Long Term Liabilities	38,503.64
Total Liabilities	42,267.64
Equity	
Retained Earnings	-4,135.53
Your Name, Capital	
Draws	-2,500.00
Investments	33,000.00
Your Name, Capital - Other	57,270.53
Total Your Name, Capital	87,770.53
Net Income	4,135.53
Total Equity	87,770.53
TOTAL LIABILITIES & EQUITY	**130,038.17**

Partial Report after Adjusting Entry

Print the **Balance Sheet** for January 2010 in **Portrait** orientation
- The Balance Sheet shows on the screen after printing is complete.

Change the **As of** date to **01/31/11**, press **Tab**
- Because you did not close the report, the title does not change
- Notice the Equity section.
- Nothing is shown for Retained Earnings or Net Income.
- The Net Income has been added to the account Your Name, Capital - Other.
- Verify this by adding the net income of 4,135.53 to 53,135.00, which was shown as the balance of the Your Name, Capital - Other account on the Balance Sheet prepared before the adjusting entry was made. The total should equal 57,270.53, which is the amount of Your Name, Capital - Other on the 2011 Balance Sheet.

Computer Consulting by Your Name	
Balance Sheet (After Transfer of Net Income)	
As of January 31, 2011	
	Jan 31, 11
Equity	
Your Name, Capital	
Draws	-2,500.00
Investments	33,000.00
Your Name, Capital - Other	57,270.53
Total Your Name, Capital	87,770.53
Total Equity	87,770.53
TOTAL LIABILITIES & EQUITY	130,038.17

Partial Report

Close the **Balance Sheet** without printing; do not close the Report Center

PRINT JOURNAL

It is always wise to have a printed or "hard copy" of the data on disk. After all entries and adjustments for the month have been made, print the Journal for January. This copy should be kept on file as an additional backup to the data stored on your disk. If something happens to your file to damage it, you will still have the paper copy of your transactions available for re-entry into the system.

▶ **DO** Print the Journal for January

With the Report Center on the screen, click **Accountant & Taxes** as the type of reports, double-click **Journal**

Enter the dates From **01/01/10** To **01/31/10**

- Notice that the report contains all the transactions from Chapters 2, 3, and 4

Verify that the final total for debits and credits is $62,055.22

- If it is not, make the necessary corrections to incorrect transactions. Frequent errors include incorrect dates, incorrect accounts used, and incorrect amounts.

Computer Consulting by Your Name
Journal
January 2010

Trans #	Type	Date	Num	Name	Memo	Account	Debit	Credit
75	Check	01/31/2010			Service Charge	Checking		8.00
					Service Charge	Bank Service Charges	8.00	
							8.00	8.00
76	Deposit	01/31/2010			Interest	Checking	66.43	
					Interest	Interest Income		66.43
							66.43	66.43
77	General Journal	01/31/2010			Transfer Net Income into Capital	Retained Earnings	4,135.53	
					Transfer Net Income into Capital	Your Name, Capital		4,135.53
							4,135.53	4,135.53
TOTAL							62,055.22	62,055.22

Partial Report

Print in **Landscape** orientation, select **Fit report to one page wide**

Close the **Journal**

EXPORTING REPORTS TO EXCEL

Many of the reports prepared in QuickBooks Pro can be exported to Microsoft® Excel. This allows you to take advantage of extensive filtering options available in Excel, hide detail for some but not all groups of data, combine information from two different reports, change titles of columns, add comments, change the order of columns, and to experiment with "what if" scenarios. In order to use this feature of QuickBooks Pro you must also have Microsoft® Excel.

▶DO Optional Exercise: Export a report from QuickBooks Pro to Excel

With Report Center on the screen, double-click **Trial Balance** in the Accountant & Taxes section

When the Trial Balance appears, enter the **From** date as **01/01/10** and the **To** date as **01/31/10**

Click the ⟦ Export… ⟧ button at the top of the report

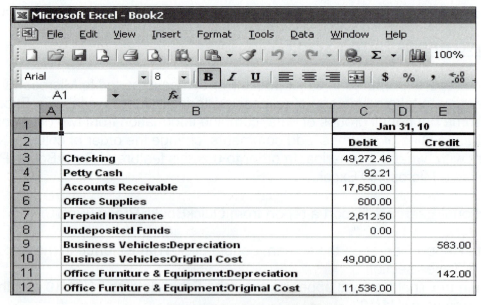

Make sure the Export QuickBooks Report to: is **a new Excel workbook**
- If necessary, click the **Include a new worksheet in the workbook that explains Excel worksheet linking** to remove the check mark

Click **Export**
- The **Trial** Balance will be displayed in Excel.
- The Book number may change depending on how many reports have been sent since you opened Excel. The following example shows Book 2.

	B	C	D	E
1		Jan 31, 10		
2		**Debit**		**Credit**
3	**Checking**	49,272.46		
4	**Petty Cash**	92.21		
5	**Accounts Receivable**	17,650.00		
6	**Office Supplies**	600.00		
7	**Prepaid Insurance**	2,612.50		
8	**Undeposited Funds**	0.00		
9	**Business Vehicles:Depreciation**			583.00
10	**Business Vehicles:Original Cost**	49,000.00		
11	**Office Furniture & Equipment:Depreciation**			142.00
12	**Office Furniture & Equipment:Original Cost**	11,536.00		

Partial Trial Balance in Excel

Click in Cell C1, change the heading by typing **JANUARY 31, 2010**
Click in Cell C2, type **DEBIT** to change Debit to all capitals
Click in Cell E2, type **CREDIT** to change Credit to all capitals

	A	B	C	D	E
1			JANUARY 31, 2010		
2			DEBIT		CREDIT

Click the **Close** button in the top right corner of the Excel title bar to close Excel
Click **No** to close Book2 without saving
Close the **Trial Balance** and the **Report Center**

END-OF-PERIOD BACKUP

Once all end-of-period procedures have been completed, a regular backup and a second backup of the company data should be made. The second backup should be filed as an archive copy. Preferably this copy will be located someplace other than on the business premises. The archive or file copy is set aside in case of emergency or in case damage occurs to the original and current backup copies of the company data.

▶ DO ▶ Back up company data and prepare an archive copy of the company data

For training purposes, use your USB drive
Follow the procedures given previously to make your backup files
Name the file **Computer (Backup Archive 1-31-10)**
- In actual practice, the company (.qbw) file would be on your hard drive and the backup (.qbb) file would be stored on separate disk or USB drive.
Once the backup has been made, click **OK** on the QuickBooks Pro Information dialog box to acknowledge the successful backup

PASSWORDS

Not every employee of a business should have access to all the financial records for the company. In some companies, only the owner will have complete access. In others, one or two key employees will have full access while other employees are provided limited access based on the jobs they perform. Passwords are secret words used to control access to data. QuickBooks Pro has several options available when assigning passwords.

In order to assign any passwords at all, you must have an administrator. The administrator has unrestricted access to all QuickBooks Pro functions, sets up users and user passwords for QuickBooks and for Windows, and assigns areas of transaction access for each user. Areas of access can be limited to transaction entry for certain types of transactions or a user may have unrestricted access into all areas of QuickBooks Pro and company data. To obtain more information regarding QuickBooks' passwords, refer to Help.

A password should be kept secret at all times. It should be something that is easy for the individual to remember, yet difficult for someone else to guess. Birthdays, names, initials, and similar devices are not good passwords because the information is too readily available. Never write down your password where it can be easily found or seen by someone else. Make sure your password is something you won't forget. Otherwise, you will not be able to access your Company file.

Since the focus of the text is in training in all aspects of QuickBooks Pro, no passwords will be assigned.

SET THE CLOSING DATE FOR THE PERIOD

A closing date assigned to transactions for a period prevents changing data from the closed period without acknowledging that a transaction has been changed. This is helpful to discourage casual changes or transaction deletions to a period that has been closed. Setting the closing date is done by accessing Preferences in QuickBooks Pro.

MEMO

DATE: January 31, 2010

Alhandra, now that the closing transactions have been performed, protect the data by setting the closing date to 1/31/10.

DO Assign the closing date of **01/31/10** to the transactions for the period

Click **Edit** on the menu bar, click **Preferences**
Scroll through the list of Preferences until you see **Accounting**
Click **Accounting**
Click **Company Preferences**
Click the **Set Date/Password** button
Enter **01/31/10** as the closing date.
Do not enter anything in the textboxes for Password, click the **OK** button

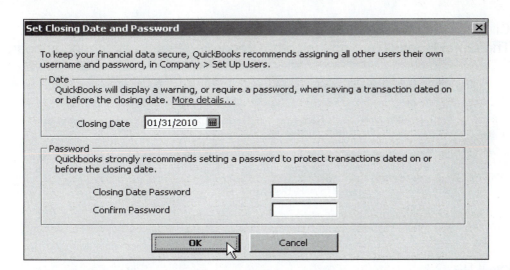

On the No Password Entered screen, click **No**.

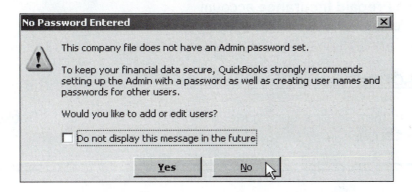

Click **OK** to close the period and to close Preferences

ACCESS TRANSACTION FOR PREVIOUS PERIOD

Even though the month of January has been "closed," transactions still appear in the account registers, the Journal, and so on. The transactions shown may not be changed unless you click Yes on the screen warning you that you have changed a transaction to a closed period.

DO Change Prepaid Insurance to 2,500

Access the **Chart of Accounts** as previously instructed
Double-click **Prepaid Insurance** to access the account Register
Click the **Increase** column showing **2,850** paid to California Insurance Company
Highlight 2,850, enter **2,500**
Click **Record**

Click **Yes** on the Recording Transaction dialog box
The **QuickBooks** warning dialog box regarding the closed period appears

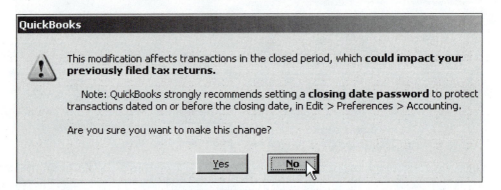

Click **No**
Click the **Restore** button to restore the transaction to the original 2,850
Close the **Prepaid Insurance** account
Do not close the **Chart of Accounts**

EDIT TRANSACTION FROM PREVIOUS PERIOD

If it is determined that an error was made in a previous period, QuickBooks Pro does allow the correction.

MEMO

DATE: February 1, 2010

After reviewing the journal and reports printed at the end of January, You find that the amount of supplies used was $325, not $350. Make the correction to the adjusting entry of January 31.

▶ DO ▶ Change Office Supplies adjusting entry to $325 from $350

Double-click the **Office Supplies** account to access the account Register
Click the **Decrease** column for the Adjusting Entry recorded to the account on 01/31/10
Change 350 to **325**
Click **Record**
Click **Yes** on the Recording Transaction dialog box
Click **Yes** on the **QuickBooks** warning dialog box
• The change to the transaction has been made.

- Notice that the Balance for the Office Supplies account now shows 625 instead of 600.

01/31/2010				325.00			625.00
	GENJRNL	Office Supplies Expense Supplies Used					

Close the **Register for Office Supplies**
- The adjusting entry used to transfer retained earnings/net income into the owner's capital account may also need to be adjusted as a result of any changes to transactions.
- Since the correction to Office Supplies decreased the amount of the expense by $25, there is an additional $25 that will need to be included in the net income.

Click **Your Name, Capital**
Click **Activities** at the bottom of the **Chart of Accounts**
Click **Make General Journal Entries**
Click **Previous** until you find the entry adjusting Retained Earnings
Change the Debit to Retained Earnings from 4135.53 to **4160.53**
Change the Credit to Your Name, Capital from 4135.53 to **4160.53**

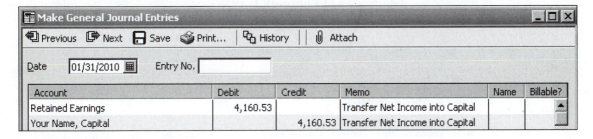

Click **Save & Close**
Click **Yes** or **OK** on all of the **QuickBooks** dialog boxes
Close the **Chart of Accounts**

PRINT POST-CLOSING TRIAL BALANCE

After "closing" has been completed, it is helpful to print a Post-Closing Trial Balance. This proves that debits still equal credits.

MEMO

DATE: February 1, 2010

Print a Post-Closing Trial Balance, a Post-Closing Profit and Loss Statement, and a Post-Closing Balance Sheet for Computer Consulting by Your Name. The dates should be as of or for 02/01/10.

DO ▶ Print a Post-Closing Trial Balance to prove debits still equal credits

Click **Accountant & Taxes** in the **Report Center**, double-click **Trial Balance**
Enter the **From** and **To** dates as **02/01/10**, tab to generate the report
Click the **Modify Report** button and change the Header so the report title is
    Post-Closing Trial Balance
Scroll through the report and study the amounts shown
- Notice that the final totals of debits and credits are equal.

Computer Consulting by Your Name
Post-Closing Trial Balance
As of February 1, 2010

	Feb 1, 10	
	Debit	Credit
Bank Service Charges	8.00	
Business Vehicles Expense	588.88	
Depreciation Expense	725.00	
Dues and Subscriptions	79.00	
Equipment Rental	25.00	
Insurance:Business Vehicles Insurance	237.50	
Interest Expense:Interest on Loans	308.61	
Office Supplies Expense	343.57	
Postage and Delivery	195.34	
Rent	1,600.00	
Telephone	0.00	
Utilities:Electricity Expense	250.00	
Utilities:Heating Expense--Gas	175.00	
Utilities:Water	35.00	
Interest Income		66.43
TOTAL	142,279.60	142,279.60

Partial Report

Print the report in **Portrait** orientation
Close the **Trial Balance**

PRINT POST-CLOSING PROFIT AND LOSS STATEMENT

Because February 1 is after the closing date of January 31, 2010, the Profit and Loss Statement for February 1 is the Post-Closing Profit and Loss Statement. To verify the closing, print a Profit and Loss statement for February 1.

DO Print a **Standard Profit and Loss Report** as the Post-Closing Profit and Loss report for February

Click **Company & Financial** in the **Report Center**, double-click **Profit & Loss Standard**
The dates are From **02/01/10** to **02/01/10**
Tab to generate the report
For clarity, change the Header so the report title is **Post-Closing Profit & Loss**
- Note the Net Income of **0.00**.

Computer Consulting by Your Name
Post-Closing Profit & Loss
February 1, 2010
◇ Feb 1, 10 ◇
Net Income ▶   0.00 ◀

Print the report in **Portrait** orientation
Close the **Post-Closing Profit and Loss Report**

PRINT POST-CLOSING BALANCE SHEET

Proof that assets are equal to liabilities and owner's equity needs to be displayed in a Post-Closing Balance Sheet. The Balance Sheet for February 1 is considered to be a Post-Closing Balance Sheet because it is prepared after the closing of the period. Most of the adjustments were for the month of January 2010. Because this report is for a month, the adjustment to Retained Earnings and Net Income will result in both accounts being included on the Balance Sheet. If, however, this report were prepared for the year, neither account would appear.

DO Prepare a **Post-Closing Balance Sheet** Report for February 1, 2010, and February 1, 2011

Prepare a **Standard Balance Sheet** as previously instructed
Tab to or click **As of**, enter **02/01/10**
Tab to generate the report
Change the Header so the report title is **Post-Closing Balance Sheet**

Scroll through the report to view the assets, liabilities, and equities listed
- Because this report is for a one-month period, both Retained Earnings and Net Income are included on this report.

Computer Consulting by Your Name
Post-Closing Balance Sheet
As of February 1, 2010

	Feb 1, 10	
Total Liabilities		42,267.64
Equity		
Retained Earnings		-4,160.53
Your Name, Capital		
Draws	-2,500.00	
Investments	33,000.00	
Your Name, Capital - Other	57,295.53	
Total Your Name, Capital		87,795.53
Net Income		4,160.53
Total Equity		87,795.53
TOTAL LIABILITIES & EQUITY		**130,063.17**

Partial Report

Print the report in **Portrait** orientation
Change the date to **02/01/11**, tab to generate the report
Scroll through the report to view the assets, liabilities, and equities listed
- Because this report is prepared after the end of the fiscal year, neither Retained Earnings nor Net Income is included on this report.

Computer Consulting by Your Name
Post-Closing Balance Sheet
As of February 1, 2011

	Feb 1, 11	
Total Liabilities		42,267.64
Equity		
Your Name, Capital		
Draws	-2,500.00	
Investments	33,000.00	
Your Name, Capital - Other	57,295.53	
Total Your Name, Capital		87,795.53
Total Equity		87,795.53
TOTAL LIABILITIES & EQUITY		**130,063.17**

Partial Report

Close the **Balance Sheet** for **February 2011** without printing

Close the **Report Center**

END-OF-CHAPTER BACKUP AND CLOSE COMPANY

As in previous chapters, you should back up your company and then close the company.

DO Follow instructions previously provided to back up company files, close the company, and make a duplicate disk

Name the backup **Computer (Backup Ch. 4)**

SUMMARY

In this chapter, end-of-period adjustments were made, a bank reconciliation was performed, backup and archive disks were prepared, and a period was closed. The use of Net Income and Retained Earnings accounts was explored and interpreted for a sole proprietorship. Account name changes were made, and the effect on subaccounts was examined. Even though QuickBooks Pro focuses on entering transactions on business forms, a Journal recording each transaction is kept by QuickBooks Pro. This chapter presented transaction entry directly into the Journal. The differences between accrual-basis and cash-basis accounting were discussed. Company preferences were established for reporting preferences. Owner withdrawals and additional owner investments were made. Many of the different report options available in QuickBooks Pro were examined, and the exporting of reports to Excel was explored. A variety of reports were printed. Correction of errors was explored, and changes to transactions in "closed" periods were made. The fact that QuickBooks Pro does not require an actual closing entry at the end of the period was examined.

END-OF-CHAPTER QUESTIONS

TRUE/FALSE

ANSWER THE FOLLOWING QUESTIONS IN THE SPACE PROVIDED BEFORE THE QUESTION NUMBER.

_____   1. Accrual-basis accounting matches the income from the period and the expenses for the period in order to determine the net income or net loss for the period.

_____   2. In QuickBooks Pro, the Journal is called the book of final entry.

_____   3. An account may be deleted at any time.

_____   4. In a sole proprietorship, an owner's name is added to the Vendor List for recording withdrawals.

_____   5. Additional investments made by an owner may be cash or noncash items.

_____   6. QuickBooks Pro records every transaction in the Journal.

_____   7. QuickBooks Pro keeps the last two Bank Reconciliation reports in memory.

_____   8. Once an account has been used in a transaction, no changes may be made to the account name.

_____   9. Anything entered as a service charge or as interest earned during a bank reconciliation will be entered automatically when the reconciliation is complete.

_____   10. A Balance Sheet is prepared to prove the equality of debits and credits.

MULTIPLE CHOICE

WRITE THE LETTER OF THE CORRECT ANSWER IN THE SPACE PROVIDED BEFORE THE QUESTION NUMBER.

_____ 1. To close a period, you must ___.
   A. have a closing password
   B. enter a closing date in the Company Preferences for Accounting
   C. enter a closing date in the Company Preferences for Reports
   D. enter the traditional closing entries in debit/credit format in the General Journal

_____ 2. When a master account name such as "cars" is changed to "automobiles," the subaccount "depreciation" ___.
   A. needs to be changed to a subaccount of automobiles
   B. is automatically changed to a subaccount of automobiles
   C. cannot be changed
   D. must be deleted and re-entered

_____ 3. The report that proves Assets = Liabilities + Owner's Equity is the ___.
   A. Trial Balance
   B. Income Statement
   C. Profit and Loss Statement
   D. Balance Sheet

_____ 4. If the adjusting entry to transfer net income/retained earnings into the owner's capital account is made prior to the end of the year, the Balance Sheet shows ___.
   A. Retained Earnings
   B. Net Income
   C. both Net Income and Retained Earnings
   D. none of the above because the income/earnings has been transferred into capital

_____ 5. The type of Profit and Loss Report showing year-to-date transactions instead of totals for each income and expense account is a(n) ___ Profit and Loss Report.
   A. Standardized
   B. YTD Comparison
   C. Prev Year Comparison
   D. Detailed

_____ 6. A bank statement may ___.
     A. show service charges or interest not yet recorded
     B. be missing deposits in transit or outstanding checks
     C. both of the above
     D. none of the above

_____ 7. The Journal shows ___.
     A. all transactions no matter where they were recorded
     B. only those transactions recorded in the General Journal
     C. only transactions recorded in account registers
     D. only those transactions that have been edited

_____ 8. A QuickBooks backup file ___.
     A. is a condensed file containing company data
     B. is prepared in case of emergencies or errors on current disks
     C. must be restored before information can be used
     D. all of the above

_____ 9. An error known as a transposition can be found by ___.
     A. dividing the amount out of balance by 9
     B. dividing the amount out of balance by 2
     C. multiplying the difference by 9, then dividing by 2
     D. dividing the amount out of balance by 5

_____ 10. The type of Balance Sheet Report showing information for today and a year ago is a(n) ___ Balance Sheet.
     A. Standard
     B. Summary
     C. Comparison
     D. Detailed

FILL-IN

IN THE SPACE PROVIDED, WRITE THE ANSWER THAT MOST APPROPRIATELY COMPLETES THE SENTENCE.

1. Bank reconciliations should be performed on a(n) _____ basis.

2. Exporting report data from QuickBooks Pro to _____ can be made in order to perform "what if" scenarios.

3. An owner's paycheck is considered a(n) _____.

4. The two types of reporting are _____ basis and _____ basis.

5. The Cash Flow Forecast _____ column shows the total in all bank accounts if all customer and bill payments are made on time.

SHORT ESSAY

Describe the four types of Balance Sheet Reports available in QuickBooks Pro.

_____

_____

_____

_____

_____

_____

_____

NAME_____

TRANSMITTAL

CHAPTER 4: COMPUTER CONSULTING BY YOUR NAME

Attach the following documents and reports:

Check No. 9: Your Name
Reconciliation Detail Report
Trial Balance, January 1-31, 2010
Cash Flow Forecast, February 1-28, 2010
Statement of Cash Flows, January 2010
Profit and Loss Statement, January 31, 2010
Balance Sheet (After Transfer of Net Income), January 31, 2010
Journal, January 1-31, 2010
Post-Closing Trial Balance, February 1, 2010
Post-Closing Profit and Loss, February 1, 2010
Post-Closing Balance Sheet, February 1, 2010

END-OF-CHAPTER PROBLEM

YOUR NAME LANDSCAPE AND POOL SERVICE

Chapter 4 continues with the end-of-period adjustments, bank reconciliation, archive disks, and closing the period for Your Name Landscape and Pool Service. The company does use a certified public accountant for guidance and assistance with appropriate accounting procedures. The CPA has provided information for use in recording adjusting entries and so on.

INSTRUCTIONS

Continue to use the company file **Landscape.qbw** that you used for Chapters 1, 2, and 3. Record the adjustments and other transactions as you were instructed in the chapter. Always read the transaction carefully and review the Chart of Accounts when selecting transaction accounts. Print the reports and journals as indicated.

RECORD TRANSACTIONS

<u>January 31</u>—Enter the following:
► Change the names of the following accounts:
  o **Student's Name, Capital** to **Your Name, Capital**
    • Remember to use your actual name
  o **Business Trucks** to **Business Vehicles** (also change the subaccounts so they reflect the name Business Vehicles)
  o **Automobile Expense** to **Business Vehicles Expense** (Delete the description)
  o **Business Trucks Loan** to **Business Vehicles Loan**
  o **Auto Insurance Expense** to **Business Vehicles Insurance**
► Make the following accounts inactive:
  o **Recruiting**
  o **Travel & Ent**
► Delete the following accounts:
  o **Sales**
  o **Services**
  o **Amortization Expenses**
  o **Contributions**
  o **Interest Expense: Mortgage**
  o **Taxes: Property**
► Print the Chart of Accounts by clicking **Reports** on the menu bar, pointing to **List**, clicking **Account Listing.** Use Landscape orientation.

January 31—Enter the following:
► Enter adjusting entries in the Journal for:
  o Office Supplies Used, $185. Memo: January Supplies Used
  o Business vehicles insurance expense for the month, $250.
    Memo: January Insurance Expense
  o Depreciation for the month (Use a compound entry),
    Memo: January Depreciation
    • Business Vehicles, $950
    • Equipment, $206.25
► Enter transactions for Owner's Equity:
  o Owner withdrawal $1,000. Memo: January Withdrawal (Print the check.)
  o Additional cash investment by you, $2,000. Memo: Investment: Cash
  o Additional noncash investment by owner, $1,500 of lawn equipment. Memo:
    Investment: Equipment (Note: The value of the lawn equipment is the original
    cost of the asset.)
► Prepare Bank Reconciliation and Enter Adjustments for the Reconciliation for
    January 31, 2010 (Be sure to enter automatic payments, service charges, and
    interest. Pay close attention to the dates.)

SANTA BARBARA BANK
1234 Coast Highway
Santa Barbara, CA 93100 (805) 555-9310

BANK STATEMENT FOR
Your Name Landscape and Pool Service
18527 State Street
Santa Barbara, CA 93103
Acct. #987-352-9152　　　　　　　　　　　　　　January 31, 2010

Beginning Balance, January 2, 2010			$23,850.00
1/18/10, Check 1		485.00	23,365.00
1/18/10, Check 2		180.00	23,185.00
1/18/10, Check 3		669.00	22,516.00
1/18/10, Check 4		375.00	22,141.00
1/31/10, Service Charge		10.00	22,131.00
1/31/10, Business Vehicles Loan Pmt.: Interest, 795.54; Principal, 160.64		956.18	21,174.82
1/31/10, Interest	59.63		21,234.45
Ending Balance, 1/31/10			$21,234.45

▶ Print a Detailed Reconciliation Report in Portrait orientation
▶ Change Preferences: Verify or change reporting preferences to accrual basis
▶ Print reports for January, 2010 or as of January 31, 2010 in Portrait orientation.
  ○ Trial Balance
  ○ Standard Profit & Loss Statement
▶ Transfer Net Income/Retained Earnings into Capital Account
▶ Prepare a Balance Sheet Standard, add **(After Transfer of Net Income)** to the header, and print
▶ Prepare the archive backup file: **Landscape (Backup Archive 01-31-10)**
▶ Close the period. The closing date is **01/31/10** (Do not use a password.)
▶ Edit a Transaction from a closed period: Discovered an error in the amount of office supplies used. The amount used should be **$175**, not $185. (Don't forget to adjust Retained Earnings and Capital.)

February 1, 2010—Print the following in Portrait orientation unless specified as Landscape:
▶ Journal for January, 2010 (Landscape orientation, Fit report to one page wide)
▶ Post-Closing Trial Balance, February 1, 2010 (Add the words **Post-Closing** to the report title)
▶ Cash Flow Forecast for February 1-28, 2010 (Landscape orientation)
▶ Statement of Cash Flows, January 1-31, 2010
▶ Post-Closing Profit & Loss Statement, February 1, 2010 (Add the words **Post-Closing** to the report title)
▶ Post-Closing Balance Sheet, February 1, 2010 (Add the words **Post-Closing** to the report title)
▶ Backup your work to **Landscape (Backup Ch. 4)**

NAME_____

TRANSMITTAL

CHAPTER 4: YOUR NAME LANDSCAPE AND POOL SERVICE

Attach the following documents and reports:

Account Listing, January 31, 2010
Check No. 8: Your Name
Reconciliation Report
Trial Balance, January 31, 2010
Profit and Loss, January 2010
Balance Sheet, January 31, 2010 (After Transfer of Net Income)
Journal, January 2010
Post-Closing Trial Balance, February 1, 2010
Cash Flow Forecast, February 2010
Statement of Cash Flows, January 2010
Post-Closing Profit and Loss, February 1, 2010
Post-Closing Balance Sheet, February 1, 2010

SECTION 1 PRACTICE SET: YOUR NAME'S HELP FOR YOU

The following is a comprehensive practice set combining all the elements of QuickBooks Pro studied in the text. In this practice set, you will keep the books for a company for one month.

Entries will be made to record invoices, receipt of payments on invoices, cash sales, receipt and payment of bills, credit memos for invoices and bills. Account names will be added, changed, deleted, and made inactive. Customer, vendor, and owner names will be added to the appropriate lists. Reports will be prepared to analyze sales, bills, and receipts. Formal reports including the Trial Balance, Profit and Loss Statement, and Balance Sheet will be prepared. Adjusting entries for depreciation, supplies used, and insurance expense will be recorded. A bank reconciliation will be prepared.

YOUR NAME'S HELP FOR YOU

Located in Beverly Hills, California, Your Name's Help for You is a service business providing assistance with errands, shopping, home repairs, simple household chores, and transportation for children and others who do not drive. Rates are on a per-hour basis and differ according to the service performed.

Your Name's Help for You is a sole proprietorship owned and operated by you. You have one assistant, Pamela Russell, helping you with errands, scheduling of duties, and doing the bookkeeping for Your Name's Help for You. In addition, a part-time employee, Alice Winston, works weekends for Your Name's Help for You.

INSTRUCTIONS

To work with transactions for Your Name's Help for You, copy the file **Help.qbw.** Follow the steps presented in Chapter 1.

The following lists are used for all sales items, customers, and vendors. You will be adding additional customers and vendors as the company is in operation. When entering transactions, you are responsible for any memos or customer messages you wish to include in transactions. Unless otherwise specified, the terms for each sale or bill will be the terms specified on the Customer or Vendor List. (View the terms for the individual customers or vendors in the Customer Center and Vendor Center.)

Customers:

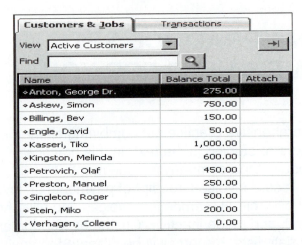

Vendors:

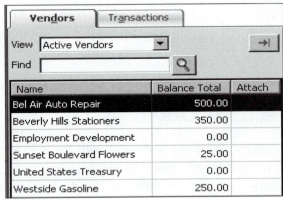

Sales Items:

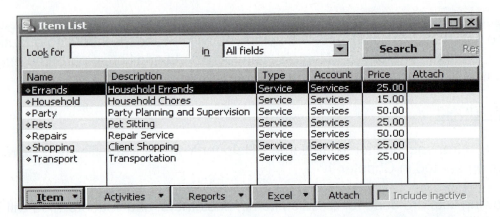

Each Item is priced per hour. Unless otherwise specified within the transactions, a minimum of one hour is charged for any service provided. As you can see, there is no difference in amount between the first hour of a service and subsequent hours of service.

RECORD TRANSACTIONS

Enter the transactions for Your Name's Help for You and print as indicated. When preparing invoices, use an Intuit Service Invoice form and a message of your choosing. Start numbering the Invoices with number 35 and Sales Receipts with the number 22. Use the standard terms provided by QuickBooks unless the transaction indicates something different. Always print invoices, sales receipts, checks, and so on as they are entered. To save time, do not print Payment Receipts unless instructed to do so by your professor.

Week 1: January 1-6, 2010:

▶ Add your name to the company name. The company name will be **Your Name's Help for You**. (Type your actual name, *not* the words *Your Name's*. For example, Joe Joseph would enter Joe Joseph's Help for You)

▶ Change Report Preferences: Reports should refresh automatically, Report Header/Footer should *not* include the Date Prepared, Time Prepared, or the Report Basis

▶ Change the Capital account to **Your Name, Capital**.

▶ Find all accounts with the name **Automobile** as part of the account name. Change every occurrence of Automobile to **Business Vehicle**.

▶ Find all accounts with the name **Office Equipment** as part of the account name. Change every occurrence of Office Equipment to **Office Furniture/Equipment**.

▶ Make the following inactive: **Interest Expense: Mortgage**, **Taxes: Property**, **Travel & Ent**

▶ Delete the following accounts: **Sales**, **Recruiting**, **Amortization Expense,** and **Professional Development**

▶ Add **Petty Cash** to the Chart of Accounts. Transfer **$100** from checking to Petty Cash to fund the account.

▶ Print an Account Listing in Portrait orientation. (Click the **Reports** button at the bottom of the Chart of Accounts, click **Account Listing**.)

▶ Prior to recording any transactions, print a Trial Balance as of January 1, 2010.

1/1/10

▶ Colleen Verhagen is having a party in two weeks. Bill Colleen Verhagen for 3 hours of party planning. Refer to the Item Detail List for the appropriate sales item. Invoice No. 35, terms, Net 30. (Remember to use an Intuit Service Invoice as the business form.) Print the invoice.

▶ Dr. Singleton has arranged for you to feed and walk his dogs every day. Bill Dr. Singleton for pet sitting, 1 hour per day for 7 days (put this all on one invoice).

▶ We were out of paper, toner cartridges for the laser printer, computer disks, and various other office supplies that we need to have on hand. Received a bill—Invoice No. 1806-1—from Beverly Hills Stationers for $350 for the office supplies we received today.

▶ Every week we put fresh flowers in the office in order to provide a welcoming environment for any customers who happen to come to the office. Received a bill— Invoice No. 887—from Sunset Boulevard Flowers for $25 for office flowers for the week. (Miscellaneous Expense)

1/2/10

▶ Dr. Anton almost forgot his anniversary. He called Your Name's Help for You with an emergency request for assistance. The store will bill the doctor for the actual gift purchased. Bill Dr. George Anton, 3 hours of shopping for his wife's birthday gift.
▶ Bev Billings needed to have her shelves relined. You did part of the house this week and will return next week to continue the work. Bill her for 5 hours of household chores for this week.

1/3/10

▶ Mr. Petrovich's mother has several doctor appointments. He has asked Your Name's Help for You to take her to these appointments. Bill Olaf Petrovich for 3 hours of transportation.

1/4/10

▶ Received a bill—Invoice No. 81056—from Westside Gasoline, $125 for the weekly gasoline charge.
▶ Received checks for payments on account from the following customers: Dr. George Anton, $275, Check No. 713; Manuel Preston, $250, Check No. 3381; Olaf Petrovich, $450, Check No. 6179; Tiko Kasseri, $1,000, Check No. 38142.

1/5/10

▶ Michelle Stein has a birthday party to attend. Her mother, Miko, has hired Your Name's Help for You to take her to the party and stay with her while she is there. Bill Miko Stein 3 hours of transportation for the birthday party. (This transportation charge also includes the time at the party.)

1/6/10

▶ Prepare Sales Receipt No. 22 to record a cash sale. Received Check No. 2894 for 1 hour of errands for a new customer: Amy Ricardo, 18062A Camden Drive, Beverly Hills, CA 90210, 310-555-7206, Fax 310-555-6027, E-mail ARicardo@abc.com, terms Net 10 days. (*Note:* Remember to key the last name first for the customer name.) Print the sales receipt.
▶ Prepare Unpaid Bills Detail Report for January 6, 2010. Print the report.

▶ Pay bills for the amount owed to Sunset Boulevard Flowers and Westside Gasoline on December 31. (Refer to the Vendor List shown on the second page of the practice set or to the Unpaid Bills Detail Report to determine the amounts for the checks. Remember that the due dates will not be 12/31/09 they will be 01/10/10.) Print the checks using a Standard check style—they may be printed on one page or individually.

▶ Make the bank deposit for the week. The date of the deposit is 1/6/10. Print a Deposit Summary.

▶ Print Trial Balance from 01/01/10 to 01/06/10.

▶ Back up your work for the week. Use **Help (Backup Week 1)** as the file name.

Week 2: January 7-13, 2010
1/7/10

▶ Colleen Verhagen is having a party and has finalized the date for January 19. Bill Colleen Verhagen for 4 hours of party planning.

▶ Mr. Petrovich's mother has several additional doctor appointments. He has asked Your Name's Help for You to take her to these appointments. Bill Olaf Petrovich for 4 hours of transportation.

▶ Dr. Singleton was pleased with the pet service we provided and has arranged to have Your Name's Help for You feed and walk his dogs every day on a permanent basis. Bill Dr. Singleton for pet sitting, 1 hour per day for 7 days.

1/8/10

▶ Melinda Kingston really likes the floral arrangements in the office of Your Name's Help for You. She has asked that flowers be brought to her home and arranged throughout the house. When you complete the placement of the flowers in the house, Melinda gives you Check No. 387 for $40. This is payment in full for 1 hour of errands and 1 hour of household chores.

1/9/10

▶ Received checks for payment on accounts from the following customers: Dr. Singleton, $500, No. 7891; Ms. Stein, $200, No. 97452; Ms. Kingston, $600, No. 395; Mr. Engle, $50, No. 178; Mr. Askew, $750, No. 3916.

▶ Received a bill—Invoice No. 943—from Sunset Boulevard Flowers for $25 for office flowers for the week.

▶ Received a bill—Invoice No. 81085—from Westside Gasoline, $100 for the weekly gasoline charge.

1/10/10
▶ Tiko Kasseri has arranged for Your Name's Help for You to supervise and coordinate the installation of new tile in his master bathroom. Bill Mr. Kasseri for 4 hours of repair service for hiring the subcontractor, scheduling the installation for 1/15 and 1/16, and contract preparation.

1/11/10
▶ Bev Billings needed to have her shelves relined. You did part of the house last week and completed the work today. Bill Ms. Billings for 5 hours of household chores for this week.
▶ Returned faulty printer cartridge that we had purchased to have on hand. Received Credit Memo No. 5 from Beverly Hills Stationers, $75.

1/13/10
▶ Pay all bills for the amounts due on or before January 13. (*Hint:* Are there any credits to apply?) There should be three checks. Print the checks–all on one page or individually.
▶ Correct the invoice issued to Bev Billings on 1/11/10. The number of hours billed should be 7 instead of 5. Print the corrected invoice.
▶ Make the bank deposit for the week. The date of the deposit is 1/13/10. Print a Deposit Summary.
▶ Back up your work for the week. Use **Help (Backup Week 2)** as the file name.

Week 3: January 14-20, 2010
1/14/10
▶ Colleen Verhagen is having a party the 19th. Bill Colleen Verhagen for 2 more hours of party planning.

1/15/10
▶ Pay postage due 64 cents. Use Petty Cash.
▶ Print Petty Cash Account QuickReport by clicking the Report button at the bottom of the Chart of Accounts. Fit report to one page wide.
▶ Melinda Kingston was really pleased with the floral arrangements you did last week. She has asked that flowers be brought to her home and arranged throughout the house on a weekly basis. This week when you complete the placement of the flowers in the house, Melinda gives you Check No. 421 for 1 hour of errands and 1 hour of household chores.

1/17/10
▶ Received a bill—Invoice No. 81109—from Westside Gasoline, $150 for the weekly gasoline charge.
▶ Received a bill—Invoice No. 979—from Sunset Boulevard Flowers for $25 for office flowers for the week.

► The bathroom tile was installed on 1/15 and 1/16. The installation was completed to Mr. Kasseri's satisfaction. Bill him for 16 hours of repair service.

1/18/10
► Melinda Kingston's neighbor, Dr. Patrick Rocklin, really liked the flowers in Melinda's house and asked you to bring flowers to his home and office. This week he gave you Check No. 90-163 for 1 hour of errands and 1 hour of household chores. Add him to the customer list: Dr. Patrick Rocklin, 236 West Canon Drive, Beverly Hills, CA 90210, 310-555-0918, Net 10.

1/19/10
► Tonight is Colleen's big party. She has arranged for both you and Alice to supervise the party from 3 p.m. until 1 a.m. Bill Colleen Verhagen for 20 hours of party planning and supervision.
► Print a Customer Balance Summary Report.

1/20/10
► Record the checks received from customers for the week: Mr. Petrovich, $175, No. 9165; Ms. Billings, $150, No. 7-303; Dr. Singleton, $175, No. 89162; Ms. Stein, $75, No. 5291.
► Make the bank deposit for the week. The date of the deposit is 1/20/10. Print a Deposit Summary.
► Back up your work for the week. Use **Help (Backup Week 3)** as the file name.

Week 4: January 21-27, 2010
1/22/10
► Melinda Kingston gave you Check No. 439 for 1 hour of errands and 1 hour of household chores in payment for the flowers that were brought to her home and arranged throughout the house this week.

1/23/10
► Use Petty Cash to pay for a box of file folders to be used immediately in reorganizing some of the files in the office, $4.23. (This is an expense.)
► Print a Petty Cash Account QuickReport. Fit the report to one page wide.
► Colleen's party went so smoothly on the 19th that You went home at 11 p.m. rather than 1 a.m. Issue a Credit Memo to Colleen Verhagen for 2 hours of party planning and supervision. Apply the credit to Invoice 48 dated January 19, 2010.
► David Engle arranged to have his pets cared for by Your Name's Help for You during the past 7 days. Bill him for 1 hour of pet sitting each day. David wants to add a doggie door and a fenced area for his dog. Bill him 20 hours of repair service for the planning and overseeing of the project.

1/24/10

▶ You arranged for theater tickets and dinner reservations for Dr. Anton to celebrate his wife's birthday. Bill him for 1 hour of errands, 3 hours shopping for the gift, and 5 hours of party planning for the after-theater surprise party.

▶ Received a bill—Invoice No. 81116—from Westside Gasoline, $110 for the weekly gasoline charge.

▶ Received a bill—Invoice No. 1002—from Sunset Boulevard Flowers for $25 for office flowers for the week.

▶ Write a check to Beverly Hills Stationers for the purchase of a new printer for the office, $500. (*Note:* If you get a warning to use Pay Bills because we owe the company money, click Continue Writing Check.) Print the check using standard-style checks.

1/27/10

▶ Dr. Singleton has arranged for Your Name's Help for You to feed and walk his dogs every day. Bill him for pet sitting, 1 hour per day for the past two weeks. In addition, Dr. Singleton is going to have a party and wants Your Name's Help for You to plan it for him. Bill him for 20 hours party planning. When the dogs were puppies they did some damage to the interior of the house. In order to prepare for the party several areas in the house need to be reorganized and repaired. Bill him for 15 hours of household chores and 15 hours of repairs.

▶ Write checks to pay bills for rent and utilities. The utility companies and the rental agent will need to be added to the Vendor List. Vendor information is provided in each transaction. Print the checks using standard-style checks. They may be printed as a batch or individually.

  o Monthly telephone bill: $192, Beverly Hills Telephone, 2015 Wilshire Boulevard, Beverly Hills, CA 90210, 310-555-8888, Net 30 days.

  o Monthly rent for office space: $1,500, Rentals for You, 3016 Robertson Boulevard, Beverly Hills, CA 90210, 310-555-1636, Net 30 days.

  o Monthly water bill: $153, California Water, 9916 Sunset Boulevard, Beverly Hills, CA 90210, 310-555-1961, Net 30 days.

  o Monthly gas and electric bill: $296, Beverly Hills Power, 10196 Olympic Boulevard, West Los Angeles, CA 90016, 310-555-9012, Net 30 days.

▶ Prepare and print in Portrait orientation an Unpaid Bills Detail Report for January 27.

▶ Pay bills for all amounts due on or before January 27. Print check(s).

▶ Prepare a Check Detail Report from 1/1/10 to 1/27/10. Use Landscape orientation and fit report to one page wide.

▶ Record payments received from customers: Ms. Verhagen, $150, No. 4692; Dr. Singleton, $175, No. 7942; Mr. Engle, $175, No. 235; Dr. Anton, $75, No. 601; Ms. Billings, $75, No. 923-10.

▶ Make the bank deposit for the week. The date of the deposit is 1/27/10. Print a Deposit Summary.

▶ Record the bill received from United Insurance, 7654 Western Avenue, Hollywood, CA 90721, 310-555-1598, Fax 310-555-8951, terms Net 30 for Business Vehicle Insurance for the year, $2,400.00, Invoice 2280.

▶ Print Customer Balance Detail Report in Portrait orientation. Fit report to one page wide.

▶ Record adjusting entries for:
   o Business Vehicle Insurance, $200
   o Office Supplies Used, $150
   o Depreciation: Business Vehicles, $500 and Office Furniture and Equipment, $92

▶ Write a check for your monthly withdrawal, $1,000.

▶ Because a fax machine is a business necessity, you decided to give your new fax machine to Your Name's Help for You. Record this additional $350 investment of equipment by you.

▶ Because they are remodeling the offices, Rentals for You decreased the amount of rent to $1,000 per month. Correct and reprint the check for rent.

▶ Back up your work for the week. Use **Help (Backup Week 4)** as the file name.

End of the Month: January 31, 2010

▶ Prepare the bank reconciliation using the following bank statement. Record any adjustments necessary as a result of the bank statement.

Beverly Hills Bank
1234 Rodeo Drive
Beverly Hills, CA 90210

Your Name's Help for You
27800 Beverly Boulevard
Beverly Hills, CA 90210

Beginning Balance, 1/1/10			$15,350.00
1/1/10, Transfer		100.00	15,250.00
1/6/10, Deposit	2,000.00		17,250.00
1/7/10, Check 1		25.00	17,225.00
1/7/10, Check 2		250.00	16,975.00
1/13/10, Check 5		25.00	16,950.00
1/13/10, Deposit	2,140.00		19,090.00
1/15/10, Check 3		500.00	18,590.00
1/16/10, Check 4		275.00	18,315.00
1/20/10, Deposit	655.00		18,970.00
1/28/10, Check 6		500.00	18,470.00
1/29/10, Check 8		1,000.00	17,470.00
1/31/10, Payment: Business Vehicle Loan: interest $445.15; principal $86.06		531.21	16,938.79
1/31/10, Payment: Office Equipment Loan: interest $53.42; principal $10.33		63.75	16,875.04
1/31/10, Service Charge		15.00	16,860.04
1/31/10, Interest	42.50		16,902.54
1/31/10, Ending Balance			$16,902.54

- ► Print a Detailed Reconciliation Report.
- ► Print the following reports as of 1/31/10:
  - o Trial Balance from 1/1/10 through 1/31/10 in Portrait orientation.
  - o Cash Flow Forecast from 2/1/10 through 2/28/10 in Landscape orientation.
  - o Statement of Cash Flows from 1/1/10 through 1/31/10 in Portrait orientation.
  - o Standard Profit and Loss Statement from 1/1/10 through 1/31/10 in Portrait orientation.
  - o Standard Balance Sheet for 1/31/10 in Portrait orientation.
- ► Transfer the net income/retained earnings to owner's capital account.
- ► Prepare a Standard Balance Sheet as of 1/31/10. Change the title to **Balance Sheet After Transfer of Net Income** and print
- ► Print the Journal from 1/1/10 through 1/31/10 in Landscape orientation and Fit to one page wide.
- ► Close the period as of 01-31-10. Do not use any passwords.
- ► Back up your work for the week. Use **Help (Backup Complete)** as the file name.

NAME _____

TRANSMITTAL

SECTION 1 PRACTICE SET: YOUR NAME'S HELP FOR YOU

Attach the following documents and reports:

Week 1
Account Listing
Trial Balance, January 1, 2010
Invoice No. 35: Colleen Verhagen
Invoice No. 36: Roger Singleton
Invoice No. 37: George Anton
Invoice No. 38: Bev Billings
Invoice No. 39: Olaf Petrovich
Invoice No. 40: Miko Stein
Sales Receipt No. 22: Amy Ricardo
Unpaid Bills Detail, January 6, 2010
Check No. 1: Sunset Boulevard Flowers
Check No. 2: Westside Gasoline
Deposit Summary, January 6, 2010
Trial Balance, January 6, 2010

Week 2
Invoice No. 41: Colleen Verhagen
Invoice No. 42: Olaf Petrovich
Invoice No. 43: Roger Singleton
Sales Receipt No. 23: Melinda Kingston
Invoice No. 44: Tiko Kasseri
Invoice No. 45: Bev Billings
Check No. 3: Bel Air Auto Repair
Check No. 4: Beverly Hills Stationers
Check No. 5: Sunset Boulevard Flowers
Invoice No. 45 (Corrected): Bev Billings
Deposit Summary, January 13, 2010

Week 3
Invoice No. 46: Colleen Verhagen
Petty Cash QuickReport, January 15, 2010 (May be in Portrait or Landscape)
Sales Receipt No. 24: Melinda Kingston
Invoice No. 47: Tiko Kasseri
Sales Receipt No. 25: Patrick Rocklin
Invoice No. 48: Colleen Verhagen
Customer Balance Summary
Deposit Summary, January 20, 2010

Week 4
Sales Receipt No. 26: Melinda Kingston
Petty Cash QuickReport, January 23, 2010 (May be in Portrait or Landscape)
Credit Memo No. 49: Colleen Verhagen
Invoice No. 50: David Engle
Invoice No. 51: George Anton
Check No. 6: Beverly Hills Stationers
Invoice No. 52: Roger Singleton
Check No. 7: Beverly Hills Telephone
Check No. 8: Rentals for You
Check No. 9: California Water
Check No. 10: Beverly Hills Power
Unpaid Bills Detail, January 27, 2010
Check No. 11: Sunset Boulevard Flowers
Check Detail, January 1-27, 2010
Deposit Summary, January 27, 2010
Customer Balance Detail
Check 12 Your Name's
Check No. 8 (Corrected): Rentals for You

End of the Month
Bank Reconciliation Report
Trial Balance, January 31, 2010
Cash Flow Forecast, February 2010
Statement of Cash Flows, January 2010
Profit and Loss, January 2010
Balance Sheet, January 31, 2010
Balance Sheet After Transfer of Net Income, January 31, 2010
Journal, January 2010

SALES AND RECEIVABLES: MERCHANDISING BUSINESS

LEARNING OBJECTIVES

At the completion of this chapter, you will be able to:

1. Enter sales transactions for a retail business.
2. Prepare invoices that use sales tax, have sales discounts, and exceed a customer's credit limit.
3. Prepare transactions for cash sales with sales tax.
4. Prepare transactions for customers using credit cards.
5. Add new accounts to the Chart of Accounts and new sales items to the Item List.
6. Add new customers and modify existing customer records.
7. Delete and void invoices.
8. Prepare credit memos with and without refunds.
9. Record customer payments on account with and without discounts.
10. Deposit checks and credit card receipts for sales and customer payments.
11. Record a transaction for a NSF check.
12. Customize report preferences and prepare and print Customer Balance Detail Reports, Open Invoice Reports, and Sales Reports.
13. View a QuickReport and use the QuickZoom feature.
14. Use the Customer Center to obtain information regarding credit customers.

ACCOUNTING FOR SALES AND RECEIVABLES IN A MERCHANDISING BUSINESS

Rather than using a traditional Sales Journal to record transactions using debits and credits and special columns, QuickBooks Pro uses an invoice to record sales transactions for accounts receivable in the Accounts Receivable Register. Because cash sales do not involve accounts receivable, a Sales Receipt is prepared, and QuickBooks Pro puts the money from a cash sale into the Undeposited Funds account until a deposit to a bank account is made. Instead of being recorded within special journals, cash receipt transactions are entered as activities. However, all transactions, regardless of the activity, are placed in the Journal behind the scenes. A new account, sales item, or customer can be added *on the fly* as transactions are entered. Customer information may be changed by editing the Customer List.

For a retail business, QuickBooks Pro tracks inventory, maintains information on reorder limits, tracks the quantity of merchandise on hand, maintains information on the value of the inventory, and can inform you of the percentage of sales for each inventory item. Early-payment discounts as well as discounts to certain types of customers can be given. Different price levels may be created for sales items and/or customers.

Unlike many computerized accounting programs, QuickBooks Pro makes error correction easy. A sales form may be edited, voided, or deleted in the same window where it was created or via an account register. If a sales form has been printed prior to correction, it may be reprinted after the correction has been made.

A multitude of reports are available when using QuickBooks Pro. Accounts receivable reports include Customer Balance Summary and Customer Balance Detail reports. Sales reports provide information regarding the amount of sales by item. Transaction Reports by Customer are available as well as the traditional accounting reports such as Trial Balance, Profit and Loss, and Balance Sheet. QuickBooks Pro also has graphing capabilities so that you can see and evaluate your accounts receivable and sales at the click of a button. Reports created in QuickBooks Pro may be exported to Microsoft® Excel.

TRAINING TUTORIAL

The following tutorial is a step-by-step guide to recording receivables (both cash and credit) for a fictitious company with fictitious employees. This company is called Your Name Mountain Sports. In addition to recording transactions using QuickBooks Pro, you will prepare several reports and graphs for Your Name Mountain Sports. The tutorial for Your Name Mountain Sports will continue in Chapters 6 and 7, when accounting for payables, bank reconciliations, financial statement preparation, and closing an accounting period for a merchandising business will be completed.

COMPANY PROFILE: YOUR NAME MOUNTAIN SPORTS

Your Name Mountain Sports is a sporting goods store located in Mammoth Lakes, California. Previously, the company was open only during the winter. As a result Your Name Mountain Sports specializes in equipment, clothing, and accessories for skiing and snowboarding. You have plans to expand into a year-round operation and will eventually provide merchandise for summer sports and activities. The company is a partnership between you and Larry Muir. Each partner has a 50 percent share of the business, and both of you devote all of your efforts to Your Name Mountain Sports. You have several part-time employees who work in the evenings and on the weekends during ski season. There is a full-time bookkeeper and manager, Ruth Morgan, who oversees purchases, maintains the inventory, and keeps the books for the company.

DATES

Throughout the text, the year used for the screen shots is 2010, which is the same year as the version of the program. You may want to check with your instructor to see if you should use 2010 as the year for the transactions. The year you use in Chapter 5 should be the same year you use in Chapters 6 and 7.

OPEN A COMPANY—YOUR NAME MOUNTAIN SPORTS

As in previous chapters, copy the Sports.qbw file as instructed in Chapter 1, access QuickBooks Pro, and open the company.

>**DO** Copy the file **Sports.qbw** as instructed in Chapter 1, open QuickBooks Pro, and open Sports

ADD YOUR NAME TO THE COMPANY NAME

As with previous companies, each student in the course will be working for the same company and printing the same documents. Personalizing the company name to include your name will help identify many of the documents you print during your training.

>**DO** Add your name to the company name

Click **Company** on the menu bar, click **Company Information**
In the Company Name textbox, drag through the words **Student's Name** to highlight
Type **your real name**
- Type your real name, *not* the words *Your Real Name*. For example, Pamela Powers would type—**Pamela Powers**.
Repeat for the Legal Name
Click **OK**
- The title bar now shows Your Name Mountain Sports

Your Name Mountain Sports - QuickBooks Pro 2010

BEGINNING THE TUTORIAL

In this chapter you will be entering both accounts receivable transactions and cash sales transactions for a retail company that sells merchandise and charges its customers sales tax. Much of the organization of QuickBooks Pro is dependent on lists. The two primary types of lists you will use in the tutorial for receivables are a Customer List and a Sales Item List.

Customer List

The names, addresses, telephone numbers, credit terms, credit limits, balances, and tax terms for all established credit customers are contained in the Customer List. The Customer List is also the Accounts Receivable Ledger. You will be using the following Customer List for established credit customers:

Customers & Jobs	Transactions	
View Active Customers ▼		→|
Find		🔍

Name	Balance Total	Attach
◆Cooper, Eileen Dr.	417.00	
◆Cunningham, Linda	455.00	
◆Daily, Gail	1,136.00	
◆Deardorff, Ramona	650.00	
◆Gardener, Monique	53.57	
◆Kandahar, Mahmet	1,085.00	
◆Mountain Schools	0.00	
◆Munoz, Francisco Dr.	95.45	
◆Perkins, Sandra	408.48	
◆Taka, Mikko	670.31	
◆Thomsen, Kevin	911.63	
◆Villanueva, Oskar	975.00	
◆Weber, Richard	85.00	

Item List

Sales are often made up of various types of income. In Your Name Mountain Sports there are several income accounts. In order to classify income regarding to the type of sale, the sales account may have subaccounts. When recording a transaction for a sale, QuickBooks requires that a Sales Item be used. When the sales item is created, a sales account is required. When the sales item is used in a transaction, the income is credited to the appropriate sales/income account. For example, Ski Boots is a sales item and uses Equipment Income, which is a subaccount of Sales, when a transaction is recorded.

QuickBooks Pro uses lists to organize sales items. Using lists for sales items allows for flexibility in billing and a more accurate representation of the way in which income is earned. If the company charges a standard price for an item, the price of the item will be included on the list. Your Name Mountain Sports sells all items at different prices, so the price given for each item is listed at 0.00. In a retail business with an inventory, the number of units on hand can be tracked; and, when the amount on hand gets to a predetermined limit, an order can be placed. The following Item List for the various types of merchandise and sales categories will be used for Your Name Mountain Sports:

Name	Description	Type	Account	On Hand	Price	Attach
◆Accessories	Sunglasses, Ski Wax, Sunscreen, Ski Holders, Boot Carriers, etc.	Inventory Part	4011 · Clothing & Accessory Sales	800	0.00	
◆Bindings-Skis	Ski Bindings	Inventory Part	4012 · Equipment Sales	50	0.00	
◆Bindings-Snow	Snowboard Bindings	Inventory Part	4012 · Equipment Sales	50	0.00	
◆Boots	After Ski Boots and Shoes	Inventory Part	4011 · Clothing & Accessory Sales	20	0.00	
◆Boots-Ski	Ski Boots	Inventory Part	4012 · Equipment Sales	15	0.00	
◆Boots-Snowbrd	Snowboard Boots	Inventory Part	4012 · Equipment Sales	12	0.00	
◆Gloves	Gloves	Inventory Part	4011 · Clothing & Accessory Sales	22	0.00	
◆Hats	Hats and Scarves	Inventory Part	4011 · Clothing & Accessory Sales	30	0.00	
◆Pants-Ski	Ski Pants	Inventory Part	4011 · Clothing & Accessory Sales	95	0.00	
◆Pants-Snowbrd	Snowboard Pants	Inventory Part	4011 · Clothing & Accessory Sales	50	0.00	
◆Parkas	Parkas and Jackets	Inventory Part	4011 · Clothing & Accessory Sales	75	0.00	
◆Poles-Ski	Ski Poles	Inventory Part	4012 · Equipment Sales	18	0.00	
◆Skis	Snow Skis	Inventory Part	4012 · Equipment Sales	50	0.00	
◆Snowboard	Snowboard	Inventory Part	4012 · Equipment Sales	30	0.00	
◆Socks	Ski and Snowboard Socks	Inventory Part	4011 · Clothing & Accessory Sales	75	0.00	
◆Sweaters	Sweaters & Shirts	Inventory Part	4011 · Clothing & Accessory Sales	75	0.00	
◆Underwear	Long Underwear	Inventory Part	4011 · Clothing & Accessory Sales	33	0.00	
◆CA Sales Tax	CA Sales Tax	Sales Tax Item	2200 · Sales Tax Payable		7.25%	
◆Out of State	Out-of-state sale, exempt from sales tax	Sales Tax Item	2200 · Sales Tax Payable		0.0%	

BASIC INSTRUCTIONS

As in previous chapters, all transactions are listed on memos. The transaction date will be the same date as the memo date unless otherwise specified within the transaction. Customer names, when necessary, will be given in the transaction. Unless otherwise specified, all terms for customers on account are Net 30 days.

Even when you are instructed to enter a transaction step by step, you should always refer to the memo for transaction details. Once a specific type of transaction has been entered in a step-by-step manner, additional transactions will be made without having instructions provided. Of course, you may always refer to instructions given for previous transactions for ideas or for steps used to enter those transactions.

CUSTOMIZE REPORT FORMAT

The report format used in one company may not be appropriate for all companies that use QuickBooks Pro. The preferences selected in QuickBooks Pro are only for the current company. In Section 1 of the text, report preferences were changed for Computer Consulting by Your Name, but those changes have no effect on Your Name Mountain Sports. The header/footer for reports in Your Name Mountain Sports must be customized to eliminate the printing of the date prepared, time prepared, and report basis as part of a report heading. In addition, QuickBooks can automatically refresh reports when a change is made. This feature may be selected as a preference as well.

MEMO

DATE: January 1, 2010

Before recording any transactions or preparing any reports, customize the report format by removing the date prepared, time prepared, and report basis from report headings. In addition, have reports refresh automatically.

DO Customize the report preferences as indicated in the memo

Click **Edit**, click **Preferences**
Click **Reports and Graphs**
On the **My Preferences** tab, click **Refresh automatically**
Click the **Company Preferences** tab
Click the **Format** button
Click the **Header/Footer** tab
Click **Date Prepared**, **Time Prepared**, and **Report Basis** to deselect

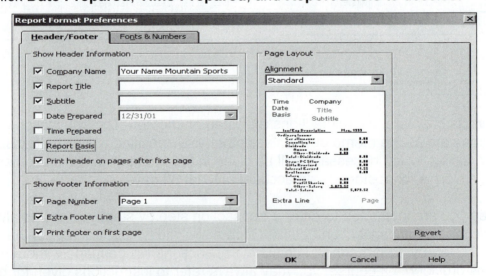

Click **OK** to save the change then click **OK** to close **Preferences**

CUSTOMIZE BUSINESS FORMS

In QuickBooks it is possible to customize the business forms used in recording transactions. Forms that may be customized include Credit Memo, Estimate, Invoice, Purchase Order, Sales Order, Sales Receipt, Statement, and Donation. In addition to customizing the forms within QuickBooks, Intuit allows users to download templates of forms without charge by accessing the Forms/Intuit Community. To do this, click Lists menu, click Templates, click the Template button, click Download.

In earlier chapters some student names included as part of the company name may not have printed on the same line as the company name. In order to provide more room for the company title, QuickBooks' Layout Designer must be used. Some business forms may be changed directly within the form, while others need to have the form duplicated. When you access an invoice, for example, QuickBooks uses a ready-made form. This is called a *template*. In order to make changes to an invoice, you must first duplicate the template and then make changes to it.

MEMO
DATE: January 2, 2010

Customize the Sales Receipt form, the Credit Memo form, and the template used for Product Invoices.

DO Customize the Sales Receipt, the Credit Memo, and the Product Invoice

Open a **Sales Receipt** as previously instructed
Click the drop-down list arrow for the Layout Designer at the top of the Sales Receipt, click **Customize Design and Layout...**

Click the **Customize Data Layout** button on the bottom of the Customize Your QuickBooks Forms screen

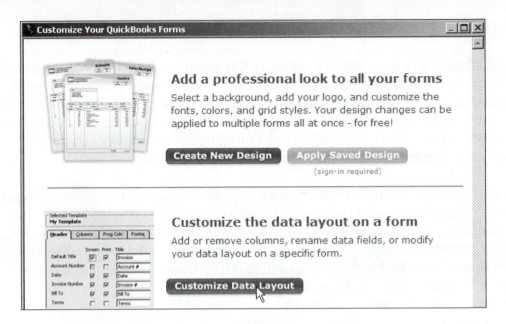

Click the **Layout Designer** button on the Additional Customization screen

Point to one of the black squares (sizing handles) on the left border of the frame around the words Sales Receipt

When the cursor turns into a double arrow, hold the primary (left) mouse button and drag until the size of the frame begins at **6** on the ruler bar

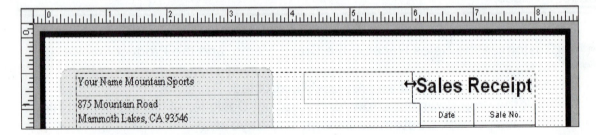

Click in the textbox for **Your Name Mountain Sports**

Drag the right border of the frame until it is a **5 ¾** on the ruler bar

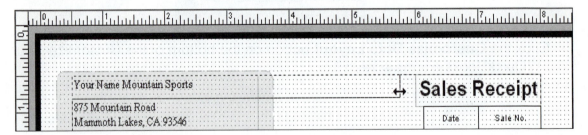

Click **OK** on Layout Designer

Click **OK** on the Additional Customization screen

Close the **Enter Sales Receipts** screen

Repeat the steps to customize the Credit Memo

When finished with the customization of the Credit Memo, click **Lists** on the menu bar

Click **Templates**

- *Note:* The Custom Sales Receipt and Custom Credit Memo have been added to the Template list

From the Templates List, click **Intuit Product Invoice**

Click the **Templates** button

Click **Duplicate**

On the Select Template Type make sure Invoice is selected and click **OK**

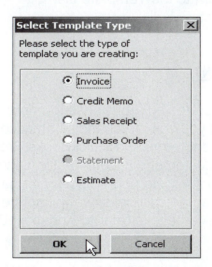

Make sure **Copy of: Intuit Product Invoice** is selected

Click the **Templates** button, click **Edit Template**

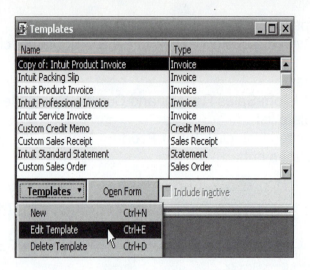

Click the **Layout Designer** button and change the layout as instructed for Sales Receipts

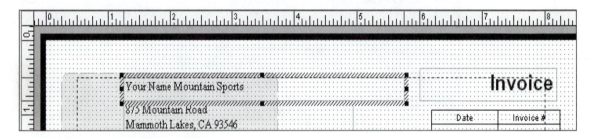

Click **OK** until you return to the Template List
Close the Template List

ENTER SALES ON ACCOUNT

Because QuickBooks Pro operates on a business form premise, a sale on account is entered via an invoice. When you sell merchandise on account, you prepare an invoice including sales tax and payment terms and QuickBooks Pro records the transaction in the Journal and updates the customer's account automatically. QuickBooks allows you to set up different price levels for customers. Since our small company has not established sales prices for each item it sells, we will not be using Price Levels in this tutorial. For information on Price Levels, refer to Appendix B.

MEMO
DATE: January 2, 2010

Bill the following: Invoice No. 1—An established customer, Richard Weber, purchased a pair of after-ski boots for $75.00 on account. Terms are Net 15.

▶ **DO** Record the sale on account shown in the transaction above.

Access a blank invoice as previously instructed in Chapter 2
Click the drop-down list arrow next to **Customer:Job**, click **Weber, Richard**
Click the drop-down list arrow next to Intuit Product Invoice
Click **Copy of: Intuit Product Invoice** to use your customized invoice
* Notice the change in the format when using a product invoice rather than a service invoice.
Tab to **Date** and enter the date of **01/02/2010**
Invoice No. 1 should be showing in the **Invoice No.** box
There is no PO No. to record
Terms should be indicated as **Net 15**
Tab to or click **Quantity**, type **1**
* The quantity is 1 because you are billing for one pair of after-ski boots.
Tab to or click the first line beneath **Item Code**
Click the drop-down list arrow next to **Item Code**
* Refer to the memo above and the Item list for appropriate billing information.
Click **Boots** to bill for one pair of after-ski boots
* The Description *After Ski Boots and Shoes* is automatically inserted.
Tab to or click **Price Each**
Type in the amount of the after-ski boots **75**
* Because the price on ski boots differs with each style, QuickBooks Pro has not been given the price in advance. It must be inserted during the invoice preparation. If you chose to set up separate sales items for each type of ski boot, sales prices could be and should be assigned. In addition, different price levels could be designated for the item.
Click in the box for **Customer Message**
* QuickBooks Pro will automatically calculate the total in the **Amount** column.
* Because this is a taxable item, QuickBooks Pro inserts **Tax** in the **Tax** column.
Click the drop-down list arrow next to **Customer Message**
Click **Thank you for your business.**
* Message is inserted in the **Customer Message** box.
* Notice that QuickBooks Pro automatically calculates the tax for the invoice and adds it to the invoice total.

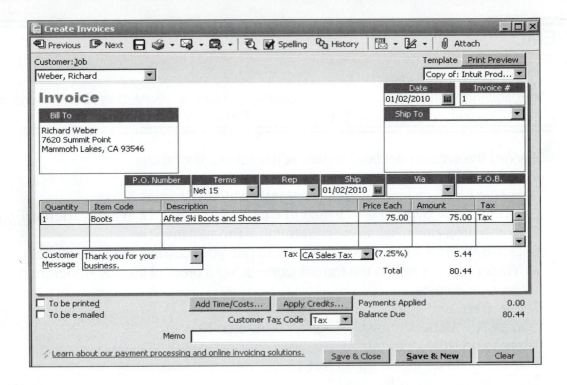

PRINT AN INVOICE

 With Invoice No. 1 on the screen, print the invoice with lines around each field immediately after entering the corrected information

Follow the instructions given previously for printing invoices
- If you get a message regarding printing Shipping Labels, click the **Do not display this message in the future** checkbox, click **OK**

Make sure that the check box for **Do not print lines around each field** does not have a check mark; if it does, click the box to remove the check mark.

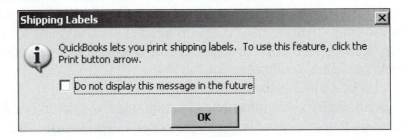

- If there is a check mark in the box, lines will not print around each field.
- If a check is not in the box, lines will print around each field.
- To save printing time and ink, your instructor may suggest that you do not print lines around each field. If this is the case, make sure there is a check mark in the check box.

When finished printing, click the **Save & New** button on the bottom of the **Create Invoices** screen to record the invoice and go to a blank invoice

ENTER TRANSACTIONS USING MORE THAN ONE SALES ITEM AND SALES TAX

Frequently, sales to customers will be for more than one item. For example, new bindings are usually purchased along with a new pair of skis. Invoices can be prepared to bill a customer for several items at once.

MEMO
DATE: January 3, 2010

Bill the following: Invoice No. 2—Every year Dr. Francisco Munoz gets new ski equipment. Bill him for his equipment purchase for this year: skis, $425; bindings, $175; ski boots, $250; and ski poles, $75.

DO Record a transaction on account for a sale involving several taxable sales items:

Click the drop-down list arrow next to **Customer:Job**
Click **Munoz, Francisco Dr.**
Verify the Template as **Copy of: Intuit Product Invoice**
Tab to or click **Date**, enter **01/03/10** as the date
Make sure the number **2** is showing in the **Invoice No.** box
There is no PO No. to record
Terms should be indicated as **2% 10 Net 30**
- The terms mean that if Dr. Munoz' payment is received within ten days, he will get a two percent discount. Otherwise, the full amount is due in 30 days.
Tab to or click **Quantity**, type **1**
Click the drop-down list arrow next to **Item Code**
Click **Skis**
- **Skis** is inserted as the item code.
- **Snow Skis** is inserted as the **Description**.
Tab to or click **Price Each,** enter **425**
- Because Dr. Munoz is a taxable customer and Skis are a taxable item, sales tax is indicated by **Tax** in the **Tax** column.

Tab to or click the second line for **Quantity**, type **1**

Click the drop-down list arrow next to **Item Code**

Click **Bindings-Skis**

- **Ski Bindings** is inserted as the **Description**.

Tab to or click **Price Each**, enter **175**

- Notice that sales tax is indicated by **Tax** in the **Tax** column.

Repeat the above steps to enter the information for the ski boots and the ski poles

Click the drop-down list arrow next to **Customer Message**

Click **Thank you for your business.**

- QuickBooks Pro automatically calculated the tax for the invoice and added it to the invoice total.

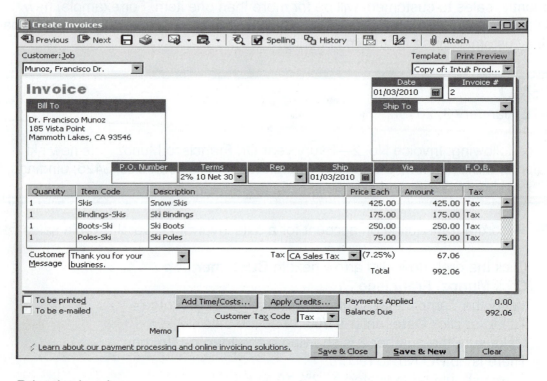

Print the invoice

Do not close the invoice

E-MAIL INVOICES

In addition to printing and mailing invoices, QuickBooks® Pro 2010 allows invoices to be sent to customers via e-mail. While this text will not actually require sending invoices by e-mail, it is important to be aware of this time-saving feature of QuickBooks. In order to use the e-mail feature of QuickBooks, you must have Microsoft Outlook installed on your computer.

| DO | Explore e-mailing an invoice:

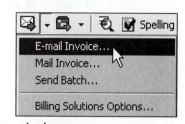

Click the drop-down list arrow next to **Send**
Click **E-mail Invoice**
- Depending on the setup of your computer, e-mail, etc. It is possible that you will not get the following screen. If that is the case, just read the example shown below.

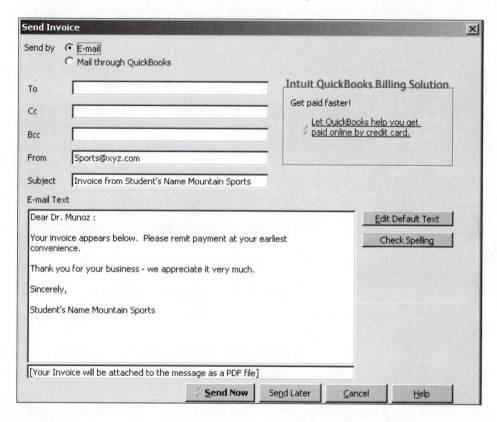

- Notice that the e-mail text has automatically been completed.
- If the name shown in the e-mail says Student's Name as part of the company name, it will need to be changed to Your Name.
- Look at the message that will accompany the electronic copy of the invoice.
Click **Cancel**
Click the **Save & New** button

PREPARE INVOICES WITHOUT STEP-BY-STEP INSTRUCTIONS

MEMO

DATE: January 3, 2010

Bill the following:

Invoice No. 3—We give Mountain Schools a special rate on equipment and clothing for the ski team. This year the school purchases 5 pairs of skis, $299 each; 5 pairs of ski bindings, $100 each; and 5 sets of ski poles, $29 each. Terms 2/10 Net 30.

Invoice No. 4—Sandra Perkins purchased a new ski outfit: 1 parka, $249; a hat, $25; a sweater, $125; 1 pair of ski pants, $129; long underwear, $68; ski gloves, $79; ski socks, $15.95; sunglasses, $89.95; and a matching ski boot carrier, $2.95. Terms Net 15.

Invoice No. 5—Kevin Thomsen broke his snowboard when he was going down his favorite run, Dragon's Back. He purchased a new one without bindings for $499.95, Terms 1/10 Net 30.

Invoice No. 6—Richard Weber decided to buy some new powder skis and bindings. Bill him for snow skis, $599, and ski bindings, $179. Terms Net 15.

▶ **DO** Prepare and print invoices without step-by-step instructions.

If Invoice 2 is still on the screen, click **Next** or **Save & New**

Enter the four transactions in the memo above. Refer to instructions given for the two previous transactions entered.

- Always use the Item List to determine the appropriate sales items for billing.
- Use *"Thank you for your business."* as the message for these invoices.
- If you make an error, correct it.
- If you get a suggestion from Spell check; i.e., **Snowboard**, and the word is spelled correctly, click **Ignore All**.
- Print each invoice immediately after you enter the information for it, and print lines around each field.
- To go from one invoice to the next, click **Save & New** at the bottom of the **Create Invoices** screen or click **Next** at the top of the invoice.
- Click **Save & New** after Invoice No. 6 has been entered and printed.

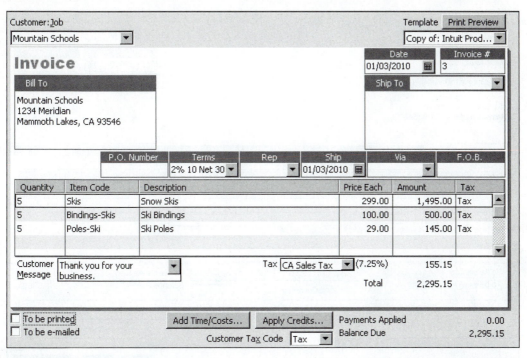

Quantity	Item Code	Description	Price Each	Amount	Tax
5	Skis	Snow Skis	299.00	1,495.00	Tax
5	Bindings-Skis	Ski Bindings	100.00	500.00	Tax
5	Poles-Ski	Ski Poles	29.00	145.00	Tax

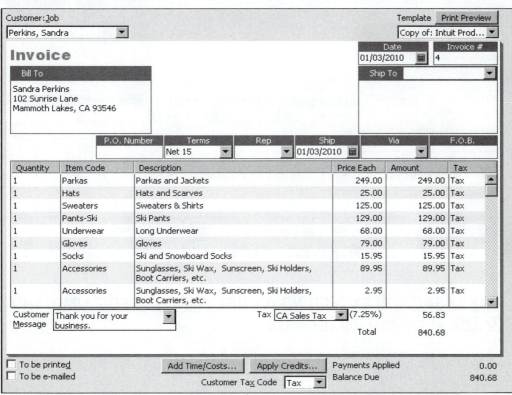

Quantity	Item Code	Description	Price Each	Amount	Tax
1	Parkas	Parkas and Jackets	249.00	249.00	Tax
1	Hats	Hats and Scarves	25.00	25.00	Tax
1	Sweaters	Sweaters & Shirts	125.00	125.00	Tax
1	Pants-Ski	Ski Pants	129.00	129.00	Tax
1	Underwear	Long Underwear	68.00	68.00	Tax
1	Gloves	Gloves	79.00	79.00	Tax
1	Socks	Ski and Snowboard Socks	15.95	15.95	Tax
1	Accessories	Sunglasses, Ski Wax, Sunscreen, Ski Holders, Boot Carriers, etc.	89.95	89.95	Tax
1	Accessories	Sunglasses, Ski Wax, Sunscreen, Ski Holders, Boot Carriers, etc.	2.95	2.95	Tax

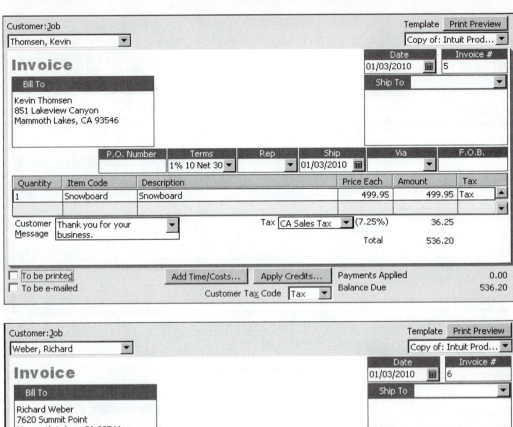

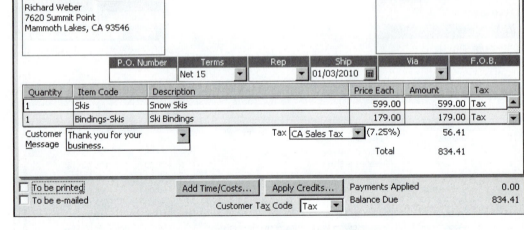

ENTER A TRANSACTION EXCEEDING A CUSTOMER'S CREDIT LIMIT AND ADD A WORD TO THE SPELLING DICTIONARY

When a customer is added to the Customer List and a complete setup is performed, the file tab for Additional Info will appear. Additional Info contains a field in which a credit limit can be established for a customer. QuickBooks Pro does allow transactions for a customer to exceed the established credit limit, but a dialog box appears with information regarding the transaction amount and the credit limit for a customer.

As was experienced in the last set of transactions, QuickBooks Pro has a spelling check. When the previous invoices were printed, QuickBooks Spell Check identified snowboard as being misspelled. In fact, the word is spelled correctly. It just needs to be added to the QuickBooks dictionary. This is done by clicking the Add button when the word is highlighted in spell check.

MEMO
DATE: January 5, 2010

Bill the following: <u>Invoice No. 7</u>—Monique Gardener decided to get a new snowboard, $489.95; snowboard bindings, $159.99; snowboard boots, $249; and a special case to carry her boots, $49.95. Terms are Net 30.

DO   Prepare Invoice No. 7 as instructed previously

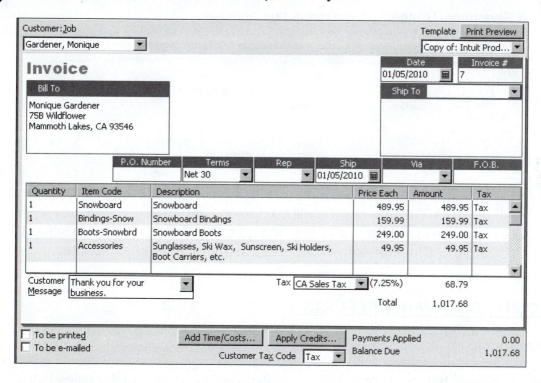

Print the invoice

When the **Check Spelling on Form** appears and the word **Snowboard** is highlighted, click the **Add** button

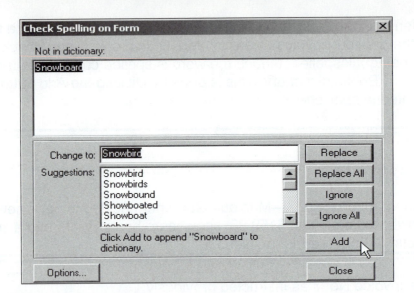

A Recording Transaction message box appears

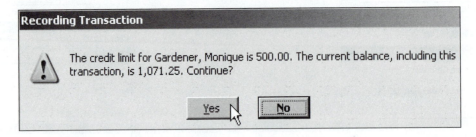

- If you click **No**, you are returned to the invoice in order to make changes.
- If you click Yes, the invoice will be printed.

Click **Yes** to exceed the credit limit and go to the Print One Invoice screen

Click **Save & Close** after Invoice No. 7 has been entered and printed

ACCOUNTS RECEIVABLE REPORTS

A variety of reports are available regarding accounts receivable. Data regarding customers may be displayed on the basis of account aging, open invoices, collections reports, customer balances, or they may be itemized according to the sales by customer. Many reports may be printed in a summarized form while other reports provide detailed information.

PREPARE CUSTOMER BALANCE DETAIL REPORT

The Customer Balance Detail Report lists information regarding each customer. The information provided includes the customer name, all invoices with a balance, the date of the invoice, the invoice number, the account used to record the invoice, the amount of each invoice, the balance after each invoice, and the total balance due from each customer.

MEMO

DATE: January 5, 2010

Prepare and print a Customer Balance Detail Report so that the owners can see exactly how much each customer owes to Your Name Mountain Sports.

DO ▶ Prepare a Customer Balance Detail Report for all customers for all transactions:

Click **Reports** on the menu bar, point to **Customers & Receivables**, and click **Customer Balance Detail**
- *Note:* When preparing a single report, it is more convenient to use the Reports menu. When preparing several reports, using the Report Center is more efficient.

Dates should be **All**
- If not, click the drop-down list arrow next to the **Dates** text box, click **All**.
- Scroll through the report. See how much each customer owes for each invoice.
- Notice that the amount owed by Monique Gardener for Invoice No. 7 is $1,017.68 and that her total balance is $1,071.25.

Do not print or close the **Customer Balance Detail Report** at this time

USE THE QUICKZOOM FEATURE

QuickZoom is a feature of QuickBooks Pro that allows you to view additional information within a report. For example, an invoice may be viewed when the Customer Balance Detail Report is on the screen simply by using the QuickZoom feature.

> **MEMO**
> **DATE:** January 5, 2010
>
> The bookkeeper, Ruth Morgan, could not remember if Invoice No. 7 was for ski equipment or snowboard equipment. With the Customer Balance Detail Report on the screen, use QuickZoom to view Invoice No. 7.

▶ **DO** Use QuickZoom to view Invoice No. 7

Position the cursor over any part of the report showing information about Invoice No. 7
• The cursor will turn into a magnifying glass with a letter **Z** inside.
Double-click
• Invoice No. 7 appears on the screen.
• Check to make sure the four items on the invoice are: Snowboard, Bindings-Snow, Boots-Snowbrd, and Accessories.
With Invoice No. 7 on the screen, proceed to the next section.

CORRECT AN INVOICE AND PRINT THE CORRECTED FORM

QuickBooks Pro allows corrections and revisions to an invoice even if the invoice has been printed. The invoice may be corrected by going directly to the original invoice or by accessing the original invoice via the Accounts Receivable Register. An invoice can be on view in QuickZoom and still be corrected.

> **MEMO**
> **DATE:** January 5, 2010
>
> While viewing Invoice No. 7 for Monique Gardener in QuickZoom, the bookkeeper, Ruth Morgan, realizes that the snowboard should be $499.95, not the $489.95 that is on the original invoice. Make the correction and reprint the invoice.

▶ **DO** Correct Invoice No. 7 while showing on the screen in QuickZoom

Click in the **Price Each** column
Change the amount to **499.95**
Press Tab to change the **Amount** calculated for the Snowboard
Print the corrected Invoice No. 7
Click **Yes** on the Recording Transaction dialog box to record the change to the transaction

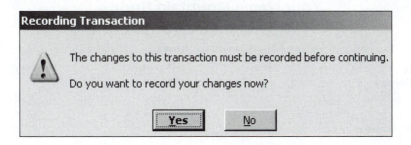

A **Recording Transaction** message box appears on the screen regarding the credit limit of $500 for Monique Gardener

Click **Yes** to accept the current balance of $1,081.98

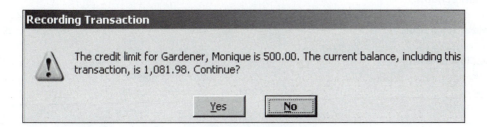

When the invoice has been printed, click **Save & Close** at the bottom of the **Create Invoice** screen to record and close the invoice

- This closes the invoice and returns you to the Customer Balance Detail Report.
- Notice that the total amount for Invoice No. 7 is $1,028.41 and that Monique Gardener's total balance is $1,081.98.
- The Total of the report is $13,549.79.

Click **Print** at the top of the **Customer Balance Detail Report** and print the report in Portrait orientation

Your Name Mountain Sports
Customer Balance Detail
All Transactions

Type	Date	Num	Account	Amount	Balance
Gardener, Monique					
Invoice	12/31/2009		1200 · Accounts Receivable	53.57	53.57
Invoice	01/05/2010	7	1200 · Accounts Receivable	1,028.41	1,081.98 ◄
Total Gardener, Monique				1,081.98	1,081.98
Kandahar, Mahmet					
Invoice	12/31/2009		1200 · Accounts Receivable	1,085.00	1,085.00
Total Kandahar, Mahmet				1,085.00	1,085.00
Mountain Schools					
Invoice	01/03/2010	3	1200 · Accounts Receivable	2,295.15	2,295.15
Total Mountain Schools				2,295.15	2,295.15
Munoz, Francisco Dr.					
Invoice	12/31/2009		1200 · Accounts Receivable	95.45	95.45
Invoice	01/03/2010	2	1200 · Accounts Receivable	992.06	1,087.51
Total Munoz, Francisco Dr.				1,087.51	1,087.51

Partial Report

After the report is printed, click **Close** to close the **Customer Balance Detail Report**

ADDING NEW ACCOUNTS TO THE CHART OF ACCOUNTS

Because account needs can change as a business is in operation, QuickBooks Pro allows you to make changes to the Chart of Accounts at any time. Some changes to the Chart of Accounts require additional changes to other lists, such as the Item List. An account may be added by accessing the Chart of Accounts. It is also possible to add an account to the Chart of Accounts while adding an item to another list.

ADD NEW ITEMS TO LIST

In order to accommodate the changing needs of a business, all QuickBooks Pro lists allow you to make changes at any time. New items may be added to the list via the Item List or *on the fly* while entering invoice information. The Item List stores information about the items Your Name Mountain Sports sells. Since Your Name Mountain Sports does not use price levels, it would be appropriate to have an item allowing for sales discounts. Having a discount item allows discounts to be recorded on the sales form. A discount can be a fixed amount or a percentage. A discount is calculated only on the line above it on the sales form. To allow the entire amount of the invoice to receive the discount, an item for a subtotal will also need to be added. When you complete the sales form, the subtotal item will appear before the discount item.

MEMO

DATE: January 5, 2010

Add an item for Sales Discounts and a Subtotal Item. Add a new expense account, 6130 Sales Discount, to the Chart of Accounts. The description for the account should be Discount on Sales.

DO Add new items and accounts

Click the **Items & Services** icon on the QuickBooks' Home Page
Click **Item** button at the bottom of the **Item List** screen
Click **New**
If you get a New Feature screen regarding Add/Edit Multiple List Entries, click
    OK
• Do not use this feature unless instructed to do so.
Item Type is **Discount**
Tab to or click **Item Name/Number**
Type **Nonprofit Discount**
Tab to or click **Description**
Type **10% Discount to Nonprofit Agencies**
Tab to or click **Amount or %**
Type in **10%**
• The % sign must be included in order to differentiate between a $10 discount
    and a 10% discount.
Click the drop-down list arrow for **Account**
Click **<Add New>**
Complete the information for a New Account:
Type should be **Expense**
• If **not**, click the drop-down list arrow next to the text box for Type.
• **Click Expense**.
• A sales discount is a cost of doing business and ultimately decreases the
    amount of Net Income. Therefore, it is categorized as an expense.
Tab to or click in the **Number** text box
Enter the Account Number **6130**
• Your Name Mountain Sports uses account numbers for all accounts.
• Numbers in the 6000 category are expenses.
Tab to or click **Account Name**
Type **Sales Discounts**
Tab to or click **Description**

Enter **Discount on Sales**

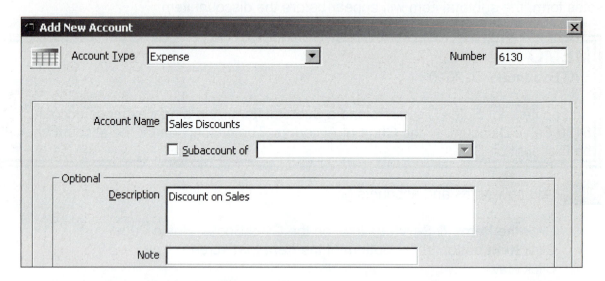

Click **Save & Close** to add the **Sales Discounts** account, close the **New Account** dialog box, and return to the New Item screen
- At the bottom of the screen you should see the Tax Code as **Tax** and the statement **Discount is applied before sales tax** should be displayed.

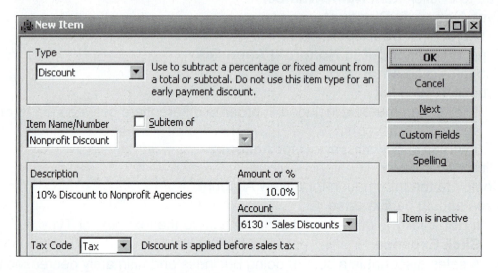

Click **Next** on the **New Item** dialog box
- A discount is calculated only on the line above it on the sales form. To allow the entire amount of the invoice to receive the discount, a subtotal needs to be calculated; so, an item for a subtotal will also need to be added.

Repeat the steps for adding a New Item to add **Subtotal**

Type should be **Subtotal**

Item Name/Number is **Subtotal**

The description is **Subtotal**

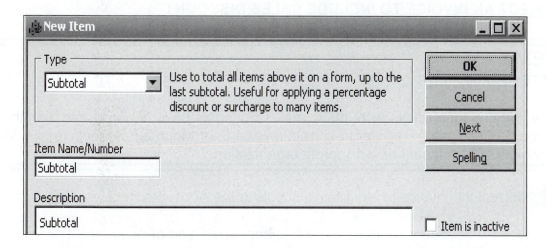

Click **OK** to add the new items and to close the **New Item** screen
- Verify the addition of Nonprofit Discount and Subtotal on the Item List. If everything is correct, close the **Item List**.
- If you find an error, click on the item with the error, click the **Item** button, click **Edit Item**, and make corrections as needed.

Name	Description	Type	Account	On Hand	Price	Attach
◆Accessories	Sunglasses, Ski Wax, Sunscreen, Ski H...	Inventory Part	4011 · Clothing & Accessory Sales	797	0.00	
◆Bindings-Skis	Ski Bindings	Inventory Part	4012 · Equipment Sales	43	0.00	
◆Bindings-Snow	Snowboard Bindings	Inventory Part	4012 · Equipment Sales	49	0.00	
◆Boots	After Ski Boots and Shoes	Inventory Part	4011 · Clothing & Accessory Sales	19	0.00	
◆Boots-Ski	Ski Boots	Inventory Part	4012 · Equipment Sales	14	0.00	
◆Boots-Snowbrd	Snowboard Boots	Inventory Part	4012 · Equipment Sales	11	0.00	
◆Gloves	Gloves	Inventory Part	4011 · Clothing & Accessory Sales	21	0.00	
◆Hats	Hats and Scarves	Inventory Part	4011 · Clothing & Accessory Sales	29	0.00	
◆Pants-Ski	Ski Pants	Inventory Part	4011 · Clothing & Accessory Sales	94	0.00	
◆Pants-Snowbrd	Snowboard Pants	Inventory Part	4011 · Clothing & Accessory Sales	50	0.00	
◆Parkas	Parkas and Jackets	Inventory Part	4011 · Clothing & Accessory Sales	74	0.00	
◆Poles-Ski	Ski Poles	Inventory Part	4012 · Equipment Sales	12	0.00	
◆Skis	Snow Skis	Inventory Part	4012 · Equipment Sales	43	0.00	
◆Snowboard	Snowboard	Inventory Part	4012 · Equipment Sales	28	0.00	
◆Socks	Ski and Snowboard Socks	Inventory Part	4011 · Clothing & Accessory Sales	74	0.00	
◆Sweaters	Sweaters & Shirts	Inventory Part	4011 · Clothing & Accessory Sales	74	0.00	
◆Underwear	Long Underwear	Inventory Part	4011 · Clothing & Accessory Sales	32	0.00	
◆Subtotal	Subtotal	Subtotal				
◆Nonprofit Discount	10% Discount to Nonprofit Agencies	Discount	6130 · Sales Discounts		-10.0%	
◆CA Sales Tax	CA Sales Tax	Sales Tax Item	2200 · Sales Tax Payable		7.25%	
◆Out of State	Out-of-state sale, exempt from sales tax	Sales Tax Item	2200 · Sales Tax Payable		0.0%	

Close the **Item List**

CORRECT AN INVOICE TO INCLUDE SALES DISCOUNT

MEMO

DATE: January 6, 2010

Now that the appropriate accounts for sales discounts have been created, use the Accounts Receivable Register to correct Invoice 3 for Mountain Schools to give the schools a 10% discount as a nonprofit organization.

DO Correct the invoice to Mountain Schools in the Accounts Receivable Register

Use the keyboard shortcut, **Ctrl+A** to open the Chart of Accounts
In the Chart of Accounts, double-click **Accounts Receivable**
- Double-clicking opens the register
- The **Accounts Receivable Register** appears on the screen with information regarding each transaction entered into the account.

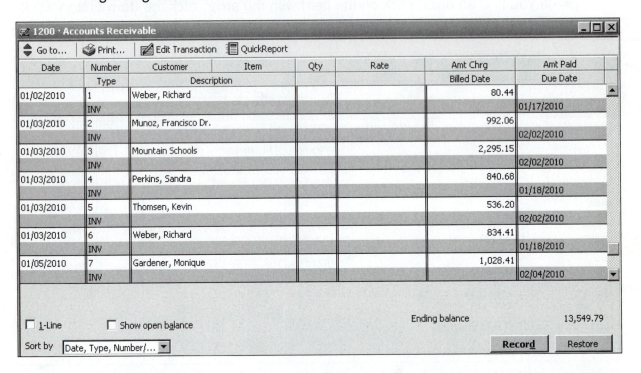

If necessary, scroll through the register until the transaction for **Invoice No. 3** is on the screen
- **Look** at the **Number/Type** column to identify the number of the invoice and the type of transaction.
- On the **Number** line you will see a <u>check number</u> or an <u>invoice number</u>.

- On **the Type** line **PMT** indicates a payment was received on account, and **INV** indicates a sale on account.

Click anywhere in the transaction for Invoice No. 3 to Mountain Schools

Click the **Edit Transaction** button at the top of the register

- Invoice No. 3 appears on the screen.

Click in **Item Code** beneath the last item, Poles-Ski

Click the drop-down list arrow for **Item Code**

Click **Subtotal**

- You may need to scroll through the Item List until you find Subtotal.

- Remember in order to calculate a discount for everything on the invoice, QuickBooks Pro must calculate the subtotal for the items on the invoice.

Tab to or click the next blank line in **Item Code**

Click **Nonprofit Discount**

- You may need to scroll through the Item List until you find Nonprofit Discount.

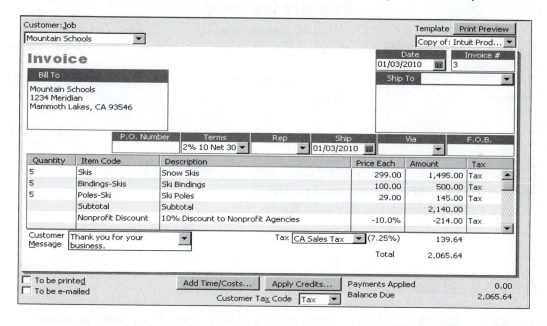

- Notice the subtotal of $2,140.00, the discount of $214, and the new invoice total of $2,065.64.

Print the corrected invoice

Click **Yes** on the **Recording Transaction** screen

After printing, click **Save & Close** on the **Create Invoices** screen to save the corrected invoice and return to the Accounts Receivable Register

- Notice the new Amt Chrg of $2,065.64 for Invoice No. 3 in the register.

Do not close the **Accounts Receivable Register**

VIEW A QUICKREPORT

After editing the invoice and returning to the register, you may get a detailed report regarding the customer's transactions by clicking the QuickReport button.

 With the cursor in Invoice No. 3, click the **QuickReport** button to view the **Mountain Schools** account

ANALYZE THE QUICKREPORT FOR MOUNTAIN SCHOOLS

 Analyze the QuickReport

Your Name Mountain Sports
Register QuickReport
All Transactions

Type	Date	Num	Memo	Account	Paid	Open Balance	Amount
Mountain Schools							
Invoice	01/03/2010	3		1200 · Accounts Receivable	Unpaid	2,065.64	2,065.64
Total Mountain Schools						2,065.64	2,065.64
TOTAL						**2,065.64**	**2,065.64**

Notice that the total of Invoice No. 3 is $2,065.64
Close the **QuickReport** without printing
Close the **Accounts Receivable Register**
Close the **Chart of Accounts**

ADD A NEW CUSTOMER

QuickBooks Pro allows customers to be added at any time. They may be added to the company records through the Customer List, through Add/Edit Multiple List entries, or they may be added *on the fly* as you create an invoice or sales receipt. When adding *on the fly*, you may choose between Quick Add (used to add only a customer's name) and Set Up (used to add complete information for a customer).

MEMO

DATE: January 8, 2010

Ruth was instructed to add a new customer. The information provided for the new customer is: Mountain Recreation Center, 985 Old Mammoth Road, Mammoth Lakes, CA 93546, Contact: Kathleene Clark, Phone: 909-555-2951, Fax: 909-555-1592, E-mail: mountainrec@abc.com, Terms: 1%10 Net 30, Tax Code is Tax, Tax Item: CA Sales Tax, Credit Limit: 5,000, as of 1/8/2010 there is a 0.00 opening balance for the customer.

DO Add a new customer

Click the **Customer Center** icon at the top of the Home Page or the **Customers** button on the left side of the Home Page

With the Customer List showing on the screen

Use the keyboard shortcut **Ctrl+N** to create a new customer

- If you get a New Feature screen to Add/Edit Multiple List Entries, click **OK**

In the **Customer** text box, enter **Mountain Recreation Center**

Tab to or click **Company Name**

Enter **Mountain Recreation Center**

Click at the end of Mountain Recreation Center in the Bill To section, press **Enter**

Enter the address listed above

Tab to or click **Contact**, enter the name of the person to contact

Tab to or click **Phone**, enter the telephone number

Tab to or click **FAX**, enter the fax number

Tab to or click **E-mail**, enter the e-mail address

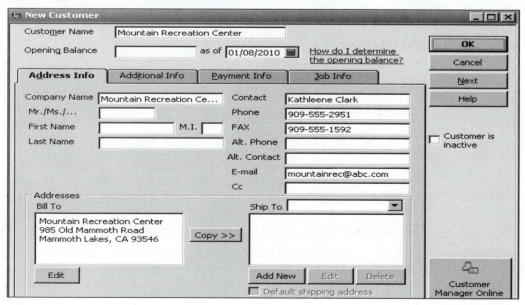

Click the **Additional Info** tab
Enter the terms and sales tax information for **Additional Info**

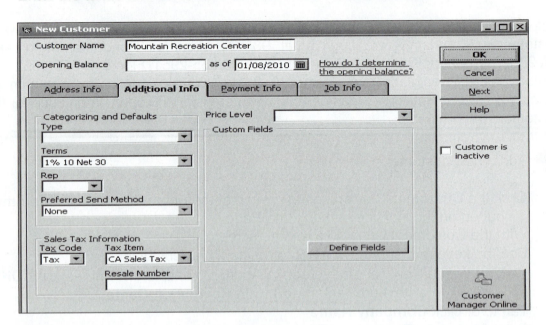

Click the **Payment Info** tab and enter the credit limit

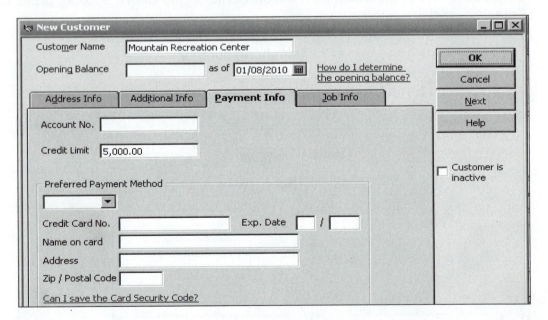

Click **OK** to complete the addition of Mountain Recreation Center as a customer
• Verify the addition of Mountain Recreation Center to the Customer:Job List.

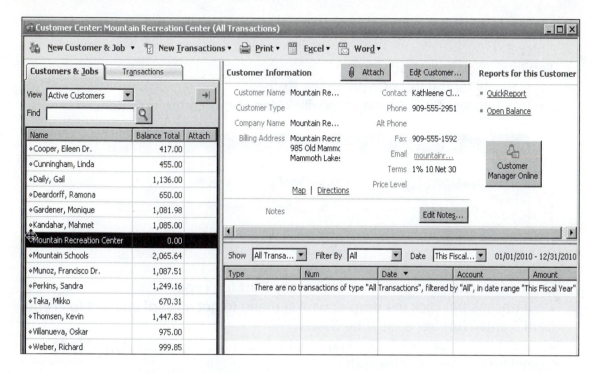

Close the **Customer Center**

RECORD A SALE TO A NEW CUSTOMER

Once a customer has been added, sales may be recorded for a customer.

MEMO

DATE: January 8, 2010

Record a sale of 5 sleds at $119.99 each and 5 toboggans at $229.95 each to Mountain Recreation Center. Because the sale is to a nonprofit organization, include a nonprofit discount.

DO Record the above sale on account to a new customer and add two new sales items

    Access a blank invoice by using the keyboard shortcut **Ctrl+I**
    Enter invoice information for **Mountain Recreation Center** as previously instructed
    Date of the invoice is **01/08/2010**
    Invoice No. is **8**

Tab to or click **Quantity**
Enter **5**
Tab to or click **Item Code**
Type **Sleds** for the **Item Code**, press **Enter**
On the Item Not Found dialog box, click **Yes** to create the new item.

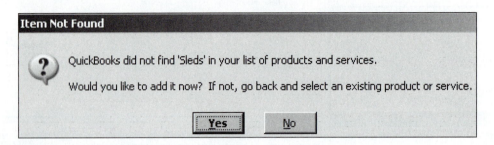

On the **New Item** screen, click **Inventory Part** for **Type**
- If necessary, click the drop-down list menu to get a list of choices for **Type**.

Item Name/Number should be **Sleds**
- If not, tab to or click in the text box for Item Name/Number, type **Sleds**.

Complete **Purchase Information**:
- This section provides information to be used for orders of sleds for Your Name Mountain Sports.

Description on Purchase Transactions: enter **Sleds**
Cost: **0.00**
- Your Name Mountain Sports has elected to keep the item list simple and not use different items for different styles and models of sleds. Thus, sleds are purchased at different prices so the Cost is left at 0.00.

COGS Account: 5000 Cost of Goods Sold
- If this account is not in the **COGS Account** text box, click the drop-down list arrow, click **5000 Cost of Goods Sold**.

Preferred Vendor: Leave blank
Complete **Sales Information**:
- This section provides the information used when Your Name Mountain Sports sells sleds to customers.

Description on Sales Transactions: Should be **Sleds**
- If Sleds was not inserted at the same time as the Purchase Information Description, enter **Sleds** for the description.

Sales Price: Leave 0.00
- Your Name Mountain Sports has elected to keep the item list simple and not use different items for different styles and models of sleds. Thus, sleds are sold at different prices; and the Sales Price remains as 0.00.

Tax Code: Should be **Tax**
- If not, click the drop-down list arrow and click **Tax**.

Click the drop-down list arrow for **Income Account**

Click **4012 Equipment Sales**

Complete the **Inventory Information**:

- QuickBooks Pro uses this information to track the amount of inventory on hand and to provide reorder information.

  Asset Account: Should be **1120 Inventory Asset**

  - If this account is not in the Asset Account text box, click the drop-down list arrow, click **1120 Inventory Asset**.

  Tab to or click **Reorder Point**

  Enter **5**

  Tab to or click **On Hand**

  Enter **10**

  Tab to or click **Total Value**

  - Five of the ten sleds were purchased by Your Name Mountain Sports for $75 each. The other five sleds were purchased for $60 each.

  Enter **675** for the **Total Value**

  Tab to or click **As of**

  Enter the As of date of **01/08/10**

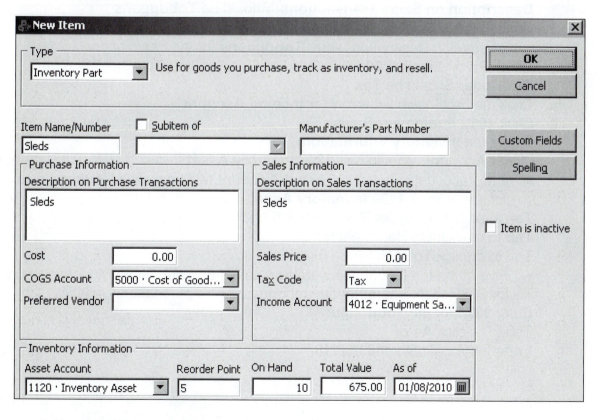

Click **OK** to add Sleds as a sales item

On the invoice, tab to or click **Price Each**

Enter **119.99**

Tab to or click the second line in **Quantity**

Enter **5**

Tab to or click **Item Code**

Click the drop-down list arrow for **Item Code**

- There is no item listed for Toboggans.

Click **<Add New>** at the top of the **Item List**

Complete the information for **New Item**

On the **New Item** screen, click **Inventory Part** for **Type**

- If necessary, click the drop-down list menu to get a list of choices for **Type**.

Tab to or click **Item Name/Number**

Enter **Toboggans**

Complete **Purchase Information**:

   Description on Purchase Transactions: Enter **Toboggans**

   Cost: **0.00**

   COGS Account: **5000 Cost of Goods Sold**

   Preferred Vendor: Leave blank

Complete **Sales Information**:

   Description on Sales Transactions: Should be **Toboggans**

   - If Toboggans was not inserted at the same time as the Purchase Information Description, enter **Toboggans** for the description.

   Sales Price: Leave **0.00**

   Tax Code: Should be **Tax**

   Click the drop-down list arrow for **Income Account**

   Click **4012 Equipment Sales**

Complete the **Inventory Information**:

   Asset Account: Should be **1120 Inventory Asset**

   - If this account is not in the **Asset Account** text box, click the drop-down list arrow, click **1120 Inventory Asset**.

   Tab to or click **Reorder Point**, enter **5**

   Tab to or click **On Hand**, enter **10**

   Tab to or click **Total Value**

   - Five of the ten toboggans were purchased by Your Name Mountain Sports for $125 each. The other five toboggans were purchased for $150 each.

   Enter **1375** for the **Total Value**

   Tab to or click **As of**

   Enter the As of date of **01/08/10**

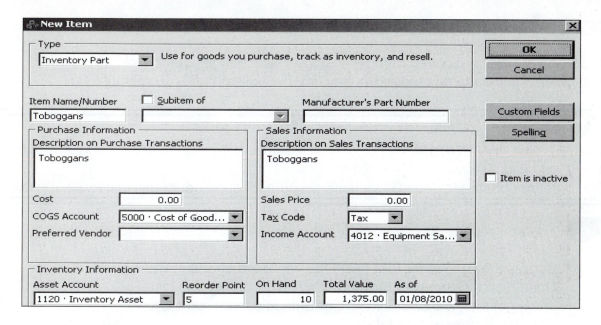

    Click **OK** to add Toboggans as a sales item

Complete the invoice

- Remember that Mountain Recreation Center is a nonprofit organization and is entitled to a Nonprofit Discount.

The message is **Thank you for your business.**

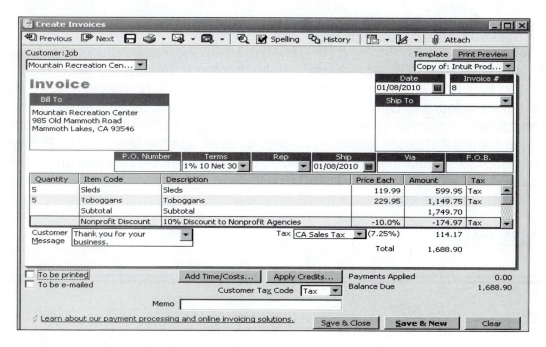

Print the invoice as previously instructed

Click **Save & Close** to record the invoice and close the transaction

MODIFY CUSTOMER RECORDS

Occasionally information regarding a customer will change. QuickBooks Pro allows customer accounts to be modified at any time by editing the Customer List.

MEMO
DATE: January 8, 2010

In order to update Monique Gardener's account, change her credit limit to $2,500.00.

DO ▶ Edit an account

> Access the **Customer List** using the keyboard shortcut: **Ctrl+J**.
> Double-click **Gardener, Monique** on the Customer:Job List.
> If you get the Add/Edit Multiple List Entries screen, click **OK**
> Click the **Payment Info** tab
> Tab to or click **Credit Limit**
> Enter **2500** for the amount
> Click **OK** to record the change and exit the information for Monique Gardener
> Close the **Customer Center**

VOID AND DELETE SALES FORMS

Deleting an invoice or sales receipt completely removes it and any transaction information for it from QuickBooks Pro. Make sure you definitely want to remove the invoice before deleting it. Once it is deleted, an invoice cannot be recovered. If you want to correct financial records for an invoice that is no longer viable, it is more appropriate to void the invoice. When an invoice is voided, it remains in the QuickBooks Pro system, but QuickBooks Pro does not count it. Voiding an invoice should be used only if there have been no payments made on the invoice. If any payment has been received, a Credit Memo would be appropriate for recording a return.

Void an Invoice

MEMO
DATE: January 8, 2010

Richard Weber returned the after-ski boots he purchased for $80.44 including tax on January 2. He had not made any payments on this purchase. Void the invoice.

DO Void the transaction for Richard Weber using **Advanced Find** to locate the invoice:

- **Advanced Find** is useful when you have a large number of invoices and want to locate an invoice for a particular customer.
- Using Advanced **Find** will locate the invoice without requiring you to scroll through all the invoices for the company. For example, if customer Sanderson's transaction was on Invoice No. 7 and the invoice on the screen was 784, you would not have to scroll through 777 invoices because Find would locate Invoice No. 7 instantly.

Click **Find** on the Edit menu, click the **Advanced** tab
In the list displayed under **Filter**, click **Name**

- A Filter allows you to specify the type of search to be performed.

In the **Name** dialog box, click the drop-down list arrow, click **Weber, Richard**
Click the **Find** button on the upper-right side of the **Find** dialog box

- QuickBooks Pro will find all transactions recorded for Richard Weber.

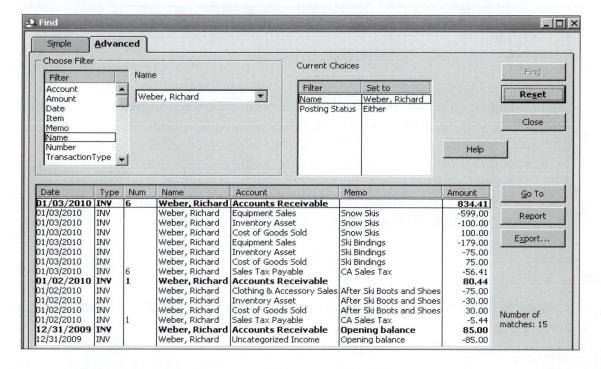

- Because there are several invoices, another filter would need to be defined in order to find the invoice with the exact amount of 80.44. This would be done by selecting a second filter.

Click **Amount** under **Filter**
Click the circle in front of the = sign
Key in **80.44** in the text box

Press the **Tab** key
- The first two lines of the Current Choices Box shows *Filter: Amount* and *Set to: 80.44*: followed by *Filter: Name* and *Set to: Weber, Richard*.

Click the **Find** button
Click the line for **Invoice No. 1**
Click **Go To** button

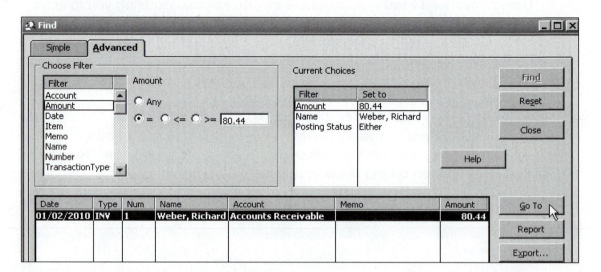

- Invoice No. 1 appears on the screen.

With the invoice on the screen, click **Edit** menu, click **Void Invoice**
- Notice that the amount and the total for Invoice No. 1 are no longer 80.44. Both are **0.00**. Also note that the Memo box contains the word Void.

Click **Save & Close** button on the **Create Invoices** screen to close the invoice
Click **Yes** on the **Recording Transaction** screen
- Invoice No. 1 is no longer displayed on the **Advanced Find** screen.

Click **Close** button to close **Find**

Delete an Invoice

MEMO

DATE: January 8, 2010

Kevin Thomsen lost his part-time job. He decided to repair his old snowboard and return the new one he purchased from Your Name Mountain Sports. Delete Invoice No. 5.

▶ DO ▶ Delete Invoice No. 5

Access Invoice No. 5 as previously instructed
Click the **Edit** menu, click **Delete Invoice**
Click **OK** in the **Delete Transaction** dialog box
- The cursor is now positioned on Invoice No. 6.
Click **Previous**
- Now the cursor is positioned on Invoice No. 4.
Click **Save & Close** on the **Create Invoices** screen to close the invoice

DO View the **Customer Balance Detail Report**

Open the **Report Center**, click **Customers & Receivables,** and double-click
Customer Balance Detail
Scroll through the report
- Look at Kevin Thomsen's account. Notice that Invoice No. 5 does not show up in the account listing. When an invoice is deleted, there is no record of it anywhere in the report.
- Notice that the Customer Balance Detail Report does not include the information telling you which amounts are opening balances.
- The report does give information regarding the amount owed on each transaction plus the total amount owed by each customer.
- Look at Richard Weber's account. The amount for Invoice No. 1 shows as **0.00**.

Your Name Mountain Sports
Customer Balance Detail
All Transactions

Type	Date	Num	Account	Amount	Balance
Thomsen, Kevin					
Invoice	12/31/2009		1200 · Accounts Receivable	911.63	911.63
Total Thomsen, Kevin				911.63	911.63
Villanueva, Oskar					
Invoice	12/31/2009		1200 · Accounts Receivable	975.00	975.00
Total Villanueva, Oskar				975.00	975.00
Weber, Richard					
Invoice	12/31/2009		1200 · Accounts Receivable	85.00	85.00
Invoice	01/02/2010	1	1200 · Accounts Receivable	0.00	85.00
Invoice	01/03/2010	6	1200 · Accounts Receivable	834.41	919.41
Total Weber, Richard				919.41	919.41
TOTAL				**14,392.54**	**14,392.54**

Close the report without printing

PREPARE THE VOIDED/DELETED TRANSACTIONS DETAIL REPORT

The report that lists the information regarding voided and deleted transactions is the Voided/Deleted Transaction Detail Report.

▶DO▶ View the Voided/Deleted Transactions Report

Click **Accountant & Taxes** in the Report Center
Double-click **Voided/Deleted Transaction Detail**
The dates are **01/01/10 - 01/08/10**
- If the report does not match the text when preparing the report with the dates of 01/08/10, use the **Current Date**.
- The Entered Last Modified column shows the actual date and time that the entry was made.
- In addition, your report may not match the one illustrated if you have voided or deleted anything else during your work session.
Scroll through the report to see the transactions

Your Name Mountain Sports
Voided/Deleted Transactions Detail
Entered/Last Modified January 8, 2010

Num	Action	Entered/Last Modified	Date	Name	Memo	Account	Split	Amount
Transactions entered or modified by Admin								
Invoice 1								
▶1	Voided Transaction	01/08/2010 11:07:28	01/02/2010	Weber, Richard	*VOID:*	1200 · Accounts Receivable	-SPLIT-	0.00 ◀
				Weber, Richard	After Ski Boots and Shoes	*4011 · Clothing & Accessory Sales*	1200 · Accounts Receivable	0.00
				State Board of Equalization	CA Sales Tax	2200 · Sales Tax Payable	1200 · Accounts Receivable	0.00
1	Added Transaction	01/02/2010 10:48:12	01/02/2010	Weber, Richard		1200 · Accounts Receivable	-SPLIT-	80.44
				Weber, Richard	After Ski Boots and Shoes	4010 · Sales:4011 · Clothing & Accessory Sales	1200 · Accounts Receivable	-75.00
				State Board of Equalization	CA Sales Tax	2200 · Sales Tax Payable	1200 · Accounts Receivable	-5.44
Invoice 5								
5	Deleted Transaction	01/08/2010 11:07:41						0.00
5	Added Transaction	01/03/2010 10:54:04	01/03/2010	Thomsen, Kevin		1200 · Accounts Receivable	-SPLIT-	536.20
				Thomsen, Kevin	Snowboard	4010 · Sales:4012 · Equipment Sales	1200 · Accounts Receivable	-499.95
				State Board of Equalization	CA Sales Tax	2200 · Sales Tax Payable	1200 · Accounts Receivable	-36.25

Close the report without printing, and close the Report Center

PREPARE CREDIT MEMOS

Credit memos are prepared to show a reduction to a transaction. If the invoice has already been sent to the customer, it is more appropriate and less confusing to make a change to a transaction by issuing a credit memo rather than voiding an invoice and issuing a new one. A credit memo notifies a customer that a change has been made to a transaction.

MEMO
DATE: January 10, 2010

Prepare Credit Memo No. 9 for Monique Gardener to show a reduction to her account for the return of the boot carrying case purchased for $49.95 on Invoice No. 7.

DO   Prepare the Credit Memo shown above

Click the **Refunds and Credit** icon on the Home Page
Click the down arrow for the drop-down list box next to **Customer:Job**
Click **Gardener, Monique**
Use the **Custom Credit Memo** Template
The **Date** of the Credit Memo is **01/10/10**
The **Credit No.** field should show the number **9**
- Because Credit Memos are included in the numbering sequence for invoices, this number matches the number of the next blank invoice.
There is no PO No.
Click the drop-down list arrow next to **Item**, click **Accessories**
Tab to or click in **Qty**, type in **1**
Tab to or click **Rate**, enter **49.95**
Press tab to enter 49.95 in the **Amount** column
The Customer Message is **Thank you for your business.**

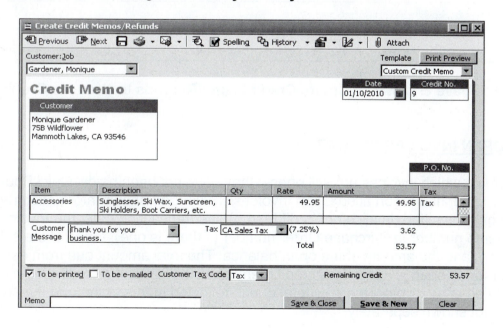

Print the credit memo with lines around each field as previously instructed
Since the return was for an item purchased on Invoice 7, it is appropriate to apply the credit to Invoice 7

To apply the credit, click the **Use Credit to** icon at the top of the Credit Memo and click **Apply to Invoice**

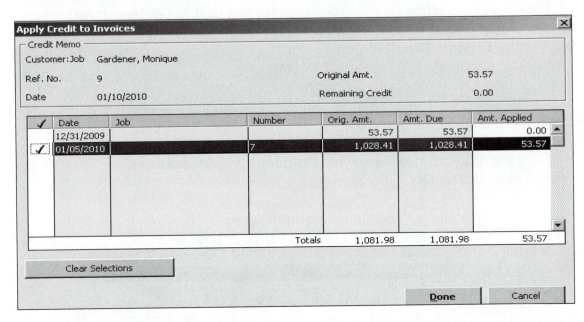

- The Apply Credit to Open Invoices screen will appear. Unless an exact match in the Amt. Due occurs, QuickBooks applies the credit to the oldest item, you will see a checkmark in the column next to the date of 12/31/2009, which is the Opening Balance.

Click the **Clear Selections** button
Click in the check column to mark Invoice 7 on 01/05/2010
Click **Done**

Click **Save & Close** on **Create Credit Memo/Refunds** to close the **Credit Memo**

PRINT OPEN INVOICES REPORT

To determine which invoices are still open—they have not been paid—QuickBooks Pro allows you to print a report titled Open Invoices. This report shows information regarding the type of transaction (Invoice or Credit Memo), the transaction date, the Invoice or Credit Memo number, a Purchase Order number (if there is one), terms of the sale, due date, aging, and the amount of the open balance. The total amount due from each customer for all open invoices less credit memos is also listed. If a credit memo has been applied to an invoice, the new total due is reflected in this report and the credit memo is not shown separately.

When you view a report, each column of information is separated by a diamond between the column headings. These diamonds may be used to change the size/width of a column for the current report. This temporary change is useful if the report is too wide to view on screen, if a column is taking up too much room, if a column is displayed too small, or a column does not contain any information.

MEMO
DATE: January 10, 2010

Ruth needs to prepare and print an Open Invoices Report to give to Larry and you, so you can see which invoices are open. When preparing the report, eliminate the column for P.O. # and adjust the width of the columns. The report should be one page wide without selecting the print option *Fit report to one page wide*.

▶ DO ▶ Prepare, resize, and print an Open Invoices Report

    Click **Reports** menu, point to **Customers & Receivables**, click **Open Invoices**
    Enter the date **011010**
    Press the **Tab** key to generate the report
- Notice the amount due for Invoice 7. It now shows $974.84 as the total rather than $1,028.41. This verifies that the credit memo was applied to Invoice 7.

    Click **Print**
- Be sure the orientation is Portrait and that *Fit report to one page wide* is not selected.

    Click **Preview**
    Click **Next Page** to see all of the pages in the report
    Click **Zoom In** to see what information is contained in the report
    Click **Close** to close the **Preview**
    Click **Cancel** to close **Print Reports**
    Hide columns or resize the width of the columns so the report will fit on one page wide
- The column for P.O. # does not contain any information.

    To hide the column from view, position the cursor on the diamond between **P.O. #** and **Terms**
- The cursor turns into a plus with arrows pointing left and right.

    Hold down the primary mouse button

Drag the cursor from the diamond between **P.O. #** and **Terms** to the diamond between **P.O. #** and **Num**

- You will see a dotted vertical line while you are dragging the mouse and holding down the primary mouse button.
- When you release the primary mouse button, the column for **P.O. #** will not show on the screen.

Look at the other columns, if any have … to represent information not shown, point to the sizing diamond and drag until the information is shown

Click **Print**

- Verify that **Fit report to one page wide** is not selected.
- If it is selected, click the check box to remove the check mark.

Click **Preview**

- The report will now fit on one page wide.

Click **Close** to close the **Preview**

Click **Print**

Your Name Mountain Sports
Open Invoices
As of January 10, 2010

Type	Date	Num	Terms	Due Date	Aging	Open Balance
Cooper, Eileen Dr.						
Invoice	12/31/2009		Net 30	01/30/2010		417.00
Total Cooper, Eileen Dr.						417.00
Cunningham, Linda						
Invoice	12/31/2009		Net 30	01/30/2010		455.00
Total Cunningham, Linda						455.00
Daily, Gail						
Invoice	12/31/2009		Net 30	01/30/2010		1,136.00
Total Daily, Gail						1,136.00
Deardorff, Ramona						
Invoice	12/31/2009		Net 30	01/30/2010		650.00
Total Deardorff, Ramona						650.00
Gardener, Monique						
Invoice	12/31/2009		Net 30	01/30/2010		53.57
Invoice	01/05/2010	7	Net 30	02/04/2010		974.84
Total Gardener, Monique						1,028.41

Partial Report

Close the **Open Invoices Report**

Click **No** if you get a Memorize Report textbox

RECORD CASH SALES WITH SALES TAX

Not all sales in a business are on account. In many instances, payment is made at the time the merchandise is purchased. This is entered as a cash sale. Sales with cash, credit cards, or checks as the payment method are entered as cash sales. When entering a cash sale, you prepare a Sales Receipt rather than an Invoice. QuickBooks Pro records the transaction in the Journal and places the amount of cash received in an account called *Undeposited Funds*. The funds received remain in Undeposited Funds until you record a deposit to your bank account.

MEMO

DATE: January 11, 2010

Record the following cash sale: Sales Receipt No. 1—Received <u>cash</u> from a customer who purchased a pair of sunglasses, $29.95; a boot carrier, $2.99; and some lip balm, $1.19. Use the message *Thank you for your business.*

▶ **DO** Enter the above transaction as a cash sale to a cash customer

Click the **Create Sales Receipts** icon on the Home Page
- If you get a message to Launch Web Browser?, click Cancel.

Enter **Cash Customer** in the **Customer:Job** text box, press Tab

Because Your Name Mountain Sports does not have a customer named Cash
   Customer, a **Customer:Job Not Found** dialog box appears on the screen.

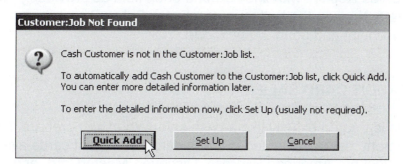

Click **Quick Add** to add the customer name Cash Customer to the Customer List
- Details regarding Cash Customer are not required, so Quick Add is the appropriate method to use to add the name to the list.
- Now that the customer name has been added to the Customer:Job List, the cursor moves to the **Template** field.

Template should be **Custom Sales Receipt**
- If not, click the drop-down list arrow and click Custom Sales Receipt.

Tab to or click **Date**, type **01/11/10**

Sales No. should be **1**

Click the drop-down list arrow next to **Payment Method**, click **Cash**

Use **Accessories** as the Item Code for each of the items sold and complete the Sales Receipt as instructed in Chapter 2

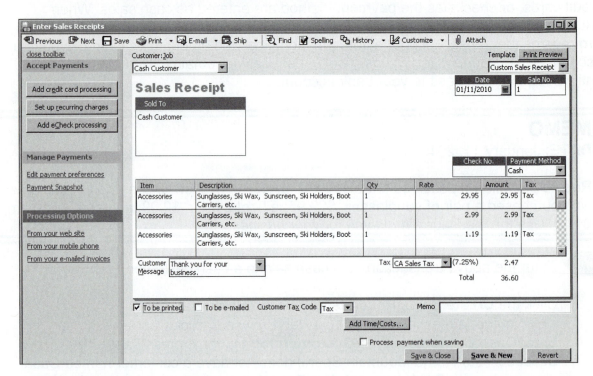

Print the Sales Receipt with lines around each field as previously instructed

Click **Save & New** on the bottom of the **Enter Sales Receipts** screen to save the Sales Receipt and go to the next one

ENTERING A CREDIT CARD SALE

A credit card sale is treated exactly like a cash sale. When you prepare the Sales Receipt, the payment method selected is credit card. The credit cards available on the Payment Method List are American Express, Discover, MasterCard, and Visa. The amount of the sale using a credit card is placed into the Undeposited Funds account. When the actual bank deposit is made, the amount is deposited into the checking or bank account. The bank fees for the charge cards are deducted directly from the bank account.

MEMO

DATE: January 11, 2010

Enter a sale to a cash customer using a Visa card. Identify the customer as Cash Customer. The sale was for a sled, $199.95. Use the message *Thank you for your business.*

DO Record the credit card sale

Click the drop-down list arrow next to **Customer:Job**, click **Cash Customer**
The date of the transaction is **01/11/10**
Sales No. should be **2**
Click the drop-down list arrow next to **Payment Method**, click **VISA**
Complete the Sales Receipt as previously instructed
- If your business subscribes to the optional QuickBooks Merchant Accounts, you may add credit card processing, set up recurring charges, add eCheck processing, and process a VISA payment when saving.
- For a low monthly fee, the QuickBooks Merchant Accounts allows all of these payment processing functions to be completed without additional software or hardware.

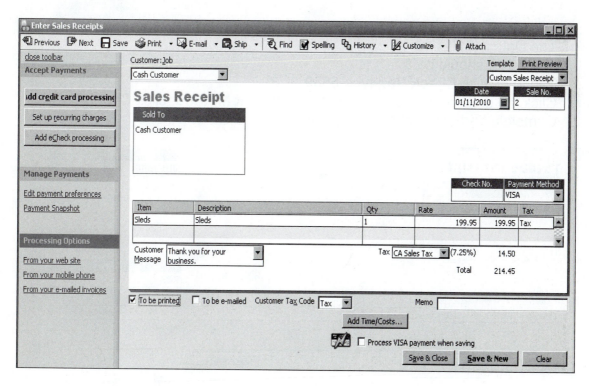

Since we do not subscribe to the QuickBooks Merchant Service, click **Close toolbar** above the Accept Payments buttons
Click **OK** on the Close Toolbar dialog box
Print the sales receipt with lines around it
Click **Next** or **Save & New** to go to Sales Receipt No. 3

RECORD SALES PAID BY CHECK

A sale paid for with a check is considered a cash sale. A sales receipt is prepared to record the sale.

MEMO

DATE: January 11, 2010

We do take checks for sales even if a customer is from out of town. Record the sale of 2 pairs of socks at $15.99 each to a cash customer using Check No. 5589. The message for the Sales Receipt is *Thank you for your business.*

DO With Sales Receipt No. 3 on the screen, enter the information for the transaction

The customer is **Cash Customer**
The Date is **01/11/10**
Sales No. should be **3**
Tab to or click **Check No.**, type **5589**
Click the drop-down list arrow next to **Payment Method**, click **Check**
Complete and print Sales Receipt No. 3

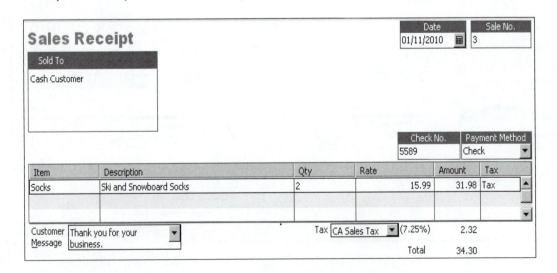

	Date	Sale No.
Sales Receipt	01/11/2010	3

Sold To
Cash Customer

	Check No.	Payment Method
	5589	Check

Item	Description	Qty	Rate	Amount	Tax
Socks	Ski and Snowboard Socks	2	15.99	31.98	Tax

Customer Message	Thank you for your business.		Tax	CA Sales Tax	(7.25%)	2.32
					Total	34.30

Click **Next** or **Save & New** to go to Sales Receipt No. 4

ENTER CASH SALES TRANSACTIONS WITHOUT STEP-BY-STEP INSTRUCTIONS

MEMO

DATE: January 12, 2010

After a record snowfall, the store is really busy. Use Cash Customer as the customer name for the transactions. Record the following cash, check, and credit card sales:

Sales Receipt No. 4—A cash customer used Check No. 196 to purchase a ski parka, $249.95; ski pants, $129.95; and a ski sweater, $89.95.

Sales Receipt No. 5—A cash customer used a Master Card to purchase a snowboard, $389.95; snowboard bindings, $189.95; and snowboard boots, $229.95.

Sales Receipt No. 6—A cash customer purchased a pair of gloves for $89.95 and paid cash.

DO Repeat the procedures used previously to record the additional transactions listed above

- Use the date 01/12/2010 (or the year you have used previously)
- Always use the Item List to determine the appropriate sales items for billing.
- Use **Thank you for your business.** as the message for these sales receipts.
- Print each Sales Receipt immediately after entering the information for it.
- If you get a Merchant Service message, click **Not Now**
- Click **Save & Close** after you have entered and printed Sales Receipt No. 6.

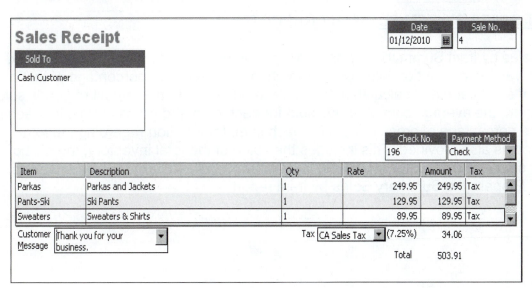

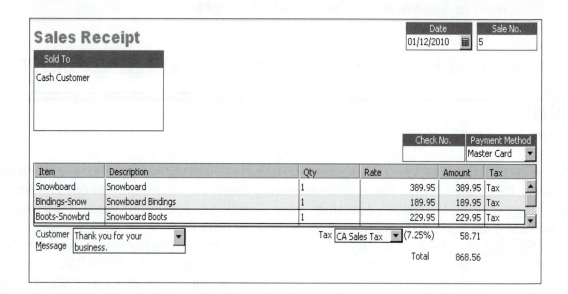

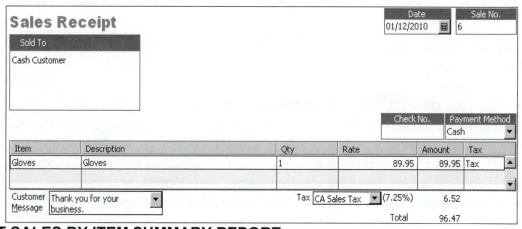

PRINT SALES BY ITEM SUMMARY REPORT

The Sales by Item Summary Report analyzes the quantity of merchandise on hand by item, gives the amount or value of the merchandise, gives the percentage of the total sales of each item, and calculates the average price per item, the cost of goods sold for each item, the average cost of goods sold for each item, the gross margin for each item, and the percentage of gross margin for each item. Information regarding the total inventory is also provided. This includes the value of the total inventory, the cost of goods sold for the inventory, and the gross margin for the inventory of merchandise.

    Prepare the Summary Sales by Item report

MEMO
DATE: January 13, 2010

Near the middle of the month, Ruth prepares a Summary Sales by Item Report to obtain information about sales, inventory, and merchandise costs. Prepare this report in landscape orientation for 1/1/2010-1/13/2010. Adjust the widths of the columns so the report prints on one page without selecting the print option *Fit report to one page wide*

Click **Reports** on the menu bar, point to **Sales**, click **Sales by Item Summary**
The report dates are From **010110** To **011310**
Tab to generate the report
Scroll through the report
Click **Print**
Click **Landscape** to select **Orientation: Landscape**
Click **Preview**
Click **Next Page**
• Notice that the report does not fit on one page wide.
Click **Close** to close the Preview
Click **Cancel** to return to the report
Position the cursor on the diamond between columns
Drag to resize the columns
• The names of the column headings should appear in full and should not have **...** as part of the heading.
If you get a **Resize Columns** dialog box wanting to know if all columns should be the same size, click **No**

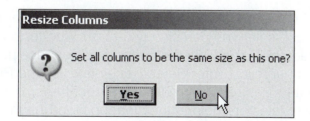

When the columns have been resized, click **Print** and **Preview**

Your Name Mountain Sports
Sales by Item Summary
January 1 - 13, 2010

	Qty	Amount	% of Sales	Avg Price	COGS	Avg COGS	Gross Margin	Gross Margin %
				Jan 1 - 13, 10				
Inventory								
Accessories	5	127.03	1.5%	25.41	18.30	3.66	108.73	85.6%
Bindings-Skis	7	854.00	10%	122.00	525.00	75.00	329.00	38.5%
Bindings-Snow	2	349.94	4.1%	174.97	150.00	75.00	199.94	57.1%
Boots	0	0.00	0.0%	0.00	0.00	0.00	0.00	0.0%
Boots-Ski	1	250.00	2.9%	250.00	75.00	75.00	175.00	70.0%
Boots-Snowbrd	2	478.95	5.6%	239.48	150.00	75.00	328.95	68.7%
Gloves	2	168.95	2%	84.48	30.00	15.00	138.95	82.2%
Hats	1	25.00	0.3%	25.00	8.00	8.00	17.00	68.0%
Pants-Ski	2	258.95	3%	129.48	60.00	30.00	198.95	76.8%
Parkas	2	498.95	5.8%	249.48	116.66	58.33	382.29	76.6%
Poles-Ski	6	220.00	2.6%	36.67	180.00	30.00	40.00	18.2%
Skis	7	2,519.00	29.5%	359.86	700.00	100.00	1,819.00	72.2%
Sleds	6	799.90	9.4%	133.32	405.00	67.50	394.90	49.4%
Snowboard	2	889.90	10.4%	444.95	200.00	100.00	689.90	77.5%
Socks	3	47.93	0.6%	15.98	9.00	3.00	38.93	81.2%
Sweaters	2	214.95	2.5%	107.48	50.00	25.00	164.95	76.7%
Toboggans	5	1,149.75	13.5%	229.95	687.50	137.50	462.25	40.2%
Underwear	1	68.00	0.8%	68.00	8.00	8.00	60.00	88.2%
Total Inventory		8,921.20	104.6%		3,372.46		5,548.74	62.2%
Discounts								
Nonprofit Discount		-388.97	-4.6%					
Total Discounts		-388.97	-4.6%					
TOTAL		8,532.23	100.0%					

When the report fits on one page wide, print and close the report

CORRECT A SALES RECEIPT AND PRINT THE CORRECTED FORM

QuickBooks Pro makes correcting errors user friendly. When an error is discovered in a transaction such as a cash sale, you can simply return to the form where the transaction was recorded and correct the error. Thus, to correct a sales receipt, you could click Customers on the menu bar, click Enter Sales Receipts, click the Previous button until you found the appropriate sales receipt, and then correct the error. Since cash or checks received for cash sales are held in the Undeposited Funds account until the bank deposit is made, a sales receipt can be accessed through the Undeposited Funds account in the Chart of Accounts. Accessing the receipt in this manner allows you to see all the transactions entered in the account for Undeposited Funds.

When a correction for a sale is made, QuickBooks Pro not only changes the form, it also changes all Journal and account entries for the transaction to reflect the correction. QuickBooks Pro then allows a corrected sales receipt to be printed.

MEMO

DATE: January 13, 2010

After reviewing transaction information, you realize that the date for Sales Receipt No. 1 was entered incorrectly. Change the date to 1/8/2010.

DO Use the Undeposited Funds account register to correct the error in the memo above, and print a corrected Sales Receipt

Open the **Chart of Accounts**, use the keyboard shortcut **Ctrl+A**
Double-click **Undeposited Funds**
- The register maintains a record of all the transactions recorded within the Undeposited Funds account.

Click anywhere in the transaction for **Sale No. 1**
- Look at the **Ref/Type** column to see the type of transaction.
- The number in the Ref column indicates the number of the sales receipt or the customer's check number.
- Type shows **RCPT** for a sales receipt.

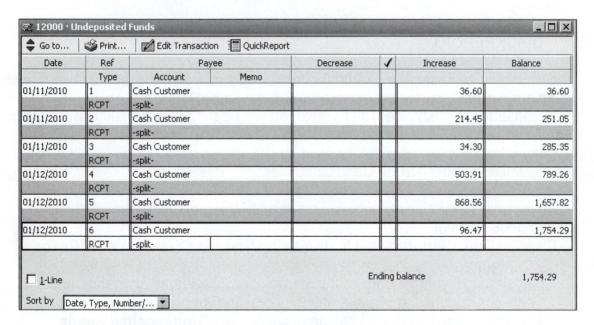

Click **Edit Transaction**
- The sales receipt appears on the screen.
Tab to or click **Date** field
Change the Date to **01/08/10**

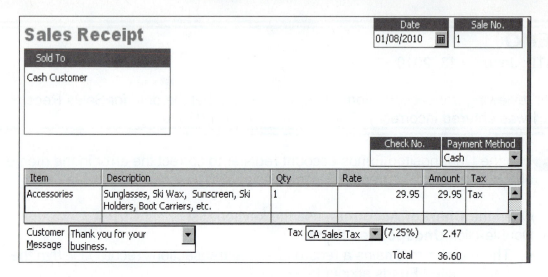

Print a corrected sales receipt as previously instructed
Click **Save & Close**
Click **Yes** on the **Recording Transactions** dialog box
Return to the **Register for Undeposited Funds**
Do not close the register

VIEW A QUICKREPORT

After editing the sales receipt and returning to the register, you may get a detailed report regarding the customer's transactions by clicking the QuickReport button. If you use Cash Customer for all cash sales, a QuickReport will be for all the transactions of Cash Customer.

DO Prepare a QuickReport for Cash Customer

After closing the sales receipt, you returned to the register for the Undeposited Funds account
Click the **QuickReport** button to display the Register QuickReport for **Cash Customer**
Because there are no entries in the Memo and Clr columns, drag the diamond between columns to eliminate the columns for **Memo** and **Clr**
Widen the **Account** column until the account name **Undeposited Funds** appears in full

Your Name Mountain Sports
Register QuickReport
All Transactions

Type	Date	Num	Account	Split	Amount
Cash Customer					
Sales Receipt	01/08/2010	1	12000 · Undeposited Funds	-SPLIT-	36.60
Sales Receipt	01/11/2010	2	12000 · Undeposited Funds	-SPLIT-	214.45
Sales Receipt	01/11/2010	3	12000 · Undeposited Funds	-SPLIT-	34.30
Sales Receipt	01/12/2010	4	12000 · Undeposited Funds	-SPLIT-	503.91
Sales Receipt	01/12/2010	5	12000 · Undeposited Funds	-SPLIT-	868.56
Sales Receipt	01/12/2010	6	12000 · Undeposited Funds	-SPLIT-	96.47
Total Cash Customer					1,754.29
TOTAL					**1,754.29**

ANALYZE THE QUICKREPORT FOR CASH CUSTOMER

▶ **DO** Analyze the QuickReport

All transactions for Cash Customer appear in the report
- Notice that the date for Sales Receipt No. 1 has been changed to **01/08/2010**.
The account used is Undeposited Funds
The Split column contains the other accounts used in the transactions
- For all the transactions you see the word **-SPLIT-** rather than an account name.
- Split means that more than one account was used for this portion of the transaction.
- In addition to a variety of sales items, sales tax was charged on all sales, so each transaction will show **-SPLIT-** even if only one item was sold as in Sales Receipt No. 2.
View the accounts used for the Split by using QuickZoom to view the actual sales receipt
Use QuickZoom by double-clicking anywhere on the information for Sales Receipt No. 2
- The accounts used are Sleds and CA Sales Tax.
Close **Sales Receipt No. 2**
Close the report without printing
Close the register for **Undeposited Funds**
Do not close the **Chart of Accounts**

VIEW SALES TAX PAYABLE REGISTER

The Sales Tax Payable Register shows a detailed listing of all transactions with sales tax. The option of 1-Line may be selected in order to view each transaction on one line rather than the standard two lines. The account register provides information regarding the vendor and the account used for the transaction.

DO View the register for the Sales Tax Payable account

Double-click **Sales Tax Payable** in the Chart of Accounts
Once the register is displayed, click **1-Line** to view the transactions

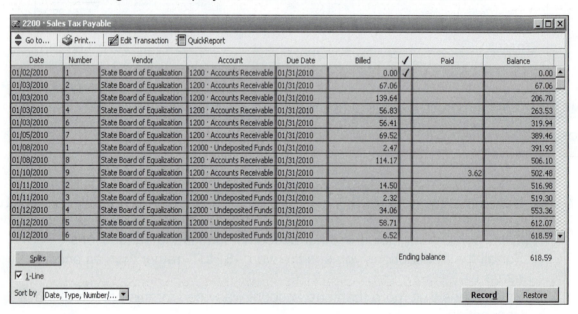

Close the register for **Sales Tax Payable**, and close the **Chart of Accounts**

RECORD CUSTOMER PAYMENTS ON ACCOUNT

Whenever money is received, whether it is for a cash sale or when customers pay the amount they owe on account, QuickBooks Pro uses the account called *Undeposited Funds* rather than a cash/checking account. The money stays in the account until a bank deposit is made. When you start to record a payment on account, you see the customer's balance, any credits or discounts, and a complete list of unpaid invoices. QuickBooks Pro automatically applies the payment received to a matching amount or the oldest invoice.

If a customer owes you money for a purchase made "on account" (an invoice) you record the payment in Receive Payments. If a customer paid you at the time the purchase was made, a sales receipt was prepared and the amount received was recorded at that time.

MEMO

DATE: January 13, 2010

Record the following receipt of Check No. 765 for $975 from Oskar Villanueva as payment in full on his account.

DO Record the above payment on account

Click the **Receive Payments** icon on the QuickBooks Home Page
Click the drop-down list for **Received From**, click **Villanueva, Oskar**
- Notice that the current date shows in the **Date** column and that the total amount owed appears as the Customer Balance.
Tab to or click **Amount**, enter **975**
Tab to or click **Date**, type **01/13/10**
Click the drop-down list arrow for **Pmt. Method**
- Notice that the cursor moves into the **Pmt. Method** text box, the invoice is checked, and the payment amount is shown as applied in the Amount for Selected Invoices section.
- When recording a payment on account, QuickBooks places a check mark in the √column to indicate the invoice for which the payment is received.
Click **Check**
Tab to or click **Check #**, enter **765**

Customer Payment

Received From	Villanueva, Oskar		Customer Balance	975.00
Amount	975.00		Date	01/13/2010
Pmt. Method	Check		Check #	765
Memo			Where does this payment go?	

☐ Process payment when saving   Find a Customer/Invoice...

✓	Date	Number	Orig. Amt.	Amt. Due	Payment
✓	12/31/2009		975.00	975.00	975.00
	Totals		975.00	975.00	975.00

Amounts for Selected Invoices

Amount Due	975.00
Applied	975.00
Discount and Credits Applied	0.00

Un-Apply Payment   Discount & Credits...

Click the **Print** button at the top of the Receive Payments screen and print the Payment Receipt

Click **Next** or **Save & New** to record this payment and advance to the next **Receive Payments** screen

RECORD CUSTOMER PAYMENT ON ACCOUNT WHEN A CREDIT HAS BEEN APPLIED

If there are any existing credits (such as a Credit Memo) on an account that have not been applied to the account, they may be applied to a customer's account when a payment is made. If a credit was recorded and applied to an invoice, the total amount due on the invoice will reflect the credit.

MEMO

DATE: January 13, 2010

Monique Gardener sent Check No. 1026 for $1,028.41 to pay her account in full. Apply unused credits when recording her payment on account.

DO ▶ Record the payment by Monique Gardener and apply her unused credits

Click the drop-down list for **Received From**, click **Gardener, Monique**
- Notice the Customer Balance shows the total amount owed by the customer.
- In the lower portion of the **Receive Payments** screen, notice the list of unpaid invoices for Monique Gardener.

Tab to or click **Amount**, enter **1028.41**

Tab to or click **Date**, type the date **01/13/10**

Check should still show as the payment method

Tab to or click **Check #**, enter **1026**

- Because the amount of the payment matched the amount due for the opening balance and Invoice 7, both have a check mark.
- Notice the Original Amount of the two transactions, the Amt. Due, and the Payment amounts. The Amt. Due for Invoice 7 reflects the $53.57 that was previously recorded on a credit memo.

Customer Payment

Received From	Gardener, Monique			Customer Balance	1,028.41
Amount	1,028.41			Date	01/13/2010
Pmt. Method	Check			Check #	1026
Memo				Where does this payment go?	

☐ Process payment when saving   Find a Customer/Invoice...

✓	Date	Number	Orig. Amt.	Amt. Due	Payment
✓	12/31/2009		53.57	53.57	53.57
✓	01/05/2010	7	1,028.41	974.84	974.84
	Totals		1,081.98	1,028.41	1,028.41

Amounts for Selected Invoices

Amount Due	1,028.41
Applied	1,028.41
Discount and Credits Applied	0.00

Un-Apply Payment

Discount & Credits...

- If you did not apply a credit directly to an invoice, you may do so now by clicking the invoice that should receive the credit (Invoice 7), clicking the Discount & Credits button, selecting the amount of credit to apply, and clicking the Done button.

Print the Payment Receipt

Click **Next** or **Save & New** to record this payment and to advance to the next **Receive Payments** screen.

RECORD PAYMENT ON ACCOUNT FROM A CUSTOMER QUALIFYING FOR AN EARLY-PAYMENT DISCOUNT

Each customer may be assigned terms as part of the customer information. When terms such as 1% 10 Net 30 or 2% 10 Net 30 are given, customers whose payments are received within ten days of the invoice date are eligible to deduct 1% or 2% from the amount owed when making their payments.

Record the receipt of the check and apply the discount to the above transaction

MEMO

DATE: January 13, 2010

Received payment from Mountain Recreation Center for Invoice No. 8. Check No. 981-13 for $1672.01 was received as full payment. Record the payment and the 1% discount for early payment under the invoice terms of 1% 10 Net 30.

Click the drop-down list for **Received From**
Click **Mountain Recreation Center**
- The total amount owed, $1,688.90, appears as the Customer Balance.
Tab to or click **Amount**, enter **1672.01**
- Notice that this amount is different from the balance of $1,688.90.
Tab to or click **Date**, type date **01/13/10**
The **Pmt. Method** should show Check
Tab to or click **Check #**, enter **981-13**
- Notice that the payment amount is entered in the **Payment** column for Invoice 8.
You will get a message in the lower portion of Receive Payments

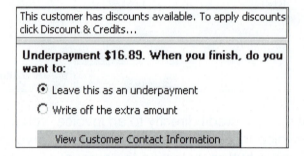

Tab to or click **Memo**, type **Includes Early Payment Discount**
- Since the column for Disc. Date is displayed, you will see that the Invoice is being paid within the discount date and is eligible to receive a discount
Click **Discounts & Credits** button
- QuickBooks displays the 1% discount amount, which was calculated on the total amount due
Click the drop-down list arrow for **Discount Account**, click **6130 Sales Discounts**

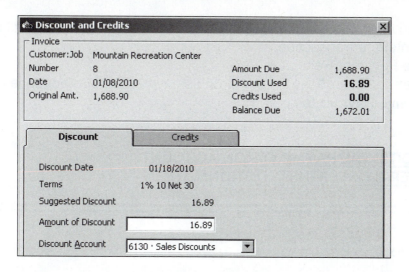

Click the **Done** button at the bottom of the Discounts and Credits screen to apply the discount of $16.89

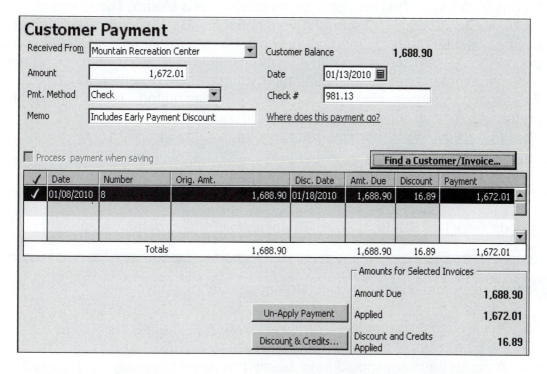

- Notice that the Original Amount stays the same, the Amount Due on Invoice No. 8 shows $1,688.90, the discount amount of $16.89 shows in the Discount column, and the Payment shows $1,672.01.
- In the area for Amounts for Selected invoices, you will see the Amount Due, 1,688.90; Amount Applied, 1,672.01; and Amount of Discounts and Credits Applied, 16.89.

- If you make an error in applying the discount, click the **Revert** button and re-enter the transaction.

Print the Payment Receipt

Click **Next** or **Save & New** to record this payment and to advance to the next **Receive Payments** screen

RECORD ADDITIONAL PAYMENTS ON ACCOUNT
WITHOUT STEP-BY-STEP INSTRUCTIONS

MEMO

DATE: January 14, 2010

Received Check No. 152 from Richard Weber for $919.41

Received Check No. 8252 dated January 11 and postmarked 1/12 for $2,024.33 from Mountain Schools. This receipt requires an item as a Memo. The memo is: *Includes Early Payment Discount.* Even though the date we are recording the payment is after the discount date, the check was postmarked within the discount period. Apply the discount for early payment to this transaction. Since the payment is being recorded after the discount date, you may need to enter the amount of the 2% discount when you click the Discounts & Credits button (use QuickMath to perform the calculation and enter the 2% discount).

Received Check No. 3951 from Dr. Francisco Munoz for $1,087.51.

Received Check No. 1051 for $500 from Gail Daily in partial payment of account. Record the memo: Partial Payment.

Received Check No. 563 from Sandra Perkins for $408.48 in payment of the 12/31/2008 balance.

Received Check No. 819 from Kevin Thomsen for $100 in partial payment of his account.

▶**DO**▶ Refer to the previous steps listed to enter the above payments:

- Any discounts or partial payments should be noted as a Memo.
- Be sure to apply any discounts.
- A partial payment should have *Leave this as an underpayment* marked.

Print a Payment Receipt for each payment recorded

Click the **Save & Close** button after all payments received have been recorded

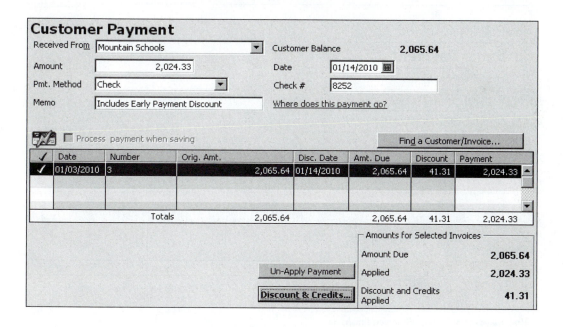

Customer Payment

Received From	Weber, Richard		Customer Balance	**919.41**
Amount	919.41		Date	01/14/2010
Pmt. Method	Check		Check #	152
Memo			Where does this payment go?	

☐ Process payment when saving   **Find a Customer/Invoice...**

✓	Date	Number	Orig. Amt.	Amt. Due	Payment
✓	12/31/2009		85.00	85.00	85.00
✓	01/03/2010	6	834.41	834.41	834.41
	Totals		919.41	919.41	919.41

Amounts for Selected Invoices

Amount Due	**919.41**
Un-Apply Payment Applied	**919.41**
Discount & Credits... Discount and Credits Applied	**0.00**

Customer Payment

Received From	Mountain Schools		Customer Balance	**2,065.64**
Amount	2,024.33		Date	01/14/2010
Pmt. Method	Check		Check #	8252
Memo	Includes Early Payment Discount		Where does this payment go?	

☐ Process payment when saving   Find a Customer/Invoice...

✓	Date	Number	Orig. Amt.	Disc. Date	Amt. Due	Discount	Payment
✓	01/03/2010	3	2,065.64	01/14/2010	2,065.64	41.31	2,024.33
	Totals		2,065.64		2,065.64	41.31	2,024.33

Amounts for Selected Invoices

Amount Due	**2,065.64**
Un-Apply Payment Applied	**2,024.33**
Discount & Credits... Discount and Credits Applied	**41.31**

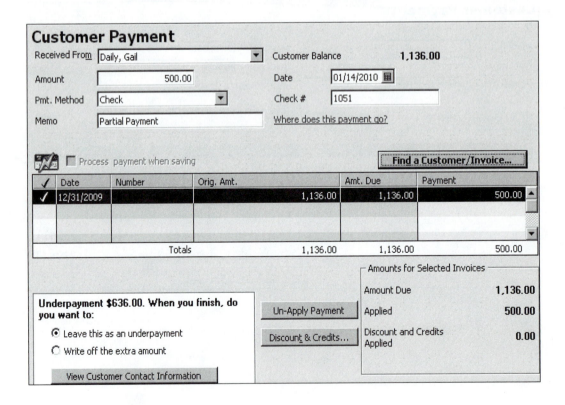

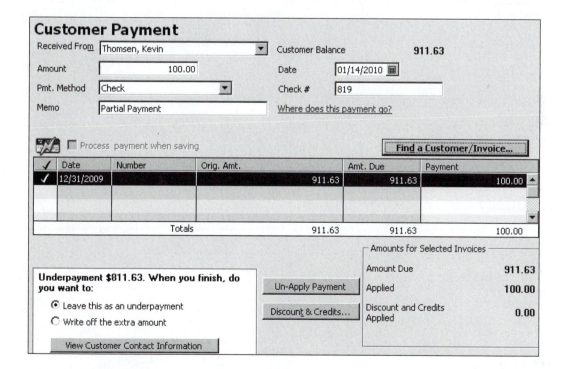

VIEW TRANSACTION LIST BY CUSTOMER

In order to see the transactions for customers, you need to prepare a report called Transaction List by Customer. This report shows all sales, credits, and payments for each customer on account and for the customer named Cash Customer. The report does not show the balance remaining on account for the individual customers.

DO ▶ View the Transaction List by Customer
Click the **Report Center** button
Click **Customers & Receivables** as the type of report
Double-click **Transaction List by Customer**
Enter the dates from **01/01/10** to **01/14/10**
Tab to generate the report
Scroll through the report
- Information is shown for the Invoices, Sales Receipts, Credit Memos, and payments made on the accounts and the Num column shows the Invoice numbers, Sales Receipt numbers, Credit Memo numbers, and Check numbers.

Your Name Mountain Sports
Transaction List by Customer
January 1 - 14, 2010

Type	Date	Num	Memo	Account	Clr	Split	Amount
Cash Customer							
Sales Receipt	01/08/2010	1		12000 · Undeposited Funds		-SPLIT-	36.60
Sales Receipt	01/11/2010	2		12000 · Undeposited Funds		-SPLIT-	214.45
Sales Receipt	01/11/2010	3		12000 · Undeposited Funds		-SPLIT-	34.30
Sales Receipt	01/12/2010	4		12000 · Undeposited Funds		-SPLIT-	503.91
Sales Receipt	01/12/2010	5		12000 · Undeposited Funds		-SPLIT-	868.56
Sales Receipt	01/12/2010	6		12000 · Undeposited Funds		-SPLIT-	96.47
Daily, Gail							
Payment	01/14/2010	1051	Partial Payment	12000 · Undeposited Funds		1200 · Accounts Receivable	500.00
Gardener, Monique							
Invoice	01/05/2010	7		1200 · Accounts Receivable		-SPLIT-	1,028.41
Credit Memo	01/10/2010	9		1200 · Accounts Receivable		-SPLIT-	-53.57
Payment	01/13/2010	1026		12000 · Undeposited Funds		1200 · Accounts Receivable	1,028.41
Mountain Recreation Center							
Invoice	01/08/2010	8		1200 · Accounts Receivable		-SPLIT-	1,688.90
Payment	01/13/2010	981-13	Includes Early Payment Discount	12000 · Undeposited Funds		1200 · Accounts Receivable	1,672.01 ◀
Mountain Schools							
Invoice	01/03/2010	3		1200 · Accounts Receivable		-SPLIT-	2,065.64
Payment	01/14/2010	8252	Includes Early Payment Discount	12000 · Undeposited Funds		1200 · Accounts Receivable	2,024.33
Munoz, Francisco Dr.							
Invoice	01/03/2010	2		1200 · Accounts Receivable		-SPLIT-	992.06
Payment	01/14/2010	3951		12000 · Undeposited Funds		1200 · Accounts Receivable	1,087.51
Perkins, Sandra							
Invoice	01/03/2010	4		1200 · Accounts Receivable		-SPLIT-	840.68
Payment	01/14/2010	563		12000 · Undeposited Funds		1200 · Accounts Receivable	408.48
Thomsen, Kevin							
Payment	01/14/2010	819	Partial Payment	12000 · Undeposited Funds		1200 · Accounts Receivable	100.00
Villanueva, Oskar							
Payment	01/13/2010	765		12000 · Undeposited Funds		1200 · Accounts Receivable	975.00
Weber, Richard							
Invoice	01/02/2010	1	VOID:	1200 · Accounts Receivable	✓	-SPLIT-	0.00
Invoice	01/03/2010	6		1200 · Accounts Receivable		-SPLIT-	834.41
Payment	01/14/2010	152		12000 · Undeposited Funds		1200 · Accounts Receivable	919.41

Close the report without printing

PRINT CUSTOMER BALANCE SUMMARY

A report that will show you the balance owed by each customer is the Customer Balance Summary. The report presents the total balance owed by each customer as of a certain date.

MEMO

DATE: January 14, 2010

Larry and you want to see how much each customer owes to Your Name Mountain Sports. Print a Customer Balance Summary Report.

DO Prepare and print a **Customer Balance Summary** follow the steps given previously for printing the report in Portrait orientation

Your Name Mountain Sports
Customer Balance Summary
All Transactions

	◇ Jan 14, 10 ◇
Cooper, Eileen Dr. ▶	417.00 ◀
Cunningham, Linda	455.00
Daily, Gail	636.00
Deardorff, Ramona	650.00
Kandahar, Mahmet	1,085.00
Perkins, Sandra	840.68
Taka, Mikko	670.31
Thomsen, Kevin	811.63
TOTAL	5,565.62

Close the report and the Report Center

DEPOSIT CHECKS AND CREDIT CARD RECEIPTS
FOR CASH SALES AND PAYMENTS ON ACCOUNT

When cash sales are made and payments on accounts are received, QuickBooks Pro places the money received in the *Undeposited Funds* account. Once the deposit is recorded, the funds are transferred from *Undeposited Funds* to the account selected when preparing the deposit.

MEMO

DATE: January 14, 2010

Deposit all cash, checks and credit card receipts for cash sales and payments on
account into the Checking account.

DO Deposit cash, checks and credit card receipts

Click the **Record Deposits** icon on the QuickBooks Home Page
The View payment method type should be **All types**
- The **Payments to Deposit** window shows all amounts received for cash sales
  (including bank credit cards) and payments on account that have not been
  deposited in the bank organized by category—Cash, Check, and finally Credit
  Cards.
- Notice that the **check** column to the left of the Date column is empty.
Click the **Select All** button
- Notice the check marks in the check column.

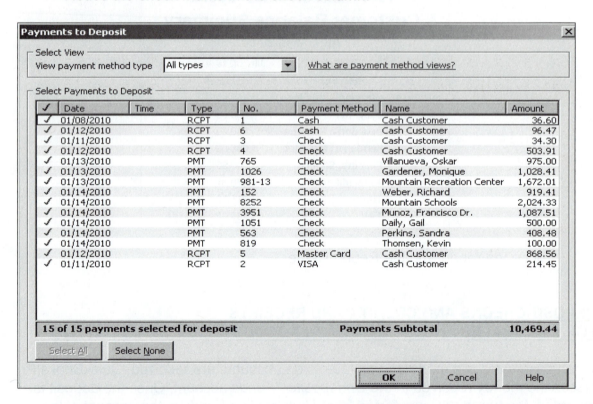

Click **OK** to close the **Payments to Deposit** screen and go to the **Make
    Deposits** screen
On the **Make Deposits** screen, **Deposit To** should be **1100 Checking**

Date should be **01/14/2010**
- Tab to date and change if not correct.

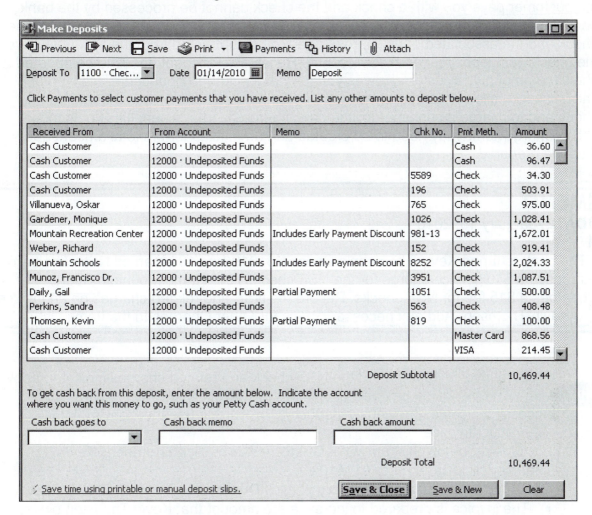

Received From	From Account	Memo	Chk No.	Pmt Meth.	Amount
Cash Customer	12000 · Undeposited Funds			Cash	36.60
Cash Customer	12000 · Undeposited Funds			Cash	96.47
Cash Customer	12000 · Undeposited Funds		5589	Check	34.30
Cash Customer	12000 · Undeposited Funds		196	Check	503.91
Villanueva, Oskar	12000 · Undeposited Funds		765	Check	975.00
Gardener, Monique	12000 · Undeposited Funds		1026	Check	1,028.41
Mountain Recreation Center	12000 · Undeposited Funds	Includes Early Payment Discount	981-13	Check	1,672.01
Weber, Richard	12000 · Undeposited Funds		152	Check	919.41
Mountain Schools	12000 · Undeposited Funds	Includes Early Payment Discount	8252	Check	2,024.33
Munoz, Francisco Dr.	12000 · Undeposited Funds		3951	Check	1,087.51
Daily, Gail	12000 · Undeposited Funds	Partial Payment	1051	Check	500.00
Perkins, Sandra	12000 · Undeposited Funds		563	Check	408.48
Thomsen, Kevin	12000 · Undeposited Funds	Partial Payment	819	Check	100.00
Cash Customer	12000 · Undeposited Funds			Master Card	868.56
Cash Customer	12000 · Undeposited Funds			VISA	214.45

Click **Print** to print **Deposit Summary**
Select **Deposit summary only** and click **OK** on the **Print Deposit** dialog box

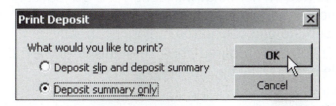

Click **Print** on the **Print Lists** dialog box
When printing is finished, click **Save & Close** on **Make Deposits**

RECORD THE RETURN OF A CHECK BECAUSE OF NONSUFFICIENT FUNDS

If a customer pays you with a check and the check cannot be processed by the bank because there are insufficient funds in the customer's bank account, the amount of the check and the associated bank charges need to be subtracted from the account where the check was deposited; and the Accounts Receivable account needs to be updated to show the amount the customer owes you for the check that "bounced." This type of check is also called *nonsufficient funds* or *NSF*. In order to track the amount of a bad check and to charge a customer for the bank charges and any penalties you impose, Other Charge items may need to be created and an invoice for the total amount due must be prepared.

MEMO
DATE: January 15, 2010

The bank returned Kevin Thomsen's Check No. 819 for $100 marked NSF. The bank imposed a $10 service charge for the NSF check. Your Name Mountain Sports charges a $15 fee for NSF checks. Record the NSF and related charges on an invoice to Kevin Thomsen. Add any necessary items for Other Charges to the Items List.

▶ **DO**   Prepare Invoice 10 to record the NSF check and related charges indicated above

Access invoices as previously instructed, be sure to use the Copy of: Intuit Product Invoice

Click the drop-down list arrow for **Customer:Job**, click **Thomsen, Kevin**

Tab to or click **Date**, enter **011510**

Click drop-down list arrow for **Terms**, click **Due on receipt**

- The invoice is prepared to increase the amount that Kevin Thomsen owes. That amount will include the bad check and the fees for the bad check.

Click the drop-down list arrow for **Item Code**

- You need to add an item that will identify the transaction as a bad check. Because you are preparing an invoice to record the NSF check, using this item will keep the bad check from being incorrectly identified as a sale.
- When the invoice is prepared, the use of this item will debit Accounts Receivable and credit Checking.

Click **<Add New>**

Click **Other Charge**

Enter **Bad Check** as the **Item Name/Number**

Tab to or click **Description**

Enter **Check Returned by Bank**

Amount or % should be **0.00**

Click the drop-down-list arrow for **Tax Code**
Click **Non-Taxable**
Click the drop-down list arrow for **Account**
Click **1100 Checking**

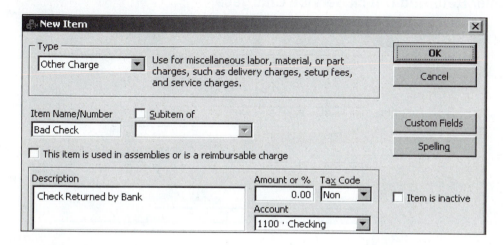

Click **OK**
Click or tab to **Price Each** on the Invoice
Enter **100**
- This is the amount of Kevin's bad check.

Tab to or click the next line for **Item Code**, click the drop-down list arrow for **Item Code**
- Another item needs be added in order to identify the amount that Kevin owes for the NSF charges from the bank and from Your Name Mountain Sports.

Click **<Add New>**
Click **Other Charge** for **Type**
Enter **Bad Check Charges** as the **Item Name/Number**
Tab to or click **Description**
Enter **Bank and Other Charges for Returned Check.**
Amount or % should be **0.00**
The **Tax Code** should be **Non-Taxable**
Click the drop-down list arrow for **Account**
Scroll through the list of accounts
- There are no appropriate accounts for this item.

Add a new account to the Chart of Accounts by clicking **<Add New>** at the top of the list for the Accounts
Type of account is **Income**
- This account is an income account because we will be receiving money for the charges. When the bank statement is reconciled, the amount of bank service charges will reduce the amount of income earned for the bad check

charges leaving only the amount actually earned by Your Name Mountain Sports.

Enter **4040** for the **Number**

Tab to or click **Name**

Enter **Returned Check Service Charges**

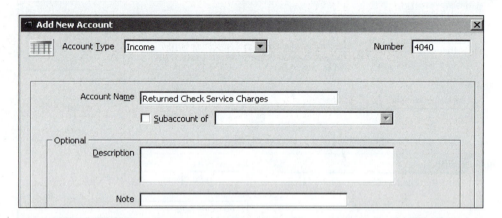

Click **Save & Close** to record the new account in the **Chart of Accounts**

Account 4040 is inserted as the **Account** for the **New Item**

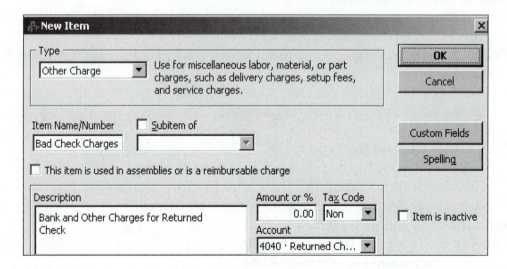

Click **OK** to add Bad Check Charges to the Item List

Tab to or click **Price Each** on the Invoice

Enter **25**

- This is the total amount of the charges Kevin has incurred for the NSF check—$10 for the bank charges and $15 for Your Name Mountain Sports charges.

Click the drop-down list arrow for **Customer Message**, click **Please remit to above address.**

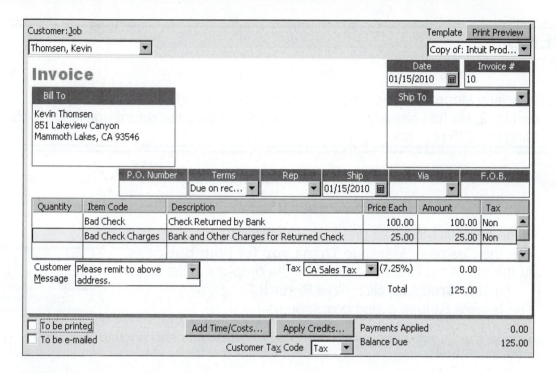

Print the Invoice

- You may get a message box regarding the change in terms for Kevin Thomsen. Click **No**

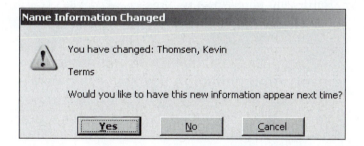

After printing, click **Save & Close** to save and exit **Create Invoices**

ISSUE A CREDIT MEMO AND A REFUND CHECK

If merchandise is returned and the invoice has been paid in full or the sale was for cash, a refund check may be issued at the same time the credit memo is prepared. Simply clicking a Check Refund button instructs QuickBooks Pro to prepare the refund check for you.

MEMO
DATE: January 15, 2010

Dr. Francisco Munoz returned the ski poles he purchased for $75 January 3 on Invoice No. 2. He has already paid his bill in full. Record the return and issue a check refunding the $75 plus tax.

DO Prepare a Credit Memo to record the return of the ski poles and issue a refund check

Issue a Credit Memo as previously instructed
Use the Customer Message **Thank you for your business.**
At the top of the Credit Memo, click the drop-down list arrow for **Use Credit to**, click **Give Refund**.
The Issue a Refund dialog box appears.

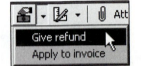

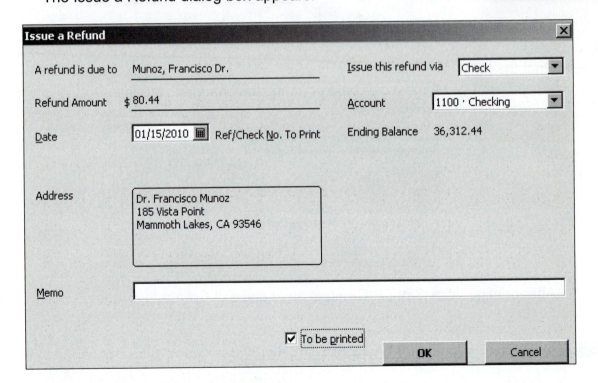

Verify the information and click **OK**.
The Credit Memo will be stamped "Refunded."

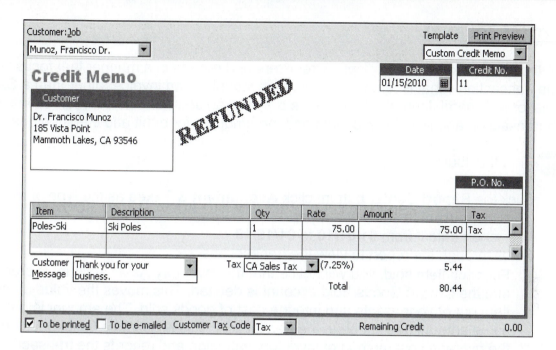

Print the Credit Memo.

Click **Save & Close** to record the **Credit Memo** and exit

Click the **Write Checks** icon on the Home Page, click **Previous** until you get to the check for Dr. Munoz

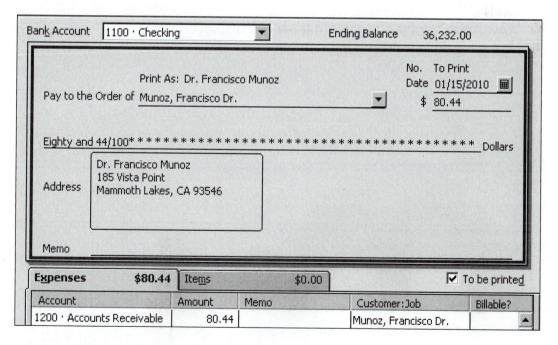

Print Check No. 1 in Standard format as previously instructed

Click **Save & Close** on the **Write Checks** screen

PRINT THE JOURNAL

Even though QuickBooks Pro displays registers and reports in a manner that focuses on the transaction—that is, entering a sale on account via an invoice rather than a Sales Journal or a General Journal—it still keeps a (General) Journal. The Journal records each transaction and lists the accounts and the amounts for debit and credit entries.

▶ DO ▶Print the Journal

> Click the **Report Center** button, click **Accountant & Taxes** as the type of report, click **Journal** to select the report
> The report date if from **01/01/10** to **01/15/10**
> Scroll through the report to view the transactions
> - For each item sold, you will notice that the Inventory Asset account is credited and the Cost of Goods Sold account is debited. This moves the value of the item out of your assets and into the cost of goods sold. The amount is not the same amount as the one in the transaction. This is because QuickBooks uses the average cost method of inventory valuation and records the transaction based on the average cost of an item rather than the specific cost of an item. The Memo column contains the Sales Item used in the transaction.
> Resize the columns by positioning the cursor on the diamond and dragging so that the report will print on one-page wide without clicking Fit to one-page wide
> - Make sure that the account names are displayed in full
> Print the report in Landscape orientation

Your Name Mountain Sports
Journal
January 1 - 15, 2010

Trans #	Type	Date	Num	Name	Memo	Account	Debit	Credit
74	Deposit	01/14/2010			Deposit	1100 · Checking	10,469.44	
				Cash Customer	Deposit	12000 · Undeposited Funds		36.60
				Cash Customer	Deposit	12000 · Undeposited Funds		96.47
				Cash Customer	Deposit	12000 · Undeposited Funds		34.30
				Cash Customer	Deposit	12000 · Undeposited Funds		503.91
				Villanueva, Oskar	Deposit	12000 · Undeposited Funds		975.00
				Gardener, Monique	Deposit	12000 · Undeposited Funds		1,028.41
				Mountain Recreation Center	Includes Early Payment Discount	12000 · Undeposited Funds		1,672.01
				Weber, Richard	Deposit	12000 · Undeposited Funds		919.41
				Mountain Schools	Includes Early Payment Discount	12000 · Undeposited Funds		2,024.33
				Munoz, Francisco Dr.	Deposit	12000 · Undeposited Funds		1,087.51
				Daily, Gail	Partial Payment	12000 · Undeposited Funds		500.00
				Perkins, Sandra	Deposit	12000 · Undeposited Funds		408.48
				Thomsen, Kevin	Partial Payment	12000 · Undeposited Funds		100.00
				Cash Customer	Deposit	12000 · Undeposited Funds		868.56
				Cash Customer	Deposit	12000 · Undeposited Funds		214.45
							10,469.44	10,469.44
75	Invoice	01/15/2010	10	Thomsen, Kevin		1200 · Accounts Receivable	125.00	
				Thomsen, Kevin	Check Returned by Bank	1100 · Checking		100.00
				Thomsen, Kevin	Bank and Other Charges for Retur...	4040 · Returned Check Service Charges		25.00
				State Board of Equalization	CA Sales Tax	2200 · Sales Tax Payable	0.00	
							125.00	125.00
76	Credit Memo	01/15/2010	11	Munoz, Francisco Dr.		1200 · Accounts Receivable		80.44
				Munoz, Francisco Dr.	Ski Poles	4012 · Equipment Sales	75.00	
				Munoz, Francisco Dr.	Ski Poles	1120 · Inventory Asset	30.00	
				Munoz, Francisco Dr.	Ski Poles	5000 · Cost of Goods Sold		30.00
				State Board of Equalization	CA Sales Tax	2200 · Sales Tax Payable	5.44	
							110.44	110.44
77	Check	01/15/2010	1	Munoz, Francisco Dr.		1100 · Checking		80.44
				Munoz, Francisco Dr.		1200 · Accounts Receivable	80.44	
							80.44	80.44
TOTAL							**34,635.38**	**34,635.38**

Partial Report

When the report is printed, close it. Do not close the Report Center

PRINT THE TRIAL BALANCE

When all sales transactions have been entered, it is important to print the trial balance and verify that the total debits equal the total credits.

▶ **DO** Click **Trial Balance** to select the type of report on the Accountant & Taxes section the Report Center

The report dates are from **01/01/2010** to **01/15/2010**

Your Name Mountain Sports
Trial Balance
As of January 15, 2010

	Jan 15, 10	
	Debit	Credit
1100 · Checking	36,232.00	
1200 · Accounts Receivable	5,690.62	
1120 · Inventory Asset	32,206.54	
12000 · Undeposited Funds	0.00	
1311 · Office Supplies	850.00	
1312 · Sales Supplies	575.00	
1340 · Prepaid Insurance	250.00	
1511 · Original Cost	5,000.00	
1521 · Original Cost	4,500.00	
2000 · Accounts Payable		8,500.00
2100 · Visa		150.00
2200 · Sales Tax Payable		613.15
2510 · Office Equipment Loan		3,000.00
2520 · Store Fixtures Loan		2,500.00
3000 · Retained Earnings	0.00	
3010 · Your Name & Muir Capital		25,459.44
3011 · Your Name, Investment		20,000.00
3012 · Larry Muir, Investment		20,000.00
4011 · Clothing & Accessory Sales		1,409.76
4012 · Equipment Sales		7,436.44
4040 · Returned Check Service Charges		25.00
5000 · Cost of Goods Sold	3,342.46	
6130 · Sales Discounts	447.17	
TOTAL	89,093.79	89,093.79

Print the Trial Balance in **Portrait** orientation
Close the report and the Report Center

CUSTOMER CENTER

In the Customer Center, you will see the customer list. As you click each customer, you will see the customer information and transaction details for the individual customer. You may also view transaction details for specific types of transactions by clicking the drop-down list arrow

DO ▶ View the Customer Center

Click the **Customer Center** button
View the information for Cash Customer

Click the drop-down list arrow next to **Show** to see the list of the types of transactions that may be displayed

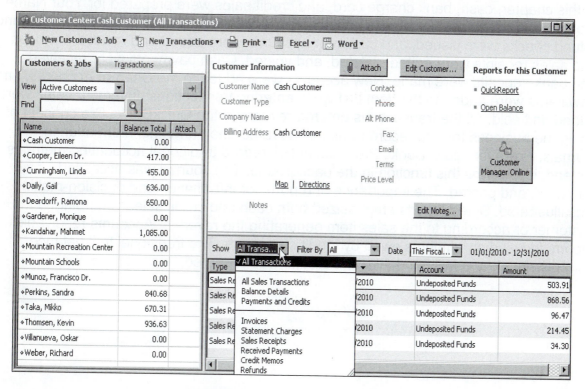

Close the Customer Center

BACK UP YOUR NAME MOUNTAIN SPORTS

Whenever an important work session is complete, you should always back up your data. If your data disk is damaged or an error is discovered at a later time, the backup disk may be restored and the information used for recording transactions. No matter what type of business, the backup procedure remains the same. In addition, it is always wise to make a duplicate of your data disk just in case the disk is damaged in some way.

▶ **DO** Follow the instructions given in Chapter 1 to back up data for Your Name Mountain Sports. If you wish to make a duplicate disk, follow the instructions provided by your professor.

SUMMARY

In this chapter, cash, bank charge card, and credit sales were prepared for Your Name Mountain Sports, a retail business, using sales receipts and invoices. Credit memos and refund checks were issued, and customer accounts were added and revised. Invoices and sales receipts were edited, deleted, and voided. Cash payments were received, and bank deposits were made. New accounts were added to the Chart of Accounts, and new items were added to the Item List while entering transactions. Inventory items were added and sold. All the transactions entered reinforced the QuickBooks Pro concept of using the business form to record transactions rather than entering information in journals. However, QuickBooks Pro does not disregard traditional accounting methods. Instead, it performs this function in the background. The Journal was accessed, analyzed, and printed. The importance of reports for information and decision-making was illustrated. Sales reports emphasized both cash and credit sales according to the customer or according to the sales item generating the revenue. Accounts receivable reports focused on amounts owed by credit customers. The traditional trial balance emphasizing the equality of debits and credits was prepared.

END-OF-CHAPTER QUESTIONS

TRUE/FALSE

ANSWER THE FOLLOWING QUESTIONS IN THE SPACE PROVIDED BEFORE THE QUESTION NUMBER.

_____ 1. If a return is made after an invoice has been paid in full, a refund check is issued along with a credit memo.

_____ 2. QuickBooks Pro automatically applies a payment received to the most current invoice.

_____ 3. Sales tax will be calculated automatically on an invoice if a customer is marked taxable.

_____ 4. A new sales item may be added only at the beginning of a period.

_____ 5. A new customer may be added *on the fly*.

_____ 6. Report formats may be customized.

_____ 7. The Discounts & Credits button on the Receive Payments window allows discounts to be applied to invoices being paid by clicking Cancel.

_____ 8. Cash sales are recorded in the Receive Payments window and marked paid.

_____ 9. If a customer issues a check that is returned marked NSF, you may charge the customer the amount of the bank charges and any penalty charges you impose.

_____ 10. Sales tax must be calculated manually and added to sales receipts.

MULTIPLE CHOICE

WRITE THE LETTER OF THE CORRECT ANSWER IN THE SPACE PROVIDED BEFORE THE QUESTION NUMBER.

_____ 1. Information regarding details of a customer's balance may be obtained by viewing __.
     A. the Trial Balance
     B. the Customer Balance Summary Report
     C. the Customer Balance Detail Report
     D. an invoice for the customer

_____ 2. Even though transactions are entered via business documents such as invoices and sales receipts, QuickBooks Pro keeps track of all transactions __.
     A. in a chart
     B. in the master account register
     C. on a graph
     D. in the Journal

_____ 3. If a transaction is __, it will not show up in the Customer Balance Detail Report.
     A. voided
     B. deleted
     C. corrected
     D. canceled

_____ 4. A credit card sale is treated exactly like a __.
     A. cash sale
     B. sale on account until reimbursement is received from a bank
     C. sale on account
     D. bank deposit

_____ 5. If the word -Split- appears in the Split column of a report rather than an account name, it means that the transaction is split between two or more __.
     A. accounts or items
     B. customers
     C. journals
     D. reports

_____ 6. When adding a customer *on the fly*, you may choose to add just the customer's name by selecting ___.
   A. Quick Add
   B. Set Up
   C. Condensed
   D. none of the above—a customer cannot be added *on the fly*

_____ 7. The Item List stores information about ___.
   A. each item that is out of stock
   B. each item in stock
   C. each customer with an account
   D. each item a company sells

_____ 8. A report prepared to obtain information about sales, inventory, and merchandise costs is a ___.
   A. Stock Report
   B. Income Statement
   C. Sales by Vendor Summary Report
   D. Sales by Item Summary Report

_____ 9. If a customer has a balance for an amount owed and a return is made, a credit memo is prepared and ___.
   A. a refund check is issued
   B. the amount of the return is applied to an invoice
   C. the customer determines whether to apply the amount to an invoice or to get a refund check
   D. all of the above

_____ 10. Purchase information regarding an item sold by the company is entered ___.
   A. in the Invoice Register
   B. when adding a sales item
   C. only when creating the company
   D. when the last item in stock is sold

FILL-IN

IN THE SPACE PROVIDED, WRITE THE ANSWER THAT MOST APPROPRIATELY COMPLETES THE SENTENCE.

1. A report showing all sales, credits, and payments for each customer on account but not the remaining balance on the account is the _____ report.

2. When a customer with a balance due on an account makes a payment, it is recorded in the _____ window.

3. If the Quantity and Price Each are entered on an invoice, pressing the _____ key will cause QuickBooks Pro to calculate and enter the correct information in the Amount column of the invoice.

4. QuickBooks Pro allows you to view additional information within a report by using the _____ feature.

5. When you receive payments from customers, QuickBooks Pro places the amount received in an account called _____.

SHORT ESSAY

Describe the use of Find to locate an invoice. Based on chapter information, what is used to instruct Find to limit its search?

_____

_____

_____

_____

_____

NAME _____

TRANSMITTAL

CHAPTER 5: YOUR NAME MOUNTAIN SPORTS

Attach the following documents and reports:

Invoice No. 1: Richard Weber
Invoice No. 2: Francisco Munoz
Invoice No. 3: Mountain Schools
Invoice No. 4: Sandra Perkins
Invoice No. 5: Kevin Thomsen
Invoice No. 6: Richard Weber
Invoice No. 7: Monique Gardener
Invoice No. 7 (Corrected): Monique Gardener
Customer Balance Detail
Invoice No. 3 (Corrected): Mountain Schools
Invoice No. 8: Mountain Recreation Center
Credit Memo No. 9: Monique Gardener
Open Invoices by Customer, January 10, 2010
Sales Receipt No. 1: Cash Customer
Sales Receipt No. 2: Cash Customer
Sales Receipt No. 3: Cash Customer
Sales Receipt No. 4: Cash Customer
Sales Receipt No. 5: Cash Customer
Sales Receipt No. 6: Cash Customer
Sales by Item Summary, January 1-13, 2010
Sales Receipt No. 1 (Revised):
    Cash Customer, January 8, 2010
Payment Receipt: Oskar Villanueva
Payment Receipt: Monique Gardener
Payment Receipt: Mountain Recreation Center
Payment Receipt: Richard Weber
Payment Receipt: Mountain Schools
Payment Receipt: Francisco Munoz
Payment Receipt: Gail Daily
Payment Receipt: Sandra Perkins
Payment Receipt: Kevin Thomsen
Customer Balance Summary
Deposit Summary

Invoice No. 10: Kevin Thomsen
Credit Memo No. 11: Francisco Munoz
Check No. 1: Francisco Munoz
Journal, January 1-15, 2010
Trial Balance, January 1-15, 2010

END-OF-CHAPTER PROBLEM

YOUR NAME RESORT CLOTHING

Your Name Resort Clothing is a men's and women's clothing store located in San Luis Obispo, California, that specializes in resort wear. The store is owned and operated by you and your partner Karen Olsen. Karen keeps the books and runs the office for the store, and you are responsible for buying merchandise and managing the store. Both partners sell merchandise in the store, and they have some college students working part time during the evenings and on the weekends.

INSTRUCTIONS

As in previous chapters, use a copy of **Clothing.qbw** that you made following the directions presented in Chapter 1. Open the company, and record the following transactions using invoices and sales receipts. Your Name Resort Clothing accepts cash, checks, and credit cards for *cash* sales. Make bank deposits as instructed. Print the reports as indicated. Add new accounts, items, and customers where appropriate. Pay attention to the dates and note that the year is **2010**. Verify the year to use with your instructor and use the same year for Clothing in Chapters 5, 6, and 7.

When recording transactions, use the Item List to determine the item(s) sold. All transactions are taxable unless otherwise indicated. Terms for sales on account are the standard terms assigned to each customer individually. If a customer exceeds his or her credit limit, accept the transaction. When receiving payment for sales on account, always check to see if a discount should be given. A customer's beginning balance is not eligible for a discount. The date of the sale begins the discount period. A check should be received or postmarked within ten days of the invoice in order to qualify for a discount. If the customer has any credits to the account because of a return, apply the credits to the appropriate invoice. If the customer makes a return and does not have a balance on account, prepare a refund check for the customer. Invoices begin with number 15, are numbered consecutively, and have lines printed around each field. Sales Receipts begin with number 25, are also numbered consecutively, and have lines printed around each field. Each invoice and sales receipt should contain a message. Use the one you feel is most appropriate.

If you write any checks, keep track of the check numbers used. QuickBooks Pro does not always display the check number you are expecting to see. Remember that QuickBooks Pro does not print check numbers on checks because most businesses use checks with the check numbers preprinted.

If a transaction can be printed, print the transaction when it is entered.

LISTS

The Item List and Customer List are displayed for your use in determining which sales item and customer to use in a transaction.

ITEM LIST

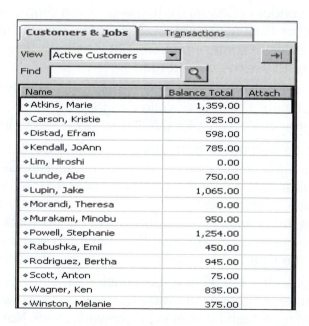

Name	Description	Type	Account	On Hand	Price	Attach
Access-Belts	Belts	Inventory Part	4010 · Sales:4013 · Accessories Sales	40	0.00	
Access-Shades	Sunglasses	Inventory Part	4010 · Sales:4013 · Accessories Sales	50	0.00	
Access-Ties	Ties and Scarves	Inventory Part	4010 · Sales:4013 · Accessories Sales	100	0.00	
Men-Pants	Men's Pants and Shorts	Inventory Part	4010 · Sales:4012 · Men's Clothing Sales	100	0.00	
Men-Shirts	Men's Shirts	Inventory Part	4010 · Sales:4012 · Men's Clothing Sales	100	0.00	
Men-Shoes	Men's Shoes	Inventory Part	4010 · Sales:4012 · Men's Clothing Sales	100	0.00	
Women-Pants	Women's Pants and Shorts	Inventory Part	4010 · Sales:4011 · Women's Clothing Sales	30	0.00	
Women-Shirts	Women's Shirts and Blouses	Inventory Part	4010 · Sales:4011 · Women's Clothing Sales	100	0.00	
Women-Shoes	Women's Shoes	Inventory Part	4010 · Sales:4011 · Women's Clothing Sales	100	0.00	
CA Sales Tax	CA Sales Tax	Sales Tax Item	2200 · Sales Tax Payable		7.25%	
Out of State	Out-of-state sale, exempt from sales tax	Sales Tax Item	2200 · Sales Tax Payable		0.0%	

CUSTOMER LIST

Name	Balance Total	Attach
Atkins, Marie	1,359.00	
Carson, Kristie	325.00	
Distad, Efram	598.00	
Kendall, JoAnn	785.00	
Lim, Hiroshi	0.00	
Lunde, Abe	750.00	
Lupin, Jake	1,065.00	
Morandi, Theresa	0.00	
Murakami, Minobu	950.00	
Powell, Stephanie	1,254.00	
Rabushka, Emil	450.00	
Rodriguez, Bertha	945.00	
Scott, Anton	75.00	
Wagner, Ken	835.00	
Winston, Melanie	375.00	

RECORD TRANSACTIONS

January 3, 2010:

▶ Add your name to the company name. The company name will be **Your Name Resort Clothing—** (Type your actual name, *not* the words *Your Name*.)

▶ Add your name to the owner's equity accounts. Replace "Student's Name" with your actual name in the capital, drawing, and investment accounts.

▶ Customize the Product Invoice, the Sales Receipt, and the Credit Memo so that there is enough room to display your name in full on the same line as the company name. Change the company preferences so that the date prepared, time prepared, and report basis do not print as part of the heading on reports. Have the reports refresh automatically.

▶ Prepare Invoice No. 15 to record the sale on account for 1 belt for $29.95, 1 pair of men's shorts for $39.95, and a man's shirt for $39.95 to Hiroshi Lim. Print the invoice.

▶ Received Check No. 3305 from Kristie Carson for $325 in payment of her account in full.

▶ Record the sale on account of 1 pair of sunglasses for $89.95 to Emil Rabushka. (Remember to approve any transaction that exceeds a customer's credit limit.)

▶ Record the sale of 1 dress on account to Stephanie Powell for $79.95. (Add a new sales item—Type: Inventory Part, Item Name: Women-Dress, Description: Women's Dresses, preferred vendor is Casual Clothes—click the drop-down arrow for Preferred Vendor, click Casual Clothes—, Tax Code: Tax, Income Account: 4011 Women's Clothing Sales, Reorder Point: 20, On Hand: 25, Total Value: $750, as of 01/01/2010—be sure to use the correct date.)

▶ Add a new customer: San Luis Obispo Rec Center, 451 Marsh Street, San Luis Obispo, CA 93407, Contact person is Katie Gregory, 805-555-2241, Credit Terms are 2% 10 Net 30, they are taxable for CA Sales Tax, Credit Limit $1,000.

▶ Sold 5 men's shirts on account to San Luis Obispo Rec Center for $29.95 each, 5 pair of men's shorts for $29.95 each. Because San Luis Rec Center is a nonprofit organization, include a subtotal for the sale and apply a 10% sales discount for a nonprofit organization. (Create any new sales items necessary by following the instructions given in the chapter. The nonprofit discount is marked Taxable so the discount is taken before adding sales tax. If you need to add an expense account for Sales Discounts to the Chart of Accounts, assign account number 6130.)

▶ Sold 1 woman's blouse for $59.95 to a cash customer, Julee Gardener. Record the sale to Cash Customer. (If necessary, refer to steps provided within the chapter for instructions on creating a cash customer.) Received Check No. 378 for the full amount including tax. Issue and print Sales Receipt No. 25 for this transaction.

▶ Received a belt returned by Ken Wagner. The original price of the belt was $49.95. Prepare a Credit Memo. Apply the credit to his Opening Balance.

▶ Sold a dress to a customer for $99.95. The customer paid with her Visa. Record the sale.

▶ Sold a scarf for $19.95 plus tax for cash. Record the sale.

▶ Received payments on account from the following customers:

- Efram Distad, $598.00, Check No. 145
- Melanie Winston, $375, Check No. 4015
- Abe Lunde, $750, Check No. 8915-02
- Ken Wagner, $781.43, Check No. 6726

January 5, 2010:
Deposit <u>all</u> cash, checks, and credit card receipts. Print a Deposit Summary.

January 15, 2010:
▶ Received an NSF notice from the bank for the check for $325 from Kristie Carson. Enter the necessary transaction for this nonsufficient funds check to be paid on receipt. The bank's charges are $15, and Your Name Resort Clothing charges $15 for all NSF checks. (If necessary, refer to steps provided within the chapter for instructions on adding accounts or items necessary to record this transaction.)

▶ Abe Lunde returned a shirt he had purchased for $54.99 plus tax. Record the return. Check the balance of his account. If there is no balance, issue a refund check.

▶ Sold 3 men's shirts to Ralph Richards, a cash customer, for $39.95 each plus tax. Ralph used his Master Card for payment.

▶ Sold on account 1 dress for $99.99, 1 pair of sandals for $79.95, and a belt for $39.95 to JoAnn Kendall.

▶ Sold 1 pair of women's shorts for $34.95 to a cash customer. Accepted Check No. 8160 for payment.

▶ Received payments on account from the following customers:

- Partial payment from Jake Lupin, $250, Check No. 2395.
- Payment in full from Anton Scott, Check No. 9802.
- Received $1,338.03 from Stephanie Powell as payment in full on account, Check No. 2311. The payment was postmarked 1/11/2010. (Because both the 12/31/2009 Invoice for $1,254 and Invoice No. 17 are being paid with this check, the payment will be applied to both invoices. In order to apply the discount to Invoice No. 17, click both the beginning balance and Invoice No. 17 to deselect; then click in the check mark column for Invoice No. 17; click the Discounts & Credits button; calculate the 2 percent discount and enter the amount on the Discounts and Credits screen, select the appropriate account for the sales discount, click Done to apply the discount; and, finally, click in the check mark column for the 12/31/2009 invoice.)

- ▶ Sold 3 pairs of men's pants for $75.00 each, 3 men's shirts for $50.00 each, 3 belts for $39.99 each, 2 pairs of men's shoes for $90.00 each, 2 ties for $55.00 each, and 1 pair of sunglasses for $75.00 to Bertha Rodriguez on account. (If the amount of the sale exceeds Bertha's credit limit, accept the sale anyway.)

- ▶ Sold on account 1 pair of sunglasses for $95.00, 2 dresses for $99.95 each, and 2 pairs of women's shoes for $65.00 each to Melanie Winston.

- ▶ Print Customer Balance Detail Report for All Transactions. Adjust column widths so the account names are shown in full and the report is one page wide without selecting Fit report to one page wide. The report length may be longer than one page.

- ▶ Print a Sales by Item Detail Report for 01/01/2010 to 01/15/2010 in Landscape orientation. Adjust column widths so the report fits on one page wide. Do not select Fit report to one page wide.

- ▶ Deposit <u>all</u> payments, checks, and charges received from customers. Print the Deposit Summary.

- ▶ Print a Journal for 01/01/2010 to 01/15/2010.

- ▶ Print a Trial Balance for 01/01/2010 to 01/15/2010.

- ▶ Backup your work.

NAME _____

TRANSMITTAL

CHAPTER 5: YOUR NAME RESORT CLOTHING

Attach the following documents and reports:

Invoice No. 15: Hiroshi Lim
Payment Receipt: Kristie Carson
Invoice No. 16: Emil Rabushka
Invoice No. 17: Stephanie Powell
Invoice No. 18: San Luis Obispo Rec Center
Sales Receipt No. 25: Cash Customer
Credit Memo No. 19: Ken Wagner
Sales Receipt No. 26: Cash Customer
Sales Receipt No. 27: Cash Customer
Payment Receipt: Efram Distad
Payment Receipt: Melanie Winston
Payment Receipt: Abe Lunde
Payment Receipt: Ken Wagner
Deposit Summary, January 5, 2010
Invoice No. 20: Kristie Carson
Credit Memo No. 21: Abe Lunde
Check No. 1: Abe Lunde
Sales Receipt No. 28: Cash Customer
Invoice No. 22: JoAnn Kendall
Sales Receipt No. 29: Cash Customer
Payment Receipt: Jake Lupin
Payment Receipt: Anton Scott
Payment Receipt: Stephanie Powell
Invoice No. 23: Bertha Rodriguez
Invoice No. 24: Melanie Winston
Customer Balance Detail
Sales by Item Detail Report, January 1-15, 2010
Deposit Summary, January 15, 2010
Journal, January 1-15, 2010
Trial Balance, January 1-15, 2010

PAYABLES AND PURCHASES: MERCHANDISING BUSINESS

LEARNING OBJECTIVES

At the completion of this chapter you will be able to:

1. Understand the concepts for computerized accounting for payables in a merchandising business.
2. Customize a Purchase Order template.
3. Prepare, view, and print purchase orders and checks.
4. Enter items received against purchase orders.
5. Enter bills, enter vendor credits, and pay bills.
6. Edit and correct errors in bills and purchase orders.
7. Add new vendors, modify vendor records, and add new accounts.
8. View accounts payable transaction history from the Enter Bills window.
9. View, use the QuickZoom feature, and/or print QuickReports for vendors, accounts payable register, and so on.
10. Record and edit transactions in the Accounts Payable Register.
11. Edit, void, and delete bills, purchase orders, and checks.
12. Use various payment options including writing checks, using Pay Bills to write checks, and company credit cards.
13. Display and print a Sales Tax Liability Report, an Accounts Payable Aging Summary Report, an Unpaid Bills Detail Report, and a Vendor Balance Summary Report.
14. Use the Vendor Detail Center to obtain information for an individual vendor.

ACCOUNTING FOR PAYABLES AND PURCHASES

In a merchandising business, much of the accounting for purchases and payables consists of ordering merchandise for resale and paying bills for expenses incurred in the operation of the business. Purchases are for things used in the operation of the business. Some transactions will be in the form of cash purchases; others will be purchases on account. Bills can be paid when they are received or when they are due. Merchandise received must be checked against purchase orders, and completed purchase orders must be closed. Rather than use cumbersome journals, QuickBooks Pro continues to focus on recording transactions based on the business document; therefore, you use the Enter Bills and Pay Bills features of the program to record the receipt and payment of bills. While QuickBooks Pro does not refer to it as such, the Vendor List is the same as the Accounts Payable Subsidiary Ledger.

QuickBooks Pro can remind you when inventory needs to be ordered and when payments are due. Purchase orders are prepared when ordering merchandise. The program automatically tracks inventory and uses the average cost method to value the inventory. QuickBooks Pro can calculate and apply discounts earned for paying bills early. Payments can be made by recording payments in the Pay Bills window or, if using the cash basis for accounting, by writing a check. Merchandise purchased may be paid for at the same time the items and the bill are received, or it may be paid for at a later date. A cash purchase can be recorded by writing a check, by using a credit card, or by using petty cash. Even though QuickBooks Pro focuses on recording transactions on the business forms used, all transactions are recorded behind the scenes in the Journal.

As in previous chapters, corrections can be made directly on the bill or within the account register. New accounts and vendors may be added *on the fly* as transactions are entered. Purchase orders, bills, or checks may be voided or deleted. Reports illustrating vendor balances, unpaid bills, accounts payable aging, sales tax liability, transaction history, and accounts payable registers may be viewed and printed.

TRAINING TUTORIAL AND PROCEDURES

The following tutorial will once again work with Your Name Mountain Sports. As in Chapter 5, transactions will be recorded for this fictitious company. Refer to procedures given in Chapter 5 to maximize training benefits. You will use the company file for Your Name Mountain Sports that contains your transactions for Chapter 5. As with the earlier training in a service company, the merchandising section of the text has you enter the transactions for all three chapters—5, 6, and 7—within the same company file.

OPEN QUICKBOOKS® PRO AND YOUR NAME MOUNTAIN SPORTS

DO▶Open QuickBooks Pro and Your Name Mountain Sports as instructed in previous chapters

DATES

Throughout the text, the year used for the screen shots is 2010, which is the same year as the version of the program. You may want to check with your instructor to see if you should use 2010 as the year for the transactions. The year you used in Chapter 5 should be the same year you use in Chapters 6 and 7.

BEGINNING THE TUTORIAL

In this chapter you will be entering purchases of merchandise for resale in the business and entering bills incurred by the company in the operation of the business. You will also be recording the payment of bills and purchases using checks and credit cards.

The Vendor List keeps information regarding the vendors with which you do business. This information includes the vendor names, addresses, telephone number, fax number, e-mail address, payment terms, credit limits, and account numbers. You will be using the following list for vendors with which Your Name Mountain Sports has an account:

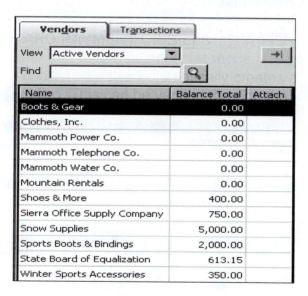

As in previous chapters, all transactions are listed on memos. The transaction date will be the same date as the memo date unless otherwise specified within the transaction. Vendor names, when necessary, will be given in the transaction. Unless otherwise specified, terms are 2% 10 Net 30. Once a specific type of transaction has been entered in a step-by-step manner, additional transactions of the same or a similar type will be made without having instructions provided. Of course, you may always refer to instructions given for previous transactions for ideas or for steps used to enter those transactions. To determine the account used in the transaction, refer to the Chart of

Accounts. When you enter account information on a bill, clicking the drop-down list arrow will show a copy of the Chart of Accounts.

VIEW THE REMINDERS LIST TO DETERMINE MERCHANDISE TO ORDER

QuickBooks Pro has a Reminders List that is used to remind you of things that need to be completed. The Company menu allows you to display the Reminders List. Information on the Reminders List may be displayed in summary (collapsed) form or in detailed (expanded) form. The information displayed is affected by the date of the computer; so, what you see on your screen may not match the text display.

MEMO
DATE: January 16, 2010

Display the Reminders List to determine which items need to be ordered.

DO Display the **Reminders List**

Click **Company** on the Menu bar, click **Reminders**
• The Reminders List appears on the screen in Summary form.

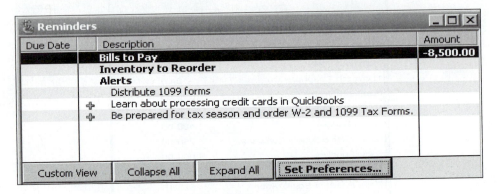

To view the list, click the **Expand All** button
• Note: Your Reminders List Summary (Collapsed) form and Reminders List Detail (Expanded) form may not match the ones displayed in the text. This is due to the fact that your computer date may be different from the date used in the chapter. Disregard any differences.
• The expanded view shows the bills that need to be paid as well as overdue invoices, inventory to reorder, any items that need to be printed, and alerts.

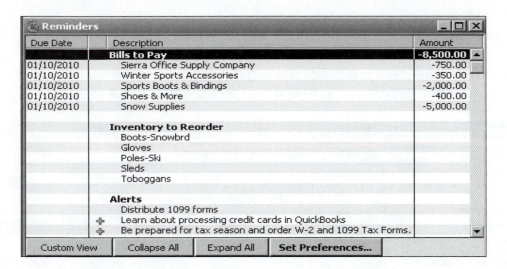

Close the Reminders List

PURCHASE ORDERS

Using the QuickBooks Pro Purchase Order feature helps you track your inventory. Information regarding the items on order or the items received may be obtained at any time. Once merchandise has been received, QuickBooks Pro marks the purchase order *Received in full*. The Purchase Order feature must be selected as a Preference when setting up the company, or it may be selected prior to processing your first purchase order. QuickBooks Pro will automatically set up an account called Purchase Orders in the Chart of Accounts. The account does not affect the balance sheet or the profit and loss statement of the company. As with other business forms, QuickBooks Pro allows you to customize your purchase orders to fit the needs of your individual company or to use the purchase order format that comes with the program.

VERIFY PURCHASE ORDERS ACTIVE AS A COMPANY PREFERENCE

Verify that the Purchase Order feature of QuickBooks Pro is active by checking the Company Preferences.

> **MEMO**
> **DATE:** January 16, 2010
>
> Prior to completing the first purchase order, verify that Purchase Orders are active.

▶ DO ▶ Verify that Purchase Orders are active by accessing the Company Preferences

Click **Edit** menu, click **Preferences**

Click **Items & Inventory** on the Preferences List, click the **Company Preferences** tab

- Make sure there is a check mark in the check box for **Inventory and purchase orders are active**. If not, click the check box to select.

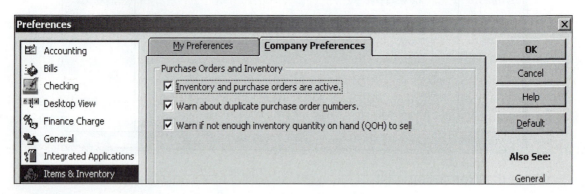

Click **OK** to accept and close

CUSTOMIZE PURCHASE ORDERS

As instructed in Chapter 5, business forms may be customized. Prior to recording your first purchase order, it should be customized.

DO Customize a Purchase Order

Click the **Purchase Orders** icon in the **Vendors** section of the Home Page

Click the drop-down list arrow for **Customize**, click **Custom Design and Layout...**

Click the **Customize Data Layout** button

On the Additional Customization screen, click the **Layout Designer** button

Change the size for **Purchase Order** to begin at **5**

Point to the black squares (sizing handles) on the frame around the words **Purchase Order**

When the cursor turns into a double arrow, hold the primary (left) mouse button and drag until the size of the frame begins at **5** on the ruler bar

- For additional information and visual references, refer to Chapter 5.

Expand the area for **Your Name Mountain Sports** to **4 ¾**

Click **OK** to close the Layout Designer

Click **OK** to close the Additional Customization screen

Do not close the Purchase Order

PREPARE PURCHASE ORDERS TO ORDER MERCHANDISE

Once the Purchase Order feature is selected, purchase orders may be prepared. Primarily, purchase orders are prepared to order merchandise; but they may also be used to order non-inventory items like supplies or services.

MEMO
DATE: January 16, 2010

With only 10 pairs of snowboard boots in stock in the middle of January an additional 25 pairs of boots in assorted sizes need to be ordered from Boots & Gear for $75 per pair. Prepare Purchase Order No. 1.

DO Prepare Purchase Order No. 1 for 25 pairs of snowboard boots

Purchase Order 1 should be on the screen
- If not, click the **Purchases Order** icon on the Home Page
Click the drop-down list arrow for **Vendor**, click **Boots & Gear**
The Template should be Custom Purchase Order, select if necessary
Tab to or click **Date**, enter **01/16/2010**
- P.O. No. should be 1. If not, enter 1 as the P.O. No.
Tab to or click **Item**, click **Boots-Snowbrd**
Tab to or click **Qty**, enter **25**
- The cost of the item was entered when Boots-Snowbrd was created. The Rate should appear automatically as **75.00**
Tab to generate Amount

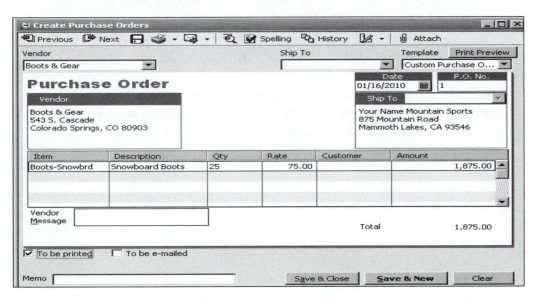

Click **Print** to print the **Purchase Order**
- If you get a message regarding shipping labels, click **OK**

Check printer settings:
- Make sure the appropriate printer is selected.
- **Printer type** is Page-oriented (Single sheets).
- **Print on** Blank paper.
- Print lines around each field.

Click **Print**

After printing, click **Next** or **Save & New** to go to the next purchase order

PREPARE A PURCHASE ORDER FOR MORE THAN ONE ITEM

If more than one item is purchased from a vendor, all items purchased can be included on the same purchase order.

MEMO

DATE: January 16, 2010

Prepare a purchase order for 3 sleds @ $50 each, and 2 toboggans @ $110 each from a new vendor: Snow Gear, 7105 Camino del Rio, Durango, CO 81302, Contact: Leo Jenkins, Phone: 303-555-7765, Fax: 303-555-5677, E-mail: SnowGear@ski.com, Terms: 2% 10 Net 30, Credit Limit: $2000.

DO Prepare a purchase order and add a new vendor

Click the drop-down list arrow for **Vendor**, click **< Add New >**
Enter **Snow Gear** for the **Vendor** name and the **Company** name
Click the second line of the address, enter **7105 Camino del Rio**
Click the third line of the address, enter **Durango, CO 81302**
Click Address Details
- Verify that **Show this window again when address is incomplete or unclear** has a check mark. This means that the **Edit Address Information** window will appear if the address is incomplete or unclear.

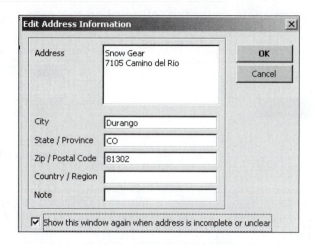

Click **OK**

Tab to or click **Contact**, enter **Leo Jenkins**

Tab to or click **Phone**, enter **303-555-7765**

Tab to or click **FAX**, enter **303-555-5677**

Tab to or click **E-mail**, enter **SnowGear@ski.com**

Click **Additional Info** tab, click the drop-down list arrow for **Terms**, and click **2% 10 Net 30**

Tab to or click **Credit Limit**, enter **2000**

Click **OK** to add Vendor

- The **Date** should be **01/16/2010**. If it is not, delete the date shown and enter **01/16/10**.
- P.O. No. should be **2**. If it is not, enter **2**.

Tab to or click the first line in the column for **Item**

Click the drop-down list arrow for **Item**, click **Sleds**

Tab to or click **Qty**, enter **3**

Tab to or click **Rate**, enter **50**

- The purchase cost was not entered when the item was created, so it must be entered on the purchase order as the Rate.

Tab to generate the total for **Amount**

- If you get a message about the change an of item cost, click **No**

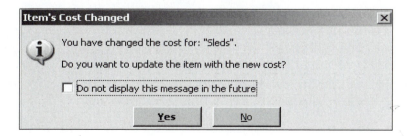

Repeat steps necessary to enter the information to order 2 toboggans at $110 each

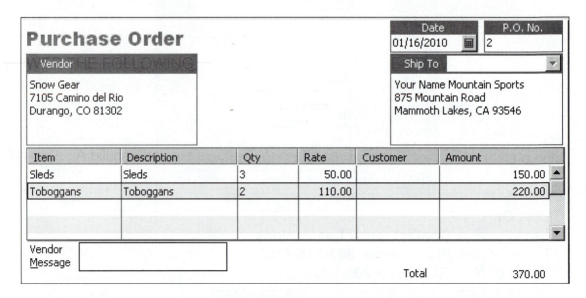

| Purchase Order | | | | Date | 01/16/2010 | P.O. No. | 2 |

Purchase Order

Date: 01/16/2010 P.O. No. 2

Ship To

Vendor
Snow Gear
7105 Camino del Rio
Durango, CO 81302

Your Name Mountain Sports
875 Mountain Road
Mammoth Lakes, CA 93546

Item	Description	Qty	Rate	Customer	Amount
Sleds	Sleds	3	50.00		150.00
Toboggans	Toboggans	2	110.00		220.00

Vendor Message

Total 370.00

Print **Purchase Order No. 2**
Click **Next** to save **Purchase Order No. 2** and go to the next purchase order

ENTER PURCHASE ORDERS WITHOUT STEP-BY-STEP INSTRUCTIONS

MEMO
DATE: January 16, 2010

Prepare purchase orders for the following:
25 pairs of gloves @ 15.00 each from Clothes, Inc.
12 sets of ski poles @ 30.00 each from Snow Supplies.

 Prepare and print the purchase orders indicated above.

Compare your completed purchase orders with the ones below:

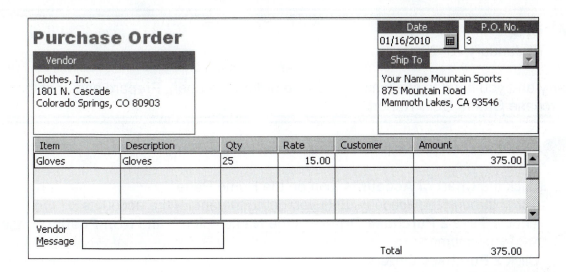

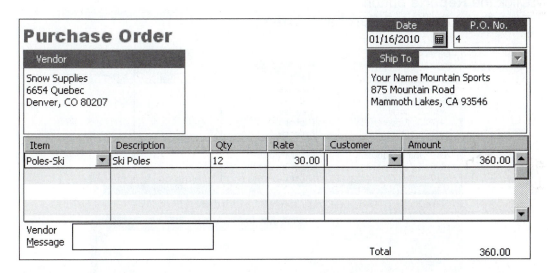

Save and **Close** after entering Purchase Order No. 4

PREPARE AND PRINT A PURCHASE ORDERS QUICKREPORT

To see a list of purchase orders that have been prepared, open the Chart of Accounts, select Purchase Orders, click the Reports button, and choose QuickReport from the menu shown.

MEMO

DATE: January 16, 2010

Larry and you need to see which purchase orders are open. Prepare and print the Purchase Orders QuickReport.

▶ **DO** View the open purchase orders for Your Name Mountain Sports

Click the **Chart of Accounts** icon on the Home Page
Scroll through the accounts until you get to the end of the accounts
Your will see **2 Purchase Orders** in the Name column and **Non-Posting** in the Type column
Click **2 Purchase Orders**
Click the **Reports** button
Click **QuickReport: 2 Purchase Orders**

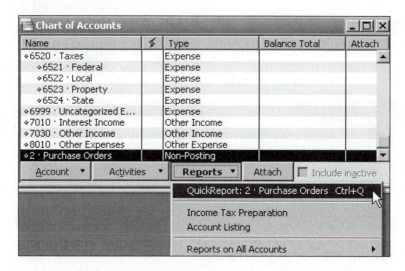

- The list shows all open purchase orders, the date of the purchase order, the number of the purchase order, and the amount of the purchase order.

The dates are from **01/01/10** to **01/16/10**
Tab to generate the report
Resize the columns as previously instructed to:
    Be able to view the account name in full in the **Split** column
    Be able to print in Portrait orientation on one page without using Fit to one page wide
Click **Print** to print the report

Your Name Mountain Sports
Account QuickReport
As of January 16, 2010

Type	Date	Num	Name	Memo	Split	Amount
2 · Purchase Orders						
Purchase Order	01/16/2010	1	Boots & Gear		1120 · Inventory Asset	-1,875.00 ◄
Purchase Order	01/16/2010	2	Snow Gear		-SPLIT-	-370.00
Purchase Order	01/16/2010	3	Clothes, Inc.		1120 · Inventory Asset	-375.00
Purchase Order	01/16/2010	4	Snow Supplies		1120 · Inventory Asset	-360.00
Total 2 · Purchase Orders						-2,980.00
TOTAL						**-2,980.00**

Close the **Purchase Order QuickReport** and the **Chart of Accounts**

CHANGE MINIMUM REORDER LIMITS FOR AN ITEM

Any time that you determine your reorder limits are too low or too high, you can change the Reorder Point by editing the Item in the Item List.

MEMO
DATE: January 16, 2010

View the Item List to see the amount on hand for each item. In viewing the list, Larry and you determine that you should have a minimum of 35 sets of long underwear on hand at all times. Currently, there are 32 sets of long underwear in stock. Change the reorder point for long underwear to 35.

▶ **DO** View the **Item List**

Click the **Items & Services** icon on the QuickBooks Home Page
Scroll through Item List, double-click **Underwear**
- If you get the Add/Edit Multiple Entries screen, click **OK**.
Click in **Reorder Point**
Change 30 to **35**

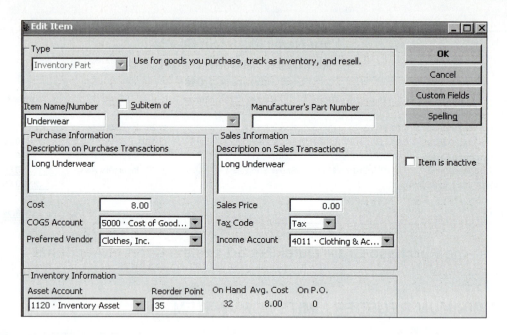

Click **OK** to save and exit
Close the **Item List**

VIEW EFFECT OF REORDER POINT ON REMINDERS LIST

Once the reorder point has been changed and the quantity on hand is equal to or falls below the new minimum, the item will be added to the Reminders List so you will be reminded to order it.

MEMO
DATE: January 16, 2010

Look at the Reminders List to see what items need to be ordered.

DO Look at the **Reminders List**

Open **Reminders** as previously instructed
Expand the list
• The items shown previously on the Reminders List (Snowboard Boots, Gloves, Ski Poles, Sleds, and Toboggans) are no longer present because they have been ordered. Underwear appears because the reorder point has been changed.

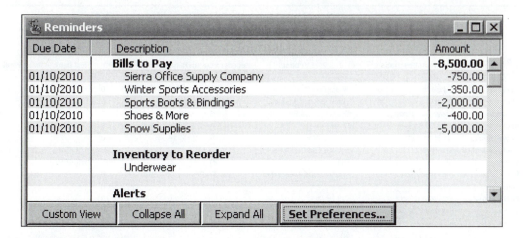

Close **Reminders**

VIEW INVENTORY STOCK STATUS BY ITEM REPORT

Several Inventory Reports are available for viewing and/or printing. One report is the Inventory Stock Status by Item report. This report provides information regarding the stock on hand, the stock on order, and the stock that needs to be reordered.

MEMO
DATE: January 16, 2010

More detailed information regarding the stock on hand, stock ordered, and stock needing to be ordered needs to be provided. View the report for Inventory Stock Status by Item.

DO View the **Inventory Stock Status by Item Report**

Click the **Reports** menu, point to **Inventory**, click **Inventory Stock Status by Item**
The dates are From **01/01/10** to **01/16/10**
Tab to generate the report

Your Name Mountain Sports
Inventory Stock Status by Item
January 1 - 16, 2010

	Item Description	Pref Vendor	Reorder Pt	On Hand	Order	On PO	Next Deliv	Sales/Week
Inventory								
Accessories	▶ Sunglasses Ski Wax Suns...	Winter Sports Accessories	100	795		0		2.2 ◀
Bindings-Skis	Ski Bindings	Sports Boots & Bindings	10	43		0		3.1
Bindings-Snow	Snowboard Bindings	Sports Boots & Bindings	5	48		0		0.9
Boots	After Ski Boots and Shoes	Shoes & More	10	20		0		0
Boots-Ski	Ski Boots	Boots & Gear	10	14		0		0.4
Boots-Snowbrd	Snowboard Boots	Boots & Gear	10	10		25	01/16/2010	0.9
Gloves	Gloves	Clothes, Inc.	20	20		25	01/16/2010	0.9
Hats	Hats and Scarves	Winter Sports Accessories	20	29		0		0.4
Pants-Ski	Ski Pants	Clothes, Inc.	10	93		0		0.9
Pants-Snowbrd	Snowboard Pants	Clothes, Inc.	10	50		0		0
Parkas	Parkas and Jackets	Clothes, Inc.	25	73		0		0.9
Poles-Ski	Ski Poles	Snow Supplies	15	13		12	01/16/2010	2.2
Skis	Snow Skis	Snow Supplies	15	43		0		3.1
Sleds	Sleds		5	4		3	01/16/2010	2.6
Snowboard	Snowboard	Snow Supplies	15	28		0		0.9
Socks	Ski and Snowboard Socks	Boots & Gear	25	72		0		1.3
Sweaters	Sweaters & Shirts	Clothes, Inc.	25	73		0		0.9
Toboggans	Toboggans		5	5		2	01/16/2010	2.2
Underwear	Long Underwear	Clothes, Inc.	35	32	✓	0		0.4

Scroll through the report
- Notice the items in stock.
- Notice the reorder point for items.
- Find the items marked as needing to be ordered. They are marked with a √.
- Notice the Next Deliv dates of the items that have been ordered.

Close the report without printing

RECEIVING ITEMS ORDERED

The form used to record the receipt of items in QuickBooks Pro depends on the way in which the ordered items are received. Items received may be recorded in three ways. If the items are received without a bill and you pay later, record the receipt on an item receipt. If the items are received at the same time as the bill, record the item receipt on a bill. If the items are received and paid for at the same time, record the receipt of items on a check or a credit card.

RECORD RECEIPT OF ITEMS NOT ACCOMPANIED BY A BILL

The ability to record inventory items prior to the arrival of the bill keeps quantities on hand, quantities on order, and the inventory up to date. Items ordered on a purchase order that arrive before the bill is received are recorded on an item receipt. When the bill arrives, it is recorded.

MEMO
DATE: January 18, 2010

The sleds and toboggans ordered from Snow Gear arrive without a bill. Record the receipt of the 3 sleds and 2 toboggans.

DO ▶ Record the receipt of the items above

Click the **Receive Inventory** icon on the Home Page
Click **Receive Inventory without Bill**
Click the drop-down list arrow for **Vendor**, click **Snow Gear**

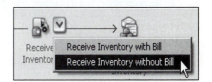

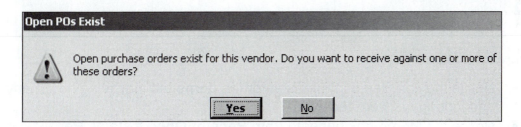

Click **Yes** on the **Open PO's Exist** message box
- An **Open Purchase Orders** dialog box appears showing all open purchase orders for the vendor, Snow Gear
Point to any part of the line for P.O. No. 2
Click to select **Purchase Order No. 2**
- This will place a check mark in the check mark column.

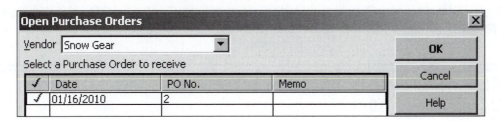

Click **OK**
Change the date to **01/18/2010**.

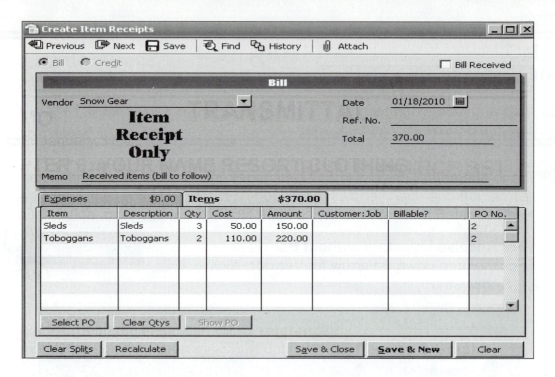

- Notice the completed information for the **Items** tab indicating how many sleds and toboggans were received.
- Notice the **Memo** box beneath **Item Receipt Only**. It states *Received items (bill to follow)*.

Click **Save & Close**

VERIFY THAT PURCHASE ORDER IS MARKED RECEIVED IN FULL

As each line on a Purchase Order is received in full, QuickBooks Pro marks it as *Clsd*. When all the items on the Purchase Order are marked *Clsd*, QuickBooks stamps the P.O. as *Received in Full*.

MEMO

DATE: January 18, 2010

View the original Purchase Order No. 2 to verify that it has been stamped Received in Full and each item received is marked Clsd.

▶ DO ▶ Verify that Purchase Order No. 2 is marked Received in Full and all items received are Closed

Access Purchase Orders as previously instructed
Click **Previous** until you get to **Purchase Order No. 2**
- Next to the **Amount** column, you will see two new columns: **Rcv'd** and **Clsd**.
  - **Rcv'd** indicates the number of the items received.
  - **Clsd** indicates that the number of items ordered was received in full so the Purchase Order has been closed for that Item
- With all the items order marked as **Clsd t**he Purchase Order is stamped **RECEIVED IN FULL**.

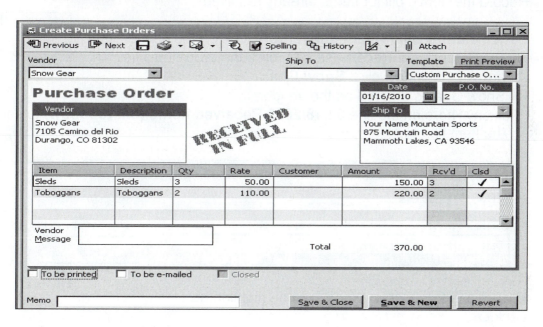

Close **Create Purchase Orders** window

ENTER RECEIPT OF A BILL FOR ITEMS ALREADY RECEIVED

For items that have been received prior to the bill, the receipt of items is recorded as soon as the items arrive. When the bill is received, it must be recorded. To do this, indicate that the bill is entered against Inventory. When completing a bill for items already received, QuickBooks Pro fills in all essential information on the bill. A bill is divided into two sections: a vendor-related section (the upper part of the bill that looks similar to a check and has a memo text box under it) and a detail section (the area that has two tabs marked Items and Expenses). The vendor-related section of the bill is where information for the actual bill is entered, including a memo with information about the transaction. The detail section is where the information regarding the items ordered, the quantity ordered and received, and the amounts due for the items received is indicated.

MEMO
DATE: January 19, 2010

Record the bill for the sleds and toboggans already received from Snow Gear,
Vendor's Invoice No. 97 dated 01/18/2010, Terms 2% 10 Net 30.

DO ▶ Record the above bill for items already received

Click the **Enter Bills Against Inventory** icon on the Home Page
On the **Select Item Receipt** screen, click the drop-down list
    arrow for **Vendor**, click **Snow Gear**

- Snow Gear is entered as the vendor.

DO ▶ Click anywhere on the line **01/18/2010 Received items (bill to follow)** to select
    the Item Receipt

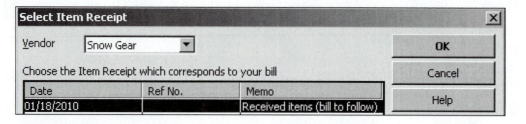

- The line for the item receipt will be highlighted.

Click **OK**

- QuickBooks Pro displays the **Enter Bills** screen and the completed bill for
  Snow Gear
- The date shown is the date of the Vendor's bill **01/18/2010**.

Tab to or click **Ref No.**, type the vendor's invoice number **97**

- Notice that the **Amount Due** of **370** has been inserted.
- Terms of **2% 10 Net 30** and the Discount Date and the Due Date are shown.

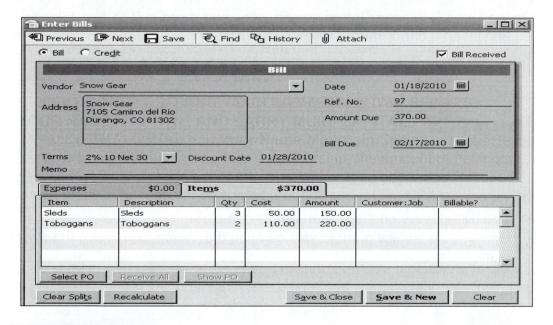

Click **Save & Close**
- If you get a Recording Transaction message box regarding the fact that the transaction has been changed, click **Yes**.

RECORD RECEIPT OF ITEMS AND A BILL

When ordered items are received and accompanied by a bill, the receipt of the items is recorded while entering the bill.

MEMO

DATE: January 19, 2010

Received 25 pairs of snowboard boots and a bill from Boots & Gear. Record the bill dated 01/18/2010 and the receipt of the items.

▶ DO ▶ Record the receipt of the items and the bill

Click **Receive Inventory** icon on the QuickBooks Home Page
Click **Receive Inventory with Bill**
Click the drop-down list for **Vendor**, click **Boots & Gear**
Click **Yes** on the **Open PO's Exist** message box

On the Open Purchase Orders screen, click anywhere in P.O. No. 1 line to select and insert a check mark in the √ column

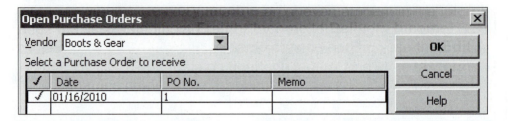

Click **OK**
- The bill appears on the screen and is complete.
- Because no invoice number was given in the transaction, leave the **Ref. No.** blank.

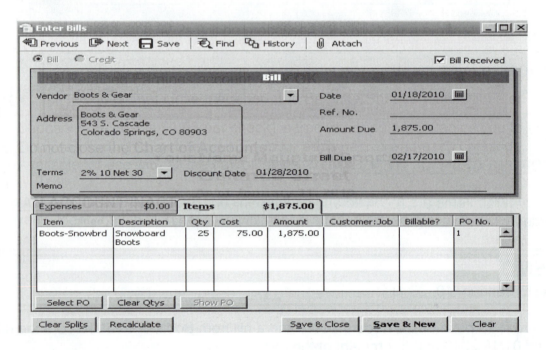

Click **Save & Close**

EDIT A PURCHASE ORDER

As with any other form, purchase orders may be edited once they have been prepared. Purchase orders may be accessed by clicking on the Purchase Order icon on the QuickBooks Home Page.

> **MEMO**
> **DATE:** January 19, 2010
>
> Ruth realized that Purchase Order No. 4 should be for 15 pairs of ski poles. Change the purchase order and reprint.

▶ **DO** Change Purchase Order No. 4

> Access Purchase Order No. 4 as previously instructed
> Click in **Qty**; change the number from 12 to **15**
> Tab to recalculate the amount due for the purchase order

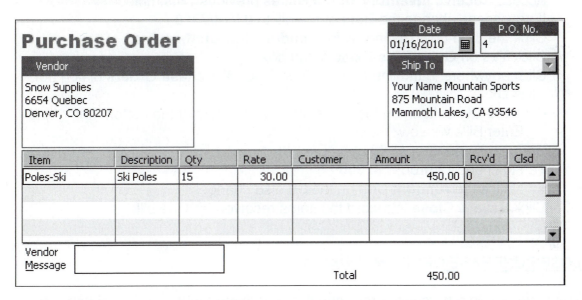

- Notice the columns for Rcv'd and Clsd. Those are included on the Purchase Order once it is saved.

Print the **Purchase Order** as previously instructed
Click **Save & Close** to record the changes and exit
Click **Yes** on the **Recording Transaction** dialog box to save the changes

RECORD A PARTIAL RECEIPT OF MERCHANDISE ORDERED

Sometimes when items on order are received, they are not received in full. The remaining items may be delivered as back-ordered items. This will usually occur if an item is out of stock, and you must wait for delivery until more items are manufactured and/or received by the vendor. With QuickBooks Pro you record the number of items you actually receive, and the bill is recorded for that amount.

MEMO

DATE: January 19, 2010

Record the bill and the receipt of 20 pairs of gloves ordered on Purchase Order No. 3. On the purchase order, 25 pairs of gloves were ordered. Clothes, Inc. will no longer be carrying these gloves, so the remaining 5 pairs of gloves on order will not be shipped. Manually close the purchase order. The date of the bill is 01/18/2010.

▶ **DO** ▶ Record the receipt of and the bill for 20 pairs of gloves from Clothes, Inc.

> Access **Receive Inventory with a Bill** as previously instructed
> If necessary, change the **Date** of the bill to **01/18/2010**
> Click the drop-down list arrow for **Vendor**, click **Clothes, Inc.**
> Click **Yes** on **Open PO's Exist** dialog box
> Click anywhere in the line for **P.O. 3** on **Open Purchase Orders** dialog box
> Click **OK**
> Click the **Qty** column on the Items tab in the middle of the bottom half of the Enter Bills window
> Change the quantity to **20**
> Tab to change **Amount** to **300**
> • Notice the **Amount Due** on the bill also changes.
> Click **Save & Close** to record the items received and the bill

CLOSE PURCHASE ORDER MANUALLY

If you have issued a purchase order and it is determined that you will not be receiving the items on order, a purchase order can be closed manually.

▶ **DO** ▶ Close Purchase Order No. 3 using **Find** to locate Purchase Order No. 3

> Click **Find** on the Edit menu, click the **Advanced Find** tab
> Scroll through **Choose Filter**
> • Filter helps to narrow the search for locating something.
> Click **Transaction Type**, click the drop-down list arrow for **Transaction Type**, click **Purchase Order**
> Click **Find**
> • A list of all purchase orders shows on the screen.

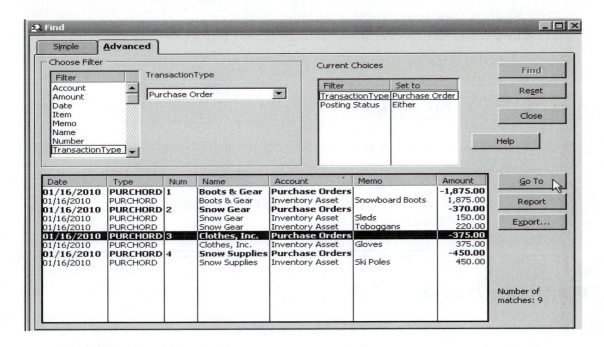

Click **Purchase Order No. 3** for **Clothes, Inc**.
Click **Go To**
P.O. 3 will show on the screen
Click the **Clsd** column for Gloves to mark and close the purchase order
- Notice that the ordered **Qty** is 25 and **Rcv'd** is 20.
- Notice the check mark in the Closed box at the bottom of the Purchase Order and the Purchase Order is stamped Closed.

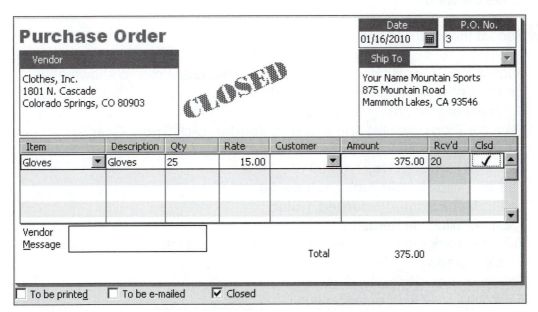

Click **Save & Close** to close the purchase order
Click **Yes** on the Recording Transactions dialog box
Close **Find**

ENTER A CREDIT FROM A VENDOR

Credit memos are prepared to record a reduction to a transaction. With QuickBooks Pro you use the Enter Bills window to record credit memos received from vendors acknowledging a return of items purchased or an allowance for a previously recorded bill and/or payment. The amount of a credit memo can be applied to the amount owed to a vendor when paying bills.

MEMO
DATE: January 21, 2010

Upon further inspection of merchandise received, Ruth Morgan found that one of the sleds received from Snow Gear, was cracked. The sled was returned. Received Credit Memo No. 9912 from Snow Gear for $50 (the full amount on the return of 1 sled).

Check the **Item List** to verify how many sleds are currently on hand

Access **Item List** as previously instructed
- Look at Sleds to verify that there are 7 sleds in stock.
Close the **Item List**

Record the return of one sled

Access the **Enter Bills** window and record the credit memo shown above
On the **Enter Bills** screen, click **Credit** to select
- The word *Bill* changes to *Credit*.
Click the drop-down list arrow next to **Vendor**, click **Snow Gear**
Tab to or click the **Date**, enter **01/21/10**
Tab to or click **Ref. No.**, type **9912**
Tab to or click **Credit Amount**, type **50**
Tab to **Memo**, enter **Returned 1 Sled**
Tab to or click the **Items** tab
Tab to or click the first line in the **Item** column, click the drop-down list arrow, click **Sleds**
Tab to or click **Qty**, enter **1**
Tab to or click **Cost**, enter **50**
Tab to enter the **50** for **Amount**

Click **No** on the Item Cost Changed message

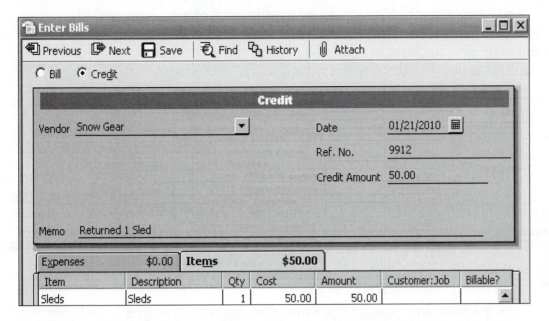

Click **Save & Close** to record the credit and exit the **Enter Bills** window
* QuickBooks Pro decreases the quantity of sleds on hand and creates a credit with the vendor that can be applied when paying the bill. The Credit Memo also appears in the Accounts Payable account in the **Paid** column, which decreases the amount owed and shows the transaction type as BILLCRED in the Accounts Payable register.

DO Verify that there are 6 sleds in stock after the return.

Access the **Item List**
Verify the number of sleds and then close the list

DO View the return in the Accounts Payable register

Access the **Chart of Accounts** as previously instructed
Double-click **Accounts Payable** to open the Register
Scroll through the register until you see the BILLCRED for Snow Gear

01/21/2010	9912	Snow Gear				50.00	10,995.00
	BILLCRED	1120 · Inv Returned					

Close the **Accounts Payable Register** and the **Chart of Accounts**

MAKE A PURCHASE USING A CREDIT CARD

Some businesses use credit cards as an integral part of their finances. Many companies have a credit card used primarily for gasoline purchases for company vehicles. Other companies use credit cards as a means of paying for expenses or purchasing merchandise or other necessary items for use in the business.

MEMO

DATE: January 21, 2010

Ruth discovered that she was out of paper. She purchased a box of paper to have on hand to be used for copies, for the laser printer, and for the fax machine from Sierra Office Supply Company for $21.98. Rather than add to the existing balance owed to the company, Ruth pays for the office supplies using the company's Visa card.

DO ▶ Purchase the above office supplies using the company's Visa card

Click the **Banking** menu, click **Enter Credit Card Charges**
Credit Card should indicate **2100 Visa**
Click the drop-down list arrow for **Purchased From**, click **Sierra Office Supply Company**
Click **OK** on the **Warning** screen

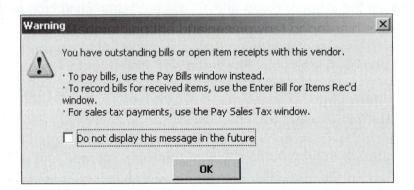

Date should be **01/21/2010**
Ref No. is blank
Tab to or click **AMOUNT**, enter **21.98**
Tab to or click **Memo**, enter **Purchase Paper**
Tab to or click the **Account** column on the **Expenses** tab, click the drop-down list arrow for **Account**, click **1311 Office Supplies**
• This transaction is for supplies to have on hand, so the asset Office Supplies is used.

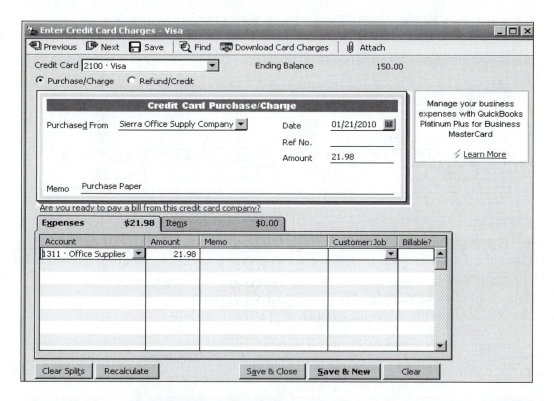

Click **Next** or **Save & New** to record the charge and go to the next credit card entry

PAY FOR INVENTORY ITEMS ON ORDER USING A CREDIT CARD

It is possible to pay for inventory items using a credit card. The payment may be made using the Pay Bills window, or it may be made by recording an entry for Credit Card Charges. If you are purchasing something that is on order, you may record the receipt of merchandise on order first, or you may record the receipt of merchandise and the credit card payment at the same time.

MEMO

DATE: January 21, 2010

Note from You: Ruth, record the receipt of 10 ski poles from Snow Supplies. Pay for the ski poles using the company's Visa credit card.

▶ **DO** Pay for the ski poles received using the company's Visa credit card

Click the drop-down list for **Purchased From** click **Snow Supplies**

Click the **Yes** button on the **Open PO's Exist** message box
To select P.O. No. 4, click the line containing information regarding P.O. No. 4 on the **Open Purchase Orders** dialog box

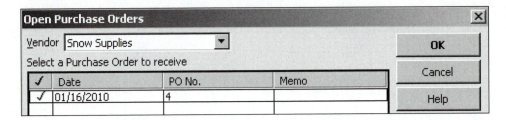

Click **OK**
- If you get a warning screen regarding outstanding bills, click **OK**.

Click the **Clear Qtys** button on the bottom of the screen to clear 15 from the Qty column
Tab to or click **Qty**, enter **10**
Tab to change the Amount to 300

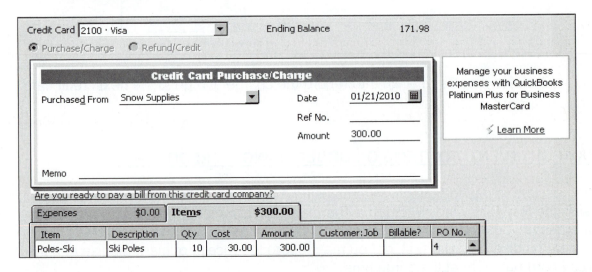

Click **Save & Close** to record and close the transaction

CONFIRM THE RECORDING OF THE SKI POLES RECEIVED ON PURCHASE ORDER NO. 4

MEMO

DATE: January 21, 2010

View Purchase Order No. 4 to determine whether or not the amount of ski poles received was recorded.

▶ **DO** ▶ Access Purchase Order No. 4 as previously instructed

- The **Rcv'd** column should show **10**.
- Notice that the **Qty** column shows **15** and **Clsd** is not marked. This indicates that 5 sets of ski poles are still on order.

Close Purchase Order No. 4 without changing

ADD A VENDOR USING ADD/EDIT MULTIPLE LIST ENTRIES

Vendors, customers, and list items may be added through the add/edit multiple list entries on the list menu. This feature is especially useful when importing data from Excel spreadsheets into QuickBooks. In addition, it may be used to quickly add one or more records to a list.

> # MEMO
> **DATE:** January 23, 2010
>
> Add a new vendor, *Mammoth News*, 1450 Main Street, Mammoth Lakes, CA 93546, Contact: Fran Lopez, Phone: 909-555-2525, Fax: 909-555-5252, E-mail: mammothnews@ski.com, Terms: Net 30.

▶ **DO** ▶ Add the new vendor using Add/Edit Multiple List Entries

Click the **Lists** menu
Click **Add/Edit Multiple List Entries**
Click the drop-down list arrow next to **List**
Click **Vendors**
Click on the Vendor Name, **Mammoth Power Co.**
Click **OK** on the Time Saving Tip
Right-click on Mammoth Power Co., click **Insert Line**
In the Vendor Name column, enter **Mammoth News**
Press, **Tab**
Enter the Company Name **Mammoth News**
Tab to or click **Contact**, key in **Fran Lopez**
Tab to or click **Phone**, enter **909-555-2525**
Tab to or click **FAX**, enter **909-555-5252**
Tab to or click **E-mail**, enter **mammothnews@ski.com**
Tab to or click **Address 1**, enter **Mammoth News**
Tab to or click **Address 2**, enter **1450 Main Street**

Tab to or click **Address 3**, enter **Mammoth Lakes, CA 93546**

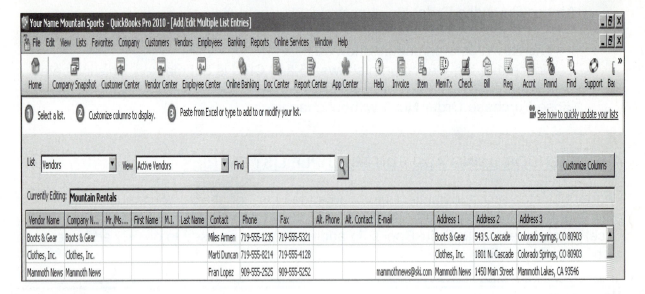

Click **Save Changes**
Click **OK** on the Record(s) Saved dialog box
Click **Close**

ENTER BILLS

Whether the bill is to pay for expenses incurred in the operation of a business or to pay for merchandise to sell in the business, QuickBooks Pro provides accounts payable tracking for all vendors to which the company owes money. Entering bills as soon as they are received is an efficient way to record your liabilities. Once bills have been entered, QuickBooks Pro will be able to provide up-to-date cash flow reports, and QuickBooks Pro will remind you when it's time to pay your bills. As previously stated, a bill is divided into two sections: a vendor-related section (the upper part of the bill that looks similar to a check and has a memo text box under it) and a detail section (the area that is divided into columns for Account, Amount, and Memo). The vendor- related section of the bill is where information for the actual bill is entered, including a memo with information about the transaction. If the bill is for paying an expense, the Expenses tab is used for the detail section. Using this tab allows you to indicate the expense accounts for the transaction, to enter the amounts for the various expense accounts, and to provide transaction explanations. If the bill is for merchandise, the Items tab will be used to record the receipt of the items ordered.

MEMO

DATE: January 23, 2010

Placed an ad in the *Mammoth News* announcing our February sale. Received a bill for $95.00 from *Mammoth News*, Terms Net 30, Invoice No. 381-22.Record the receipt of the bill from *Mammoth News*.

▶ **DO** Enter the bill

Click the **Enter Bills** icon on the Home Page
Click the drop-down list arrow for Vendor, and click **Mammoth News**
Tab to Date, enter **01/23/10** as the date
Tab to **Ref No.**, type the vendor's invoice number **381-22**
Tab to **Amount Due**, type **95**
Tab to **Terms**, click the drop-down list arrow next to **Terms**, click **Net 30**
- QuickBooks Pro automatically changes the Bill Due date to show 30 days from the transaction date.
- Since the terms are Net 30, there is no Discount Date.
- At this time no change will be made to the Bill Due date, and nothing will be inserted as a memo.
Complete the **Detail Section** of the bill:
- If necessary, click the **Expenses** tab so it is the area of the detail section in use.
Tab to or click in the column for **Account**, click the drop-down list arrow next to **Account**, scroll through the list to find **Advertising Expense**
Because the account does not appear, click **<Add New>**
- **Type** of account should show **Expense**. If not, click drop-down list arrow and click **Expense**.
Click **Continue**
Enter **6140** as the account number in **Number**
Tab to or click **Name**, enter **Advertising Expense**

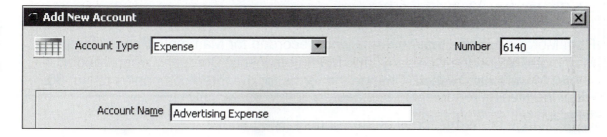

Click **Save & Close**

6140 Advertising Expense shows as the Account
- Based on the accrual method of accounting, **Advertising Expense** is selected as the account for this transaction because this expense should be matched against the revenue of the period.
- The Amount column already shows **95.00**—no entry required
- Tab to or click the first line in the column for **Memo**

Enter the transaction explanation of **Ad for February Sale**

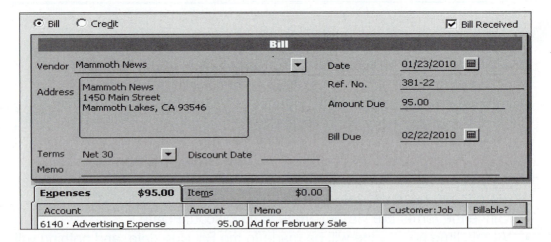

Click **Save & Close**

Since no terms were assigned when the company was added to the Vendor List, click **Yes** On the **Name Information Changed** dialog box

CHANGE EXISTING VENDORS' TERMS

Once a vendor has been established, changes can be made to the vendor's account information. The changes will take effect immediately and will be reflected in any transactions recorded for the vendor.

MEMO

DATE: January 23, 2010

Ruth Morgan realizes that no terms were recorded for Mammoth Power Company, Mammoth Telephone Company, and Mammoth Water Company when vendor accounts were established. Change the terms for the three companies to Net 30.

> **DO** Change the terms for all of the vendors listed above

Access the **Vendor List** in the Vendor Center as previously instructed

Double-click on **Mammoth Power Co.**
Click **OK** on the Add/Edit Multiple List Entries screen
Click **Additional Info** tab
Click the drop-down list arrow for terms, click **Net 30**
Click **OK**
Repeat for the other vendors indicated in the memo above
- Also, check Mammoth News to verify that the terms are Net 30
Close the **Vendor Center** when all changes have been made

PREPARE BILLS WITHOUT STEP-BY-STEP INSTRUCTIONS

It is more efficient to record bills in a group or batch than it is to record them one at a time. If an error is made while preparing the bill, correct it. Your Name Mountain Sports uses the accrual basis of accounting. In the accrual method of accounting the expenses of a period are matched against the revenue of the period. Unless otherwise instructed, use the accrual basis of accounting when recording entries.

MEMO
DATE: January 25, 2010

Record the following bills:
Mammoth Power Company electrical power for January: Invoice No. 3510-1023, $359.00, Net 30.
Mammoth Telephone Company telephone service for January: Invoice No. 7815-21, $156.40, Net 30.
Mammoth Water Company water for January: Invoice No. 3105, $35.00, Net 30.

DO Enter the three transactions in the memo above.

- Refer to the instructions given for previous transactions.
- Remember, when recording bills, you will need to determine the accounts used in the transaction. To determine the appropriate accounts to use, refer to the Chart of Accounts as you record the transactions.
- Enter information for Memos where transaction explanation is needed for clarification.
- To go from one bill to the next, click the **Next** button at the top of the bill or the **Save & New** button at the bottom of the bill.
- After entering the last bill, click **Save & Close** to record and exit the **Enter Bills** screen.

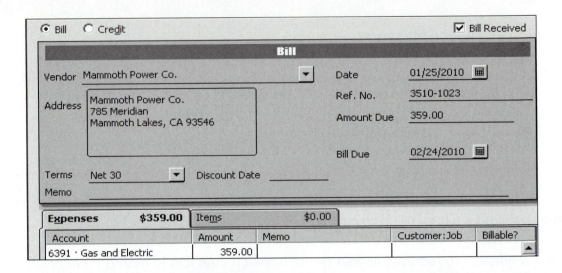

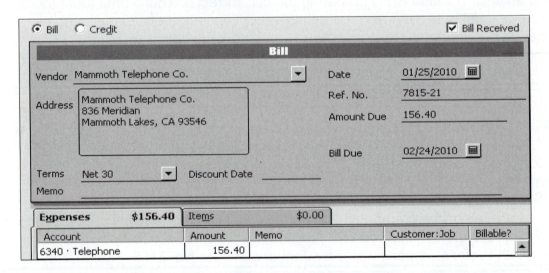

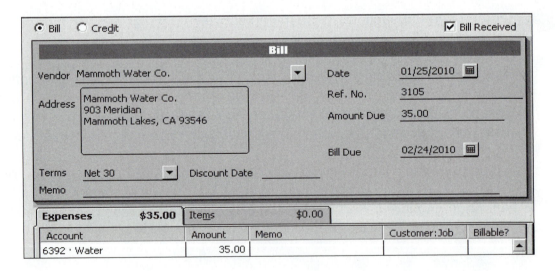

ENTER A BILL USING THE ACCOUNTS PAYABLE REGISTER

The Accounts Payable Register maintains a record of all the transactions recorded within the Accounts Payable account. Not only is it possible to view all of the account activities through the account's register, it is also possible to enter a bill directly into the Accounts Payable register. This can be faster than filling out all of the information through Enter Bills.

MEMO
DATE: January 25, 2010

Received a bill for the rent from Mountain Rentals. Use the Accounts Payable Register and record the bill for rent of $950, Invoice No. 7164, due February 4, 2010.

DO Use the Accounts Payable Register to record the above transaction:

Use the keyboard shortcut, **Ctrl+A** to access the Chart of Accounts
Double-click **Accounts Payable** to open the Accounts Payable register
Click in the blank entry at the end of the register
The date is highlighted, key in **01/25/10** for the transaction date
The word *Number* is in the next column
Tab to or click **Number**
- The word *Number* disappears.
Enter the Vendor's Invoice Number **7164**
Tab to or click **Vendor**, click the drop-down list arrow for the Vendor, click
   Mountain Rentals
Tab to or click **Due Date**; and, if necessary, enter the due date **02/04/10**
Tab to or click **Billed**, enter the amount **950**
Tab to or click **Account**, click the drop-down list arrow for **Account**
Determine the appropriate account to use for rent
- If all of the accounts do not appear in the drop-down list, scroll through the accounts until you find the one appropriate for this entry.
Click **6300 Rent**
Tab to or click Memo, key **Rent**
Click **Record** to record the transaction

01/25/2010	7164	Mountain Rentals	02/04/2010	950.00		12,590.40
	BILL	6300 · Rent Rent				

Do not close the register

EDIT A TRANSACTION IN THE ACCOUNTS PAYABLE REGISTER

Because QuickBooks Pro makes corrections extremely user friendly, a transaction can be edited or changed directly in the Accounts Payable Register as well as on the original bill. By eliminating the columns for Type and Memo, it is possible to change the register to show each transaction on one line. This can make the register easier to read.

MEMO

DATE: January 25, 2010

Upon examination of the invoices and the bills entered, Ruth discovers an error: The actual amount of the bill from the water company was **$85**, not $35. Change the transaction amount for this bill.

DO ▶ Correct the above transaction in the Accounts Payable Register

Click the check box for **1-line** to select
- Each Accounts Payable transaction will appear on one line.

Click the transaction for Mammoth Water Co.

Change the amount of the transaction from $35.00 to **$85.00**

To record the change in the transaction, click the **Record** button at the bottom of the register and click **Yes** on the Record Transaction dialog box

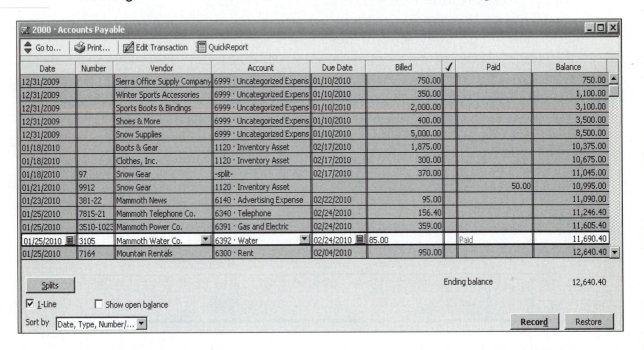

Do not close the register

PREVIEW AND PRINT A QUICKREPORT
FROM THE ACCOUNTS PAYABLE REGISTER

After editing the transaction, you may want to view information about a specific vendor. Clicking the vendor's name within a transaction and clicking the QuickReport button at the top of the register can do this quickly and efficiently.

MEMO

DATE: January 25, 2010

More than one transaction has been entered for Snow Gear. Larry and you like to view transaction information for all vendors that have several transactions within a short period of time.

▶ **DO** Prepare a QuickReport for Snow Gear

Click any field in any transaction for Snow Gear
Click the **QuickReport** button at the top of the Register
- The Register QuickReport for All Transactions for Snow Gear appears on the screen.
Resize the columns so the Account is shown in full and the report will print on one page in Landscape orientation
Click **Print**
Click **Preview** to view the report before printing
- The report appears on the screen as a full page.
- A full-page report usually cannot be read on the screen.
To read the text in the report, click the **Zoom In** button at the top of the screen
Use the scroll buttons and bars to view the report columns
Click the **Zoom Out** button to return to a full-page view of the report
When finished previewing the report, click **Close**
- You will return to the Print Reports Screen.
- If necessary, click **Cancel** and resize the columns so the reports will print on one-page wide.
When the columns are shown appropriately, print the report

Your Name Mountain Sports

Register QuickReport

All Transactions

◇	Type	◇	Date	◇	Num	◇	Memo	◇	Account	◇	Paid	◇	Open Balance	◇	Amount	◇
Snow Gear																
▶	Bill		01/18/2010		97				2000 · Accounts Payable		Unpaid		370.00		370.00	◀
	Credit		01/21/2010		9912		Returned 1 Sled		2000 · Accounts Payable		Unpaid		-50.00		-50.00	
	Total Snow Gear												320.00		320.00	
TOTAL													320.00		320.00	

        Click the **Close** button to close the report
        Close the Accounts Payable register and the Chart of Accounts

PREPARE AND PRINT UNPAID BILLS DETAIL REPORT

It is possible to get information regarding unpaid bills by simply preparing a report. No more digging through tickler files, recorded invoices, ledgers, or journals. QuickBooks Pro prepares an Unpaid Bills Detail Report listing each unpaid bill grouped and subtotaled by vendor.

MEMO

DATE: January 25, 2010

Ruth Morgan prepares an Unpaid Bills Report for you and Larry each week. Because Your Name Mountain Sports is a small business, you like to have a firm control over cash flow so you can determine which bills will be paid during the week.

DO ▶ Prepare and print an **Unpaid Bills Detail Report**

        Click **Reports** on the menu bar, point to **Vendors & Payables**, click **Unpaid Bills Detail**
        Enter the date of **01/25/10** as the report date
        Tab to generate report
        Adjust column size as necessary to display all data in the columns in full

Your Name Mountain Sports
Unpaid Bills Detail
As of January 25, 2010

Type	Date	Num	Due Date	Aging	Open Balance
Sierra Office Supply Company					
Bill	12/31/2009		01/10/2010	15	750.00
Total Sierra Office Supply Company					750.00
Snow Gear					
Credit	01/21/2010	9912			-50.00
Bill	01/18/2010	97	02/17/2010		370.00
Total Snow Gear					320.00
Snow Supplies					
Bill	12/31/2009		01/10/2010	15	5,000.00
Total Snow Supplies					5,000.00
Sports Boots & Bindings					
Bill	12/31/2009		01/10/2010	15	2,000.00
Total Sports Boots & Bindings					2,000.00
Winter Sports Accessories					
Bill	12/31/2009		01/10/2010	15	350.00
Total Winter Sports Accessories					350.00
TOTAL					**12,640.40**

Partial Report

Print in Portrait orientation
Click **Close** to close the report

PAYING BILLS

When using QuickBooks Pro, you may choose to pay your bills directly from the Pay Bills command and let QuickBooks Pro write your checks for you, or you may choose to write the checks yourself. If you recorded a bill, you should use the Pay Bills feature of QuickBooks Pro to pay the bill. If no bill was recorded, you should pay the bill by writing a check in QuickBooks Pro. Using the Pay Bills window enables you to determine which bills to pay, the method of payment—check, or credit card—and the appropriate account. When you are determining which bills to pay, QuickBooks Pro allows you to display the bills by due date, discount date, vendor, or amount. All bills may be displayed, or only those bills that are due by a certain date may be displayed. In addition, when a bill has been recorded and is paid using the Pay Bills feature of QuickBooks Pro, the bill will be marked *Paid in Full* and the amount paid will no longer be shown as a liability. If you record a bill and pay it by writing a check and *not* using the Pay Bills feature of QuickBooks, the bill won't be marked as paid and it will show up as a liability.

MEMO
DATE: January 25, 2010

Whenever possible, Ruth Morgan pays the bills on a weekly basis. Show all the bills in the Pay Bills window. Select the bills, except the bill for Snow Gear, with discounts dates of 1/28/2010 for payment.

DO ▶ Pay the bills that are eligible for a discount

> Click **Pay Bills** on the QuickBooks Home Page
> Click **Show All Bills** to select
> Filter By **All vendors**
> Sort Bills By **Due Date**
> At the bottom of the **Pay Bills** window, verify and/or select the following items:
>> **Payment Date** is **01/25/10**
>> **Payment Method** is **Check**
>> **To be printed** should be selected
>> **Account** is **1100 Checking**
> Scroll through the list of bills
> • The bills will be shown according to the date due.

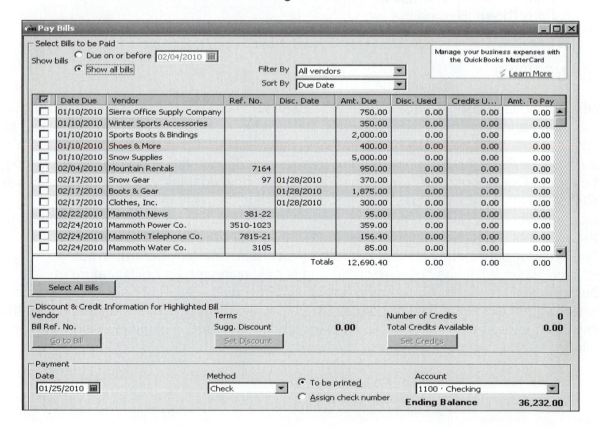

Select the bills to be paid and apply the discounts:

Click in the check mark column for the transaction for **Boots & Gear** with a due date of 2/17/2010

Click the **Set Discount** button

- Verify the Suggested Discount of **37.50**.

Click the drop-down list arrow for the Discount Account

- Scroll through the list of accounts.
- There is account 4030 Purchases Discounts but it is not appropriate for this transaction. It is used for purchases of things used by the business not for merchandise.
- There is 6130 Sales Discounts. This expense account is used when we give discounts to customers.
- The bill payment is for merchandise purchased to sell in the business. A cost of goods sold discount account needs to be created for merchandise discounts

Click **<Add New>**

Click **Cost of Goods Sold** as the type of account

Enter **5100** as the account number

Enter the account name **Merchandise Discounts**

Click **Subaccount** and select **5000 Cost of Goods Sold** as the account

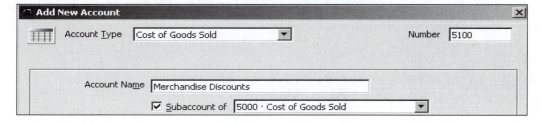

Click **Save & Close**

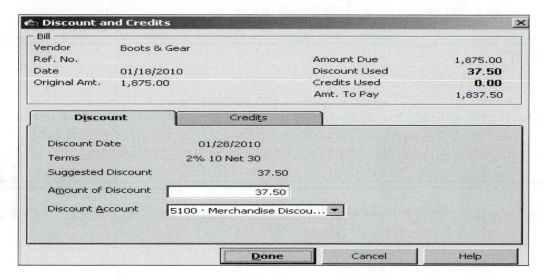

Click **Done** to record the discount
Repeat the steps for the bill from Clothes, Inc. that is eligible for a discount

✓	Date Due	Vendor	Ref. No.	Disc. Date	Amt. Due	Disc. Used	Credits U...	Amt. To Pay
☐	01/10/2010	Sierra Office Supply Company			750.00	0.00	0.00	0.00
☐	01/10/2010	Winter Sports Accessories			350.00	0.00	0.00	0.00
☐	01/10/2010	Sports Boots & Bindings			2,000.00	0.00	0.00	0.00
☐	01/10/2010	Shoes & More			400.00	0.00	0.00	0.00
☐	01/10/2010	Snow Supplies			5,000.00	0.00	0.00	0.00
☐	02/04/2010	Mountain Rentals	7164		950.00	0.00	0.00	0.00
☐	02/17/2010	Snow Gear	97	01/28/2010	370.00	0.00	0.00	0.00
✓	02/17/2010	Boots & Gear		01/28/2010	1,875.00	37.50	0.00	1,837.50
✓	02/17/2010	Clothes, Inc.		01/28/2010	300.00	6.00	0.00	294.00
☐	02/22/2010	Mammoth News	381-22		95.00	0.00	0.00	0.00
☐	02/24/2010	Mammoth Power Co.	3510-1023		359.00	0.00	0.00	0.00
☐	02/24/2010	Mammoth Telephone Co.	7815-21		156.40	0.00	0.00	0.00
☐	02/24/2010	Mammoth Water Co.	3105		85.00	0.00	0.00	0.00
				Totals	12,690.40	43.50	0.00	2,131.50

- Once you click **Done** to accept the discount, the amount due and amount paid amounts change to reflect the amount of the discount taken.
- Notice the totals provided indicating the Disc. Used and the Amt. To Pay for the two selected bills

Click the **Pay Selected Bills** button, and then click the **Pay More Bills** button on the **Payment Summary** screen

PAY A BILL QUALIFYING FOR A PURCHASE DISCOUNT
AND APPLY CREDIT AS PART OF PAYMENT

When paying bills, it is a good idea to apply credits received for returned or damaged merchandise to the accounts as payment is made.

MEMO

DATE: January 25, 2010

As she is getting ready to pay bills, Ruth looks for any credits that may be applied to the bill as part of the payment. In addition, Ruth looks for bills that qualify for an early-payment discount. Apply the credit received from Snow Gear, as part of the payment for the bill, then apply the discount, and pay the bill within the discount period.

▶ DO ▶ Apply the credit received from Snow Gear, as part of the payment for the bill and pay bill within the discount period

Look at the bottom of the screen and verify:
  Payment Date of **01/25/2010**
  Payment Method is **Check**
  To be printed is marked
  1100 Checking is the **Payment Account**
Select **Show all bills**
Click the drop-down list for **Sort Bills By**, click **Vendor**
Scroll through transactions until you see the transaction for Snow Gear
Click the check mark column next to the transaction to select it
- *Note:* This must be completed before applying the discount or credit to the bill.
- Notice that both the Set Credits and Set Discount buttons are now active and that information regarding credits and discounts is displayed.

☐	01/10/2010	Sierra Office Supply Company			750.00	0.00	0.00	0.00
☑	02/17/2010	Snow Gear	97	01/28/2010	370.00	0.00	0.00	370.00
☐	01/10/2010	Snow Supplies			5,000.00	0.00	0.00	0.00
☐	01/10/2010	Sports Boots & Bindings			2,000.00	0.00	0.00	0.00
☐	01/10/2010	Winter Sports Accessories			350.00	0.00	0.00	0.00
				Totals	10,515.40	0.00	0.00	370.00

Clear Selections

Discount & Credit Information for Highlighted Bill

Vendor	**Snow Gear**	Terms	**2% 10 Net 30**	Number of Credits	1
Bill Ref. No. 97		Sugg. Discount	7.40	Total Credits Available	50.00
Go to Bill		Set Discount		Set Credits	

Click the **Set Discount** button
- Verify the amount of the discount **7.40** and the discount account **5100 Merchandise Discounts**
Click the **Credits** tab
Click the Check Mark column for the credit amount of **50.00**
- On the Discounts and Credits screen, verify the amount due of **370**, the discount used of **7.40**, and the credit used of **50.00**, leaving an amount to pay of **312.60**
- QuickBooks calculates the discount on the original amount of the invoice rather than the amount due after subtracting the credit. If you need to recalculate the discount on the amount due after the credit, you may change the amount of the discount on the Discount screen. At this point in training, we will accept the discount calculated by QuickBooks.
Click the **Done** button

☑	02/17/2010	Snow Gear		97	01/28/2010	370.00	7.40	50.00	312.60
☐	01/10/2010	Snow Supplies				5,000.00	0.00	0.00	0.00
☐	01/10/2010	Sports Boots & Bindings				2,000.00	0.00	0.00	0.00
☐	01/10/2010	Winter Sports Accessories				350.00	0.00	0.00	0.00
					Totals	10,515.40	7.40	50.00	312.60

Click **Pay Selected Bills** then click **Done** on the payment summary screen.

VERIFY THAT BILLS ARE MARKED PAID

▶ **DO** Access **Enter Bills** as previously instructed

Click **Previous** and view all the bills that were paid in Pay Bills to verify that they are marked as paid
- Notice that the Credit for Snow Gear is *not* marked in any way to indicate that it has been used.

Close the Enter Bills screen

PRINT CHECKS TO PAY BILLS

Once bills have been selected for payment and any discounts taken or credits applied, the checks should be printed, signed, and mailed. QuickBooks Pro has two methods that may be used to print checks. Checks may be accessed and printed one at a time using the Write Checks window. This allows you to view the Bill Payment Information for each check. A more efficient way to print checks is to click the File menu and select checks from the Print Forms menu. This method will print all checks that are marked *To be printed* but will not allow you to view the bill payment information for any of the checks as you would if you printed each check separately. QuickBooks does not separate checks it writes in Pay Bills from the checks that are written when using the Write Checks feature of the program.

MEMO

DATE: January 25, 2010

Ruth needs to print the checks for bills that have been paid. Since she did not print them at the time she paid the bills, she decides to print checks individually so she can view bill payment information for each check while printing. When she finishes with the checks, she will give them to you for approval and signature.

DO Print the checks for bills that have been paid

Access the Write Checks window using the keyboard shortcut **Ctrl+W**
- A blank check will show on the screen.
Click **Previous** until you get to the check for **Boots & Gear**
Click **Print** at the top of the window to print the check
Click **OK** on the Print Check screen to select Check No. 2
- Check No. 1 was issued in Chapter 5 to Dr. Francisco Munoz for a return. If Check No. 2 is not on the Print Check screen, change the screen so that the check number is 2.

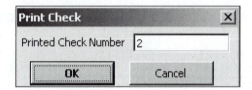

- On the **Print Checks** screen, verify the printer name, printer type, and the selection of Standard check style.
Print Company Name and Address should be selected
- If is not marked with a check, click the check box to insert a check mark and select.

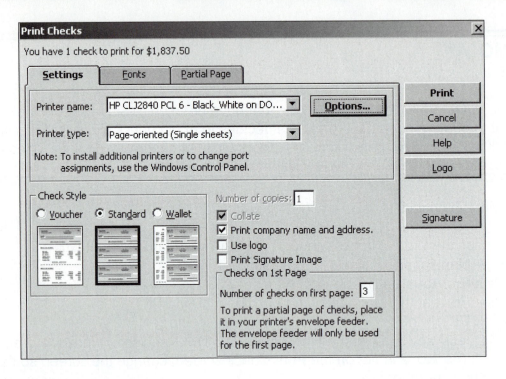

Click **Print** to print the check

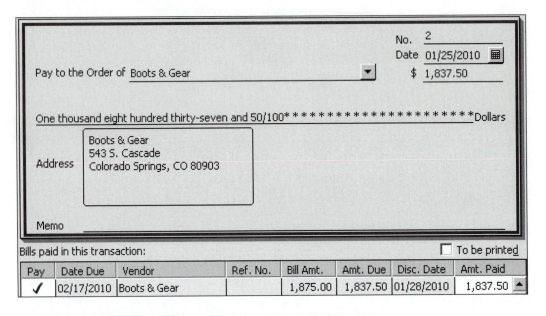

Click **OK** on the **Print Checks – Confirmation** screen
- If you get a **Set Check Reminder** screen, click **No**

Click **Previous** or **Next** and repeat the steps to print Check No. 3 for Clothes, Inc., and Check No. 4 for Snow Gear

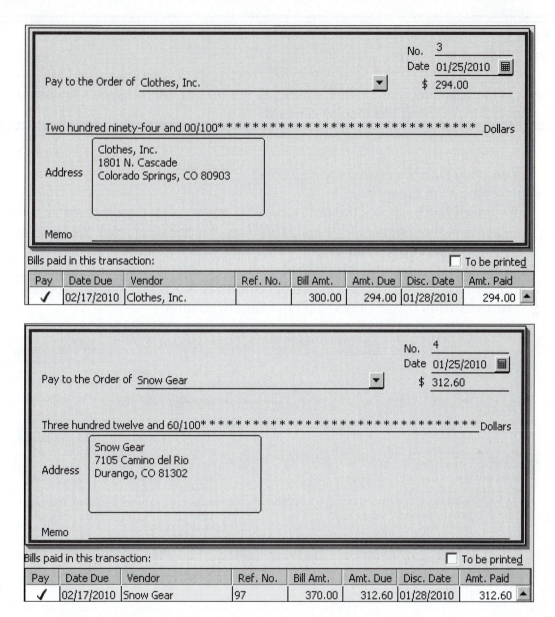

- Notice that the amount of the check to Snow Gear is $312.60. This allows for the original bill of $370 less the return of $50 and the discount of $7.40. Close the **Write Checks** window.

PAY BILLS USING A CREDIT CARD

A credit card may be used to pay a bill rather than a check. Use the Pay Bills feature, but select Pay By Credit Card rather than Pay By Check.

Pay the above bills with a credit card

MEMO

DATE: January 25, 2010

In viewing the bills due, you direct Ruth to pay the bills to Winter Sports Accessories and Shoes & More using the Visa credit card.

Access **Pay Bills** as previously instructed

Select **Show all bills**

In **Payment Method** click the drop-down list arrow, click **Credit Card** to select

- Payment Account should show 2100 Visa. If it does not, click the drop-down list arrow and click **2100 Visa**.

Payment Date should be **01/25/2010**

Scroll through the list of bills and select **Shoes & More** and **Winter Sports Accessories** by clicking in the check mark column

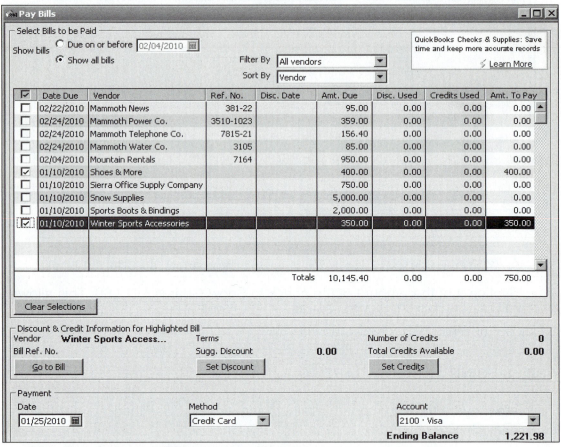

Click **Pay Selected Bills** to record the payment

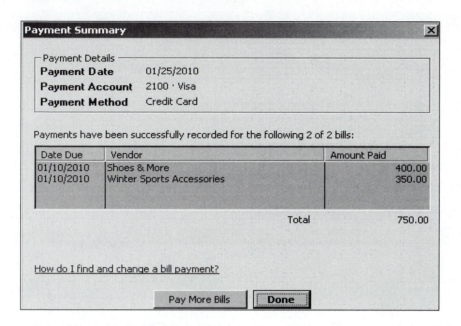

Verify the payments and click **Done**

VERIFY THE CREDIT CARD PAYMENT OF BILLS

Paying bills with a credit card in Pay Bills automatically creates a Credit Card transaction in QuickBooks Pro. This can be verified through the Visa account register in the Chart of Accounts and through Enter Credit Card Charges. The entry into QuickBooks does not actually charge the credit card. It only records the transaction.

MEMO

DATE: January 25, 2010

Verify the credit card charges for Winter Sports Accessories and Shoes & More.

▶ **DO** Verify the credit card charges

Access the Visa account register in the **Chart of Accounts**
Scroll through the register to see the charges for Shoes & More and Winter Sports Accessories

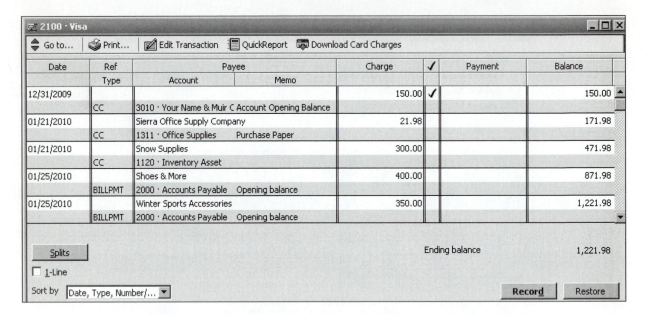

Close the **Accounts Payable** register and the **Chart of Accounts**

SALES TAX

When a company is set up in QuickBooks Pro, a Sales Tax Payable liability account is automatically created if the company indicates that it charges sales tax on sales. The Sales Tax Payable account keeps track of as many tax agencies as the company needs. As invoices are written, QuickBooks Pro records the tax liability in the Sales Tax Payable account. To determine the sales tax owed, a Sales Tax Liability Report is prepared.

PRINT SALES TAX LIABILITY REPORT

The Sales Tax Liability Report shows your total taxable sales, the total nontaxable sales, and the amount of sales tax owed to each tax agency.

MEMO

DATE: January 25, 2010

Prior to paying the sales tax, Ruth prepares the Sales Tax Liability Report.

▶ **DO** Prepare the Sales Tax Liability Report

Click **Reports** on the Menu bar, point to **Vendors & Payables** as the type of report, click **Sales Tax Liability**

The Report Dates are **From 01/01/2010 To 01/25/2010**

- If necessary, adjust the column widths so the report will fit on one page.
- If you get a message box asking if all columns should be the same size as the one being adjusted, click **No**.

Your Name Mountain Sports
Sales Tax Liability
January 1 - 25, 2010

	◇ Total Sales	◇ Non-Taxable Sales	◇ Taxable Sales	◇ Tax Rate	◇ Tax Collected	◇ Sales Tax Payable As of Jan 25, 10 ◇
State Board of Equalization						
CA Sales Tax	▶ 8,582.23	◀ 125.00	8,457.23	7.25%	613.15	613.15
Total State Board of Equalization	8,582.23	125.00	8,457.23		613.15	613.15
TOTAL	**8,582.23**	**125.00**	**8,457.23**		**613.15**	**613.15**

Print in Landscape orientation
Close the report after printing

PAYING SALES TAX

Use the Pay Sales Tax window to determine how much sales tax you owe and to write a check to the tax agency. QuickBooks Pro will update the sales tax account with payment information.

MEMO
DATE: January 25, 2010

Note from Larry: Ruth, pay the sales taxes owed.

▶ DO ▶ Pay the sales taxes owed

Click the **Manage Sales Tax** icon, and then click the **Pay Sales Tax** button on the Manage Sales Tax screen.

Pay From Account is **1100 Checking**

Check Date is **01/25/2010**

Show sales tax due through is **01/25/2010**

Starting Check No. should be **To be printed**

Click the **Pay All Tax** button or click in the Pay column to mark the transaction

- Once the transaction has been marked, the Pay All Tax button changes to Clear Selections

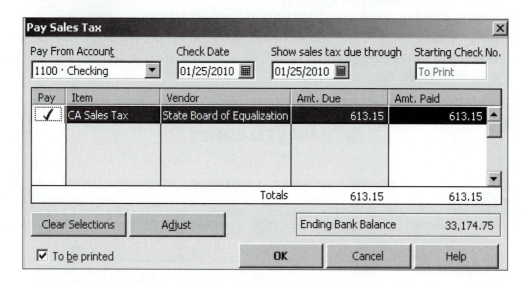

- Once **Pay All Tax** has been clicked and the Sales Tax item is selected, the **Ending Bank Balance** changes to reflect the amount in checking after the tax has been paid.

Click **OK**, and then click **Close** on the Manage Sales Tax screen

▶DO▶ Print Check No. 5 for the payment of the Sales Tax

Click **File**, point to **Print Forms**, click **Checks**
- Verify the Bank Account 1100 Checking, the First Check No. 5, and the check mark in front of State Board of Equalization.

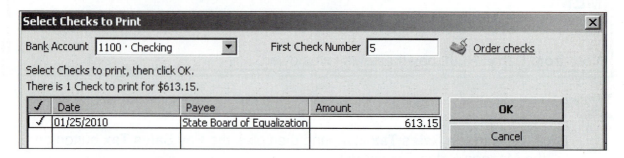

Click **OK**, click **Print**, click **OK** on the **Print Checks – Confirmation** screen

VOIDING AND DELETING PURCHASE ORDERS, BILLS, CHECKS, AND CREDIT CARD PAYMENTS

QuickBooks Pro is so user friendly it allows any business form to be deleted. In some accounting programs, once an entry has been made error corrections are not allowed except as adjusting entries. As you learned in earlier chapters, QuickBooks Pro allows a purchase order, a bill, a credit card payment, or a check to be voided or deleted. If a business form is voided, the form remains as a transaction. The transaction shows as a zero amount. This is useful when you want a record to show that an entry was made. If the form is deleted, all trace of the form is deleted. QuickBooks Pro keeps an audit trail of all transactions entered. The audit trail includes information regarding deleted transactions as well as transactions that appear on business forms, in the Journal, and in reports. An audit trail helps to eliminate misconduct such as printing a check and then deleting the check from the company records. In addition, you may print voided/deleted transaction reports that indicate when a transaction was recorded and when it was voided/deleted.

The procedures for voiding and deleting business forms are the same whether the business is a retail business or a service business. For actual assignments and practice in voiding and deleting business forms, refer to Chapters 2, 3, and 5.

VENDOR CENTER

The Vendor Center is used to obtain information regarding individual vendors. Once you open the Vendor Center, clicking on a vendor in the Vendor List will display the Vendor Contact Information for the selected vendor. Click Edit/More Info to see further information about the vendor or to edit the information.

In the lower-right section of the Vendor Center, you will see transaction information displayed for the selected vendor.

DO Open the Vendor Center

Click the **Vendor Center** button
Click the vendor **Snow Supplies** in the Vendor List
Click the **Edit Vendor** button to change the vendor information for the company
Change the following information for Snow Supplies
Company Name: **Snow Supplies**
Address: **1274 Boulder Avenue, Lafayette, CO 80026**
Contact: **Robert Carrillo**
Telephone: **303-555-1263**
FAX: **303-555-6321**

E-mail: **supplies@co.com**
Click **OK**
View the changes to the Vendor
Show **All Transactions**, Filter By **All**, Date **All**
- Click the drop-down list arrow for **Date** and click **All**.
Look at the transactions and Vendor Information displayed for Snow Supplies

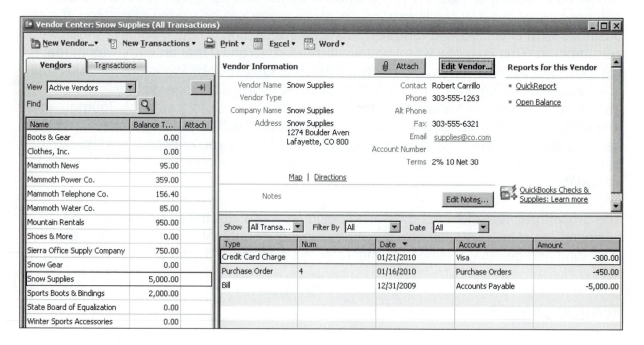

Close the **Vendor Center**

PRINT JOURNAL

The Journal records each transaction and lists the accounts and the amounts for debit and credit entries. The Journal is very useful; especially if you are trying to find errors. Always check the transaction dates, the account names, and the items listed in the Memo column. If a transaction does not appear in the Journal, it may be due to using an incorrect date. Remember, only the transactions entered within the report dates will be displayed.

DO Print the Journal for Chapter 6 transactions

Open the **Report Center** as previously instructed
Click **Accountant & Taxes** as the Report type
Double-click **Journal**
The dates for Chapter 6 transactions are from **01/18/10** to **01/25/10**

Your Name Mountain Sports
Journal
January 18 - 25, 2010

Trans #	Type	Date	Num	Name	Memo	Account	Debit	Credit
94	Bill Pmt -Check	01/25/2010	3	Clothes, Inc.		1100 · Checking		294.00
				Clothes, Inc.		2000 · Accounts Payable	294.00	
				Clothes, Inc.		2000 · Accounts Payable	6.00	
				Clothes, Inc.		5100 · Merchandise Discounts		6.00
							300.00	300.00
95	Bill Pmt -Check	01/25/2010	4	Snow Gear		1100 · Checking		312.60
				Snow Gear		2000 · Accounts Payable	312.60	
				Snow Gear		2000 · Accounts Payable	7.40	
				Snow Gear		5100 · Merchandise Discounts		7.40
							320.00	320.00
96	Bill Pmt -CCard	01/25/2010		Shoes & More	Opening balance	2100 · Visa		400.00
				Shoes & More	Opening balance	2000 · Accounts Payable	400.00	
							400.00	400.00
97	Bill Pmt -CCard	01/25/2010		Winter Sports Accessories	Opening balance	2100 · Visa		350.00
				Winter Sports Accessories	Opening balance	2000 · Accounts Payable	350.00	
							350.00	350.00
98	Sales Tax Payment	01/25/2010	5	State Board of Equalization		1100 · Checking		613.15
				State Board of Equalization		2200 · Sales Tax Payable	613.15	
							613.15	613.15
TOTAL							**8,430.53**	**8,430.53**

Partial Report

Print the Journal in Landscape orientation
Close the **Journal** and the **Report Center**

BACK UP YOUR NAME MOUNTAIN SPORTS

DO Follow the instructions given in previous chapters to back up data for Your Name Mountain Sports, use the file name **Sports (Backup Ch. 6)**.

SUMMARY

In this chapter, purchase orders were completed, inventory items were received, and bills were recorded. Payments for purchases and bills were made by cash and by credit card. Sales taxes were paid. Vendors, inventory items, and accounts were added while transactions were being recorded. Various reports were prepared to determine unpaid bills, account and vendor QuickReports, and sales tax liability.

END-OF-CHAPTER QUESTIONS

TRUE/FALSE

ANSWER THE FOLLOWING QUESTIONS IN THE SPACE PROVIDED BEFORE THE QUESTION NUMBER.

_____   1.   Receipt of purchase order items is never recorded before the bill arrives.

_____   2.   A bill can be paid by check or credit card.

_____   3.   The Cost of Goods Sold account Merchandise Discounts is used to record discounts to customers.

_____   4.   Voiding a purchase order removes every trace of the purchase order from the company records.

_____   5.   The Vendor Center displays the vendor list and information about individual vendors.

_____   6.   A single purchase order can be prepared and sent to several vendors.

_____   7.   A Sales Tax account is automatically created if a company indicates that it charges sales tax on sales.

_____   8.   A credit received from a vendor for the return of merchandise can be applied to a payment to the vendor.

_____   9.   A new vendor cannot be added while recording a transaction.

_____ 10.   A purchase order is closed automatically when a partial receipt of merchandise is recorded.

MULTIPLE CHOICE

WRITE THE LETTER OF THE CORRECT ANSWER IN THE SPACE PROVIDED
BEFORE THE QUESTION NUMBER.

_____ 1. If you change the minimum quantity for an item, it becomes effective ___.
A. immediately
B. the beginning of next month
C. as soon as outstanding purchase orders are received
D. the beginning of the next fiscal year

_____ 2. If an order is received with a bill but is incomplete, QuickBooks Pro will ___.
A. record the bill for the full amount ordered
B. record the bill only for the amount received
C. not allow the bill to be prepared until all the merchandise is received
D. close the purchase order

_____ 3. The Purchase Order feature must be selected as a preference ___.
A. when setting up the company
B. prior to recording the first purchase order
C. is automatically set when the first purchase order is prepared
D. either A or B

_____ 4. A faster method of entering bills can be entering the bills ___.
A. while writing the checks for payment
B. in the Pay Bills window
C. in the Accounts Payable Register
D. none of the above

_____ 5. When items ordered are received with a bill, you record the receipt ___.
A. on an item receipt form
B. on the bill
C. on the original purchase order
D. in the Journal

_____ 6. Sales tax is paid by using the ___ window.
A. Pay Bills
B. Manage Sales Tax
C. Write Check
D. Credit Card

_____ 7. A Purchase Order may be customized using the ___.
    A. Layout Designer
    B. Drawing menu
    C. Customize Form button on the Home Page
    D. a form may not be changed

_____ 8. Checks to pay bills may be printed ___.
    A. individually
    B. all at once
    C. as the checks are written
    D. all of the above

_____ 9. When recording a bill for merchandise received, you click the ___ tab on the vendor section of the bill.
    A. Memo
    B. Expenses
    C. Items
    D. Purchase Order

_____ 10. The ___ basis of accounting matches income for the period against expenses for the period.
    A. cash
    B. credit
    C. accrual
    D. debit/credit

FILL-IN

IN THE SPACE PROVIDED, WRITE THE ANSWER THAT MOST APPROPRIATELY COMPLETES THE SENTENCE.

1. Orders for merchandise are prepared using the QuickBooks Pro _____ form.

2. Information on the Reminders List may be displayed in _____ or _____ form.

3. The _____ Report shows the total taxable sales and the amount of sales tax owed.

4. A purchase order can be closed _____ or _____.

5. To see the bill payment information, checks must be printed _____.

SHORT ESSAY

Describe the cycle of obtaining merchandise. Include the process from ordering the merchandise through paying for it. Include information regarding the QuickBooks Pro forms prepared for each phase of the cycle, the possible ways in which an item may be received, and the ways in which payment may be made.

_____

_____

_____

_____

_____

NAME_____

TRANSMITTAL

CHAPTER 6: YOUR NAME MOUNTAIN SPORTS

Attach the following documents and reports:

Purchase Order No. 1: Boots & Gear
Purchase Order No. 2: Snow Gear
Purchase Order No. 3: Clothes, Inc.
Purchase Order No. 4: Snow Supplies
Account QuickReport, Purchase Orders, January 16, 2010
Purchase Order No. 4 (Corrected): Snow Supplies
Register Quick Report, Snow Gear
Unpaid Bills Detail, January 25, 2010
Check No. 2: Boots & Gear
Check No. 3: Clothes, Inc.
Check No. 4: Snow Gear
Sales Tax Liability Report, January 1-25, 2010
Check No. 5: State Board of Equalization
Journal, January 18-25, 2010

END-OF-CHAPTER PROBLEM

YOUR NAME RESORT CLOTHING

Chapter 6 continues with the transactions for purchase orders, merchandise receipts, bills, bill payments, and sales tax payments. Your partner, Karen Olsen, prints the checks, purchase orders, and any related reports; and you sign the checks. This procedure establishes cash control procedures and lets both owners know about the checks being processed.

INSTRUCTIONS

Continue to use the copy of Your Name Resort Clothing you used in Chapter 5. Open the company—the file used is **Clothing.qbw**. Record the purchase orders, bills, payments, and other purchases as instructed within the chapter. Always read the transactions carefully and review the Chart of Accounts when selecting transaction accounts. Print reports and graphs as indicated. Add new vendors and minimum quantities where indicated. Print all purchase orders and checks issued. The first purchase order used is Purchase Order No. 1. When paying bills, always check for credits that may be applied to the bill, and always check for discounts.

In addition to the Item List and the Chart of Accounts, you will need to use the Vendor List when ordering merchandise and paying bills.

Name	Balance Total	Attach
Accessories for All Seasons, Inc.	0.00	
Casual Clothes	3,053.00	
Resort Clothing Supply, Inc.	2,598.00	
Shades, Inc.	500.00	
Shoes by Ricardo	450.00	
State Board of Equalization	165.58	

RECORD TRANSACTIONS

January 5, 2010:
► Customize a Purchase Order template so the Company Name is expanded to **5 ¼** and Purchase Order begins at **5 ½**.
► Change the reorder point for dresses from 20 to 25.

▶ Change the reorder point for women's pants to 30.
▶ Prepare and print an Inventory Stock Status by Item Report for January 1-5, 2010 in Landscape orientation. Manually adjust column widths so the item descriptions and the vendors' names are shown in full and the report prints on one page.
▶ Prepare Purchase Orders for all items marked Order on the Stock Status by Item Inventory Report. Refer to the Stock Status by Item Report for vendor information. The quantity for each item ordered is 10. The rate is $35 for dresses and $20 for pants. Print purchase orders with lines around each field.
▶ Order an additional 10 dresses from a new vendor: Clothes Time, 9382 Grand Avenue, San Luis Obispo, CA 93407, Contact person is Mitchell Rogers, 805-555-5512, Fax is 805-555-2155, E-mail is clothestime@slo.com, Credit terms are 2% 10 Net 30, Credit limit is $2000. The rate for the dresses is $25.
▶ Print a Purchase Order QuickReport in Landscape orientation for January 1-5. Adjust column widths so all columns are displayed in full and the report prints on one page.

January 8, 2010:
▶ Received pants ordered from Resort Clothing Supply, Inc. without the bill. Enter the receipt of merchandise. The transaction date is 01/08/2010.
▶ Received dresses from Casual Clothes with Bill C309. Enter the receipt of the merchandise and the bill.
▶ Received 8 dresses from Clothes Time. Enter the receipt of the merchandise and Bill 406. Manually close the Purchase Order.
▶ After recording the receipt of merchandise, view the three purchase orders. Notice which ones are marked *Received in Full* and *Clsd*.

January 9, 2010:
▶ Received Bill 239 from Resort Clothing Supply, Inc. for the pants received on 01/08/10. The bill was dated 01/08/2010 (use this date for the bill).
▶ Pay for the dresses from Clothes Time with a credit card. (Take a purchase discount if the transaction qualifies for one. Use a Cost of Goods Sold account 5100 Merchandise Discounts for the discount.)

January 10, 2010:
▶ Discovered unstitched seams in two pairs of women's pants ordered on PO 2. Return the pants for credit. Use 2340 as the Reference number.

January 15, 2010:
▶ Record bill for rent of $1150. (Vendor is SLO Rental Company, 301 Marsh Street, San Luis Obispo, CA 93407, Contact person is Matt Ericson, 805-555-4100, Fax 805-555-0014, Terms Net 30.)

▶ Record bill for telephone service of $79.85. (Vendor is SLO Telephone Co., 8851 Hwy. 58, San Luis Obispo, CA 93407, 805-555-1029. No terms or credit limits have been given.)

January 18, 2010:
▶ Pay all bills that are eligible for a discount. Take any discounts for which you are eligible. Take the full amount of the discount calculated by QuickBooks even if you have a credit to apply. If there are any credits to an account, apply the credit prior to paying the bill. Pay the bill(s) by check.
▶ Print Check Nos. 2 and 3 for the bills that were paid.

January 25, 2010:
▶ Purchase office supplies to have on hand for $250 with a credit card from Office Masters, 8330 Grand Avenue, Arroyo Grande, CA 93420, Contact person is Larry Thomas, 805-555-9915, Fax 805-555-5199, E-mail OfficeMasters@slo.com, Terms Net 30, Credit limit $500.
▶ Print Unpaid Bills Detail Report in Portrait orientation.
▶ Pay bills for rent and telephone. Print the checks prepared for these bills.

January 30, 2010:
▶ Prepare Sales Tax Liability Report from 01/01/2010 to 01/30/2010. Print the report in Landscape orientation. Change columns widths, if necessary, so the report will fit on one page.
▶ Pay Sales Tax for the amount due through 01/30/10, and print the check.
▶ Prepare a Vendor Balance Detail Report for All Transactions. Print in Portrait orientation. Adjust column widths so the report will display the account names in full and will print on one page without selecting Fit report on one page wide.
▶ Print a Trial Balance for 01/01/2010 to 01/30/2010.
▶ Print a Journal for 01/01/2010 to 01/30/2010
▶ Back up data.

NAME_____

TRANSMITTAL

CHAPTER 6: YOUR NAME RESORT CLOTHING

Attach the following documents and reports:

Inventory Stock Status by Item, January 1-5, 2010
Purchase Order No. 1: Casual Clothes
Purchase Order No. 2: Resort Clothing Supply, Inc.
Purchase Order No. 3: Clothes Time
Account QuickReport, Purchase Orders
Check No. 2: Casual Clothes
Check No. 3: Resort Clothing Supply, Inc.
Unpaid Bills Detail, January 25, 2010
Check No. 4: SLO Rental Company
Check No. 5: SLO Telephone Company
Sales Tax Liability Report
Check No. 6: State Board of Equalization
Vendor Balance Detail, January 30, 2010
Trial Balance, January 1-30, 2010
Journal, January 1-30, 2010

GENERAL ACCOUNTING AND END-OF-PERIOD PROCEDURES: MERCHANDISING BUSINESS

7

LEARNING OBJECTIVES

At the completion of this chapter, you will be able to:

1. Complete the end-of-period procedures.
2. Change the name of existing accounts in the Chart of Accounts, view the account name change, and view the effect of an account name change on subaccounts.
3. Delete an existing account from the Chart of Accounts.
4. Enter the adjusting entries required for accrual-basis accounting.
5. Record depreciation and an adjustment for Purchases Discounts.
6. Understand how to record owners' equity transactions for a partnership.
7. Enter a transaction for owner withdrawals, and transfer owner withdrawals and net income to the owners' capital accounts.
8. Reconcile the bank statement, record bank service charges, and mark cleared transactions.
9. Reconcile a credit card statement.
10. Undo a reconciliation and customize the layout of the reconciliation screen.
11. Print the Journal.
12. Print reports such as Trial Balance, Profit and Loss Statement, and Balance Sheet.
13. Export a report to Microsoft® Excel and import data from Excel
14. Perform end-of-period backup, close a period, record transactions in a closed period, and adjust inventory quantities.

GENERAL ACCOUNTING AND END-OF-PERIOD PROCEDURES

As stated in previous chapters, QuickBooks Pro operates from the standpoint of the business document rather than an accounting form, journal, or ledger. While QuickBooks Pro does incorporate all of these items into the program, in many instances they operate behind the scenes. Many accounting programs require special closing procedures at the end of a period. QuickBooks Pro does not require special closing procedures at the end of a period. At the end of the fiscal year, QuickBooks Pro transfers the net income into the Retained Earnings account and allows you to protect the data for the year by assigning a closing date to the period. All of the transaction detail is maintained and viewable, but it will not be changed unless OK is clicked on a warning screen.

Even though a formal closing does not have to be performed within QuickBooks Pro, when using accrual-basis accounting, several transactions must be recorded in order to reflect all expenses and income for the period accurately. For example, bank statements and credit cards must be reconciled; and any charges or bank collections need to be recorded. Adjusting entries such as depreciation, office supplies used, and so on will also need to be made. These adjustments may be recorded by the CPA or by the company's accounting personnel. At the end of the year, net income for the year and the owner withdrawals for the year should be transferred to the owners' capital accounts.

As in a service business, the CPA for the company will review things such as account names, adjusting entries, depreciation schedules, owner's equity adjustments, and so on.

If the CPA makes the changes and adjustments, they may be made on the Accountant's Copy of the business files. An Accountant's Copy is a version of your company file that your accountant can use to make changes. You record the day-to-day business transactions; and, at the same time, your accountant works using the Accountant's Copy. The changes made by the CPA are imported into your company file. There are certain restrictions to the types of transactions that may be made on an Accountant's Copy of the company file. There are also restrictions regarding the types of entries that may be made in the company file that you are using.

Once necessary adjustments have been made, reports reflecting the end-of-period results of operations should be prepared. For archive purposes, at the end of the fiscal year, an additional backup is prepared and stored.

TRAINING TUTORIAL AND PROCEDURES

The following tutorial will once again work with Your Name Mountain Sports. As in Chapters 5 and 6, transactions will be recorded for this fictitious company. Refer to procedures given in Chapter 5 to maximize training benefits.

As in the other chapters in the text, the year used for the screen shots is 2010, which is the same year as the version of the program. You may want to check with your instructor to see if you should use 2010 as the year for the transactions. Be sure to use the same year for all the transactions in Chapters 5, 6, and 7.

OPEN QUICKBOOKS® PRO AND YOUR NAME MOUNTAIN SPORTS

 Open **QuickBooks Pro** and **Your Name Mountain Sports** as instructed in previous chapters

BEGINNING THE TUTORIAL

In this chapter you will be recording end-of-period adjustments, reconciling bank and credit card statements, changing account names, and preparing traditional end-of-period reports. Because QuickBooks Pro does not perform a traditional closing of the books, you will learn how to close the period to protect transactions and data recorded during previous accounting periods.

As in previous chapters, all transactions are listed on memos. The transaction date will be the same as the memo date unless otherwise specified within the transaction. To determine the account used in the transaction, refer to the Chart of Accounts.

CHANGE THE NAME OF EXISTING ACCOUNTS IN THE CHART OF ACCOUNTS

Even though transactions have been recorded during the month of January, QuickBooks Pro makes it a simple matter to change the name of an existing account. Once the name of an account has been changed, all transactions using the old name are updated and show the new account name.

MEMO
DATE: January 31, 2010

On the recommendation of the company's CPA, you decided to change the account named Freight Income to Delivery Income.

DO Change the account name of Freight Income

Access the Chart of Accounts using the keyboard shortcut **Ctrl+A**
Scroll through accounts until you see Freight Income, click **Freight Income**

Use the keyboard shortcut **Ctrl+E**

On the **Edit Account** screen, highlight **Freight Income**

Enter the new name **Delivery Income**

Change the description from **Freight Income** to **Delivery Income**

Click **Save & Close** to record the name change and to close the **Edit Account** screen

- Notice that the name of the account appears as Delivery Income in the Chart of Accounts.

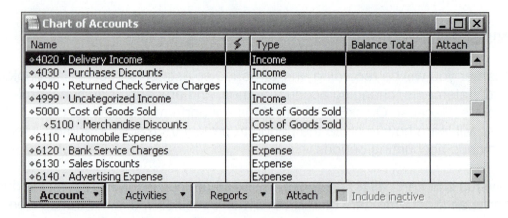

Do not close the **Chart of Accounts**

MAKE AN ACCOUNT INACTIVE

If you are not using an account and do not have plans to do so in the near future, the account may be made inactive. The account remains available for use, yet it does not appear on your Chart of Accounts unless you check the Show All check box.

MEMO

DATE: January 31, 2010

At this time, Your Name Mountain Sports does not plan to rent any equipment. The account Equipment Rental should be made inactive. In addition, the company does not plan to use Franchise Fees. Make these accounts inactive.

DO Make the accounts listed above inactive

Click **Equipment Rental**

Click the **Account** button at the bottom of the Chart of Accounts, click **Make Account Inactive**
- The account no longer appears in the Chart of Accounts.

Make **Franchise Fees** inactive

Click **Franchise Fees**

Use the keyboard shortcut **Ctrl+E**

On the Edit Account screen, click the **Account is inactive** check box in the lower-left portion of the screen

Click **Save & Close**
- If you wish to view all accounts, including the inactive ones, click the **Include Inactive** check box at the bottom of the Chart of Accounts, and all accounts will be displayed.
- Notice the icons that mark Equipment Rental and Franchise Fees as inactive accounts.

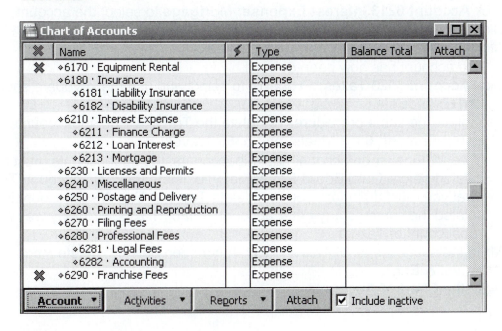

Do not close the **Chart of Accounts**

DELETE AN EXISTING ACCOUNT FROM THE CHART OF ACCOUNTS

If you do not want to make an account inactive because you have not used it and do not plan to use it at all, QuickBooks Pro allows the account to be deleted at anytime. However, as a safeguard, QuickBooks Pro does prevent the deletion of an account once it has been used even if it simply contains an opening or an existing balance.

> **MEMO**
> **DATE:** January 31, 2010
>
> In addition to previous changes to account names, you find that you do not use nor will you use the expense accounts: Account 6213 Interest Expense: Mortgage, Account 6523 Taxes: Property, and Account 6350 Travel & Ent. and its subaccounts. Delete these accounts from the Chart of Accounts.

DO ▶ Delete the accounts listed in the memo

> Scroll through Chart of Accounts until you see Account 6213 Interest Expense: Mortgage
> Click **Account 6213 Interest Expense: Mortgage** to select the account
> Click the **Account** button at the bottom of the Chart of Accounts, click **Delete**
> Click **OK** on the **Delete Accounts** dialog box
> - The account has now been deleted.
> Click **Account 6523 Taxes: Property** to select and use the keyboard shortcut **Ctrl+D** to delete
> Also follow the same procedures to delete the Travel & Ent. subaccounts: **6351 Entertainment**, **6352 Meals**, and **6353 Travel**
> - *Note:* Whenever an account has subaccounts, the subaccounts must be deleted before QuickBooks Pro will let you delete the main account. This is what you must do before you can delete Travel & Ent. A subaccount is deleted the same as any other account. In fact, Taxes: Property was a subaccount of Taxes.
> When the subaccounts of Travel & Ent. have been deleted; delete **Account 6350 Travel & Ent.**
> Close the **Chart of Accounts**

FIXED ASSET MANAGEMENT

QuickBooks Pro enables you to keep a record of your company's fixed assets. In the Fixed Asset List, you may record information about your company's fixed assets including the purchase date and price, whether the item new or used when purchased, and the sales price if the item is sold. Note that Depreciation and Book Value are not calculated or stored in the Fixed Asset List.

The Accountant or Enterprise versions of QuickBooks includes a more a Fixed Asset Manager that is more comprehensive than a list of fixed assets. When used, the Fixed Asset Manager pulls information about the fixed assets from an open company file. The accountant can determine the depreciation for the assets and post a journal entry back to the company file. The Fixed Asset Manager also integrates with Intuit's ProSeries Tax products.

The Fixed Asset List provides a way to keep important information about your assets in one convenient place. This is useful to do whether or not your accountant uses the Fixed Asset Manager.

You can create an item to track a fixed asset at several points during the asset's life cycle; however, it is recommended that you create the item when you buy the asset or setup the company.

You can create a fixed asset item from the Fixed Asset List or from a Transaction.

MEMO

DATE: January 31, 2010

When Your Name Mountain Sports was setup in QuickBooks, Office Equipment and Store Fixtures were designated as Fixed Assets but were not added to the Fixed Asset List. To work with the Fixed Asset List, the Fixed Assets need to be added to the list.

DO Create a fixed asset list

> Click **Lists** on the menu bar
> Click **Fixed Asset Item List**
> Use the keyboard shortcut **Ctrl+N** to create a new item
> Complete the information for the new item:
> The **Asset Name** is **Store Fixtures**
> The Item is **new**
> The **Purchase Description** should be **Store Fixtures**
> The **Date** is **12/31/09**
> The **Cost** is **4500**
> The **Asset Account** is **1520**
> The **Asset Description** is **Store Fixtures**

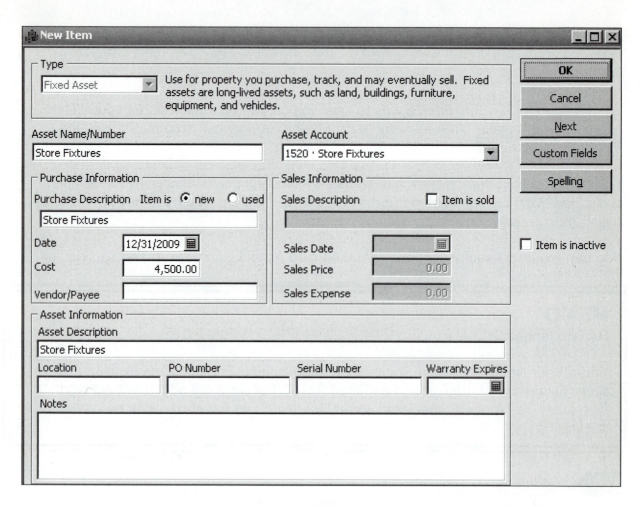

- Look at the bottom of the screen. If you want to add information for the items location, PO Number, Serial Number, and Warranty, fields are provided. There is also room to add Notes about the item.

When the information is entered for Store Fixtures, click **Next**

Repeat to add the Office Equipment with a cost of $5,000.00 to the list

- Be sure to use the appropriate account for Office Equipment

Click **OK**

Close the Fixed Asset List

ADJUSTMENTS FOR ACCRUAL-BASIS ACCOUNTING

In accrual-basis accounting, the income from a period is matched against the expenses of a period in order to arrive at an accurate figure for net income. Thus, the revenue is earned at the time the service is performed or the sale is made regardless of when the cash is actually received. The same holds true when a business buys things or pays bills. In the accrual basis of accounting, the expense is recorded at the time the bill is received or the product or service is delivered regardless of the actual payment date. The cash basis of accounting records income or revenue at the time cash is received regardless of when the sale was made or the service performed. In cash-basis accounting, the expense is not recorded until it is paid.

There are several internal transactions that must be recorded when using the accrual basis of accounting. These entries are called adjusting entries. For example, equipment does wear out and will eventually need to be replaced. Rather than waiting until replacement to record the use of the equipment, an adjusting entry is made to allocate the use of equipment as an expense for a period. This is called *depreciation*. Certain items used in a business are paid for in advance. As these are used, they become expenses of the business. For example, insurance for the entire year would be used up month by month and should, therefore, be a monthly expense. Commonly, the insurance is billed and paid for the entire year. Until the insurance is used, it is an asset. Each month the portion of the insurance used becomes an expense for the month. Another similar adjustment is made to record the amount of supplies that have been used during the month. Supplies on hand are assets and the amount of the supplies used during the period is the expense.

ADJUSTING ENTRIES—PREPAID EXPENSES

During the operation of a business, companies purchase supplies to have on hand for use in the operation of the business. In accrual-basis accounting, the supplies are considered to be assets (something the business owns) or prepaid expenses until they are used in the operation of the business. As the supplies are used, the amount used becomes an expense for the period. The same rationale applies to other things paid for in advance, such as insurance. At the end of the period, an adjusting entry must be made to allocate correctly the amount of prepaid assets to expenses.

The transactions for these adjustments may be recorded in the account register or they may be entered in the General Journal.

MEMO
DATE: January 31, 2010

The monthly adjustment for Prepaid Insurance needs to be recorded. The $250 is the amount we paid for two months of liability insurance coverage. Also, we have a balance of $521.98 in office supplies and a balance of $400 in sales supplies. Please adjust accordingly.

DO ▶Record the adjusting entries for insurance expense, office supplies expense, and sales supplies expense in the General Journal.

Access the **General Journal**:
Click **Company,** click **Make General Journal Entries**
Record the adjusting entry for Prepaid Insurance
Click **OK** on the Assigning Numbers to Journal Entries screen
Enter **01/31/10** as the **Date**

- Entry No. is left blank unless you wish to record a specific number.
- Because all transactions entered for the month have been entered in the Journal as well as on an invoice or a bill, all transactions automatically have a Journal entry number. When the Journal is printed, your transaction number may be different from the answer key. Disregard the transaction number because it can change based on how many times you delete transactions, etc.

Tab to or click the **Account** column, click the drop-down list arrow for **Account**, click **6181 Liability Insurance Expense**
Tab to or click **Debit**

- The $250 given in the memo is the amount for two months.

Use the QuickBooks Calculator to determine the amount of the adjustment for the month:
Enter **250** in the Debit column
Press **/** for division
Key **2**
Press **Enter**

- The calculation is performed and the amount is entered in the Debit column.

Tab to or click the **Memo** column, type **Adjusting Entry, Insurance**
Tab to or click **Account**, click the drop-down list arrow for Account, click **1340 Prepaid Insurance**

- The amount for the **Credit** column should have been entered automatically. If not, enter **125**.

Enter the Memo information by using the copy command:
Click the **Memo** column for the Debit entry
Drag through the memo **Adjusting Entry, Insurance**
When the memo is highlighted, use the keyboard command **Ctrl+C** to copy the memo
Click in the **Memo** column for the Credit entry
Use the keyboard command **Ctrl+V** to paste the memo into the column

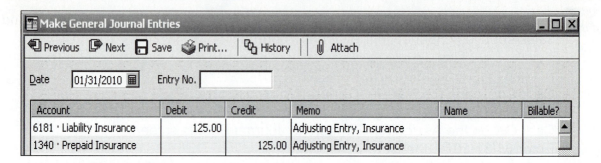

Click **NEXT** or **Save & New** to record the adjustment and to advance to the next General Journal Entry screen

Repeat the above procedures to record the adjustment for the office supplies used

- The amount given in the memo is the balance of the account after the supplies have been used.
- The actual amount of the supplies used in January must be calculated.

Determine the balance of the Office Supplies account by using the keyboard shortcut **Ctrl+A** to access the Chart of Accounts

Use the QuickBooks Calculator or the Windows Calculator to determine the amount of the adjustment

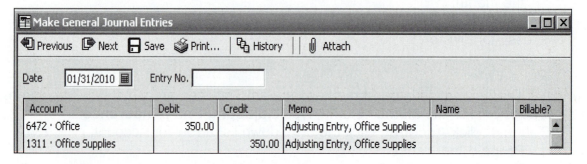

When the entry is complete, click **Next**

Repeat the above procedures to record the adjustment for the sales supplies used

- The amount given in the memo is the balance of the account after the supplies have been used. The actual amount of the supplies used in January must be calculated. Remember to subtract the $400 balance in the memo from the account total in order to get the amount of supplies used.

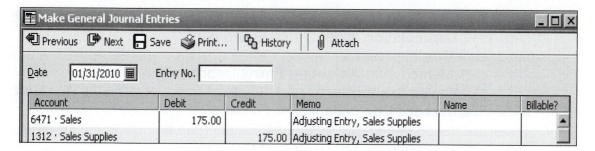

Account	Debit	Credit	Memo	Name	Billable?
6471 · Sales	175.00		Adjusting Entry, Sales Supplies		
1312 · Sales Supplies		175.00	Adjusting Entry, Sales Supplies		

When the entry is complete, click **Save & New** or **Next**

ADJUSTING ENTRIES—DEPRECIATION

Using the accrual basis of accounting requires companies to record an expense for the amount of equipment used in the operation of the business. Unlike supplies, where you can actually see the paper supply diminishing, it is very difficult to see how much of a cash register has been used up during the month. To account for the fact that machines do wear out and need to be replaced, an adjustment is made for depreciation. This adjustment correctly matches the expenses of the period against the revenue of the period.

The adjusting entry for depreciation can be made in the depreciation account register, or it can be made in the General Journal.

MEMO
DATE: January 31, 2010

Having received the necessary depreciation schedules from the accountant, Ruth records the adjusting entry for depreciation:

Office Equipment, $85 per month
Store Fixtures, $75 per month

DO Record a compound adjusting entry for depreciation of the office equipment and the store fixtures in the General Journal:

The Date is **01/31/10**
Entry No. is left blank
- In order to use the automatic calculation feature of QuickBooks Pro, the credit entries will be entered first.

Tab to or click the **Account** column, click the drop-down list arrow for **Account**, click **1512 Depreciation** under **Office Equipment**

Tab to or click **Credit**, enter **85**

Tab to or click **Memo**, enter **Adjusting Entry, Depreciation**

Tab to or click the **Account** column, click the drop-down list arrow for **Account**, click **1522 Depreciation** under **Store Fixtures**

- Disregard the 85 that shows as a debit. Entering an amount in the credit column and pressing the tab key will eliminate the debit.

Tab to or click **Credit**, enter **75**

Tab to or click **Memo**, enter **Adjusting Entry, Depreciation**

Tab to or click the **Account** column, click the drop-down list arrow for **Account**, click **6150 Depreciation Expense**

Debit column should automatically show **160**

Tab to or click **Memo**, enter **Adjusting Entry, Depreciation**

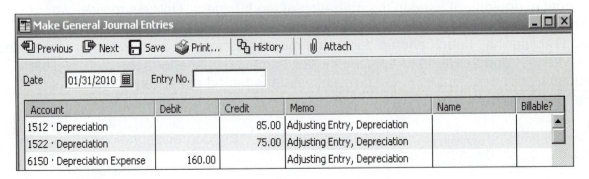

Verify that you entered Credits to accounts 1512 and 1522 and a Debit to account 6150

Click **Save & Close** to record the adjustment and close the General Journal

- If you get a message regarding tracking fixed assets on journal entries, click **OK**.

VIEW GENERAL JOURNAL

Once transactions have been entered in the General Journal, it is important to view them. QuickBooks Pro also refers to the General Journal as the Journal and allows it to be viewed or printed at any time. Even with the special ways in which transactions are entered in QuickBooks Pro through invoices, bills, checks, and account registers, the Journal is still considered the book of original entry. All transactions recorded for the company may be viewed in the Journal even if they were entered elsewhere.

DO View the Journal for January

Click **Reports** on the menu bar, point to **Accountant & Taxes**, and click **Journal**
The Dates are from **01/01/10** to **01/31/10**
Tab to generate the report

Your Name Mountain Sports
Journal
January 2010

Trans # ◊	Type ◊	Date ◊	Num ◊	Name ◊	Memo ◊	Account ◊	Debit ◊	Credit ◊
99	General Journal	01/31/2010			Adjusting Entry, Insurance	6181 · Liability Insurance	125.00	
					Adjusting Entry, Insurance	1340 · Prepaid Insurance		125.00
							125.00	125.00
100	General Journal	01/31/2010			Adjusting Entry, Office Supplies	6472 · Office	350.00	
					Adjusting Entry, Office Supplies	1311 · Office Supplies		350.00
							350.00	350.00
101	General Journal	01/31/2010			Adjusting Entry, Sales Supplies	6471 · Sales	175.00	
					Adjusting Entry, Sales Supplies	1312 · Sales Supplies		175.00
							175.00	175.00
102	General Journal	01/31/2010			Adjusting Entry, Depreciation	1512 · Depreciation		85.00
					Adjusting Entry, Depreciation	1522 · Depreciation		75.00
					Adjusting Entry, Depreciation	6150 · Depreciation Expense	160.00	
							160.00	160.00
TOTAL							**43,875.91**	**43,875.91**

Partial Report

Scroll through the report to view all transactions recorded in the Journal
- Only the transactions made from January 1 through January 31, 2010 are displayed. Since opening balances were entered during the creation of the company, note that the first transaction shown is 48—Invoice No. 1.
- Viewing the Journal and checking the accounts used in transactions, the dates entered for transactions, the sales items used, and the amounts recorded for the transactions is an excellent way to discover errors and determine corrections that need to be made.

Close the report without printing

DEFINITION OF A PARTNERSHIP

A partnership is a business owned by two or more individuals. Because it is unincorporated, each partner owns a share of all the assets and liabilities. Each partner receives a portion of the profits based on the percentage of his or her investment in the business or according to any partnership agreement drawn up at the time the business was created. Because the business is owned by the partners, they do not receive a salary. Any funds obtained by the partners are in the form of withdrawals against their share of the profits. QuickBooks Pro makes it easy to set up a partnership and create separate accounts, if desired, for each partner's equity, investment, and withdrawals.

OWNER WITHDRAWALS

In a partnership, owners cannot receive a paycheck because they own the business. An owner withdrawing money from a business—even to pay personal expenses—is similar to an individual withdrawing money from a savings account. A withdrawal simply decreases the owners' capital. QuickBooks Pro allows you to establish a separate account for owner withdrawals for each owner. If a separate account is not established, owner withdrawals may be subtracted directly from each owner's capital or investment account.

MEMO
DATE: January 31, 2010

Because both partners work in the business full time, they do not earn a paycheck. Prepare checks for your monthly withdrawal of $1,000 and Larry's monthly withdrawal of $1,000.

DO Write the checks for the owner withdrawals

> Use the keyboard shortcut **Ctrl+W** to open the **Write Checks - Checking** window:
> Click the check box **To be printed**, the Check No. should be **To Print**
> **Date** should be **01/31/10**
> Enter **Your Name** on the **Pay to the Order of** line, press the **Tab** key
> - Because your name was not added to any list when the company was created, the **Name Not Found** dialog box appears on the screen.

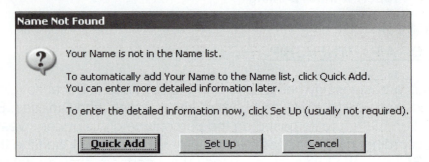

> Click **Quick Add** to add your name to a list
> The **Select Name Type** dialog box appears

Click **Other** and click **OK**

- Your name is added to a list of *Other* names, which is used for owners, partners, and other miscellaneous names.

Tab to or click in the area for the amount of the check

- If necessary, delete any numbers showing for the amount (0.00).

Enter **1000**

Tab to or click **Memo**, enter **Owner Withdrawal for January**

Tab to or click in the Account column at the bottom of the check, click the drop-down list arrow, click the Equity account **3013 Your Name, Drawing**

- The amount 1,000.00 should appear in the Amount column.
- If it does not, tab to or click in the Amount column and enter 1000.
- Make sure To be printed is selected.

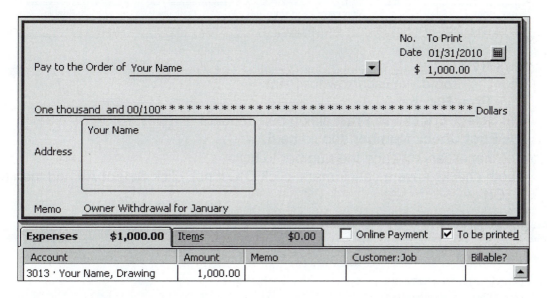

Click **Next** to record the check and advance to the next check

Repeat the above procedures to prepare Check No. 7 for Larry Muir for $1,000 withdrawal

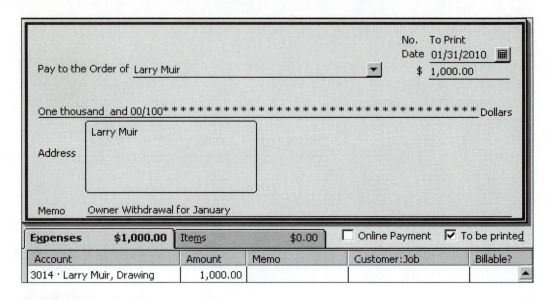

Click **Next**

Click the drop-down list arrow for **Print**

Click **Print Batch**

The **Select Checks to Print** dialog box appears

The **First Check Number** should be **6**

- If necessary, change the number to **6**.

If both checks have a check mark, click **OK**, if not, click **Select All** and then click **OK**

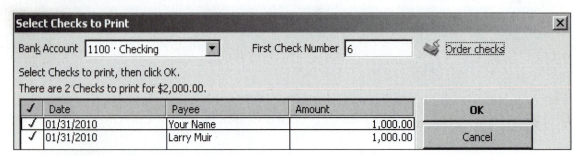

The Check style should be Standard

Once the check has printed successfully, click **OK** on the **Print Checks – Confirmation** dialog box

Close **Write Checks - Checking**

PREPARE BALANCE SHEET

A balance sheet proves that assets equal liabilities plus owners' equity; however, the owners' equity in a partnership may be organized in a manner that is more meaningful than is currently shown.

DO ▶ View the Balance Sheet for January 31, 2010

Click **Reports** on the menu bar, point to **Company & Financial**, and then click **Balance Sheet Standard**
Enter **01/31/10** for the date
Tab to generate the report
Scroll through the report
- Notice the Equity section, especially the Investment and Drawing accounts for each owner.
- Also notice the Your Name & Muir Capital account balance. When the capital for both owners is combined into one account, the report does not indicate how much of the capital is for each owner.

Your Name Mountain Sports
Balance Sheet
As of January 31, 2010

	Jan 31, 10
Equity	
3010 · Your Name & Muir Capital	
3011 · Your Name, Investment	20,000.00
3012 · Larry Muir, Investment	20,000.00
3013 · Your Name, Drawing	-1,000.00
3014 · Larry Muir, Drawing	-1,000.00
3010 · Your Name & Muir Capital - Other	25,459.44
Total 3010 · Your Name & Muir Capital	63,459.44
Net Income	2,667.07
Total Equity	66,126.51
TOTAL LIABILITIES & EQUITY	82,243.89

Partial Report

Do not close the report

CREATE AN INDIVIDUAL CAPITAL ACCOUNT FOR EACH OWNER

A better display of owners' equity would be to show all equity accounts for each owner grouped together by owner. In addition, each owner should have an individual capital account.

MEMO
DATE: January 31, 2010

Change the account number of Your Name & Muir, Capital, to 3100. Create separate Capital accounts for Your Name and Larry Muir. Name the accounts 3110 Your Name, Capital, and 3120 Larry Muir, Capital. In addition, renumber Your Name Investment account to 3111 and your Drawing account to 3112. Make these subaccounts of Your Name, Capital. Do the same for Larry's accounts: 3121 Investment and 3122 Drawing.

DO Create separate Capital accounts and change subaccounts for existing owners' equity accounts

Access the **Chart of Accounts** as previously instructed
Click **3010 Your Name & Muir, Capital**
Click **Account** at the bottom of the **Chart of Accounts**, click **Edit**
Change the account number to **3100**
- To be consistent, make sure to use just your last name in Your Name & Muir, Capital. If you did not do this previously, change it now.
Click **Save & Close**
Click **Account** at the bottom of the **Chart of Accounts**, click **New**
Click **Equity** as the account type, click **Continue**
Tab to or click **Number**, enter **3110**
Tab to or click **Name**, enter **Your Name, Capital**
- Remember to use your real name.
Click **Subaccount**, click the drop-down list arrow next to **Subaccount**, click
     3100 Your Name & Muir, Capital
Click **Save & Close**
Click the account **Your Name, Investment**
Edit the account following steps previously listed
Change the account number to **3111**
Make this a subaccount of **3110 Your Name, Capital**
Click **Save & Close** when the changes have been made
Make the following changes to **Your Name, Drawing**: Account number is **3112**,
     Subaccount of **3110**
Create the Equity account **3120 Larry Muir, Capital**: Account 3120 is a
     subaccount of **3100**
Change **3012 Larry Muir, Investment** to **3121**: Account 3121 is a subaccount of
     3120
Change **3014 Larry Muir, Drawing** to **3122**: Account 3122 is a subaccount of
     3120

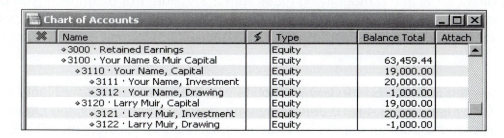

Close the **Chart of Accounts**
- Since the Balance Sheet is still on the screen, the changes made to the Capital accounts will be shown in the report. If you get a screen asking if you would like to refresh the report, click **Yes**.
- Notice the change in the Equity section of the Balance Sheet.
- Observe how much easier it is to determine the value of equity for each owner.
- Notice that there is an amount shown for 3100-Your Name & Muir, Capital – Other of $25,459.44.

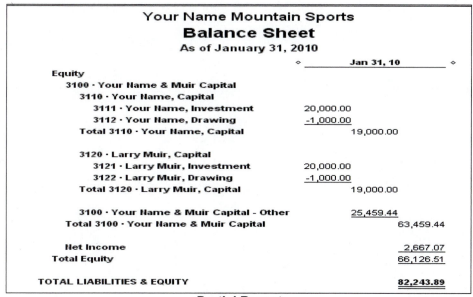

Partial Report

Do not close the report

USE QUICKZOOM TO VIEW THE CAPITAL – OTHER ACCOUNT

QuickZoom is a QuickBooks Pro feature that allows you to make a closer observation of transactions, amounts, etc. With QuickZoom you may zoom in on an item when the mouse pointer turns into a magnifying glass with a Z inside. For example, if you point to Store Fixtures Loan, you will see the magnifying glass with the Z inside. If you point to an item and you do not get a magnifying glass with a Z inside, you cannot zoom in on the item.

As you view the Balance Sheet, you will notice that the balance for Your Name & Muir, Capital - Other is $25,459.44. To determine why there is an amount in the Other Capital, use QuickZoom to see the Transactions by Account report. You will see that the amounts for the beginning balances of the assets, liabilities, and the owners' equity have been entered in this account. Thus, the value of the Other Capital account proves the fundamental accounting equation of Assets = Liabilities + Owner's Equity.

> **DO** Use QuickZoom to view in the Your Name & Muir Capital – Other account
> Point to the amount 25,459.44, and double-click the primary mouse button
> Change the report dates **From** is **12/01/09** and **To** is **01/31/10**, press Tab to
>   generate the report

Your Name Mountain Sports
Transactions by Account
As of January 31, 2010

Type	Date	Num	Name	Memo	Clr	Split	Amount	Balance
3100 · Your Name & Muir Capital								0.00
Inventory Adjust	12/31/2009			Pants Opening balance	✓	1120 · Inventory Asset	1,750.00	1,750.00
Inventory Adjust	12/31/2009			Accessories Opening balance	✓	1120 · Inventory Asset	2,925.00	4,675.00
Inventory Adjust	12/31/2009			Bindings-Skis Opening balance	✓	1120 · Inventory Asset	3,750.00	8,425.00
Inventory Adjust	12/31/2009			Bindings-Snow Opening balance	✓	1120 · Inventory Asset	3,750.00	12,175.00
Inventory Adjust	12/31/2009			Boots Opening balance	✓	1120 · Inventory Asset	600.00	12,775.00
Inventory Adjust	12/31/2009			Boots-Ski Opening balance	✓	1120 · Inventory Asset	1,125.00	13,900.00
Inventory Adjust	12/31/2009			Boots-Snowbrd Opening balance	✓	1120 · Inventory Asset	900.00	14,800.00
Inventory Adjust	12/31/2009			Gloves Opening balance	✓	1120 · Inventory Asset	330.00	15,130.00
Inventory Adjust	12/31/2009			Hats Opening balance	✓	1120 · Inventory Asset	240.00	15,370.00
Inventory Adjust	12/31/2009			Pants-Ski Opening balance	✓	1120 · Inventory Asset	2,850.00	18,220.00
Inventory Adjust	12/31/2009			Parkas Opening balance	✓	1120 · Inventory Asset	4,375.00	22,595.00
Inventory Adjust	12/31/2009			Poles-Ski Opening balance	✓	1120 · Inventory Asset	540.00	23,135.00
Inventory Adjust	12/31/2009			Skis Opening balance	✓	1120 · Inventory Asset	5,000.00	28,135.00
Inventory Adjust	12/31/2009			Snowboard Opening balance	✓	1120 · Inventory Asset	3,000.00	31,135.00
Inventory Adjust	12/31/2009			Socks Opening balance	✓	1120 · Inventory Asset	225.00	31,360.00
Inventory Adjust	12/31/2009			Sweaters Opening balance	✓	1120 · Inventory Asset	1,875.00	33,235.00
Inventory Adjust	12/31/2009			Underwear Opening balance	✓	1120 · Inventory Asset	264.00	33,499.00
Credit Card Charge	12/31/2009			Account Opening Balance		2100 · Visa	-150.00	33,349.00
General Journal	12/31/2009			Account Opening Balance		2510 · Office Equipment Loan	-3,000.00	30,349.00
General Journal	12/31/2009			Account Opening Balance		2520 · Store Fixtures Loan	-2,500.00	27,849.00
Deposit	12/31/2009			Account Opening Balance		1100 · Checking	25,943.00	53,792.00
Deposit	12/31/2009			Account Opening Balance		1311 · Office Supplies	850.00	54,642.00
General Journal	12/31/2009			Account Opening Balance		1511 · Original Cost	5,000.00	59,642.00
General Journal	12/31/2009			Account Opening Balance		1521 · Original Cost	4,500.00	64,142.00
Deposit	12/31/2009			Account Opening Balance		1340 · Prepaid Insurance	250.00	64,392.00
General Journal	12/31/2009			Account Opening Balance		3111 · Your Name, Investment	-20,000.00	44,392.00
General Journal	12/31/2009			Account Opening Balance		3121 · Larry Muir, Investment	-20,000.00	24,392.00
Deposit	12/31/2009			Account Opening Balance		1312 · Sales Supplies	575.00	24,967.00
General Journal	12/31/2009					4999 · Uncategorized Income	6,942.44	31,909.44
General Journal	12/31/2009					6999 · Uncategorized Expenses	-8,500.00	23,409.44
Inventory Adjust	01/08/2010			Sleds Opening balance	✓	1120 · Inventory Asset	675.00	24,084.44
Inventory Adjust	01/08/2010			Toboggans Opening balance	✓	1120 · Inventory Asset	1,375.00	25,459.44
Total 3100 · Your Name & Muir Capital							25,459.44	25,459.44
TOTAL							**25,459.44**	**25,459.44**

- Notice that the amounts shown include the amounts for the opening balances of all the assets including each inventory item, all the liabilities, the original investment amounts (equity), and uncategorized income and expenses.
- Uncategorized Income and Expenses reflect the income earned and expenses incurred prior to the current period. This prevents previous income/expenses being included in the calculation for the net income or loss for the current period.

Close the Transactions by Account report without printing

Do not close the Balance Sheet

DISTRIBUTE CAPITAL TO EACH OWNER

The Balance Sheet does not indicate how much of the Other Capital should be distributed to each partner because Your Name & Muir, Capital, is a combined Capital account. In order to clarify this section of the report, the capital should be distributed between the two owners. Each owner has contributed an equal amount as an investment in the business, so the Other Capital should be divided equally between Larry and you.

DO ▶ Make an adjusting entry to distribute capital between the two owners

Access the **General Journal Entry** screen as previously instructed

Transfer the amount in the account **3100 Your Name & Muir, Capital –Other** to the owners' individual capital accounts by debiting Account **3100** for **25459.44**

Memo for all entries in the transaction is **Transfer Capital to Individual Accounts**

Transfer one-half of the amount debited to **3110 Your Name, Capital**, by crediting this account

- To determine one-half of the amount use QuickMath as follows: Click after the credit amount, press **/**, enter **2**, and press **Enter**.

Credit **3120 Larry Muir, Capital**, for the other half of the amount

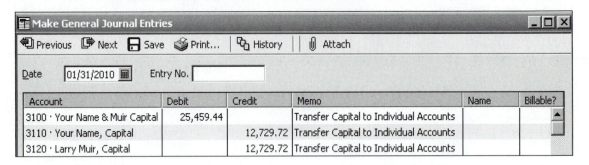

Click **Save & Close** to record and return to the Balance Sheet

- If the report does not automatically refresh, click **Yes**
- Notice the change in the Equity section of the Balance Sheet.
- The total of 3100 Your Name & Muir, Capital, is still 63,459.44. There is no longer a 3100 Your Name & Muir, Capital – Other account. Now, each owner has a Capital-Other account that shows 12,729.72.

Your Name Mountain Sports
Balance Sheet
As of January 31, 2010

		Jan 31, 10	
Equity			
3100 · Your Name & Muir Capital			
3110 · Your Name, Capital			
3111 · Your Name, Investment	20,000.00		
3112 · Your Name, Drawing	-1,000.00		
3110 · Your Name, Capital - Other	12,729.72		
Total 3110 · Your Name, Capital		31,729.72	
3120 · Larry Muir, Capital			
3121 · Larry Muir, Investment	20,000.00		
3122 · Larry Muir, Drawing	-1,000.00		
3120 · Larry Muir, Capital - Other	▶ 12,729.72		◀
Total 3120 · Larry Muir, Capital		31,729.72	
Total 3100 · Your Name & Muir Capital		63,459.44	
Net Income		2,667.07	
Total Equity		66,126.51	
TOTAL LIABILITIES & EQUITY		82,243.89	

Partial Report

Close the report without printing

BANK RECONCILIATION

Each month the Checking account should be reconciled with the bank statement to make sure both balances agree. The bank statement will rarely have an ending balance that matches the balance of the Checking account. This is due to several factors: outstanding checks, deposits in transit, bank service charges, interest earned on checking accounts, collections made by the bank, errors made in recording checks and/or deposits by the company or by the bank, etc.

In order to have an accurate amount listed as the balance in the Checking account, it is important that the differences between the bank statement and the Checking account be reconciled. If something such as a service charge or a collection made by the bank appears on the bank statement, it needs to be recorded in the Checking account.

Reconciling a bank statement is an appropriate time to find any errors that may have been recorded in the Checking account. The reconciliation may be out of balance because a transposition was made, a transaction was recorded backwards, a transaction was recorded twice, or a transaction was not recorded at all.

Bank Statement

OLD MAMMOTH BANK
12345 Old Mammoth Road
Mammoth Lakes, CA 93546
(909) 555-3880

Your Name Mountain Sports
875 Mountain Road
Mammoth Lakes, CA 93546

Acct. # 123-456-7890   **January 2010**

Beginning Balance 1/1/10	25,943.00		$25,943.00
1/18/10 Deposit	10,469.44		36,412.44
1/20/10 NSF Returned Check		100.00	36,312.44
1/20/10 Check 1		80.44	36,232.00
1/25/10 Check 3		294.00	35,938.00
1/25/10 Check 2		1,837.50	34,100.50
1/25/10 Check 4		312.60	33,787.90
1/25/10 Check 5		613.15	33,174.75
1/31/10 Office Equip. Loan Pmt.: $10.33 Principal, $53.42 Interest		63.75	33,111.00
1/31/10 Store Fixtures Loan Pmt.: $8.61 Principal, $44.51 Interest		53.12	33,057.88
1/31/10 Service Chg.		8.00	33,049.88
1/31/10 NSF Charge		10.00	33,039.88
1/31/10 Interest	54.05		33,093.93
Ending Balance 1/31/10			33,093.93

ENTER BANK STATEMENT INFORMATION AND COMPLETE BEGIN RECONCILIATION

The Begin Reconciliation screen initiates the account reconciliation. On this screen, information regarding the ending balance, service charges, and interest earned is entered.

MEMO

DATE: January 31, 2010

Received the bank statement from Old Mammoth Bank dated January 31, 2010.
Reconcile the bank statement and print a Reconciliation Report for Larry and you.

DO Use the bank statement on the previous page to reconcile the bank statement for January

Open the **Reconcile - Checking** window and enter preliminary information on the Begin Reconciliation screen
Click the **Reconcile** icon on the QuickBooks Home Page
- *Note:* If you need to exit the Begin Reconciliation screen before it is complete, click **Cancel**.

The **Account To Reconcile** should be **1100 Checking**
- If not, click the drop-down list arrow, click **Checking**.

The **Statement Date** should be **01/31/10**
Beginning Balance should be **25,943.00**
- This is the same amount as the Checking account starting balance.

Enter the **Ending Balance** from the bank statement, **33,093.93**
Tab to or click **Service Charge**, enter the **Service Charge**, **18.00**
- Note that this includes both the service charge of $8.00 and the $10.00 charge for Kevin Thomsen's NSF check in Chapter 5.

Tab to or click Service Charge **Date**, the date should be **01/31/10**; if not, change it
Tab to or click **Account**, click the drop-down list arrow for **Account**, click **6120 Bank Service Charges**
Tab to or click **Interest Earned**, enter **54.05**
Tab to or click Interest Earned **Date**, the date should be **01/31/10**; if not, change it
Tab to or click **Account**, enter the account number **7010** for **Interest Income**

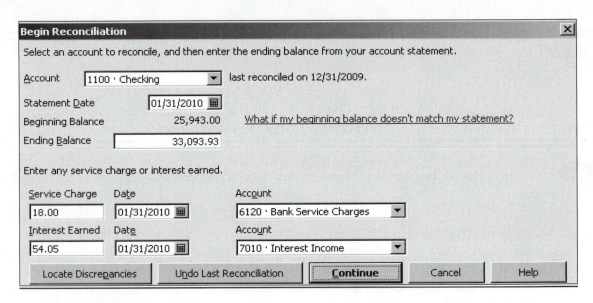

Click **Continue**

MARK CLEARED TRANSACTIONS FOR BANK RECONCILIATION

Once bank statement information for the ending balance, service charges, and interest has been entered, compare the checks and deposits listed on the statement with the transactions for the Checking account. If a deposit or a check is listed correctly on the bank statement and in the Reconcile - Checking window, it has cleared and should be marked. An item may be marked individually by positioning the cursor on the deposit or the check and clicking the primary mouse button. If all deposits and checks match, click the Mark All button to mark all the deposits and checks at once. To remove all the checks, click the Unmark All button. To unmark an individual item, click the item to remove the check mark.

▶ DO ▶ Mark cleared checks and deposits

- *Note:* If you need to exit the Reconcile - Checking screen before it is complete, click **Leave**. If you click **Reconcile Now**, you must Undo the reconciliation and start over.
- If you need to return to the Begin Reconciliation window, click the **Modify** button.
- Notice the selection of Highlight Marked. When an item has been selected, the background color changes.

Compare the bank statement with the **Reconcile - Checking** window

Click the items that appear on both statements

Look at the bottom of the **Reconcile - Checking** window

You have marked cleared:

1 Deposits and Other Credits for 10,469.44
6 Checks and Payments for 3,237.69
The Service Charge of -18.00 and Interest Earned of 54.05 are shown
The Ending Balance is 33,093.93
The Cleared Balance is 33,210.80
There is a Difference of -116.87

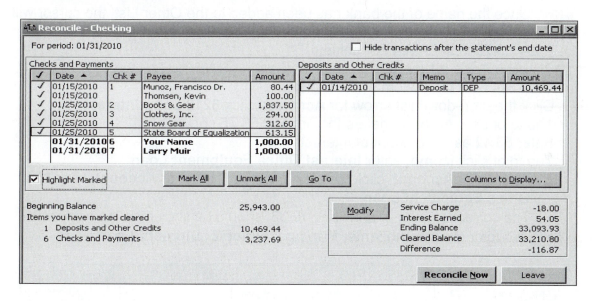

The bank statement should remain on the screen while you complete the next section

ADJUSTING AND CORRECTING ENTRIES—BANK RECONCILIATION

As you complete the reconciliation, you may find errors that need to be corrected or transactions that need to be recorded. Anything entered as a service charge or interest earned will be entered automatically when the reconciliation is complete and the Reconcile Now button is clicked. To correct an error such as a transposition, click on the entry then click the Go To button. The original entry will appear on the screen. The correction can be made and will show in the Reconcile - Checking window. If there is a transaction, such as an automatic loan payment to the bank, access the register for the account used in the transaction and enter the payment.

DO Enter the automatic loan payments shown on the bank statement

Use the keyboard shortcut **Ctrl+R** to open the register for the **1100 Checking** account:
In the blank transaction at the bottom of the register, enter the **Date**, **01/31/10**
Tab to or click **Number**, enter **Transfer**

Tab to or click **Payee**, enter **Old Mammoth Bank**
Tab to or click the **Payment** column
- Because Old Mammoth Bank does not appear on any list, you will get a **Name Not Found** dialog box when you move to another field.

Click the **Quick Add** button to add the name of the bank to the Name List
Click **Other**, and click **OK**
- Once the name of the bank has been added to the Other List, the cursor will be positioned in the **Payment** column.

Enter **63.75** in the **Payment** column
Click the **Account** column
Click **Splits** at the bottom of the register
Click the drop-down list arrow for **Account**, click **6212 Loan Interest**
Tab to or click **Amount**, delete the amount 63.75 shown
Enter **53.42** as the amount of interest
Tab to or click **Memo**, enter **Interest Office Equipment Loan**
Tab to or click **Account**, click the drop-down list arrow for **Account**, click **2510 Office Equipment Loan**
- The correct amount of principal, 10.33, should be shown as the amount.
- Tab to or click **Memo**, enter **Principal Office Equipment Loan**

Account	Amount	Memo	Customer:Job	Billable?	
6212 · Loan Interest	53.42	Interest Office Equipment Loan			Close
2510 · Office Equipment Loan	10.33	Principal Office Equipment Loan			Clear

Click **Close** on the Splits window
- This closes the window for the information regarding the way the transaction is to be "split" between accounts.

For the **Memo** in the Checking Register, record **Loan Payment Office Equipment**
Click the **Record** button to record the transaction
- Transfers are shown before checks prepared on the same date; thus, the loan payment does not appear as the last transaction in the register.

| 01/31/2010 | Transfer | Old Mammoth Bank | | 63.75 | | 33,111.00 |
| | CHK | -split- | Loan Payment Office Equipment | | | |

Repeat the procedures to record the loan payment for store fixtures
- When you enter the Payee as Old Mammoth Bank, the amount for the previous transaction (63.75) appears in amount.

Enter the new amount **53.12**
Click **Splits**
Click the appropriate accounts and enter the correct amount for each item

- The accounts used for the office equipment loan payment may appear. Click the drop-down list arrow and select the appropriate accounts for the store fixture loan payment.
- Refer to the bank statement for details regarding the amount of the payment for interest and the amount of the payment applied to principal.

Account	Amount	Memo	Customer:Job	Billable?	
6212 · Loan Interest	44.51	Interest Store Fixtures Loan			Close
2520 · Store Fixtures Loan	8.61	Principal Store Fixtures Loan		▲	Clear

Click **Close** to close the window for the information regarding the "split" between accounts

Enter the transaction **Memo**

Click **Record** to record the loan payment

01/31/2010	Transfer	Old Mammoth Bank		53.12		33,057.88
	CHK	-split- Loan Payment Store Fixtures				

Close the **Checking Register**
- You should return to **Reconcile - Checking**.

Scroll to the top of **Checks and Payments**
- Notice the two entries for the payments in Checks and Payments.

Mark the two entries
- At this point the Ending Balance and Cleared Balance should be equal—$33,093.93 with a difference of 0.00.

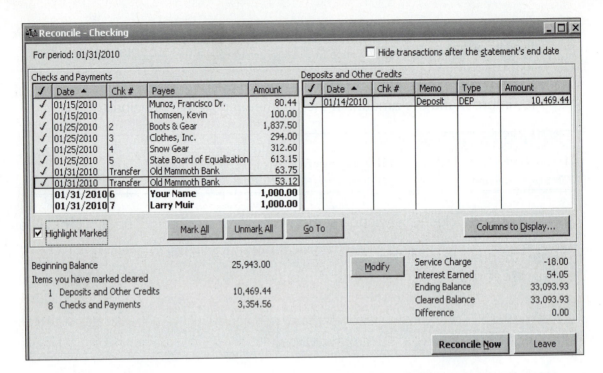

If your entries agree with the above, click **Reconcile Now** to finish the reconciliation

- If your reconciliation is not in agreement, do not click **Reconcile Now** until the errors are corrected.
- Once you click **Reconcile Now**, you may not return to this **Reconciliation - Checking** window. You would have to Undo the reconciliation and start over.

PRINT A RECONCILIATION REPORT

As soon as the Ending Balance and the Cleared Balance are equal or when you finish marking transactions and click Reconcile Now, a screen appears allowing you to select the level of Reconciliation Report you would like to print. You may select Detail, which shows all the transactions that were reconciled, or Summary, which shows the beginning balance, the totals of the deposits and checks, and the ending balance. You may print the report at the time you have finished reconciling the account, or you may print the report later by returning to the Reconciliation window. QuickBooks Pro keeps your last two Reconciliation Reports in memory. If you think you may want to print the report after it is no longer one of the two reconciliation reports in memory, you can print the report to a file to save it permanently.

DO ▶ Print a Detail Reconciliation report

On the **Reconciliation Complete** screen, click **Detail**, click **Display**

Adjust the column widths so the report will print on one page and all information is displayed in full

Your Name Mountain Sports
Reconciliation Detail
1100 · Checking, Period Ending 01/31/2010

Type	Date	Num	Name	Clr	Amount	Balance
Beginning Balance						25,943.00
Cleared Transactions						
Checks and Payments - 9 items						
▶ Invoice	01/15/2010	10	Thomsen, Kevin	✓	-100.00	-100.00 ◄
Check	01/15/2010	1	Munoz, Francisco Dr.	✓	-80.44	-180.44
Bill Pmt -Check	01/25/2010	2	Boots & Gear	✓	-1,837.50	-2,017.94
Sales Tax Payment	01/25/2010	5	State Board of Equalization	✓	-613.15	-2,631.09
Bill Pmt -Check	01/25/2010	4	Snow Gear	✓	-312.60	-2,943.69
Bill Pmt -Check	01/25/2010	3	Clothes, Inc.	✓	-294.00	-3,237.69
Check	01/31/2010	Transfer	Old Mammoth Bank	✓	-63.75	-3,301.44
Check	01/31/2010	Transfer	Old Mammoth Bank	✓	-53.12	-3,354.56
Check	01/31/2010			✓	-18.00	-3,372.56
Total Checks and Payments					-3,372.56	-3,372.56
Deposits and Credits - 2 items						
Deposit	01/14/2010			✓	10,469.44	10,469.44
Deposit	01/31/2010			✓	54.05	10,523.49
Total Deposits and Credits					10,523.49	10,523.49
Total Cleared Transactions					7,150.93	7,150.93
Cleared Balance					7,150.93	33,093.93
Uncleared Transactions						
Checks and Payments - 2 items						
Check	01/31/2010	7	Larry Muir		-1,000.00	-1,000.00
Check	01/31/2010	6	Your Name		-1,000.00	-2,000.00
Total Checks and Payments					-2,000.00	-2,000.00
Total Uncleared Transactions					-2,000.00	-2,000.00
Register Balance as of 01/31/2010					5,150.93	31,093.93
Ending Balance					**5,150.93**	**31,093.93**

Print as previously instructed in Portrait orientation
When the report finishes printing, close the report

VIEW THE CHECKING ACCOUNT REGISTER

Once the bank reconciliation has been completed, it is wise to scroll through the Check Register to view the effect of the reconciliation on the account. You will notice that the check column shows a check mark for all items that were marked as cleared during the reconciliation. If at a later date an error is discovered, the transaction may be changed, and the correction will be reflected in the Beginning Balance on the reconciliation.

DO ▶ View the register for the Checking account

Access the register as previously instructed
To display more of the register, click the check box for **1-Line**

Scroll through the register
- Notice that the transactions are listed in chronological order. Even though the bank reconciliation transactions were recorded after the checks written on January 31, the bank reconciliation transactions appear before the checks because they were recorded as a Transfer.

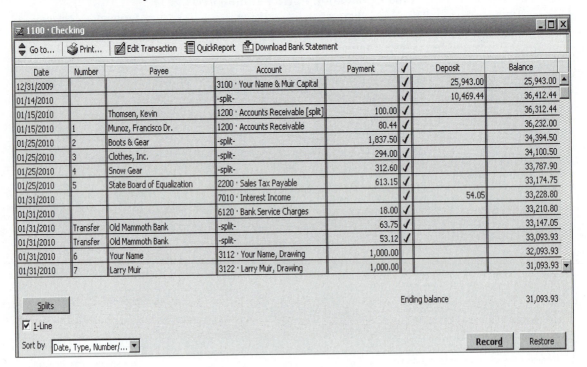

Date	Number	Payee	Account	Payment	✓	Deposit	Balance
12/31/2009			3100 · Your Name & Muir Capital		✓	25,943.00	25,943.00
01/14/2010			-split-		✓	10,469.44	36,412.44
01/15/2010		Thomsen, Kevin	1200 · Accounts Receivable [split]	100.00	✓		36,312.44
01/15/2010	1	Munoz, Francisco Dr.	1200 · Accounts Receivable	80.44	✓		36,232.00
01/25/2010	2	Boots & Gear	-split-	1,837.50	✓		34,394.50
01/25/2010	3	Clothes, Inc.	-split-	294.00	✓		34,100.50
01/25/2010	4	Snow Gear	-split-	312.60	✓		33,787.90
01/25/2010	5	State Board of Equalization	2200 · Sales Tax Payable	613.15	✓		33,174.75
01/31/2010			7010 · Interest Income		✓	54.05	33,228.80
01/31/2010			6120 · Bank Service Charges	18.00	✓		33,210.80
01/31/2010	Transfer	Old Mammoth Bank	-split-	63.75	✓		33,147.05
01/31/2010	Transfer	Old Mammoth Bank	-split-	53.12	✓		33,093.93
01/31/2010	6	Your Name	3112 · Your Name, Drawing	1,000.00			32,093.93
01/31/2010	7	Larry Muir	3122 · Larry Muir, Drawing	1,000.00			31,093.93

Ending balance   31,093.93

Splits

☑ 1-Line

Sort by Date, Type, Number/... ▼   Record   Restore

- Notice that the final balance of the account is $31,093.93.

Close the register and the Chart of Accounts

CREDIT CARD RECONCILIATION

Any account used in QuickBooks Pro may be reconciled. As with a checking account, it is a good practice to reconcile the Credit Card account each month. When the credit card statement is received, the transactions entered in QuickBooks Pro should agree with the transactions shown on the credit card statement. A reconciliation of the credit card should be completed on a monthly basis.

MEMO
DATE: January 31, 2010

The monthly bill for the Visa has arrived and is to be paid. Prior to paying the monthly credit card bill, reconcile the Credit Card account.

DO ▶ Reconcile and pay the credit card bill

Click the **Reconcile** icon on the Home Page
Click the drop-down list arrow for Account
Click **2100 Visa** to select the account

OLD MAMMOTH BANK
VISA
12345 Old Mammoth Road
Mammoth Lakes, CA 93546
(619) 555-3880

Your Name Mountain Sports
875 Mountain Road
Mammoth Lakes, CA 93546   **Acct. # 098-776-4321**

Beginning Balance 1/1/10		150.00	$150.00
1/23/10 Sierra Office Supply Company		21.98	171.98
1/23/10 Snow Supplies		300.00	471.98
1/25/10 Winter Sports Accessories		350.00	821.98
1/25/10 Shoes & More		400.00	1,221.98
Ending Balance 1/31/10			1,221.98

Minimum Payment Due: $50.00   Payment Due Date: February 15, 2010

Compare the credit card statement with the **Reconcile Credit Card - Visa**
Enter the **Statement Date** of **01/31/10**
Enter the **Ending Balance** of **1,221.98** in the **Begin Reconciliation** window

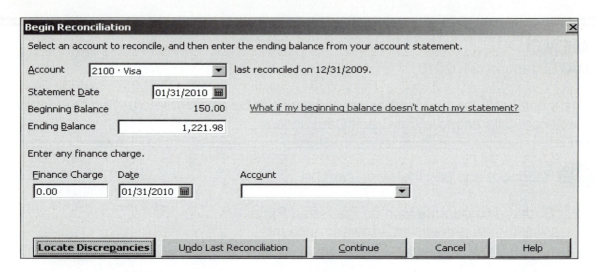

Click the **Continue** button
Mark each item that appears on both the statement and in the reconciliation
      EXCEPT for the $**400** transaction for Shoes & More

RECORD AN ADJUSTMENT TO A RECONCILIATION

In QuickBooks Pro 2010, adjustments to reconciliations may be made during the reconciliation process. In addition, account reconciliations may be eliminated by clicking an Undo button.

DO Verify that all items are marked EXCEPT the charge for $**400** for Shoes & More

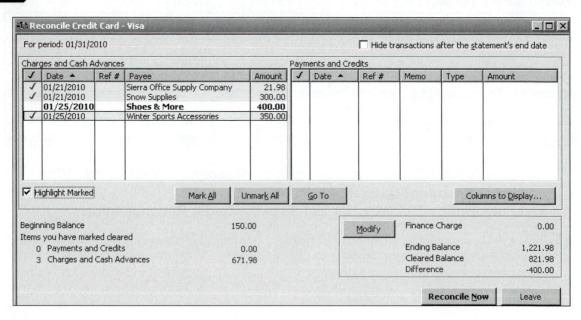

Click **Reconcile Now**

- The Reconcile Adjustment screen appears because there was a $400 Difference shown at the bottom of the reconciliation.
- Even though the error on the demonstration reconciliation is known, an adjustment will be entered and then deleted at a later time.

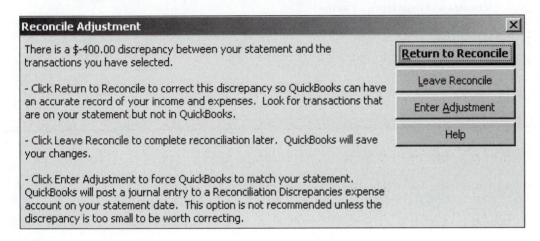

Click **Enter Adjustment**

Click **Cancel** on the Make Payment screen

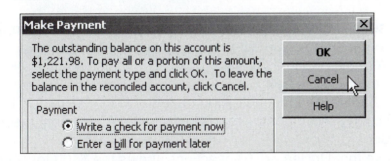

- The Reconciliation report is generated

Display the Detail report

Your Name Mountain Sports
Reconciliation Detail
2100 · Visa, Period Ending 01/31/2010

Type	Date	Num	Name	Clr	Amount	Balance
Beginning Balance						150.00
Cleared Transactions						
Checks and Payments - 4 items						
▶ Credit Card Charge	01/21/2010		Snow Supplies	✓	-300.00	-300.00 ◀
Credit Card Charge	01/21/2010		Sierra Office Supply Company	✓	-21.98	-321.98
Bill Pmt -CCard	01/25/2010		Winter Sports Accessories	✓	-350.00	-671.98
General Journal	01/31/2010			✓	-400.00	-1,071.98
Total Checks and Payments					-1,071.98	-1,071.98
Total Cleared Transactions					-1,071.98	-1,071.98
Cleared Balance					1,071.98	1,221.98
Uncleared Transactions						
Checks and Payments - 1 item						
Bill Pmt -CCard	01/25/2010		Shoes & More		-400.00	-400.00
Total Checks and Payments					-400.00	-400.00
Total Uncleared Transactions					-400.00	-400.00
Register Balance as of 01/31/2010					1,471.98	1,621.98
Ending Balance					**1,471.98**	**1,621.98**

- Because the date of your computer may be different from the date used in the text, there may be some differences in the appearance of the Reconciliation Detail report. As long as the appropriate transactions have been marked, disregard any discrepancies.
- Notice that there is a General Journal entry for $400 in the Cleared Transactions section of the report. This is the Adjustment made by QuickBooks.
- Also note that Uncleared Transactions shows the $400 for Shoes & More.
Close the Reconciliation Detail report without printing
- When you return to the chart of Accounts, you will see a new account, **66900 Reconciliation Discrepancies**

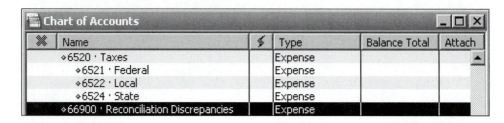

UNDO A PREVIOUS RECONCILIATION, DELETE AN ADJUSTMENT, AND REDO A RECONCILIATION

If an error is discovered after an account reconciliation has been completed, the reconciliation may be removed by using the Undo Reconciliation feature located on the Locate Discrepancies screen. If an adjusting entry for a reconciliation has been made, it may be deleted. This is useful if you had a discrepancy when making the reconciliation and found the error at a later date.

 Undo the credit card reconciliation and delete the adjusting entry made by QuickBooks

Access the **Reconcile Credit Card** window as previously instructed
Click **Locate Discrepancies** on the Begin Reconciliation screen

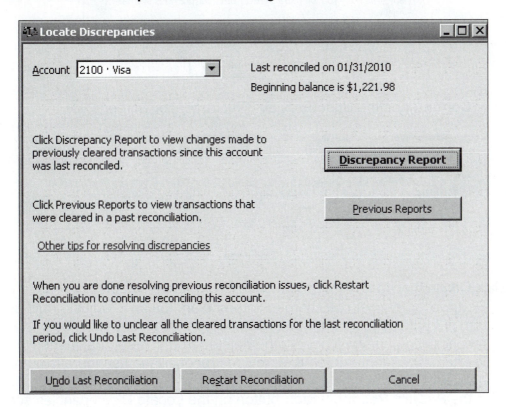

Click the **Undo Last Reconciliation** button

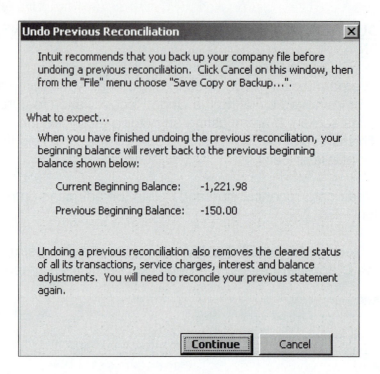

Click **Continue** on the Undo Previous Reconciliation screen

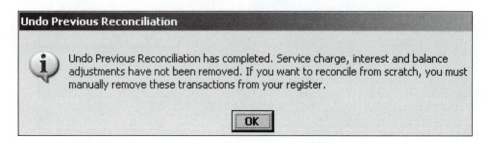

Click **OK** on the Undo Previous Reconcile Complete screen
- Remember that service charges, interest, and balance adjustments are not removed. If you have entered any of these items on the previous reconciliation, they will need to be deleted from the Journal manually. None of the items were entered on the previous reconciliation so there is nothing to be deleted.

Click the **Restart Reconciliation** button on the Locate Discrepancies screen
- You will return to the Begin Reconciliation screen.

Make sure the **Statement Date** is **01/31/10**
Enter the **Ending Balance** of **1221.98**
Click **Continue**
Click **Mark All**
- All of the items listed on the Credit Card Statement <u>INCLUDING</u> the $400 for Shoes & More will be marked.

Click the Adjusting entry for 01/31/10

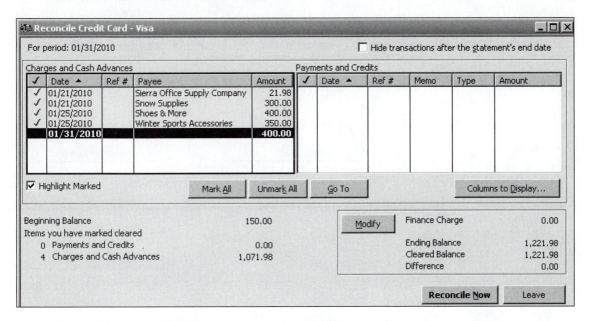

Click **Go To**
- You will go to the Make General Journal Entries screen

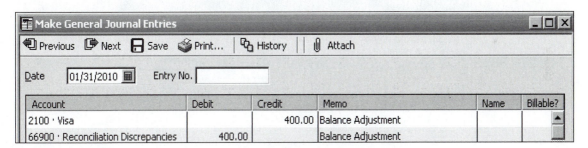

Use the keyboard shortcut **Ctrl+D** to delete the entry
After the adjustment has been deleted, close the Journal
Verify that the adjusting entry has been deleted and that the Ending and Cleared
    Balances are 1,221.98 and the Difference is 0.00

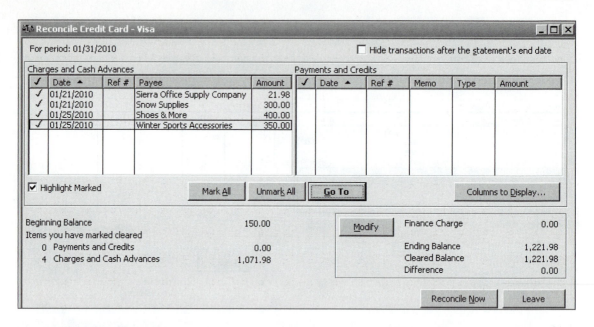

Click **Reconcile Now**
When the **Make Payment** dialog box appears on the screen
Make sure **Write a check for payment now** is selected, click **OK**

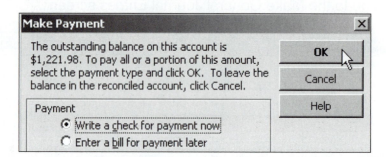

Display and print a **Reconciliation Detail Report** following the procedures given
for the Bank Reconciliation Report

Your Name Mountain Sports
Reconciliation Detail
2100 · Visa, Period Ending 01/31/2010

Type	Date	Num	Name	Clr	Amount	Balance
Beginning Balance						**150.00**
Cleared Transactions						
Checks and Payments - 4 items						
▶ Credit Card Charge	01/21/2010		Snow Supplies	✓	-300.00	-300.00 ◀
Credit Card Charge	01/21/2010		Sierra Office Supply Company	✓	-21.98	-321.98
Bill Pmt -CCard	01/25/2010		Shoes & More	✓	-400.00	-721.98
Bill Pmt -CCard	01/25/2010		Winter Sports Accessories	✓	-350.00	-1,071.98
Total Checks and Payments					-1,071.98	-1,071.98
Total Cleared Transactions					-1,071.98	-1,071.98
Cleared Balance					1,071.98	1,221.98
Register Balance as of 01/31/2010					1,071.98	1,221.98
Ending Balance					**1,071.98**	**1,221.98**

Close the Reconciliation Detail report
The payment check should appear on the screen
Enter **8** as the check number
The **Date** of the check should be **01/31/10**
Click the drop-down list next to **Pay to the Order of**, click **Old Mammoth Bank**
- If you get a dialog box for **Auto Recall**, click **No**.

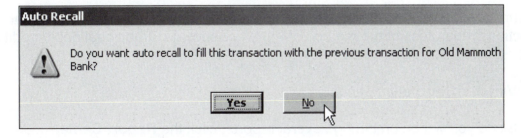

Tab to or click **Memo** on the bottom of the check
Enter **January Visa Payment** as the memo

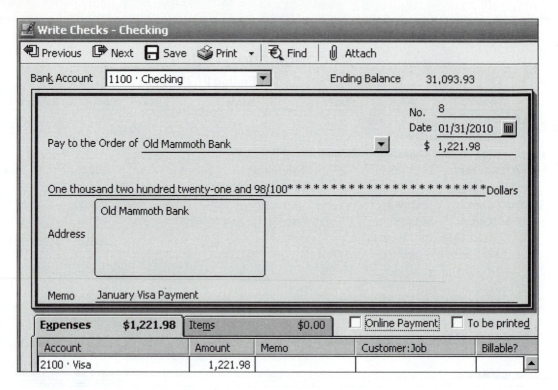

Print the standard-style check as previously instructed
When the check has printed successfully, click **Save & Close** to record and exit
    Write Checks
Close the Chart of Accounts

VIEW THE JOURNAL

After entering several transactions, it is helpful to view the Journal. In the Journal all transactions regardless of the method of entry are shown in traditional debit/credit format.

DO View the **Journal** for January

    Since you will be preparing several reports, click the **Report Center** button
    Click **Accountant & Taxes** as the type of report, double-click **Journal**
    The dates are from **01/01/10** to **01/31/10**, press **Tab**
    Scroll through the Journal and view all the transactions that have been made

Your Name Mountain Sports
Journal
January 2010

Trans #	Type	Date	Num	Name	Memo	Account	Debit	Credit
106	Check	01/31/2010	Transfer	Old Mammoth Bank	Loan Payment Office Equipment	1100 · Checking		63.75
				Old Mammoth Bank	Interest Office Equipment Loan	6212 · Loan Interest	53.42	
				Old Mammoth Bank	Principal Office Equipment Loan	2510 · Office Equipment Loan	10.33	
							63.75	63.75
107	Check	01/31/2010	Transfer	Old Mammoth Bank	Loan Payment Store Fixtures	1100 · Checking		53.12
				Old Mammoth Bank	Interest Store Fixtures Loan	6212 · Loan Interest	44.51	
				Old Mammoth Bank	Principal Store Fixtures Loan	2520 · Store Fixtures Loan	8.61	
							53.12	53.12
108	Check	01/31/2010			Service Charge	1100 · Checking		18.00
					Service Charge	6120 · Bank Service Charges	18.00	
							18.00	18.00
109	Deposit	01/31/2010			Interest	1100 · Checking	54.05	
					Interest	7010 · Interest Income		54.05
							54.05	54.05
111	Check	01/31/2010	8	Old Mammoth Bank	January Visa Payment	1100 · Checking		1,221.98
				Old Mammoth Bank	January Visa Payment	2100 · Visa	1,221.98	
							1,221.98	1,221.98
TOTAL							**72,746.25**	**72,746.25**

Partial Report

Close the **Journal** without printing
The **Report Center** should remain on the screen

PREPARE TRIAL BALANCE

After all adjustments have been recorded and the bank reconciliation has been completed, it is wise to prepare the Trial Balance. As in traditional accounting, the QuickBooks Pro Trial Balance proves that debits equal credits.

MEMO
DATE: January 31, 2010

Because adjustments have been entered, prepare a Trial Balance.

▶ DO   Prepare a trial balance using the Report Center

Verify that the type of report is **Accountant & Taxes**
Double-click **Trial Balance**

- If necessary, enter the dates **From 01/01/10** and **To 01/31/10**
Scroll through the report and study the amounts shown

Your Name Mountain Sports
Trial Balance
As of January 31, 2010

	Jan 31, 10	
	Debit	Credit
1100 · Checking	29,871.95	
1200 · Accounts Receivable	5,690.62	
1120 · Inventory Asset	34,991.54	
12000 · Undeposited Funds	0.00	
1311 · Office Supplies	521.98	
1312 · Sales Supplies	400.00	
1340 · Prepaid Insurance	125.00	
1511 · Original Cost	5,000.00	
1512 · Depreciation		85.00
1521 · Original Cost	4,500.00	
1522 · Depreciation		75.00
2000 · Accounts Payable		9,395.40
2100 · Visa	0.00	
2200 · Sales Tax Payable	0.00	
2510 · Office Equipment Loan		2,989.67
2520 · Store Fixtures Loan		2,491.39
3000 · Retained Earnings	0.00	
3100 · Your Name & Muir Capital	0.00	
3110 · Your Name, Capital		12,729.72
3111 · Your Name, Investment		20,000.00
3112 · Your Name, Drawing	1,000.00	
3120 · Larry Muir, Capital		12,729.72
3121 · Larry Muir, Investment		20,000.00
3122 · Larry Muir, Drawing	1,000.00	
4011 · Clothing & Accessory Sales		1,409.76
4012 · Equipment Sales		7,436.44
4040 · Returned Check Service Charges		25.00
5000 · Cost of Goods Sold	3,352.46	
5100 · Merchandise Discounts		50.90
6120 · Bank Service Charges	18.00	
6130 · Sales Discounts	447.17	
6140 · Advertising Expense	95.00	
6150 · Depreciation Expense	160.00	
6181 · Liability Insurance	125.00	
6212 · Loan Interest	97.93	
6300 · Rent	950.00	
6340 · Telephone	156.40	
6391 · Gas and Electric	359.00	
6392 · Water	85.00	
6471 · Sales	175.00	
6472 · Office	350.00	
7010 · Interest Income		54.05
TOTAL	89,472.05	89,472.05

- Notice that the final totals of debits and credits are equal: $89,472.05. Do not close the report

USE QUICKZOOM IN TRIAL BALANCE

DO Use QuickZoom to view the details of Office Supplies:

Scroll through the Trial Balance until you see **1311 Office Supplies**
Position the mouse pointer over the amount of Office Supplies, **521.98**
- Notice that the mouse pointer changes to a magnifying glass with a Z.
Double-click the primary mouse button

- A **Transactions by Account Report** appears on the screen showing the two transactions entered for office supplies.

Scroll through the report

			Your Name Mountain Sports					
			Transactions by Account					
			As of January 31, 2010					
◊ Type ◊	Date ◊	Num ◊	Name ◊	Memo	◊ Clr ◊	Split	◊ Amount ◊	Balance ◊
1310 · Supplies								**850.00**
1311 · Office Supplies								**850.00**
Credit Card Charge	01/21/2010		Sierra Office Supply Company	Purchase Paper		2100 · Visa	21.98	871.98 ◀
General Journal	01/31/2010			Adjusting Entry, Office Supplies		6472 · Office	-350.00	521.98
Total 1311 · Office Supplies							-328.02	521.98
Total 1310 · Supplies							-328.02	521.98
TOTAL							**-328.02**	**521.98**

Close the Transactions by Account report

PRINT THE TRIAL BALANCE

Once the trial balance has been prepared, it may be printed.

DO ▶ Print the **Trial Balance** in Portrait orientation as previously instructed
Click **Preview** to view a miniature copy of the report
- This helps determine the orientation, whether you need to select the feature to print one page wide, or whether you need to adjust the column widths.
Print in Portrait orientation
Close the **Trial Balance**
Do not close the **Report Center**

SELECT ACCRUAL-BASIS REPORTING PREFERENCE

QuickBooks Pro allows a business to customize the program and select certain preferences for reports, displays, graphs, accounts, and so on. There are two report preferences available in QuickBooks Pro: Cash and Accrual. You need to select the preference you prefer. If you select Cash as the report preference, income on reports will be shown as of the date payment is received, and expenses will be shown as of the date you pay the bill. If Accrual is selected, QuickBooks Pro shows the income on the report as of the date of the invoice and expenses as of the bill date. Prior to printing end-of-period reports, it is advisable to verify which reporting basis is selected. If Cash has been selected and you are using the Accrual method, it is imperative that you change your report basis.

MEMO
DATE: January 31, 2010

Prior to printing the Balance Sheet, Profit and Loss or Income Statement, or any other reports, check the report preference. If necessary, choose Accrual. After the selection has been made, print a Standard Profit and Loss and a Standard Balance Sheet for Your Name Mountain Sports.

DO Select **Accrual** as the Summary Report Basis

Click **Edit** on the menu bar, click **Preferences**
Scroll through the Preferences List until you see **Reports & Graphs**
Click **Reports & Graphs** and the **Company Preferences** tab
- If necessary, click **Accrual** to select the Summary Reports Basis

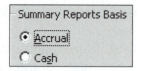

Click **OK** to close the **Preferences** window

PRINT STANDARD PROFIT AND LOSS STATEMENT

Because all income, expenses, and adjustments have been made for the period, a Profit and Loss Statement can be prepared. This statement is also known as the Income Statement. QuickBooks Pro has several different types of Profit and Loss Statements available: Standard—summarizes income and expenses; Detail—shows year-to-date transactions for each income and expense account; YTD Comparison—like the Standard Profit and Loss but summarizes your income and expenses for this month and compares them to your income and expenses for the current fiscal year; Prev Year Comparison—summarizes your income and expenses for both this month and this month last year and shows $ change and % change; By Job—like the Standard Profit and Loss statement, but with columns for each customer and job and amounts for this year to date; and By Class—like the Standard Profit and Loss statement, but with columns for each class and subclass with the amounts for this year to date. Unclassified shows how much you are making or losing within segments of your business that are not assigned to a QuickBooks class.

▶ **DO** Print a **Standard Profit and Loss Report**

> In the Report Center, click **Company & Financial** as the type of report, double-click **Profit & Loss Standard**
> The dates are from **01/01/10** to **01/31/10**, press **Tab** to generate the report

Your Name Mountain Sports	
Profit & Loss	
January 2010	
	◇ ____Jan 10____ ◇
Total Expense	3,018.50
Net Ordinary Income	2,551.14
Other Income/Expense	
Other Income	
7010 · Interest Income	54.05
Total Other Income	54.05
Net Other Income	54.05
Net Income	**2,605.19**

Partial Report

> Scroll through the report to view the income and expenses listed
> Print the report using **Portrait** orientation
> Close the **Profit and Loss Report**

VIEW A STANDARD BALANCE SHEET

The Balance Sheet proves the fundamental accounting equation: Assets = Liabilities + Owners' Equity. When all transactions and adjustments for the period have been recorded, a Balance Sheet should be prepared. QuickBooks Pro has several different types of Balance Sheet statements available: Standard—shows as of today the balance in each Balance Sheet account with subtotals provided for assets, liabilities, and equity; Detail—This report is a more detailed version of the Standard Balance Sheet Report, Summary—shows amounts for each account type but not for individual accounts; and Prev Year Comparison—has columns for today, a year ago today, $ change, and % change;. For each account, the report shows the starting balance at the beginning of last month, transactions entered in the account for this month to date, and the ending balance as of today.

▶ **DO** View a **Standard Balance Sheet Report**

Double-click **Balance Sheet Standard**
Tab to or click **As of,** enter **01/31/10**, tab to generate the report
Scroll through the report to view the assets, liabilities, and equities listed

- Notice the Net Income account listed in the **Equity** section of the report. This is the same amount of Net Income shown on the Profit and Loss Statement.

Your Name Mountain Sports
Balance Sheet
As of January 31, 2010

	Jan 31, 10
Equity	
3100 · Your Name & Muir Capital	
3110 · Your Name, Capital	
3111 · Your Name, Investment	20,000.00
3112 · Your Name, Drawing	-1,000.00
3110 · Your Name, Capital - Other	12,729.72
Total 3110 · Your Name, Capital	31,729.72
3120 · Larry Muir, Capital	
3121 · Larry Muir, Investment	20,000.00
3122 · Larry Muir, Drawing	-1,000.00
3120 · Larry Muir, Capital - Other	12,729.72
Total 3120 · Larry Muir, Capital	31,729.72
Total 3100 · Your Name & Muir Capital	63,459.44
Net Income	2,605.19
Total Equity	66,064.63
TOTAL LIABILITIES & EQUITY	**80,941.09**

Partial Report

Do not close the report

CLOSING ENTRIES

In traditional accrual-basis accounting, there are four entries that need to be made at the end of a fiscal year. These entries close income, expenses, and the drawing accounts and transfer the net income into owners' equity.

Income and Expense accounts are closed when QuickBooks is given a closing date. This will occur later in this chapter. When preparing reports during the next fiscal year, QuickBooks Pro will not show any amounts in the income and expense accounts for the previous year once the closing date has been entered.

However, QuickBooks Pro does not close the owners' drawing accounts, nor does it transfer the net income into the owners' Capital accounts. If you prefer to use the power of the program and omit the last two closing entries, QuickBooks Pro will keep a running account of the owner withdrawals, and it will put net income into a Retained Earnings account. However, transferring the net income and drawing into the owners' Capital accounts provides a clearer picture of the value of the owners' equity.

ADJUSTMENT TO TRANSFER NET INCOME/RETAINED EARNINGS INTO YOUR NAME, CAPITAL, AND LARRY MUIR, CAPITAL:

Because Your Name Mountain Sports is a partnership, the amount of net income should appear as part of each owner's capital account rather than appear as Retained Earnings. In many instances, this is the type of adjustment the CPA makes on the Accountant's Copy of the QuickBooks Pro company files. The adjustment may be made before the closing date for the fiscal year, or it may be made after the closing has been performed. Because QuickBooks Pro automatically transfers the amount in the Net Income account into Retained Earnings, the closing entry for a partnership will transfer the net income into each owner's capital account. This adjustment is made by debiting Retained Earnings and crediting the owners' individual capital accounts. When you view a report before the end of the year, you will see an amount in Net Income and the same amount as a negative in Retained Earnings. If you view a report after the end of the year, you will not see any information regarding Retained Earnings or Net Income because the adjustment correctly transferred the amount to the owners' capital accounts.

On the Balance Sheet, Retained Earnings and/or Net Income appear as part of the equity section. The owners' Drawing and Investment accounts are kept separate from Retained Earnings at all times

DO ▶ Evenly divide and transfer the net income into the Your Name, Capital, and Larry Muir, Capital, accounts after year end:

Open the **General Journal** as previously instructed
The **Date** is **01/31/10**
The first account used is **3000 Retained Earnings**
Debit **3000 Retained Earnings**, **2,605.19**
For the Memo record **Transfer Net Income into Capital**
The other accounts used are **3110 Your Name, Capital**, and **3120 Larry Muir, Capital**
Use QuickMath to divide the 2,605.19 in half
   Click after the 2,605.19 in the credit column, type **/**, type **2**, press **Enter**
- **1,302.60** should be entered as the credit amount for **3110 Your Name, Capital**
- QuickBooks Pro enters **1,302.59** as the credit amount for **3120 Larry Muir, Capital**.

- Because QuickBooks Pro accepts only two numbers after a decimal point, the cents must be rounded. Thus, there is a 1¢ difference in the distribution between the two owners. If there is an uneven amount in the future, Larry will receive the extra amount.

Enter the same Memo as entered for Retained Earnings

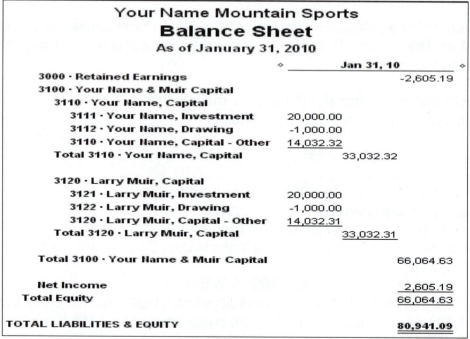

Click **Save & Close** to record and close the **General Journal**
- If you get a Retained Earnings dialog box regarding posting a transaction to the Retained Earnings account, click **OK**
- Since you did not close the report, the Balance Sheet should still be on the screen.

Your Name Mountain Sports
Balance Sheet
As of January 31, 2010

	Jan 31, 10
3000 · Retained Earnings	-2,605.19
3100 · Your Name & Muir Capital	
3110 · Your Name, Capital	
3111 · Your Name, Investment	20,000.00
3112 · Your Name, Drawing	-1,000.00
3110 · Your Name, Capital - Other	14,032.32
Total 3110 · Your Name, Capital	33,032.32
3120 · Larry Muir, Capital	
3121 · Larry Muir, Investment	20,000.00
3122 · Larry Muir, Drawing	-1,000.00
3120 · Larry Muir, Capital - Other	14,032.31
Total 3120 · Larry Muir, Capital	33,032.31
Total 3100 · Your Name & Muir Capital	66,064.63
Net Income	2,605.19
Total Equity	66,064.63
TOTAL LIABILITIES & EQUITY	80,941.09

Partial Report

- Notice the change in the **Equity** section of the Balance Sheet.

- Not all companies have a profit each month. If your business has a negative amount for net income, the appropriate adjustment would be to debit each owner's individual capital account and to credit Retained Earnings. For example, if Net Income was -500.00, you would record the following: 3110 Your Name, Capital—debit 250; 3120 Larry Muir, Capital—debit 250; and 3000 Retained Earnings—credit 500.

Do not close the report

PRINT STANDARD BALANCE SHEET

Once the adjustment for Net Income/Retained Earnings has been performed, viewing or printing the Balance Sheet will show you the status of the Owners' Equity.

DO To see the effect of the adjustment, print a **Standard Balance Sheet** for **January 2011**

Change the **As of** date to **01/31/2011**, press **Tab**

Your Name Mountain Sports
Balance Sheet
As of January 31, 2011

	Jan 31, 11
Equity	
3100 · Your Name & Muir Capital	
3110 · Your Name, Capital	
3111 · Your Name, Investment	20,000.00
3112 · Your Name, Drawing	-1,000.00
3110 · Your Name, Capital - Other	14,032.32
Total 3110 · Your Name, Capital	33,032.32
3120 · Larry Muir, Capital	
3121 · Larry Muir, Investment	20,000.00
3122 · Larry Muir, Drawing	-1,000.00
3120 · Larry Muir, Capital - Other	14,032.31
Total 3120 · Larry Muir, Capital	33,032.31
Total 3100 · Your Name & Muir Capital	66,064.63
Total Equity	66,064.63
TOTAL LIABILITIES & EQUITY	**80,941.09**

Partial Report

Print the report in Portrait Orientation
- The Balance Sheet still appears on the screen after printing is complete.
- Notice the Equity section. Nothing is shown for Retained Earnings or Net Income.

- The net income has been added to the owners' Capital accounts.

Do not close the report

Change the **As of** date for the Balance Sheet to **01/31/10**

CLOSE DRAWING AND TRANSFER INTO OWNERS' CAPITAL ACCOUNTS

The entry transferring the net income into the owners' Capital accounts has already been made. While this is not the actual end of the fiscal year for Your Name Mountain Sports, the closing entry for the Drawing accounts will be entered at this time so that you will have experience in recording this closing entry.

MEMO

DATE: January 31, 2010

Record the closing entry to close 3112 Your Name, Drawing, and 3122 Larry Muir, Drawing, into each owner's Capital account.

DO Record the closing entry for each owner's Drawing account

Access the **General Journal** as previously instructed
Debit **3110 Your Name, Capital**, for the amount of the drawing account **1,000**
The Memo for the transaction is **Close Drawing**
Credit **3112 Your Name, Drawing**, for **1,000**
Use the same Memo for this portion of the transaction

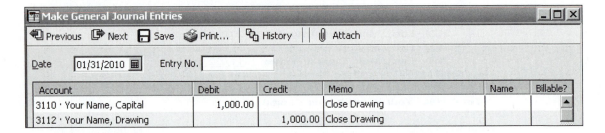

Click **Next**
Repeat the above steps to close **3122 Larry Muir, Drawing**

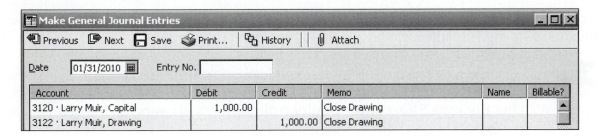

Click **Save & Close** and return to the Balance Sheet
- Notice the change in the **Equity** section of the Balance Sheet.

Change the Header/Footer so the title is **Balance Sheet After Equity Adjustments**

Your Name Mountain Sports
Balance Sheet After Equity Adjustments
As of January 31, 2010

	Jan 31, 10
Equity	
3000 · Retained Earnings	-2,605.19
3100 · Your Name & Muir Capital	
3110 · Your Name, Capital	
3111 · Your Name, Investment	20,000.00
3110 · Your Name, Capital - Other	13,032.32
Total 3110 · Your Name, Capital	33,032.32
3120 · Larry Muir, Capital	
3121 · Larry Muir, Investment	20,000.00
3120 · Larry Muir, Capital - Other	13,032.31
Total 3120 · Larry Muir, Capital	33,032.31
Total 3100 · Your Name & Muir Capital	66,064.63
Net Income	2,605.19
Total Equity	66,064.63
TOTAL LIABILITIES & EQUITY	**80,941.09**

Partial Report

Print the **Balance Sheet**
Do not close the report if you are going to do the following optional exercise

EXPORTING REPORTS TO EXCEL (OPTIONAL)

Many of the reports prepared in QuickBooks Pro can be exported to Microsoft® Excel. This allows you to take advantage of extensive filtering options available in Excel, hide detail for some but not all groups of data, combine information from two different reports, change titles of columns, add comments, change the order of columns, and experiment with "what if" scenarios. In order to use this feature of QuickBooks Pro you must also have Microsoft Excel available for use on your computer.

DO Optional Exercise: Export a report from QuickBooks Pro to Excel

> With the **Balance Sheet After Equity Adjustments** showing on the screen, click the **Export** button

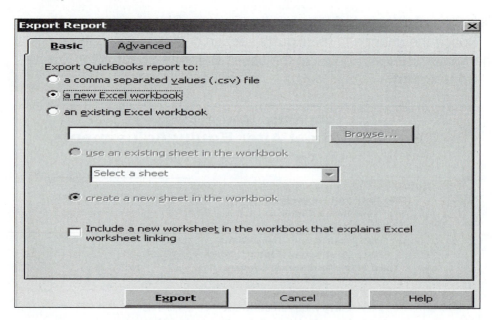

> Make sure the Export Report screen has **a new Excel workbook** selected as the File option and that **Include a new worksheet in the workbook that explains Excel worksheet linking** is <u>not</u> selected

Click **Export**

• The Balance Sheet will be displayed in Excel.

	A	B	C	D	E	F
1						Jan 31, 10
2	ASSETS					
3		Current Assets				
4			Checking/Savings			
5					1100 · Checking	29,871.95
6			Total Checking/Savings			29,871.95
7			Accounts Receivable			
8					1200 · Accounts Receivable	5,690.62
9			Total Accounts Receivable			5,690.62
10			Other Current Assets			
11					1120 · Inventory Asset	34,991.54
12					1310 · Supplies	
13					1311 · Office Supplies	521.98
14					1312 · Sales Supplies	400.00
15				Total 1310 · Supplies		921.98
16					1340 · Prepaid Insurance	125.00
17			Total Other Current Assets			36,038.52
18		Total Current Assets				71,601.09

Scroll through the report and click in Cell A60
Type **BALANCE SHEET EXPORTED TO EXCEL**

	A	B	C	D	E	F
1						Jan 31, 10
42		Equity				
43			3000 · Retained Earnings			-2,605.19
44			3100 · Your Name & Muir Capital			
45				3110 · Your Name, Capital		
46					3111 · Your Name, Investment	20,000.00
47					3110 · Your Name, Capital - Other	13,032.32
48				Total 3110 · Your Name, Capital		33,032.32
49				3120 · Larry Muir, Capital		
50					3121 · Larry Muir, Investment	20,000.00
51					3120 · Larry Muir, Capital - Other	13,032.31
52				Total 3120 · Larry Muir, Capital		33,032.31
53			Total 3100 · Your Name & Muir Capital			66,064.63
54			Net Income			2,605.19
55		Total Equity				66,064.63
56	TOTAL LIABILITIES & EQUITY					80,941.09
57						
58						
59						
60	BALANCE SHEET EXPORTED TO EXCEL					

Click the **Close** button in the upper right corner of the Excel title bar to close **Excel**

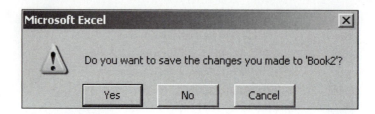

Click **No** to close **Book2** without saving
- The Book number changes depending on how many times you export reports to Excel.

Return to QuickBooks, close the Balance Sheet, and the Report Center

IMPORTING DATA FROM EXCEL

You may have Excel or .csv (comma separated value) files that contain important business information about customers, vendors, and sales that are not contained in your QuickBooks Company File. That information can now be imported directly into QuickBooks and customized as desired. An import file must conform to a specific structure for QuickBooks to interpret the data in the file correctly.

It is recommended that you set up your import file correctly in order to transfer the data properly and avoid errors. This includes preparing the file for import into QuickBooks, mapping the data from your file to QuickBooks, and previewing the imported data. QuickBooks has a built in Reference Guide for Importing Files that may be accessed and printed through Help.

JOURNAL FOR JANUARY

It is always wise to have a printed or hard copy of the data on disk. After all entries and adjustments for the month have been made, print the Journal for January. This copy should be kept on file as an additional backup to the data stored on your disk. If something happens to your disk to damage it, you will still have the paper copy of your transactions available for re-entry into the system. Normally, the Journal would be printed before closing the period; however, we will print the Journal at the end of the chapter so that all entries are included.

END-OF-PERIOD BACKUP

Once all end-of-period procedures have been completed, in addition to a regular backup copy of company data and a duplicate disk, a second duplicate disk of the company data should be made and filed as an archive disk. Preferably, this copy will be located someplace other than on the business premises. The archive disk or file copy is set aside in case of emergency or in case damage occurs to the original and current backup copies of the company data.

▶ DO ▶ Back up company data and prepare an archive copy of the company data

    Prepare a Back Up as previously instructed
- In the **File Name** text box enter **Sports (Archive 1-31-10)** as the name for the backup

    Also prepare a duplicate disk as instructed by your professor
- Label this disk **Sports Archive, 1-31-10**

PASSWORDS

Not every employee of a business should have access to all the financial records. In some companies, only the owner(s) will have complete access. In others, one or two key employees will have full access while other employees are provided limited access based on the jobs they perform. Passwords are secret words used to control access to data. QuickBooks Pro has several options available to assign passwords.

In order to assign any passwords at all, you must have an administrator. The administrator has unrestricted access to all QuickBooks Pro functions and sets up users, user passwords, and assigns areas of transaction access for each user. Areas of access can be limited to transaction entry for certain types of transactions or a user may have unrestricted access into all areas of QuickBooks Pro and company data.

A password should be kept secret at all times. It should be something that is easy for the individual to remember, yet difficult for someone else to guess. Birthdays, names, initials, and other similar devices are not good passwords because the information is too readily available. Never write down your password where it can be easily found or seen by someone else.

Even though the password feature is available, we will not be assigning passwords during training. If a password is forgotten, QuickBooks cannot be accessed until the appropriate password is entered.

SET THE CLOSING DATE FOR THE PERIOD

A closing date assigned to transactions for a period prevents changing data from the closed period without acknowledging that a transaction from a previous period has been changed. This is helpful to discourage casual changes or transaction deletions to a period that has been closed. Setting the closing date is done by accessing Accounting Preferences in QuickBooks Pro.

MEMO

DATE: January 31, 2010

Now that the closing transactions have been performed, you want to protect the data by setting the closing date to 1/31/10.

DO Assign the closing date of **01/31/10** to the transactions for the period ending 1/31/10

Click **Edit** on the menu bar, click **Preferences**
Click **Accounting**
Click **Company Preferences**
Click the **Set Date/Password** button.
Enter **01/31/10** as the closing date in the Closing Date section of the Company Preferences for Accounting
Do not set any passwords at this time

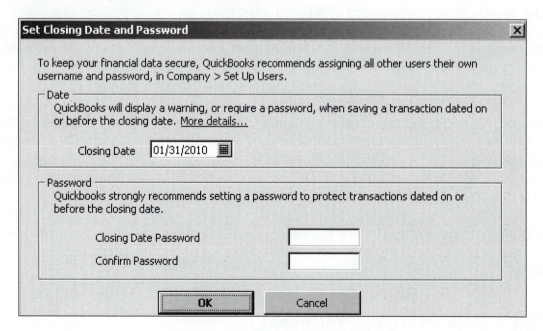

Click **OK**
Click **No** on the No Password Entered dialog box

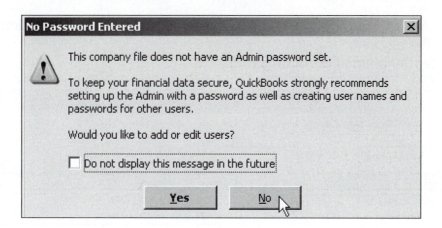

Click **OK** to close Preferences

ENTER A CORRECTION TO A CLOSED PERIOD

If it is determined that an error was made in a previous period, QuickBooks Pro does allow the correction. Before it will record any changes for previous periods, QuickBooks Pro requires that Yes is clicked on the dialog box warning of the change to a transaction date that is prior to the closing date for the company.

MEMO

DATE: January 31, 2010

After entering the closing date, Ruth reviews the Journal and reports printed at the end of January. She finds that $25 of the amount of Office Supplies should have been recorded as Sales Supplies. Record an entry in the Journal to transfer $25 from Office Supplies to Sales Supplies.

DO ▸ Transfer $25 from Office Supplies to Sales Supplies

 Access the **General Journal** as previously instructed
 Enter the date of **01/31/10**
 Tab to or click **Account**, click the drop-down list arrow for **Account**, click **1312 Sales Supplies**
 Enter the debit of **25.00**
 Enter the Memo **Correcting Entry**
 Tab to or click **Account**, click the drop-down list arrow for Account, click **1311 Office Supplies**

- A credit amount of 25.00 should already be in the credit column. If not, enter the amount.

Enter the Memo **Correcting Entry**

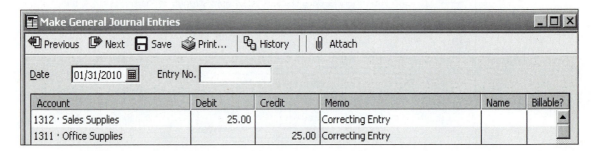

Click **Save & Close**
Click **Yes** on the **QuickBooks** dialog box

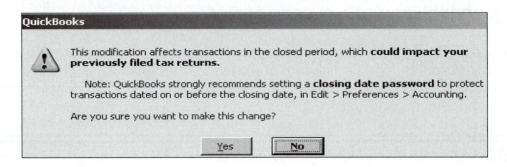

VERIFY THE CORRECTION TO OFFICE AND SALES SUPPLIES

Once the correction has been made, it is important to view the change in the accounts. The transfer of an amount of one asset into another will have no direct effect on the total assets in your reports. The account balances for Office Supplies and Sales Supplies will be changed. To view the change in the account, open the Chart of Accounts and look at the balance of each account. You may also use the account register to view the correcting entry as it was recorded in each account.

MEMO
DATE: January 31, 2010

Access the Chart of Accounts and view the change in the account balances and the correcting entry in each account's register.

DO View the correcting entry in each account

Open the **Chart of Accounts** as previously instructed
- Notice that the balance for Office Supplies has been changed from 521.98 to 496.98.
- Notice that the balance for Sales Supplies has been changed from 400.00 to 425.00.

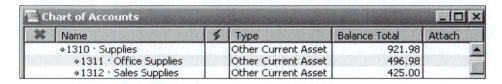

⚿ Chart of Accounts				_ □ ×
✕	Name	✎	Type	Balance Total	Attach
	◆1310 · Supplies		Other Current Asset	921.98	▲
	◆1311 · Office Supplies		Other Current Asset	496.98	
	◆1312 · Sales Supplies		Other Current Asset	425.00	

Double-click **Office Supplies** to open the account register
- Verify that the correcting entry was recorded for Office Supplies.

⚿ 1311 · Office Supplies							_ □ ×
⬍ Go to...		🖨 Print...		📝 Edit Transaction	📄 QuickReport		
Date	Ref	Payee		Decrease	✓	Increase	Balance
	Type	Account	Memo				
01/21/2010		Sierra Office Supply Company				21.98	871.98 ▲
	CC	2100 · Visa					
01/31/2010				350.00			521.98
	GENJRNL	6472 · Office	Adjusting Entry, Office				
01/31/2010				25.00			496.98
	GENJRNL	1312 · Sales Supplies	Correcting Entry				

Close the **Office Supplies Register**
Repeat the steps to view the correcting entry in Sales Supplies

⚿ 1312 · Sales Supplies							_ □ ×
⬍ Go to...		🖨 Print...		📝 Edit Transaction	📄 QuickReport		
Date	Ref	Payee		Decrease	✓	Increase	Balance
	Type	Account	Memo				
12/31/2009					✓	575.00	575.00
	DEP	3100 · Your Name & Muir Capit.	Account Opening Balance				
01/31/2010				175.00			400.00
	GENJRNL	6471 · Sales	Adjusting Entry, Sales Supplies				
01/31/2010						25.00	425.00
	GENJRNL	1311 · Office Supplies	Correcting Entry				

Close the **Sales Supplies Register**
Close the **Chart of Accounts**

INVENTORY ADJUSTMENTS

In a business that has inventory, it is possible that the number of items on hand is different from the quantity shown in QuickBooks Pro when a physical inventory is taken. This can be caused by a variety of items: loss due to theft, fire, or flood; damage to an item in the stockroom; an error in a previous physical inventory. Even though QuickBooks Pro uses the average cost method of inventory valuation, the value of an item can be changed as well. For example, assume that several pairs of after-ski boots are discounted and sold for a lesser value during the summer months. QuickBooks Pro allows the quantity and value of inventory to be adjusted.

MEMO

DATE: January 31, 2010

After taking a physical inventory, you discover two hats were placed next to the cleaning supplies and are discolored because bleach was spilled on them. These hats must be discarded. Record this as an adjustment to the quantity of inventory. Use the Expense account 6190 Merchandise Adjustments to record this adjustment.

▶ **DO** ▶ Adjust the quantity of hats

QuickBooks values inventory using the Average Cost Method.
Open the Item List as previously instructed, double-click **Hats**

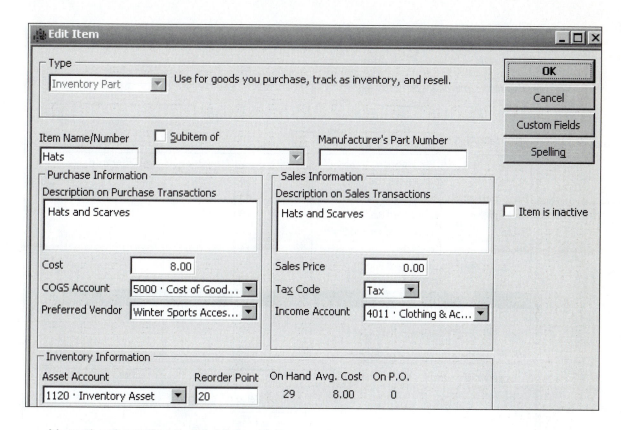

- Note the Avg. Cost of 8.00 for Hats

Close the Edit Item screen and the Item List

Click the **Adjust Qty on Hand** icon on the QuickBooks Home Page

Enter the adjustment date of **013110**

Click the drop-down list arrow next to **Adjustment Account**

Click **<Add New>**

Enter the new account information:

Type **Expense**

Number **6190**

Name **Merchandise Adjustments**

Click **Save & Close** to add the account

Click in the **New Qty** column for Hats

Enter **27**

Tab to enter the change

- Notice that the Total Value of the Adjustment is -16.00, which is -8.00 for each hat.

Adjust Quantity On Hand

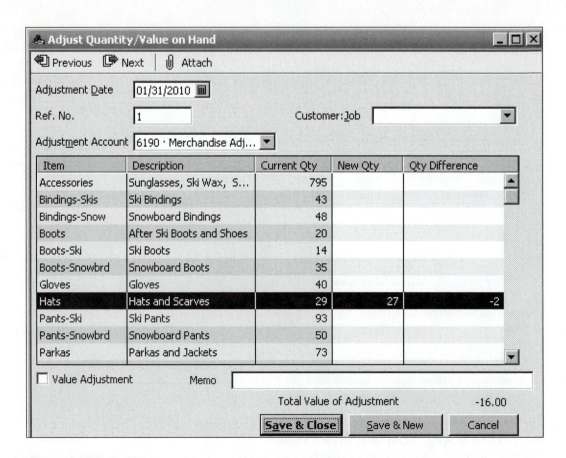

Click **Save & Close**
Click **Yes** on the **QuickBooks** dialog box regarding changing a transaction for a
closed period

ADJUST THE JOURNAL ENTRY FOR NET INCOME/RETAINED EARNINGS

The adjustment to inventory reduced the value of the inventory asset by $16.00 and
increased the expenses of the business by $16.00. The change decreased the net
income by $16.00; thus, the adjusting entry for net income/retained earnings made
previously needs to be changed.

DO Adjust the net income

Access **General Journal** transactions as previously instructed
Click **Previous** until you get to the entry debiting Retained Earnings for 2,605.19
Reduce the amount by $16.00 so change the debit to Retained Earnings to
2,589.19
Change the credit amount for Your Name to **1,294.60**
Change the credit amount for Larry Muir to **1,294.59**

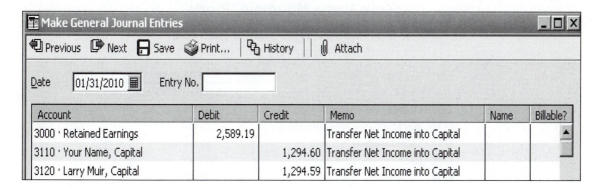

Click **Save & Close**
Click **Yes** or **OK** on all the dialog boxes for saving a changed transaction, recording a transaction for a closed period, and posting a transaction to Retained Earnings

PRINT POST-CLOSING TRIAL BALANCE

After closing has been completed, it is helpful to print a Post-Closing Trial Balance. This proves that debits still equal credits. Preparing the Trial Balance as of February 1 is preparing the Post-Closing Trial Balance for January 31.

MEMO
DATE: February 1, 2010

Print a Post-Closing Trial Balance, a Post-Closing Profit and Loss Statement, and a Post-Closing Balance Sheet for Your Name Mountain Sports. The dates should be as of or for 02/01/10.

▶ DO ▶ Print a **Post-Closing Trial Balance** to prove debits still equal credits

Prepare a **Trial Balance** as previously instructed
The dates are from **02/01/10** to **02/01/10**
Scroll through the report and study the amounts shown
• Notice that the final totals of debits and credits are equal.
Change the Header/Footer so the report title is **Post-Closing Trial Balance**

Your Name Mountain Sports
Post-Closing Trial Balance
As of February 1, 2010

	Feb 1, 10	
	Debit	Credit
6181 · Liability Insurance	125.00	
6190 · Merchandise Adjustments	16.00	
6212 · Loan Interest	97.93	
6300 · Rent	950.00	
6340 · Telephone	156.40	
6391 · Gas and Electric	359.00	
6392 · Water	85.00	
6471 · Sales	175.00	
6472 · Office	350.00	
7010 · Interest Income		54.05
TOTAL	90,061.24	90,061.24

Partial Report

Print in Portrait orientation
Close the **Trial Balance**

PRINT POST-CLOSING PROFIT AND LOSS STATEMENT

Because February 1 is after the closing date of January 31, 2010, the Profit and Loss Statement for February 1 is the Post-Closing Profit and Loss Statement. To verify the closing, print a Profit and Loss Statement for February 1.

DO ▶ Print a **Standard Profit and Loss Report** for February

Prepare a Standard Profit and Loss Report as previously instructed
The dates are from **02/01/10** to **02/01/10**
Change the Header/Footer so the report title is **Post-Closing Profit & Loss**
- The Net Income is **0.00**.

Your Name Mountain Sports
Post-Closing Profit & Loss
February 1, 2010

	Feb 1, 10
Net Income ▶	0.00 ◀

Print the report in **Portrait** orientation and close the Report

PRINT POST-CLOSING BALANCE SHEET

The proof that assets equal liabilities and owners' equity after the closing entries have been made needs to be displayed in a Post-Closing Balance Sheet. The Balance Sheet for February 1 is considered to be a Post-Closing Balance Sheet because it is prepared after the closing of the period. Most of the adjustments were for the month of January 2010. Because this report is for a month, the adjustment to Retained Earnings and Net Income will result in both of the accounts being included on the Balance Sheet. If, however, this report were prepared for the year, neither account would appear.

> **DO** ▶ Print a Standard Balance Sheet report for February 1, 2010

Prepare a **Standard Balance Sheet** as previously instructed
If necessary, enter the as of date as **02/01/10**
Change the Header/Footer so the report title is **Post-Closing Balance Sheet**
Scroll through the report to view the assets, liabilities, and equities listed
- Because this report is for a one-month period, both Retained Earnings and Net Income are included on this report.

Your Name Mountain Sports
Post-Closing Balance Sheet
As of February 1, 2010

	Feb 1, 10
Equity	
3000 · Retained Earnings	-2,589.19
3100 · Your Name & Muir Capital	
3110 · Your Name, Capital	
3111 · Your Name, Investment	20,000.00
3110 · Your Name, Capital - Other	13,024.32
Total 3110 · Your Name, Capital	33,024.32
3120 · Larry Muir, Capital	
3121 · Larry Muir, Investment	20,000.00
3120 · Larry Muir, Capital - Other	13,024.31
Total 3120 · Larry Muir, Capital	33,024.31
Total 3100 · Your Name & Muir Capital	66,048.63
Net Income	2,589.19
Total Equity	66,048.63
TOTAL LIABILITIES & EQUITY	80,925.09

Partial Report

Print the report, orientation is **Portrait**
Close the **Balance Sheet**

PRINT JOURNAL

Since the Journal was not printed before closing the period, it should be printed at this time. This will give a printed copy of all the transactions made in Chapters 5, 6, and 7.

DO ▶Print the **Journal** for January

Access the Journal as previously instructed
The dates are from **01/01/10** to**01/31/10**
Tab to generate the report
Resize the columns so all names and accounts are shown in full and the report prints on one-page wide

Your Name Mountain Sports
Journal
January 2010

Trans #	Type	Date	Num	Name	Memo	Account	Debit	Credit
111	Check	01/31/2010	8	Old Mammoth Bank	January Visa Payment	1100 · Checking		1,221.98
				Old Mammoth Bank	January Visa Payment	2100 · Visa	1,221.98	
							1,221.98	1,221.98
112	General Journal	01/31/2010			Transfer Net Income into Capital	3000 · Retained Earnings	2,589.19	
					Transfer Net Income into Capital	3110 · Your Name, Capital		1,294.60
					Transfer Net Income into Capital	3120 · Larry Muir, Capital		1,294.59
							2,589.19	2,589.19
113	General Journal	01/31/2010			Close Drawing	3110 · Your Name, Capital	1,000.00	
					Close Drawing	3112 · Your Name, Drawing		1,000.00
							1,000.00	1,000.00
114	General Journal	01/31/2010			Close Drawing	3120 · Larry Muir, Capital	1,000.00	
					Close Drawing	3122 · Larry Muir, Drawing		1,000.00
							1,000.00	1,000.00
115	General Journal	01/31/2010			Correcting Entry	1312 · Sales Supplies	25.00	
					Correcting Entry	1311 · Office Supplies		25.00
							25.00	25.00
116	Inventory Adjust	01/31/2010	1			6190 · Merchandise Adjustments	16.00	
					Hats Inventory Adjustment	1120 · Inventory Asset		16.00
							16.00	16.00
TOTAL							77,376.44	77,376.44

Partial Report

Print the report in **Landscape** orientation
Close the **Journal** and the **Report Center**

BACKUP YOUR NAME MOUNTAIN SPORTS

As in previous chapters, you should back up your company and then close the company.

Follow instructions previously provided to back up company files, close the company, and make a duplicate disk

Name the backup **Sports (Backup Ch. 7)**

SUMMARY

In this chapter, end-of-period adjustments were made, a bank reconciliation and a credit card reconciliation were performed, backup (duplicate) and archive disks were prepared, and adjusting entries were made. The use of Drawing, Net Income, and Retained Earnings accounts were explored and interpreted for a partnership. The closing date for a period was assigned. Account names were changed, and new accounts were created. Even though QuickBooks Pro focuses on entering transactions on business forms, a Journal recording each transaction is kept by QuickBooks Pro. This chapter presented transaction entry directly into the Journal. The difference between accrual-basis and cash-basis accounting was discussed. Company preferences were established for accrual-basis reporting preferences. Owner withdrawals and distribution of capital to partners were examined. Many of the different report options available in QuickBooks Pro were explored, and a report was exported to Microsoft® Excel. A variety of reports were printed. Correction of errors was analyzed, and corrections were made after the period was closed and adjustments were made to inventory. The fact that QuickBooks Pro does not require an actual closing entry at the end of the period was addressed.

END-OF-CHAPTER QUESTIONS

TRUE/FALSE

ANSWER THE FOLLOWING QUESTIONS IN THE SPACE PROVIDED BEFORE THE QUESTION NUMBER.

_____ 1. The owner's drawing account should be transferred to capital each week.

_____ 2. Even if entered elsewhere, all transactions are recorded in the Journal.

_____ 3. You must access the General Journal in order to close a period.

_____ 4. If Show All is selected, inactive accounts will not appear in the Chart of Accounts.

_____ 5. When you reconcile a bank statement, anything entered as a service charge will automatically be entered as a transaction when the reconciliation is complete.

_____ 6. Once an account has been used, the name cannot be changed.

_____ 7. The adjusting entry for depreciation may be made in the Depreciation account register.

_____ 8. At the end of the year, QuickBooks Pro transfers the net income into retained earnings.

_____ 9. A withdrawal by an owner in a partnership reduces the owner's capital.

_____ 10. As with other accounting programs, QuickBooks Pro requires that a formal closing be performed at the end of each year.

MULTIPLE CHOICE

WRITE THE LETTER OF THE CORRECT ANSWER IN THE SPACE PROVIDED
BEFORE THE QUESTION NUMBER.

_____ 1. To print a Reconciliation Report that lists only totals, select ___.
A. none
B. summary
C. detail
D. complete

_____ 2. The report that proves debits equal credits is the ___.
A. Sales Graph
B. Balance Sheet
C. Profit and Loss Statement
D. Trial Balance

_____ 3. If reports are prepared for the month of January, net income will appear in the ___.
A. Profit and Loss Statement
B. Balance Sheet
C. both A and B
D. neither A nor B

_____ 4. In QuickBooks Pro, you export reports to Microsoft® Excel in order to ___.
A. print the report
B. explore "what if" scenarios with data from QuickBooks Pro
C. prepare checks
D. all of the above

_____ 5. QuickBooks Pro uses the ___ method of inventory valuation
A. LIFO
B. average cost
C. FIFO
D. Actual Cost

_____ 6. If a transaction is recorded in the Journal, it may be viewed ___.
A. in the Journal
B. in the register for each account used in the transaction
C. by preparing an analysis graph
D. in both A and B

_____ 7. Entries for bank collections of automatic payments ___.
   A. are automatically recorded at the completion of the bank reconciliation
   B. must be recorded after the bank reconciliation is complete
   C. should be recorded when reconciling the bank statement
   D. should be recorded on the first of the month

_____ 8. The account(s) that may be reconciled is (are) ___.
   A. Checking
   B. Credit Card
   C. both A and B
   D. the Customer list account

_____ 9. The closing entry for drawing transfers the balance of an owner's drawing account into the ___ account.
   A. Retained Earnings
   B. Net Income
   C. Capital
   D. Investment

_____ 10. A Balance Sheet that shows amounts for each account type but not for individual accounts is the ___ Balance Sheet.
   A. Standard
   B. Summary
   C. Detail
   D. Comparison

FILL-IN

IN THE SPACE PROVIDED, WRITE THE ANSWER THAT MOST APPROPRIATELY COMPLETES THE SENTENCE.

1. _____-basis accounting matches income and expenses against a period, and _____-basis accounting records income when the money is received and expenses when the purchase is made or the bill is paid.

2. The _____ proves that Assets = Liabilities + Owners' Equity.

3. In a partnership, each owner has a share of all the _____ and _____ based on the percentage of his or her investment in the business or according to any partnership agreements.

4. In order to close a period, a closing _____ must be provided.

5. No matter where transactions are recorded, they all appear in the _____.

SHORT ESSAY

Describe the entry that is made to transfer net income into the owner's capital account. Include the reason this entry should be made and how income will be listed if it is not made.

_____

_____

_____

_____

_____

NAME_____

TRANSMITTAL

CHAPTER 7: YOUR NAME MOUNTAIN SPORTS

Attach the following documents and reports:

Check No. 6: Your Name
Check No. 7: Larry Muir
Bank Reconciliation Detail Report, January 30, 2010
Credit Card Reconciliation Detail Report, January 31, 2010
Check No. 8: Old Mammoth Bank
Trial Balance, January 31, 2010
Standard Profit and Loss Statement, January 2010
Standard Balance Sheet, January 31, 2011
Standard Balance Sheet, January 31, 2010 (After Equity Adjustments)
Post-Closing Trial Balance, February 1, 2010
Post-Closing Profit and Loss, February 1, 2010
Post-Closing Balance Sheet, February 1, 2010
Journal, January, 2010

END-OF-CHAPTER PROBLEM

YOUR NAME RESORT CLOTHING

Chapter 7 continues with the end-of-period adjustments, bank and credit card reconciliations, archive disks, and closing the period for Your Name Resort Clothing. The company does use a certified public accountant for guidance and assistance with appropriate accounting procedures. The CPA has provided information for Karen to use for adjusting entries, etc.

INSTRUCTIONS

Continue to use the copy of Your Name Resort Clothing you used in the previous chapters. Open the company—the file used is **Clothing.qbw**. Record the adjustments and other transactions as you were instructed in the chapter. Always read the transaction carefully and review the Chart of Accounts when selecting transaction accounts. Print the reports and journals as indicated.

RECORD TRANSACTIONS

January 31, 2010—Enter the following:
▶ Change the names and/or the account numbers of the following accounts. Make sure the account description is appropriate for the new account name.
   o **6260 Printing and Reproduction** to **6260 Printing and Duplication**
   o **6350 Travel & Ent** to **6350 Travel**
   o **3010 Your Name & Olsen, Capital** to **3100 Your Name & Olsen, Capital**
      ▪ Remember to use just your last name.
▶ Add the following accounts:
   o Equity account **3110 Your Name, Capital** (subaccount of **3100**)
   o Equity account **3120 Karen Olsen, Capital** (subaccount of **3100**)
▶ Change the following accounts:
   o **3011 Your Name, Investment** to **3111 Your Name, Investment** (subaccount of **3110**)
      (Note: Since 3110 is a subaccount of 3100, you may not see the entire name of the subaccount listing. Cursor through the subaccount name to read it completely.)
   o **3013 Your Name, Drawing** to **3112 Your Name, Drawing** (subaccount of **3110**)
   o **3012 Karen Olsen, Investment** to **3121 Karen Olsen, Investment** (subaccount of **3120**)

- o **3014 Karen Olsen, Drawing** to **3122 Karen Olsen, Drawing** (subaccount of **3120**)
- ▶ Make the following accounts inactive:
  - o **6291 Building Repairs**
  - o **6351 Entertainment**
- ▶ Delete the following accounts:
  - o **6182 Disability Insurance**
  - o **6213 Mortgage**
  - o **6823 Property**
- ▶ Print an Account Listing in Landscape orientation (Do *not* show inactive accounts. Use the Report menu to print the Account Listing. Resize the columns to display the Account Names in full—including subaccounts—and to hide the columns for Description, and Tax Line.)
- ▶ Create a Fixed Asset Item List for:
  - o Office Equipment, New, Date is 12/31/09, Cost is $8,000, Account is 1510
  - o Store Fixtures, New, Date is 12/31/09, Cost is $9,500, Account is 1520
- ▶ Enter adjusting entries in the Journal and use the memo Adjusting Entry for the following:
  - o Office Supplies Used, the amount used is $35
  - o Sales Supplies Used, account balance (on hand) at the end of the month is $1,400
  - o Record a compound entry for depreciation for the month: Office Equipment, $66.67 and Store Fixtures, $79.17
  - o The amount of insurance remaining in the Prepaid Insurance account is for six months of liability insurance. Record the liability insurance expense for the month
- ▶ Each owner withdrew $500. (Memo: Withdrawal for January) Print Check Nos. 7 and 8 for the owners' withdrawals.
- ▶ Prepare Bank Reconciliation and Enter Adjustments for the Reconciliation: (Refer to the chapter for appropriate Memo notations)

CENTRAL COAST BANK
1234 Coast Highway
San Luis Obispo, CA 93407
(805) 555-9300

Your Name Resort Clothing
784 Marsh Street
San Luis Obispo, CA 93407

Acct. # 987-352-9152   January 31, 2010

Beginning Balance, January 1, 2010			$32,589.00
1/15/10, Deposit	3,022.33		35,611.33
1/15/10, Deposit	1,829.05		37,440.38
1/15/10, NSF Returned Check		325.00	37,115.38
1/15/10, Check 1		58.98	37,056.40
1/18/10, Check 3		156.00	36,900.40
1/18/10, Check 2		343.00	36,557.40
1/25/10, Check 4		1,150.00	35,407.40
1/25/10, Check 5		79.85	35,327.55
1/31/10, Service Charge 10.00, NSF Charge 15.00		25.00	35,302.55
1/31/10, Office Equipment Loan Pmt.: $44.51 Interest, $8.61 Principal		53.12	35,249.43
1/31/10, Store Fixtures Loan Pmt.: $53.42 Interest, $10.33 Principal		63.75	35,185.68
1/31/10, Interest	73.30		35,258.98
Ending Balance, 1/31/10			35,258.98

► Print a Detailed Reconciliation Report. Adjust column widths so the report fits on one page
► Reconcile the Visa account using the statement on the following page
► Print a Detailed Reconciliation Report. Pay Central Coast Bank for the Visa bill using Check No. 9. Print Check No. 9

CENTRAL COAST BANK
1234 Coast Highway
San Luis Obispo, CA 93407

Your Name Resort Clothing
784 Marsh Street
San Luis Obispo, CA 93407
VISA Acct. # 9187-52-9152   **January 31, 2010**

		Balance
Beginning Balance, January 2, 2010		0.00
1/9/10, Clothes Time	196.00	196.00
1/18/10, Office Masters	250.00	446.00
Ending Balance, 1/31/10		446.00

Minimum Payment Due: $50.00   **Payment Due Date: February 5, 2010**

▶ After completing the Visa reconciliation, distribute capital to each owner: divide the balance of 3100 Your Name & Olsen, Capital - Other equally between the two partners. (View a Standard Balance Sheet to see the balance of the Capital – Other account.) Record an entry to transfer each owner's portion of the Capital Other to the individual capital accounts. (Memo: Transfer Capital to Individual Accounts)
▶ Verify or change reporting preferences to accrual basis
▶ Print the following for January 1-31, 2010, or as of January 31, 2010:
   o Trial Balance
   o Standard Profit and Loss Statement
▶ Divide in half and transfer Net Income/Retained Earnings into owners' individual Capital accounts.
▶ Close Drawing accounts into owner's individual Capital accounts
▶ Print a Standard Balance Sheet
▶ Prepare an archive copy of the company file
▶ Close the period as of January 31, 2010 (Do not assign passwords)
▶ After closing the period on 01/31/10, discovered an error in the amount of Office Supplies and Sales Supplies: Transfer $40 from Office Supplies to Sales Supplies
▶ After closing the period on 01/31/10, found one damaged tie. Adjust the quantity of ties on 01/31/10 using the Expense account 6190 Merchandise Adjustments
▶ Change the net income/retained earnings adjustment to reflect the merchandise adjustment for the ties
▶ Backup the company

Print Reports for February 1, 2010 and February 1, 2011
   o Journal for January, 2010 (Landscape orientation, Fit to one page wide)
   o Post-Closing Trial Balance, February 1, 2010
   o Post-Closing Standard Profit and Loss Statement, February 1, 2010
   o Post-Closing Standard Balance Sheet, February 1, 2010
   o Standard Balance Sheet, February 1, 2011

NAME_____

TRANSMITTAL

CHAPTER 7: YOUR NAME RESORT CLOTHING

Attach the following documents and reports:

Account Listing
Check No. 7: Your Name
Check No. 8: Karen Olsen
Bank Reconciliation, January 31, 2010
Visa Reconciliation, January 31, 2010
Check No. 9: Central Coast Bank
Trial Balance, January 31, 2010
Standard Profit and Loss, January 2010
Standard Balance Sheet, January 31, 2010
Journal, January, 2010
Post-Closing Trial Balance, February 1, 2010
Post-Closing Profit and Loss, February 1, 2010
Post-Closing Balance Sheet, February 1, 2010
Balance Sheet, February 1, 2011

YOUR NAME'S GOLF WORLD PRACTICE SET: MERCHANDISING BUSINESS

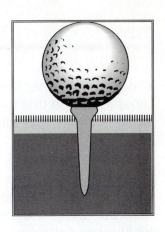

The following is a comprehensive practice set combining all the elements of QuickBooks Pro studied in the merchandising section of the text. Since the version of QuickBooks is 2010, the text shows the year as 2010. In this practice set, you are instructed to keep the books for a company for the month of January 2010. Check with your instructor to find out what year you should use when recording transactions. Entries will be made to record invoices, receipt of payments on invoices, cash sales, credit card sales, receipt and payment of bills, orders and receipts of merchandise, credit memos for invoices and bills, sales tax payments, and credit card payments. Account names will be added, changed, deleted, and made inactive. Customers, vendors, owners, and fixed assets will be added to the appropriate lists. Reports will be prepared to analyze sales, bills, receipts, and items ordered. Formal reports including the Trial Balance, Profit and Loss Statement, and Balance Sheet will be prepared. Adjusting entries for depreciation, supplies used, insurance expense, and automatic payments will be recorded. Both bank and credit card reconciliations will be prepared. Entries to display partnership equity for each partner will be made. The owners' drawing accounts will be closed and the period will be closed.

YOUR NAME'S GOLF WORLD

Located in Palm Springs, California, Your Name's Golf World is a full-service golf shop that sells golf equipment and golf clothing. Your Name's Golf World is a partnership owned and operated by Valerie Childers and you. Each partner contributed an equal amount to the partnership. You buy the equipment and manage the store. Valerie buys the clothing and accessory items and keeps the books for Your Name's Golf World. There are several part-time employees working for the company selling merchandise.

INSTRUCTIONS

Copy the file **Golf.qbw** as previously instructed.

When entering transactions, you are responsible for any memos you wish to include in transactions. Unless otherwise specified, the terms for each sale or bill will be the term specified on the Customer or Vendor List. (Choose edit for the individual customers or vendors and select the Additional Info tab to see the terms for each customer or vendor.) Customer Message is usually *Thank you for your business*. However, any other message that is appropriate may be used. If a customer's order exceeds the established credit limit, accept the order and process it.

If the terms allow a discount for a customer, make sure to apply the discount if payment is made within the discount period. Use 6130 Sales Discounts as the discount account. On occasion, a payment may be made within the discount period but not received or recorded within the discount period. Information within the transaction will indicate whether or not the payment is equivalent to a full payment. For example, if you received $98 for an invoice for $100 shortly after the discount period and the transaction indicated payment in full, apply the discount. If a customer has a credit and has a balance on the account, apply the credit to the appropriate invoice for the customer. If there is no balance for a customer and a return is made, issue a credit memo and a refund check.

Always pay bills in time to take advantage of purchase discounts. Use the Cost of Goods Sold Account 5010 Merchandise Discounts for the discount account. Remember that the discount due date will be ten days from the date of the bill.

Invoices, purchase orders, and other business forms should be printed as they are entered. To save time, you do not need to print Payment Receipts unless your professor requests that you do so. Print with lines around each field. Most reports will be printed in Portrait orientation; however, if the report (such as the Journal) will fit across the page using Landscape, use Landscape orientation. Whenever possible, adjust the column widths so that reports fit on one page wide *without* selecting Fit report to one page wide.

Back up your work at the end of each week.

The following lists are used for all sales items, customers, and vendors. You will be adding additional customers and vendors as the company is in operation.

Sales Items:

Name	Description	Type	Account	On Hand	Price	Attach
◆Bags	Golf Bags	Inventory Part	4010 · Accessory Sales	15	0.00	
◆Clubs-Irons	Golf Clubs: Irons	Inventory Part	4030 · Equipment Sales	150	0.00	
◆Clubs-Sets	Golf Clubs: Sets	Inventory Part	4030 · Equipment Sales	50	0.00	
◆Clubs-Woods	Golf Clubs: Woods	Inventory Part	4030 · Equipment Sales	150	0.00	
◆Gift Sets	Golf Gift Sets	Inventory Part	4010 · Accessory Sales	10	0.00	
◆Gloves	Golf Gloves	Inventory Part	4010 · Accessory Sales	35	0.00	
◆Golf Balls	Golf Balls	Inventory Part	4010 · Accessory Sales	60	0.00	
◆Hats	Golf Hats	Inventory Part	4010 · Accessory Sales	20	0.00	
◆Men's Jackets	Men's Jackets	Inventory Part	4020 · Clothing Sales	12	0.00	
◆Men's Pants	Men's Pants	Inventory Part	4020 · Clothing Sales	15	0.00	
◆Men's Shirts	Men's Shirts	Inventory Part	4020 · Clothing Sales	15	0.00	
◆Men's Shoes	Men's Shoes	Inventory Part	4020 · Clothing Sales	18	0.00	
◆Men's Shorts	Men's Shorts	Inventory Part	4020 · Clothing Sales	12	0.00	
◆Tees	Golf Tees	Inventory Part	4010 · Accessory Sales	30	0.00	
◆Towels	Golf Towels	Inventory Part	4010 · Accessory Sales	10	0.00	
◆Women's Jacket	Women's Jackets	Inventory Part	4020 · Clothing Sales	12	0.00	
◆Women's Pants	Women's Pants	Inventory Part	4020 · Clothing Sales	12	0.00	
◆Women's Shirt	Women's Shirts	Inventory Part	4020 · Clothing Sales	12	0.00	
◆Women's Shoes	Women's Shoes	Inventory Part	4020 · Clothing Sales	20	0.00	
◆Women's Short	Women's Shorts	Inventory Part	4020 · Clothing Sales	15	0.00	
◆CA Sales Tax	CA Sales Tax	Sales Tax Item	2200 · Sales Tax Payable		7.25%	
◆Out of State	Out-of-state sale, exempt from sales tax	Sales Tax Item	2200 · Sales Tax Payable		0.0%	

Note: Individual golf clubs are categorized as irons or woods. A complete set of clubs would be categorized as a set. The type of material used in a golf club makes no difference in a sales item. For example, graphite is a material used in the shaft of a golf club. A set of graphite clubs would refer to a set of golf clubs. Titanium is a type of metal used in the head of a golf club. A titanium wood would be sold as a wood. Golf balls are sold in packages called sleeves; thus, a quantity of one would represent one package of golf balls.

Vendors:

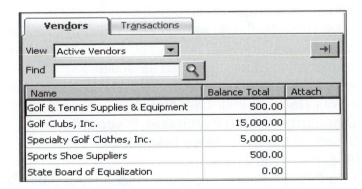

Name	Balance Total	Attach
Golf & Tennis Supplies & Equipment	500.00	
Golf Clubs, Inc.	15,000.00	
Specialty Golf Clothes, Inc.	5,000.00	
Sports Shoe Suppliers	500.00	
State Board of Equalization	0.00	

Customers:

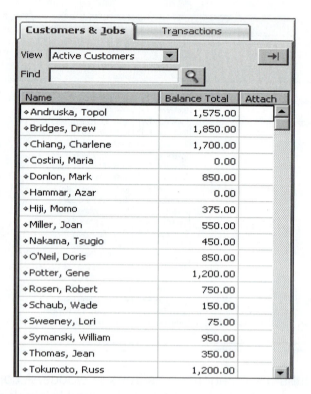

RECORD TRANSACTIONS:

Enter the transactions for Your Name's Golf World and print as indicated.

Week 1—January 2-8, 2010:
▶ Add your name to the company name. Even though this is a partnership, the company name will be **Your Name's Golf World**. (Type your actual name *not* the words Student's Name. Don't forget the apostrophe s after your last name. For example, Sue Smith would be Sue Smith's Golf World.)
▶ Change Preferences: Reports should refresh automatically, the Report Header/Footer should *not* include the Date Prepared, Time Prepared, or Report Basis. Inventory and purchase orders should be active
▶ Change the names and, if necessary, the descriptions of the following accounts:
  ○ **3000** change Your Name to your **Last Name**
  ○ **4200 Sales Discounts** to **4200 Purchases Discounts**
  ○ **6130 Cash Discounts** to **6130 Sales Discounts**
  ○ **6350 Travel & Ent** to **6350 Travel**
  ○ **6381 Marketing** to **6381 Sales** (this is a subaccount of 6380 Supplies Expense)
▶ Delete the following accounts:
  ○ **4050 Reimbursed Expenses**
  ○ **4070 Resale Discounts**

- o **4090 Resale Income**
- o **4100 Freight Income**
- o **6140 Contributions**
- o **6182 Disability Insurance**
- o **6213 Mortgage**
- o **6265 Filing Fees**
- o **6285 Franchise Fees**
- o **6351 Entertainment**

▶ Make the following accounts inactive:
- o **6311 Building Repairs**
- o **6413 Property**

▶ Add the following accounts:
- o Re-add the deleted expense account **6140 Contributions**
- o Equity account: **3010 Your Name, Capital** (subaccount of **3000**)
- o Equity account: **3020 Valerie Childers, Capital** (subaccount of **3000**)
- o Cost of Goods Sold account: **5010 Merchandise Discounts** (subaccount of **5000**)

▶ Change the following accounts:
- o **Student's Name, Investment** to **3011 Your Name, Investment** (subaccount of **3010**)
- o **Student's Name, Drawing** to **3012 Your Name, Drawing** (subaccount of **3010**)
- o **Valerie Childers, Investment** to **3021 Valerie Childers, Investment** (subaccount of **3020**)
- o **Valerie Childers, Drawing** to **3022 Valerie Childers, Drawing** (subaccount of **3020**)

▶ Use the Report Menu to access the List reports. Print the Account Listing in portrait orientation. Re-size the columns so the Account Names, Type, and Balance Total show in full. Do *not* show the Description, Acct. #, or Tax Line columns. Click the Modify Report button and on the Header/Footer tab, change the report date to January 2, 2010.

▶ Create Fixed Asset Item List
- o Office Equipment, New, Description Office Equipment, Purchase Date 12/31/(use the end of previous year), Cost 5,000.00, Asset Account 1510 Office Equipment
- o Store Fixtures, New, Description Store Fixtures, Purchase Date 12/31/(use the end of previous year), Cost 6,000.00, Asset Account 1520 Store Fixtures

▶ Prior to recording any transactions, print a Trial Balance as of January 1, 2010.

▶ Customize Sales Receipts, Product Invoices, and Purchase Orders so your name will print on the same line as the company name.

▶ Print invoices, checks, and other items as they are entered in the transactions.

1/2/2010
▶ Sold 2 pairs of women's shorts @ $64.99 each, 2 women's shirts @ $59.99 each, 1 women's jacket @ $129.99, and 1 pair of women's shoes @ $179.99 to Tamara

Yanov. (Remember: Use your Copy of: Intuit Product Invoice. Print Invoice No. 1 when the transaction is entered.)

▶ Having achieved her goal of a handicap under 30, Maria treated herself to the new clubs she had been wanting. Sold on account 1 set of graphite clubs for $750, 1 golf bag for $129.95, and 5 sleeves (packages) of golf balls @ $6.95 each to Maria Costini. (Remember to accept sales that are over the credit limit.)

▶ Azar heard that titanium would give him extra yardage with each shot. Sold 4 titanium woods on account to Azar Hammar @ $459.00 each.

▶ Sold 5 golf bags @ $59.99 each and 5 sets of starter clubs @ $159.99 each to Palm Springs Schools on account for the high school golf team. Palm Springs Schools located at 99-4058 South Palm Canyon Drive, Palm Springs, CA 92262 is a nonprofit organization. The telephone number is 760-555-4455, and the contact person is Claudia Colby. The terms are Net 30. Even though this is a nonprofit organization, it does pay California Sales Tax on all purchases. The credit limit is $1,500. Include a subtotal for the sale and apply a 10% sales discount for a nonprofit organization. (Create any new sales items necessary.)

▶ Correct the invoice to Maria Costini. The price of the golf bag should be $179.95. Reprint the invoice.

▶ Received Check No. 2285 from Topol Andruska in full payment of his account.

▶ Received Check No. 102-33 from Russ Tokumoto, $600, in partial payment of his account.

1/3/2010

▶ Sold 3 gift sets @ $14.99 each and 3 sleeves (packages) of golf balls @ $8.95 each to Lori Sweeney on account to be given away as door prizes at an upcoming ladies' club tournament.

▶ Sold 2 pairs of men's shorts @ $49.95 each, 2 men's shirts @ $59.99 each, and 1 pair of golf shoes @ $119.99 to Wade Schaub on account.

▶ Received Check No. 815 from Mark Donlon for $850 in full payment of his account.

▶ Sold 2 golf towels @ $9.95 each to a cash customer. (Cash is the payment method. Remember to print Sales Receipt No. 1.)

▶ Sold on account 1 pair of women's golf shoes @ $149.95 to a new customer: Laura Hansen (Remember, last name first in the Customer List), 45-2215 PGA Drive, Rancho Mirage, CA 92270, 760-555-3322, Terms 1% 10 Net 30, taxable customer for California Sales Tax, Credit Limit $1,000

▶ Received Check No. 2233 for $950 from Gene Potter in partial payment of his account.

▶ Sold a golf bag for $99.95 to a cash customer using a Visa card.

<u>1/5/2010</u>
▶ Prepare and print an Inventory Stock Status by Item Report for January 1-5 in Landscape orientation.
▶ Prepare Purchase Orders for all items marked Order on the Inventory Stock Status by Item Report. Place all orders with the preferred vendors. Prepare only one purchase order per vendor. For all items ordered, the Qty on Hand should exceed the Reorder Point by 10 when the new merchandise is received. (For example, if the reorder point is 5 and you have 4 items on hand, you will need to order 11 items. This would make the quantity 15 when the order is received. This would exceed the reorder point by 10.) The cost of golf bags are $40 each, gift sets are $3 each, men's shorts are $20 each, towels are $2 each, and women's shirts are $20 each. (Remember to print the purchase orders.)
▶ Order 5 women's hats @ $10.00 each from a new vendor: Head Gear, Inc., 45980 West Los Angeles Street, Los Angeles, CA 90025, Contact Sally Lockhart, Phone 310-555-8787, Fax 310-555-7878, E-mail HeadGear@la.com, Terms 2% 10 Net 30, Credit Limit $500. Add a new inventory sales item: Women's Hats. The purchase and sales description is Women's Golf Hats. Leave the purchase and sales price at 0.00. The COGS account is 5000. Head Gear, Inc. is the preferred vendor (Click the drop-down list arrow for Vendor, click Head Gear, Inc.). The hats are taxable. The Income account is 4000-Sales: 4010-Accessory Sales. The Asset account is 1120-Inventory Asset. The reorder point is 10. Quantity on Hand is 0 as of 01/05/2010.
▶ Change the current sales item Hats from Item Name: Hats to Men's Hats. The purchase and sales descriptions should be Men's Golf Hats. Change the reorder point from 15 to 12.
▶ Print a Purchase Order QuickReport in Landscape orientation for January 1-5.

<u>1/8/2010</u>
▶ Received Check No. 1822 for a cash sale of 2 men's golf hats @ $49.95 each.
▶ Deposit all receipts (checks, credit cards, and/or cash) for the week. Print the Deposit Summary.
▶ Backup your work for Week 1. Name your backup file **Golf (Backup Week 1)**

<u>Week 2—January 9-15:</u>
<u>1/10/2010</u>
▶ Received the order from Head Gear, Inc. without the bill.
▶ Received the orders from Golf & Tennis Supplies & Equipment and Specialty Golf Clothes, Inc., along with the bills for the merchandise received. All items were received in full except the golf bags. Of the 12 bags ordered, only 8 were received. Use 01/10/2010 for the bill date for both transactions.
▶ Lori Sweeney returned 1 of the gift sets purchased on January 3. Issue a credit memo and apply to Invoice 5.

▶ Mark Donlon returned 1 pair of men's golf shorts that had been purchased for $59.95. (The shorts had been purchased previously and were part of his $850 opening balance.) Issue the appropriate items.

▶ Sold 1 complete set of golf clubs on account to Tsugio Nakama for $1,600.00.

▶ Sold a graphite sand wedge and a graphite gap wedge @ $119.95 each to a customer using a Visa card. (Both clubs are classified as irons.)

1/12/2010

▶ Received the telephone bill for the month, $85.15 from Desert Telephone Co., 11-092 Highway 111, Palm Springs, CA 92262, 760-555-9285. The bill is due January 25.

▶ Purchased $175 of office supplies to have on hand from Indio Office Supply, 3950 46th Avenue, Indio, CA 92201, Contact Cheryl Lockwood, Phone 760-555-1535, Fax 760-555-5351. Used the company Visa card for the purchase.

1/14/2010

▶ Received the bill for the order from Head Gear, Inc. Use 01/14/2010 for the bill date.

▶ Received a bill from the Sunshine Electric Co., 995 Date Palm Drive, Cathedral City, CA 92234, 760-555-4646 for the monthly electric bill. The bill is for $275.00 and is due January 30.

▶ Received the monthly water bill for $65 from Indian Wells Water, 84-985 Jackson Street, Indian Wells, CA 92202, 760-555-5653. The bill is due January 30.

▶ Sold a set of golf clubs on account to Laura Hansen for $895.00.

▶ Received Check No. 3801 for $1,949.42 from Azar Hammar in full payment of his bill. (The transaction date is 01/14/10. The payment appropriately includes the discount since the check was dated 01/10/10.)

▶ Received Check No. 783 for $594.53 from Tamara Yanov in full payment of her bill. (The payment includes the discount since the check was dated 01/11/10.)

▶ Deposit all receipts (checks, credit cards, and/or cash) for the week. Print the Deposit Summary.

▶ Back up your work for Week 2. Name the file **Golf (Backup Week 2)**.

Week 3—January 16-22:
1/17/2010

▶ Received Check No. 1822 back from the bank. This check was for $107.14 from a cash customer: William Jones, 8013 Desert Drive, Desert Hot Springs, CA 92270, 760-555-0100. Payment is due on receipt. Charge William the bank charge of $15 plus Your Name's Golf World's own NSF charge of $15. Add any necessary customers, items and/or accounts. (Returned check service charges should be Income account 4040.)

▶ Received Check No. 67-086 for $135.95 from Lori Sweeney in full payment of her account.

▶ Received the remaining 4 golf bags and the bill from Golf & Tennis Supplies & Equipment on earlier purchase order. The date of the bill is 01/16/2010.

1/18/2010

▶ Pay all bills that are eligible to receive a discount if paid between January 18 and 22. Use account 5010 Merchandise Discounts as the Discount Account. (Print the checks. To print the checks, you may use Print Forms or you may print them individually.)

▶ Sold 1 golf bag @ $199.95, 1 set of graphite golf clubs @ $1,200.00, 1 putter @ $129.95 (record the putter as Golf Clubs: Irons), and 3 sleeves of golf balls @ $9.95 each on account to Lori Sweeney.

▶ Returned 2 men's shirts that had poorly stitched seams at a cost of $20 each to Specialty Golf Clothes, Inc. Received a credit memo from the company.

1/20/2010

▶ Sold 1 men's golf hat @ $49.95 and 1 men's golf jacket at $89.95 to a customer using a Master Card.

▶ Sold 1 towel @ $9.95, 2 packages of golf tees @ $1.95 each, and 1 sleeve of golf balls at $5.95 to a customer for cash.

▶ Received Check No. 1256 in full payment of account from Charlene Chiang.

▶ Gene Potter bought a starter set of golf clubs on account for his son @ $250.00 and a new titanium driver for himself @ $549.95 (a driver is a Golf Club: Woods).

▶ A businessman in town with his wife bought them each a set of golf clubs @ $1,495.00 per set and a new golf bag for each of them @ $249.95 per bag. He purchased 1 men's jacket for $179.95. His wife purchased 1 pair of golf shoes for $189.99 and 1 women's jacket for $149.99. He used his Visa to pay for the purchases.

▶ Prepare and print an Inventory Stock Status by Item Report for January 1-20.

▶ Prepare Purchase Orders to order any inventory items indicated on the report. As with earlier orders, use the preferred vendor, issue only one purchase order per vendor, and order enough to have 10 more than the minimum quantity of the ordered items on hand. (Golf balls cost $3.50 per sleeve, men's and women's jackets cost $20 each, and women's hats cost $10 each.)

▶ Deposit all receipts (checks, credit cards, and/or cash) for the week. Print the Deposit Summary.

▶ Back up your work for Week 3. Name the file **Golf (Backup Week 3)**.

Week 4 and End of Period—January 23-31:
1/23/2010

▶ Pay all bills eligible to receive a discount if paid between January 23 and 30 and pay the telephone bill in full.

▶ Lori Sweeney was declared Club Champion and won a prize of $500. She brought in the $500 cash as a payment to be applied to the amount she owes on her account.

▶ Sold on account to Lori Sweeney 5 Women's Golf Hats @ $25.99 each to give away as prizes at her next ladies' club tournament.

1/24/2010
▶ Received the bill and all the items ordered from Specialty Golf Clothes, Inc., and Golf & Tennis Supplies & Equipment. The bills are dated 01/23/2010.
▶ Received Check No. 5216 from Drew Bridges as payment in full on his account.
▶ Received Check No. 1205 from Maria Costini as payment in full on her account.
▶ Received a letter of apology for the NSF check and a new check for $137.14 from William Jones to pay his account in full. The new check is Check No. 9015.

1/25/2010
▶ Received the bill and all the hats ordered from Head Gear, Inc. The date of the bill is 01/23/2010.
▶ Received the bill for $3,000 rent from Palm Springs Rentals, 11-2951 Palm Canyon Drive, Palm Springs, CA 92262, Contact Tammi Moreno, Phone 760-555-8368, Fax 760-555-8638. The rent is due February 4.
▶ Purchased sales supplies to have on hand for $150 from Indio Office Supply. Used the company Visa for the purchase.
▶ Prepare an Unpaid Bills Detail Report for January 25, 2010. Print the report.
▶ Pay Bills (Note: Bills for 12/31/2009 will have a due date of 01/10/10.)
   o $1,000 to Specialty Golf Clothes, Inc., for the amount owed on 12/31/2009. (NOTE: Select the bill you want to pay. Apply the credit you have from Specialty Golf Clothes, Inc., because of returned merchandise. You want to pay $1,000 plus use the $40 credit and reduce the amount owed by $1,040, *not* $960. Once the credit is applied, you will see the amount owed as $4,960. Since you are not paying the full amount owed, click in Amt. To Pay column and enter the amount you are paying. In this case, enter 1,000 as the amount you are paying. When the payment is processed, $1,000 will be deducted from cash to pay for this bill and the $40 credit will be applied.)
   o Pay $5,000 to Golf Clubs, Inc. toward the amount owed on 12/31/2009
   o Pay $500 to Golf & Tennis Supplies & Equipment to pay the amount owed on 12/31/2009
   o Pay $500 to Sports Shoe Suppliers to pay the amount owed on 12/31/2009
   o Pay the rent
   o Pay the electric bill
   o Pay the water bill.

1/26/2010
▶ Prepare and print an Unpaid Bills Detail Report for January 26, 2010. (*Note:* check Specialty Golf Clothes, Inc., the amount owed should be $4,360. If your report does not show this, check to see how you applied the credit when you paid bills. If necessary, QuickBooks Pro does allow you to delete the previous bill payment and

redo it. If this is the case, be sure to apply the credit, and record $1,000 as the payment amount.)

▶ Received $1,000 from Tsugio Nakama, Check No. 3716, in partial payment of his account.

▶ Received payment in full from Russ Tokumoto, Check No. 102-157.

▶ Sold 15 sleeves of golf balls @ $5.95 each to a cash customer to use as prizes in a retirement golf tournament for an employee of his company. Paid with Check No. 2237.

1/29/2010

▶ Deposit all checks and credit card receipts for the week.

1/30/2010

▶ Prepare Sales Tax Liability Report from January 1-30, 2010. Adjust the column widths and print the report in Landscape orientation. The report should fit on one page.

▶ Pay sales tax due as of January 30, 2010 and print the check.

▶ Print a Sales by Item Summary Report for January 1-30. Use Landscape orientation and, if necessary, adjust column widths so the report fits on one page wide.

▶ Print a Trial Balance for January 1-30 in Portrait orientation.

▶ Enter the following adjusting entries:
   o Office Supplies Used for the month is $125.
   o The balance of the Sales Supplies is $650 on January 30.
   o The amount of Prepaid Insurance represents the liability insurance for 12 months. Record the adjusting entry for the month of January.
   o Depreciation for the month is: Office Equipment, $83.33, Store Fixtures, $100.

▶ Record the transactions for owner's equity:
   o Each owner's withdrawal for the month of January is $2,000.
   o Divide the amount in account 3000-Your Name & Childers, Capital - Other, and transfer one-half the amount into each owner's individual Capital account. Prepare a Standard Balance Sheet for January 30 to determine the amount to divide.

▶ Back up your work for Week 4. Name the file **Golf (Backup Week 4)**.

01/31/2010

▶ Use the following bank statement to prepare a bank reconciliation. Enter any adjustments.

DESERT BANK 1234-110 Highway 111 Palm Springs, CA 92270			
Your Name's Golf World 55-100 PGA Boulevard Palm Springs, CA 92270 Acct. # 9857-32-922		(760) 555-3300 January 2010	
Beginning Balance, January 1, 2010			$35, 275.14
1/8/2010, Deposit	4,210.68		39,485.82
1/10/2010, Check 1		64.30	39,421.52
1/14/2010, Deposit	2,801.24		42,222.76
1/16/2010, NSF Check		107.14	42,115.62
1/18/2010, Check 2		365.54	41,750.08
1/25/2010, Check 3		392.00	41,358.08
1/23/2010, Check 4		85.15	41,272.93
1/23/2010, Check 5		156.80	41,116.13
1/23/2010, Check 6		49.00	41,067.13
1/25/2010, Deposit	6,307.77		47,374.90
1/25/2010, Check 11		1,000.00	46.374.90
1/25/2010, Check 13		275.00	46,099.90
1/25/2010, Check 12		500.00	45,599.90
1/25/2010, Check 10		3,000.00	42,599.90
1/25/2010, Check 8		5,000.00	37,599.90
1/25/2010, Check 7		500.00	37,099.90
1/25/2010, Check 9		65.00	37,034.*0
1/31/2010, Service Charge, $15, and NSF Charge, $15		30.00	37,004.90
1/31/2010, Store Fixtures Loan Pmt.: Interest, $89.03; Principal, $17.21		106.24	36,898.66
1/31/2010, Office Equipment Loan Pmt:.: Interest, $53.42; Principal, $10.33		63.75	36,834.91
1/31/2010, Interest	76.73		36,911.64
Ending Balance, 1/31/2010			36,911.64

▶ Print a Reconciliation Detail Report.

▶ Received the Visa bill. Prepare a Credit Card Reconciliation and pay the Visa bill.

<table>
<tr><td colspan="4">DESERT BANK
VISA DEPARTMENT
1234-110 Highway 111
Palm Springs, CA 92270</td><td>(760) 555-3300</td></tr>
<tr><td colspan="4">Your Name's Golf World
55-100 PGA Boulevard
Palm Springs, CA 92270
VISA Acct. # 9287-52-952</td><td>January 2010</td></tr>
<tr><td>Beginning Balance, January 1, 2010</td><td></td><td></td><td></td><td>0.00</td></tr>
<tr><td>1/12/2010, Indio Office Supply</td><td></td><td></td><td>175.00</td><td>175.00</td></tr>
<tr><td>1/25/2010, Indio Office Supply</td><td></td><td></td><td>150.00</td><td>325.00</td></tr>
<tr><td>Ending Balance, 1/25/2010</td><td></td><td></td><td></td><td>325.00</td></tr>
<tr><td colspan="2">Minimum Payment Due, $50.00</td><td colspan="3">Payment Due Date: February 7, 2010</td></tr>
</table>

▶ Print the check for payment to Desert Bank and a Reconciliation Summary Report
▶ Make sure the reporting preference is for accrual basis.
▶ Print the following reports for January 1-31, 2010, or as of January 31, 2010:
  ○ Standard Profit & Loss Statement
  ○ Standard Balance Sheet
▶ Divide the Net Income/Retained Earnings in half and transfer one-half into each owner's individual capital account.
▶ Close the drawing account for each owner into the owner's individual capital account.
▶ Print a Standard Balance Sheet for January 31, 2010. Use the title **Balance Sheet—After Owner Equity Adjustments** for the report.
▶ Prepare an Archive Backup named **Golf (Archive 01-31-10)**
▶ Close the period using the closing date of 01/31/2010. Do not use a password.
▶ Edit a transaction from the closed period: Discovered an error in the Supplies accounts. Transfer $50 from 1320-Sales Supplies to 1310-Office Supplies.
▶ Adjust the number of tees on hand to 24. Use the expense account 6190 for Merchandise Adjustments. Be sure to correct the adjustment for net income/ retained earnings.

Print Reports and Back Up
▶ Print the following:
  ○ Journal (Landscape orientation, Fit on one page wide) for January , 2010
  ○ Post-Closing Trial Balance, February 1, 2010 (Portrait orientation)
  ○ Post-Closing Standard Profit and Loss Statement, February 1, 2010
  ○ Post-Closing Standard Balance Sheet, February 1, 2010
  ○ Change the year on the report to 2011 and print a Standard Balance Sheet for February 1, 2011
▶ Back up your work to **Golf (Backup Complete)**.

NAME_____

TRANSMITTAL

YOUR NAME'S GOLF WORLD: PRACTICE SET MERCHANDISING BUSINESS

Attach the following documents and reports:

Week 1
Account Listing
Trial Balance, January 1, 2010
Invoice No. 1: Tamara Yanov
Invoice No. 2: Maria Costini
Invoice No. 3: Azar Hammar
Invoice No. 4: Palm Springs Schools
Invoice No. 2 (Corrected): Maria Costini
Invoice No. 5: Lori Sweeney
Invoice No. 6: Wade Schaub
Sales Receipt No. 1: Cash Customer
Invoice No. 7: Laura Hansen
Sales Receipt No. 2: Cash Customer
Inventory Stock Status by Item Report, January 1-5, 2010
Purchase Order No. 1: Golf & Tennis Supplies & Equipment
Purchase Order No. 2: Specialty Golf Clothes, Inc.
Purchase Order No. 3: Head Gear, Inc.
Purchase Order QuickReport, January 5, 2010
Sales Receipt No. 3: Cash Customer
Deposit Summary, January 8, 2010

Week 2
Credit Memo No. 8: Lori Sweeney
Credit Memo No. 9: Mark Donlon
Check No. 1: Mark Donlon
Invoice No. 10: Tsugio Nakama
Sales Receipt No. 4: Cash Customer
Invoice No. 11: Laura Hansen
Deposit Summary, January 14, 2010

Week 3
Invoice No. 12: William Jones
Check No. 2: Golf & Tennis Supplies & Equipment
Check No. 3: Specialty Golf Clothes, Inc.
Invoice No. 13: Lori Sweeney
Sales Receipt No. 5: Cash Customer
Sales Receipt No. 6: Cash Customer
Invoice No. 14: Gene Potter
Sales Receipt No. 7: Cash Customer
Inventory Stock Status by Item, January 1-20, 2010
Purchase Order No. 4: Golf & Tennis Supplies & Equipment
Purchase Order No. 5: Specialty Golf Clothes, Inc.
Purchase Order No. 6: Head Gear, Inc.
Deposit Summary, January 20, 2010

Week 4 and End of Period
Check No. 4: Desert Telephone
Check No. 5: Golf & Tennis Supplies & Equipment
Check No. 6: Head Gear, Inc.
Invoice No. 15: Lori Sweeney
Unpaid Bills Detail, January 25, 2010
Check No. 7: Golf & Tennis Supplies & Equipment
Check No. 8: Golf Clubs, Inc.
Check No. 9: Indian Wells Water
Check No. 10: Palm Springs Rentals
Check No. 11: Specialty Golf Clothes, Inc.
Check No. 12: Sports Shoe Suppliers
Check No. 13: Sunshine Electric Co.
Unpaid Bills Detail, January 26, 2010
Sales Receipt No. 8: Cash Customer
Deposit Summary, January 29, 2010
Sales Tax Liability Report, January 1-30, 2010
Check No. 14: State Board of Equalization
Sales by Item Summary, January 1-30, 2010
Trial Balance, January 30, 2010
Check No. 15: Your Name
Check No. 16: Valerie Childers
Bank Reconciliation, January 31, 2010
Credit Card Reconciliation, January 31, 2010
Check No. 17: Desert Bank
Standard Profit and Loss, January 2010
Standard Balance Sheet, January 31, 2010
Standard Balance Sheet After Owner Equity Adjustments, January 31, 2010
Journal, January 2010
Post-Closing Trial Balance, February 1, 2010
Post-Closing Standard Profit and Loss Statement, February 1, 2010
Post-Closing Standard Balance Sheet, February 1, 2010
Standard Balance Sheet, February 1, 2011

PAYROLL

8

LEARNING OBJECTIVES

At the completion of this chapter, you will be able to:

1. Create, preview, and print payroll checks.
2. Adjust pay stub information.
3. Correct, void, and delete paychecks.
4. Change employee information and add a new employee.
5. Print a Payroll Summary by Employee Report.
6. View an Employee Earnings Summary Report.
7. Print a Payroll Liabilities Report.
8. Pay Taxes and Other Liabilities.
9. Print a Journal

PAYROLL

Many times, a company begins the process of computerizing its accounting system simply to be able to do the payroll using the computer. It is much faster and easier to let QuickBooks Pro look at the tax tables and determine how much withholding should be deducted for each employee than to have an individual perform this task. Because tax tables change frequently, QuickBooks Pro requires its users to enroll in a payroll service plan. In order to enroll in a payroll service plan, you must have a company tax identification number and a registered copy of QuickBooks. QuickBooks Pro has a variety of payroll service plans that are available for an additional charge. If you do not subscribe to a payroll plan, you must calculate and enter the payroll taxes manually.

At the time of writing, QuickBooks has the following Payroll Plans available on a subscription basis:

Basic Payroll: ($129-229 per year depending on the number of employees) a payroll option for companies. Subscribing to this plan enables you to download up-to-date tax tables into QuickBooks. If you use this, you enter your employee information once, and QuickBooks will use this information each payday to automatically calculate deductions and prepare paychecks for your employees each pay period. To prepare your federal and state tax forms, you will work with your accountant; or use QuickBooks reports to generate the data you need in order to fill in tax forms by hand.

Enhanced Payroll: ($199-349 per year depending on the number of employees) a more comprehensive do-it-yourself payroll solution used to calculate deductions, earnings, and payroll taxes using QuickBooks. Enhanced payroll includes federal and state tax forms, tools for tracking workers compensation costs, tools for calculating bonuses, and tools for entering hours for a large number of employees more quickly. Enhanced payroll automatically fills in your data on quarterly federal and state tax forms. Just print, sign & mail your tax filings or use E-File to file and pay payroll taxes electronically with QuickBooks. In addition, the QuickBooks Enhanced Payroll also comes in an accountant's version and allows payroll to be processed for up to 50 businesses

Assisted Payroll: (Starting at $60 per month) Assistance from an Intuit payroll specialist is available for help during the setup procedures and when running your first payroll. You calculate earnings, deductions, and net pay and print paychecks using your QuickBooks software, and then your federal and state payroll taxes will be filed, tax deposits will be made, and W-2s will be processed for you. You are guaranteed that, if you provide accurate information, everything submitted for you will be accurate and on-time. And, if any issues come up with the IRS or state tax agencies, you will receive help to resolve them.

Direct Deposit: (The cost is $1.05 per check) is free to set up and enables you to pay your employees through direct deposit. Fees for each payroll and each check deposited apply. Available for use with all the payroll plans.

Since all of our businesses in this text are fictitious and we do not have a FEIN, (Federal Employee's Identification Number), we will not be subscribing to any of the QuickBooks Pro Payroll Services. As a result, we will be entering all tax information for paychecks manually based on data provided in the text. Calculations will be made for vacation pay, sick pay, medical and dental insurance deductions, and so on. Paychecks will be created, printed, corrected, and voided. Tax reports, tax payments, and tax forms will be explored.

Payroll is an area of accounting that has frequent changes; for example, tax tables are frequently updated, changes in withholding or tax limits are made, etc. As a result, QuickBooks is modified via updates to implement changes to payroll. As a word of caution, the materials presented in this chapter are current at the time of writing. It may be that as Intuit updates QuickBooks some of the things displayed in the chapter may change. If this happens, please read the information and ask your professor how to proceed.

TRAINING TUTORIAL AND PROCEDURES

The tutorial will work with Student's Name Fitness Solutions. You should use the company file **Fitness**. Once you open your copy of the company file, transactions will be recorded for the fictitious company. To maximize training benefits, you should follow the procedures listed in earlier chapters.

You have four employees Mikhail Branchev, who provides the management and supervision of the gym; Stan Mendelson, who is a personal trainer; Leslie Shephard, who manages the boutique shop and is the bookkeeper; and Laura Waters, who is the Pilates instructor.

Mikhail Branchev and Leslie Shephard are salaried employees. Stan Mendelson and Laura Waters are paid on an hourly basis, and any hours in excess of 160 for the pay period will be paid as overtime. Paychecks for all employees are issued on a monthly basis.

DATES

Throughout the text, the year used for the screen shots is 2010, which is the same year as the version of the program. You may want to check with your instructor to see if you should use 2010 as the year for the transactions.

ADD YOUR NAME TO THE COMPANY NAME

As with previous companies, each student in the course will be working for the same company and printing the same documents. Personalizing the company name to include your name will help identify many of the documents you print during your training.

> **DO** Add your name to the Company Name and Legal Name

> Follow the instructions presented in Chapter 1

CHANGE THE NAME OF THE CAPITAL ACCOUNTS

Since the owner's equity accounts have the words Student's Name as part of the account name, replace *Student's Name* with your actual name.

> **DO** Change the owner equity account names as previously instructed

Change the following:

> **Student's Name Capital** to **Your Name Capital** (remember to use your real name)
> **Student's Name Investment** to **Your Name Investment**
> **Student's Name Withdrawals** to **Your Name Withdrawals**

SELECT A PAYROLL OPTION

Before entering any payroll transactions, QuickBooks Pro must be informed of the type of payroll service you are selecting. Once QuickBooks Pro knows what type of payroll process has been selected for the company, you will be able to create paychecks. In order to create paychecks manually, you must go through the Help menu to designate this choice.

DO ▶ Select a **Manual** payroll option

> Press **F1** to access Help
> Click the **Search** tab
> Type **Manual Payroll**; click the right-arrow button

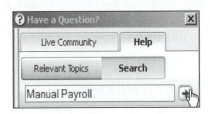

> Click **Process payroll manually (without a subscription to QuickBooks Payroll)**

> In the **"Set your company file to use the manual payroll calculations setting"** section, click the words <u>**manual payroll calculations**</u>

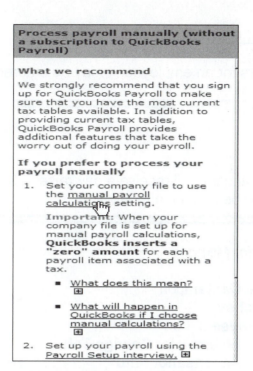

In the section **"Are you sure you want to set your company file to use manual calculations"**, click <u>**Set my company file to use manual calculations**</u>

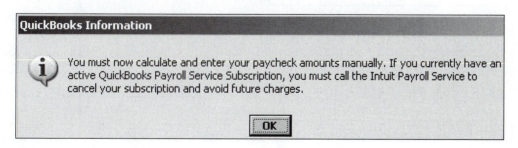

Once QuickBooks processes the selection, you will get a message

QuickBooks Information

> You must now calculate and enter your paycheck amounts manually. If you currently have an active QuickBooks Payroll Service Subscription, you must call the Intuit Payroll Service to cancel your subscription and avoid future charges.

OK

Click **OK**
Close Help

CHANGE EMPLOYEE INFORMATION

Whenever a change occurs for an employee, it may be entered at any time.

MEMO
DATE: January 30, 2010

Effective today, Mikhail Branchev will receive a pay raise to $30,000 annually. In addition, all employees will be paid on a monthly basis.

DO ▶ Change the salary for Mikhail

> Click the **Employee Center** icon
> Click **Mikhail Branchev**
> Click the **Edit Employee** button
> Click the drop-down list arrow for **Change Tabs**
> Click **Payroll and Compensation Info**
> On the **Payroll Info** tab, change the **Hourly/Annual Rate** to **30,000**
> Click the drop-down list arrow for Pay Frequency, click **Monthly**

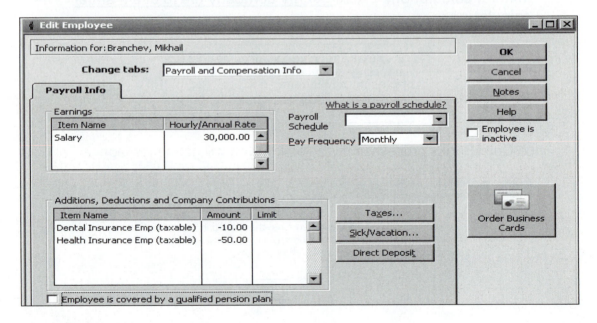

> Click **OK**
> Do *not* close the **Employee Center**

DO ▶ Change the other three employees to a monthly Pay Frequency

Edit each employee and change the pay frequency to Monthly by following the procedures listed above

ADD A NEW EMPLOYEE

As new employees are hired, they should be added.

MEMO

DATE: January 30, 2010

Effective 01/30/10 hired a part-time employee to teach yoga classes. Ms. Pamela Gale, SS. No. 100-55-6936, Female, Birth date 02/14/80, 2379 Bayshore Drive, Venice, CA 90405, 310-555-6611. Paid an hourly rate of $15.00 and an overtime rate of $22.50. Pay frequency is monthly. Federal and state withholding: Single, 0 Allowances. No local taxes, dental insurance, medical insurance, sick time, or vacation time.

DO ▶ Add the new employee, Pamela Gale

Click the **New Employee** button at the top of the Employee Center
On the **Personal** tab, click in the text box for **Mr./Ms./...**, enter **Ms.**
Using the information provided, tab to or click in each field and enter the
    information for the **Personal** tab

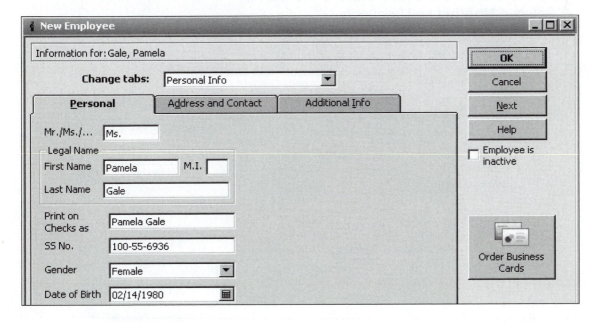

Click the **Address and Contact** tab and continue to enter the information provided

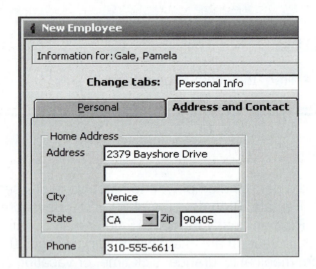

Click the drop-down list arrow for Change Tabs and select **Payroll and Compensation Info**

Click **Item Name** column under **Earnings**, click the drop-down list arrow that appears, and click **Hourly Rate**

Tab to or click **Hourly/Annual Rate**, enter the hourly rate she will be paid

Click **Item Name** column under **Hourly Rate**, click the drop-down list arrow that appears, click **Overtime Rate**

- QuickBooks enters the rate of 22.50.

Select a **Monthly** pay frequency

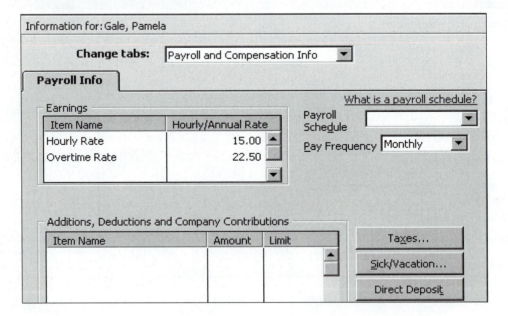

Click the **Taxes** button and complete the tax information
Federal taxes should show Filing Status: **Single,** Allowances: **0,** Extra
    Withholding: **0.00,** Subject to **Medicare**, **Social Security**, and **Federal**
    Unemployment Tax (Company Paid) should have a check mark

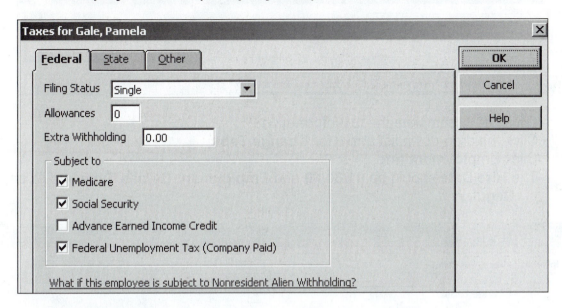

Click the **State** tab
State Worked: **CA**, **SUI** and **SDI** should be selected
State Subject to Withholding: **CA**, Filing Status: **Single**, Allowances: **0**, Extra
    Withholding: **0.00**; Estimated Deductions: **0**

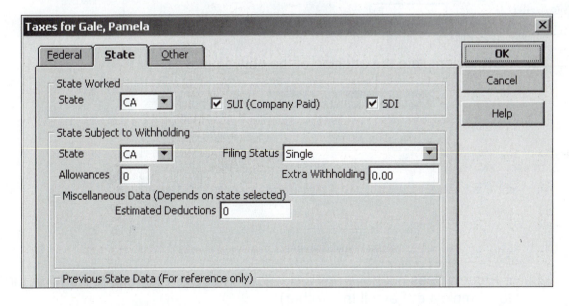

Click the **Other** tab

If CA-Employment Training Tax is not shown, click the drop-down list arrow for **Item Name**, and click **CA-Employment Training Tax**

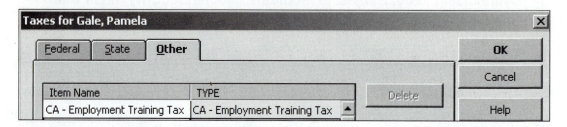

Click **OK** to complete the tax information
Click the drop-down list arrow for **Change Tabs**
Click **Employment Info**
The **Hire Date** should be **01/30/10** and **Employment Details Type** should be **Regular**

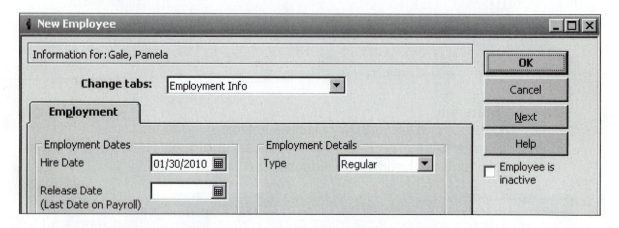

Click **OK** to complete the addition of the new employee

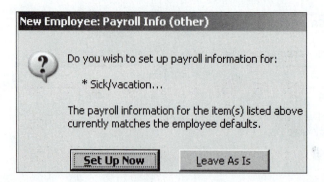

Since Pamela does not have any sick/vacation hours, click **Leave As Is** on the New Employee: Payroll Info (other)
Close the Employee Center

VIEW THE PAYROLL ITEM LIST

Prior To processing employee paychecks, it is helpful to view the Payroll Item list. The payroll Item list contains a listing of all payroll items, the type of item, amount and annual limit for deductions (if applicable), tax tracking, vendor for payment, and the account id.

View the Payroll Item List

> Click **Employees** on the Menu bar
> Click **Manage Payroll Items**, click **View/Edit Payroll Item List**
> Click **No** on the Payroll Service Message regarding signing up for payroll services

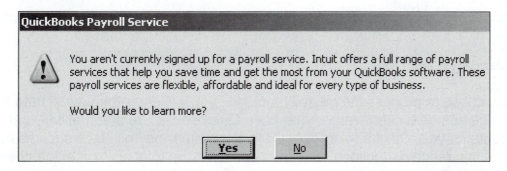

QuickBooks Payroll Service

You aren't currently signed up for a payroll service. Intuit offers a full range of payroll services that help you save time and get the most from your QuickBooks software. These payroll services are flexible, affordable and ideal for every type of business.

Would you like to learn more?

[Yes]   [No]

- Since you have not signed up for Payroll Services through QuickBooks, you will frequently see this message. Whenever it appears, click **No.**
- The Payroll Item List is displayed.

Payroll Item List

Item Name	Type	Amount	Annual Limit	Tax Tracking	Payable To	Account ID
Salary	Yearly Salary			Compensation		
Sick Salary	Yearly Salary			Compensation		
Vacation Salary	Yearly Salary			Compensation		
Hourly Rate	Hourly Wage			Compensation		
Overtime Rate	Hourly Wage			Compensation		
Sick Hourly Rate	Hourly Wage			Compensation		
Vacation Hourly Rate	Hourly Wage			Compensation		
Dental Insurance Emp (taxable)	Deduction	0.00		None	Medical and Dental Insurance Co.	
Health Insurance Emp (taxable)	Deduction	0.00		None	Medical and Dental Insurance Co.	
Advance Earned Income Credit	Federal Tax			Advance EIC Payment	United States Treasury	12-3456789
Federal Unemployment	Federal Tax	0.8%	7,000.00	FUTA	United States Treasury	12-3456789
Federal Withholding	Federal Tax			Federal	United States Treasury	12-3456789
Medicare Company	Federal Tax	1.45%		Comp. Medicare	United States Treasury	12-3456789
Medicare Employee	Federal Tax	1.45%		Medicare	United States Treasury	12-3456789
Social Security Company	Federal Tax	6.2%	106,800.00	Comp. SS Tax	United States Treasury	12-3456789
Social Security Employee	Federal Tax	6.2%	-106,800.00	SS Tax	United States Treasury	12-3456789
CA - Withholding	State Withholding Tax			SWH	EDD	123-4567-8
CA - Disability Employee	State Disability Tax	1.1%	-90,669.00	SDI	EDD	123-4567-8
CA - Unemployment Company	State Unemployment Tax	4.0%	7,000.00	Comp. SUI	EDD	123-4567-8
CA - Employment Training Tax	Other Tax	0.1%	7,000.00	Co. Paid Other Tax	EDD	123-4567-8

[**Payroll Item** ▾] [Activities ▾] [Reports ▾] ☐ Include inactive

View the Payroll Item list to see the item names, types, amounts, annual limits, tax tracking, payable to, and account id
- As you learned when printing reports, you may point to the line between columns, hold down the primary mouse button, and drag to resize the column. Close the list without printing

CREATE PAYCHECKS

Once the manual payroll option has been selected, paychecks may be created. You may enter hours and preview the checks before creating them, or, if using a payroll service, you may create the checks without previewing. Once the payroll has been processed, checks may be printed.

MEMO
DATE: January 31, 2010

Since you chose to process the payroll manually, you will enter the payroll data for withholdings and deductions rather than have QuickBooks Pro automatically calculate the amounts for you. QuickBooks Pro will still enter other payroll items such as medical and dental insurance deductions, and it will calculate the total amount of the checks. Create and print paychecks for January 31, 2010. Use the above date as the pay period ending date and the check date. Pay all employees using the hours and deductions listed in the following table.

▶ DO ▶ Use the following information to record the payroll for January

PAYROLL TABLE: JANUARY 31, 2010

	Mikhail Branchev	Pamela Gale	Stan Mendelson	Leslie Shephard	Laura Waters
HOURS					
REGULAR	160	8	72	140	160
OVERTIME					8
SICK			8		
VACATION				20	
DEDUCTIONS OTHER PAYROLL ITEMS: EMPLOYEE					
DENTAL INS.	10.00			10.00	
MEDICAL INS.	50.00			50.00	
DEDUCTIONS: COMPANY					
CA-EMPLOYMENT TRAINING TAX	2.50	0.00	2.00	1.67	2.58
SOCIAL SECURITY	155.00	7.44	124.00	103.33	159.96
MEDICARE	36.25	1.74	29.00	24.17	37.41
FEDERAL UNEMPLOYMENT	20.00	0.00	16.00	13.33	20.64
CA-UNEMPLOYMENT	100.00	4.80	80.00	66.67	103.20
DEDUCTIONS: EMPLOYEE					
FEDERAL WITHHOLDING	375.00	18.00	300.00	249.90	387.00
SOCIAL SECURITY	155.00	7.44	124.00	103.33	159.96
MEDICARE	36.25	1.74	29.00	24.17	37.41
CA-WITHHOLDING	100.00	4.80	80.00	66.64	103.20
CA-DISABILITY	27.00	1.30	21.60	17.99	27.86

DO ▶ Create checks for the above employees

Click **Pay Employees** on the **Employees** menu
If you get a message regarding QuickBooks Payroll Service, click **No**
The **Enter Payroll Information** screen appears
Enter the **Pay Period Ends** date of **01/31/10**
Enter the **Check Date** of **01/31/10**
The bank account is **Checking**
Click the **Check All** button

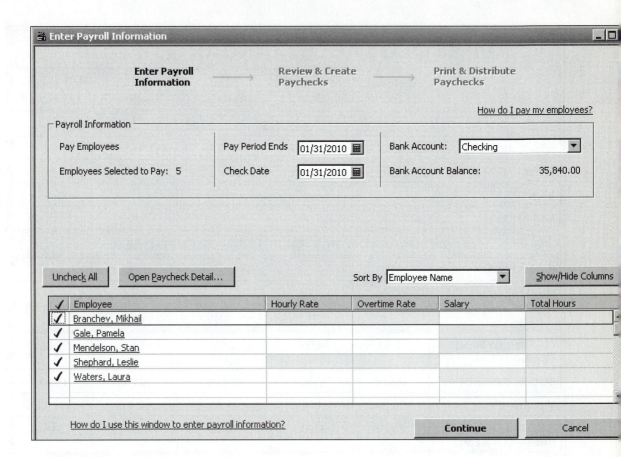

- Notice the check mark in front of each employee name.

Click the **Continue** button

On the **Review & Create Paychecks** screen, make sure that **Print Paychecks from QuickBooks** is selected

- Notice the amounts given for each employee. There is nothing listed for taxes or employer tax contributions. This information needs to be entered because we are doing payroll manually.

- Remember, if you do subscribe to a QuickBooks Pro payroll service, you will not enter the taxes manually. QuickBooks Pro will calculate them and enter them for you. Since tax tables change frequently, the taxes calculated by QuickBooks Pro may not be the same as the amounts listed on the Payroll Table in the text.

- As you record the information for each employee, refer to the payroll chart listed earlier in the chapter.

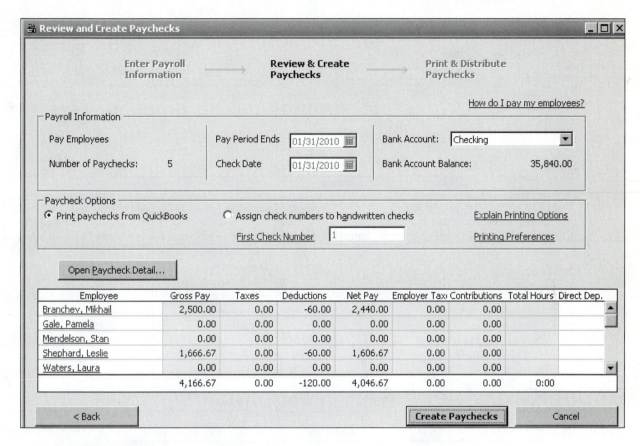

Click the **Open Paycheck Detail...** button
The **Preview Paycheck** screen for Mikhail Branchev appears.
Tab to or click **Hours**, enter **160**
Because these deductions were set up previously for Mikhail, the section for
    Other Payroll Items is completed by QuickBooks Pro
Complete the Company Summary (adjusted) information:
    Click in the **Amount** column for **CA-Employment Training Tax,** enter **2.50**
    Click in the **Amount** column for **Social Security Company**, enter **155.00**
    For **Medicare Company** enter **36.25**
    Federal Unemployment is **20.00**
    CA-Unemployment Company is **100.00**
Complete the Employee Summary information:
    Click in the **Amount** column for **Federal Withholding**, enter **375.00**
    For **Social Security Employee** enter **155.00**
    Medicare Employee is **36.25**
    CA-Withholding is **100.00**
    CA-Disability Employee is **27.00**, press **Tab**
- Notice that QuickBooks calculated the monthly salary based on the annual
  salary and automatically entered the amount of Dental and Health Insurance
  paid by the employee.

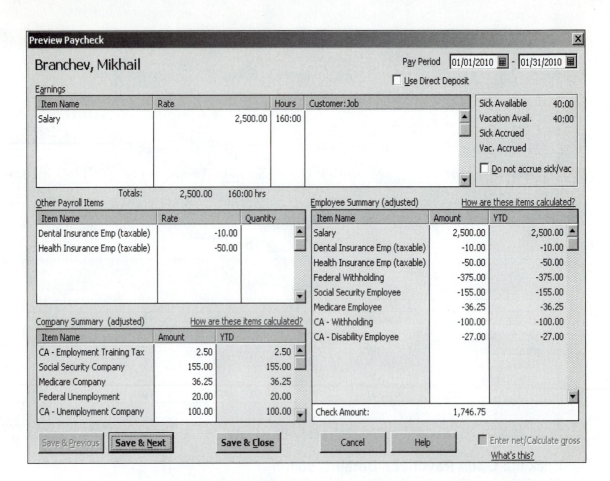

After verifying that everything was entered correctly, click **Save & Next**
The next Preview Paycheck screen should be for **Pamela Gale**
Tab to or click the **Hours** column next to **Hourly Rate** for **Pamela Gale**, enter **8**
Refer to the Payroll Table for January 31, 2010, and enter the company and
   employee deductions for Pamela

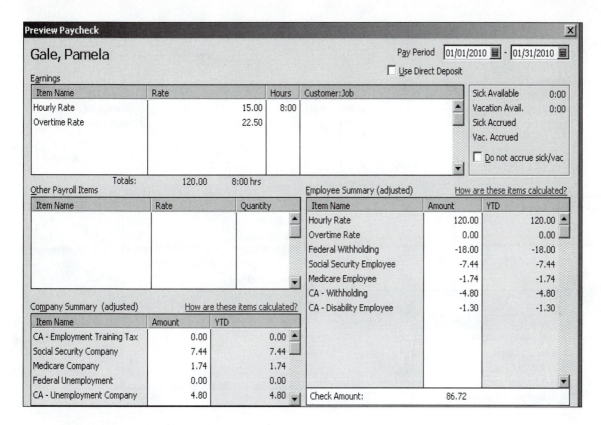

Click **Save & Next**
Pay **Stan Mendelson** for **72** hours of **Hourly Regular Rate**
Click in the **Item Names** section for **Earnings**
Click the drop-down list arrow, click **Sick Hourly Rate**
Enter **8** for the number of hours Stan was out sick
Enter the company and employee deductions from the Payroll Table for
    January 31, 2010

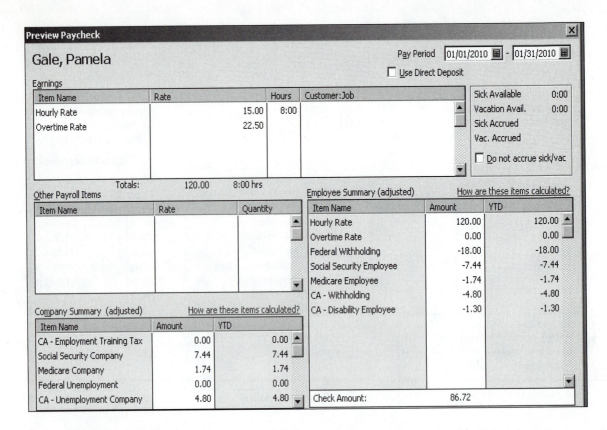

Click **Save & Next**

Pay **Leslie Shephard** for **140** hours of **Salary**

- Notice that the number of Vacation Hours listed in **Vacation Available** is **20.00**.

In the **Item Name** column under **Earnings**, click on the blank line beneath Salary, click the drop-down list arrow that appears, click **Vacation Salary**, tab to or click the **Hours** column, enter **20**

- The Vacation Hours will show 0.00 and the Rates for Salary and Vacation Salary will change to reflect the amount paid for vacation.

Complete the paycheck information

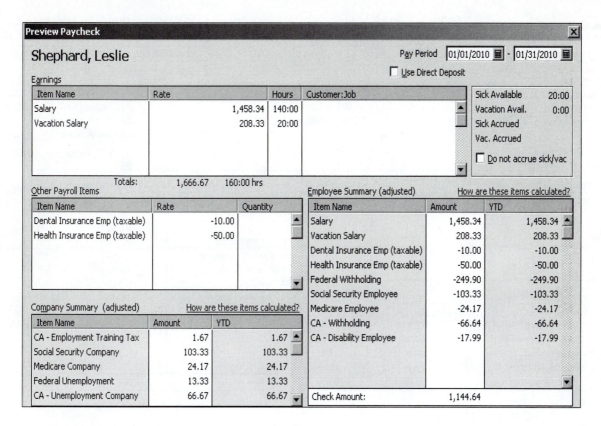

Click **Save & Next**
Process the paycheck for **Laura Waters**
Record **160** for her Hourly Rate Hours
Record **8** as her Overtime Rate Hours
Enter the remaining payroll information as previously instructed

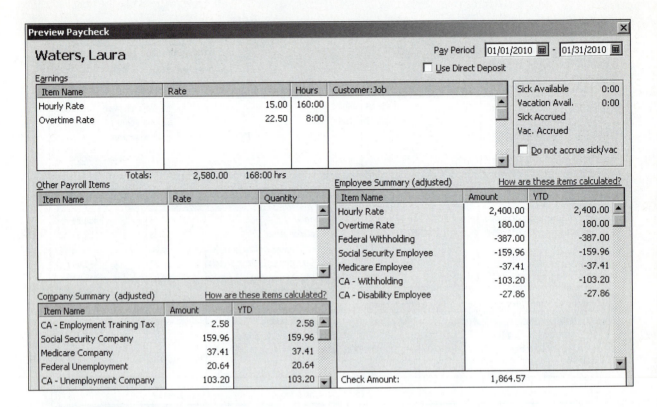

Click **Save & Close**

The Review and Create Paychecks screen appears with the information for
   Taxes and Deductions completed

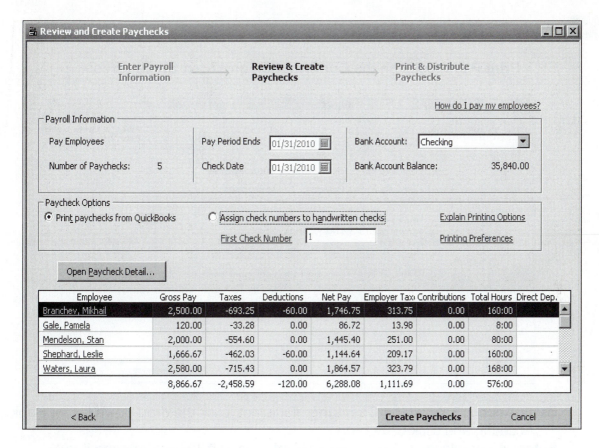

Click **Create Paychecks**

PRINT PAYCHECKS

Paychecks may be printed one at a time or all at once. You may use the same printer setup as your other checks in QuickBooks Pro or you may print using a different printer setup. If you use a voucher check, the pay stub is printed as part of the check. If you do not use a voucher check, you may print the pay stub separately. The pay stub information includes the employee's name, address, Social Security number, the pay period start and end dates, pay rate, the hours, the amount of pay, all deductions, sick and vacation time used and available, net pay, and year-to-date amounts.

MEMO

DATE: January 31, 2010

Print the paychecks for all employees using a voucher-style check with 2 parts. Print the company name on the checks.

DO Print the January 31 paychecks

Click **Print Paychecks** on the **Confirmation and Next Steps** screen

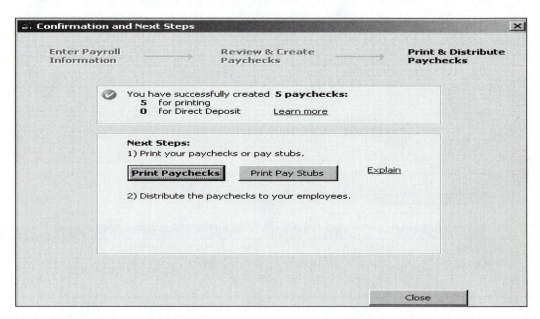

Bank Account should be **Checking**; if it is not, click the drop-down list for Bank
   Account, and click **Checking**
Select All employees, **First Check Number** is **1**; if it is not, change it to 1
• Notice that there are 5 Paychecks to be printed for a total of $6,288.08.
• QuickBooks can process payroll for direct deposit or printed paychecks. Even
   though we are not processing direct deposit paychecks, leave **Show** as **Both**.

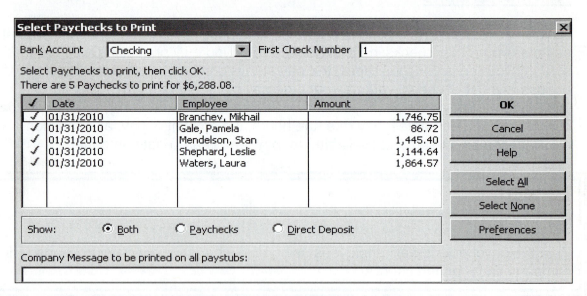

Click the **Preferences** button
Verify that all items for Payroll Printing Preferences for Paycheck Vouchers and
    Pay stubs have been selected

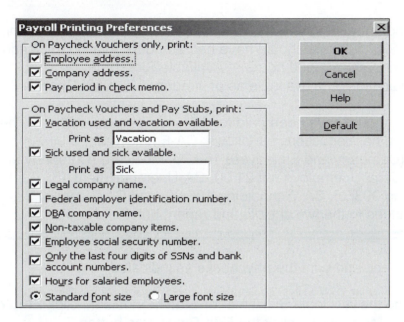

Click **OK**
Click **OK** on the Select Paychecks to Print screen
- Printer Name and Printer Type will be the same as in the earlier chapters.
Click **Voucher Checks** to select as the check style
- If necessary, click **Print company name and address** to select. There
  should not be a check mark in Use logo. **Number of copies** should be **1**.
Click **Print**, click **OK** on the **Print Checks Confirmation** screen
- *Note*: The pay stub information may be printed on the check two times. This is
  acceptable.
When the checks have been printed, click **Close** on the **Confirmation and Next
Steps** screen

VIEW CHECKS, MAKE CORRECTIONS, AND PRINT CHECKS INDIVIDUALLY

As in earlier chapters, checks may be viewed individually and printed one at a time. A
paycheck differs from a regular check. Rather than list accounts and amounts, it
provides a Payroll Summary and an option to view Paycheck Detail at the bottom of the
screen. When you are viewing the paycheck detail, corrections may be made and will
be calculated for the check.

MEMO
DATE: January 31, 2010

After reviewing the printed checks, you notice that Stan Mendelson shows -8.00 for
   Available Sick time. He should have had 20 hours Available. Change his employee
   information to show 12.00 hours of Available Sick Time. He should also have 20
   hours of vacation time available as of January 31, 2010. Change this to 20 hours as
   well.

Laura Waters should have been paid for 10 hours overtime. Change her overtime hours
   and change her deductions as follows: CA-Employment Training Tax 2.63, Social
   Security (Company and Employee) 162.75, Medicare (Company and Employee)
   38.25, Federal Unemployment 21.00, CA-Unemployment 105.00, Federal
   Withholding 393.75, CA Withholding 105.00, and CA Disability 28.35.

View the changes to the two checks and reprint both.

▶ DO ▶ View, correct, and print the paychecks as indicated

To change the Available Sick time for Stan Mendelson, click **Employee Center**
Click **Stan Mendelson**, click the **Edit Employee** button
Click the drop-down list arrow for Change tabs
Click **Payroll and Compensation Info**
Click the **Sick/Vacation** button
Enter **12:00** for the Sick Hours available as of **01/31/10**
If necessary, enter the date of **01/01/10** for **Begin accruing sick time on**
Enter **20:00** for the Vacation Hours available as of **01/31/10**
If necessary, enter the date of **01/01/10**for **Begin accruing sick time on**

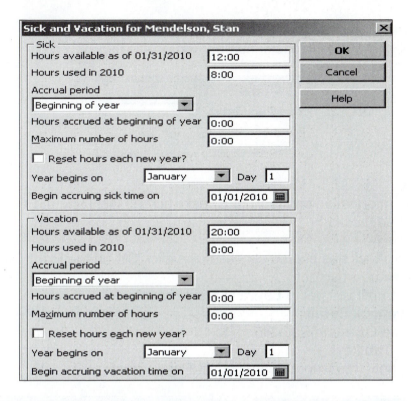

Click **OK** for Sick/Vacation, and click **OK** on the Edit Employee Screen

Close the Employee Center

To view the paychecks, click **Write Checks** in the Banking section of the Home
   Page

Click **Previous** until you get to the check for **Stan Mendelson** for **01/31/10**

Click **Paycheck Detail** button to view the withholding details

• Notice that the Sick Available shows 12:00 rather than -8:00.
• Vacation Avail. Shows 20:00.

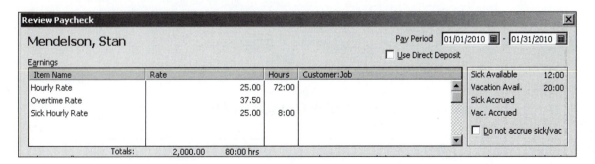

Click **OK**

• Even though the amount of the check is not changed by this adjustment, the
   check should be reprinted so the correct sick leave information is shown.

Reprint Check **3**

Click **Print**
If 3 is not shown as the check number, enter **3**

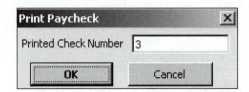

Click **OK**
Verify the information on the Print Checks screen including the selection of
    Voucher checks
Click **Print**
When the check has printed successfully, click **OK** on the **Print Checks
    Confirmation** screen
Click **Next** until you get to **Laura Waters'** paycheck
Click **Paycheck Detail**
Change the Overtime Rate Hours to **10**
Press the **Tab** key
You may get a message regarding Net Pay Locked

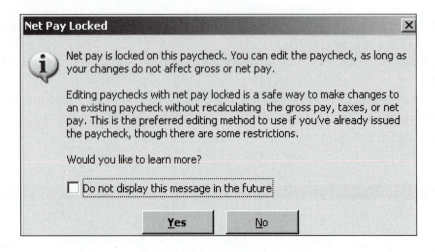

Click **No**
At the bottom of the paycheck, click **Unlock Net Pay**

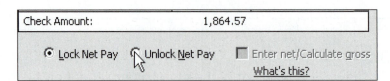

Once you click Unlock Net Pay, you get a Special Paycheck Situation screen

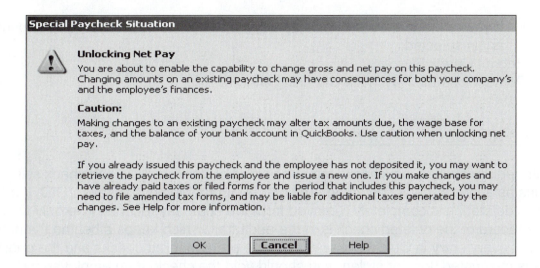

- Since paychecks have not been distributed to the employees until after they are reviewed, it is acceptable to change this paycheck rather than voiding and reissuing a new one.

Click **OK** on the Special Paycheck Situation screen

Enter the changes to the tax amounts as indicated in the Memo

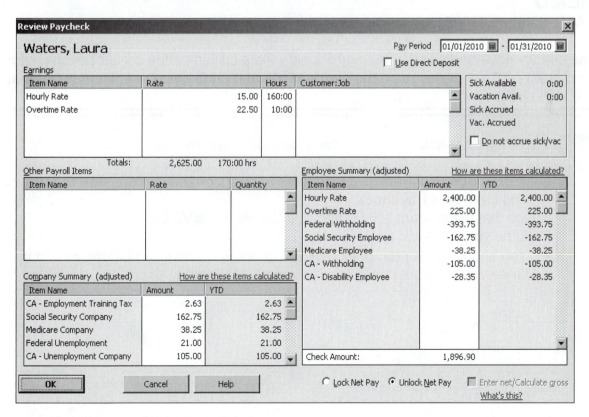

Click **OK**

- If you return to the Paycheck Detail, you will find that Lock Net Pay is once again selected.

Reprint Check 5

Do not close the Paycheck-Checking window

VOIDING AND DELETING CHECKS

As with regular checks, paychecks may be voided or deleted. A voided check still remains as a check, but it has an amount of 0.00 and a Memo that says VOID. If a check is deleted, it is completely removed from the company records. The only way to have a record of the deleted check is in the audit trail, which keeps a behind the scenes record of every entry in QuickBooks. If you have prenumbered checks and the original check is misprinted, lost, or stolen, you should void the check. If an employee's check is lost or stolen and needs to be replaced and you are not using prenumbered checks, it may be deleted and reissued. For security reasons, it is better to void a check than to delete it.

MEMO

DATE: January 31, 2010

The checks have been distributed and Pamela Gale spilled coffee on her paycheck for the January 31 pay period. Void the check, issue and print a new one. Remember that she worked 8 hours.

▶ **DO** ▶ Void Pamela's January 31 paycheck and issue a new one

Click **Previous** until Pamela's paycheck appears on the screen, click **Edit** menu, and click **Void Paycheck**

Notice that the amount is 0.00 and that the Memo is VOID:.

Print the voided check as Check No. 2

- You should get a prompt to save the changed transaction before you print. Once you save the check, it will be marked Cleared.

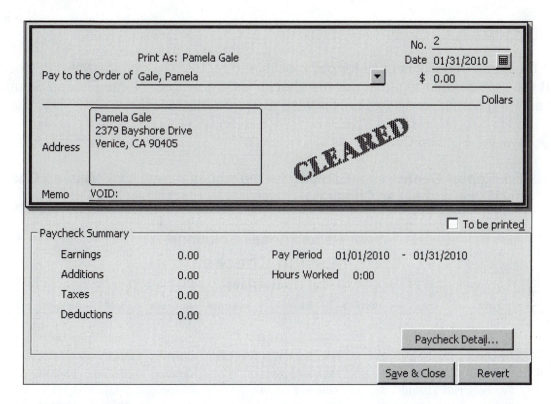

To issue Pamela's replacement check, click **Save & Close** on Paycheck-Checking screen, click **Pay Employees** in the Employees section of the Home Page

The Pay Period Ends **01/31/10** and the Check Date is **01/31/10**

The Bank Account is **Checking**

Click in the check column for **Pamela Gale** to select her

Click **Continue**

Click the **Open Paycheck Detail** button

Pay Period is **01/01/10 - 01/31/10**

Pamela worked **8** hours at the Hourly Regular Rate

Enter the deductions listed on the Payroll Table for January 31, 2010

Click **Save & Close**

Click the **Create Paychecks** button

Click **Print Paychecks**

Print the replacement check as Check No. **6**

Click **OK** on the **Confirmation and Next Steps** screen

Print the Voucher-style check

After the check has been printed successfully, click **OK**

Click **Close**

MISSING CHECK REPORT

Since the same account is used for paychecks and regular checks, the Missing Check report will provide data regarding all the checks issued by Your Name Fitness Solutions After entering a number of checks, it is wise to review this report.

DO View the Missing Check report

Click **Report Center**, click **Banking** for the type of report, click **Missing Checks** Specify the account as **Checking**

Your Name Fitness Solutions
Missing Checks
All Transactions

Type	Date	Num	Name	Memo	Account	Split	Amount
Paycheck	01/31/2010	1	Branchev, Mikhail		Checking	-SPLIT-	-1,746.75 ◀
Paycheck	01/31/2010	2	Gale, Pamela	VOID:	Checking	-SPLIT-	0.00
Paycheck	01/31/2010	3	Mendelson, Stan		Checking	-SPLIT-	-1,445.40
Paycheck	01/31/2010	4	Shephard, Leslie		Checking	-SPLIT-	-1,144.64
Paycheck	01/31/2010	5	Waters, Laura		Checking	-SPLIT-	-1,896.90
Paycheck	01/31/2010	6	Gale, Pamela		Checking	-SPLIT-	-86.72

Review the report and close without printing
Do not close the Report Center

PAYROLL SUMMARY REPORT

The Payroll Summary Report shows gross pay, sick and vacation hours and pay, deductions from gross pay, adjusted gross pay, taxes withheld, deductions from net pay, net pay, and employer-paid taxes and contributions for each employee individually and for the company.

DO Print the Payroll Summary Report for January

Since the Report Center is on the screen, click **Employees & Payroll** to select the type of report
Double-click **Payroll Summary**
Enter the report dates from **01/01/10** to **01/31/10**
• View the information listed for each employee and for the company.
Remove the Date Prepared and Time Prepared from the header

Print the report in Landscape orientation
Close the report

PREPARE THE EMPLOYEE EARNINGS SUMMARY REPORT

The Employee Earnings Summary Report lists the same information as the Payroll Summary Report above. The information for each employee is categorized by payroll items.

> **DO** Prepare the Employee Earnings Summary report

Double-click **Employee Earnings Summary** as the report
Use the dates from **01/01/10** to **01/31/10**
Scroll through the report
- Notice the way in which payroll amounts are grouped by item rather than employee.
Do not print the report

PAYROLL LIABILITY BALANCES REPORT

Another payroll report is the Payroll Liability Balances Report. This report lists the company's payroll liabilities that are unpaid as of the report date. This report should be prepared prior to paying any payroll taxes.

> **DO** Prepare and print the Payroll Liability Balances report

Double-click **Payroll Liability Balances** as the report
The report dates should be **01/01/10** to **01/31/10**
Remove the Date Prepared and Time Prepared from the header
Print the report in Portrait orientation

```
                    Your Name Fitness Solutions
                   Payroll Liability Balances
                           January 2010
                                          ◇ BALANCE ◇

        Payroll Liabilities
            Federal Withholding        ▶  1,336.65 ◀
            Medicare Employee               129.41
            Social Security Employee        552.52
            Federal Unemployment             70.33
            Medicare Company                129.41
            Social Security Company         552.52
            CA - Withholding                356.44
            CA - Disability Employee         96.24
            CA - Unemployment Company       356.47
            CA - Employment Training Tax      8.80
            Dental Insurance Emp (taxable)   20.00
            Health Insurance Emp (taxable)  100.00
        Total Payroll Liabilities         3,708.79
```

Close the report and the Report Center

PAY TAXES AND OTHER LIABILITIES

QuickBooks Pro keeps track of the payroll taxes and other payroll liabilities that you owe. When it is time to make your payments, QuickBooks Pro allows you to choose to pay all liabilities or to select individual liabilities for payment. When the liabilities to be paid have been selected, QuickBooks Pro will consolidate all the amounts for one vendor and prepare one check for that vendor.

MEMO

DATE: January 31, 2010

Based on the information in the Payroll Liabilities Report, pay all the payroll liabilities.

▶ DO ▶ Pay all the payroll liabilities

Click **Pay Liabilities** in Employees section of the Home Page
Enter the dates of **01/01/10** to **01/31/10** on the **Select Date Range For Liabilities** screen

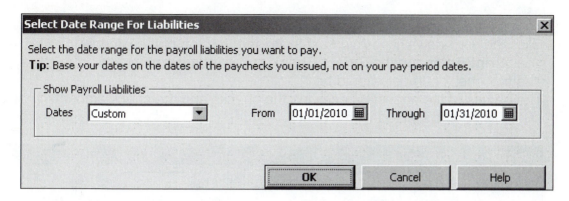

Click **OK**

If necessary, select **To be printed**

Bank Account should be **Checking**; if it is not, select it from the drop-down list.

Check Date is **01/31/10**

Sort by **Payable To**

Show payroll liabilities from **01/01/10** to **01/31/10**

Create liability check without reviewing should be selected

Click in the check column to place a check mark next to each liability listed; be
   sure to scroll through the list to view and mark each liability

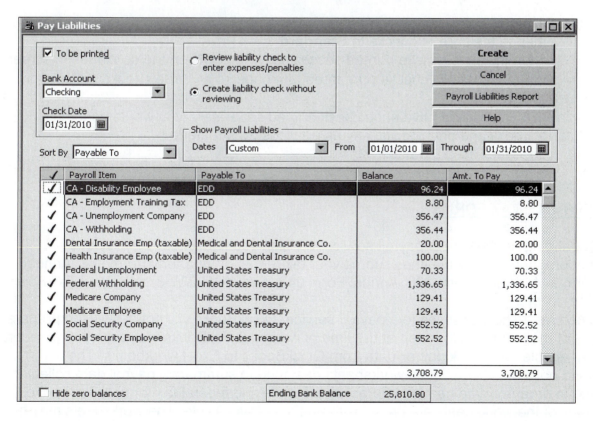

Click **Create**

To print the checks, access **Write Checks** as previously instructed
Click the drop-down list arrow next to **Print** at the top of the window
Click **Print Batch**, on the **Select Checks to Print** screen
The first check number should be **7**
The names of the agencies receiving the checks and the check amounts should
    be listed and marked with a check.

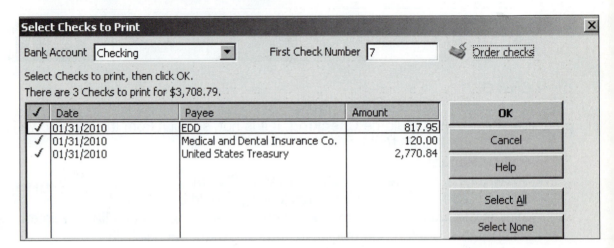

Click **OK**
Change the style of checks to **Standard**, click **Print**
When the checks have printed successfully, click **OK** on the confirmation screen

- Standard style checks print three to a page so all three checks will print on
  one page.
- If you wish to have each check printed separately, you would go to each
  check and print individually as previously instructed.

Close the Checks window

PAYROLL TAX FORMS

Depending on the type of payroll service to which you subscribe, QuickBooks will
prepare, print, and sometimes submit your tax forms for Quarterly Form 941, Annual
Form 944, Annual Form 940, Annual Form 943, Annual W-2/W-3, and State Tax Forms.

Since we do not subscribe to a payroll service, QuickBooks will not allow us to prepare
any of these forms. However, at the time of writing, QuickBooks includes several reports
that enable you to link payroll data from QuickBooks to Excel workbooks. The
workbooks provided contain worksheets designed to summarize payroll data collected
and to organize data needed to prepare the state and federal tax forms listed above.
Many of the worksheets are preset with an Excel Pivot Table. The worksheets may be
used as designed or they may be modified to suit your reporting needs. You may only

prepare these Excel reports if you have entered payroll data; i.e., paychecks and withholding, in QuickBooks and have Microsoft Excel 2000 or later installed on your computer.

Since QuickBooks continually updates payroll, please note that your screens may not be an exact match to those displayed in the text. If at anytime your materials do not match, please check with your instructor to see if you should just read the book or to see if there are changes that you should make in order to complete the chapter.

OPTIONAL: TRANSFER PAYROLL DATA FOR FORM 941 TO EXCEL

If you have Excel available, your instructor may wish to have you complete the optional exercise to transfer payroll data to an Excel worksheet. The report summarizes information so that Tax Forms may be prepared manually.

MEMO
DATE: January 31, 2010

Transfer payroll data for Form 941—Employer's Quarterly Federal Tax Return to Excel.

▶DO▶ Transfer data for Form 941 to Excel

> Click **Reports** on the Menu bar
> Point to **Employees & Payroll**
> Click **More Payroll Reports in QuickBooks**
> Click **Tax Form Worksheets**

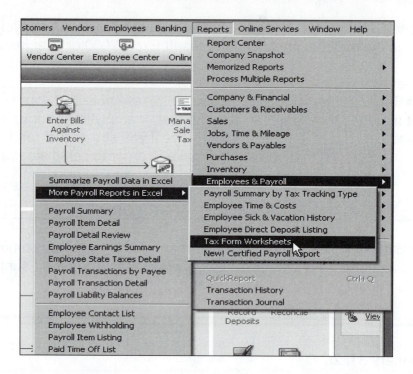

- The first time you use Excel for tax forms, you may get:

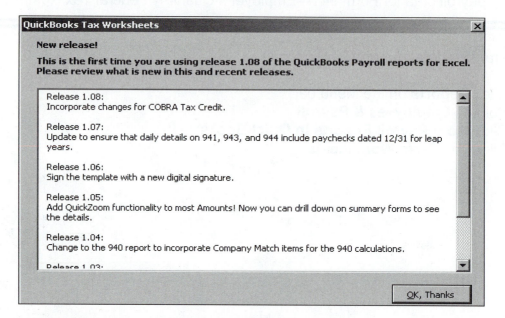

Click **OK, Thanks**
Click **Quarterly 941** to select the type of form you want to prepare
Click **Custom** for the dates
Enter the dates From **01/01/10** and To **01/31/10**

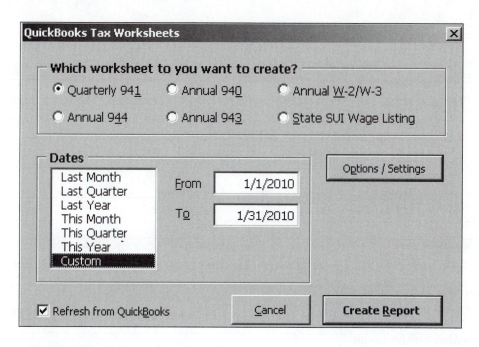

Click **Create Report**

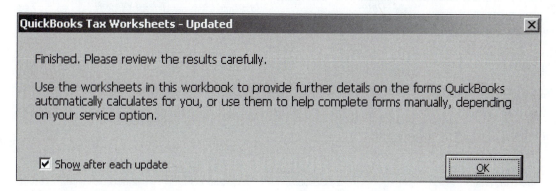

Click **OK** on the QuickBooks Tax Worksheets – Updated dialog box
The 941 Summary data is shown
Review the report

941 Summary

Wages, Tips, and other Compensation

Payroll Category	Item Type	Tax Tracking Type	Amount
Hourly Rate	Hourly salary	Compensation	4,320.00
Overtime Rate	Hourly salary	Compensation	225.00
Sick Hourly Rate	Hourly salary	Compensation	200.00
Salary	Salary	Compensation	3,958.34
Vacation Salary	Salary	Compensation	208.33
			8,911.67

Federal Tax Withholding	Subject Income	Taxed Wages		Tax
Federal Withholding	8,911.67	8,911.67		1,336.65

Social Security & Medicare	Subject Income	Taxed Wages	Tax Rate	Tax
Social Security	8,911.67	8,911.67	0.124	1,105.05
Medicare	8,911.67	8,911.67	0.029	258.44
				1,363.49

Total Tax (Calculated)				2,700.14

Advance Earned Income Credit	Subject Income	Taxed Wages		Tax Credit
				0.00

Total Tax After AEIC (Calculated)				2,700.14

COBRA Earned Credit				Tax Credit
				0.00

Total Due After COBRA Credit				2,700.14

Daily Wage Summary

Item	Date	Subject Income	Taxed Wages	Tax
Federal Withholding	1/31/2010	8,911.67	8,911.67	1,336.65
Social Security Company	1/31/2010	8,911.67	8,911.67	552.52
Social Security Employee	1/31/2010	8,911.67	8,911.67	552.52
Medicare Company	1/31/2010	8,911.67	8,911.67	129.41
Medicare Employee	1/31/2010	8,911.67	8,911.67	129.41
				2,700.51

Monthly Total - January				2,700.51

Total Tax - Actual				2,700.51

Taxed Wages by Employee

Employee	SSec. Wages	SSec. Tax	Medicare Wages	Medicare Tax
Branchev, Mikhail	2,500.00	310.00	2,500.00	72.50
Gale, Pamela	120.00	14.88	120.00	3.48
Mendelson, Stan	2,000.00	248.00	2,000.00	58.00
Shephard, Leslie	1,666.67	206.66	1,666.67	48.34
Waters, Laura	2,625.00	325.50	2,625.00	76.50
	8,911.67	1,105.04	8,911.67	258.82

Close the report without saving and close Excel

PRINT THE JOURNAL

As in the previous chapters, it is always a good idea to print the Journal to see all of the transactions that have been made. If, however, you only want to see the transactions for a particular date or period of time, you can control the amount of data in the report by restricting the dates.

DO Print the Journal for January 31 in landscape orientation

Prepare the report as previously instructed
Use the dates from **01/31/10** to **01/31/10**
Remove the Date Prepared and Time Prepared from the Header
Adjust column widths so the information in each column is displayed in full
Print in Landscape orientation

BACK UP

Follow the instructions provided in previous chapters to make a backup file.

SUMMARY

In this chapter, paychecks were generated for employees who worked their standard number of hours, took vacation time, took sick time, and were just hired. Rather than have QuickBooks Pro calculate the amount of payroll deductions, a table was provided and deductions to paychecks were inserted manually. Changes to employee information were made, and a new employee was added. Payroll reports were printed and/or viewed, and payroll liabilities were paid. Exporting payroll data to Excel workbooks was explored.

END-OF-CHAPTER QUESTIONS

TRUE/FALSE

ANSWER THE FOLLOWING QUESTIONS IN THE SPACE PROVIDED BEFORE THE QUESTION NUMBER.

_____ 1. You cannot process payroll manually.

_____ 2. Once a paycheck has been printed, you may not edit it.

_____ 3. Paychecks may be printed only as a batch.

_____ 4. A payroll check may never be deleted.

_____ 5. Once an employee is hired, you may not change the pay period from semi-monthly to monthly.

_____ 6. An employee may be added at anytime.

_____ 7. If several taxes are owed to a single agency, QuickBooks Pro generates a separate check to the agency for each tax liability item.

_____ 8. If a salaried employee uses vacation pay, QuickBooks Pro will automatically distribute the correct amount of earnings to Vacation Salary once the number of vacation hours has been entered.

_____ 9. Processing the Payroll Liabilities Balances Report also generates the checks for payment of the liabilities.

_____ 10. All payroll reports must be printed before payroll liabilities may be paid.

MULTIPLE CHOICE

WRITE THE LETTER OF THE CORRECT ANSWER IN THE SPACE PROVIDED BEFORE THE QUESTION NUMBER.

_____ 1. When completing paychecks manually, you ___.
  A. provide the information about hours worked
  B. provide the amounts for deductions
  C. provide the number of sick and/or vacation hours used
  D. all of the above

_____ 2. To change the amount of a deduction entered on an employee's check that has been created, you ___.
  A. must void the check and issue a new one
  B. adjust the next check to include the change
  C. change the Paycheck Detail for the check and reprint it
  D. must delete the check

_____ 3. When paying tax liabilities, you may ___.
  A. pay all liabilities at one time
  B. select individual tax liabilities and pay them one at a time
  C. pay all the tax liabilities owed to a vendor
  D. all of the above

_____ 4. A new employee may be added ___.
  A. at any time
  B. only at the end of the week
  C. only at the end of the pay period
  D. only when current paychecks have been printed

_____ 5. Pay stub information may be printed ___.
  A. as part of a voucher check
  B. separate from the paycheck
  C. only as an individual employee report
  D. both A and B

_____ 6. The Employee Earnings Summary Report lists payroll information for each employee categorized by ___.
  A. employee
  B. department
  C. payroll item
  D. date paid

_____ 7. A voided check ___.
A. shows an amount of 0.00
B. has a Memo of VOID
C. remains as part of the company records
D. all of the above

_____ 8. When the payroll liabilities to be paid have been selected, QuickBooks Pro will ___.
A. create a separate check for each liability
B. consolidate the liabilities paid and create one check for each vendor
C. automatically process a Payroll Liability Balances Report
D. prepare any tax return forms necessary

_____ 9. The Journal may be prepared ___.
A. for any range of dates
B. for a specific month
C. for a specific day
D. all of the above

_____ 10. Changes made to an employee's pay rate will become effective ___.
A. immediately
B. at the end of the next payroll period
C. at the end of the quarter
D. after a W-2 has been prepared for the employee

FILL-IN

IN THE SPACE PROVIDED, WRITE THE ANSWER THAT MOST APPROPRIATELY COMPLETES THE SENTENCE.

1. In the _____, the individual employees name, address, and telephone number is displayed in the Employee Information area.

2. The _____ is the report that lists transactions in debit/credit format.

3. The reports that show an employee's gross pay, sick and vacation hours and pay, deductions, taxes, and other details are the _____ and the _____.

4. When the Employee Center is on the screen, the _____ button is used to add a new employee.

5. The report listing the company's unpaid payroll liabilities as of the report date is the _____ Report.

SHORT ESSAY

What is the difference between voiding a paycheck and deleting a paycheck? Why should a business prefer to void paychecks rather than delete them?

_____

_____

_____

_____

_____

_____

NAME _____

TRANSMITTAL

CHAPTER 8: YOUR NAME FITNESS SOLUTIONS

Attach the following documents and reports:

Check No. 1: Mikhail Branchev
Check No. 2: Pamela Gale
Check No. 3: Stan Mendelson
Check No. 4: Leslie Shephard
Check No. 5: Laura Waters
Check No. 3: Stan Mendelson After Editing Sick Time
Check No. 5: Laura Waters After Editing Overtime
Check No. 2: Pamela Gale Voided Check
Check No. 6: Pamela Gale Replacement Check
Payroll Summary, January 2010
Payroll Liability Balances, January 2010
Check No. 7: EDD
Check No. 8: Medical and Dental Insurance Co.
Check No. 9: United States Treasury
Journal, January 31, 2010

END-OF-CHAPTER PROBLEM

YOUR NAME POOL & SPA

You will be working with a company called Your Name Pool & Spa. Transactions for employees, payroll, and payroll liabilities will be completed.

INSTRUCTIONS

For Chapter 8 download the company file **Pool.qbw** as previously instructed. You will select a manual payroll option; record the addition of and changes to employees; create, edit, and void paychecks; pay payroll liabilities; and prepare payroll reports.

RECORD TRANSACTIONS:

January 30, 2010
▶ Add your name to the company name and the owner equity accounts
▶ Turn off the Date Prepared, Time Prepared, and Report Basis in the Header/Footer
▶ Select Manual processing for payroll
▶ Add a new employee, Sara Atkins to help with pool supply sales. Social Security No. 100-55-2145; female, Date of Birth 04/23/1977. Her address is: 2325 Summerland Road, Summerland, CA 93014, 805-555-9845. Sara is an hourly employee with a Regular Rate of $7.00 per hour with an Overtime Hourly Rate 1 of $10.50. She is paid monthly and is not eligible for medical or dental insurance. She is single, claims no exemptions or allowances, and is subject to Federal Taxes: Medicare, Social Security, and Federal Unemployment Tax, State Taxes for CA: SUI, and SDI; Other Taxes: CA-Employment Training Tax. Sara does not accrue vacation or sick leave.
▶ Dori Stevens changed her telephone number to 805-555-5111. Edit the employee on the employee list and record the change.

January 31, 2010
▶ Use the following Payroll Table to prepare and print checks for the monthly payroll. The pay period ends January 31, 2010 and the check date is also January 31, 2010: Checking is the appropriate account to use. (Remember, you may get a screen regarding signing up for QuickBooks Payroll service. You should say No.)

PAYROLL TABLE: JANUARY 31, 2010

	Dori Stevens	Joe Masterson	Morrie Miller	Sara Atkins
HOURS				
Regular	120	152	160	8
Overtime			20	
Sick		8		
Vacation	40			
DEDUCTIONS OTHER PAYROLL ITEMS: EMPLOYEE				
Dental Ins.	25.00	25.00	25.00	
Medical Ins.	25.00	25.00	25.00	
DEDUCTIONS: COMPANY				
CA-Employment Training Tax	2.60	2.42	1.71	0.00
Social Security	161.20	149.83	106.00	3.47
Medicare	37.70	35.04	24.80	.81
Federal Unemployment	20.80	19.33	13.68	0.00
CA-Unemployment	104.00	96.67	68.40	2.24
DEDUCTIONS: EMPLOYEE				
Federal Withholding	390.00	362.50	256.50	0.00
Social Security	161.20	149.83	106.00	3.47
Medicare	37.70	35.04	24.80	.81
CA-Withholding	104.00	96.67	68.40	0.00
CA-Disability	28.08	26.10	18.47	0.00

► Print the company name and address on the voucher checks. Checks begin with number 1.

▶ Change Morrie Miller's check to correct the overtime hours. (Remember to Unlock Net Pay before recording the changes.) He worked 12 hours overtime. Because of the reduction in overtime pay, his deductions change as follows: CA-Employment Training Tax: 1.60; Social Security Company and Employee: 99.32; Medicare Company and Employee: 23.23; Federal Unemployment: 12.82; CA-Unemployment: 64.08; Federal Withholding: 240.30; CA-Withholding: 64.08; and CA-Disability: 17.30. Reprint Check No. 3.

▶ Sara spilled coffee on her check. Void her Check No. 4 for January 31, print the voided check, reissue the paycheck, and print it using Check No. 5. Remember to use 01/31/10 as the check and pay period ending date. The pay period is 01/01/10 to 01/31/10.

▶ Prepare and print the Payroll Summary Report for January 1-31, 2010 in Landscape orientation.

▶ Prepare and print the Payroll Liability Balances Report for January 1-31, 2010 in Portrait orientation.

▶ Pay all the taxes and other liabilities for January 1-31, 2010. The Check Date is 01/31/10. Print the checks using a Standard check style with the company name and address.

▶ Prepare and print the Journal for January 31, 2010 in Landscape orientation.

NAME _____

TRANSMITTAL

CHAPTER 8: YOUR NAME POOL & SPA

Attach the following documents and reports:

Check No. 1: Dori Stevens
Check No. 2: Joe Masterson
Check No. 3: Morrie Miller
Check No. 4: Sara Atkins
Check No. 3: Morrie Miller (Corrected)
Check No. 4: Sara Atkins (Voided)
Check No. 5: Sara Atkins
Payroll Summary, January, 2010
Payroll Liability Balances, January 2010
Check No. 6: Dental and Medical Ins.
Check No. 7: Employment Development Department
Check No. 8: United States Treasury
Journal, January 31, 2010

CREATING A COMPANY IN QUICKBOOKS

LEARNING OBJECTIVES

At the completion of this chapter, you will be able to:

1. Set up a company using the EasyStep Interview.
2. Establish a Chart of Accounts for a company.
3. Set up Company Info and start dates.
4. Create lists for receivables, payables, items, customers, vendors, employees, and others.
5. Complete the Payroll setup and create payroll items and employee defaults.
6. Customize reports and company preferences.

COMPUTERIZING A MANUAL SYSTEM

In previous chapters, QuickBooks Pro was used to record transactions for businesses that were already set up for use in the program. In this chapter, you will actually set up a business, create a chart of accounts, create various lists, add names to lists, and delete unnecessary accounts. QuickBooks Pro makes setting up the records for a business user-friendly by going through the process using the EasyStep Interview. Once the basic accounts, items, lists, and other items are established via the EasyStep Interview, you will make some refinements to accounts, add detail information regarding customers and vendors, transfer Uncategorized Income and Expenses to the owner's equity account, customize report and company preferences, and customize a business form.

TRAINING TUTORIAL AND PROCEDURES

The following tutorial is a step-by-step guide to setting up the fictitious company Your Name Movies & More. Company information, accounts, items, lists, and other items must be provided before transactions may be recorded in QuickBooks Pro. The EasyStep Interview will be used to set up company information. Once the basic company information has been entered via the EasyStep Interview, changes and modifications to the company data will be made. As in earlier chapters, information for the company setup will be provided in memos. Information may also be shown in lists or within the step-by-step instructions provided.

Please note that QuickBooks is updated on a regular basis. If your screens are not always an exact match to the text, check with your instructor to see if you should select something that is similar to the text. For example, QuickBooks has been known to change the type of businesses or industries that it uses in the Easy Step Interview. If that happens, your instructor may suggest that you select the company type closest to Your Name Movies & More. A different company type may result in a different chart of accounts. This would mean adjusting the chart of accounts to match the one given in the text.

DATES

Throughout the text, the year used for the screen shots is 2010, which is the same year as the version of the program. You may want to check with your instructor to see if you should use 2010 as the year for the transactions. Sometimes, QuickBooks' screens will display in a slightly different manner than the text. This is due to the fact that the date of your computer is not the same as the date of the text. Instructions are given where this occurs. The main criterion is to be consistent with the year you use throughout the chapter. On certain screens, the difference in the computer and text dates will cause a slight variation in the way things are displayed. If you cannot change a date that is provided by QuickBooks, accept it and continue with your training.

COMPANY PROFILE: YOUR NAME MOVIES & MORE

Your Name Movies & More is a fictitious company that sells and rents DVDs. In addition, Your Name Movies & More has a repair department that cleans, conditions, and repairs DVD players. Your Name Movies & More is located in San Diego, California, and is a sole proprietorship owned by you. You are involved in all aspects of the business. Your Name Movies & More has one full-time employee who is paid a salary: Alice Brooks, whose duties include placing all the orders, managing the office, and keeping the books. There is one full-time hourly employee: Greg Hanson, who works in the store and performs all the services in the repairs department,

CREATE A NEW COMPANY

Since Your Name Movies & More is a new company, it does not appear as a company file if you select Open Company on the File menu. A new company may be created by clicking New Company on the File menu.

Open QuickBooks Pro as previously instructed

MEMO

DATE: January 1, 2010

Because this is the beginning of the fiscal year for Your Name Movies & More, it is an appropriate time to set up the company information in QuickBooks Pro. Use the EasyStep Interview in QuickBooks Pro.

Insert a USB drive as previously instructed or use the storage location you have been using throughout the text

Click **File** menu, click **New Company** or click the **Create a new Company** icon on the **No Company Open** dialog box

The first screen of the EasyStep Interview will appear on the screen.

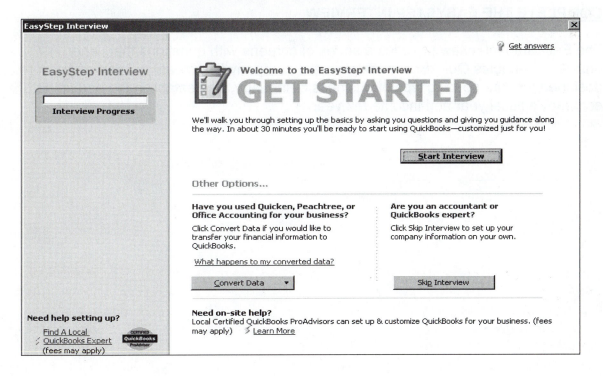

THE EASYSTEP INTERVIEW

The EasyStep Interview is a step-by-step guide to entering your company information as of a single date called a start date. It also provides tips regarding a chart of accounts, standard industry practices, and other items for the type of company indicated. During the Interview, general company information is entered; you may select a preset Chart of

Accounts; indicate preferences such as payroll, inventory, time tracking, and employees; and select a start date.

Once a screen has been read and any required items have been filled in or questions answered, the Next button is clicked to tell QuickBooks Pro to advance to the next screen. If you need to return to a previous screen, click the Previous button. If you need to stop the Interview before completing everything, you may exit by clicking the Leave button in the bottom right corner of the screen or by clicking the close button at the top right corner of the EasyStep Interview screen

> **DO** Begin the Interview

Click the **Start Interview** button

COMPLETE THE EASYSTEP INTERVIEW

The EasyStep Interview provides a series of screens with questions that, when answered, enables QuickBooks to set up the company file, create a Chart of Accounts designed for your specific type of business or industry, and establish the beginning of a company's fiscal year and income tax year.

MEMO

DATE: January 1, 2010

Use the following information to complete the EasyStep Interview for Your Name Movies & More:

Company and Legal Name: Your Name's Movies & More (*Key in your actual name*)
Federal Tax ID: 159-88-8654
Address: 8795 Mission Bay Drive, San Diego, CA 92109
Telephone: 760-555-7979; Fax: 760-555-9797
E-mail: YourNameMovies@info.com (use *your actual name*Movies@info.com)
Web: www.Movies.com
Type of Business: Retail Shop or Online Commerce
Company Organization: Sole Proprietorship
Do not use Passwords
File Name: Your Name Movies & More
File Type: .qbw
Sell both services and products
Record each sale individually, do charge sales tax
Do not sell online
Do use sales receipts and invoices (do not use progress invoicing)
Do accept credit cards and debit cards
Do not use estimates, statements, or track time
Do track bills and inventory
Do print checks
Employees: Yes, W-2 Employees
Use QuickBooks to set up the Chart of Accounts
Start Date: 01/01/2010
Bank account name Checking, account number 123-456-78910, opened before
    01/01/2010. Last bank statement 12/31/2007, ending balance 29,385.00
First Month in Tax and Fiscal Year: January
Income Tax form: None

DO Complete the Company Info screen

Enter the Company Name **Your Name's Movies & More**, press the Tab key
- Your Name Movies & More is entered as the Legal name when the Tab key is pressed. Do not actually enter the words "Your Name's" as part of the company name. Instead, type your own name. For example, Selma Anderson would have **Selma Anderson's Movies & More**. This makes it easier for you to identify your work when you print.

Tab to or click **Tax ID number**, enter **159-88-8654**

Enter the Company Address information in the spaces provided, tab to or click in the blanks to move from item to item

For the state, California, type C and QuickBooks Pro will fill in the rest or click the drop-down list arrow for State and click CA.

- The country is automatically filled in as US.

Enter the telephone number, fax number, e-mail address, and Web address as given in the Memo

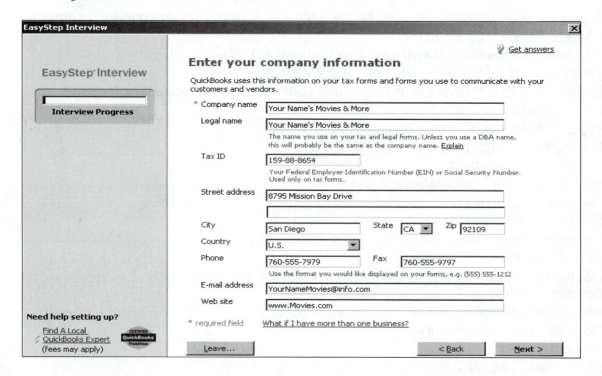

Click **Next**

Scroll through the list of industries

Click **Retail Shop or Online Commerce**, click **Next**

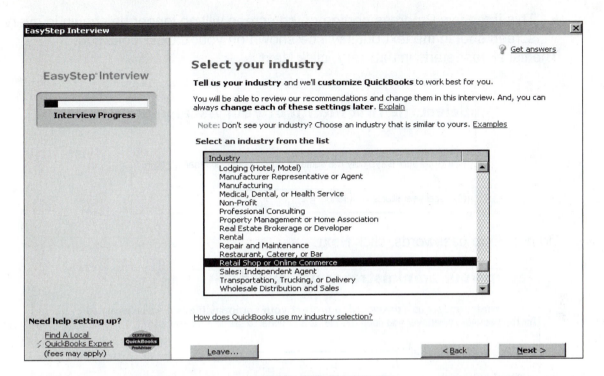

The company is a Sole Proprietorship, select this, and then click **Next**

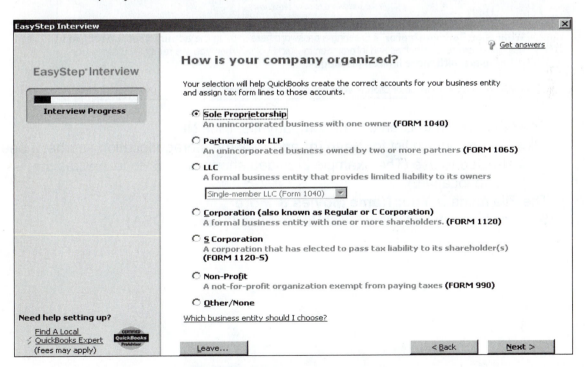

- Notice the Interview Progress in the upper-left side of the interview. This shows how much of the EasyStep Interview has been completed.

- This Interview Progress portion of the screen will no longer be shown in every screen shot in the text but it will be shown on your QuickBooks screen.

The fiscal year starts in **January**, click **Next**.

Select the first month of your fiscal year

Your fiscal year is typically the same as your income tax year. Explain

My fiscal year starts in   January   ▼

Do not setup passwords, click **Next**.

Set up your administrator password   (optional)

We recommend you set up a **password to protect your company file**. You will be prompted for this password whenever you open this file. It is optional to set up a password.

Administrator password   [   ]

Retype password   [   ]

Your password is case-sensitive.

What is an "administrator"? Entering a password here sets up the **administrator user**, who has full access to all activities and information in QuickBooks. When you are ready, you can set up **other users with more limited privileges**.

Note: You can also set up or change your administrator password later.

Read the screen to Create your company file, click **Next**

Click the drop-down list for **Save in:** and click the storage location you have been instructed to use (The example provided shows a USB drive in K: as the storage location.)

The File name is **Your Name Movies & More**

Save as type: should show QuickBooks Files (*.QBW, *.QBA)

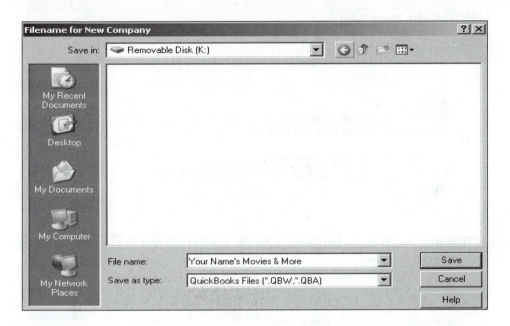

Click **Save**

Read the screen regarding Customizing QuickBooks for your business

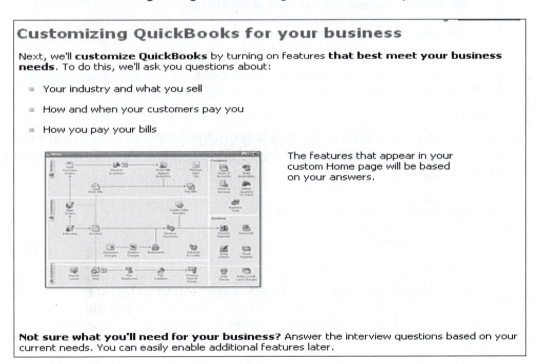

Click **Next**

Click **Both services and products** on the "What do you sell?" screen

What do you sell?

○ **Services only**
Such as consulting, rentals, gym memberships, hair styling services, event services, construction and labor.

○ **Products only**
Such as lamps, fertilizer, books, hardware, tickets, insurance policies. Manufacturers and distributors should also select this option.

◉ **Both services and products**
Such as a bicycle repair shop that sells bikes, a carpet installation company that sells carpet.

Click **Next**

Click **Record each sale individually** on the "How will you enter sales in QuickBooks" screen

How will you enter your sales in QuickBooks?

◉ **Record each sale individually**
You can also print sales receipts to give customers.

○ **Record only a summary of your daily or weekly sales**
If you use a cash register to ring up individual sales, you can enter the sales totals (for the day, week, etc.) into QuickBooks.

○ **Use QuickBooks Point of Sale**
You can send the details of each individual sale into QuickBooks—with just one click.

Click **Next**

At this point you are not planning to sell products online so click **I don't sell online and I am not interested in doing so** on the "Do you sell products online?" screen,

Do you sell products online?

○ I currently sell online.

○ I don't sell online, but I may want to someday.

◉ I don't sell online and I am not interested in doing so.

QuickBooks will use this answer to display information about services that can help you sell your products on the Web.

Click **Next**

You do plan to charge sales tax, click **Yes** on the "Do you charge sales tax?" screen

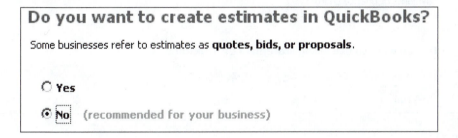

Do you charge sales tax?

⊙ Yes (recommended for your business)

○ No

Click **Next**

Click **No** on the "Do you want to create estimates in QuickBooks?" screen

Do you want to create estimates in QuickBooks?

Some businesses refer to estimates as **quotes, bids, or proposals**.

○ Yes

⊙ No (recommended for your business)

Click **Next**

Click **Yes** on the "Using sales receipts in QuickBooks" screen

Using sales receipts in QuickBooks

Use a **sales receipt** when your **customers pay in full** at the time of sale. This is especially common in retail businesses.

Some examples:

- A bookstore provides a sales receipt when the customer buys a book.

- A TV repair shop provides a sales receipt when a customer picks up and pays for a repaired TV.

Do you want to use sales receipts in QuickBooks?

⊙ Yes (recommended for your business)

○ No

Click **Next**

You do not plan to send statements, click **No** on the "Using statements in QuickBooks" screen

---

Using statements in QuickBooks

Billing statements are sent to customers to list **charges accumulated over a period of time**. Statements may be sent at regular intervals, as in a monthly statement, or when a customer payment is past due.

Some examples:

- An attorney **invoices** a client for multiple services provided. If the invoice isn't paid, the attorney can then send the client a **reminder statement**.

- A gym sends each member a **monthly statement** that includes fees and any overdue payments or finance charges.

Do you want to use billing statements in QuickBooks?

○ Yes

◉ No (recommended for your business)

Click **Next**

Since you plan to use invoices to record sales on account, click **Yes** on the "Using invoices in QuickBooks" screen

---

Using invoices in QuickBooks

Use an invoice when you **do not receive full payment** at the time you provide your product or service. Using invoices will help you keep track of what your customers owe you.

Some examples:

- A consultant sends an invoice to receive payment **when a project is complete.**

- A general contractor invoices the customer **at each stage** of a construction project.

- A caterer receives a **down payment** and later invoices the customer for the remaining balance.

Do you want to use invoices in QuickBooks?

◉ Yes (recommended for your business)

○ No

Note: If you use an estimate or a sales order you must use an invoice in QuickBooks to bill a customer.

Click **Next**

Click **No** on the "Using progress invoicing" screen

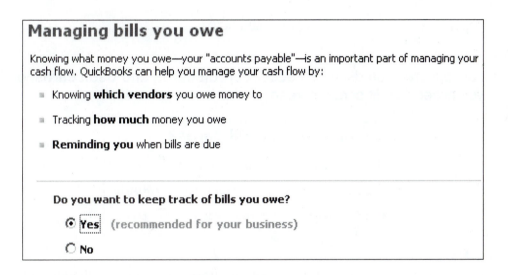

Click **Next**

You do want to keep track of the bills you owe, click **Yes** on the "Managing bills you owe" screen

Click **Next**

Click **I print checks**, and **Next**

You have inventory and plan to use QuickBooks to track it, click **Yes** on the "Tracking inventory in QuickBooks" screen

Tracking inventory in QuickBooks

Use inventory in QuickBooks to keep track of items in stock, items on order from vendors, or items to be built for customers.

Some examples:

- An importer **stocks and resells** products, and tracks items on order from vendors.

- An electronics manufacturer keeps inventory for both raw **materials and finished products**, and tracks products to be built for customer orders.

- A construction contractor purchases materials as they are needed. Because no items are kept in stock, there is **no need to track inventory** in QuickBooks.

QuickBooks uses average costing to determine the value of your inventory.

Do you want to track inventory in QuickBooks?

- ⦿ Yes
- ◯ No

Click **Next**

You accept credit cards, click **I accept credit cards and debit cards.** on the "Do you accept credit cards" screen

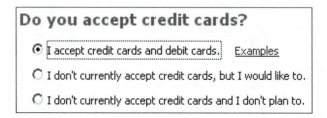

Click **Next**

Tracking time is used to keep track of the time spent on a particular job or with a particular client, which is not done in your company; so click **No** on the "Tracking time in QuickBooks" screen

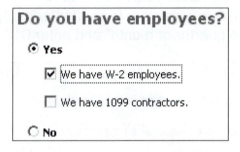

Click **Next**

There are two employees who work for us so click **Yes** and **We have W-2 employees.** On the "Do you have employees?" screen

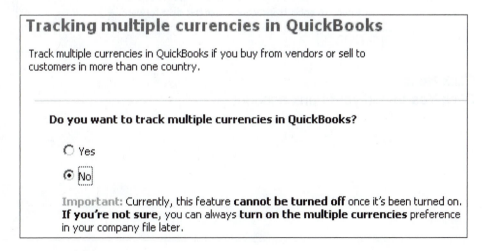

Click **Next**

You do not to track multiple currencies, so click **No**

Click **Next**
You want to use QuickBooks to set up the Chart of Accounts

Using accounts in QuickBooks

Next, we'll help you set up your **Chart of Accounts**, which are categories of income, expenses and more that you'll use to track your business.

Why is the chart of accounts important?

To set up your chart of accounts, you'll need to:

- Decide on a date to use as the starting point to track your business finances in QuickBooks (e.g., beginning of fiscal year, first of this month, etc.)

- Understand how you want to categorize your business' income and expenses. (You may want to discuss this with your accountant, if you have one.)

Click **Next**
Click **Beginning of this fiscal year: 01/01/2010**
- If the beginning of this fiscal year is not 01/01/2010, click Use today's date or the first day of the quarter or month" and enter 01/01/10

Select a date to start tracking your finances

The date you select will be your **start date** in QuickBooks.

⦿ **Beginning of this fiscal year: 01/01/2010**
- In order to complete this year's tax returns, you'll need to enter transactions from the beginning of this fiscal year to today.

○ **Use today's date or the first day of the quarter or month.**
- You'll need to enter transactions from this date forward.

  01/01/2010 📧

Click **Next**
Click **Yes** to add your bank account

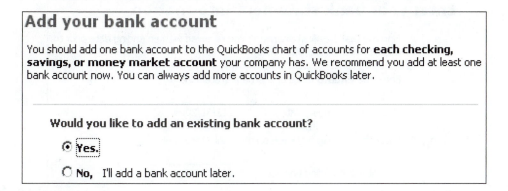

Click **Next**

Enter the bank account information: name is **Checking**, the number is **123-456-78910**, opened **Before 01/01/2010**

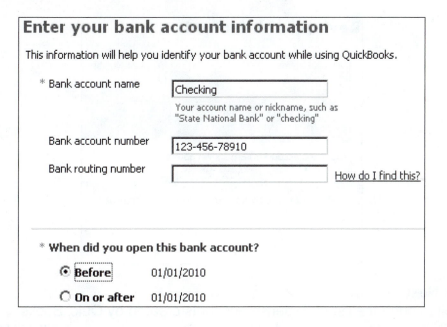

Click **Next**

Enter the ending date of the last bank statement **12/31/2009** and the ending balance **29,385**

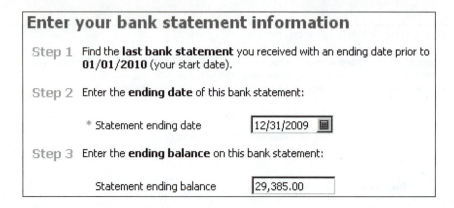

Click **Next**

Review the bank account name, **No** should be selected for adding another bank account

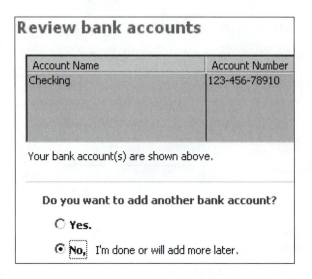

Click **Next**

Scroll through the list of Expense accounts created by QuickBooks

• The accounts recommended by QuickBooks are marked with a check. These accounts may or may not match your chart of accounts. You may make changes at this time to add and delete from this account list or you may customize your chart of accounts later.

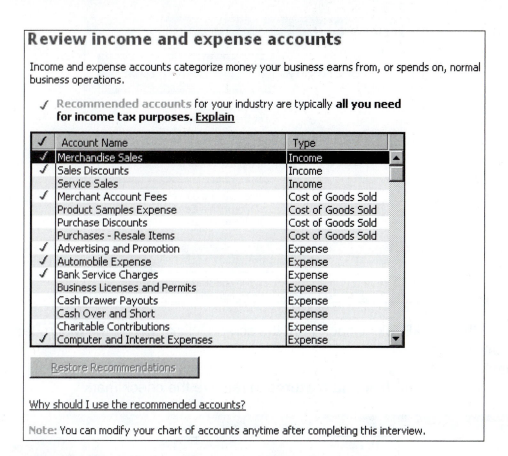

Click **Next**

On the **Congratulations** screen, click **Finish**

You will see the QuickBooks Coach displayed

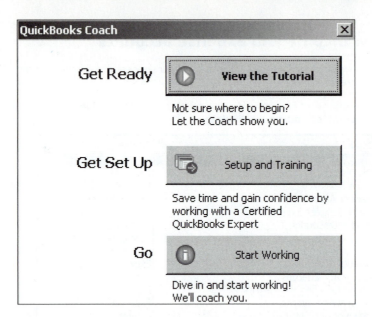

To remove the QuickBooks Coach from the screen, click **Edit** on the Menu Bar
Click **Preferences**
Click **Desktop View**
Click **Show Coach window and features** to remove the check mark

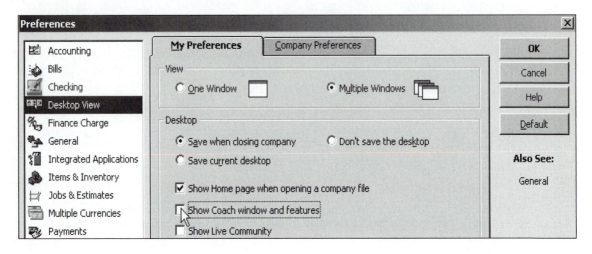

Click **OK** on the Preferences screen

COMPLETE COMPANY INFORMATION

Once the EasyStep Interview has been completed, other information for the company must be entered. Information such as tax forms, Federal Employer Identification numbers, and payroll processing information may need to be provided. Customers, vendors, employees, sales items, and preferences need to be entered. In addition, the chart of accounts will need to be refined.

MEMO
DATE: January 1, 2010

The information necessary to complete the Company information is the Federal Employer Identification number. The number is 15-9888654.

▶ DO ▶ Enter the Federal Employer Identification number

Click **Company Info** on the Company menu
Click in the Federal Employer Identification number text box, enter **15-9888654**

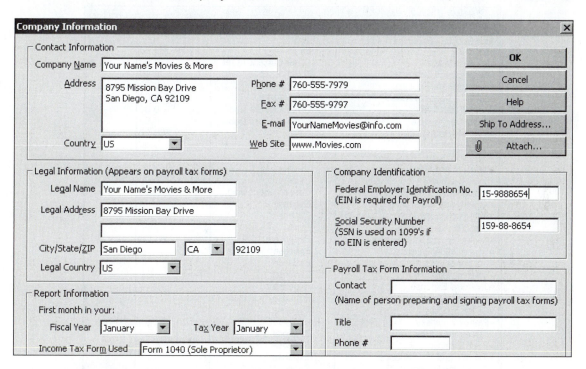

- View the other information on the page. Notice that the Report Information shows the Fiscal Year and Tax Year as January. The Income Tax Form Used is Form 1040 (Sole Proprietor). The Contact Information and Legal Information appear as it was entered during the EasyStep Interview. Do not make any other changes to the Company Information.
Click **OK**

CHART OF ACCOUNTS

Using the EasyStep Interview to set up a company is a user-friendly way to establish the basic structure of the company. However, the Chart of Accounts created by QuickBooks Pro may not be the exact Chart of Accounts you wish to use in your business. In order to customize your chart of accounts, additional accounts need to be created, balances need to be entered for balance sheet accounts, some account names need to be changed, and some accounts need to be deleted or made inactive

The Chart of Accounts is not only a listing of the account names and balances but also the General Ledger used by the business. As in textbook accounting, the General Ledger/Chart of Accounts is the book of final entry.

At the completion of the EasyStep Interview, you have the following Chart of Accounts:

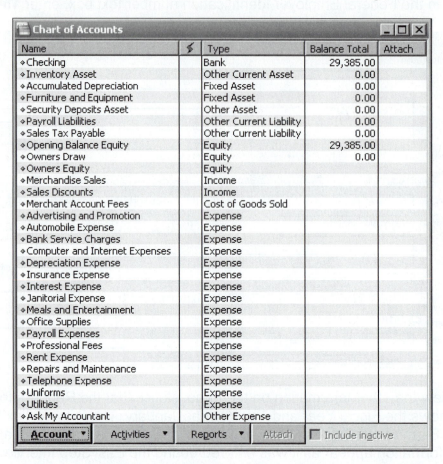

Name	$	Type	Balance Total	Attach
⬥Checking		Bank	29,385.00	
⬥Inventory Asset		Other Current Asset	0.00	
⬥Accumulated Depreciation		Fixed Asset	0.00	
⬥Furniture and Equipment		Fixed Asset	0.00	
⬥Security Deposits Asset		Other Asset	0.00	
⬥Payroll Liabilities		Other Current Liability	0.00	
⬥Sales Tax Payable		Other Current Liability	0.00	
⬥Opening Balance Equity		Equity	29,385.00	
⬥Owners Draw		Equity	0.00	
⬥Owners Equity		Equity		
⬥Merchandise Sales		Income		
⬥Sales Discounts		Income		
⬥Merchant Account Fees		Cost of Goods Sold		
⬥Advertising and Promotion		Expense		
⬥Automobile Expense		Expense		
⬥Bank Service Charges		Expense		
⬥Computer and Internet Expenses		Expense		
⬥Depreciation Expense		Expense		
⬥Insurance Expense		Expense		
⬥Interest Expense		Expense		
⬥Janitorial Expense		Expense		
⬥Meals and Entertainment		Expense		
⬥Office Supplies		Expense		
⬥Payroll Expenses		Expense		
⬥Professional Fees		Expense		
⬥Rent Expense		Expense		
⬥Repairs and Maintenance		Expense		
⬥Telephone Expense		Expense		
⬥Uniforms		Expense		
⬥Utilities		Expense		
⬥Ask My Accountant		Other Expense		

| Account ▼ | Activities ▼ | Reports ▼ | Attach | ☐ Include inactive |

Please be aware that the Chart of Accounts created in the Easy-Step Interview may be different from the one shown above. Notice that there are some accounts, such as, Accounts Receivable, Accounts Payable, and Cost of Goods Sold that are not part of the account listing. QuickBooks will automatically add these accounts and their balances when customers, vendors, and sales items are added.

Use the following chart of accounts and balances to customize Your Name Movies & More chart of accounts. Instructions will be given to add, delete, edit, and/or make accounts inactive after the complete listing of the final Chart of Accounts. When the charts of accounts, customer list, vendor list, and sales items have been entered, your chart of accounts should match the following:

YOUR NAME MOVIES & MORE CHART OF ACCOUNTS				
ACCOUNT	**TYPE**	**BALANCE**	**ACCOUNT**	**TYPE**
Checking	Bank	29,385.00	Sales	Inc.
Accounts Receivable (QB)	Accts. Rec.	***	Merchandise	Inc.
Inventory Asset	Other C.A.	***	Rental	Inc.
Office Supplies	Other C.A.	350.00	Service	Inc.
Sales Supplies	Other C.A.	500.00	Sales Discounts	Inc.
Prepaid Insurance	Other C.A.	1,200.00	Cost of Goods Sold (QB)	COGS
Store Equipment	Fixed Asset	***	Advertising and Promotion	Exp.
Original Cost	Fixed Asset	8,000.00	Automobile Expense	Exp.
Depreciation	Fixed Asset	-800.00	Bank Service Charges	Exp.
Store Fixtures	Fixed Asset	***	Computer and Internet Expenses	Exp.
Original Cost	Fixed Asset	15,000.00	Depreciation Expense	Exp
Depreciation	Fixed Asset	-1,500.00	Insurance Expense	Exp.
Accounts Payable (QB)	Other C.L.	***	Interest Expense	Exp.
Payroll Liabilities	Other C.L.	0.00	Office Supplies Expense	Exp.
Sales Tax Payable	Other C.L.	0.00	Payroll Expenses	Exp.
Store Equipment Loan	Long Term L.	2,000.00	Professional Fees	Exp.
Store Fixtures Loan	Long Term L.	2,500.00	Rent Expense	Exp.
Retained Earnings (QB*)	Equity	***	Repairs and Maintenance	Exp.
Your Name, Capital	Equity	***	Sales Supplies Expense	Exp.
Withdrawals	Equity	0.00	Telephone Expense	Exp.
Investment	Equity	25,000.00	Utilities	Exp.
			Other Income	Other Inc
			Other Expenses	Other Exp

Chart Abbreviations:
(QB)=Account Created by QuickBooks
(QB*)=Account Created by QuickBooks. Name change required.
Indented Account Names indicate that the account is a subaccount
*** means that QuickBooks will enter the account balance
C.A.=Current Asset, F.A.=Fixed Asset; C.L.=Current Liability; Long Term L.=Long Term Liability; COGS=Cost of Goods Sold, Inc.=Income, Exp.=Expense.

MEMO

DATE: January 1, 2010

Since Your Name Movies & More the Chart of Accounts/General Ledger needs to be customized, make the following changes to the accounts:

<u>Delete</u>: Accumulated Depreciation, Furniture and Equipment, Security Deposits Assets, Owners Draw, Owners Equity, Uniforms, and Ask My Accountant

<u>Make inactive</u>: Merchant Account Fees, Janitorial Expense, and Meals and Entertainment

<u>Edit Equity Accounts</u>: Change Opening Balance Equity to **Your Name, Capital**

<u>Add Equity Accounts</u>: **Your Name, Investment**; Subaccount of Your Name, Capital; Opening Balance $25,000 as of 01/01/10

Your Name, Withdrawals; Subaccount of Your Name, Capital; Opening Balance, $0.00 as of 01/01/10

<u>Add Income Accounts</u>: **Sales**; add **Rental** a Subaccount of Sales, add **Service** a subaccount of Sales, add **Other Income**

<u>Add Expense Accounts</u>: **Sales Supplies Expense**, and **Other Expenses**

<u>Edit Income Accounts</u>: Rename Merchandise Sales to **Merchandise** make a subaccount of Sales, Make **Sales Discounts** a subaccount of Sales

<u>Edit Expense Accounts</u>: Rename Office Supplies to **Office Supplies Expense**

<u>Delete Account Descriptions</u>: Check each account and delete the descriptions entered by QuickBooks.

▶ **DO** Make the changes indicated above

Click **Chart of Accounts** in the Company section of the Home Page

Click the account **Accumulated Depreciation** to highlight, use the keyboard **Ctrl+D** to delete the account, click **OK** to delete

Repeat to delete the other accounts listed in the memo

Position the cursor on **Merchant Account Fees**, click the **Account** button, and click **Make Inactive**

Repeat the procedures to make Janitorial Expense and Meals and Entertainment inactive

Position the cursor on **Opening Balance Equity**, click the **Account** button, click **Edit**, enter **Your Name, Capital** as the account name, delete the account description, and click **Save & Close**

Click the **Account** button, click **New**, account type is **Equity**, enter the account name **Your Name, Investment**, click **Subaccount**, click **Your Name, Capital**

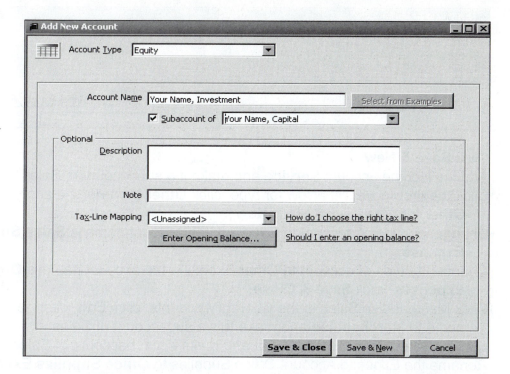

Click the **Enter Opening Balance** button, enter **25,000** as of **01/01/10**, click **OK**

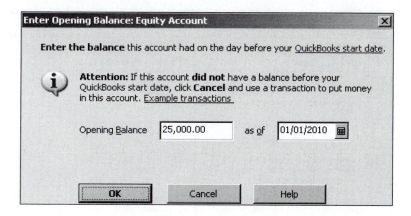

Click **Save & New** on the Your Name, Investment Add New Account screen
- If you get a screen warning about a transaction being 30 days in the future or 90 days in the past, click **Yes**

Add **Your Name, Withdrawals** using the information provided in the memo, click **Save & New**

Click the drop-down list arrow for type, click **Income**, the account name is **Sales**

Add the Income account **Rental**, make this a subaccount of Sales

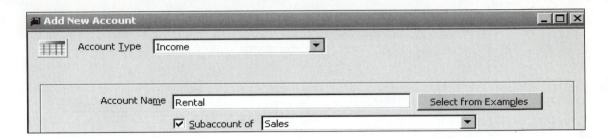

Click **Save & New**

Add the income account **Service** and make it a subaccount of Sales

Click the drop-down list arrow for type, click **Other Income**, the account name is **Other Income**, click **Save & New**

Change the type of account to Expense, the account name is **Sales Supplies Expense**

Change the type of account to Other Expense, the account name is **Other Expenses**, click **Save & Close**

Click Merchandise Sales in the Chart of Accounts, click **Edit**, change the account name to **Merchandise** and make this a subaccount of Sales

Edit the **Sales Discounts** account and make it a subaccount of Sales

Rename the Expense Account Office Supplies to **Office Supplies Expense**

At this point, the Chart of Accounts appears as follows:

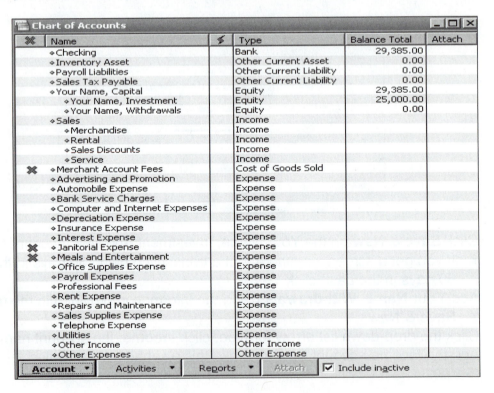

- As you can see, income and expense accounts do not have opening balances. Only balance sheet accounts—assets, liabilities, and owner's equity accounts—have opening balances.
- As you review the Chart of Accounts above, note that a number of balance sheet accounts and their balances need to be added.

MEMO

DATE: January 1, 2010

Set up the following Balance Sheet accounts and balances. The as of dates for opening balances is 01/01/10.

Other Current Asset: Prepaid Insurance, Opening Balance $1,200
Other Current Asset: Office Supplies, Opening Balance $350
Other Current Asset: Sales Supplies, Opening Balance $500
Fixed Asset: Store Equipment
Fixed Asset: Original Cost, Subaccount of Store Equipment, Opening Balance $8,000
Fixed Asset: Depreciation, Subaccount of Store Equipment, Opening Balance -$800
Fixed Asset: Store Fixtures
Fixed Asset: Original Cost, Subaccount of Store Fixtures, Opening Balance $15,000
Fixed Asset: Depreciation, Subaccount of Store Fixtures, Opening Balance -$1,500
Long-term liability: Store Equipment Loan, Opening Balance $2,000,
Long-term liability: Store Fixtures Loan, Opening Balance $2,500,

---

▶ **DO** Add the accounts and balances listed above

Click the **Account** button at the bottom of the Chart of Accounts
Click **New**
Click the drop-down list arrow for **Other Account Types**, click **Other Current Asset**, and click **Continue**.
Enter **Prepaid Insurance** as the Account Name

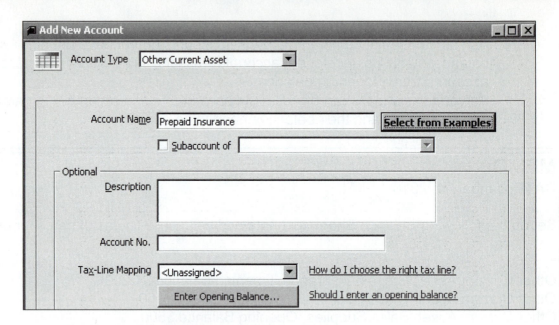

Click the **Enter Opening Balance** button
Enter **1,200** as of **01/01/10**, and then click **OK**

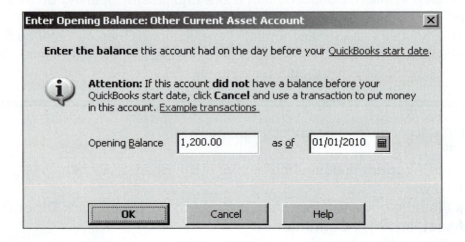

Click **Save & New**

Add the Other Current Asset accounts: Office Supplies and Sales Supplies and the opening balances listed in the Memo, click **Save & New** after adding each account

Click the drop-down list arrow for Type, click **Fixed Asset**

Tab to or click in the textbox for **Account Name**, enter **Store Equipment**

Click **Save & New**

The type of account is still Fixed Asset, enter **Original Cost** as the Name

Click **Subaccount of** to enter a check mark

Click the drop-down list arrow for Subaccount, click **Store Equipment**

Click the **Enter Opening Balance** button, enter **8,000** as of **01/01/10**, click **OK**

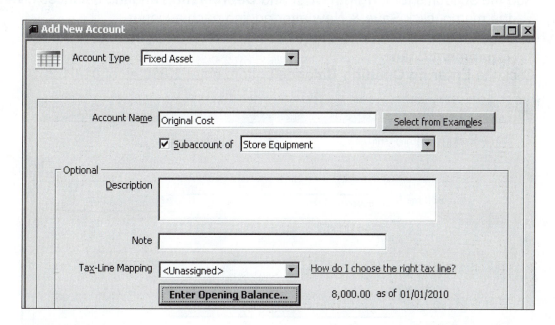

Click **Save & New** and repeat the procedure to add **Depreciation** as a
Subaccount of Store Equipment with an Opening Balance of **-800** as of
01/01/10

* Be sure to use a minus (-) sign in front of the 800. Remember, depreciation
reduces the value of the asset.

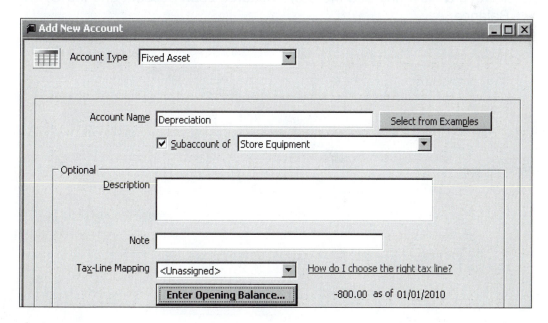

Add the other fixed asset, **Store Fixtures**

Add the accounts for **Original Cost** and **Depreciation** and the balances given in the memo, click **Save & New** after adding each account

Change the account Type to **Long Term Liability**, enter the name **Store Equipment Loan**

Click the **Entering Opening Balance** button; enter **2,000** as of **01/01/2010**

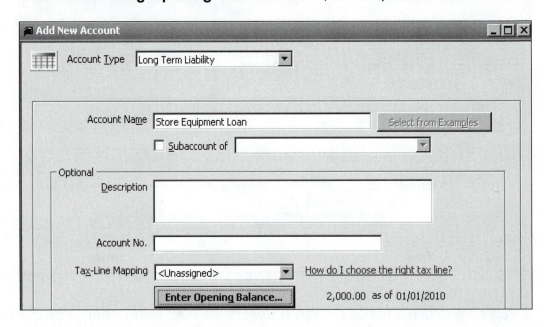

Click **Save & New** and add the Store Fixtures Loan account and the Opening Balance

When finished, click **Save & Close**, and review the Chart of Accounts

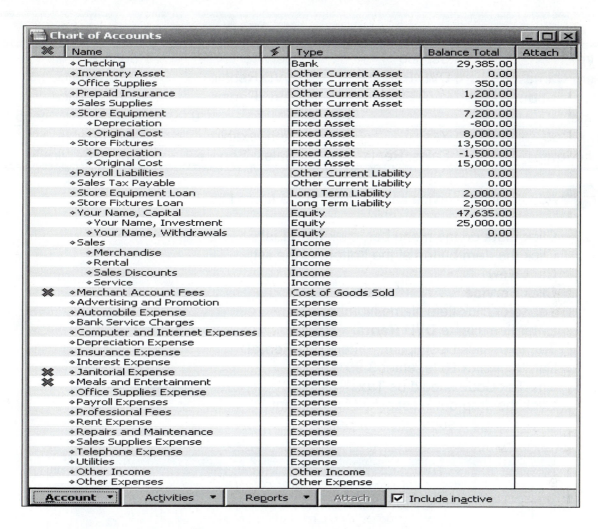

Name	Type	Balance Total	Attach
Checking	Bank	29,385.00	
Inventory Asset	Other Current Asset	0.00	
Office Supplies	Other Current Asset	350.00	
Prepaid Insurance	Other Current Asset	1,200.00	
Sales Supplies	Other Current Asset	500.00	
Store Equipment	Fixed Asset	7,200.00	
Depreciation	Fixed Asset	-800.00	
Original Cost	Fixed Asset	8,000.00	
Store Fixtures	Fixed Asset	13,500.00	
Depreciation	Fixed Asset	-1,500.00	
Original Cost	Fixed Asset	15,000.00	
Payroll Liabilities	Other Current Liability	0.00	
Sales Tax Payable	Other Current Liability	0.00	
Store Equipment Loan	Long Term Liability	2,000.00	
Store Fixtures Loan	Long Term Liability	2,500.00	
Your Name, Capital	Equity	47,635.00	
Your Name, Investment	Equity	25,000.00	
Your Name, Withdrawals	Equity	0.00	
Sales	Income		
Merchandise	Income		
Rental	Income		
Sales Discounts	Income		
Service	Income		
Merchant Account Fees	Cost of Goods Sold		
Advertising and Promotion	Expense		
Automobile Expense	Expense		
Bank Service Charges	Expense		
Computer and Internet Expenses	Expense		
Depreciation Expense	Expense		
Insurance Expense	Expense		
Interest Expense	Expense		
Janitorial Expense	Expense		
Meals and Entertainment	Expense		
Office Supplies Expense	Expense		
Payroll Expenses	Expense		
Professional Fees	Expense		
Rent Expense	Expense		
Repairs and Maintenance	Expense		
Sales Supplies Expense	Expense		
Telephone Expense	Expense		
Utilities	Expense		
Other Income	Other Income		
Other Expenses	Other Expense		

- Note the value of Store Equipment and Store Fixtures.
- Nothing shows for Accounts Receivable, Accounts Payable, Cost of Goods Sold. No balance is shown for Inventory Asset. These accounts and their balances will be added by QuickBooks when the Item, Customer, and Vendor Lists are entered.

Close the Chart of Accounts

ITEMS LIST

The Items list contains information about all of the items sold or services performed by the business. The Items used to track services performed and products sold for income are created. The Items List is used in conjunction with the income accounts previously created.

January 1, 2010			
Type	Service	Service	Service
Item Name	DVD Rental	DVD Repair	DVD Service
Description	DVD Rental	DVD Repair	DVD Service
Rate	3.95	0.00	39.95
Tax Code	Yes	Non-taxable	Non-taxable
Account	Sales: Rental	Sales: Service	Sales: Service

DO ▸ Add the three service items above to the Items List

Click **Lists** on the menu bar, click **Item List**
Click the **Item** button at the bottom of the list
Click **New**
Click **Service**
Tab to or click Item Name/Number
Enter Item Name **DVD Rental**
Tab to or click Description, enter **DVD Rental**
Tab to or click Rate, enter **3.95**
The Tax Code should be **Tax**
Click the drop-down list arrow for Account
Click **Rental** a subaccount of Sales

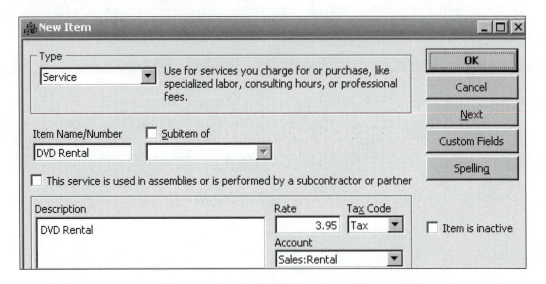

The information for DVD Rental is complete, click the **Next** button to add the
    sales item for DVD repair
DVD does not appear in QuickBooks spell check so the Check Spelling on Form
    screen appears

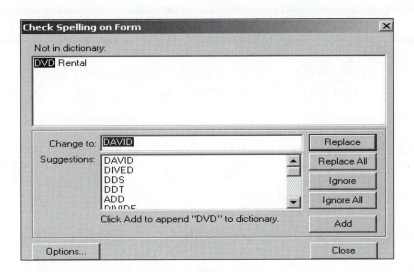

Click **Add** to add the word to the dictionary

Complete the information for DVD Repair and DVD Service using the information
provided in the memo

When the service items have been added return to the Item List

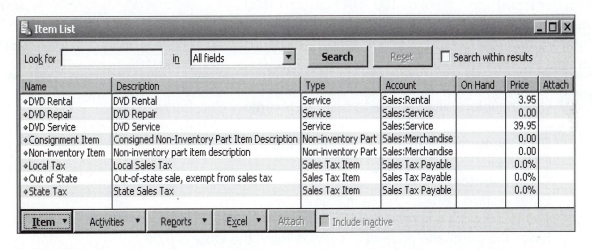

Now that the service items have been added, the Inventory part items should be
entered. Inventory part items are the things you purchase, hold in inventory, and then
sell.

January 1, 2010				
Type	Inventory Part	Inventory Part	Inventory Part	Inventory Part
Item Name	Action DVD	Children DVD	Comedy DVD	Drama DVD
Purchase Description	Action DVD	Children DVD	Comedy DVD	Drama DVD
Cost	0.00	0.00	0.00	0.00
COGS Account	Cost of Goods Sold	Cost of Goods Sold	Cost of Goods Sold	Cost of Goods Sold
Preferred Vendor				
Sales Description	Action DVD	Children DVD	Comedy DVD	Drama DVD
Sales Price	0.00	0.00	0.00	0.00
Tax Code	Tax	Tax	Tax	Tax
Income Account	Sales: Merchandise	Sales: Merchandise	Sales: Merchandise	Sales: Merchandise
Asset Account	Inventory Asset	Inventory Asset	Inventory Asset	Inventory Asset
Reorder Point	100	100	100	100
On-Hand	2550	1250	1500	1450
Total Value	12,750	6,250	7,500	7,250
As Of	01/01/10	01/01/10	01/01/10	01/01/10

▶ **DO** Use the information above to add the Inventory Part Items

Click the **Item** button at the bottom of the Item List screen
Click **New**
Click **Inventory Part**
Enter **Action DVD** as the Item Name
Tab to or click Description on Purchase Transactions, enter **Action DVD**
Since the purchase price of the DVDs vary, the Cost is **0.00**
The COGS Account is **Cost of Goods Sold**
• There is no Preferred Vendor, so leave this blank
Enter the Description on Sales Transactions **Action DVD**
Because DVDs are sold for different amounts, Sales Price remains **0.00**
The Tax Code should be **Tax**
Click the drop-down list arrow for Income Account, click **Merchandise,** which is a
    subaccount of Sales
The Asset Account is **Inventory Asset**
Enter the Reorder Point of **100**
Tab to On Hand, enter **2,550**
Enter the Total Value of **12,750**, and the As of date **01/01/2010**

- The only time a Total Value may be entered is at the time the Inventory Part item is created.

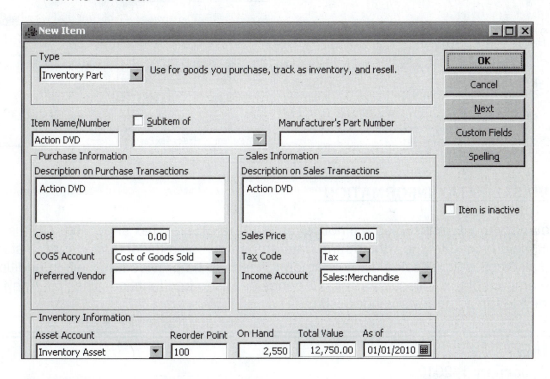

Click **Next** and enter the information for Children DVD, Comedy DVD, and Drama DVD

When the last Inventory Item has been entered, click **OK** to return to the Item List

The Item List shows some items that we will not be using. These items need to be deleted.

DO Delete the following sales items: Consignment Item and Non-Inventory Item

Click **Consignment Item** in the Item list
Click the **Item** button at the bottom of the Item List
Click **Delete Item**, click **OK** on the Delete Item dialog box
Repeat the procedures for Non-inventory Item
Your Item List should match the following:

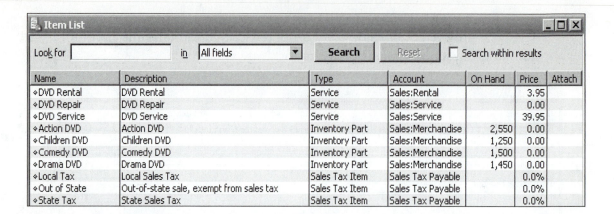

ENTER SALES TAX INFORMATION

As you view the Item List, you will notice that the State Sales Tax shows 0.0%. This should be changed to show the appropriate amount of sales tax deducted for the state. If you also collect local sales tax, this amount needs to be provided as well. In addition to the amount of tax collected, the Tax Agency needs to be identified. The Tax Agency is added to the company's vendor list.

MEMO
DATE: January 1, 2010

The information necessary to complete the CA Sales Tax: A tax rate of 7.25% paid to State Board of Equalization, 7800 State Street, Sacramento, CA 94267.

 Enter the amount of sales tax and the sales tax agency information for CA Sales Tax

Click **State Tax** in the Item List
Use the keyboard shortcut **Ctrl+E** to edit the State Tax Item
Change the Item Name and Description to **CA Sales Tax**
Enter **7.25%** as the tax rate
Click the drop-down list arrow for Tax Agency
Click **<Add New>**
Enter **State Board of Equalization** as the Vendor name and Company name
Tab to or click in the address text box, if necessary enter **State Board of Equalization**, press Enter
Enter **7800 State Street**, press Enter, type **Sacramento, CA 94265**, press Tab

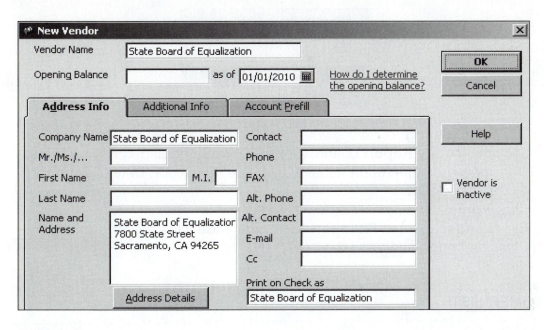

Click **OK**

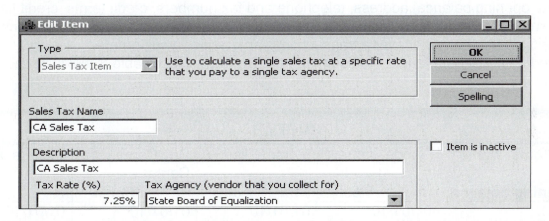

Click **OK** to close the Sales Tax Item

Name	Description	Type	Account	On Hand	Price	Attach
◆DVD Rental	DVD Rental	Service	Sales:Rental		3.95	
◆DVD Repair	DVD Repair	Service	Sales:Service		0.00	
◆DVD Service	DVD Service	Service	Sales:Service		39.95	
◆Action DVD	Action DVD	Inventory Part	Sales:Merchandise	2,550	0.00	
◆Children DVD	Children DVD	Inventory Part	Sales:Merchandise	1,250	0.00	
◆Comedy DVD	Comedy DVD	Inventory Part	Sales:Merchandise	1,500	0.00	
◆Drama DVD	Drama DVD	Inventory Part	Sales:Merchandise	1,450	0.00	
◆CA Sales Tax	CA Sales Tax	Sales Tax Item	Sales Tax Payable		7.25%	
◆Local Tax	Local Sales Tax	Sales Tax Item	Sales Tax Payable		0.0%	
◆Out of State	Out-of-state sale, exempt from sales tax	Sales Tax Item	Sales Tax Payable		0.0%	

- Note the change to the State Tax on the Item List

To print the List, click the **Reports** button at the bottom of the screen

Click **Item Listing**

Click the **Modify Report** button, click Date Prepared and Time Prepared to remove from the report heading, Change the Report Date to **January 1, 2010**, click **OK**

Click **Print**

Click **Landscape** and **Fit report to 1 page wide**, click the **Print** button, Close the report and close the Item List

CUSTOMER LIST

The Customer List is created in the Customer Center. The list includes a customer's name, opening balance, address, telephone and fax numbers, credit terms, credit limits, and sales tax information. The Customer List is also known as the Accounts Receivable Subsidiary Ledger. Whenever a transaction is entered for a customer, it is automatically posted to the General Ledger account and the Accounts Receivable Subsidiary Ledger account.

January 1, 2010				
Customer Name	Goode, Jeffrey	Morse, Ellen	Day Care Center	Winters, Ben
Opening Balance	500	800	1,500	150
As Of	01/01/10	01/01/10	01/01/10	01/01/10
Address	1980 A Street	719 4th Avenue	2190 State Street	2210 Columbia Street
City, State, Zip	San Diego, CA 92101	San Diego, CA 92101	San Diego, CA 92101	San Diego, CA 92101
Telephone	760-555-8763	760-555-8015	760-555-1275	760-555-2594
Terms	Net 30	Net 30	Net 30	Net 30
Tax Code	Tax	Tax	Tax	Tax
Tax Item	CA Sales Tax	CA Sales Tax	CA Sales Tax	CA Sales Tax
Credit Limit	500	1,000	1,500	500

DO ▶ Add the customers and their information to create the Customer List

Click the icon for **Customer Center**
Click **New Customer & Job**
Click **New Customer**
Enter **Goode, Jeffrey**

- QuickBooks will organize the Customer List by alphabetizing the first letter shown for the Customer Name.

Enter the Opening Balance of **500** as of **01/01/10**

- When you enter the opening balance for your customers, you are creating the opening balance for the Accounts Receivable account.

Enter **Jeffrey** in the text box for First Name
Enter **Goode** in the text box for Last Name
Tab to or click in the text box for Address
The cursor should appear after Jeffrey Goode in the first line of the address, press Enter
Enter the street address **1980 A Street**, press Enter
Enter the city, state and Zip **San Diego, CA 92101**
Press **Tab** until your cursor is positioned in the **Phone** textbox
Enter the telephone number **760-555-8763**

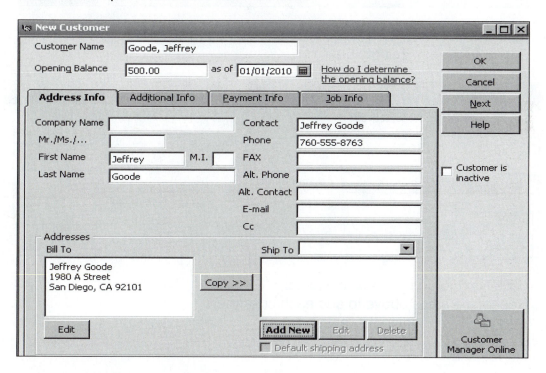

Click the **Additional Info** tab
Click the drop-down list arrow for Terms, click **Net 30**
Click the drop-down list arrow for Tax Code, click **Tax**
Click the drop-down list arrow for Tax Item, click **CA Sales Tax**

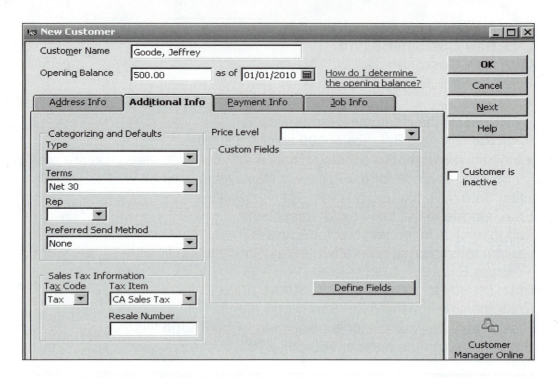

Click the **Payment Info** tab
Enter the Credit Limit of **500**

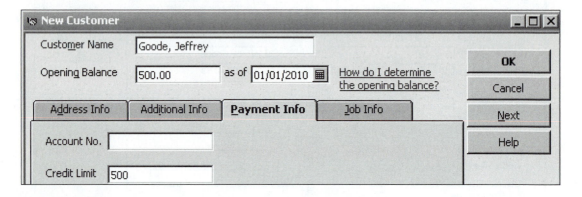

Click **Next** to add the next customer
Repeat the steps above to add each customer
Click **OK** after adding the last customer

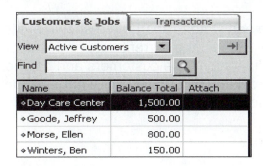

Print the Customer:Job List in Portrait orientation, click **Print** at the top of the
screen, click **Customer & Job List**,

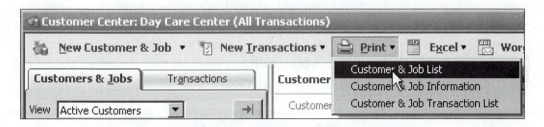

Click **OK** on the List Reports screen

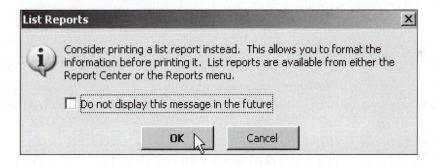

Check the print to information, select **Portrait** orientation and make sure you are
not using **Fit report to 1 page wide**
Click **Print**

	Your Name's Movies & More		
12:04 PM	**Customer & Job List**		
01/01/10	January 1, 2010		

Customer	Balance Total	At...
Day Care Center	1,500.00	No
Goode, Jeffrey	500.00	No
Morse, Ellen	800.00	No
Winters, Ben	150.00	No

- Notice the Time and Date Prepared are shown at the top of the report. Your time and date will reflect the current date and time of your computer and may not match the illustration. The customers and balances should match the illustration. The column heading for Attachment is only partially displayed.

Close the report and close the Customer Center

VENDOR LIST

QuickBooks Pro keeps detailed information regarding vendors. This includes the vendor's name, opening balance, address, contact person, telephone and fax numbers, credit terms, and credit limits. The Vendor List is also known as the Accounts Payable Subsidiary Ledger. Whenever a transaction is entered for a vendor, it is automatically posted to the General Ledger account and the Accounts Payable Ledger account. Some vendors are those from whom you purchase merchandise, while others are vendors you use to pay tax and withholding payments

January 1, 2010			
Vendor Name	Movie & DVD Supplies	Disks Galore	DVD Sales
Opening Balance	3,000	2,000	0.00
As Of	01/01/10	01/01/10	01/01/10
Address	10855 Western Avenue	7758 Broadway Avenue	1970 College Boulevard
City, State, Zip	Los Angeles, CA 90012	San Diego, CA 92101	Hollywood, CA 90028
Contact Person	Virginia Gonzalez	Delores Cooper	Carol Lewis
Phone	310-555-6971	760-555-2951	310-555-6464
Fax	310-555-1796	760-555-1592	310-555-4646
Terms	2% 10, Net 30	2% 10, Net 30	Net 30
Credit Limit	1,500	10,000	5,000

DO Add the vendors that sell us merchandise and their information to create part of the Vendor List

Click the icon for **Vendor Center**
- Notice that the State Board of Equalization already appears as a vendor.

Click **New Vendor**

Enter **Movie & DVD Supplies** for the Vendor Name

Enter the Opening Balance of **3,000** as of **01/01/10**

- When you enter the opening balance for your vendors, you are creating the opening balance for the Accounts Payable account.

Enter **Movie & DVD Supplies** as the Company Name

Click after Movie & DVD Supplies in the Address, press Enter

Enter **10855 Western Avenue**, press Enter

Enter **Los Angeles, CA 90012**

Tab to Contact, enter **Virginia Gonzalez**

Tab to or click Phone, enter **310-555-6971**

Tab to or click Fax, enter **310-555-1796**

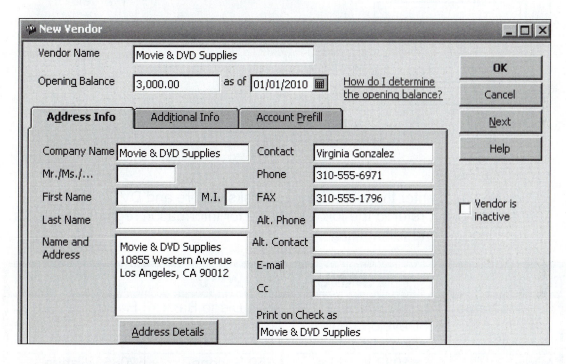

Click the **Additional Info** tab

Click the drop-down list arrow for Terms, click **2% 10 Net 30**

Enter the Credit Limit **1,500**

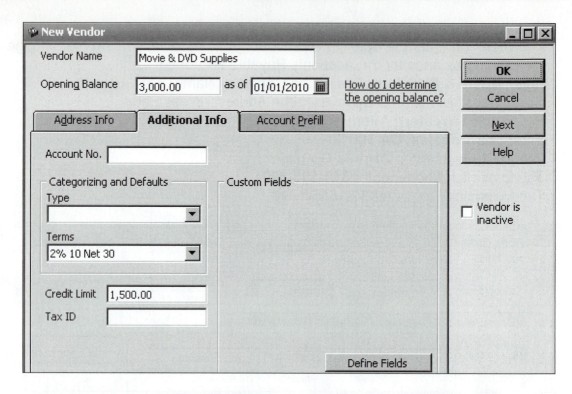

Click **Next** and enter the information for Disks Galore and DVD Sales
When complete, refer to the following table for information regarding vendors
used for tax and withholding payments

JANUARY 1, 2010			
Vendor Name	Employment Development Department	San Diego Bank	Health Insurance, Inc.
Address	11033 Wilshire Boulevard	350 Second Street	2085 Wilshire Boulevard
City, State, Zip	Los Angeles, CA 90007	San Diego, CA 92114	Los Angeles, CA 90007
Phone	310-555-8877	760-555-9889	310-555-7412
Fax	310-555-7788	760-555-9988	310-555-2147

► **DO** Add the vendors that we use for tax and withholding payments to the Vendor List

Follow the steps previously provided to enter the vendors
Click **OK** after adding the last vendor

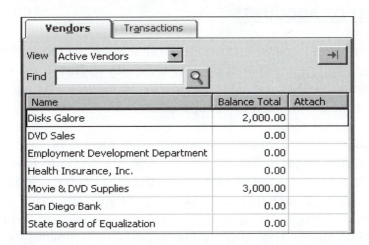

Print the Vendor List in Portrait orientation, click **Print** at the top of the screen, click **Vendor List**

Click **OK** on the List Reports screen

Check the print to information, select **Portrait** orientation and make sure you are not using **Fit report to 1 page wide**

Click **Print**

12:17 PM	Your Name's Movies & More		
01/01/10	**Vendor List**		
	January 1, 2010		

Vendor	Balance Total	At...
Disks Galore	2,000.00	No
DVD Sales	0.00	No
Employment Development Department	0.00	No
Health Insurance, Inc.	0.00	No
Movie & DVD Supplies	3,000.00	No
San Diego Bank	0.00	No
State Board of Equalization	0.00	No

- Notice the Time and Date Prepared are shown at the top of the report. Your time and date will reflect the current date and time of your computer and may not match the illustration. The vendors and balances should match the illustration. The Attach column heading is shown partially.

Close the report and close the Vendor Center

PRINT THE CHART OF ACCOUNTS

DO When all items, customers, and vendors have been added to the Chart of Accounts, change the title of **Owner's Equity** to **Retained Earnings**; and, then, delete the QuickBooks account descriptions for all accounts and print the **Account Listing** in Landscape orientation

Open the Chart of Accounts as previously instructed

Edit the account **Owner's Equity** and change the name to **Retained Earnings**

Edit each account and delete the account description provided by QuickBooks

- Lengthy account descriptions are provided by QuickBooks when it establishes the Chart of Accounts. These descriptions are designed to help those with limited accounting. They will print on reports so removing them helps to streamline QuickBooks reports.

Click the **Report** button at the bottom of the Chart of Accounts, click **Account Listing**

Click the **Modify Report** button, click the **Header/Footer** button, change the report date to January 1, 2010, click **Date Prepared** and **Time Prepared** to remove from the heading, click **OK**

Click the **Print** button, select **Landscape** orientation, click **Fit report to 1 page wide**

When finished printing, close the Account Listing report and the Chart of Accounts

Your Name's Movies & More
Account Listing
January 1, 2010

Account	Type	Balance Total	Description	Tax Line
Checking	Bank	29,385.00		<Unassigned>
Accounts Receivable	Accounts Receivable	2,950.00		<Unassigned>
Inventory Asset	Other Current Asset	33,750.00		<Unassigned>
Office Supplies	Other Current Asset	350.00		<Unassigned>
Prepaid Insurance	Other Current Asset	1,200.00		<Unassigned>
Sales Supplies	Other Current Asset	500.00		<Unassigned>
Store Equipment	Fixed Asset	7,200.00		<Unassigned>
Store Equipment:Depreciation	Fixed Asset	-800.00		<Unassigned>
Store Equipment:Original Cost	Fixed Asset	8,000.00		<Unassigned>
Store Fixtures	Fixed Asset	13,500.00		<Unassigned>
Store Fixtures:Depreciation	Fixed Asset	-1,500.00		<Unassigned>
Store Fixtures:Original Cost	Fixed Asset	15,000.00		<Unassigned>
Accounts Payable	Accounts Payable	5,000.00		<Unassigned>
Payroll Liabilities	Other Current Liability	0.00		<Unassigned>
Sales Tax Payable	Other Current Liability	0.00		<Unassigned>
Store Equipment Loan	Long Term Liability	2,000.00		<Unassigned>
Store Fixtures Loan	Long Term Liability	2,500.00		<Unassigned>
Retained Earnings	Equity			<Unassigned>
Your Name, Capital	Equity	81,385.00		<Unassigned>
Your Name, Capital:Your Name, Investment	Equity	25,000.00		<Unassigned>
Your Name, Capital:Your Name, Withdrawals	Equity	0.00		<Unassigned>
Sales	Income			<Unassigned>
Sales:Merchandise	Income			Schedule C: Gross receipts or sales
Sales:Rental	Income			<Unassigned>
Sales:Sales Discounts	Income			Schedule C: Gross receipts or sales
Sales:Service	Income			<Unassigned>
Uncategorized Income	Income			<Unassigned>
Cost of Goods Sold	Cost of Goods Sold			<Unassigned>
Advertising and Promotion	Expense			Schedule C: Advertising
Automobile Expense	Expense			Schedule C: Car and truck expenses
Bank Service Charges	Expense			Schedule C: Other business expenses
Computer and Internet Expenses	Expense			Schedule C: Other business expenses
Depreciation Expense	Expense			<Unassigned>
Insurance Expense	Expense			Schedule C: Insurance, other than health
Interest Expense	Expense			Schedule C: Interest expense, other
Office Supplies Expense	Expense			Schedule C: Office expenses
Payroll Expenses	Expense			Schedule C: Wages paid
Professional Fees	Expense			Schedule C: Legal and professional fees
Rent Expense	Expense			Schedule C: Rent/lease other bus. prop.
Repairs and Maintenance	Expense			Schedule C: Repairs and maintenance
Sales Supplies Expense	Expense			<Unassigned>
Telephone Expense	Expense			Schedule C: Utilities
Uncategorized Expenses	Expense			<Unassigned>
Utilities	Expense			Schedule C: Utilities
Other Income	Other Income			<Unassigned>
Other Expenses	Other Expense			<Unassigned>

PREFERENCES

Many preferences used by QuickBooks Pro are selected during the EasyStep Interview. However, there may be some preferences you would like to select in addition to those marked during the interview. The Preferences section has tabs where you may indicate your preferences or company preferences. Some areas that may be customized include: Accounting, Bills, Checking, Desktop View, Finance Charge, General,

Integrated Applications, Items & Inventory, Jobs & Estimates, Multiple Currencies, Payroll & Employees, Reminders, Reports & Graphs, Sales & Customers, Sales Tax, Send Forms, Service Connection, Spelling, Tax: 1099, Time & Expenses. Not all the possible changes will be discussed in this chapter; however, some changes will be made.

MEMO

DATE: January 1, 2010

Open the Preferences screen and explore the choices available for each of the areas. When you get to the following preferences, make the changes indicated below:

<u>Checking Preferences</u>: My Preferences—Select Default Accounts to use should be Checking for Open Write Checks, Open Pay Bills, Open Pay Sales Tax, and Open Make Deposits; Company Preferences— Select Default Accounts to use should be Checking for Create Paychecks and Pay Payroll Liabilities

<u>Payroll & Employees</u>: Company Preferences—Display Employee List by Last Name

<u>Reports & Graphs</u>: My Preferences—Refresh reports automatically, Company Preferences—modify the report Format for the Header/Footer to remove the Date Prepared, Time Prepared, and Report Basis from reports

<u>Sales Tax</u>: Company Preferences—Most common sales tax is CA Sales Tax

---

▶ **DO**   Access Preferences from the Edit menu

In the following sections the Preferences are shown in the exact order listed on the Preferences screen. Click the icons for each category and explore the choices available on both the My Preferences tabs and the Company tabs. When you get to a Preference that needs to be changed, make the changes indicated in the textbox above.

ACCOUNTING PREFERENCES

On the Accounting Preferences screen the Company Preferences tab is accessed to select the use of account numbers. Selecting Use Account Numbers provides an area for each account to be given a number during editing. This screen instructs QuickBooks to automatically assign general journal entry numbers and to warn when posting a transaction to Retained Earnings. There are two check boxes for warning when transactions are 90 days within the past or 30 days within the future. The closing date for a period is entered after clicking the Set Date/Password button on this screen.

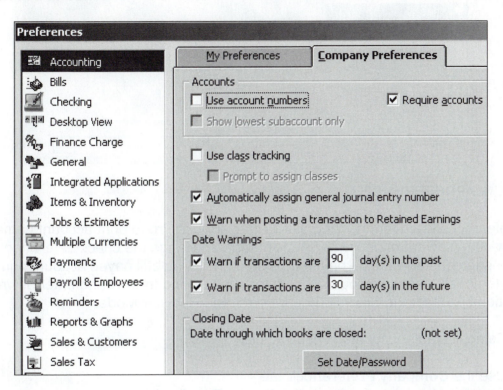

BILLS PREFERENCES

Bills Preferences has the selections on the Company Preferences tab for Entering Bills and Paying Bills. You may tell QuickBooks the number of days after the receipt of bills that they are due. You may also select to be warned about duplicate bill numbers from the same vendor. When paying bills, you may tell QuickBooks to use discounts and credits automatically.

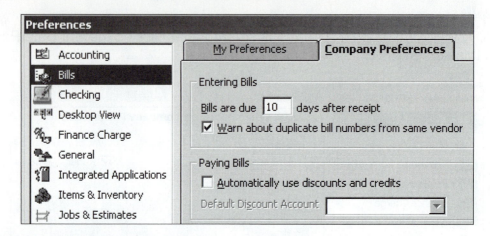

CHECKING PREFERENCES

The preferences listed for checking allows QuickBooks Pro to print account names on check vouchers, warn of duplicate check numbers, change the check date when a check is printed, start with the payee field on a check, autofill payee account number in check memo, set default accounts to use for checks, and to view and enter downloaded transactions in either the Side-by-Side Mode or the Register Mode.

DO Select Default Accounts to use Checking

Use the **Company Preferences** tab
Click the check box for **Open the Create Paychecks**,
Click **Checking** on the drop-down list for account
Repeat for **Pay Payroll Liabilities**

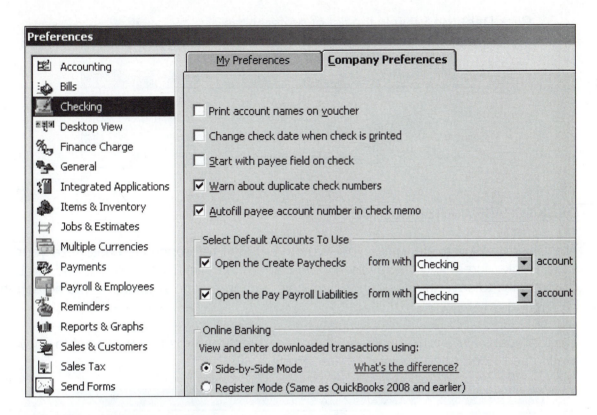

Click **My Preferences Tab**
Click the Check box for Open the Write Checks to select
Click the drop-down list arrow for Account
Click **Checking**
Repeat for Open the Pay Bills, Open the Pay Sales Tax, and Open the Make
    Deposits

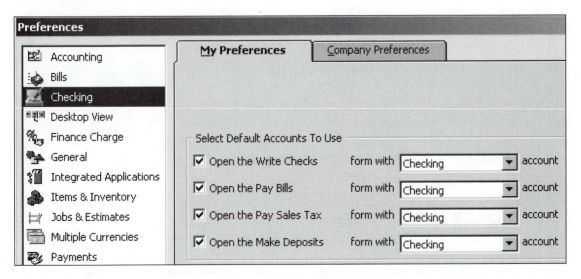

Click **Desktop View** in the list of preferences
If you get a dialog box to save changes to Checking preferences, click **Yes**

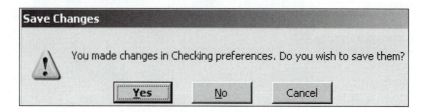

DESKTOP VIEW PREFERENCES

The Desktop View preference allows you to set My Preferences to customize your QuickBooks screens to display the Home Page, the QuickBooks Coach, and the Live Community; to save the desktop; select color schemes and sounds, and to detach the Help Window.

The Company Preferences tab allows you to select features that you want to show on the Home Page and to explore Related Preferences.

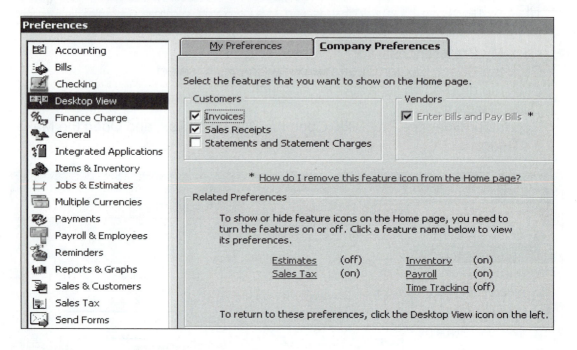

FINANCE CHARGE PREFERENCES

This preference allows you to tell QuickBooks Pro if you want to collect finance charges and to provide information about finance charges. The information you may provide includes the annual interest rate, the minimum finance charge, the grace period, the finance charge account, and whether to calculate finance charges from the due date or from the invoice/billed date.

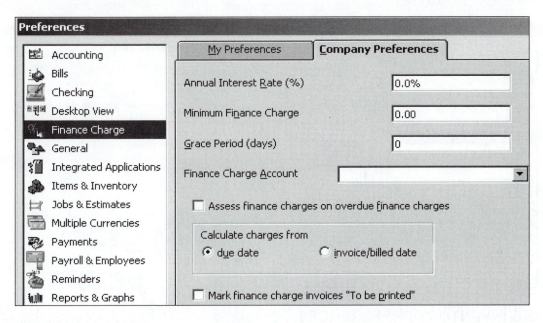

GENERAL PREFERENCES

General preferences use the Company Preferences tab to set the time format, to display the year as four digits. My Preferences tab is used to indicate decimal point placement, to set warning screens and beeps, to turn on messages, and to automatically recall the last transaction for a name.

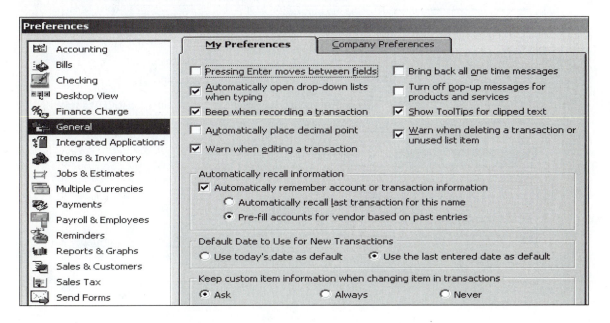

INTEGRATED APPLICATIONS PREFERENCES

Integrated preferences are used to manage all applications that interact with the current QuickBooks company file.

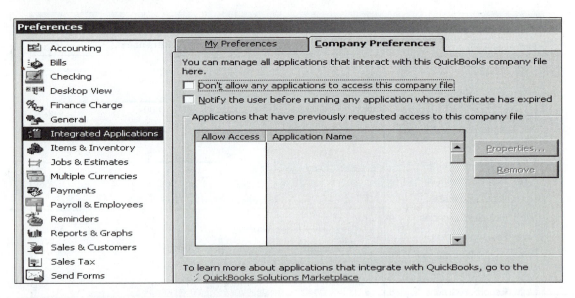

ITEMS & INVENTORY PREFERENCES

This section allows you to activate the inventory and purchase orders features of the program, have QuickBooks provide warnings if there is not enough inventory to sell, and to warn if there are duplicate purchase order numbers.

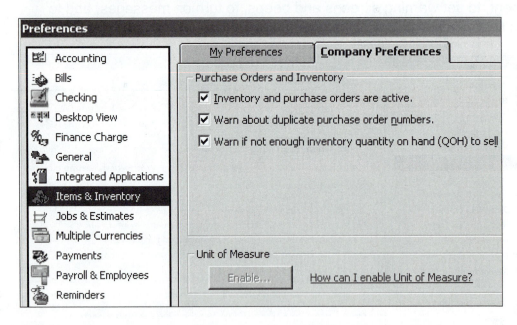

JOBS & ESTIMATES PREFERENCES

This preference allows you to indicate the status of jobs and to choose whether or not to use estimates.

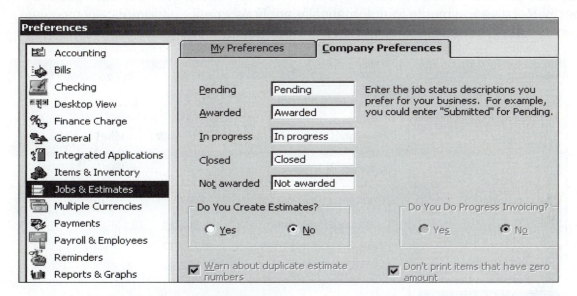

MULTIPLE CURRENCIES PREFERENCES

Using the Company Preferences tab, you may select to use more than one currency. You can assign a currency to customers, vendors, price levels, bank and credit card accounts as well as accounts receivable and accounts payable accounts. You must designate a home currency that will be used for income and expense accounts. Once you choose to use multiple currencies, you may not change the preference to discontinue the use of multiple currencies

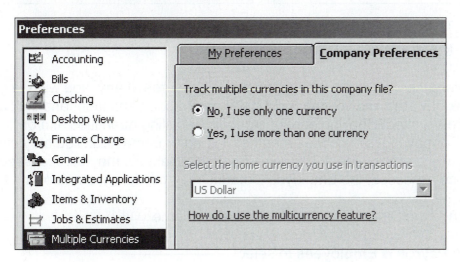

PAYMENTS PREFERENCES

On the Company Preferences tab of the Payments preference, you may specify Integrated Payment Processing with Intuit Payment Solutions that include credit card processing, paper check processing, and eCheck processing. In addition, you may specify Receive Payments to automatically apply payments, automatically calculate payments, and to use Undeposited Funds as a default deposit to account.

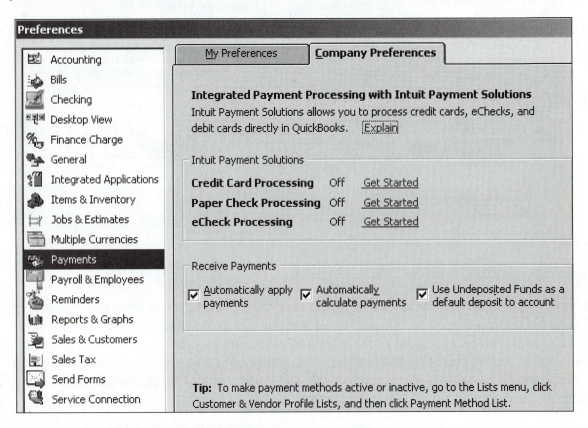

PAYROLL & EMPLOYEES PREFERENCES

Payroll preferences include selecting the payroll features, if any, you wish to use. Preferences pay stub and voucher printing, workers compensation, and sick and vacation are selected. Copying earnings details, recalling quantities and/or hours, and job costing for paycheck expenses may be marked or unmarked. You may choose the method by which employees are sorted. Employee Defaults may be accessed from this screen. Once accessed, the Employee Defaults may be changed and/or modified.

▷ **DO** Change the Display Employee List to Last Name

Click **Payroll & Employees** to select

Click the **Company Preferences** tab
Click **Last Name** in the section for Display Employee List by

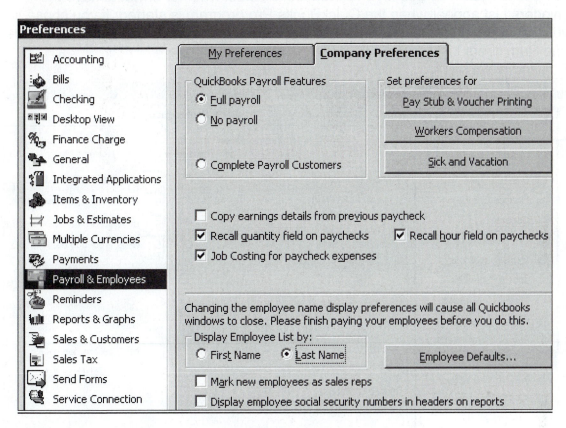

Click **Reminders** to go to the next Preference area
Click **Yes** on the Save Changes dialog box
Click **OK** on the Warning screen

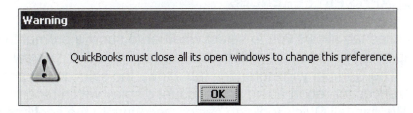

- Preferences should reopen automatically. If it does not, click the Edit menu, click Preferences, click Reminders

REMINDERS PREFERENCES

In this section you may use My Preferences to select whether or not to have the Reminders List appear when the QuickBooks Pro program is started. If you chose to have Reminders displayed, Company Preferences is used to select the items included on the Reminders List.

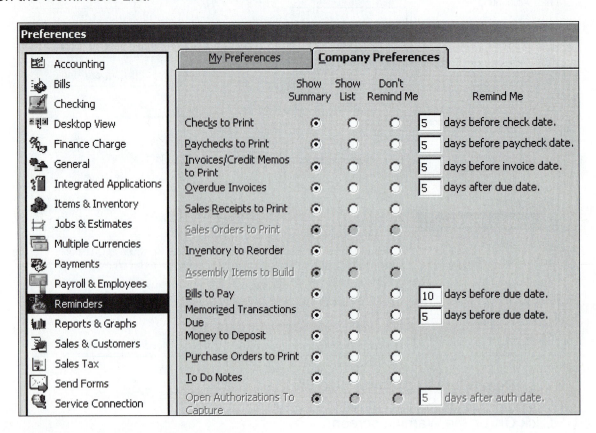

REPORTS & GRAPHS PREFERENCES

The My Preferences tab allows you to select whether to show a prompt to refresh reports and graphs or to refresh them automatically and whether to draw graphs in 2D or use patterns. The Company Preferences tab allows the selection of accrual or cash reporting. Preferences for report aging and account display within reports are selected in this section. We can tell QuickBooks to assign accounts to the sections of the Statement of Cash Flows. In addition, report formats may be customized using this screen.

▶ DO ▶ Change My Preferences to have the reports refresh automatically

> Click **My Preferences** tab
> Click **Refresh Automatically**

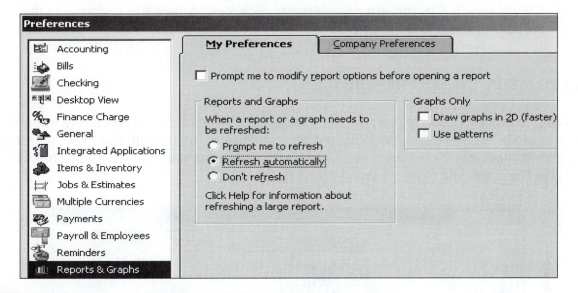

DO ▶ Modify the report format to remove the Date Prepared, Time Prepared, and Report Basis

Click **Company Preferences** tab
Click the **Format** button
On the Header/Footer tab, click **Date Prepared**, **Time Prepared**, and **Report Basis** to remove the check marks

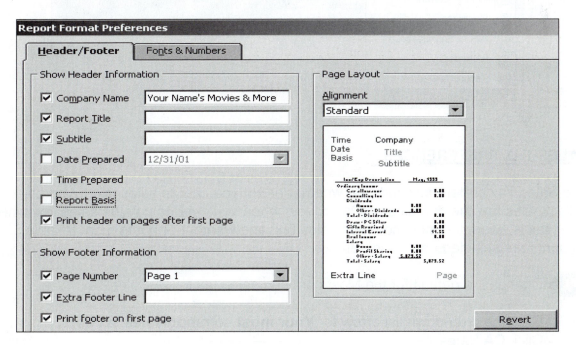

Click **OK**
Click **Sales & Customers** preferences, click **Yes** to save the changes to the
Reports & Graphs preferences

SALES & CUSTOMERS PREFERENCES

Shipping methods, markup percentages, usual FOB (free on board) preferences, and
the use of Price Levels may be indicated on this screen. In addition, the My Preferences
tab allows Available Time/Costs to Invoices to be selected and the Payment Toolbar on
Receive Payment and Sales Receipt forms to be shown.

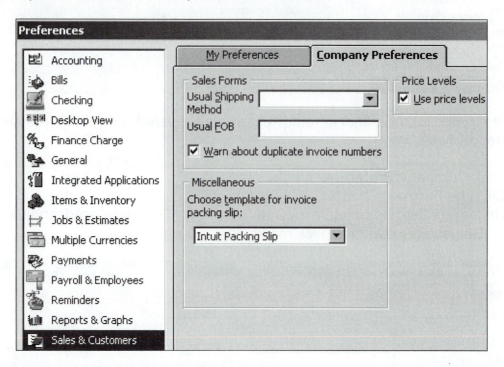

SALES TAX PREFERENCES

The Sales Tax preferences indicate whether or not you charge sales tax. If you do
collect sales tax, the default sales tax codes, when you need to pay the sales tax, when
sales tax is owed, the most common sales tax, and whether or not to mark taxable
amounts are selected on this screen.

DO ▶ Change the default for the Most common sales tax to CA Sales Tax

  Click the drop-down list arrow for **Your most common sales tax item**
  Click **CA Sales Tax**

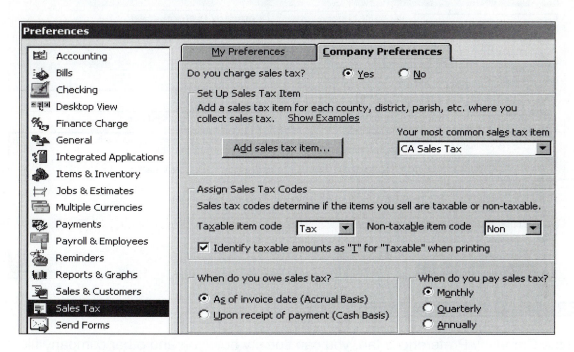

Click **Send Forms** preferences and click **Yes** to save the change

SEND FORMS PREFERENCES

Default text is provided and may be changed for invoices, estimates, statements, sales orders, sales receipts, credit memos, purchase orders and reports for business documents that are sent by e-mail. The My Preferences tab allows auto-check to determine if the customer's preferred send method is e-mail.

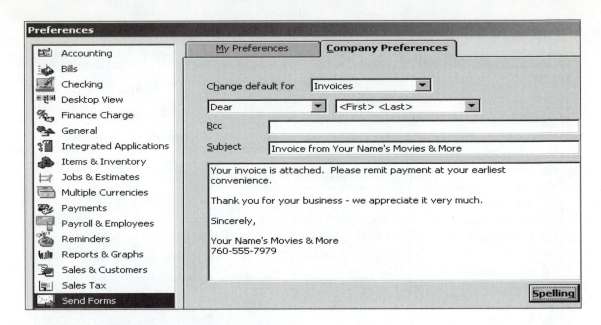

SERVICE CONNECTION PREFERENCES

On the Company Preferences tab, you can specify how you and other company file users log in to QuickBooks Business Services. You may select to automatically connect to QuickBooks Business Services network without passwords or require passwords before connecting. This preference is used to select whether or not Service updates are automatically downloaded from the Intuit server to your computer. The My Preferences tab allows settings for saving a file whenever Web Connect data is downloaded and leaving your browser open after Web Connect is done.

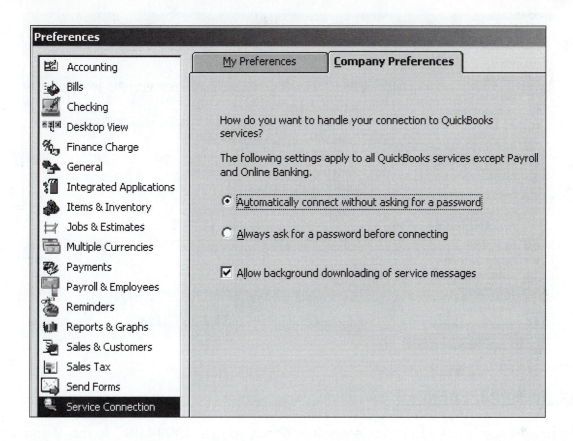

SPELLING PREFERENCES

You can check the spelling in the fields of most sales forms including invoices, estimates, sales receipts, credit memos, purchase orders, and lists. You can run Spell Checker automatically or change the preference and run the Spell Checker manually. There is also a selection for words to ignore.

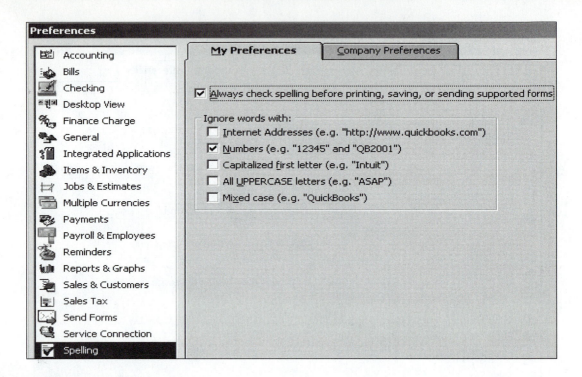

TAX: 1099 PREFERENCES

This preference is used to indicate whether or not you file 1099-MISC forms. If you do file 1099s, you are given categories; you may select accounts and thresholds for the categories on this screen.

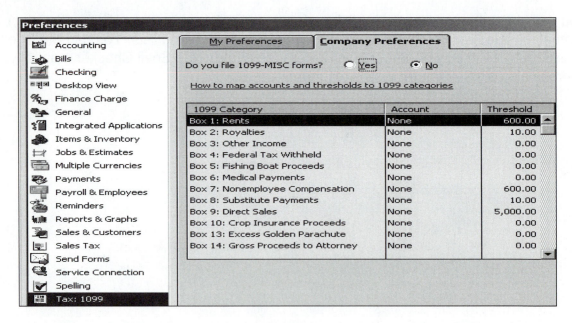

TIME & EXPENSES PREFERENCES

The Time Tracking preference is used to tell QuickBooks Pro to track time. Tracking time is useful if you bill by the hour.

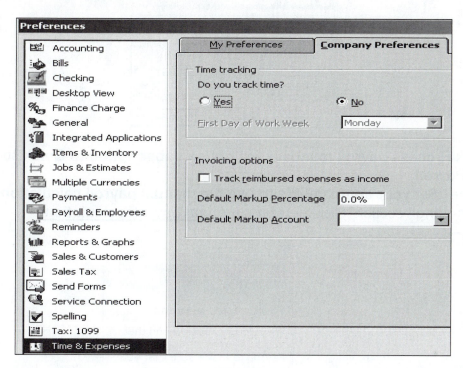

      To close the Preferences screen, click **OK**

PAYROLL

When you completed the tutorial in Chapter 8, you paid the employees who worked for the company. In order to use QuickBooks to process payroll, you need to complete the Payroll Set up Interview and add your employees.

SELECT A PAYROLL OPTION

Before entering any payroll transactions, QuickBooks Pro must be informed of the type of payroll service you are selecting. Once QuickBooks Pro knows what type of payroll process has been selected for the company, you will be able to create paychecks. As in you did in Chapter 8, you must go through the Help menu to designate the selection of the Manual payroll option.

▶ DO   Select a **Manual** payroll option

Press **F1** to access Help
Click the **Search** tab
Type **Manual Payroll** and click the **Start Search** button

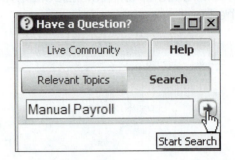

Click **Process payroll manually (without a subscription to QuickBooks Payroll)**
In the **"Set your company file to use the manual payroll calculations setting"** section, click the words <u>**manual payroll calculations**</u>

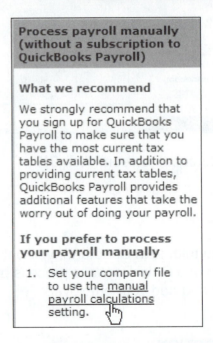

In the section **"Are you sure you want to set your company file to use manual calculations"**, click <u>**Set my company file to use manual calculations**</u>

> If you are sure you want to
> manually calculate your
> payroll taxes in QuickBooks,
> click here: <u>Set my company file to
> use manual calculations</u>

Once QuickBooks processes the selection, you will get a message

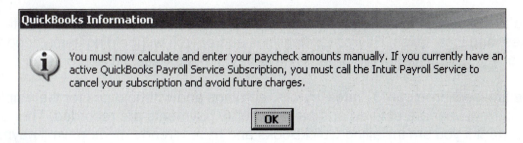

Click **OK**
Close Help

GENERAL NOTES ON PAYROLL SETUP

Before adding employees, you complete the payroll setup interview. QuickBooks is setup with Automatic Update turned on. Periodically, Intuit will send out program updates via the Internet that will be downloaded to your computer. It is important to note that sometimes information in the program changes. If your screens differ from the ones shown, do not be alarmed, you will enter the same information; but, perhaps, in a slightly different format or order.

You may find that some of your screens are different from the ones shown in the text. This is due to the fact that the computer date used when writing the text is January 1, 2010 and your computer will use the current date. If you see a different year on your screen, and you are not able to change it, just continue with the training and leave the date as it appears.

THE PAYROLL SETUP INTERVIEW

There are six sections in the Payroll Setup to guide you through the process of setting up the payroll in QuickBooks.

The first section is an introductory screen. The second section is the Company Setup for payroll. This section helps you identify and setup your methods of compensation, benefits your company offers, and additions and deductions your employees might have.

The third section leads you through setting up individual employees. When establishing the Employee Defaults, you will specify which payroll items apply to all or most of the employees of the company. Payroll items are used to identify and/or track the various amounts that affect a paycheck. There are items for salaries and wages, each kind of tax, each type of other deduction, commissions, and company-paid benefits.

The fourth section, Taxes, automatically sets up the payroll items for federal taxes, state taxes, and local taxes. Payroll tax liabilities and payroll withholding items need to be associated with a vendor in order to have payments processed appropriately.

The fifth section, Year-to-Date Payrolls, earnings and withholdings for the employees for the current year are entered and payroll liability payments are recorded. This is important if you are installing QuickBooks and have already made payroll payments during the calendar year.

The final section, Finishing Up, takes companies that subscribe to QuickBooks Payroll Services to the Payroll Center. Since we do not subscribe to a payroll service, we will go to the Employee Center or to the Home Page.

If at anytime you exit the payroll setup, be sure to click the Finish Later button. If you exit the payroll setup by any other method, you may lose all of the information you have entered. Sometimes, QuickBooks will retain the information and will re-enter it for you as you click through each of the sections in the Payroll Setup. Otherwise, you will need to re-enter all of your information.

BEGIN THE PAYROLL SETUP

▶ **DO** ▶ Click the **Employees** menu, click **Payroll Setup**

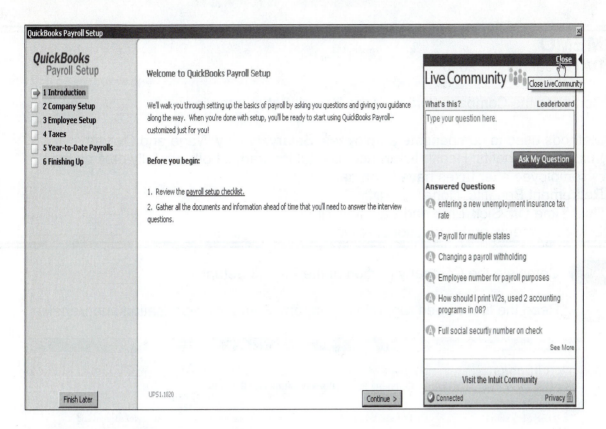

Read the Introduction screen
- If your screen shows Live Community, click <u>Close</u> on the Live Community screen.
- If you click <u>payroll setup checklist</u> you will go to an Adobe pdf file that contains information about all of the information you need to gather in order to setup your payroll.

Click **Continue**

COMPANY SECTION OF THE PAYROLL SETUP

In this section of the Payroll Setup, information about the methods of paying employees, deductions, and benefits is entered.

MEMO

DATE: January 1, 2010

Complete the Company portion of the Payroll Setup Interview:

Methods used to compensate employees: Salary, Hourly Wage and Overtime
Insurance Benefits: Health Insurance, Dental Insurance both are fully paid by the
    employee after taxes have been deducted
Retirement Benefits: None
Paid Time Off: Sick Time and Vacation Time
Other Payments and Deductions: None

> **DO** ▶ Complete the Company portion of the Payroll Setup

Read the first screen regarding Company Setup: Compensation and Benefits

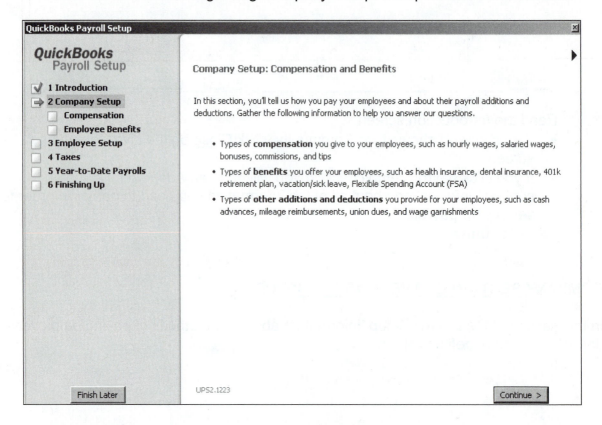

Click **Continue**
Click **Bonus, award, or one-time compensation** to unmark

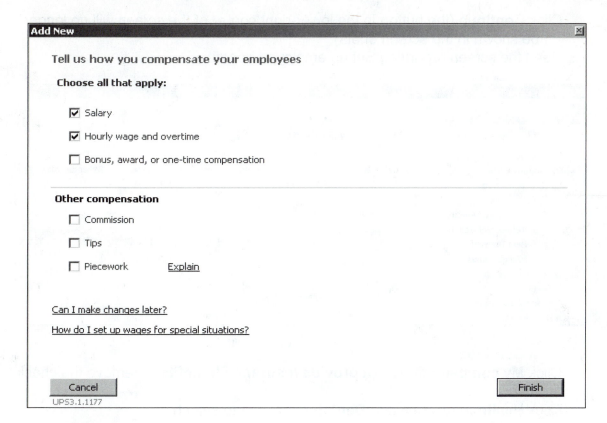

Click **Finish**

Review the Compensation List

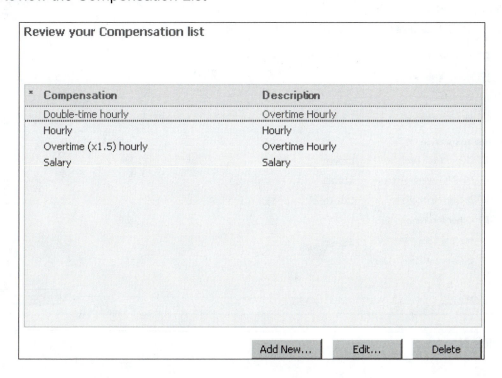

Click **Continue** (the button in the lower-right corner of the screen will no longer
　　be shown in the screen shots)
Read the screen regarding Set up employee benefits

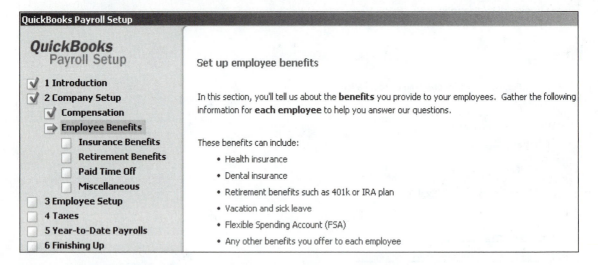

Click **Continue**
Click **My company does not provide insurance benefits** to remove the check
　　mark
Click **Health insurance** and **Dental insurance** to select

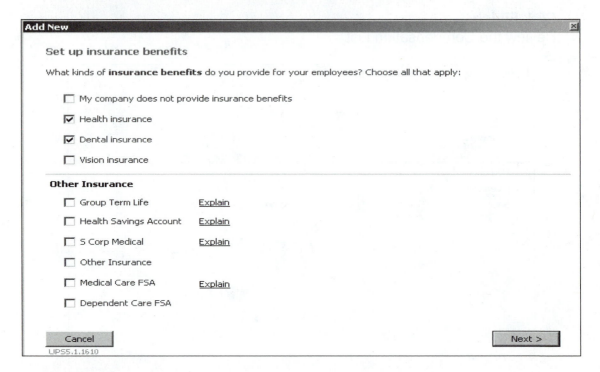

Click **Next**

On the Health Insurance screen, click **Employee pays for all of it**
Payment is deducted after taxes should appear and be selected

```
┌─────────────────────────────────────────────────────────────────────────┐
│ Add New                                                                    │
├─────────────────────────────────────────────────────────────────────────┤
│                                                                            │
│    Tell us about health insurance                                          │
│                                                                            │
│    How is Health Insurance paid?                                           │
│                                                                            │
│       ○  Company pays for all of it                                        │
│       ○  Both the employee and company pay portions                        │
│       ◉  Employee pays for all of it                                       │
│                                                                            │
│    Is the employee portion deducted before or after taxes are calculated?  │
│                                                                            │
│       ◉  Payment is deducted after taxes            Help me decide which one│
│                                                     to choose.             │
│       ○  Payment is deducted BEFORE taxes (section 125)                    │
│                                                                            │
└─────────────────────────────────────────────────────────────────────────┘
```

Click **Next**
Click the drop-down list arrow, click **Health Insurance, Inc.** to select the Vendor
that receives payment for health insurance premiums,

```
┌─────────────────────────────────────────────────────────────────────────┐
│ Add New                                                                    │
├─────────────────────────────────────────────────────────────────────────┤
│                                                                            │
│    Set up the payment schedule for health insurance                        │
│                                                                            │
│                                                                            │
│   Payee (Vendor)    Health Insurance, Inc.                    ▼   Explain   │
│                                                                            │
│   Account #         [                                    ]                  │
│                     (The number the payee uses to identify you. Example: 99-99999X)│
│                                                                            │
│   Payment frequency  ○ Weekly, on    Monday        ▼  for the previous week's liabilities│
│                                                                            │
│                      ○ Monthly, on the  1  ▼  day of the month for the previous month's liabilities│
│                                                                            │
│                      ○ Quarterly, on the  1  ▼  day of the month for the previous quarter's liabilities│
│                                                                            │
│                      ○ Annually, on   January   ▼  1  ▼  for the previous year's liabilities│
│                                                                            │
│                      ◉ I don't need a regular payment schedule for this item│
│                                                                            │
└─────────────────────────────────────────────────────────────────────────┘
```

Click **Next**
On The Dental Insurance screen, click **Employee pays for all of it** and **Payment
is deducted after taxes**

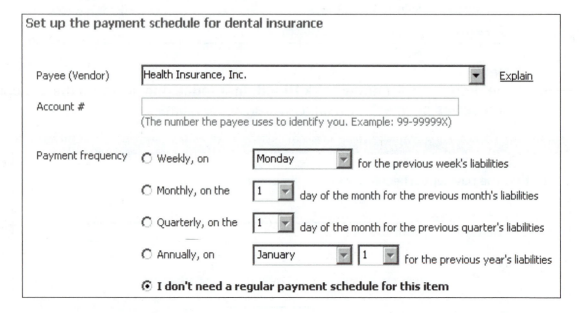

Tell us about dental insurance

How is Dental Insurance paid?

○ Company pays for all of it

○ Both the employee and company pay portions

◉ Employee pays for all of it

Is the employee portion deducted before or after taxes are calculated?

◉ **Payment is deducted after taxes**

○ Payment is deducted BEFORE taxes (section 125)

Help me decide which one to choose.

Click **Next**

The Payee for Dental Insurance is **Health Insurance, Inc.**

Set up the payment schedule for dental insurance

Payee (Vendor)	Health Insurance, Inc. ▾ Explain
Account #	[ ]
	(The number the payee uses to identify you. Example: 99-99999X)

Payment frequency

○ Weekly, on   Monday ▾ for the previous week's liabilities

○ Monthly, on the   1 ▾ day of the month for the previous month's liabilities

○ Quarterly, on the   1 ▾ day of the month for the previous quarter's liabilities

○ Annually, on   January ▾ 1 ▾ for the previous year's liabilities

◉ **I don't need a regular payment schedule for this item**

Click **Finish**

Review your Insurance Benefits list

Review your Insurance Benefits list

* Insurance Item	Description
Dental Insurance (taxable)	After-Tax Employee-Paid Dental
Health Insurance (taxable)	After-Tax Employee-Paid Health

Click **Continue**

The next screen allows you to select retirement benefits.
We do not provide any retirement benefits for our employees

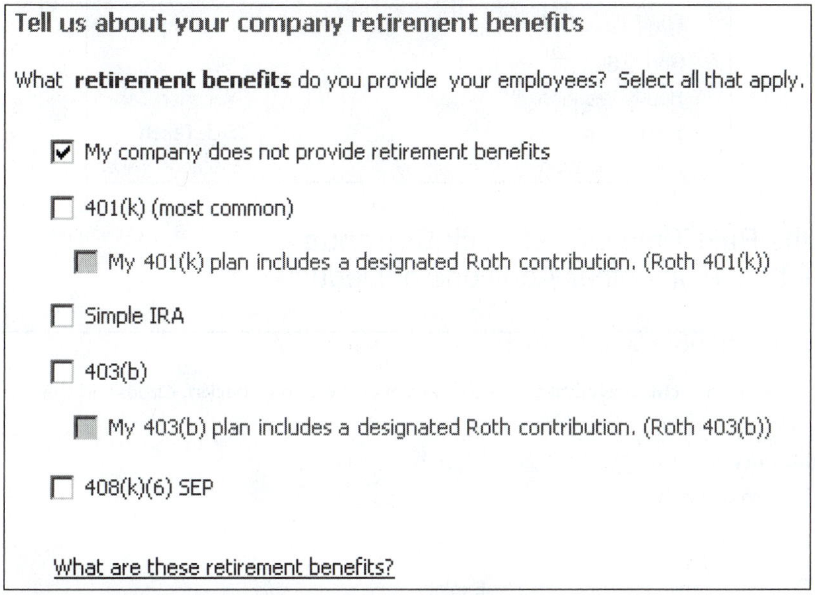

Tell us about your company retirement benefits

What **retirement benefits** do you provide your employees? Select all that apply.

☑ My company does not provide retirement benefits

☐ 401(k) (most common)

☐ My 401(k) plan includes a designated Roth contribution. (Roth 401(k))

☐ Simple IRA

☐ 403(b)

☐ My 403(b) plan includes a designated Roth contribution. (Roth 403(b))

☐ 408(k)(6) SEP

What are these retirement benefits?

Click **Finish**, and then click **Continue**
For Paid Time Off, we do provide paid time off for Sick Leave and Vacation
Leave, click **Paid sick time off** and **Paid vacation time off** to select

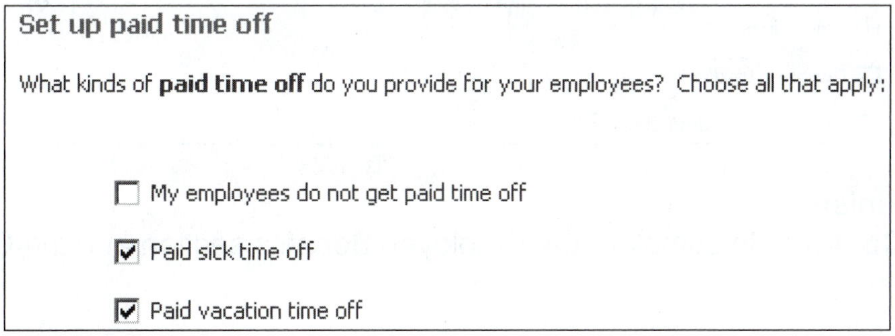

Set up paid time off

What kinds of **paid time off** do you provide for your employees? Choose all that apply:

☐ My employees do not get paid time off

☑ Paid sick time off

☑ Paid vacation time off

Click **Finish**

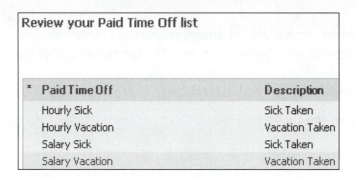

Review the Paid Time Off list, click **Continue**
We do not have any other Additions or Deductions

Click **Finish**
Click **Continue** to complete the Employee Benefits section and the Company Setup

EMPLOYEE SECTION OF THE PAYROLL SETUP

During the Employee section of the Payroll Setup, individual employees are added and information about their payroll items will be identified.

- When you print the Summary for each employee, check the beginning date for accruing sick and vacation time. It should show the Hire date; however, if it does not, change it by editing the employee(s) in the Employee Center after the Payroll Setup Interview is complete.

CHAPTER 9: CREATING A COMPANY IN QUICKBOOKS

EMPLOYEES January 1, 2010 Alice Brooks and Greg Hanson		
Name	Alice Brooks	Greg Hanson
Status	Active	Active
Street Address	1077 Columbia Street	2985 A Street
City, State Zip	San Diego, CA 92101	San Diego, CA 92101
Employee Tax Type	Regular	Regular
Social Security No.	100-55-2525	100-55-9661
Hire Date	04/23/1996	06/30/2004
Birth Date	12/28/1949	04/23/1977
Gender	Female	Male
Pay Period	Monthly	Monthly
Salary	$26,000 per year	$15.50 per hour $31.00 Double-time hourly $23.25 Overtime (x1.5) hourly
Dental Insurance	$10 per month, annual maximum $120	$10 per month, annual maximum $120
Health Insurance	$50 per month, annual maximum $600	$25 per month, annual maximum $300
Sick Time Earns	40:00 per year	40:00 per year
Unused Hours	Have an accrual limit	Have an accrual limit
Maximum Hours	120:00	120:00
Earns	Time off currently	Time off currently
Hours Available as of 01/01/10	20:00	50:00
Vacation Time Earns	40:00 per year	40:00 per year
Unused Hours	Have an accrual limit	Have an accrual limit
Maximum Hours	120:00	120:00
Earns	Time off currently	Time off currently
Hours Available as of 01/01/10	20:00	40:00
Direct Deposit	No	No
State Subject to Withholding	CA	CA
State Subject to Unemployment Tax	CA	CA
Live or Work in Another	No	No

EMPLOYEES
January 1, 2010
Alice Brooks and Greg Hanson

State in 2010		
Federal Filing Status	Single	Married
Allowances	0	2
Subject to	Medicare Social Security Federal Unemployment	Medicare Social Security Federal Unemployment
State Filing Status	Single	Married (2 incomes)
Regular Withholding Allowances	0	2
Subject to	CA-Unemployment CA-Employment Training Tax CA-Disability	CA-Unemployment CA-Employment Training Tax CA-Disability
Local Taxes	No	No
Wage Plan Code	S	S

DO Complete the Employee portion of the Payroll Setup using the chart above

Read the screen about the Employee Setup

QuickBooks
Payroll Setup

☑ 1 Introduction
☑ 2 Company Setup
➡ 3 Employee Setup
  ☐ Employee List
☐ 4 Taxes
☐ 5 Year-to-Date Payrolls
☐ 6 Finishing Up

Set up your employees

In this section, you'll tell us about your employees. Gather the following information to help you answer our questions.

- Employee's completed **W-4 form**
- **Pay rate** (hourly, salary, commission, etc.)
- **Paycheck deductions** (401(k), insurance, garnishments, etc.)
- **Sick/vacation hours** balance (if applicable)
- **Direct deposit** information (use a voided check, not deposit slip, of the employee's bank account)
- **Hire date**
- Termination date (if applicable)

Click **Continue**
Enter the name, address, and phone for Alice Brooks using the information provided in the chart

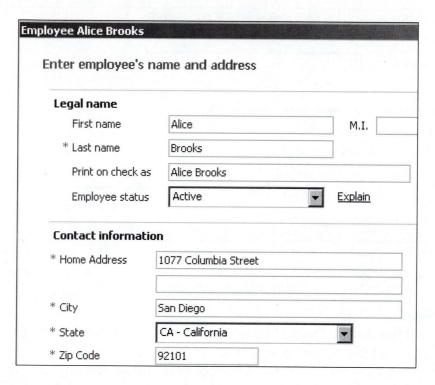

Click **Next**

Enter Alice's hiring information as given in the memo

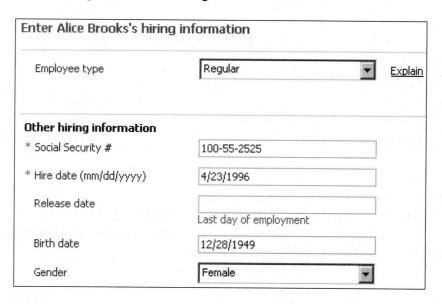

Click **Next**

Alice is paid monthly and has a salary of $26,000 per year, complete the screen for compensation

Tell us about wages and compensation for Alice Brooks

Pay frequency | Monthly ▾ |

What regular compensation does Alice Brooks receive?

○ Employee is paid hourly
● **Employee is paid on salary**
○ Employee does not have any base compensation

Salary amount | 26,000.00 | Per | Year ▾ |

Regular wages	Amount	Description
☐ Double-time hourly		$ per hour
☐ Overtime (x1.5) hourly		$ per hour

Click **Next**

Click the **Use** box for **Dental Insurance**; enter **10** as the amount per paycheck and **120** as the annual maximum

Click the **Use** box for **Health Insurance**; enter **50** as the amount per paycheck and **600** as the annual maximum

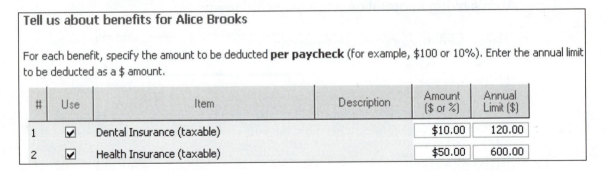

Tell us about benefits for Alice Brooks

For each benefit, specify the amount to be deducted **per paycheck** (for example, $100 or 10%). Enter the annual limit to be deducted as a $ amount.

#	Use	Item	Description	Amount [$ or %]	Annual Limit [$]
1	☑	Dental Insurance (taxable)		$10.00	120.00
2	☑	Health Insurance (taxable)		$50.00	600.00

Click **Next**

Enter the information about Alice's sick time

- In the Current balances section of the screen you may not see the dates of 1/1/2010. Use whatever date is automatically inserted by QuickBooks. The date shown may be the date of the computer.

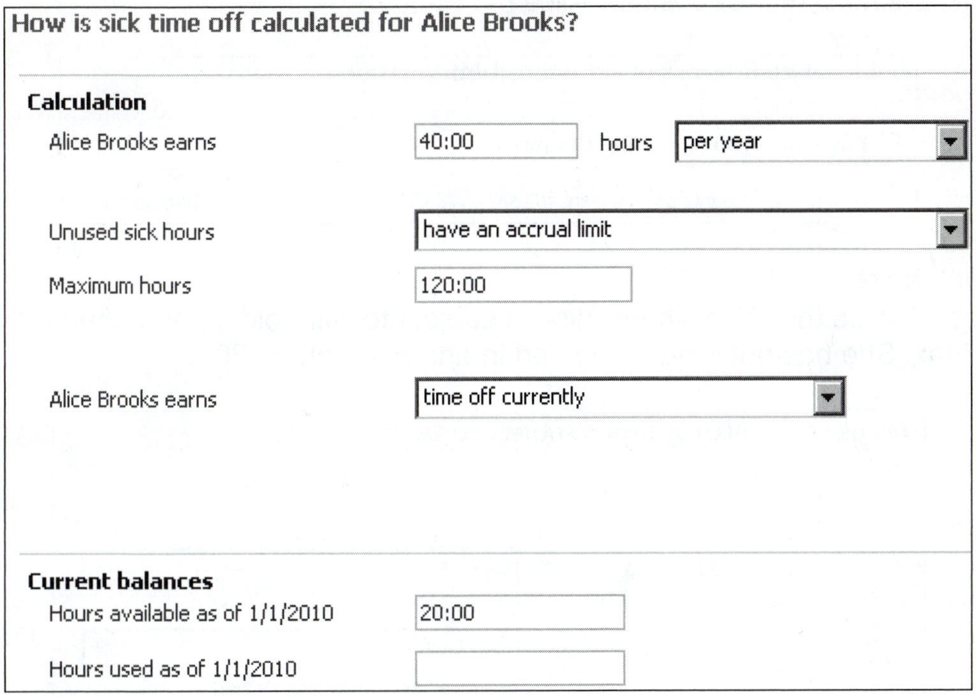

How is sick time off calculated for Alice Brooks?

Calculation

Alice Brooks earns · 40:00 · hours · per year ▾

Unused sick hours · have an accrual limit ▾

Maximum hours · 120:00

Alice Brooks earns · time off currently ▾

Current balances

Hours available as of 1/1/2010 · 20:00

Hours used as of 1/1/2010 · [ ]

Click **Next**

Enter the information regarding Alice's vacation time

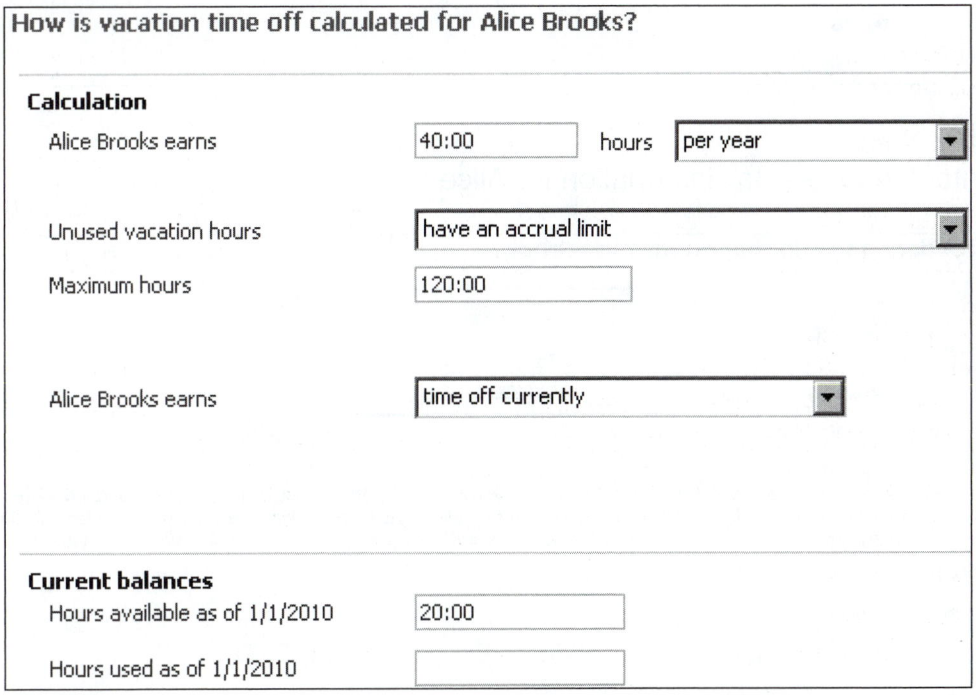

How is vacation time off calculated for Alice Brooks?

Calculation

Alice Brooks earns · 40:00 · hours · per year ▾

Unused vacation hours · have an accrual limit ▾

Maximum hours · 120:00

Alice Brooks earns · time off currently ▾

Current balances

Hours available as of 1/1/2010 · 20:00

Hours used as of 1/1/2010 · [ ]

Click **Next**

There is no Direct Deposit for Alice

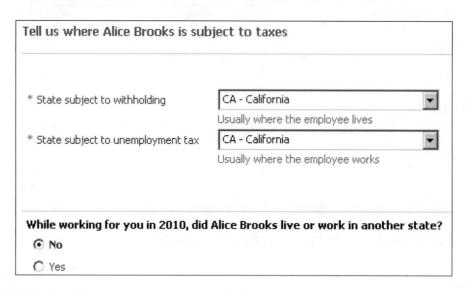

Click **Next**

Enter **CA** as the state where Alice is subject to withholding and unemployment tax. She has not lived or worked in another state in 2010

Click **Next**

Enter the federal tax information for Alice

Click **Next**

Enter the state tax information for Alice

Enter state tax information for Alice Brooks

CA - California state taxes

Filing Status   Single ▾   Explain

Regular Withholding Allowances   0   Explain

Estimated Deductions   Explain

Extra Withholding

Most employees' wages are **subject to** the following withholdings. Incorrectly changing the selections below will cause your taxes to be calculated incorrectly, resulting in penalties; be sure to check with your tax agency or accountant if you are unsure.

☑ Subject to CA - Unemployment

☑ Subject to CA - Employment Training Tax

☑ Subject to CA - Disability

Is this employee subject to any special local taxes not shown above?

◉ No

○ Yes   Some of the taxes for employees who changed locations aren't listed here. Why?

Click **Next**

The California Employment Development Department agency requires employers who file electronically to select a Wage Plan Code. Since you do participate in the state unemployment and disability insurance programs, select **S** as the code.

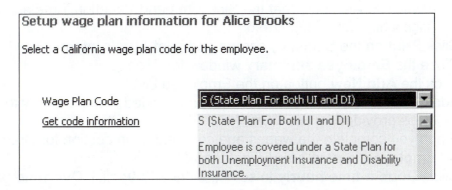

Setup wage plan information for Alice Brooks

Select a California wage plan code for this employee.

Wage Plan Code   S (State Plan For Both UI and DI) ▾

Get code information   S (State Plan For Both UI and DI)

Employee is covered under a State Plan for both Unemployment Insurance and Disability Insurance.

Click **Finish**

Click the **Summary** button to view the information entered for Alice Brooks

Alice Brooks

Summary

Contact information	
Print as	Alice Brooks
Active	Active
Email	(none)
Address	1077 Columbia Street San Diego, CA 92101
Phone	(none)

Hiring information	
State Work/Live	CA/CA
Social Security #	100-55-2525
Hire Date	4/23/1996
Release Date	(none)
Birth Date	12/28/1949
Gender	Female
Employee Type	Regular

Direct Deposit	
Primary account	(no direct deposit)
Secondary account	(no direct deposit)

Paid time off	
Sick Time	effective 4/23/1996 3:20 hrs per paycheck 120:00 max 20:00 avail, 0:00 used
Vacation	effective 4/23/1996 3:20 hrs per paycheck 120:00 max 20:00 avail, 0:00 used

Compensation	
Pay frequency	Monthly
Salary	$26,000.00

Taxes	
Federal Withholding	Allowances:0 Filing Status:Single Special Rate:Does not apply
Federal Unemployment	Subject to
Medicare Company	Subject to
Medicare Employee	Subject to
Social Security Company	Subject to
Social Security Employee	Subject to
CA - Disability	Subject to
CA - Unemployment	Subject to
CA - Withholding	Allowances:0 Filing Status:Single
CA - Employment Training Tax	Subject to

Other paycheck items	
Dental Insurance (taxable)	$10.00
Health Insurance (taxable)	$50.00

- Notice that the Sick Time and Vacation time are shown as hours per paycheck. Also note that the Sick Time and Vacation Time are effective as of Alice's hire date 04/23/1996.

Click **Print** on the Summary screen and print Alice's information

Close the **Employee summary** window for Alice

Click the **Add New** button on the Employee List

Add Greg Hanson using the information provided in the chart by following the steps provided for Alice Brooks

When you complete the wages and compensation section for Greg, click **Employee is paid hourly**, enter **15.50**

Click, **Double-time hourly** to select, enter **31.00**; click **Overtime (x1.5) hourly** to select, enter the amount **23.25**

Tell us about wages and compensation for Greg Hanson

Pay frequency   Monthly ▼

What regular compensation does Greg Hanson receive?
⦿ **Employee is paid hourly**
○ Employee is paid on salary
○ Employee does not have any base compensation

Hourly wage   15.50

	Regular wages	Amount	Description
☑	Double-time hourly	$31.00	$ per hour
☑	Overtime (x1.5) hourly	$23.25	$ per hour

Complete the employee setup for Greg Hanson
Review the Employee List

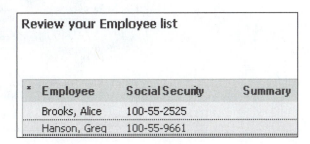

Review your Employee list

*	Employee	Social Security	Summary
	Brooks, Alice	100-55-2525	
	Hanson, Greg	100-55-9661	

With Greg Hanson highlighted in the employee list, click the **Summary** button

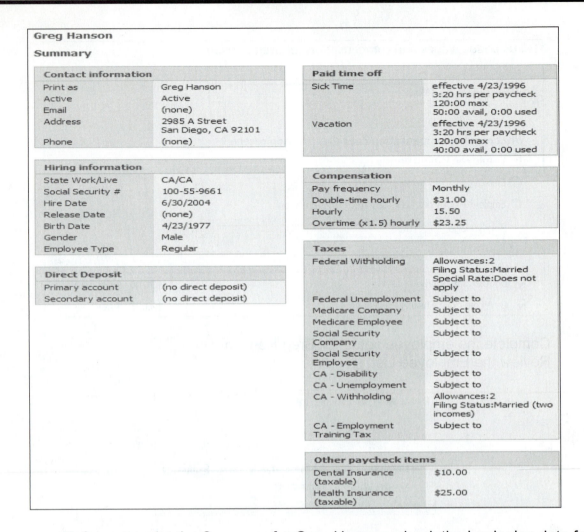

- Before you print the Summary for Greg Hanson, check the beginning date for accruing sick and vacation time. It should show his Hire date; however, in this example it shows the effective date of 04/23/1996, which is Alice's hire date. Since it does not show the correct effective date, we will change it by editing the employee(s) in the Employee Center after the Payroll Setup Interview is complete.

Print Greg's Summary, close the Summary

Click **Continue**

TAXES SECTION OF THE PAYROLL SETUP

The Taxes section of the Payroll setup allows you to identify federal, state, and local tax payments and agencies.

▶ **DO** Complete the Taxes section of the Payroll setup

Read the screen for "Set up your payroll taxes"

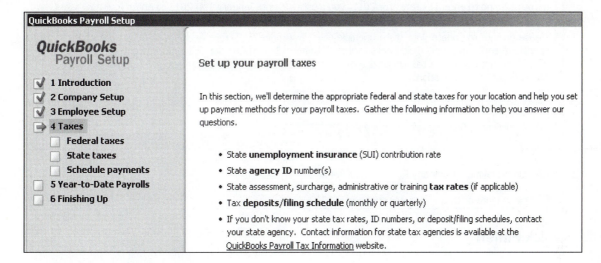

Click **Continue**
Review the list of taxes

Click **Continue**
Enter the California-Unemployment Company Rate of **3.4%**
- The rate for CA-Disability Employee Rate should be shown as 1.1% and the rate for CA-Employment Training Tax Company Rate should be shown as 0.1%, if not change as necessary

CA - EDD payments

If you're trying to enter tax rates for 2011, you must wait until January 1st, 2011 to enter your new rates.

Please be sure to update your state unemployment insurance (SUI) rate each year. Because each rate is specific to each employer, QuickBooks cannot automatically update your SUI rate. To get your SUI rate, please contact your state tax agency; visit the QuickBooks Payroll Tax Information website for your state agency's contact information.

* CA - Disability Employee Rate   `1.1%` ▼

* CA - Employment Training Tax Company Ra `0.1%` ▼

Tax Year 2010

* CA - Unemployment Company Rate: `3.4%`   Explain

☐ One or more of these tax rates changed in 2010

Click **Finish**

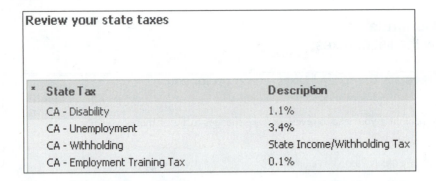

Review your state taxes

* State Tax	Description
CA - Disability	1.1%
CA - Unemployment	3.4%
CA - Withholding	State Income/Withholding Tax
CA - Employment Training Tax	0.1%

Review the state taxes, click **Continue**
Read the screen regarding Review your Scheduled Tax Payments list

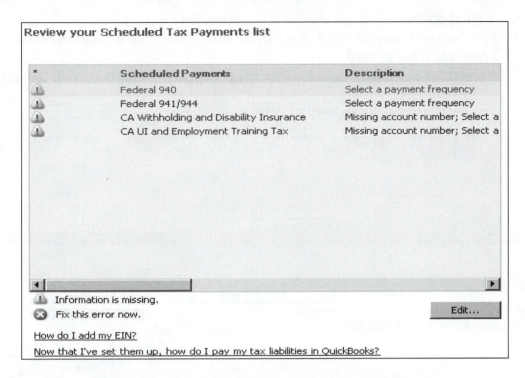

- Notice that each item is marked with Information is missing.
The Schedule Payments window for Federal 940 should appear
- If not, click Edit.
- For Federal Form 940, the Payee should be United States Treasury, the deposit frequency is Quarterly. Enter these if necessary.

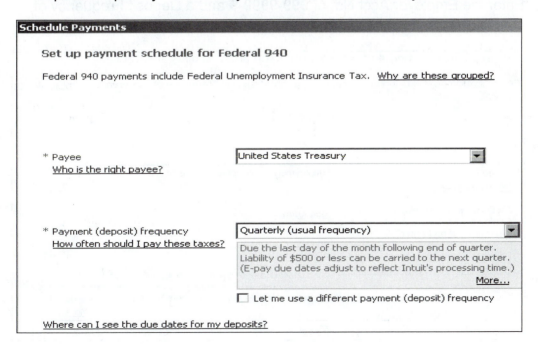

Click **Next** on the Schedule Payments window for Federal 940

- For Federal Form 941/944, the Payee should be United States Treasury, enter this if necessary.

Click the drop-down list arrow for Payment (deposit) frequency, click **Quarterly**

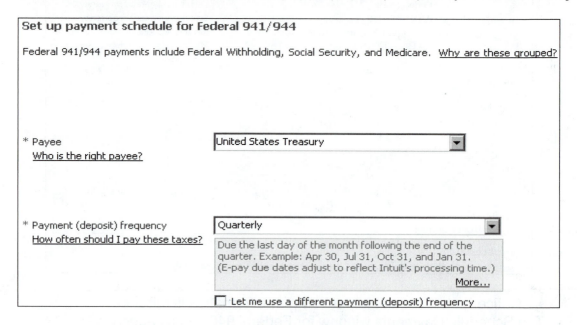

Click **Next**

For CA UI and Employment Training Tax, click the drop-down list arrow for Payee, click **Employment Development Department**

Enter the Employer Acct No. of **999-9999-9** and a Deposit Frequency of **Quarterly.**

Click **Next**
Complete the information for CA Withholding and Disability Insurance
Payee is **Employment Development Department**
 Employer Acct No. is **999-9999-9**
Deposit Frequency is **Quarterly**

Set up payment schedule for CA UI and Employment Training Tax

CA UI payments include Unemployment Insurance and Employment Training Tax. Why are these grouped?

* Payee Who is the right payee?	Employment Development Department ▾
* CA Employment Development Dept Employer Acct No. What number do I enter?	999-9999-9
* Payment (deposit) frequency How often should I pay these taxes?	Quarterly (usual frequency) ▾

Due the last day of the month following the end of the
quarter. Example: Apr 30, Jul 31, Oct 31, and Jan 31.
(E-pay due dates adjust to reflect Intuit's processing time.)

More...

☐ Let me use a different payment (deposit) frequency

Click **Finish**, click **Continue**

YEAR-TO-DATE PAYROLLS SECTION OF THE PAYROLL SETUP

The Year-to-Date Payrolls is completed to enter year-to-date amounts for employees and to identify liability payments you made. Since there have been no payroll payments processed or paid for 2010, there is no payroll history to enter.

▶ DO Read the screen, click **Continue**

- Depending on the date of your computer, your screens for Payroll History may not be an exact match for the following screen shots. Your screen may show all four quarters listed under payroll history. This will not affect your setup. (Some examples of screens that you might see, appear below.)

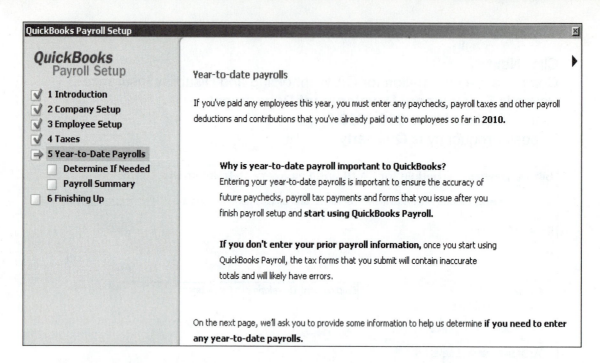

Click **Continue**

On the screen to determine whether you need to add payroll history, click **No** when asked if your company issued paychecks this year

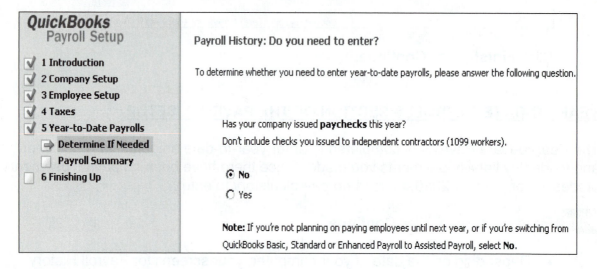

Click **Continue**

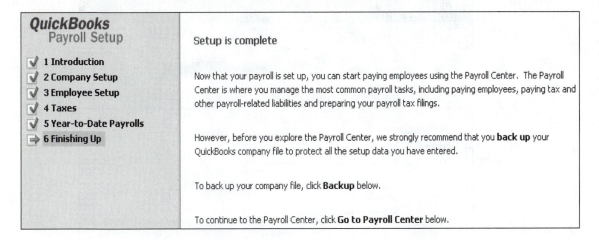

Difference due to computer dates not being January 1, 2010:

- If your screen shows from one to four quarters for processing, you may get the following. If it does, click **OK**

Click the **Go to Payroll Center** button

- You will go to the Employee Center.

ENTER EMPLOYEE TELEPHONE NUMBERS

During the Payroll Setup Interview, telephone numbers for employees were not entered. Since you go directly to the Employee Center, edit the employees information.

DO Enter the telephone numbers for the employees

Open the Employee Center
Double-click **Alice Brooks**
Click the **Address and Contact** tab for Personal Info
Enter **760-555-1232** for Phone

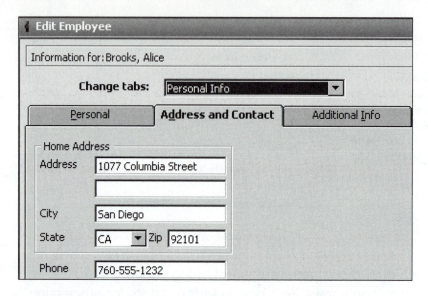

Repeat to enter Greg Hanson's phone number **760-555-9874**
Continue to edit Greg Hanson's employee information

CORRECT EFFECTIVE DATE OF SICK AND VACATION TIME

> **DO** If the Effective Date of sick and vacation time for Greg Hanson is shown as
> anything other than his hire date of 06/30/2004, change his effective date of sick
> and vacation time

Click the drop-down list arrow for **Change Tabs**
Click **Payroll and Compensation Info**
Click the **Sick/Vacation** button
Change **Begin accruing sick time on** to **06/30/2004**
Change **Begin accruing vacation time on** to **06/30/2004**

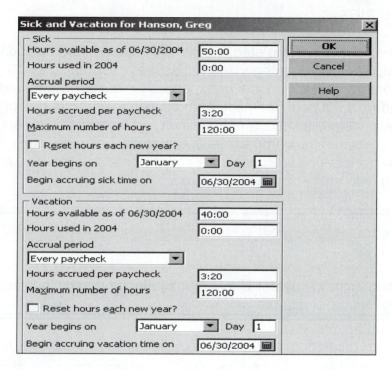

Click **OK**
Close the Employee Center

PRINT THE PAYROLL ITEM LISTING

To verify the payroll items used and the information regarding the employees entered, it is wise to print a listing of the Payroll Items and the Employees Contact List. There are also reports available to print information regarding the employees withholding and paid time off.

▶ **DO** Print the **Payroll Item Listing** for January 1, 2010

Click **Report Center** at the top of the Home Page
Click **List** as the report type
Click **Payroll Item Listing**
Click **No** on the Payroll Services screen
Adjust the column widths and print the report in landscape orientation
Close the report and the Report Center

ADJUSTING ENTRIES

When the company setup is completed, all existing balances are placed into the Uncategorized Income and Uncategorized Expenses accounts so that the amounts listed will not be interpreted as income or expenses for the current period. This adjustment transfers the amount of income and expenses recorded prior to the current period into the owner's capital account. In actual practice this adjustment would be made at the completion of the company setup. In traditional accounting, Income is credited to the owner's capital account and expenses are debited. The same process is used in recording a Journal entry in QuickBooks.

MEMO

DATE: January 1, 2010

Make the adjusting entry to transfer Uncategorized Income and Uncategorized Expenses to Your Name, Capital.

DO Transfer the Uncategorized Income and Expenses to the owner's capital account

Click **Chart of Accounts** in the Company Section of the Home Page
Double-click on the account **Uncategorized Income**, enter the to and from dates as **01/01/10**, tab to generate the report, note the amount of Uncategorized Income **$2,950.00**

Your Name's Movies & More
Account QuickReport
January 1, 2010

Type	Date	Num	Name	Memo	Split	Amount
Uncategorized Income						
Invoice	01/01/2010		Goode, Jeffrey	Opening balance	Accounts Receivable	500.00 ◀
Invoice	01/01/2010		Morse, Ellen	Opening balance	Accounts Receivable	800.00
Invoice	01/01/2010		Day Care Center	Opening balance	Accounts Receivable	1,500.00
Invoice	01/01/2010		Winters, Ben	Opening balance	Accounts Receivable	150.00
Total Uncategorized Income						2,950.00
TOTAL						**2,950.00**

Close the QuickReport
Repeat the steps given to determine the balance of the Uncategorized Expenses account

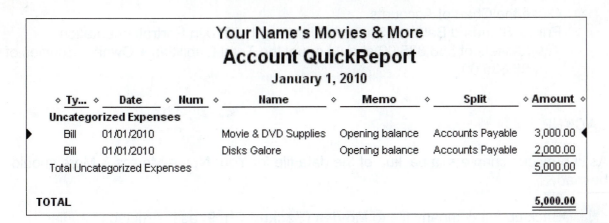

Your Name's Movies & More
Account QuickReport
January 1, 2010

◇ Ty... ◇	Date ◇	Num ◇	Name ◇	Memo ◇	Split ◇	Amount ◇
Uncategorized Expenses						
Bill	01/01/2010		Movie & DVD Supplies	Opening balance	Accounts Payable	3,000.00
Bill	01/01/2010		Disks Galore	Opening balance	Accounts Payable	2,000.00
Total Uncategorized Expenses						5,000.00
TOTAL						**5,000.00**

Close the QuickReport

Click the **Activities** button at the bottom of the Chart of Accounts, click **Make General Journal Entries**

Enter the date **01/01/10**

Tab to or click **Account**, click the drop-down list arrow, click **Uncategorized Income**, tab to or click **Debit** enter **2950**, tab to or click **Account**, click the drop-down list arrow, click **Your Name, Capital**

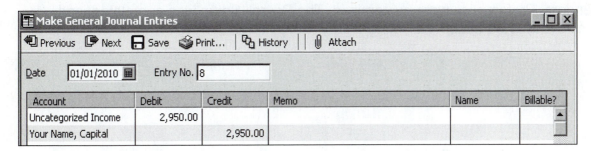

Account	Debit	Credit	Memo	Name	Billable?
Uncategorized Income	2,950.00				
Your Name, Capital		2,950.00			

Date: 01/01/2010   Entry No. 8

Click **Save & New**

Enter the adjustment to transfer the amount of **Uncategorized Expenses** to **Your Name, Capital**

- Remember, you will debit the Capital account and credit the Uncategorized Expenses account.

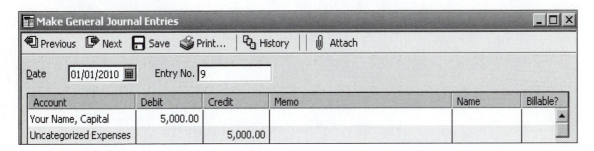

Account	Debit	Credit	Memo	Name	Billable?
Your Name, Capital	5,000.00				
Uncategorized Expenses		5,000.00			

Date: 01/01/2010   Entry No. 9

Click **Save & Close**

Close the Chart of Accounts
Print a Standard Balance Sheet for January 1, 2010 in Portrait orientation
Total Assets of $88,835.00 should equal the Total Liabilities + Owners Equities of
    $88,835.00

BACKUP

As in previous chapters, a backup of the data file for Your Name Movies & More should
be made.

DO Back up the company file to **Movies (Backup Ch. 9)** as instructed in earlier
    chapters and make a duplicate disk as instructed by your professor.

SUMMARY

In this chapter a company was created using the EasyStep Interview provided by
QuickBooks Pro. Once the interview was complete, the Chart of Accounts/General
Ledger was customized. Detailed information was given for items, customers and
vendors. Preferences were customized. The Payroll Setup was completed, and
employees were added. Adjusting entries were made.

END-OF-CHAPTER QUESTIONS

TRUE/FALSE

ANSWER THE FOLLOWING QUESTIONS IN THE SPACE PROVIDED BEFORE THE QUESTION NUMBER.

_____ 1. You must use the EasyStep Interview to add customers and vendors.

_____ 2. The EasyStep Interview is used to add employees and year-to-date earnings.

_____ 3. If you setup a company using the EasyStep Interview, you will enter the company name, address, and Tax ID number as part of the Interview.

_____ 4. Permanently removing the date prepared and time prepared from a balance sheet heading is done the first time you complete a balance sheet.

_____ 5. The start date is the date you select to give QuickBooks Pro the financial information for your company.

_____ 6. The EasyStep Interview allows you to have QuickBooks generate a chart of accounts.

_____ 7. When the EasyStep Interview is complete, the Uncategorized Expenses account contains a balance that reflects the total amount of all receivables accounts.

_____ 8. When using the EasyStep Interview to set up income and expenses, you must type in the name of every income and expense account you use.

_____ 9. The Item List is automatically generated in the Easy Step Interview.

_____ 10. Customer names, addresses, credit terms, and credit limits are entered after the EasyStep Interview.

MULTIPLE CHOICE

WRITE THE LETTER OF THE CORRECT ANSWER IN THE SPACE PROVIDED
BEFORE THE QUESTION NUMBER.

_____ 1. Send Forms preferences contain default text for business documents sent
            by ___.
            A. Fax
            B. E-mail
            C. Fed-Ex
            D. All of the above

_____ 2. Adjusting entries that must be made after the company setup are ___.
            A. Close Uncategorized Income to Capital
            B. Close Uncategorized Expenses to Capital
            C. Both of the above
            D. None of the above

_____ 3. When creating the employee list, you use the ___.
            A. Payroll Setup Interview
            B. Employee File
            C. Employee Roster
            D. Payroll Menu

_____ 4. The EasyStep Interview is accessed on the ___.
            A. File menu
            B. QuickBooks Company Preferences screen
            C. Activities menu
            D. all of the above

_____ 5. In order to create paychecks manually, you must go through the __ to
            designate this choice.
            A. Payroll menu
            B. Help menu
            C. EasyStep Interview
            D. Company Configuration

_____ 6. The Company File has a _____ extension.
            A. .qbb
            B. .qbi
            C. .qbp
            D. .qbw

_____ 7. When a(n) ___ account is created, you must provide an opening balance.
     A. Income
     B. Expense
     C. Asset
     D. Posting

_____ 8. Select to display employee names by last name on the ___.
     A. Payroll & Employees Preferences
     B. Employee List
     C. Employee Center
     D. none of the above

_____ 9. Employee deductions for medical and dental insurance may be created ___.
     A. during the EasyStep Interview
     B. during the Payroll Setup Interview
     C. by clicking the Reports button at the bottom of the employee list
     D. on the Employee Menu

_____ 10. Sales tax is listed on the ___..
     A. Vendor List
     B. Company List
     C. Banking List
     D. Item List

FILL-IN

IN THE SPACE PROVIDED, WRITE THE ANSWER THAT MOST APPROPRIATELY COMPLETES THE SENTENCE.

1. The asset account used for Inventory sales items is _____.

2. In the Chart of Accounts, only _____ accounts have opening balances.

3. Accounts that are listed individually but are grouped together under a main account are called _____.

4. _____ Preferences warns you of duplicate check numbers

5. The _____ section of the Payroll Setup Interview allows information for earnings, withholding, and payroll liabilities to be entered for the year-to-date.

SHORT ESSAY

List the six sections in the Payroll Setup and describe the purpose of each section.

_____

_____

_____

_____

NAME_____

TRANSMITTAL

► CHAPTER 9: YOUR NAME MOVIES & MORE

Attach the following documents and reports:

Item Listing
Customer:Job List
Vendor List
Account Listing
Alice Brooks Employee Summary
Greg Hanson Employee Summary
Payroll Item Listing
Balance Sheet, January 1, 2010

END-OF-CHAPTER PROBLEM

YOUR NAME COFFEE CORNER

Your Name Coffee Corner is a fictitious company that sells coffee and pastries. You also provide catering service for meetings and lunches. The company is located in San Francisco, California, and is a sole proprietorship owned by you. You are involved in all aspects of the business. There is one full-time employee, Barbara Olsen, who is paid a salary. She manages the store, is responsible for the all the employees, and keeps the books. There is one full-time hourly employee, Cheryl Almeda, who works in the shop and provides the catering service.

CREATE A NEW COMPANY

▶ Use the following information to complete the EasyStep Interview for Your Name Coffee Corner.
  o **Your Name Coffee Corner** (*Use your actual name*) is the Company Name and the Legal Name
  o Federal Tax ID 45-6221346
  o Address: 550 Powell Street, San Francisco, CA 94102
  o Phone: 415-555-4646; Fax: 415-555-6464
  o E-mail: YourNameCoffeeCorner@info.com (*Use your actual name*)
  o Web: www.YourNameCoffeeCorner.com (*Use your actual name*)
  o Type of business: Retail shop or online commerce
  o The company is a Sole Proprietorship
  o The Fiscal Year starts in January
  o Do not use passwords
  o File Name: Your Name Coffee Corner.qbw
  o You sell both products and services.
  o Record each sale individually
  o You do not sell online and are not interested in doing so
  o You do charge sales tax
  o Do not use estimates, statements, or track time
  o Do use sales receipts and invoices (do not use progress invoicing)
  o Do track bills and print checks
  o Inventory: Yes
  o Do accept credit cards and debit cards,
  o Employees: Yes, W-2 Employees
  o Do not track multiple currencies
  o Use QuickBooks to set up the chart of Accounts (Accept all the accounts provided by QuickBooks. They will be edited later.)

- o The date to start tracking finances is: 01/01/2010
- o Bank account name: Checking; account number 123-654-98755; opened before 01/01/2010; last bank statement 12/31/2009; ending balance $35,871
- o Accept the income and expense accounts created by QuickBooks
- o After the Easy-Step Interview is complete, go to Desktop Preferences and turn off the QuickBooks Coach

COMPANY INFORMATION

▶ Verify the company information. Make sure the Federal Employer Identification number is 45-6221346, First Month in Tax and Fiscal Year: January

CHART OF ACCOUNTS

After the EasyStep Interview has been completed, you have created a partial Chart of Accounts. The Chart of Accounts must be customized to reflect the actual accounts used by Your Name Coffee Corner. After the balance sheet accounts and balances have been entered, you will set up your item list, customer list, and vendor list. Some accounts and their balances will be created automatically by QuickBooks. These include Accounts Receivable, Accounts Payable, and Cost of Goods Sold.

▶ Customize the Chart of Accounts provided by QuickBooks.
- o Delete: Accumulated Depreciation, Furniture and Equipment, Security Deposits, Owners Draw, Owners Equity, Uniforms, and Ask My Accountant
- o Make Inactive: Merchant Account Fees, Janitorial Expense, and Meals and Entertainment
- o Edit Equity Account: Change the name of Opening Balance Equity to **Your Name, Capital** and delete the description.
- o Add Equity Accounts: **Your Name, Investment**; Subaccount of Your Name, Capital; Opening Balance $35,000 as of 01/01/10.
  Your Name, Withdrawals; Subaccount of Your Name, Capital; Opening Balance, $0.00 as of 01/01/10
- o Add Income Accounts: Add **Sales**; add **Coffee Sales** a subaccount of Sales, and add **Catering Sales** a subaccount of Sales
- o Add Other Income Account: **Other Income**
- o Add Expense Accounts: **Store Supplies Expense**
- o Add Other Expense Account: **Other Expenses**
- o Edit Income Accounts: Rename Merchandise Sales to **Pastry Sales** make it a subaccount of Sales, make **Sales Discounts** a subaccount of Sales
- o Edit Expense Accounts: Rename Office Supplies to **Office Supplies Expense**

▶ Set up the following Balance Sheet accounts and balances. The Opening Balance date is **01/01/2010**.

CHART OF ACCOUNTS

Account Type	Account Name	Sub-Account of	Opening Balance
Other Current Asset	Prepaid Insurance		$1,200.00
Other Current Asset	Office Supplies		$950.00
Other Current Asset	Store Supplies		$1,800.00
Fixed Asset	Store Fixtures		
Fixed Asset	Original Cost	Store Fixtures	$18,000
Fixed Asset	Depreciation	Store Fixtures	$-1,800
Long-Term Liability	Store Fixtures Loan		$2,000.00

▶ Close the Chart of Accounts

ITEMS LIST

▶ Add the service item

SERVICE ITEM

Type	Service
Item Name	Catering
Description	Catering
Rate	$50 per hour
Tax Code	Non-taxable
Account	Catering Sales

▶ Add the inventory items

INVENTORY ITEMS		
Type	Inventory Part	Inventory Part
Item Name	Coffee	Pastry
Purchase Description	Coffee	Pastry
Cost	0.00	0.00
COGS Account	Cost of Goods Sold	Cost of Goods Sold
Preferred Vendor		
Sales Description	Coffee	Pastry
Sales Price	0.00	0.00
Tax Code	Tax	Tax
Income Account	Coffee Sales	Pastry Sales
Asset Account	Inventory Asset	Inventory Asset
Reorder Point	100	100
On-Hand	1,500	1,750
Total Value	12,000	1,750
AS Of	01/01/10	01/01/10

▶ Delete the following sales items: Consignment Item, and Non-Inventory Item

COMPLETE SALES TAX INFORMATION

▶ Edit the State Sales Tax item. The name and description should be **CA Sales Tax**
The rate is 7.25% and is paid to the State Board of Equalization, 7800 State Street,
Sacramento, CA 94267
▶ Print the Item List in Landscape orientation. Modify the Header so the Date Prepared
and Time Prepared are not shown and the report date prints as January 1, 2010.

CUSTOMER LIST

▶ Use the following information to add customers. Remember to use Jenkins, Sally,
Inc. as the customer name and use Sally Jenkins, Inc. in the Bill To address.

CUSTOMER LIST		
Customer Name	Jenkins, Sally, Inc.	Training, Inc.
Opening Balance	1,500.00	5,245.00
As Of	01/01/2010	01/01/2010
Company Name	Sally Jenkins, Inc.	Training, Inc.
Address	785 Mason Street	490 Harvard Street
City, State Zip	San Francisco, CA 94102	San Francisco, CA 94102
Phone	415-555-1248	415-555-8762
Terms	Net 30	Net 30
Tax Code	Tax	Tax
Tax Item	CA Sales Tax	CA Sales Tax
Credit Limit	2,000.00	8,000.00

▶ Print the Customer:Job List in Portrait orientation. (Since you are printing from the Customer Center, you will have the date and time prepared as the header. Your date and time may not be the same as the one shown in the answer key.)

VENDOR LIST

▶ Use the following Vendor List as you add individual vendors

VENDOR LIST		
Vendor Name	Coffee Royale	Pastries Divine
Opening Balance	1,000.00	500.00
As Of	01/01/2010	01/01/2010
Address	195 N. Market Street	701 7th Street
City, State Zip	San Francisco, CA 94103	San Francisco, CA 94104
Contact Person	Ron Richards	Katie Collins
Phone	415-555-3614	415-555-8712
Fax	415-555-4163	415-555-2178
Terms	2% 10, Net 30	2% 10, Net 30
Credit Limit	3,000.00	2,500.00

▶ Use the following information to add vendors who receive tax and withholding payments. There are no credit terms.

VENDOR LIST		
Vendor and Company Name	Employment Development Department	Union Square Bank	Insurance Organization of California
Address	10327 Washington Street	205 Hill Street	20951 Oakmont Avenue
City, State Zip	San Francisco, CA 94107	San Francisco, CA 94104	San Francisco, CA 94103
Phone	415-555-5248	415-555-9781	415-555-2347
Fax	415-555-8425	415-555-1879	415-555-7432

▶ Print the Vendor List in Portrait orientation. (Since you are printing from the Vendor Center, you will have the date and time prepared as the header. Your date and time may not be the same as the one shown in the answer key.)

CHART OF ACCOUNTS

Now that the item lists, customers, and vendors have been created and the Chart of Accounts has been customized, your Chart of Accounts should match the following:

Name	⚡	Type	Balance Total	Attach
◆ Checking		Bank	35,871.00	
◆ Accounts Receivable		Accounts Receivable	6,745.00	
◆ Inventory Asset		Other Current Asset	13,750.00	
◆ Office Supplies		Other Current Asset	950.00	
◆ Prepaid Insurance		Other Current Asset	1,200.00	
◆ Store Supplies		Other Current Asset	1,800.00	
◆ Store Fixtures		Fixed Asset	16,200.00	
◆ Depreciation		Fixed Asset	-1,800.00	
◆ Original Cost		Fixed Asset	18,000.00	
◆ Accounts Payable		Accounts Payable	1,500.00	
◆ Payroll Liabilities		Other Current Liability	0.00	
◆ Sales Tax Payable		Other Current Liability	0.00	
◆ Store Fixtures Loan		Long Term Liability	2,000.00	
◆ Your Name, Capital		Equity	67,771.00	
◆ Your Name, Investment		Equity	35,000.00	
◆ Your Name, Withdrawals		Equity	0.00	
◆ Sales		Income		
◆ Catering Sales		Income		
◆ Coffee Sales		Income		
◆ Pastry Sales		Income		
◆ Sales Discounts		Income		
◆ Uncategorized Income		Income		
◆ Cost of Goods Sold		Cost of Goods Sold		
◆ Advertising and Promotion		Expense		
◆ Automobile Expense		Expense		
◆ Bank Service Charges		Expense		
◆ Computer and Internet Expenses		Expense		
◆ Depreciation Expense		Expense		
◆ Insurance Expense		Expense		
◆ Interest Expense		Expense		
◆ Office Supplies Expense		Expense		
◆ Payroll Expenses		Expense		
◆ Professional Fees		Expense		
◆ Rent Expense		Expense		
◆ Repairs and Maintenance		Expense		
◆ Store Supplies Expense		Expense		
◆ Telephone Expense		Expense		
◆ Uncategorized Expenses		Expense		
◆ Utilities		Expense		
◆ Other Income		Other Income		
◆ Other Expenses		Other Expense		

Account ▾   Activities ▾   Reports ▾   Attach   ☐ Include inactive

► Edit each account and delete all account descriptions provided by QuickBooks.
► Print an Account Listing in Landscape orientation. Use the Report Center to print a List report for Account Listing. Remove the Date and Time Prepared from the Header and change the Report Date to January 1, 2010

CUSTOMIZE PREFERENCES

► Make the following changes to Preferences.
  o Checking Preferences: Company Preferences—Select Default Accounts for Create Paychecks and Pay Payroll Liabilities to Checking;
  o Checking Preferences: My Preferences—Select Default Accounts for Open the Write Checks, Open the Pay Bills, Open the Pay Sales Tax, and Open the Make Deposits to Checking
  o Payroll & Employees: Company Preferences—Display Employee List by Last Name
  o Reports & Graphs: My Preferences—Refresh reports automatically
  o Reports & Graphs: Company Preferences—modify the report Format for the Header/Footer to remove the Date Prepared, Time Prepared, and Report Basis from reports
  o Sales Tax: Company Preferences—Most common sales tax is CA Sales Tax

PAYROLL SETUP

► Prior to completing the Payroll Setup Interview, select a **Manual** payroll option
► Begin the Payroll Setup Interview

PAYROLL SETUP INTERVIEW

► Complete the **Company** portion of the Payroll Setup Interview.
  o Payroll List Items for Wages, Tips, and Taxable Fringe Benefits: Salary, Hourly Wage, and Overtime (Keep all overtime items provided by QuickBooks. If any other items appear on the list, delete them.)
  o Insurance Benefits: Health Insurance, Dental Insurance (both are fully paid by the employee after taxes have been deducted) (The vendor for Health and Dental insurance is Insurance Organization of California. You do not need a payment schedule.
  o Retirement Benefits: None
  o Paid Time Off: Sick Time and Vacation Time
  o Other Payments and Deductions: None

▶ Use the following information to complete the **Employee** portion of the Payroll Setup Interview. Print a Summary Report for each employee

EMPLOYEES January 1, 2010 Barbara Olsen and Cheryl Almeda		
Name	Barbara Olsen	Cheryl Almeda
Status	Active	Active
Street Address	9077 Harvard Avenue	1808 17th Street
City, State Zip	San Francisco, CA 94101	San Francisco, CA 94103
Employee Tax Type	Regular	Regular
Social Security No.	100-55-5201	100-55-9107
Hire Date	02/19/2001	06/30/2007
Birth Date	09/29/1975	07/17/1980
Gender	Female	Female
Pay Period	Monthly	Monthly
Salary	$21,000 per year	$9.50 per hour $19.00 Double-time $14.25 Overtime (x1.5)
Dental Insurance	$10 per month, annual maximum $120	$10 per month, annual maximum $120
Health Insurance	$35 per month, annual maximum $420	$25 per month, annual maximum $300
Sick Time Earns	40:00 per year	40:00 per year
Unused Hours	Have an accrual limit	Have an accrual limit
Maximum Hours	120:00	120:00
Earns	Time off currently	Time off currently
Hours Available as of 01/01/10	30:00	20:00
Vacation Time Earns	40:00 per year	40:00 per year
Unused Hours	Have an accrual limit	Have an accrual limit
Maximum Hours	120:00	120:00
Earns	Time off currently	Time off currently
Hours Available as of 01/01/10	40:00	20:00

EMPLOYEES January 1, 2010 Barbara Olsen and Cheryl Almeda		
Direct Deposit	No	No
State Subject to Withholding	CA	CA
State Subject to Unemployment Tax	CA	CA
Live or Work in Another State in 2010	No	No
Federal Filing Status	Single	Married
Allowances	0	2
Subject to	Medicare Social Security Federal Unemployment	Medicare Social Security Federal Unemployment
State Filing Status	Single	Married (2 incomes)
Regular Withholding Allowances	0	2
Subject to	CA-Unemployment CA-Employment Training Tax CA-Disability	CA-Unemployment CA-Employment Training Tax CA-Disability
Local Taxes	No	No
Wage Plan Code	S	S

► Print the Summary for each employee.
► Complete the **Taxes** section of the Payroll Setup Interview.
  o State Payroll Tax Rates— CA-Disability Employee Rate: 1.1%, CA-Employment Training Tax Company Rate: 0.1%; California-Unemployment Company Rate: 3.4%;
  o Federal Payroll Taxes— Schedules 940 and 941/944: Payee: United States Treasury, Frequency: Quarterly
  o State Payroll Taxes—Payee: Employee Development Department; California Withholding, SDI, Unemployment, and Employee Training Tax: California Employment Development Department, Account Number 999-9999-9, Quarterly
► Complete the **Year-to-Date Payrolls** section of the Payroll Setup Interview. No payroll has been paid this year
► After completing the Payroll Setup, print the Payroll Item Listing in Landscape orientation using the Report menu or Report Center

MAKE ADJUSTMENTS, PRINT THE BALANCE SHEET, AND PREPARE BACKUP

► Enter the telephone numbers for the employees:
  o Cheryl Almeda: 415-555-7364
  o Barbara Olsen: 415-555-7801
► Change the effective date for sick and vacation time for Cheryl Almeda to 06/30/2007.
► Record the adjusting entry to transfer Uncategorized Income and Uncategorized Expenses to Your Name, Capital
► Print the Balance Sheet for January 1, 2010 in Portrait orientation
► Backup your company file to **Your Name Coffee Corner (Backup Ch. 9)**

NAME_____

TRANSMITTAL

CHAPTER 9: YOUR NAME COFFEE CORNER

Attach the following documents and reports:

Item Listing
Customer: Job List
Vendor List
Account Listing
Barbara Olsen Employee Summary
Cheryl Almeda Employee Summary
Payroll Item Listing
Balance Sheet, January 1, 2010

COMPREHENSIVE PRACTICE SET: YOUR NAME BOOK STORE

The following is a comprehensive practice set that combines all the elements of QuickBooks studied throughout the text. In this practice set you will set up a company and keep the books for January 2010 (or the year that your instructor specifies). You will use the EasyStep Interview to create Your Name Book Store. Once the company has been created, detailed information will be provided for items, customers, vendors, and employees. The Payroll Setup Interview will be completed. Adjustments will be made to accounts and various items, and transactions will be recorded.

During the month, new customers, vendors, and employees will be added. When entering transactions, you are responsible for any memos you wish to include in transactions. Unless otherwise specified, the terms for each sale or bill will be the term specified on the Customer or Vendor List. The Customer Message is usually *Thank you for your business*. However, any other message that is appropriate may be used. If a customer's order exceeds the established credit limit, accept the order and process it. If the terms allow a discount for a customer, make sure to apply the discount if payment is received in time for the customer to take the discount. Remember, the discount period starts with the date of the invoice. If an invoice or bill date is not provided, use the transaction date to begin the discount period. Use Sales Discounts as the discount account. If a customer has a credit and has a balance on the account, apply the credit to the invoice used for the sale. If there is no balance for a customer and a return is made, issue a credit memo and a refund check. Always pay bills in time to take advantage of purchase discounts.

Invoices, purchase orders, and other similar items should be printed. You do not need to print Payment Receipts unless instructed to do so by your professor. It is your choice whether or not to print lines around each field. Most reports will be printed in Portrait orientation; however, if the report (such as the Journal) will fit across the page using Landscape orientation, use Landscape. Whenever possible, adjust the column widths so that reports fit on one-page wide <u>without</u> selecting Fit report to one page wide.

<u>YOUR NAME BOOK STORE</u>

Your Name Book Store is a fictitious company that provides a typing service and sells books and educational supplies. Your Name Book Store is located in Sacramento,

California, and is a sole proprietorship owned by you. You do all the purchasing and are involved in all aspects of the business. Your Name Book Store has one full-time employee who is paid a salary, Ms. Afshana Newcomb, who manages the store, is responsible for the all the employees, and keeps the books. Cassie Egkan is a full-time hourly employee who works in the shop. The store is currently advertising for a part-time employee who will provide word processing/typing services.

CREATE A NEW COMPANY

▶ Use the following information to complete the EasyStep Interview:
o   Company and Legal Name: **Your Name Book Store** (*Key in your actual name*)
o   Federal Tax ID: **466-52-1446**
o   Address: **1055 Front Street, Sacramento, CA 95814**
o   Telephone: **916-555-9876**; Fax: **916-555-6789**
o   E-mail: **Books@reader.com**, Web: **www.Books.com**
o   Type of Business: **Retail Shop or Online**
o   Company Organization: **Sole Proprietorship**
o   Fiscal Year Starts: **January**
o   Passwords: **No**
o   File Name: **Your Name Book Store.qbw**
o   Sell **Both Services and Products**, record each sale **individually**
o   Sell online: **No**
o   Charge Sales tax: **Yes**
o   Sales receipts and invoices: **Yes**
o   Estimates, statements, progress invoicing, or track time: **No**
o   Track bills: **Yes**
o   Print checks: **Yes**
o   Track Inventory: **Yes**
o   Accept credit cards and debit cards: **Yes**
o   Employees: **Yes, W-2 Employees**
o   Multiple Currencies: No
o   Use QuickBooks to set up the **Chart of Accounts**
o   Start Date: **01/01/2010** (or the year you have been instructed to use)
o   Bank account name **Checking**, account number **123-456-78910**, opened before **01/01/2010**. Last bank statement **12/31/2009**, ending balance **35,870.25**
o   Review Income and Expense Accounts: If an account has a check and you do not want the account, click it to remove it. If you want an account and there is no check, click the account to add it.
  ▪ Remove Merchant Account Fees, Computer and Internet Expenses, Janitorial Expenses, Meals and Entertainment, Uniforms, Ask My Accountant by clicking

the √ column to remove the checkmark or delete the accounts after completing the EasyStep Interview.

- Add: Dues and Subscriptions, Equipment Rental, Health Insurance, Postage and Delivery, Printing and Reproduction, Interest Income by clicking in the √ column to add a checkmark or add the accounts after completing the EasyStep Interview.

CHANGE PREFERENCES

▶ Change the following preferences:
- <u>Accounting</u>: Delete the Date Warnings for past and future transactions
- <u>Checking</u>: My Preferences—Default Accounts to use should be Checking for Open Write Checks, Open Pay Bills, Open Pay Sales Tax, and Open Make Deposits; Company Preferences— Select Default Accounts to use should be Checking for Create Paychecks and Pay Payroll Liabilities
- <u>Desktop View</u>: Do not show the QuickBooks Coach
- <u>Payroll & Employees</u>: Company Preferences—Display Employee List by Last Name
- <u>Reports & Graphs</u>: My Preferences—Refresh reports automatically, Company Preferences—modify the report Format for the Header/Footer to remove the Date Prepared, Time Prepared, and Report Basis from reports
- <u>Sales Tax</u>: Company Preferences—Most common sales tax is State Tax

COMPLETE THE COMPANY INFORMATION

▶ Add the Federal Employer Identification number 46-6521146 to the Company Information

CHART OF ACCOUNTS

▶ Use the following chart of accounts and balances to customize the chart of accounts for Your Name Book Store:
- To save space when printing, delete account descriptions for all accounts.
- Use whatever tax form QuickBooks suggests
- First, rename accounts where appropriate, make inactive or delete any unused accounts (if you did not delete accounts in the EasyStep Interview, delete them now)
- Second, add appropriate Income, Cost of Goods Sold, and Expense accounts (if you did not add accounts in the EasyStep Interview, add them now)
- Finally, add Asset, Liability, and Owner's Equity accounts and balances as of 01/01/10
- Chart Abbreviations:
    - (QB)=Account Created by QuickBooks—Do not do anything for these
    - *** means that QuickBooks will enter the account balance
    - Indented Account Names indicate that the account is a subaccount

- C.A.=Current Asset, F.A.=Fixed Asset, C.L.=Current Liability, Long Term L.=Long Term Liability, COGS=Cost of Goods Sold

YOUR NAME BOOK STORE CHART OF ACCOUNTS				
ACCOUNT	**TYPE**	**BALANCE**	**ACCOUNT**	**TYPE**
Checking	Bank	35,870.25	Equipment Rental	Expense
Accounts Receivable(QB)	Accts. Rec.	***	Insurance Expense	Expense
Inventory Asset	Other C.A	***	Disability Insurance	Expense
Office Supplies	Other C.A.	450.00	Fire Insurance	Expense
Prepaid Insurance	Other C.A.	1,200.00	Health Insurance	Expense
Sales Supplies	Other C.A.	900.00	Liability Insurance	Expense
Undeposited Funds (QB)	Other C.A.	***	Interest Expense	Expense
Store Equipment	F.A.	***	Marketing and Advertising	Expense
Depreciation	F.A.	0.00	Miscellaneous	Expense
Original Cost	F.A.	6,000.00	Office Expenses	Expense
Store Fixtures	F.A.	***	Postage and Delivery	Expense
Depreciation	F.A.	0.00	Printing and Reproduction	Expense
Original Cost	F.A.	10,000.00	Payroll Expenses	Expense
Accounts Payable (QB)	Acct. Pay.	***	Professional Fees	Expense
MasterCard (12/31/09)	Credit Card	50.00	Rent Expense	Expense
Payroll Liabilities	Other C.L.	0.00	Repairs	Expense
Sales Tax Payable	Other C.L.	0.00	Building	Expense
Store Equipment Loan	Long Term L.	1,500.00	Computer	Expense
Store Fixtures Loan	Long Term L.	4,500.00	Equipment	Expense
Retained Earnings (QB)	Equity	***	Sales Discounts	Expense
Your Name, Capital	Equity	***	Supplies Expense	Expense
Your Name, Investment	Equity	10,000.00	Office	Expense
Your Name, Withdrawals	Equity	0.00	Sales	Expense
Purchases Discounts	Income		Taxes	Expense
Sales and Services	Income		Federal	Expense
Book Sales	Income		State	Expense
Supplies Sales	Income		Telephone Expense	Expense
Word Processing/Typing Service	Income		Uncategorized Expenses (QB)	Expense
Uncategorized Income (QB)	Income		Utilities	Expense
Cost of Goods Sold (QB)	COGS		Gas and Electric	Expense
Merchandise Discounts (Create after entering Items List)	COGS		Water	Expense
Bank Service Charges	Expense		Interest Income	Other Income
Depreciation Expense	Expense		Other Income	Other Income
Dues and Subscriptions	Expense		Other Expenses	Other Expense

VENDOR LIST

▶ Use the following Vendor Lists to add vendors that sell us merchandise and that are used for tax and withholding payments. Enter any opening balances provided when the vendor is created. An opening balance is not eligible for a discount. The terms given are for future purchases from a vendor.

o   Use the following list to add the vendors that sell merchandise to us:

VENDOR LIST			
Vendor Name	Textbook Co.	Exotic Pens	Supplies Co.
Opening Balance	$1,000	$500	$800
As Of	01/01/10	01/01/10	01/01/10
Address	559 4th Street	2785 Market Street	95 8th Street
City, State, Zip	Sacramento, CA 95814	San Francisco, CA 94103	Sacramento, CA 95814
Contact Person	Al Daruty	Dennis Johnson	Raymond Ahrens
Phone	916-555-2788	415-555-3224	916-555-5759
Fax	916-555-8872	415-555-4223	916-555-9575
Terms	2% 10, Net 30	2% 10, Net 30	2% 10, Net 30
Credit Limit	$15,000	$5,000	$15,000

o   Use the following list to add the vendors that are used for tax and withholding payments:

VENDOR LIST			
Vendor Name	Employment Development Department	Sacramento State Bank	Medical Ins., Inc.
Address	1037 California Street	102 8th Street	20865 Oak Street
City, State, Zip	Sacramento, CA 95814	Sacramento, CA 95814	San Francisco, CA 94101
Phone	916-555-8877	916-555-9889	415-555-4646
Fax	916-555-7788	916-555-9988	415-555-6464

ITEMS LIST

▶ Create the Items List
o   There is only one service item for Your Name Book Store: Item Name: WP/Typing, Sales Description: Word Processing/Typing Service, Rate: 0.00, Non-Taxable, Income Account: Word Processing/Typing Service.
o   Use the following Inventory Items List and balances to add inventory items.

INVENTORY ITEMS					
Item Name	Textbooks	Paperback Books	Paper	Stationery	Pens, etc.
Purchase Description	Textbooks	Paperback Books	Paper Supplies	Stationery	Pens, etc.
Cost	0.00	0.00	0.00	0.00	
COGS Account	Cost of Goods Sold	Cost of Goods Sold	Cost of Goods Sold	Cost of Goods Sold	Cost of Go Sold
Preferred Vendor	Textbook Co.	Textbook Co.	Supplies Co.	Supplies Co.	Exotic Per
Sales Description	Textbooks	Paperback Books	Paper Supplies	Stationery	Pens, etc.
Sales Price	0.00	0.00	0.00	0.00	
Tax Code	Tax	Tax	Tax	Tax	Tax
Income Account	Book Sales	Book Sales	Supplies Sales	Supplies Sales	Supplies S
Asset Account	Inventory Asset	Inventory Asset	Inventory Asset	Inventory Asset	Inventory /
Reorder Point	100	30	100	25	
Quantity on Hand	2,000	45	200	30	
Value	10,000	180	3,000	150	
As of	01/01/10	01/01/10	01/01/10	01/01/10	01/01/1

o   Delete: the following sales items: Consignment, Non-inventory Item, and Local Tax.
o   Edit: the State Sales Tax Item, change the name and description to CA Sales Tax, tax rate of 7.25%, paid to State Board of Equalization, 7800 State Street, Sacramento, CA 94267
o   Change: the description for Out of State to Exempt from sales tax
o   Add: the account Merchandise Discounts as a subaccount of Cost of Goods Sold

CUSTOMER LIST

► Use the following Customer List to add customers. Those customers who are individuals should be added last name first for Customer:Job but first name then last name on the Bill to address. Enter any opening balances provided when the customer is created. An opening balance is not eligible for a discount. The terms given are for future sales to a customer.

CUSTOMER LIST						
Customer Name	Complete Training, Inc.	Nazid, Ellahe	Wong, Jai Jin	Sacramento Schools	Sanchez, Sergio Dr.	Yu, Charlie
Opening Balance	$1,450	$100	$0.00	$1,000	$0.00	$350
As Of	01/01/10	01/01/10	01/01/10	01/01/10	01/01/10	01/01/10
Address	785 Harvard Street	8025 Richmond Street	6784 Front Street	1085 2nd Street	158 16th Street	253 Mason Street
City, State, Zip	Sacramento, CA 95814	Sacramento, CA 95814	Sacramento, CA 95814	Sacramento, CA 95814	Sacramento, CA 95814	Sacramento, CA 95814
Contact	Sharon Jackson	Ellahe Nazid	Jai Jin Wong	Alicia Vincent	Dr. Sergio Sanchez	Charlie Yu
Telephone	916-555-8762	916-555-8961	916-555-6487	916-555-1235	916-555-3693	916-555-2264
Fax	916-555-2678					
Terms	Net 30	2% 10 Net 30	Net 30	2% 10 Net 30	Net 30	Net 30
Tax Code	Tax	Tax	Tax	Tax	Tax	Tax
Tax Item	CA State Tax	CA State Tax	CA State Tax	CA State Tax	CA State Tax	CA State Tax
Credit Limit	$1,500	$500	$100	$5,000	$100	$350

PRINT LISTS

▶ Print a Vendor List
▶ Print an Item Listing (If necessary use Fit to 1-page wide)
▶ Print a Customer List
▶ Prepare an Account Listing for the Chart of Accounts, delete any descriptions added to the accounts by QuickBooks, and print in Landscape orientation

PAYROLL

▶ Select Manual as the payroll option
▶ Complete the Payroll Setup (Remember that on some screens QuickBooks will show you the current computer date or current year. This should not make a difference as long as you use the same year as the EasyStep Interview whenever you enter a date.)
o Complete the Company portion of the setup
 • Payroll List Items for Wages, Tips, and Taxable Fringe Benefits: **Salary, Hourly Wage and Overtime**
 • Insurance Benefits: **Health Insurance**, **Dental Insurance**. Both are fully **paid by the employee after taxes** have been deducted. The Payee/Vendor is **Medical Ins., Inc.**, you do not need a payment schedule.

- Retirement Benefits: **None**
- Paid Time Off: **Sick Time** and **Vacation Time**
- Other Payments and Deductions: **None**
  - o Use the Employee List to enter the employees and the appropriate information

EMPLOYEE LIST Cassie Egkan and Afshana Newcomb		
Name	Cassie Egkan	Afshana Newcomb
Employee Status	Active	Active
Street Address	833 Oak Avenue	1777 Watt Avenue
City, State Zip	Sacramento, CA 95814	Sacramento, CA 95814
Employee Tax Type	Regular	Regular
Social Security No.	100-55-6886	100-55-5244
Hire Date	04/03/96	02/17/95
Birth Date	12/07/70	11/28/49
Gender	Female	Female
Pay Period	Monthly	Monthly
Salary	$10.00 per hour $20.00 Double-time hourly $15.00 Overtime (x1.5) hourly	$26,000 per year
Dental Insurance	$20 per month, annual maximum $240	$30 per month, annual maximum $360
Health Insurance	$20 per month, annual maximum $240	$30 per month, annual maximum $360
Sick Time Earns	40:00 per year	40:00 per year
Unused Hours	Have an accrual limit	Have an accrual limit
Maximum Hours	120:00	120:00
Earns	Time off currently	Time off currently
Hours Available as of 01/01/10	40:00	40:00
Sick Time Effective (Edit via the Employee List after Payroll Setup)	04/03/96	02/17/95
Vacation Time Earns	40:00 per year	40:00 per year
Unused Hours	Have an accrual limit	Have an accrual limit
Maximum Hours	120:00	120:00
Earns	Time off currently	Time off currently
Hours Available as of 01/01/10	40:00	40:00

EMPLOYEE LIST Cassie Egkan and Afshana Newcomb		
Vacation Time Effective (Edit via the Employee List after Payroll Setup)	04/03/96	02/17/95
Direct Deposit	No	No
State Subject to Withholding	CA	CA
State Subject to Unemployment Tax	CA	CA
Live or Work in Another State in 2010	No	No
Federal Filing Status	Married	Single
Allowances	1	0
Subject to	Medicare Social Security Federal Unemployment	Medicare Social Security Federal Unemployment
State Filing Status	Married (one income)	Single
Regular Withholding Allowances	1	0
Subject to	CA-Unemployment CA-Employment Training Tax CA-Disability	CA-Unemployment CA-Employment Training Tax CA-Disability
Local Taxes	No	No
Wage Plan Code	S	S

- Print the Summary for each employee
o Enter Payroll Tax information
  - California-Unemployment Company Rate is **3.4%**, the rate for CA-Employment Training Tax Company Rate is 0.1% and the rate for CA-Disability Employee Rate 1.1 %
  - Federal Payroll Taxes: Payee **United States Treasury**, **Quarterly** deposits; California State Taxes: Payee: is **Employment Development Department**, the Employer Account is **999-9999-9**, use **Quarterly** deposits
o Determine if you need to enter the Year-to-Date Payrolls
  - No paychecks have been

MAKE ADJUSTMENTS

▶ Enter the telephone numbers for Cassie 916-555-7862 and Afshana 916-555-1222 on the Address and Contact tab of Personal Info.

▶ Verify and if necessary change the beginning accrual date for vacation and sick time for Cassie Egkan of 4/03/96 and Afshana Newcomb of 02/17/95.

▶ Transfer the Uncategorized Income and Uncategorized Expenses to the owner's capital account

▶ Print a Balance Sheet as of January 1, 2010.

▶ Customize business forms: Use a duplicate of a Product Invoice. Use Layout Designer to make the area for the company name wide enough for your name. Customize Sales Receipts, and Purchase Orders so they have the same format as the invoice. Finally, duplicate and customize a Return Receipt (used for Credit Memos). Duplicate the Return Receipt in the Templates list. Go to the form. On the **Additional Customization Header** tab, replace the Default Title of Return Receipt with **Credit Memo**. Then click the **Layout Designer** button and adjust the sizes of the title and the area for the company name.)

ENTER TRANSACTIONS

▶ Print invoices, sales receipts, purchase orders, checks, and other items as they are entered in the transactions.

▶ Use the customized product invoice for all invoices, and the customized credit memo for customer returns, voucher checks for payroll, and standard checks for all other checks. Create new items, accounts, customers, vendors, etc., as necessary. Refer to information given at the beginning of the problem for additional transaction details and information.

▶ Prepare an Inventory Stock Status by Item Report every five days as the last transaction of the day to see if anything needs to be ordered. If anything is indicated, order enough so you will have 10 more than the minimum number of items. (For example, if you needed to order textbooks and the minimum number on hand is 100, you would order enough books to have 110 on hand.) For this problem, the price per book ordered is $15 per textbook and $5 per paperback; pens are $2.50 each, paper is $2.00 per ream, stationery is $4.00 per box, and gift ware is $5.00 each.

▶ Full-time employees usually work 160 hours during a payroll period. Hourly employees working in excess of 160 hours in a pay period are paid overtime. In this problem, use the regular checking account to pay employees.

▶ Check every five days to see if any bills are due and eligible for a discount. If any bills can be paid and a discount received, pay the bills; otherwise, wait for instructions to pay bills. Remember that an opening balance is not eligible for a discount.

▶ Backup the company file every five days. Create your first backup file before recording transactions. Name the file **Your Name Book Store (Backup Company)**, name subsequent files with the date. For example, your first backup that includes transactions would be named **Your Name Book Store (Backup 01-05-10)**. The final backup should be made at the end of the practice set. Name it **Your Name Book Store (Backup Complete)**.

January 1
► Add a new part-time hourly employee:
o Personal Info:
  ▪ Katie Kellor
  ▪ Social Security No. 100-55-3699
  ▪ Gender Female
  ▪ Birthday 1/3/76
  ▪ 1177 Florin Road, Sacramento, CA 95814
  ▪ 916-555-7766
o Payroll and Compensation Info:
  ▪ Hourly: $6.50, Overtime (x1.5) hourly: $9.75, Double-time hourly: $13.00
  ▪ Pay Frequency: Monthly
  ▪ Dental and Health Insurance: None
  ▪ Sick and Vacation Hours
    • Available and Used: 0
    • Accrual Period: Beginning of the year
    • Sick and Vacation Hours Accrued at the beginning of the year: 20
    • Maximum Sick and Vacation Hours: 40
    • Year begins on: January 1
    • Begin accruing Sick and Vacation time on: 01/01/10
  ▪ Federal Taxes:
    • Filing Status and Allowance: Single, 0
    • Subject to: Medicare, Social Security, Federal Unemployment
  ▪ State Taxes:
    • State Worked and State Subject to Withholding: California
    • Subject to, CA Unemployment (SUI), CA Disability taxes (SDI)
    • Filing Status and Allowance: Single, 0
  ▪ Other Taxes:
    • CA Employment Training Tax
o Employment Info:
  ▪ Hire Date: 01/01/10
  ▪ Type: Regular

January 2:
► Cash sale to Cash Customer of one $40 textbook.
► Complete Training purchased 30 copies of a textbook on account for $40 each.

▶ Sold three paperback books at $6.99 each to a cash customer.
▶ Received Check No. 1096 from Ellahe Nazid for $100 as payment in full on her account. (An opening balance is not eligible for a discount.)
▶ Sold 25 pens on account at $8.99 each to Sacramento Schools for awards to students.
▶ Sold five textbooks at $39.99 each for the new quarter to a student using a Visa.
▶ Prepare and print an Inventory Stock Status by Item report to see if anything needs to be ordered.
▶ Prepare and print Purchase Orders for any merchandise that needs to be ordered.
▶ Check bills for discount eligibility between January 1-4. Pay any bills that qualify for a discount. (Opening balances do not qualify for an early payment discount.)

January 3:
▶ Received Check No. 915 for $350 from Charlie Yu for the full amount due on his account.
▶ Sold five pens on account at $12.99 each to Ellahe Nazid.
▶ Received payment of $1,450 from Complete Training, Inc., Check No. 7824.

January 4:
▶ Katie typed a five-page paper for a student at the rate of $5 per page. Received Check No. 2951 for $25 as full payment.
▶ Sold two textbooks on account at $40 each to a new customer: Hector Gomez, 478 Front Street, Sacramento, CA 95814, Phone: 916-555-6841, E-mail: HGomez@email.com, Terms Net 10 (Do you need to add a new Standard Term for Net 10?), Taxable, Credit Limit $100.

January 5:
▶ Received the pens ordered from Exotic Pens with the bill.
▶ Sold five boxes of stationery at $10.99 per box to Jai Jin Wong on account.
▶ Sold on account five reams of paper at $4.99 per ream to Sacramento Schools.
▶ Prepare and print Inventory Stock Status by Item Report for January 1-5, 2010. Order any items indicated.
▶ Check bills for discount eligibility. Pay any bills that qualify for a discount between January 5-9.
▶ Deposit all cash, checks, and credit card payments received.
▶ Backup the company file.

January 7:
▶ The nonprofit organization, State Schools, bought a classroom set of 30 computer training textbooks on account for $40.00 each. Add the new customer: State Schools, 451 State Street, Sacramento, CA 95814, Contact Allison Hernandez, 916-555-8787, Fax 916-555-7878, Terms Net 30, Taxable, Credit Limit $2000. Include a subtotal for

the sale and apply a 10% sales discount for a nonprofit organization. (Create any new sales items necessary.)
▶ Add a new inventory part sales item for Gift Ware, Purchase Description: Gift Ware, Cost: 0.00, COGS Account: Cost of Goods Sold, Preferred Vendor: Gifts Galore (125 Oak Street, Sacramento, CA 95814, Contact: Mary Ellen Morrison, 916-555-5384, Fax: 916-555-4835, E-mail: gifts@abc.com, Terms: Net 30, Credit Limit: $500), Sales Description: Gift Ware, Sales Price: 0.00, Tax Code: Tax, Income Account: Supplies Sales, Asset Account: Inventory Asset, Reorder Point: 15, Quantity on Hand: 0, Value: 0.00,
▶ Order 15 gift ware items at $5.00 each from the Gifts Galore.

January 8:
▶ Sold ten reams of paper on account to Dr. Sergio Sanchez at $3.99 per ream.
▶ Ellahe Nazid returned two pens purchased on January 3. She did not like the color. Apply the credit to the invoice and print after you apply the credit to the invoice.
▶ Paid Textbook Co. full amount owed on account. This is the opening balance for the vendor. Print Check No. 1 using Standard Checks. (Remember, no discounts are available for opening balances.)

January 10:
▶ Sold three pens at $14.95 each, two sets of stationery at $9.99 each, and three paperback books at $6.99 each to a cash customer.
▶ Katie typed a 15-page report at $5.00 per page on account for Jai Jin Wong.
▶ Sold eight additional computer textbooks on account to Sacramento Schools at $40 each.
▶ Received Check No. 825 as payment from Sacramento Schools for the 01/02/10 transaction for $236.22, the full amount due, less discount.
▶ Received Check No. 10525 from Complete Training, Inc., $1,000 as partial payment on account.
▶ Deposit all cash, checks, and credit card receipts.
▶ Prepare Inventory Stock Status by Item Report for January 1-10, 2010. Order any items indicated. (If an item is marked to order but a purchase order has already been prepared, do not re-order the item.)
▶ Check bills for discount eligibility. Pay any bills that qualify for a discount between January 10-14. (Remember opening balances do not qualify for a discount.)
▶ Backup the company file.

January 11:
▶ Sold ten paperback books at $6.99 each and two pens at $5.99 each to a customer using a Visa.
▶ Sold ten reams of paper to a cash customer at $4.99 each. Received Check No. 8106.

January 12:

► Received gift ware ordered from Gifts Galore. A bill was not included with the order.

► Sold one pen at $8.99 and a box of stationery at $9.99 to a cash customer.

► Katie typed a one-page letter with an envelope for Charlie Yu, $8.00. (Qty is 1.)

January 13:

► Received Check No. 1265 from Ellahe Nazid in payment for full amount due, $40.41. Apply any discounts.

► Received a notice from the bank that Check No. 915 from Charlie Yu was marked NSF and returned. Record the NSF check and charge Charlie the bank's $25 fee for the bad check plus Your Name Book Store's fee of $15. Payment is due on receipt. Add any necessary items and/or accounts. The income account used to record the charges for bad checks is Returned Check Service Charges.

January 14:

► Received Check No. 870 from Sacramento Schools for $26.22 as payment in full for Invoice No. 6.

► Received Check No. 10-283 for $85.80 from Hector Gomez in payment of Invoice No. 4.

January 15:

► Received all but three boxes of stationery ordered. The bill was included with the stationery and the three missing boxes are on back order. (Was your Purchase Order for 10 boxes?)

► Received Charlie Yu's new Check No. 304 for payment in full of his account including all NSF charges.

► Sold five paperback books to a customer using a Visa. The books were $6.99 each.

► Deposit all cash, checks, and credit card receipts.

► Check to see if any bills qualify for a discount between January 15 and 19. If any qualify, take the discount and pay them. (Remember, no discounts are available for opening balances.)

► Prepare and print an Inventory Stock Status by Item Report for January 1-15 in Landscape orientation. Prepare Purchase Orders for all items marked Order on the Inventory Stock Status by Item Report. Place all orders with preferred vendors.

► Backup the company file.

January 17:

► Sold eight textbooks on account at $50 each to State Schools, which is a nonprofit organization.

► Hector Gomez returned one textbook he had purchased for $40.

▶ Received Credit Memo No. 721 from Supplies Co. for the return of ten reams of paper. (Be sure to apply the credit when you pay your bill.)

January 18:
▶ Print a Stock Status by Item Report after recording the return of the paper. Print in Landscape.
▶ Sold three paperback books on account to Charlie Yu at $8.99 each.

January 20:
▶ Received the bill and the three boxes of stationery that were on back order with Supplies Co..
▶ A cash customer purchased four textbooks at $59.99 each using Check No. 289.
▶ Received Check No. 891 from Sacramento Schools for $336.34 for payment in full of Invoice No. 11.
▶ Prepare Inventory Stock Status by Item Report. Order any items indicated.
▶ Check to see if any bills qualify for a discount between January 20 and 24. If any qualify, pay them. (Remember, no discounts are available for opening balances.)
▶ Backup the company file.

January 21:
▶ Sold one textbook for $89.95. Customer used a VISA card to pay for the purchase.
▶ Katie typed an eight-page exam for a professor at $5 per page. Add Professor James Sanders, 1052 Florin Avenue, Sacramento, CA 95814, 916-555-8741, Terms Net 30, Taxable, Credit Limit $100.
▶ Received the bill from Gifts Galore for the gift ware ordered and received January 12. Date the bill January 21.
▶ Forgot to record the bank deposit on January 20. Deposit all cash, checks , and credit card receipts.

January 22:
▶ Sold one gift ware item at $15.99 to a cash customer. Received Check No. 105.
▶ Sold five gift ware items at $9.99 each to Ellahe Nazid on account.

January 24:
▶ Sold three pens at $8.99 each to Hector Gomez.
▶ Received Check No. 127 for $42.79 as payment in full from Dr. Sergio Sanchez.

January 25:
▶ Prepare Inventory Stock Status by Item Report. Order any items indicated.
▶ Check to see if any bills qualify for a discount between January 25 and 29. If any qualify, accept the discount offered by QuickBooks, and pay them. If there are any credits to apply to any bill payments, be sure to use them. (Remember, no discounts are available for opening balances.)
▶ Deposit all cash, checks, and credit card receipts.
▶ Backup the company file.

January 27:
▶ Received the bill and all of the paperback books ordered from Textbook Co..

January 29:
▶ Received Check No. 4325 for $133.93 from Jai Jin Wong.
▶ Received Bill No. 1092-5 and pens on order from Exotic Pens.
▶ Sold 60 textbooks on account to Complete Training, Inc., for $59.95 each.
▶ Sold 45 textbooks on account to Sacramento Schools for $49.99 each.

January 30:
▶ Prepare Inventory Stock Status by Item Report. Order any items indicated.
▶ Deposit all checks, cash, and credit card receipts.
▶ Pay balance due to Supplies Co. as well as any bills eligible for a discount between January 30 and February 4. Print using a standard style check.
▶ Pay $900 rent to the Sacramento Rental Agency, 1234 Front Street, Sacramento, CA 95814, Contact: Gail Ruiz, 916-555-1234, Fax 916-555-4321, Terms Net 30.
▶ Pay gas and electricity bill of $257 to CA State Utilities, 8905 Richmond, Sacramento, CA 95814, 916-555-8523, Terms Net 30.
▶ Pay the telephone bill of $189 to State Telephone Company, 3899 Oak Avenue, Sacramento, CA 95814, 916-555-8741, Terms Net 30.
▶ Backup the company file.

January 31:
▶ Pay the payroll: The pay period is 01/01/10 through 01/31/10. The check date is 01/31/10. Use the information in the following table and print the paychecks using a voucher-style check.

PAYROLL TABLE: JANUARY 31, 2010			
	Cassie Egkan	Katie Kellor	Afshana Newcomb
HOURS			
Regular	144	80	158
Overtime	3		
Sick	16		2
Vacation			
DEDUCTIONS OTHER PAYROLL ITEMS: EMPLOYEE			
Dental Ins.	20.00		30.00
Medical Ins.	20.00		30.00
DEDUCTIONS: COMPANY			
CA Employment Training Tax	2.58	1.40	2.50
Social Security	97.53	63.33	134.34
Medicare	23.20	18.77	31.42
Federal Unemployment	9.33	6.75	9.33
CA-Unemployment	46.67	30.40	46.67
DEDUCTIONS: EMPLOYEE			
Federal Withholding	126.00	56.00	292.00
Social Security	52.39	46.12	67.17
Medicare	23.20	18.77	31.42
CA-Withholding	56.05	37.00	63.30
CA-Disability	8.00	6.30	10.00

► Before distributing paychecks, you realize that the Social Security Employee Deductions for each employee are incorrect. Go to the checks, unlock them and change the amount of Social Security Employee Deductions for Cassie to 97.53, for Katie to 63.33, and for Afshana to 134.34. Reprint the checks using Voucher style.

► Prepare and print the Payroll Summary Report for January in Landscape orientation. (Adjust column widths to print the report on one page.)

► Prepare and print the Payroll Liabilities Balances Report for January in Portrait orientation.

▶ Pay all the payroll taxes payroll liabilities for January 1-31, 2010. Print the standard checks.

▶ Prepare Sales Tax Liability Report for January 1-31, 2010. Print in Landscape orientation. Adjust column widths so the report fits on one page, maintains the same font, and has column headings shown in full.

▶ Pay Sales Tax for January 31, 2010 and print the check.

▶ Print a Sales by Item Summary Report for January in Landscape orientation. Adjust column widths so report fits on one-page wide.

▶ Print a Trial Balance for January 1-31 in Portrait orientation.

▶ Enter adjusting entries: Depreciation—Store Equipment $100, Store Fixtures $166.66. Supplies used—Office Supplies $150, Sales Supplies $250. Insurance a total of $100—$50 fire Insurance, $50 Liability Insurance. (Use a compound entry to record insurance adjustment.)

▶ Record the owner withdrawal for the month $1,500.

▶ Prepare a bank reconciliation and record any adjustments. Be sure to use the date of 01/31/10 for the bank statement date, service charges, and interest earned.

SACRAMENTO STATE BANK
102 8th Street
Sacramento, CA 95814
(916) 555-9889

BANK STATEMENT FOR:

Your Name Book Store
1055 Front Street
Sacramento, CA 95814   Acct. # 97-1132-07922   January 2010

Beginning Balance, January 1, 2010			$35,870.25
1/5/2010, Deposit	2,204.84		38,075.09
1/9/2010, Check 1		1,000.00	37,075.09
1/10/2010, Deposit	1,328.24		38,403.33
1/13/2010, NSF Check		350.00	38,053.33
1/15/2010, Deposit	749.61		38,802.94
1/16/2010, Check 2		85.75	38,717.19
1/18/2010, Check 3		42.90	38,674.29
1/21/2010, Deposit	690.17		39,364.46
1/25/2010, Check 4		7.44	39,357.02
1/25/2010, Deposit	59.94		39,416.96
1/31/2010, Service Charge, $15, and NSF Charge, $25		40.00	39,379.96
1/31/2010, Store Fixtures Loan Pmt.: $80.12 Interest, $15.49 Principal		95.61	39,281.35
1/31/2010, Store Equipment Loan Pmt.: $26.71 Interest, $5.16 Principal		31.87	39,249.48
1/31/2010, Interest	94.03		39,343.51
Ending Balance, 1/31/2010			$39,343.51

▶ Print the Detail Reconciliation Report.
▶ Print a Standard Profit and Loss Statement.
▶ Close the Drawing account
▶ Transfer the Net Income/Retained Earnings into the capital account. (If necessary, change the name of the account Owners Equity to Retained Earnings.)
▶ Print a Standard Balance Sheet for January
▶ Print a Statement of Cash Flows for January
▶ Adjust the Merchandise Item of Gift Ware for 1 Gift Set that was damaged. (Use the expense account Merchandise Adjustments.)
▶ Correct the Amount of Net Income to reflect the merchandise adjustment
▶ Print a Standard Balance Sheet

► Close the period with a closing date of 01/31/10 (Do not use passwords.)
► Print the Journal (Use the dates from 12/31/2009 to 01/31/2010. Landscape orientation, adjust column width to fit to one-page wide with the standard font). The order in which your transactions appear may be different from any answer keys provided. As long as all of the transactions have been entered, the order of entry does not matter.
► Backup the company file.

NAME_____

TRANSMITTAL

COMPREHENSIVE PRACTICE SET: YOUR NAME BOOK STORE

Attach the following documents and reports:

Customer:Job List
Vendor List
Item Listing
Account Listing
Employee Summary for Cassie Egkan
Employee Summary for Afshana Newcomb
Standard Balance Sheet, January 1, 2010
Sales Receipt No. 1: Cash Customer
Invoice No. 1: Complete Training, Inc.
Sales Receipt No. 2: Cash Customer
Invoice No. 2: Sacramento Schools
Sales Receipt No. 3: Cash Customer
Inventory Stock Status by Item, January 1, 2010
Purchase Order No. 1: Exotic Pens
Invoice No. 3: Ellahe Nazid
Sales Receipt No. 4: Cash Customer
Invoice No. 4: Hector Gomez
Invoice No. 5: Jai Jin Wong
Invoice No. 6: Sacramento Schools
Inventory Stock Status by Item, January 1-5, 2010
Purchase Order No. 2: Supplies Co.
Deposit Summary, January 5, 2010
Invoice No. 7: State Schools
Purchase Order No. 3: Gifts Galore
Invoice No. 8: Sergio Sanchez
Credit Memo No. 9: Ellahe Nazid
Check No. 1: Textbook Co.
Sales Receipt No. 5: Cash Customer
Invoice No. 10: Jai Jin Wong

Invoice No. 11: Sacramento Schools
Deposit Summary, January 10, 2010
Inventory Stock Status by Item, January 1-10, 2010
Sales Receipt No. 6: Cash Customer
Sales Receipt No. 7: Cash Customer
Sales Receipt No. 8: Cash Customer
Invoice No. 12: Charlie Yu
Invoice No. 13: Charlie Yu
Sales Receipt No. 9: Cash Customer
Deposit Summary, January 15, 2010
Check No. 2: Exotic Pens
Inventory Stock Status by Item, January 1-15, 2010
Purchase Order No. 4: Gifts Galore
Purchase Order No. 5: Textbook Co.
Invoice No. 14: State Schools
Credit Memo No. 15: Hector Gomez
Check No. 3: Hector Gomez
Inventory Stock Status by Item, January 1-18, 2010
Invoice No. 16: Charlie Yu
Sales Receipt No. 10: Cash Customer
Inventory Stock Status by Item, January 1-20, 2010
Sales Receipt No. 11: Cash Customer
Invoice No. 17: James Sanders
Deposit Summary, January 21, 2010
Sales Receipt No. 12: Cash Customer
Invoice No. 18: Ellahe Nazid
Invoice No. 19: Hector Gomez
Inventory Stock Status by Item, January 1-25, 2010
Purchase Order No. 6: Exotic Pens
Check No. 4: Supplies Co.
Deposit Summary, January 25, 2010
Invoice No. 20: Complete Training, Inc.
Invoice No. 21: Sacramento Schools
Inventory Stock Status by Item, January 1-30, 2010
Deposit Summary, January 30, 2010
Check No. 5: Supplies Co.
Check No. 6: Sacramento Rental Agency
Check No. 7: CA State Utilities
Check No. 8: State Telephone Company
Check No. 9: Cassie Egkan
Check No. 10: Katie Kellor
Check No. 11: Afshana Newcomb

Check No. 9: Cassie Egkan (Corrected)
Check No. 10: Katie Kellor (Corrected)
Check No. 11: Afshana Newcomb (Corrected)
Payroll Summary, January 2010
Payroll Liability Balances, January 30, 2010
Check No. 12: Employment Development Department
Check No. 13: Medical Ins., Inc.
Check No. 14: United States Treasury
Sales Tax Liability Report, January 2010
Check No. 15: State Board of Equalization
Sales by Item Summary, January 2010
Trial Balance, January 31, 2010
Check No. 16: Your Name
Bank Reconciliation Report
Standard Profit and Loss, January 2010
Balance Sheet After Adjustments, January 31, 2010
Statement of Cash Flows, January 2010
Balance Sheet, January 31, 2010, (After Adjustment of Merchandise Inventory)
Journal, December 31, 2009 - January 31, 2010

QUICKBOOKS PROGRAM INTEGRATION WITH MICROSOFT® WORD, EXCEL, AND OUTLOOK

QuickBooks Pro is integrated to work in conjunction with Microsoft Word and Excel to prepare many different types of letters or send QuickBooks reports directly to an Excel workbook. In order to use the integration features of the program, you must have Microsoft Word 2000 (or higher) and Microsoft Excel 2000 (or higher) installed on your computer. This appendix will use the sample company, Larry's Landscaping & Garden Supply, to provide information regarding the features mentioned in the appendix title. Since saving the demonstration transactions will make permanent changes to the sample company, you will not need to do the demonstration transactions unless they are assigned by your instructor.

QUICKBOOKS LETTERS

There are many times in business when you need to write a letter of one type or another to your customers. This is an important feature because QuickBooks will insert information, such as the amount a customer owes, from your customer files directly into a letter. We will use the sample service-based company, Larry's Landscaping & Garden Supply, to work with QuickBooks Letters and prepare a collection letter for Susie Rummens.

▶ **DO** Prepare a Collection Letter for Susie Rummens

To open the Sample Company file for a Service Business, open QuickBooks
On the **No Company Open** window, click the button for **Open a Sample File**
Click **Sample service-based business**

A notification regarding QuickBooks Information appears

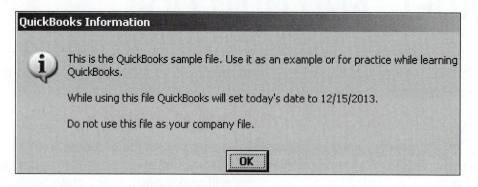

Click **OK** on the QuickBooks Information screen
Click the **Customers Center** icon
- If necessary, click the **Customers & Jobs** tab
Click the **Word** button
Click **Prepare Collection Letters**
- If you get a screen regarding the lack of available templates, click **Copy**
Complete the screen to Choose the Recipients
- Include listed customers or jobs that are: **Both**
- Create a letter for each: **Customer**
- Limit letters to customers or jobs with payments overdue by: **1 Day or More**

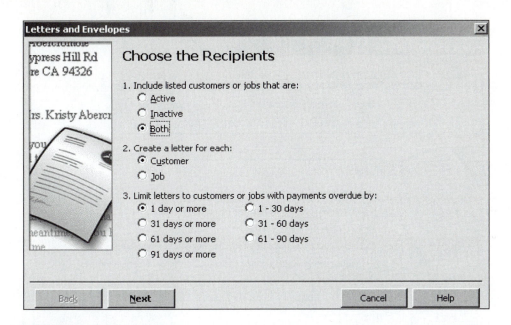

Click **Next**
Click **Unmark All** button
Click in the check column to select **Susie Rummens**
Click **Next**
Click **Friendly Collection** as the type of letter

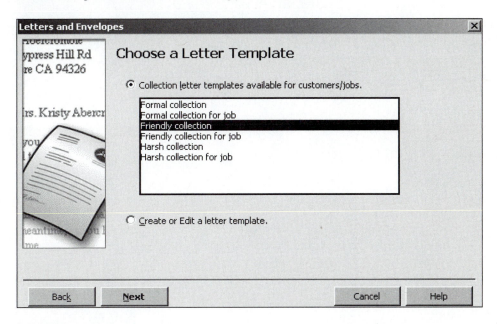

Click **Next**
Enter **Your Name** (your actual name not the words your name) for the name at the end of the letter
Enter your title as **President**

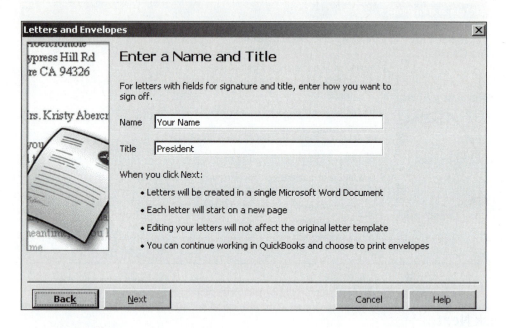

Click **Next**.

- When the letter is created, Microsoft Word will be opened and the collection letter for Susie Rummens will appear on the screen.

Larry's Landscaping & Garden Supply
1045 Main Street
Bayshore, CA 94326
(415) 555-4567

December 15, 2013

Susie Rummens
2877 S. Rosebush
Middlefield, CA 98731

Dear Susie,

Just a friendly reminder that you have 1 overdue invoice(s), with an overdue balance of $1,438.56. If you have any questions about the amount you owe, please give us a call and we'll be happy to discuss it. If you've already sent your payment, please disregard this reminder.

We appreciate your continuing business, and we look forward to hearing from you shortly.

Sincerely,

Your Name
President
Larry's Landscaping & Garden Supply

To make the short letter appear more balanced:
Press **Ctrl+A** to select the entire document
Click **File** menu, **Page Setup**
Change the Top and Bottom margins to **1"**
Change the Left and Right margins to **2"**

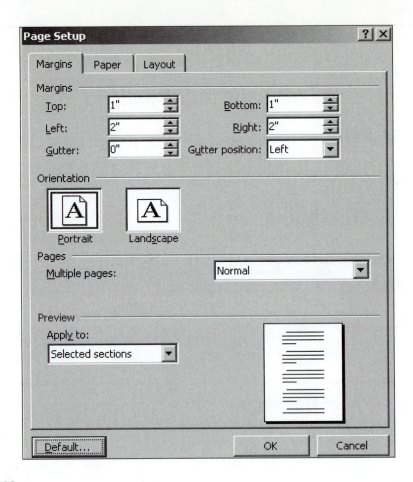

Click **OK**

Position the cursor between the date and the letter address

Press the **Enter** until there are 8 blank lines between the date and the letter address

Delete one of the blank lines between the letter address and the salutation (Dear Susie)

Click ⬚ icon on the Toolbar to display the letter.

• Your letter should look like the following.

Larry's Landscaping & Garden Supply
1045 Main Street
Bayshore, CA 94326
(415) 555-4567

December 15, 2013

Susie Rummens
2877 S. Rosebush
Middlefield, CA 98731

Dear Susie,

Just a friendly reminder that you have 1 overdue invoice(s), with
an overdue balance of $1,438.56. If you have any questions about
the amount you owe, please give us a call and we'll be happy to
discuss it. If you've already sent your payment, please disregard
this reminder.

We appreciate your continuing business, and we look forward to
hearing from you shortly.

Sincerely,

Your Name
President
Larry's Landscaping & Garden Supply

- Notice that Susie's overdue balance of $1,438.56 was automatically inserted in the letter.

Close View, and close Word without saving the letter

Click **Cancel** to cancel the Letters to Customers, close the **Customer Center**

EXPORTING REPORTS TO EXCEL

Many of the reports prepared in QuickBooks Pro can be exported to Microsoft® Excel. This allows you to take advantage of extensive filtering options available in Excel, hide detail for some but not all groups of data, combine information from two different reports, change titles of columns, add comments, change the order of columns, and experiment with *what if* scenarios. In order to use this feature of QuickBooks Pro you must also have Microsoft Excel 2000 or higher.

DO Continue to use the sample company: Larry's Landscaping and Export a report to Excel
Click **Reports Menu**
Click **Company and Financial** on the Reports Menu
Click **Balance Sheet Standard**
If necessary, enter the date **12/15/13**
Click the **Export** button at the top of the report

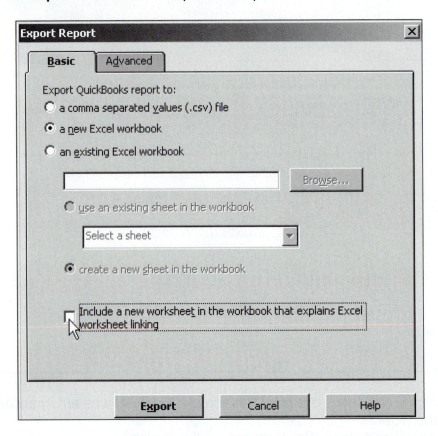

Make sure the Export QuickBooks Report to has **a new Excel workbook** selected as the File option
Click **Include a new worksheet in the workbook that explains Excel worksheet linking** to remove the check
Click **Export**
• The Balance Sheet will be displayed in Excel.

	A	B	C	D	E	F	G
1							Dec 15, 13
2	ASSETS						
3		Current Assets					
4			Checking/Savings				
5				Checking			99,250.02
6				Cash Expenditures			225.23
7				Savings			5,987.50
8			Total Checking/Savings				105,462.75
9			Accounts Receivable				
10				Accounts Receivable			35,810.02
11			Total Accounts Receivable				35,810.02
12			Other Current Assets				
13				Prepaid Insurance			500.00
14				Employee advances			100.00
15				Inventory Asset			6,937.08
16				Undeposited Funds			110.00
17			Total Other Current Assets				7,647.08
18		Total Current Assets					148,919.85

Scroll through the report and click in Cell A61
Type **BALANCE SHEET IMPORTED TO EXCEL**

	A	B	C	D	E	F	G
1							Dec 15, 13
59	TOTAL LIABILITIES & EQUITY						160,944.85
60							
61	BALANCE SHEET IMPORTED TO EXCEL						

Click the **Close** button in the upper right corner of the Excel title bar to close
   Excel
Click **No** to close **Book1** without saving

IMPORTING DATA FROM EXCEL

Another feature of QuickBooks is the ability to import data from Excel into QuickBooks.
You may have Excel or .csv (comma separated value) files that contain important
business information about customers, vendors, sales items, and other lists that are not
contained in your QuickBooks Company File. That information can be imported directly

into QuickBooks and customized as desired. An import file must conform to a specific structure for QuickBooks to interpret the data in the file correctly.

You may import your data from Excel in three ways. First, you may use an advanced import method to modify and use an existing Excel or CVS file, use a specially formatted spreadsheet and then add it to QuickBooks, or you may copy and paste your data from Excel directly into QuickBooks using the Add/Edit Multiple List Entries window.

Since importing data is not reversible, a backup should be made prior to importing data. An example of procedures to follow when using a spreadsheet to import a customer is shown below:

- In the Customer Center, select the Customers & Jobs or Vendors tab.
  - o Click the drop-down list arrow for the Excel menu, and click Import from Excel.
  - o Complete the Wizard

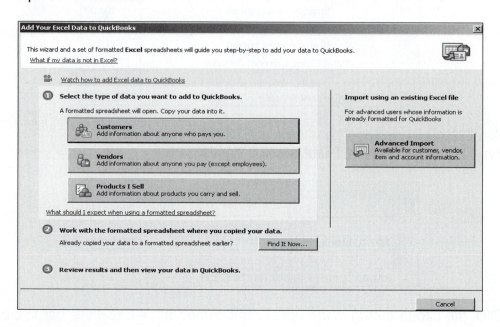

  - o Click **Customers**
  - o Click **Yes** on the Import textbox.
  - o You are taken to a pre-formatted spreadsheet that is ready for data entry.
  - o Enter the customer data

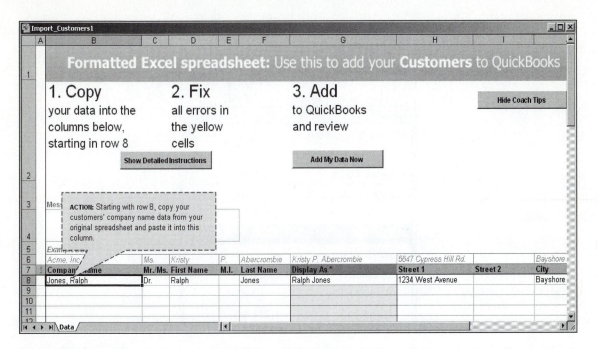

o   When you have entered the data, save the file
o   Click the **Add My Data Now** button

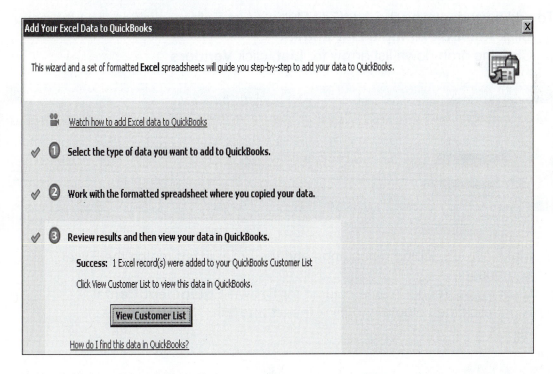

o   To see the customer that was added in the example, click **View Customer List**

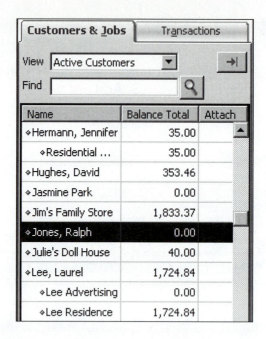

QuickBooks makes it possible import customers, vendors, and sales items by using the Add/Edit Multiple List Entries feature.

- To add a vendor using the Add/Edit Multiple List Entries, click on the **List** menu
  - ○ Click **Add/Edit Multiple List Entries**
  - ○ Click the drop-down list arrow for **List**, click **Vendors**

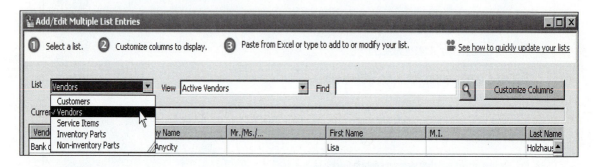

  - ○ Make sure the column headings and the order listed match the Excel spreadsheet.
  - ○ Click in the Vendor Name column for **Brown Equipment Rental**
  - ○ Right-click the column and click **Insert line**

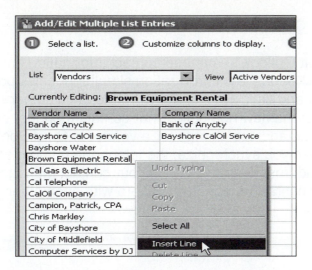

o   Enter the vendor information for **Beacon Utilities** on the blank line

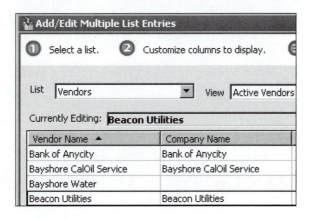

o   Click the **Save Changes** button

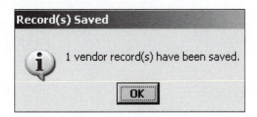

This method may also be used to copy and paste information from an Excel spreadsheet and is a great time saver when working with several vendors, customers, and sales items.

MICROSOFT OUTLOOK

You may use Microsoft Outlook to manage contact information and synchronize your contact data with QuickBooks. Synchronization simultaneously updates data in both your contact manager and QuickBooks. For example, a customer's telephone number changes and you enter the new number in your contact manager but not in QuickBooks. In addition, you enter an address change for a vendor in QuickBooks but not your contact manager. When you synchronize, the telephone number gets updated in QuickBooks and the address gets updated in your contact manager. This brings QuickBooks and your contact manager up to date with each other.

QUICKBOOKS® FEATURES: NOTES, TIME TRACKING, JOB COSTING AND TRACKING, MAILING SERVICES, SHIPPING, AND PRICE LEVELS

B

The QuickBooks Program contains many areas that were not explored during the training chapters of the text. Some of these areas are time tracking, job costing and tracking, price levels, and notes. To Do Notes, customer notes, vendor notes, employee notes, other names notes, and customer:job classifications are available in all versions of QuickBooks while the other features listed are available only in QuickBooks Pro and QuickBooks Premier. This appendix will use the sample company, Rock Castle Construction, to provide information regarding the features mentioned in the appendix title. Since saving the demonstration transactions will make permanent changes to the sample company, you will not need to do the demonstration transactions unless they are assigned by your instructor.

QUICKBOOKS NOTES

QuickBooks allows you to use several types of notes. These are To Do List, Customer notes, Vendor notes, Employee notes, and Time Tracking notes.

To Do List

To Do List contains notes regarding things to do. To Do notes are available in all the versions of QuickBooks. To Do's are accessed by clicking To Do List on the Company menu. The To Do List is QuickBooks version of a tickler file, which is used to remind you to do something on a particular date.

Steps to Create a To Do Note:

Click **To Do List** on the Company menu
Click **To Do** button, click **New**
Enter the text of the note
Enter the **Remind me on date**

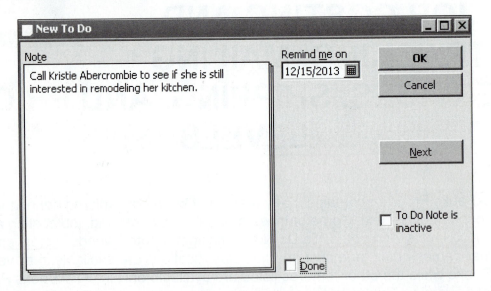

Click **OK**
- The note will be added to the list of To Do notes

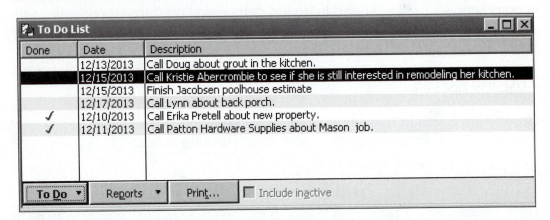

Customer Notes

The customer list contains information about each customer and/or job. One of the columns available is the Notes column. QuickBooks provides a notepad for recording notes about a customer or job. Approximately ten windows worth of text can be displayed on each customer's notepad. You can also write on the customer notepad when viewing a customer's record or when entering a transaction. When using the customer notepad, an entry may be date stamped, To Do notes may be accessed, and the note may be printed.

Steps to Create Customer or Job Notes

Open the **Customer Center**
Click on the Customer you wish to view or add notes (Kristie Abercrombie)
Click the **Edit Notes** button
Click at the bottom of the list of notes, press **Enter**, click the **Date Stamp** button and
   QuickBooks will enter the date of the note, then you type the note

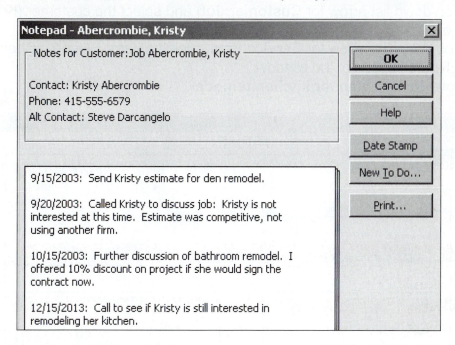

Click **OK** to save and exit the notepad

Vendor, Employee, and Other Names Notes

Vendor notes are recorded on the notepad for individual vendors in the Vendor Center. As with customer notes, this is where important conversations and product information would be recorded. The vendor notepad can be accessed from the Vendor Center. When using the vendor notepad, an entry may be date stamped, To Do notes may be accessed, and the note may be printed. Each entry on your Vendor, Employee, and Other Names lists has its own notepad where you can keep miscellaneous notes to yourself about that vendor, employee, or name. The procedures followed for vendors, employees, or other names are the same as illustrated for customers.

Notes for Time Tracking

The Timer is a separate program that is installed and works in conjunction with QuickBooks Pro and Premier. Time Tracking will be discussed separately later in this appendix. Notes regarding the time spent working on a task are entered when using the stopwatch.

Steps to Create Notes for Time Tracking

Click the **Employees** menu, point to **Enter Time**
Click **Time/Enter Single Activity**
Click the drop-down list arrow for **Name** and select the employee (Dan T. Miller)
Click the drop-down list arrow for **Customer:Job** and select the customer (Kristie Abercrombie)
Click the drop-down list arrow for **Service Item**, click the item (Blueprint Changes)
Click in the **Notes** section of the window
Enter the note: **Revise plan for kitchen remodel**

Do not close the Time/Enter Single Activity screen

TRACKING TIME

Many businesses bill their customers or clients for the actual amount of time they spend working for them. In this case you would be tracking billable time. When you complete the invoice to the customer, you can add the billable time to the invoice with a few clicks. In other situations, you may not want to bill for the time; but you may want to track it. For example, you may want to find out how much time you spend working on a job that was negotiated at a fixed price. This will help you determine whether or not you estimated the job correctly. Also, you may want to track the amount of time employees spend on various jobs, whether or not you bill for the time.

Both QuickBooks Pro and Premier come with a separate Timer program. Timer can be run on any computer whether or not it has QuickBooks. You have a choice between tracking time via the Timer and then transferring the time data to QuickBooks, using the Stopwatch on the Time/Enter Single Activity window, or entering time directly into QuickBooks manually on the Weekly Timesheet window or the Time/Enter Single Activity window.

Steps to Track Time as a Single Activity

With the Time/Enter Single Activity screen showing the time for Dan T. Miller and the blueprint changes for Kristie Abercrombie, indicate whether or not the time recorded is billable
- A check in the billable box means that this is recorded as billable time. No check means that the time is being tracked but not billed.

Click **Start** on the timer
When finished with the work, click **Stop** on the timer
- If work is stopped at any time, you may click Pause when stopping and click Start when resuming work.

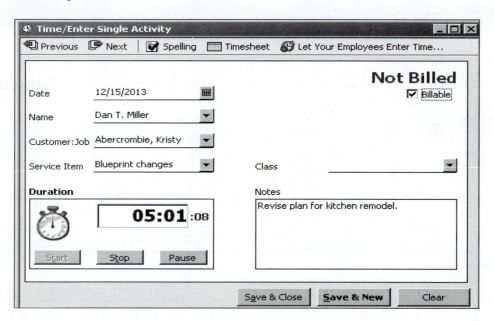

When finished, click **Stop** and **Save & Close**

Steps to Track Time on a Timesheet

Click **Employees** menu, point to **Enter Time**
Click **Use Weekly Timesheet**
Click the drop-down list arrow for **Name**, and click the name of the employee doing the work (Dan T. Miller)
- Accept the date the computer provides
  - o If you want to change the date of the time sheet, click the calendar button, and click the date for the time sheet.
- Any work completed as a Single Activity will appear on the time sheet
If you need to enter the information for the time period, in the Customer column, click the drop-down list arrow for **Customer:Job**
Click the name of the customer for whom work is being performed
Click the drop-down list arrow for **Service Item**
Click the name of the service item
Enter any notes regarding the work
Enter the number of hours worked in the appropriate columns for the days of the week
- If the information is the same as the previous timesheet, click Copy Last Sheet
  - o The information for the previous timesheet will be entered for this time period.
Indicate whether or not the hours are billable
- QuickBooks Timer records all hours as billable unless otherwise indicated. The icons in the last column indicate whether or not the items are billable, have been billed on a previous invoice, or are not billable.

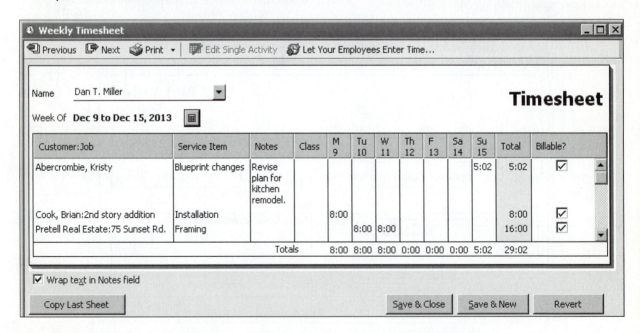

- Notice the Blueprint changes were recorded when using the Timer

When the timesheet is complete, click **Save & Close**

<u>Prepare an Invoice Using Billable Hours</u>

Click the **Create Invoices** icon on the Home Page
Enter the name of the **Customer:Job**

- QuickBooks will search for any estimates to be billed to the Customer:Job. If necessary, select the estimate to be billed. Indicate whether the estimate should be billed in full or in part. Complete this section of the invoice.

Since we do not want to bill for estimates, click **Cancel** to go to the invoice and not bill
The Billable Time and Costs screen appears after cancelling .the Estimates screen.
"Select the outstanding billable time and costs to add to this invoice?" should be selected, click **OK**.
Scroll through the list of Time and Costs for the customer
Click the time you wish to bill

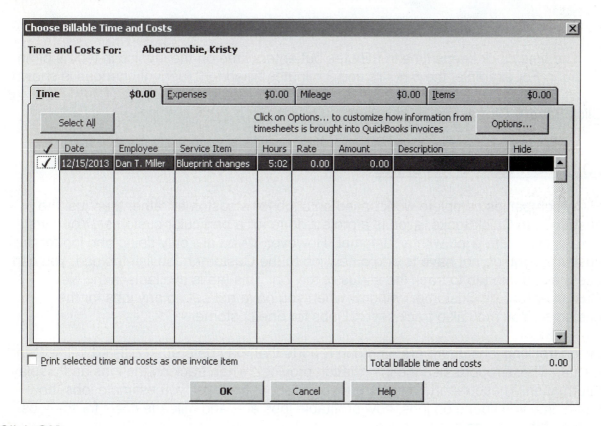

Click **OK**

- The time will be entered on the invoice.

Complete the invoice as previously instructed

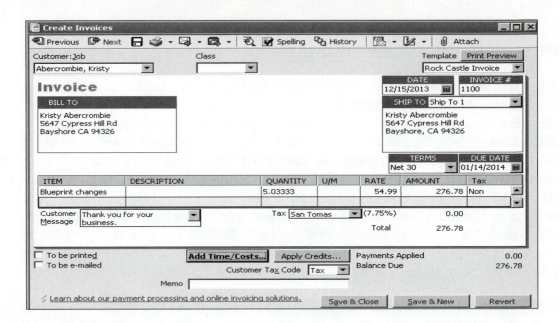

- The time clock keeps time in minutes but enters time on the invoice in tenths of an hour. For example, the 5 hours and 3 minutes billed for blueprint changes is shown as 5:03333

Click **Save & Close**

JOB COSTING AND TRACKING

Many companies complete work based on a job for a customer rather than just the customer. In QuickBooks, a job is a project done for a particular customer. You must always associate a job with a customer. However, if you are only doing one job for the customer, you do not have to add a new job to the Customer:Job list. Instead, you can use the Job Info tab to track the status of the job. This tab is available in the New Customer (or Edit Customer) window when you have not set up any jobs for the customer. You may also track several jobs for one customer.

When tracking jobs, there are nineteen reports that may be prepared listed in the Report Center. These reports use the information provided when tracking the jobs and display information. These reports answer questions about how well you estimate jobs, how much time you spend on jobs, how profitable jobs are, and mileage costs for the jobs. Some of the reports available are:

Job Profitability Summary: This report summarizes how much money your company has made or lost on each job for each customer
Job Profitability Detail: This report shows how much money your company has made to date on the customer or job whose name you entered. The report lists costs and

revenues for each item you billed to the customer so you can see which parts of the job were profitable and which parts were not.

Job Estimates vs. Actuals Summary: This report summarizes how accurately your company estimated job-related costs and revenues. The report compares estimated cost to actual cost and estimated revenue to actual revenue for all customers.

Job Estimates vs. Actuals Detail: This report shows how accurately your company estimated costs and revenues for the customer or job whose name you entered. The report compares estimated and actual costs and estimated and actual revenues for each item that you billed. That way, you can see which parts of the job you estimated accurately and which parts you did not.

Time by Job Summary: This report shows how much time your company spent on various jobs. For each customer or job, the report lists the type of work performed (service items). Initially, the report covers all dates from your QuickBooks records, but you can restrict the period covered by choosing a different date range from the Dates list.

Time by Job Detail: This report lists each time activity (that is, work done by one person for a particular customer or job on a specific date) and shows whether the work is billed, unbilled, or not billable. The report groups and subtotals the activities first by customer and job and then by service item.

Mileage by Job Detail: This report shows the miles for each trip per customer:job and includes the trip date, billing status, item, total miles, sales price and amount.

Steps to Create a Job for a Customer

Open the **Customer Center**
Select the customer for whom you want to add a job
Click the **New Customer & Job** button, click **Add Job**

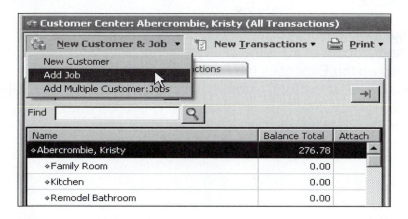

In the New Job window, enter a name for this job
On the **Job Info** tab, choose a job status (Pending, Awarded, etc.) from the drop-down list.
(Optional) Enter a start date and an end date (projected or actual) for the job

(Optional) Enter a job description and a job type

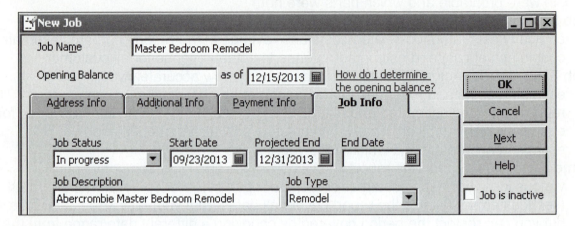

Click **OK** to record the new job.
The job is added to the customer or the Customer List

Name	Balance Total	Attach
◆Abercrombie, Kristy	276.78	
◆Master Bedroom Remodel	0.00	
◆Family Room	0.00	
◆Kitchen	0.00	
◆Remodel Bathroom	0.00	

Steps to Create a Bill Received for Expenses Incurred on a Job and Items Purchased for a Job

Enter the bill information as instructed in Chapter 6
Enter the date and amount of the bill
Enter the expense on the Expenses tab
Click the drop-down list arrow for Customer:Job in the Customer:Job column on the Expenses tab
Click the appropriate Customer:Job

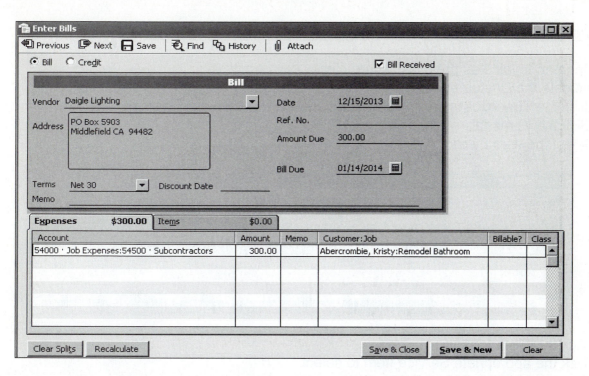

To complete a bill for both expenses and items, click the Items tab and enter the appropriate information.

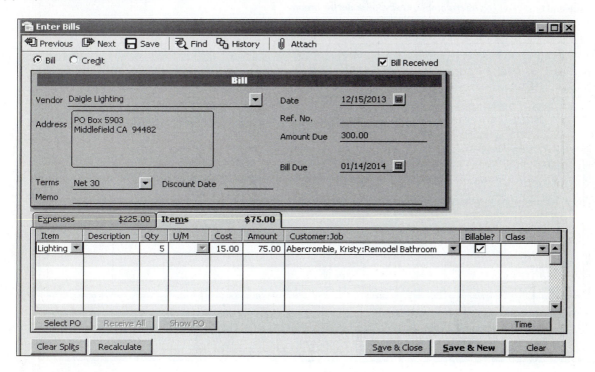

Click **Save & Close**

Steps to Create an Invoice for Items and Time Billed for a Job

Open an Invoice as previously instructed
Indicate the Customer:Job as previously instructed
Click the **Time/Costs** button at the bottom of the Create Invoices window
Click the **Items** tab
Select the Item by clicking in the Check column

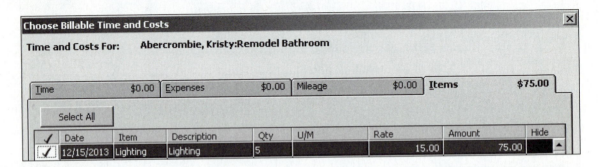

Click the **Time** tab
Click the appropriate Service Item to select

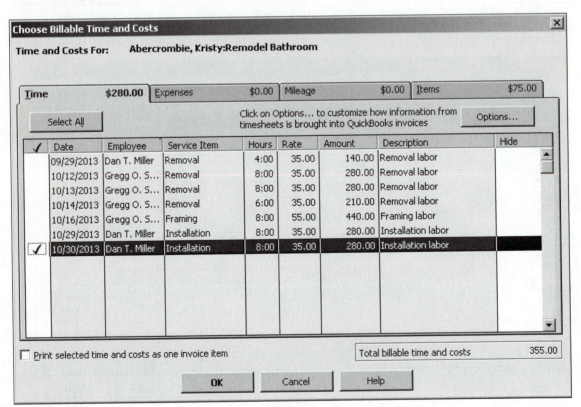

Click **OK**

Complete the Invoice

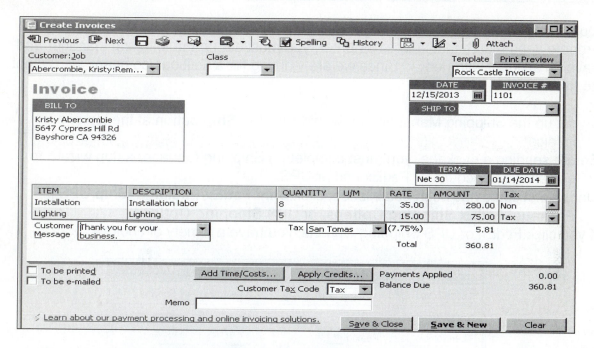

Notice that the Balance Due includes the amount for the lighting fixtures and the Installation labor

Click **Save & Close**

Creating Reports Using Jobs and Time

Use **Report Center** or the Reports Menu
Click **Jobs, Time & Mileage**
Click the report you wish to prepare
If preparing the report from the menu, enter the Dates as a range or enter the **From** and **To** dates at the top of the report and Tab

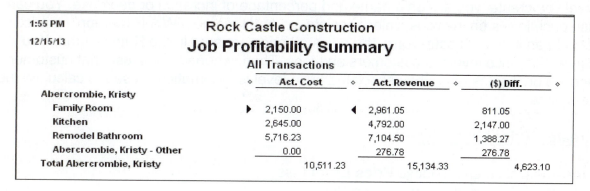

Scroll through the report to evaluate the information

SENDING MERCHANDISE USING QUICKBOOKS SHIPPING MANAGER

QuickBooks has a shipping manager that works in conjunction with FedEx or UPS. In order to send merchandise to a customer, you must set up the shipping manager and have an account with FedEx. Since we are working for a fictitious company we will not do this.

To set up the Shipping Manager, you would click the **Ship** button at the top of an invoice

Before sending a package, you must complete a Shipping Manager setup wizard to establish an account for FedEx and/or UPS.

Once an account has been established, click **Ship FedEx Package**, **Ship UPS Package**, **FedEx Shipping Options**, or **UPS Shipping Options**

If you click FedEx or UPS Shipping Options, you have a variety of choices

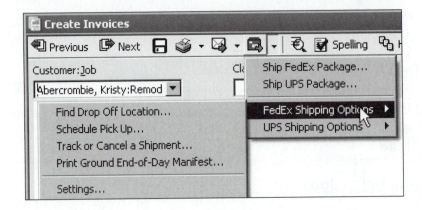

PRICE LEVELS

In QuickBooks Pro and Premier you can create price levels. Price levels are created to increase or decrease inventory, non-inventory, and service item prices. For each price level you create, you assign a name and percentage of increase or decrease. You can use price levels on invoices, sales receipts, or credit memos. When you apply a price level to an item on a sales form, the adjusted price appears in the Rate column. You can assign price levels to customers and jobs. Then, whenever you use that customer and job on a sales form, the associated price level is automatically used to calculate the item price.

Create a Price Level List

From the Lists menu, choose **Price Level List**

From the Price Level menu, choose **New**

In the New Price Level window, enter the name of the new price level

In the area for **This price level will**, select either **increase** or **decrease** for **item prices by**

In the Percentage % field, enter the percent number by which the item price will be increased or reduced.

Indicate whether QuickBooks should round numbers.

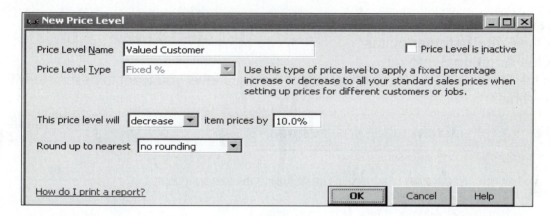

Click **OK** to go back to the Price Levels list.

Apply a Price Level on an Invoice

Fill out the invoice as previously instructed
In the Rate column, click the drop-down button

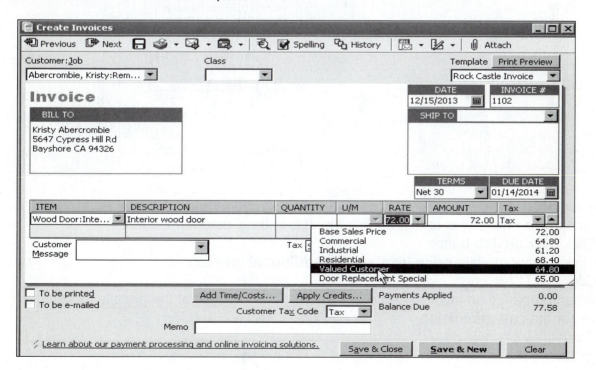

Choose a price level to apply to the item
• The amount shown next to each price level is the adjusted amount of the item
Save the invoice

Associate a Price Level with a Customer/Job

Access the Customer Center, select the **Customer**
Click the **Edit Customer** button
Click the **Additional Info** tab
From the Price Level drop-down list, select the price level you want to associate with the
    customer

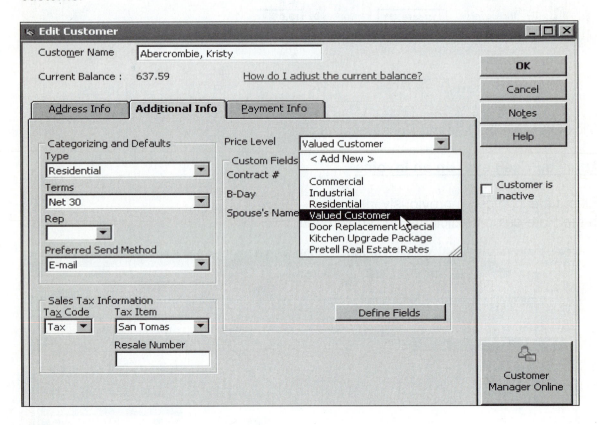

Click **OK**
To apply a Price Level to a Job, click the **Job** in the Customer Center
Click the **Edit Job** button
Click the appropriate **price level** on the **Additional Info** tab
Click **OK**
When preparing an invoice, items will automatically appear at the price level selected
    for the customer or job

To verify this, click the drop-down list arrow for Price Each and notice that the price for the interior wood door has been entered at the price level selected for the customer (Residential).

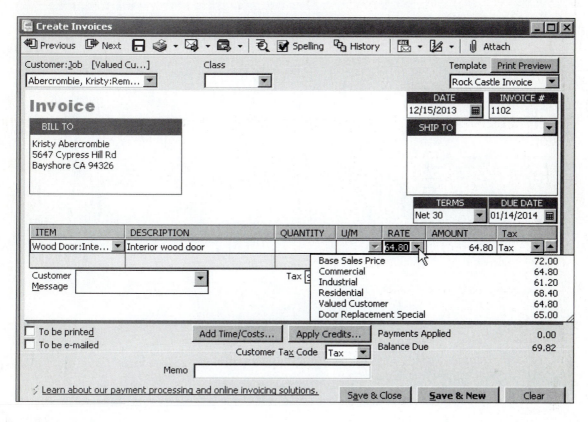

Click **Save & Close**

QUICKBOOKS® PRO ONLINE FEATURES

QuickBooks Pro uses the Internet as an integral part of the program. Some of the uses it performs are online updates to the program, subscribers to the Payroll Services can receive online updates to tax tables, and online banking can be performed within the program. In addition, you can subscribe to online backup services, obtain product support, access training resources, find a professional advisor in your area, access user-to-user forums, obtain information about business resources, access Intuit's Home Page, and order checks and business forms online.

In addition to the included online items, there are several online subscription programs that may be used in conjunction with QuickBooks. These include customer manager, e-mail marketing, Website services, search advertising, incorporation services, processing credit card payments, e-check processing, set up recurring charges, a QuickBooks credit card, a shipping manager, bill pay, time tracking, and others. Intuit also offers the Live Community where you may post questions, give advice, participate in a Webinar, and get suggestions for resources for your business. QuickBooks Solutions Marketplace that brings together over 100 companies that have integrated their software products with QuickBooks Pro, Premier and QuickBooks Enterprise Solutions.

This Appendix will explore some of the online options listed above.

INTUIT AND THE INTERNET

At Intuit's Web site you may get up-to-date information about QuickBooks Pro and other products by Intuit. You can access the Intuit Web site at www.Intuit.com through your browser.

QUICKBOOKS® PRO UPDATES

Intuit has a service that is free of charge and allows you to check the Web site to download messages and updates for QuickBooks Pro. You may have QuickBooks Pro do this automatically, or it will remind you to update periodically. QuickBooks Pro provides two methods for updating—automatic and immediate. Both methods require an Internet connection and may be used concurrently.

Update QuickBooks Pro Automatically

With this method, updates of your choice are automatically downloaded from the Intuit server to your computer. QuickBooks Pro periodically checks the Intuit server for new updates, and proceeds to download information gradually at times when your open Internet connection is not being used by another process or application.

The advantages of updating QuickBooks Pro automatically are:

- Updates are downloaded to your computer unobtrusively, without interrupting a QuickBooks Pro session or other tasks that you perform with your computer.
- Updating occurs whether or not QuickBooks Pro is running.
- You can disconnect from the Internet anytime and not worry about updating. When you reconnect to the Internet, QuickBooks Pro resumes downloading updates at the point where it was previously halted.

QuickBooks Pro continues to download updates automatically until you turn off the Automatic Update option. Even with the Automatic Update option turned on, you can still download all available updates immediately whenever you choose to do so.

If you have several different copies of QuickBooks Pro running and you share data, it is essential that computers be updated at the same time so they all have the same exact version of the program in operation. If you update QuickBooks Pro on one computer and not another, QuickBooks Pro may not be able to read the company file on the computer that did not receive the update.

In addition, whenever Intuit updates QuickBooks it includes refinements and enhancements to the program. Having an updated program may mean that the screen shots illustrated in the text will not match your computer screen.

Update QuickBooks Pro Immediately

With this method, updates of your choice are downloaded immediately from the Intuit server to your computer. You can use this method at any time—even when your computer is configured to download updates automatically.

To download immediately, click the **Help** menu, click **Update QuickBooks**, click the **Update Now** tab

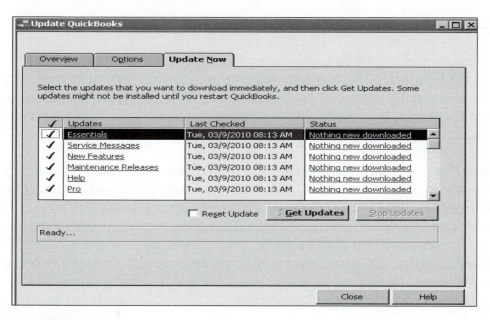

Click **Get Updates**

• Notice the lightening bolt on the Get Updates button. This indicates that you will access Intuit via the Internet.

Select or Deselect Automatic Updates

To select or deselect automatic updates, click the **Help** menu, click **Update QuickBooks**, click the **Options** tab
To select Automatic Update, click **Yes**, click **Mark All**

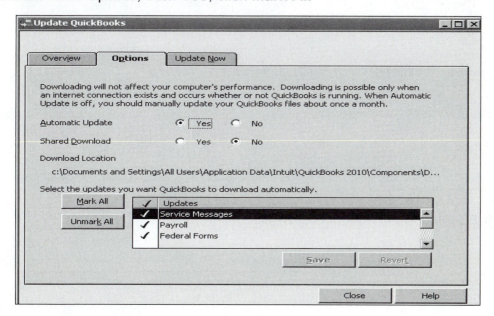

To deselect automatic update, click **No** and **Save**

CONNECTING TO INTUIT INTERNET IN QUICKBOOKS® PRO

Before connecting to Intuit's Web Site using QuickBooks, you must have the QuickBooks Pro program and a company open. In addition, you must have a modem for your computer, and the modem must be connected to a telephone line or cable. Once the modem is connected and QuickBooks Pro and a company are open, you may establish your Internet connection.

QuickBooks Pro has a step-by-step tutorial that will help you do this. Clicking Internet Connection Setup on the Help menu allows you to identify an internet connection and complete the setup. The first screen you see informs QuickBooks Pro of your choice for your Internet connection. You may tell QuickBooks Pro that you have an existing dial-up Internet connection, that you plan to use a direct connection through a network at school or work, or that you want to sign up for an Internet account with limited access.

To Use an Established Internet Connection

Click the **Help** menu, click **Internet Connection Setup**
Click **Use the following connection**, click **Other Internet connection**, click **Next**

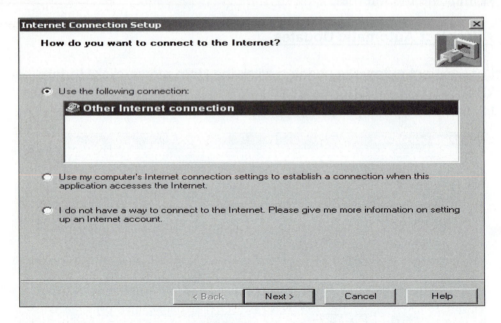

Verify the information provided, click **Done**

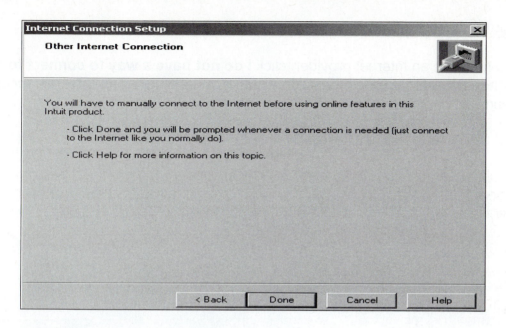

To Use a Computer's Internet Connection

If you have a direct Internet connection, select **Use my computer's Internet connection settings to establish a connection when this application accesses the Internet**, click **Next**

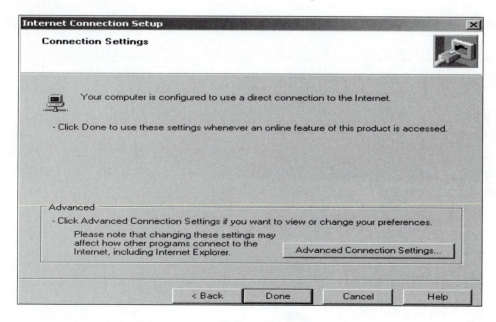

Verify the information, click **Done**

To Establish an Internet Provider and Connection

If you do not have an Internet provider, click **I do not have a way to connect to the Internet. Please give me more information on setting up an Internet account** Click **Next**

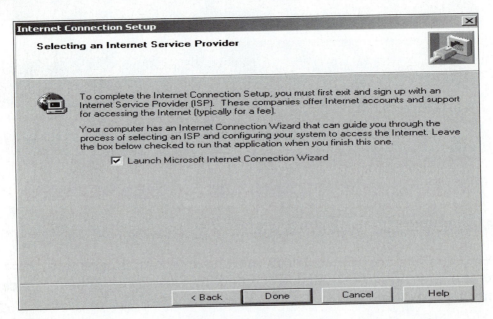

Click **Done** and complete the steps listed in the Microsoft Internet Connection Wizard

ACCESS QUICKBOOKS' ONLINE FEATURES

Anytime you see a lightning bolt, this denotes information or services that require an Internet connection. Click on the lightning bolt. If you have a direct Internet connection, you will go directly to the QuickBooks Web site. When you are connected, you will go to the areas requested. For example, I clicked Order Checks & Business Cards in the Do More with QuickBooks section of the Home Page

QuickBooks connected to the Web and brought up a screen describing QuickBooks Checks, Business Cards, and More

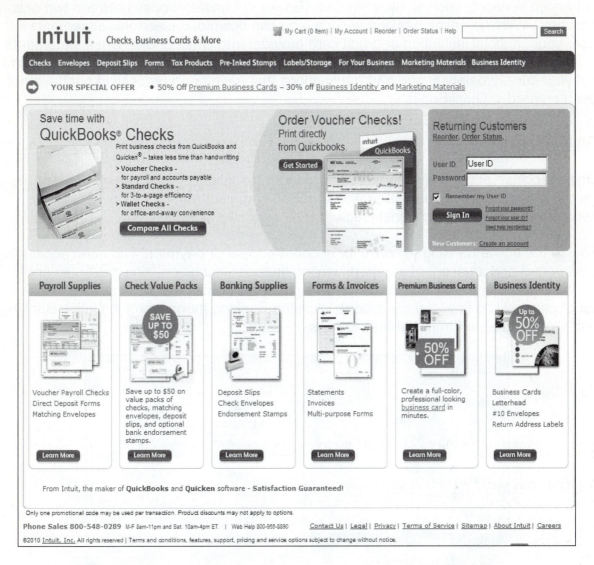

You may select and order forms and other items that are setup to work with QuickBooks.

ONLINE BANKING AND PAYMENTS

Online banking and payment services are offered through QuickBooks Pro in conjunction with a variety of financial institutions. This is also called online account access. To use this, you must apply for this service through your financial institution. If you bank with or make payments to more than one institution, you must sign up with each institution separately. Most banks will charge a fee for online services and may not offer both online banking and online payment services. Some institutions provide enhanced services, such as allowing QuickBooks to transfer money between two online accounts. With the online banking service, you can download electronic statements from your financial institution or credit card provider into QuickBooks. Once statements have been downloaded, you can see what transactions have cleared your account, find out your current balance, and add transactions that have been processed but have not been entered in QuickBooks.

Online Banking

Online account access allows you to download transactions from a checking, savings, money market, or credit or charge account. You can also transfer money online and send e-mail to your financial institution.

To use the online banking services for account access or payment, you need access to the Internet and an account at a participating financial institution. You must also apply for the service through QuickBooks or through a participating financial service. To see a list of participating financial institutions, click the Banking menu, point to Online Banking, and click **Available Financial Institutions**

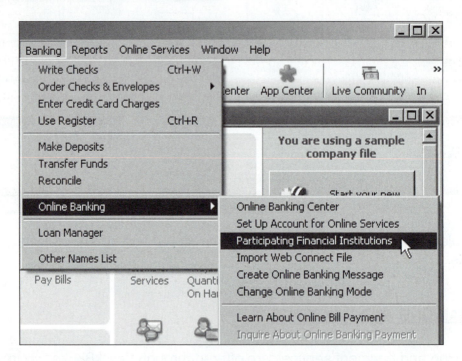

QuickBooks connects to the Internet and a list of banks appears

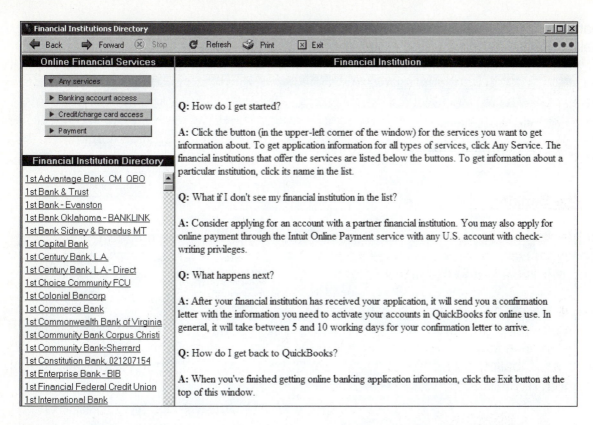

In order to provide security and confidentiality in online services, QuickBooks uses state-of-the-art encryption and authentication security features. All of your online communications with your financial institution require a Personal Identification Number (PIN) or password, which only you possess. You may also use passwords within QuickBooks Pro.

Set Up Online Banking

Since we do not have an actual company, we are unable to setup an online banking account.

To create an online banking account for your own business, click the **Banking** menu
Point to Online Banking, click **Setup Account for Online Banking Access**
Complete the Online Setup Interview

Using Online Banking

Online banking allows you to download current information from and send messages to your financial institution. This can include transactions, balances, online messages, and transfer of funds. To use online banking, click **Banking** on the menu bar, point to Online Banking, click **Online Banking Center**. You may view and work with your online banking transactions in either the Side-by-Side mode or Register mode. The screen below shows the Side-by-Side Mode.

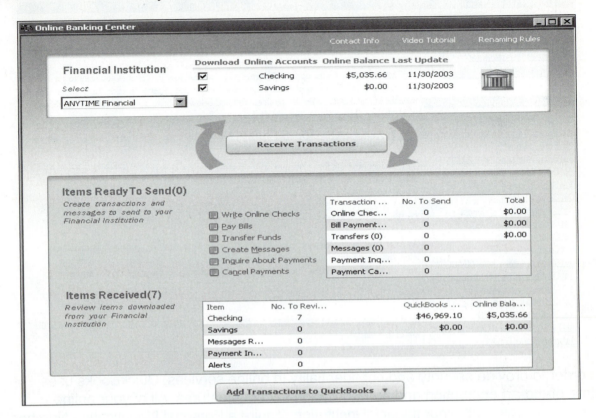

To download transactions, click the account you wish to download.
In this example, I clicked Checking.

Once the download is complete, you can automatically compare the downloaded transactions with those in your register. QuickBooks Pro will match downloaded transactions to those in your register and note any unmatched transactions so that they may be entered into your register.

The downloaded transactions shown lists the transactions that occurred since your last download and any transactions that were not matched from previous downloads.

Note: Even though the year for the sample company is 2013, many of the transactions have the year 2003.

To record the transactions, click each individual item, and mark it accordingly.

For example, click the transaction labeled as a bank service charge

Click the drop-down list arrow and select Great Statewide Bank as the payee

Click the drop-down list arrow and select Bank Service Charges for the account

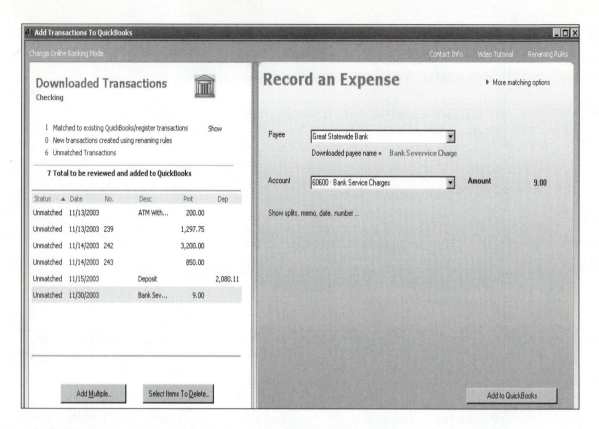

When finished, click the **Add to QuickBooks** button
The transaction is no longer shown on the Downloaded Transactions list
Click the **Finish Later** button to exit
Verify that the service charge was deducted from the checking account by opening the checking account register.

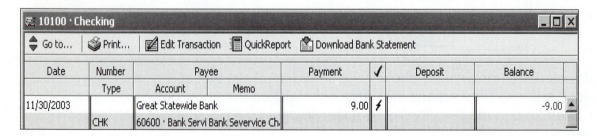

Online Payments

If your financial institution provides this service, you may use the online payment services to create online payment instructions for one or more payments, then send the instructions via your modem. You may schedule a payment to arrive on a certain date, inquire about online payments, and cancel them if need be. You can record and pay your bills at the same time, all from within QuickBooks.

Online banking through QuickBooks uses state-of-the-art encryption technology and requires a PIN to send transactions. You can use online payment with any U.S. bank account with check-writing privileges.

With online payment you can:
- Pay bills without writing checks or going to the post office.
- Attach additional information to the payment (such as invoice number and invoice date) so your vendor knows which bill to apply it to.
- Schedule a payment in advance, to be delivered on or before the date you specify.
- Apply for online payment services online.

There are three ways to send an online payment:
- From the Pay Bills window
- From the Write Checks window
- From an online account register

You use these methods the same way you always do, except that you designate the transaction as an online transaction and send the payment instructions to your financial institution.

To use online payments, you need to set up a payee. Once the payee is set up, you may either send an electronic funds transfer (EFT) to the payee's institution or have your financial institution print a check and send it to the payee. An electronic funds transfer deducts money from your account and transfers it into the payee's account electronically. This usually takes one or two business days, however, payments should be scheduled four days before they are due. This is called lead time and must be considered when sending online payments. If you have your institution mail checks to payees, you should allow five days lead time.

A check used to send an online payment will use Send as the No. and will have a checkmark for Online Bank Payment.

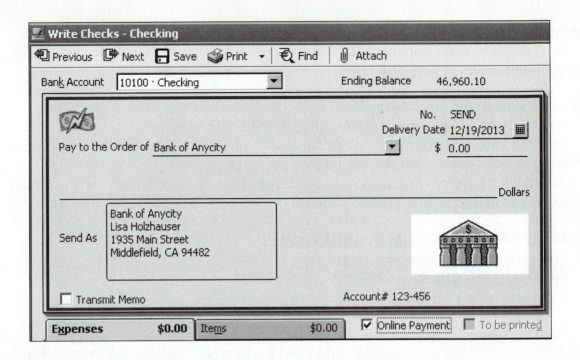

QUICKBOOKS BILLING SOLUTIONS

QuickBooks offers an invoice e-mail service that will instantly e-mail easy-to-read PDF files of invoices, statements, estimates, and payment reminders from QuickBooks. It also has a mailing service that will print, fold, and mail invoices to customers. In addition, payment reminders, online e-mail tracking, and customer online payment options are also included. Customers can pay invoices and statements online by entering their credit card information in a secure Web site hosted by Intuit. Charges are processed through the QuickBooks Merchant Service. Customers may view their account information on line and you can track when customers view your e-mails. This requires signing up for the optional QuickBooks Billing Solutions and QuickBooks Merchant Service.

QUICKBOOKS MERCHANT SERVICES

QuickBooks Merchant Services allows your business to accept credit cards from customers. As a subscriber to QuickBooks Merchant Services, credit card charges are processed and deposited into your designated bank account. Everything needed to process credit cards is built right into QuickBooks. This enables you to offer customers more payment options, process credit cards in QuickBooks or remotely. Credit card payments may be entered manually into QuickBooks or by swiping the credit card by using a card reader purchased separately. You can also process recurring charges and bill customers online.

Enter credit card transactions

When a transaction is processed for a credit card payment, sales receipt, or customer payment, it is recorded as usual. The checkbox for "Process payment when saving" should be checked.

When receiving payments by credit card, enter the payment information as usual. Pmt. Method should be Master Card or Visa, click Process Master Card or Visa payment when saving

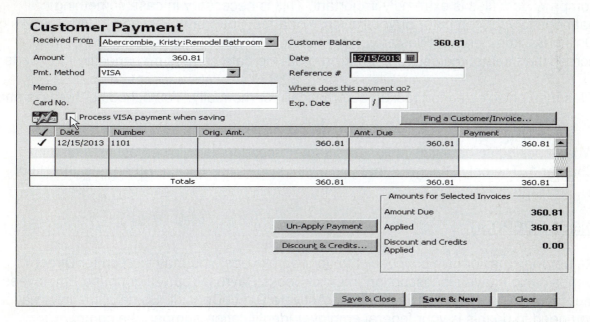

You may also sign up for and attach a credit card reader that will enable you to swipe a card and have the transaction entered directly into QuickBooks.

Once a credit card transaction has been entered, you will get a notice of approval.

In addition, you may download transaction information directly into QuickBooks using an internet-accessible mobile device.

You may set up automatic recurring charges and integrate with Billing Solutions so customers can also pay online. QuickBooks credit card processing also enables credit card fees to be included on the Make Deposits window.
There is also an option for processing E-Checks in QuickBooks. This, too, is a feature available in Merchant Services.

Automatic Credit Card Billing

QuickBooks Merchant Account Services also has an Automatic Credit Card Billing feature that allows you to bill a customer's credit card a fixed amount at regular intervals for recurring services, such as membership fees, insurance premiums, or subscriptions. Prior to setting up a recurring charge, you must have written authorization from your customer.

ONLINE BACKUP SERVICES

In addition to having a backup stored in the office, having an offsite backup copy of your company data files is extremely important. This is necessary in case something happens to your computer or your office. For a fee, you may subscribe to QuickBooks Online Backup Service. Files are compressed, encrypted, and securely transferred across the Internet then stored at mirrored off-site data centers managed by IT experts.

Files may be selected for backup automatically or manually. You schedule the days and times for your backups.

When backing up data files online, the same procedure is followed as instructed in Chapter 1. The only change is that you click Online backup rather than Local backup.

DIRECT DEPOSIT

Rather than mail or give paychecks to your employees, you may sign up for Direct Deposit if you have a subscription to QuickBooks Payroll. You will go to the Employees menu and click My Payroll Service and Activate Direct Deposit. Some of the information you need to do this is your federal employer identification number, the company's principal name, the company's legal name and address, your financial institution routing and account numbers, and your QuickBooks registration number.

You also need to set up those employees who wish to receive their checks by direct deposit. This is done by:

- Accessing the Employee Center.
- Double-click the employee you want to set up for direct deposit.
- In the Edit Employee window, click the "Change Tabs" drop-down list and choose Payroll and Compensation Info.
- Click the Direct Deposit button.
- Select Use Direct Deposit for this employee.

- Select whether to deposit the paycheck into one or two accounts.
- Enter the employee's financial institution information.

GOOGLE DESKTOP AND INTUIT MARKETING TOOLS

Google Desktop Search

Use Google Desktop to search your Desktop to find files related to your search that are outside of QuickBooks data, such as, e-mails, documents, and files. Entering a few words or phrases will enable you to search for a list of the most likely matches. Once you've identified the information you want, you can click the link to go directly to the data in QuickBooks or to the file on your desktop. You can search within QuickBooks using Google Desktop to find an amount, a customer name, forms, and even information in a notes field. You can search for multiple words, exclude items from your search results, and even search for information on your computer. You may search for anything you have permission to view in QuickBooks. For example, if your permissions do not allow you to view payroll information, no payroll information will be returned in your search results.

Marketing Tools

Intuit provides several marketing tools including:

Intuit Websites: Create your own Website by customizing a professionally-designed website or have a Website designed for you, create a personalized domain name, use Email addresses that work with your domain name, website hosting, site traffic reports, and other web services that are provided depending upon the plan selected.

WebListings: Online postings on a network of local search sites without requiring a website.

Email Marketing: QuickBooks can send your QuickBooks contacts high-impact email containing newsletters and promotions. Monthly fees are based on the email list size.

Custom Logo Design: Working in conjunction with Logoworks, you may have a logo custom designed. Depending on the package you select, you will have several initial concepts, work with designers, and have the ability to make revisions.

Trademark Search: To confirm that no one else is using your name or slogan, QuickBooks works with MyCorporation to provide a search regarding trademarks. You may also apply for a trademark to protect your logo or brand name.

Index